# THE USBORNE POCKET DICTIONARY

Edited by Rachel Wardley.

Abridged by Rebecca Heddle
and Rachel Wardley.

Designed by Susie McCaffrey.
Page layout: Sue Grobecker, Isaac Quaye, Rod Ellis

Illustrations by Ian Jackson, Sean Wilkinson,
Gerald Wood, Nicholas Hewetson, Peter Dennis,
Michelle Ross, Chris Shields, Kuo Kang Chen,
David Goldston, Dan Courtney, Andrew Beckett,
Nick Gibbard, David Wright, Chris Lyon,
Steven Kirk, Malcolm McGregor.

Photography by Mark Mason Studio.

Senior editor: Jane Bingham

Definitions by John McIlwain, Sheila Dignen,
Jessica Feinstein, Andrew Delahunty.

Advisors: Colin Hope, Richard Hatton, John Rostron,
Margaret Rostron, Bill Chambers, Anne Millard

# YOUR DICTIONARY: *A USER'S GUIDE*

This dictionary contains over eleven thousand definitions and more than two hundred and fifty pictures, many of them surrounded by picture labels.

## Finding a word

All of the **entries** in the dictionary are listed in alphabetical order. To find your word, make a guess at its first few letters, for example for "dinosaur", first find "din", then try different ways of spelling the next part.

## If you can't find a word

◆ You may have chosen the wrong first letters. Try some alternative spellings and look out for **spelling guides** at the bottom of the page.

◆ You may be able to find a word that is related to your word. For example, you would find the word "raucously" at the end of the entry for "raucous".

## Looking at pages

**Guide letters** help you to find the right letter section.

**Guide words** help you to find the right page.

d

diligent 68

**diligent** *(adj)* hard-working.

**dilute diluting diluted** *(v)* to make a liquid weaker by adding water.

**dimension** *(n)* The **dimensions** of an object are its measurements or its size.

**diminish diminishes diminishing diminished** *(v)* If something **diminishes**, it becomes smaller or weaker.

**dinghy dinghies** *(n)* a small, open boat.

**dingy** *(din-jee)* **dingier dingiest** *(adj)* dull and shabby. *A dingy room.*

**dinner** *(n)* the main meal of the day, eaten at midday or in the evening.

**dinosaur** *(n)* the general name for the large, land-living reptiles that existed in prehistoric times.

**dinosaurs**

*travelled in a westerly direction.* 2 **directions** *(plural n)* instructions.

**directory directories** *(n)* a book which gives addresses, phone numbers etc. in alphabetical order.

**dirty dirtier dirtiest** 1 *(adj)* not clean. **dirt** *(n)*. 2 *(adj)* unfair. *A dirty trick.*

**disabled** *(adj)* People who are **disabled** are restricted in what they can do, usually because of illness or injury. **disability** *(n)*.

**disadvantage** *(n)* something which causes a problem or makes life difficult.

**disagree disagreeing disagreed** *(v)* to think differently from someone else.

**dip dipping dipped** 1 *(v)* to push something briefly into a liquid. *Dip your brush in the water.* 2 *(v)* to slope downwards. 3 *(n)* a short swim.

**diplomat** *(n)* a person who represents their country's government in a foreign country. **diplomacy** *(n)*.

**diplomatic** 1 *(adj)* If you are **diplomatic**, you are tactful and good at dealing with people. **diplomacy** *(n)*. 2 *(adj)* to do with being a diplomat. *The diplomatic service.*

**dire direr direst** *(adj)* disastrous.

**direct directing directed** 1 *(adj)* in a straight line, or by the shortest route. 2 *(v)* to supervise people, especially in a play or film. 3 *(v)* to tell someone the way to go.

**direction** 1 *(n)* the way that someone or something is moving or pointing. *We*

**disappear disappearing disappeared** *(v)* to go out of sight. **disappearance**

**disappoint disappointing disappointed** *(v)* to let someone down by failing to do what they expected.

**disapprove disapproving disapproved** *(v)* If you **disapprove** of something, you think it is bad or wrong. **disapproval**

**disaster** 1 *(n)* a very serious accident, earthquake, etc. in which many die. **disastrous** *(adj)*. 2 *(n)* something that has gone completely wrong. **disastrous**

**disbelief** *(n)* refusal to believe something. *My story met with disbelief.*

**disc** or **disk** 1 *(n)* a flat, circular shape. 2 *(n)* a piece of plastic, used for recording music or information. *Compact disc.*

*Some words that begin with a "di" sound are spelt "dy".*

**Spelling guides** suggest other spellings.

## Looking at entries

**Headwords** show how a word is spelt.

**Pronunciation guides** show how a word is said.

**Parts of speech** identify what a word does in a sentence (see page 3).

**Definitions** explain what a word means.

**Changing forms** show how words change their spelling when they are used in different ways.

**raucous** *(raw-kus)* *(adj)* harsh, or loud. **raucously** *(adv)*.
**rave raving raved 1** *(v)* to speak in a wild, uncontrolled way. **2** *(v)* *(informal)* to be very enthusiastic about something. *Gary raves about football.*

**Related words** introduce words from the same family.

**Numbers** indicate a separate sense of a word.

**Usage guides** show that a word is old-fashioned, poetic, informal or slang. Informal words are used in everyday speech, but not in formal or official writing. Slang is usually only spoken.

**Example sentences** show how a word is used.

---

Weights, measures, numbers, days and months are listed on page 256.

# PARTS OF SPEECH: *THE PARTS THAT WORDS PLAY*

**noun** *(n)* Nouns give the name of a person, animal or thing. They tell you who or what a sentence is about.

*Bobo is juggling. Practice is essential.*

**pronoun** *(pronoun)* Pronouns refer to a person or thing without naming it. They act like nouns.

*(Annie is good at skiing.)*
*She is good at skiing.*

*(The weather is cold.)*
*It is cold.*

**verb** *(v)* Verbs are action words. They say what someone or something does, thinks, or feels. All sentences need verbs to tell you what is happening.

*Spike loves his motorbike. It goes really fast.*

**adjective** *(adj)* Adjectives are descriptive words which tell you more about a person or thing. They are used with nouns and pronouns.

*Toucans have enormous beaks. They are very colourful.*

**adverb** *(adv)* Adverbs tell you how, when, where or why something happens. They are used with verbs.

*The horse is bucking wildly. Its rider may soon fall off.*

**conjunction** *(conj)* Conjunctions are linking words. They join parts of sentences.

*Penguins have wings, but cannot fly. They breed on land and hunt in water.*

**preposition** *(prep)* Prepositions show where people or things are, or what relation they have to each other.

*A Chinese dragon weaves through the streets. People are dancing under the dragon.*

**interjection** *(interject)* Interjections are used to show surprise, delight or pain, or to get attention. They are sometimes known as exclamations and often have an exclamation mark.

*"Wow!" cried the crowd as the baseball player hit the ball. "Yippee!" yelled the fielder as he caught it.*

**Note** - Some words in the dictionary are not given a part of speech. This is because they are used with other words or in a phrase.

# WRITING ENGLISH: *SOME HINTS AND GUIDELINES*

## Spelling English

It is sometimes difficult to spell English correctly because it is a mixture of so many languages.

Some basic spelling rules are shown here, but watch out for exceptions and always use a dictionary to check your spelling.

### Making plurals

dinosaur

Most nouns gain an **s** to become plural.

*dinosaur - dinosaurs*
*book - books*
*garden - gardens*
*zoo - zoos*
*day - days*
*house - houses*

dinosaurs

Some words, however, change differently. Here are some word groups for you to remember.

fox

If a word ends in **ch**, **sh**, **s**, **ss**, **x** or **z**, add **es**.

*arch - arches*
*dish - dishes*
*bus - buses*
*dress - dresses*
*fox - foxes*
*waltz - waltzes*

foxes

berry

If a word ends in **y** and the letter before the y is not a, e, i, o or u, replace the y with **ies**.

*berry - berries*
*baby - babies*
*party -parties*
*country - countries*
*city - cities*
*puppy - puppies*

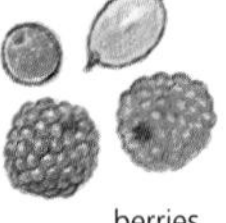
berries

leaf

Many words ending in **f** drop their final f and gain **ves**.

*leaf - leaves*
*loaf - loaves*
*shelf - shelves*
*wife - wives*
*thief - thieves*
*wolf - wolves*

leaves

buffalo

Many words ending in **o** gain **es**.

*buffalo - buffaloes*
*cargo - cargoes*
*tomato - tomatoes*
*potato - potatoes*
*echo - echoes*
*hero - heroes*

buffaloes

### Odd plurals

Some words change their spelling dramatically when they become plural. These plurals need to be learnt.

*woman - women*
*child - children*
*man - men*
*mouse - mice*
*foot - feet*
*tooth - teeth*

**i and e**

It is very easy to get these two letters the wrong way round, but this rule should help you.

"i before e, except after c,
when the sound is ee."

| **i** before **e** | **e** before **i** |
|---|---|
| *field* | *ceiling* |
| *believe* | *receive* |
| *thief* | *conceited* |

Note - there are some exceptions to this rule, such as *seize, weir, weird.*

## Punctuation

Without punctuation to break them up, your sentences would be impossible to read. These guidelines will help you to use some tricky punctuation marks.

### Apostrophes

Apostrophes show the owner of something:

If the owner is singular, add an **apostrophe s**
*Ben's hat*
*Charles's hat*

If the owner is plural and ends in s, add an **apostrophe only**
*The boys' hats*

If the owner is plural, but does not end in s, add an **apostrophe s**
*The children's hats*

**Never** use an apostrophe s to make a plural.

Apostrophes also mark missing letters:

*I'd = I would or I had*
*haven't = have not*
*she'll = she will*

**it's and its**

**it's** is only used to show that a letter has been missed out from **it is**.
*I'm glad it's a sunny day.*
*The kangaroo carries its baby in its pouch.*

### Colons and semi-colons

**Colons** can be used to introduce a statement or a list.
*At last Harry revealed the secret of his success: three raw carrots every day.*
*For this trick you need: a pack of cards, a silk scarf and a wand.*

**Semi-colons** are useful for breaking up lists when the items in the list are long and complicated.
*We visited the zoo and saw: two giraffes; an elephant with a baby; some performing seals; and a very mischievous monkey.*

### Inverted commas

You use inverted commas, or speech marks, to show that someone is speaking. Always start someone's spoken words with a capital letter and use a comma to separate speech from the rest of the sentence.
*"The view is amazing," said the astronaut.*
*The astronaut said, "The view is amazing."*
*"The view," said the astronaut, "is amazing."*

# Aa

**aardvark** *(n)* an African mammal with a long, sticky tongue, that it uses to search for insects.

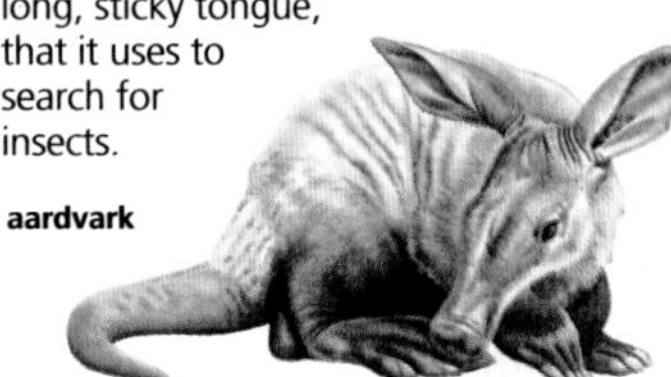
**aardvark**

**abacus abacuses** *or* **abaci** *(n)* a frame with beads on wires, used for counting.

**abandon abandoning abandoned** 1 *(v)* to leave something or someone forever. *Abandon ship!* 2 *(v)* to give something up. *Never abandon hope.*

**abattoir** *(ab-er-twar) (n)* a place where animals are killed for their meat.

**abbey** *(n)* a group of buildings where monks or nuns live and work.

**abbreviation** *(n)* a short way of writing a word. *CD is an abbreviation of compact disc.* **abbreviated** *(adj).*

**abduct abducting abducted** *(v)* to kidnap someone. **abduction** *(n).*

**abide abiding abode** *or* **abided 1** *(v) (old-fashioned)* to stay or live somewhere. **2** *(v)* If you **cannot abide** something, you cannot put up with it.

**ability abilities 1** *(n)* the power to do something. *I know I have the ability to do better.* **2** *(n)* skill. *Jo has great ability in art.*

**able abler ablest 1** *(adj)* If you are **able** to do something, you can do it. **2** *(adj)* skilful, or clever. **ably** *(adv).*

**abnormal** *(adj)* unusual, or not normal.

**aboard** *(prep)* on or into a train, ship, or aircraft. **aboard** *(adv).*

**abolish abolishes abolishing abolished** *(v)* to put an end to something officially. *We voted to abolish school uniform.*

**Aborigine** *(ab-or-ij-in-ee) (n)* one of the native people of Australia who lived there before Europeans arrived. **Aboriginal** *(adj).*

**abort aborting aborted 1** *(v)* to remove a fetus from its mother's womb so that the pregnancy ends. **abortion** *(n).* **2** *(v)* to stop something from happening.

**abound abounding abounded** *(v)* to have a large amount of something. *The forest abounds with wildlife.*

**above board** *(adj)* If an action is **above board**, it is completely honest and legal.

**abreast** *(adv)* side by side. *We walked three abreast.*

**abridged** *(adj)* shortened. *An abridged novel.* **abridge** *(v).*

**abroad** *(adv)* in or to another country. *We are going abroad this summer.*

**abrupt 1** *(adj)* sudden and unexpected. *An abrupt halt.* **2** *(adj)* rude and short-tempered. *An abrupt reply.*

**abseil** *(ab-sail)* **abseiling abseiled** *(v)* to lower yourself down a steep cliff or mountain face by holding on to a rope.

**absent** *(adj)* not present. **absence** *(n).*

**absent-minded** *(adj)* If you are **absent-minded**, you are forgetful and do not think about what you are doing.

**absolute 1** *(adj)* complete, or total. *Ben looks an absolute idiot.* **absolutely** *(adv).* **2** *(adj)* without any limit. *Absolute power.*

**absolve absolving absolved** *(v)* to pardon someone, or free them from blame. **absolution** *(n).*

**absorb absorbing absorbed 1** *(v)* to soak up liquid. *The sponge absorbed the juice.* **absorbent** *(adj).* **2** *(v)* to take in information. *The students quickly absorbed all the facts.*

**abstain abstaining abstained** *(v)* to stop yourself from doing something. *The prisoners abstained from eating until their demands were met.* **abstention** *(n).*

**abstract** *(adj)* based on ideas rather than things. *Abstract artists paint shapes rather than people or objects.*

**absurd absurder absurdest** *(adj)* silly, or ridiculous. **absurdity** *(n),* **absurdly** *(adv).*

**abundant** *(adj)* If there is an **abundant** supply of something, there is plenty of it. **abundance** *(n),* **abundantly** *(adv).*

**abuse abusing abused 1** *(ab-yuce) (n)* rude or unkind words. **abuse** *(ab-yooze) (v),* **abusive** *(adj).* **2** *(ab-yooze) (v)* to treat a person or creature cruelly. **abuse** *(ab-**yuce**) (n).* 3 *(ab-**yuce**) (n)* wrong or harmful use of something. *Alcohol abuse.*

**abysmal** *(ab-**iz**-mal) (adj)* very bad, or terrible. **abysmally** *(adv).*

**abyss** *(ab-**iss**)* **abysses** *(n)* a very deep hole that seems to have no bottom.

**academic** 1 *(adj)* to do with study and learning. *Academic work.* 2 *(n)* someone who teaches in a university or college, or someone who does research.

**accelerate** **accelerating accelerated** *(v)* to get faster and faster. **acceleration** *(n).*

**accent** 1 *(n)* the way that you pronounce words. *Helmut speaks with a German accent.* 2 *(n)* a mark put over a letter in some languages to show how it is pronounced, for example, café.

**accentuate** **accentuating accentuated** *(v)* to emphasize or draw attention to something.

**accept** **accepting accepted** 1 *(v)* to take something that you are offered. 2 *(v)* to agree to something.

**access** **accesses** 1 *(n)* an entrance or approach to a place. **accessible** *(adj).* 2 *(n)* the right to see someone. *Lucy's father has access at weekends.*

**accessory** **accessories** 1 *(n)* an extra part for something. *Computer accessories.* 2 *(n)* something, like a belt or a scarf, that goes with your clothes.

**accident** *(n)* something that takes place unexpectedly, and which often involves people being hurt. **accidental** *(adj).*

**acclimatize** *or* **acclimatise** **acclimatizing acclimatized** *(v)* to get used to a different climate or to new surroundings. **acclimatization** *(n).*

**accommodation** *(n)* a place where people live. **accommodate** *(v).*

**accompany** **accompanies accompanying accompanied** 1 *(v)* to go somewhere with someone. 2 *(v)* to support a musician or singer by playing a musical instrument. **accompanist** *(n).*

**accomplice** *(ak-**um**-pliss) (n)* someone who helps a person to commit a crime.

**accomplish** **accomplishes accomplishing accomplished** *(v)* to do something successfully.

**according to** 1 *(prep)* as someone has said or written. *According to Amy, all boys are stupid!* 2 *(prep)* in a way that is suitable. *You'll be paid according to how much work you do.* **accordingly** *(adv).*

**account** 1 *(n)* a description of something that has happened. 2 *(n)* money in a bank or building society that you can add to or take from, when needed.

**accountant** *(n)* an expert in finance and keeping accounts.

**accumulate** **accumulating accumulated** *(v)* to collect things or let them pile up. **accumulation** *(n).*

**accurate** *(adj)* exactly correct. **accuracy** *(n),* **accurately** *(adv).*

**accuse** **accusing accused** *(v)* to say that someone has done something wrong. **accusation** *(n),* **accuser** *(n).*

**accustomed** 1 *(adj)* When you are **accustomed to** something, you are used to it. 2 *(adj)* usual. *My accustomed seat.*

**ace** 1 *(n)* a playing card with only one symbol on it. 2 *(n)* a serve in tennis that is impossible to hit back.

**ache** *(rhymes with take) (n)* a dull pain that goes on and on. **ache** *(v).*

**achieve** *(ach-**eev**)* **achieving achieved** *(v)* to do something successfully, especially after a lot of effort. **achievement** *(n).*

**acid** 1 *(n)* a substance that turns blue litmus paper red. **acidic** *(adj).* 2 *(adj)* sour, or bitter. **acidic** *(adj).*

**acid rain** *(n)* rain that is polluted by acid in fumes and damages the environment.

**acknowledge** **acknowledging acknowledged** 1 *(v)* to admit to something. *I acknowledged my mistake.* 2 *(v)* to show that you have seen and recognized somebody. *Toby walked straight past without acknowledging me.*

**acne** *(**ak**-nee) (n)* lots of red pimples on the skin, especially on the face.

**acoustic** *(a-**koo**-stik)* 1 *(adj)* to do with sound or hearing. 2 **acoustics** *(plural n)* If a place has good **acoustics**, you can hear sounds and music very clearly inside it.

**acquaintance** *(n)* someone you have met, but do not know very well.

**acquire** **acquiring acquired** *(v)* to obtain or get something.

**acrobatics** *(plural n)* difficult and exciting gymnastic acts. *The picture shows a "human column", an example of acrobatics.* **acrobat** *(n),* **acrobatic** *(adj).*

**acronym** *(n)* a word made from the first or first few letters of the words of a phrase. *Radar is an acronym for radio detecting and ranging.*

**acrylic** *(ak-**rill**-ik) (n)* a chemical substance used to make fibres and paints.

**act acting acted 1** *(v)* to do something. *We must act now to save the rainforests.* **act** *(n).* **2** *(v)* to perform in a play, film, etc. **3** *(v)* to have an effect. *This drug acts very quickly.* **4** *(n)* a short performance. *A comedy act.* **5** *(n)* a part of a play.

**action 1** *(n)* something that you do to achieve a result. *Kamran's rapid action prevented an accident.* **2** When you **take action**, you do something for a purpose.

**active** *(adj)* energetic and busy.

**activity activities 1** *(n)* action, or movement. *The playground was full of activity.* **2** *(n)* something that you do for pleasure. *Leisure activities.*

**actor** *(n)* someone who performs in the theatre, films, television, etc.

**actual** *(adj)* real, or true. **actually** *(adv).*

**acupuncture** *(**ak**-yoo-punk-cher) (n)* a way of treating illness by pricking parts of the body with small needles.

**acute acuter acutest 1** *(adj)* sharp, or severe. *Acute pain.* **2** *(adj)* able to detect things easily. *Dogs have an acute sense of smell.* **3** *(adj)* An **acute** angle is an angle of less than 90°.

**AD** the initials of the Latin phrase *Anno Domini*, which means "in the year of Our Lord". AD is used to show that a date comes after the birth of Christ. *Columbus discovered America in AD1492.*

**adapt adapting adapted 1** *(v)* to make something suitable for a different purpose. *We have adapted our garage to make a games room.* **2** *(v)* to change because you are in a new situation. *It can be hard to adapt to a new school.*

**adapter** *or* **adaptor** *(n)* a type of electrical plug that you use to connect two or more plugs to one socket.

**add adding added 1** *(v)* to put one thing with another. *Add the eggs to the flour.* **2** *(v)* to put numbers together.

**adder** *(n)* a small poisonous snake, sometimes called a viper.

**addictive** *(adj)* very hard to give up. *Smoking is addictive.* **addict** *(n).*

**additive** *(n)* something added to a substance to change it in some way. *The additives give my yogurt colour.*

**address addresses addressing addressed 1** *(n)* details of the place where someone lives. **2** *(v)* to write an address on a letter, card, or package. **3** *(v)* to give a speech. *Mo addressed the meeting on racial equality.* **address** *(n).*

**adenoids** *(**ad**-in-oyds) (plural n)* spongy lumps of flesh at the back of your nose.

**adequate** *(adj)* just enough, or good enough. **adequately** *(adv).*

**adhesive** *(n)* a substance, such as glue, that makes things stick together.

**adjective** *(n)* a word that describes someone or something. *In the phrase "A tall, handsome stranger", "tall" and "handsome" are adjectives.* *See* page 3.

**adjudicate adjudicating adjudicated** *(v)* to judge something, like a competition.

**adjust adjusting adjusted 1** *(v)* to move or change something slightly. **adjustment** *(n).* **2** *(v)* to get used to something new and different. **adjustment** *(n).*

**ad lib ad libbing ad libbed** *(v)* to speak in public without preparing first.

**administrate administrating administrated** *(v)* to manage and control an organization. **administration** *(n).*

**admiral** *(n)* an officer who holds a very high rank in the British navy.

**admire admiring admired 1** *(v)* to like and respect someone. **admiration** *(n).* **2** *(v)* to look at something and enjoy it.

**admit admitting admitted 1** *(v)* to confess to something, or agree that something is true, often reluctantly.

admission *(n)*. 2 *(v)* to allow someone or something to enter. **admission** *(n)*.

**admonish admonishes admonishing admonished** *(v)* to tell someone off, or to warn someone. **admonishment** *(n)*.

**adolescent** *(n)* a young person who is more grown-up than a child, but is not yet an adult. **adolescence** *(n)*, **adolescent** *(adj)*.

**adopt adopting adopted** *(v)* When a couple **adopt** a child, they take it into their family and become its legal parents. **adoption** *(n)*.

**adore adoring adored** *(v)* to love someone or something very much. **adoration** *(n)*.

**adorned** *(adj)* decorated. **adorn** *(v)*.

**adrenaline** *(n)* a chemical produced by your body when you are excited, frightened, or angry.

**adult** *(n)* a fully-grown person or animal. **adulthood** *(n)*, **adult** *(adj)*.

**adulterate adulterating adulterated** *(v)* to spoil something by adding something less good to it.

**adultery** *(n)* If someone commits **adultery**, they are unfaithful to their husband or wife by having sexual intercourse with somebody else.

**advance advancing advanced 1** *(v)* to move forward, or to make progress. **advancement** *(n)*. 2 *(adj)* happening before something else. *Advance warning.* 3 *(v)* to lend money. **advance** *(n)*. 4 *(n)* a movement forward by a group of soldiers.

**advanced 1** *(adj)* If something is at an **advanced** stage, it is nearly finished. 2 *(adj)* **Advanced** work is not elementary or easy. *Advanced level science.*

**advantage 1** *(n)* something that helps you or is useful to you. 2 If you **take advantage of** a person or situation, you use them for your own benefit.

**advent 1** *(n)* the beginning of something important. *The advent of civilization.* 2 **Advent** *(n)* the weeks leading up to Christmas in the Christian church's year.

**adventure** *(n)* an exciting or dangerous experience. **adventurous** *(adj)*.

**adverb** *(n)* a word usually used to describe a verb. Adverbs tell how, when, where, how often, or how much something happens. *"Slowly", "late", and "soon" are all adverbs. See* page 3.

**adversary adversaries** *(n)* someone who fights or argues against you.

**adverse** *(adj)* unfavourable, or difficult. *Adverse weather.* **adversely** *(adv)*.

**advertise advertising advertised** *(v)* to give information about something that you want to sell. **advertisement** *(n)*.

**advice** *(n)* suggestions about what someone should do. *Shahid gave me good advice on how to mend my bike.*

**advisable** *(adj)* sensible and worth doing. **advisably** *(adv)*.

**advise advising advised** *(v)* to give someone information or suggestions, so that they can decide what to do. *Tom advised me to stay at home.* **adviser** *(n)*.

**aerial** *(air-ee-ul)* **1** *(n)* a piece of wire that receives television or radio signals. **2** *(adj)* happening in the air. *Aerial refuelling.*

**aerobatics** *(plural n)* skilful or dangerous movements made by aircraft in the sky. *The picture shows a plane performing the positive flick roll, an example of aerobatics.* **aerobatic** *(adj)*.

**aerobics** *(plural n)* energetic exercises performed to music. **aerobic** *(adj)*.

**aerodynamic** *(adj)* designed to move through the air very easily and quickly.

**aeroplane** *(n)* a machine with wings and an engine, that flies through the air.

**aerosol** *(n)* a can containing liquid which is forced out in a fine spray.

**affair 1** *(n)* a special event. *The wedding was a grand affair.* **2 affairs** *(plural n)* business connected with private or public life. *Personal affairs. Business affairs.*

**affect affecting affected** *(v)* to change or influence someone or something. *Lance's accident affected him badly.*

**affection** *(n)* a great liking for someone or something.

**affectionate** *(adj)* very loving.

**affirmative** *(adj)* giving the answer "yes". *Joe answered in the affirmative.*

**affluent** *(adj)* If you are **affluent**, you have plenty of money. **affluence** *(n).*

**afford** **affording afforded** 1 *(v)* If you can **afford** something, you have enough money to buy it. 2 *(v)* to have enough time or ability to do something. *I'm so far ahead, I can afford to relax.*

**afloat** *(adj)* floating on water.

**afraid** 1 *(adj)* frightened, or worried. 2 *(adj)* sorry. *I'm afraid I can't come.*

**aft** *(adv)* towards the back of a ship or an aeroplane.

**after** 1 *(prep)* later than. *After lunch.* 2 *(prep)* following. *The puppy ran after her.* 3 *(prep)* trying to catch someone or something. *The police are after him.*

**afternoon** *(n)* the time of day between midday and about five o'clock in the evening.

**against** 1 *(prep)* next to and touching. *Put your ear against the wall.* 2 *(prep)* competing with. *It's the Dodgers against the Vikings tonight.* 3 *(prep)* opposed to. *I'm against killing whales.*

**age** **ageing** *or* **aging aged** 1 *(n)* the number of years that someone has lived or that something has existed. 2 *(n)* a period of time in history. *The Stone Age.* 3 *(v)* to become or seem older.

**aged** 1 *(rhymes with caged) (adj)* being a particular number of years old. *Anyone aged 12 can join our club.* 2 *(**ay**-jid) (adj)* Someone who is **aged** is very old.

**ageism** *or* **agism** *(n)* discrimination or prejudice because of age. **ageist** *(adj).*

**agenda** *(a-**jen**-der) (n)* a list of things that need to be done or discussed.

**agent** 1 *(n)* someone who arranges things for other people. *Travel agent.* **agency** *(n).* 2 *(n)* a spy. *Secret agent.*

**aggravate** **aggravating aggravated** 1 *(v)* to make a difficult situation even worse. 2 *(v)* to annoy someone.

**aggression** *(n)* fierce or threatening behaviour. **aggressive** *(adj),* **aggressively** *(adv).*

**aghast** *(ur-**gast**) (adj)* shocked, or dismayed. *Al was aghast at our plans.*

**agile** *(adj)* able to move fast and easily. **agility** *(n).*

**agism** *see* **ageism**.

**agitate** **agitating agitated** *(v)* to make someone nervous and worried. **agitation** *(n),* **agitated** *(adj).*

**agnostic** *(n)* someone who believes that you cannot know that God exists.

**ago** *(adv)* before now, or in the past. *Three days ago.*

**agony** **agonies** *(n)* great pain or suffering. *David was screaming in agony.*

**agree** **agreeing agreed** 1 *(v)* to say yes to something. *I agreed to Sally's plan.* **agreement** *(n).* 2 *(v)* to share the same opinions. *Dan and I always agree on politics.* **agreement** *(n).*

**agriculture** *(n)* farming. **agricultural** *(adj),* **agriculturally** *(adv).*

**aground** *(adv)* If a boat runs **aground**, it gets stuck on the bottom in shallow water.

**ahead** 1 *(adv)* in front. *Go on ahead.* 2 *(adv)* in the future. *Think ahead.*

**aid** **aiding aided** 1 *(v)* to help someone. **aid** *(n).* 2 *(n)* money or equipment for people in need. *Foreign aid.*

**AIDS** *(n)* a fatal illness in which the body's ability to protect itself against disease is destroyed. AIDS stands for acquired immune deficiency syndrome.

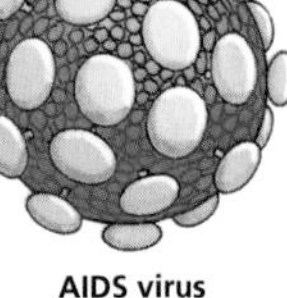
**AIDS virus**
(magnified)

**ailment** *(n)* an illness, though not usually a serious one.

**aim** **aiming aimed** 1 *(v)* to hit, throw, or shoot something in a particular direction. **aim** *(n).* 2 *(v)* to intend to achieve something. *I aim to become a chef.*

**air** **airing aired** 1 *(n)* the invisible mixture of gases around you that you need to breathe. 2 *(v)* to let air into a room. 3 *(n)* an appearance, or manner. *Wanda has an air of mystery.*

**air conditioning** *(n)* a system for keeping the air in a building cool and clean when it is hot outside.

**aircraft** *(n)* a vehicle that can fly.

**aircraft-carrier** *(n)* a warship with a flat deck where aircraft take off and land.

**air force** *(n)* a part of a country's fighting force that can attack or defend from the air.

**airline** *(n)* a company that owns and flies aircraft, carrying people and goods by air.

**airmail** *(n)* a postal service by which letters, packages, etc. are carried abroad by aircraft.

**airport** *(n)* a place where aircraft take off and land and where people get on and off planes.

**airship** *(n)* a large air balloon with engines and a passenger compartment hanging underneath it.

**airtight** *(adj)* If a container is **airtight**, it is sealed so that no air can get in or out.

**aisle** *(rhymes with pile) (n)* the passage that runs between the rows of seats in a church, cinema, aircraft, etc.

**ajar** *(adj)* If a door is **ajar**, it is partly open. **ajar** *(adv).*

**alarm alarming alarmed 1** *(n)* a device, containing a bell, buzzer, or siren, that wakes someone or warns them of danger. **2** *(n)* a sudden fear that something bad will happen. *Don't worry, there's no cause for alarm.* **3** *(v)* to make someone afraid that something bad might happen. *I don't want to alarm you, but I can smell smoke.*

**albino** *(al-**bee**-no) (n)* a person or animal born without any natural colouring in their skin, hair, or eyes.

**album 1** *(n)* a book in which you keep photographs, stamps, etc. **2** *(n)* a collection of pieces of music recorded on a CD, tape, or record.

**alcohol** *(n)* a colourless liquid found in drinks such as wine, whisky, and beer, which can make people drunk.

**alcoholic 1** *(adj)* containing alcohol. **2** *(n)* **Alcoholics** cannot stop themselves from drinking alcohol. **alcoholism** *(n).*

**alert alerting alerted 1** *(adj)* If you are **alert**, you pay attention to what is happening and are ready for action. **2** *(v)* to warn someone that there might be danger. *Alert the fire brigade!* **3** *(n)* a warning of danger. *A nuclear alert.*

**algae** *(**al**-jee) (plural n)* small plants that grow without roots or stems in water or on damp surfaces.

**algebra** *(**al**-jer-bra) (n)* a type of mathematics in which signs and letters are used to represent numbers, for example, 2x + y = 7.

**alias** *(**ay**-lee-uss)* **aliases** *(n)* a false name.

**alibi** *(**al**-ee-bye) (n)* a claim that a person accused of a crime was somewhere else when the crime was committed.

**alien** *(**ay**-lee-un)* **1** *(n)* a creature from another planet. **2** *(adj)* different and strange. *An alien culture.*

**alike 1** *(adj)* looking or acting the same. *The twins are alike.* **2** *(adv)* in a similar way. *All the children were treated alike.*

**alive 1** *(adj)* living. **2** *(adj)* full of life.

**alkali** *(**al**-ka-**lye**) (n)* a substance which turns red litmus paper blue. **alkaline** *(adj).*

**Allah** *(n)* the Muslim name for God.

**allegiance** *(a-**lee**-jenss) (n)* loyal support for someone or something.

**allergic** *(adj)* If you are **allergic** to something, it makes you ill. **allergy** *(n).*

**alliance** *(n)* a friendly agreement to work together.

**alligator** *(n)* a large reptile with strong jaws and very sharp teeth.

**alligator**

**alliteration** *(n)* repeated use of the same sound at the beginning of a group of words, for example, "The gruesome ghost gave a ghastly groan." **alliterative** *(adj).*

**allocate allocating allocated** *(v)* to decide that something should be used for a particular purpose. *We allocated half the money to charity.* **allocation** *(n).*

**allotment** *(n)* a small piece of land that people can rent and use to grow vegetables, fruit, or flowers.

**allow allowing allowed** *(v)* to let someone have or do something.

**allowance** *(n)* money given to someone regularly.

**alloy** *(n)* a mixture of two or more metals.

**all right** 1 *(adj)* good enough, or acceptable. 2 *(adj)* not hurt, or not ill. 3 *(interject)* You say **all right** when you agree to do something.

**ally** *(al-eye)* **allies** *(n)* a person or country that gives support to another.

**almighty** 1 *(adj)* very big. *An almighty crash.* 2 *(adj)* possessing total power.

**almost** *(adv)* very nearly.

**alone** *(adj)* by yourself. **alone** *(adv).*

**along** 1 *(prep)* from one end to the other. *We drove along the street.* 2 **all along** *(adv)* all the time. *I knew all along that Hal was lying.*

**aloud** *(adv)* in a voice that other people can hear. *Reading aloud.*

**alphabet** *(n)* all the letters of a language arranged in order. **alphabetical** *(adj).*

**already** *(adv)* before now. *I've seen that film already.*

**altar** *(n)* a large table in a church or temple, used for religious ceremonies.

**alter altering altered** *(v)* to change something. *We've altered our plans.*

**alternate** *(ol-ter-nat) (adj)* If something happens on **alternate** days, it happens every second day.

**alternative** 1 *(n)* something that you can choose to have or do instead of something else. **alternative** *(adj),* **alternatively** *(adv).* 2 *(adj)* different from what is usual. *Alternative medicine.*

**alternative energy** *(n)* energy from natural sources, such as the Sun, waves, and wind. *See* **wind turbine**.

**although** 1 *(conj)* in spite of something. *Although it was raining, we all enjoyed ourselves.* 2 *(conj)* but. *Natalie is only nine, although she seems much older.*

**altitude** *(n)* the height of something above the ground. *This plane can fly at very high altitudes.*

**altogether** 1 *(adv)* in total. *Pippa has seven hats altogether.* 2 *(adv)* completely, or entirely. *What I told you wasn't altogether true.* 3 *(adv)* on the whole. *Altogether, it was a very good party.*

**aluminium** *(n)* a light, silver-coloured metal.

**always** *(adv)* If something is **always** happening, it happens all the time or very many times.

**a.m.** the initials of the Latin phrase *ante meridiem*, which means "before midday". *I get up at 7 a.m.*

**amateur** *(n)* someone who takes part in a sport or other activity for pleasure rather than for money.

**amaze amazing amazed** *(v)* to make someone feel very surprised. **amazement** *(n),* **amazing** *(adj),* **amazingly** *(adv).*

**ambidextrous** *(adj)* able to use both hands equally well, especially for writing.

**ambiguous** *(am-**big**-yoo-uss) (adj)* If something is **ambiguous,** it can be understood in more than one way. *Conrad gave an ambiguous answer.*

**ambition** 1 *(n)* something you really want to do. *My ambition is to be a film star.* 2 *(n)* a strong wish to be successful. *Ed is driven by ambition.* **ambitious** *(adj).*

**amble ambling ambled** *(v)* to walk slowly because you are not in a hurry.

**ambulance** *(n)* a vehicle that takes people to hospital when they are ill.

**ambush ambushes ambushing ambushed** *(v)* to hide and then attack someone. **ambush** *(n).*

**ammunition** *(n)* things that can be fired from weapons, such as bullets or arrows.

**amoeba** *(am-ee-ber)* **amoebas** *or* **amoebae** *(n)* a microscopic creature made of only one cell.

**among** *or* **amongst** 1 *(prep)* surrounded by other people or things. 2 *(prep)* If you share something **among** several people, you divide it between them.

**amount amounting amounted** 1 *(n)* The **amount** of something is how much of it there is. 2 *(v)* If something **amounts to** a total, it adds up to it.

**amphibian** 1 *(n)* an animal that lives on land, but breeds in water. **amphibious** *(adj).* 2 *(n)* a vehicle that can travel on land and in water. **amphibious** *(adj).*

**amphitheatre** *(n)* a large, open-air building, built in Roman times, with rows of seats in a high circle around an arena.

**ample ampler amplest** 1 *(adj)* more than enough. *There was ample food for* *everyone.* **amply** *(adv).* 2 *(adj)* large. *Moira has an ample figure.*

**amplifier** *(n)* a piece of equipment that makes sound louder. **amplification** *(n).*

**amputate amputating amputated** *(v)* to cut off someone's arm or leg because it is damaged or diseased. **amputation** *(n).*

**amuse amusing amused** 1 *(v)* to make someone laugh or smile. **amusing** *(adj).* 2 *(v)* to keep someone happy and stop them from being bored. **amusement** *(n).*

**anaemic** *(a-nee-mik) (adj)* If you are **anaemic**, you become easily tired and weak because your blood does not contain enough iron. **anaemia** *(n).*

**anaesthetic** *(an-iss-thet-ik) (n)* a drug or gas given to someone before an operation to prevent them from feeling pain.

**anagram** *(n)* a word or phrase made by changing the order of letters in another word or phrase. *Pea is an anagram of ape.*

**analyse analysing analysed** *(v)* to examine something carefully in order to understand it. **analysis** *(n).*

**anarchy** *(n)* a situation with no order and no one in control. **anarchist** *(n).*

**anatomy** 1 *(n)* The **anatomy** of a person or an animal is the structure of their body. 2 *(singular n)* the study of how the bodies of people and animals fit together.

**ancestor** *(n)* Your **ancestors** are members of your family who lived a long time ago. **ancestry** *(n),* **ancestral** *(adj).*

**anchor** *(n)* a heavy metal hook which is lowered from a ship or boat to stop it drifting. **anchor** *(v).*

**ancient** *(ayn-shent)* 1 *(adj)* very old. 2 *(adj)* belonging to a time long ago. *An ancient monument. Ancient Rome.*

**android** *(n)* a robot that acts and looks like a human being.

**anecdote** *(n)* a short, funny story about something that has happened.

**angel** 1 *(n)* a messenger of God. **angelic** *(adj).* 2 *(n)* a very kind, gentle person. **angelic** *(adj).*

**anger** *(n)* the feeling of being very annoyed.

**angle** 1 *(n)* the space between two lines at the point where they touch. *Angles are measured in degrees, for example, 90°.* 2 *(n)* a way of looking at something. *Leroy approached the problem from a different angle.* 3 If something is **at an angle**, it is sloping and not straight.

**angling** *(n)* the sport of fishing with a fishing rod rather than a net. **angler** *(n).*

**angora** *(n)* fluffy wool made from the hair of angora rabbits and sheep's wool.

**angry angrier angriest** *(adj)* If you are **angry**, you feel that you want to argue or fight with someone. **angrily** *(adv).*

**anguish** *(n)* a strong feeling of misery or distress. **anguished** *(adj).*

**angular** *(adj)* Something that is **angular** has a lot of straight lines and sharp corners. *Foxy had a thin, angular face.*

**animal** *(n)* any living creature that can breathe and move about.

**animated** 1 *(adj)* lively. *An animated conversation.* **animation** *(n).* 2 *(n)* An **animated film** is made by filming a series of drawings very quickly, one after the other, so that the characters in the drawings seem to move. **animation** *(n).*

**ankle** *(n)* the joint that connects your foot to your leg.

**annex annexes annexing annexed** *(v)* When one country **annexes** another, it takes control of it by force.

**annexe** *(n)* an extra building which joins on to or stands near a main building.

**annihilate** *(an-eye-ill-ate)* **annihilating annihilated** *(v)* to destroy something completely. **annihilation** *(n).*

**anniversary anniversaries** *(n)* a date which people remember because something important happened on that date in the past.

**annotate annotating annotated** *(v)* to write notes explaining a piece of writing.

**announce announcing announced** *(v)* to say something officially or publicly. **announcement** *(n).*

**announcer** *(n)* someone who introduces programmes on television or radio.

**annoy annoying annoyed** *(v)* to make someone feel angry. **annoyance** *(n).*

**annual** 1 *(adj)* happening once every year or over a period of one year. *An annual competition. An annual subscription.* 2 *(n)* a book published once a year.

**anon** *short for* **anonymous**.

**anonymous** *(adj)* written, done, or given by a person whose name is not known. *An anonymous letter.* **anonymity** *(n).*

**anorak** *(n)* a waterproof jacket with a hood.

**anorexia** *(n)* If someone suffers from **anorexia**, they think they are too fat and so they eat very little and become dangerously thin. **anorexic** *(adj).*

**another** 1 *(adj)* one more of the same kind. *Have another sweet.* 2 *(pronoun)* a different one. *I didn't like the red dress, so I chose another.*

**answer** **answering answered** 1 *(v)* to say or write something as a reply to a question. **answer** *(n).* 2 *(n)* the solution to a problem. *Is there an answer to world poverty?* 3 *(v)* If you **answer back**, you make a rude or cheeky reply. 4 If someone has **a lot to answer for**, they have caused a lot of trouble.

**answering machine** *(n)* a machine connected to or built into a telephone, which records messages from people who telephone while you are out.

**ant** *(n)* a small insect with no wings that lives in a group called a colony.

**antagonize** *or* **antagonise** **antagonizing antagonized** *(v)* If you **antagonize** someone, you make them feel very angry with you. **antagonism** *(n).*

**Antarctic** *(n)* the area around the South Pole. **Antarctic** *(adj).*

**anteater** *(n)* a South American mammal with a very long tongue that it uses to search for ants and other small insects.

**antelope** *(n)* a large animal like a deer, that runs very fast. Antelopes are found in Africa and parts of Asia.

**antenna** **antennas** *or* **antennae** 1 *(n)* a feeler on the head of an insect. 2 *(n)* a piece of wire that receives radio and television signals.

**anthem** *(n)* a religious or national song, usually sung by a choir.

**anthology** **anthologies** *(n)* a collection of poems or stories by different writers which are all printed in the same book.

**antibiotic** *(n)* a drug, such as penicillin, that kills bacteria and cures infections.

**antibody** **antibodies** *(n)* Your blood makes **antibodies** to fight against infection.

**anticipate** **anticipating anticipated** *(v)* to expect something to happen and be prepared for it. *The police anticipate trouble after the match.* **anticipation** *(n).*

**anticlimax** **anticlimaxes** *(n)* If something is an **anticlimax**, it is not as exciting as you expected.

**anticlockwise** *(adv)* in the opposite direction from that of the hands of a clock. **anticlockwise** *(adj).*

**antidote** *(n)* something that stops a poison from working.

**antique** *(an-teek)* 1 *(n)* a very old object that is valuable because it is rare or beautiful. 2 *(adj)* very old.

**antiseptic** *(n)* a substance that kills germs and prevents infection.

**antisocial** 1 *(adj)* If someone behaves in an **antisocial** way, they do something that upsets or harms other people. 2 *(adj)* If somebody is **antisocial**, they do not enjoy being with other people.

**antler** *(n)* one of the two large, branching structures on a stag's head.

**anxiety** *(ang-**zye**-it-ee)* **anxieties** *(n)* a feeling of worry or fear.

**anxious** *(**ank**-shuss)* 1 *(adj)* worried. *Mum gets anxious when I'm late.* **anxiously** *(adv).* 2 *(adj)* very keen to do something. *Sid is anxious to succeed.*

**anyhow** 1 *(adv)* in any case. *I didn't want to come anyhow.* 2 *(adv)* carelessly. *She threw her things down just anyhow!*

**anyway** *(adv)* in any case. *I never liked him anyway.*

**anywhere** *(adv)* in or to any place. *I'd follow Jason anywhere.*

**apart** *(adv)* If two people or things are **apart**, they are separated from each other.

**apartheid** *(a-**part**-ate)* *(n)* a political system in which people of different races are kept apart from each other.

**apartment** *(n)* the American word for a flat.

**apathetic** *(adj)* If you are **apathetic**, you do not care about anything or want to do anything. **apathy** *(n).*

**ape** *(n)* a large animal like a monkey, but with no tail. Gorillas, gibbons, and chimpanzees are all kinds of ape. *The picture shows an ape searching for food.*

**chimpanzee**

**apex** apexes *(n)* the highest point of something. *The apex of a triangle.*

**apologize** *or* **apologise** apologizing apologized *(v)* to say that you are sorry about something. **apology** *(n).*

**apostle** *(n)* one of the twelve men chosen by Christ to spread his teaching.

**apostrophe** *(a-poss-trer-fee) (n)* a punctuation mark (') used to show ownership, for example, "Jane's bag", or to show that letters have been missed out, for example, "can't".

**appalling** *(adj)* horrifying and shocking.

**apparatus** 1 *(n)* equipment used for performing sports, especially gymnastics. 2 *(n)* equipment or machines used to do a job or laboratory experiment.

**apparent** 1 *(adj)* obvious, or clear. *Bill's guilt was apparent to us all.* 2 *(adj)* seeming real or true. *Claudia's apparent confidence is a sham.* **apparently** *(adv).*

**appeal** appealing appealed 1 *(v)* to ask for something urgently. 2 *(v)* to ask for a decision made by a court to be changed. 3 *(v)* If something **appeals** to you, you like it or find it interesting.

**appear** appearing appeared 1 *(v)* to come into sight. **appearance** *(n).* 2 *(v)* to seem. **appearance** *(n).*

**appendicitis** *(n)* If someone has **appendicitis**, their appendix is infected and very painful.

**appendix** appendices *or* appendixes 1 *(n)* a small, closed tube attached to your large intestine. 2 *(n)* extra information at the end of a book.

**appetite** 1 *(n)* desire for food. 2 *(n)* great enjoyment of something. *Sadjit has a real appetite for work.*

**appetizing** *or* **appetising** *(adj)* looking and smelling good to eat.

**applaud** applauding applauded *(v)* to show that you like something, usually by clapping your hands. **applause** *(n).*

**apple** *(n)* a round, usually crispy fruit.

**application** 1 *(n)* a written request for something, like a job. **applicant** *(n).* 2 *(n)* a way of using something. *Our computer system has many applications.*

**apply** applies applying applied 1 *(v)* to ask for something in writing. 2 *(v)* to be relevant. *These rules don't apply to us.*

**appointment** 1 *(n)* an arrangement to meet someone at a fixed time. 2 *(n)* a job.

**appreciate** appreciating appreciated 1 *(v)* to enjoy or value somebody or something. **appreciation** *(n).* 2 *(v)* to understand something. *I appreciate your point of view.*

**apprehensive** *(adj)* worried and slightly afraid. *Dolores was apprehensive about making her speech.* **apprehension** *(n).*

**apprentice** *(n)* someone who learns a trade or craft by working with a craftsman and going to college. **apprenticeship** *(n).*

**approach** approaches approaching approached 1 *(v)* to move nearer. 2 *(v)* If you **approach** somebody, you go up to them and talk to them.

**approachable** *(adj)* friendly and easy to talk to.

**appropriate** *(ap-ro-pree-ut) (adj)* suitable, or right. **appropriately** *(adv).*

**approve** approving approved 1 *(v)* If you **approve of** someone or something, you think that they are acceptable or good. **approval** *(n).* 2 *(v)* to accept a plan or an idea. **approval** *(n).*

**approximate** *(adj)* more or less accurate or correct. *An approximate price.*

**apricot** *(n)* a small, soft fruit with an orange skin.

**apron** *(n)* a piece of clothing that you wear to protect your clothes when you are cooking, painting, etc.

**apt** 1 *(adj)* very suitable. *An apt reply.* 2 *(adj)* quick to learn things. 2 *(adj)* If you are **apt** to do something, you are likely to do it.

**aptitude** *(n)* a natural ability to do something well. *Gerald has an aptitude for looking after animals.*

**aquarium** **aquariums** *or* **aquaria** *(n)* a glass tank in which you can keep fish.

**aqueduct** *(n)* a large bridge built to carry water across a valley. *The Roman aqueduct shown below was built in France in AD14.*

aqueduct

**Arabic** 1 *(n)* a language spoken by many people in the Middle East and North Africa. 2 *(n)* **Arabic numerals** are the sort of figures, such as 1,2,3, that we use today.

**arable** *(adj)* **Arable** land is used for growing crops.

**arbitrate** **arbitrating** **arbitrated** *(v)* to help two sides to reach an agreement. **arbitration** *(n)*, **arbitrator** *(n)*.

**arc** *(n)* a curved line.

**arcade** 1 *(n)* a row of arches in a building. 2 **amusement arcade** *(n)* a covered area with machines, such as video games, that you pay to play on. 3 **shopping arcade** *(n)* a covered passageway with shops or stalls.

**arch** **arches** **arching** **arched** 1 *(n)* a curved structure. Arches often support a building or bridge. 2 *(v)* to curve. *The cat arched its back and spat.* **arched** *(adj)*. 3 *(adj)* chief. *Karen is my arch-enemy.*

**archaeology** *or* **archeology** *(ar-kee-**ol**-oh-jee) (n)* a way of learning about the past by digging up old buildings and objects and examining them carefully. **archaeologist** *(n)*, **archaeological** *(adj)*.

**archbishop** *(n)* one of the most important leaders in the Christian church.

**archeology** *see* **archaeology**.

**archery** *(n)* the sport of shooting at targets, using a bow and arrow. **archer** *(n)*.

**architect** *(**ar**-ki-tekt) (n)* someone who designs buildings and checks that they are built correctly.

**architecture** 1 *(n)* the activity of designing buildings. 2 *(n)* the style in which buildings are designed. *Modern architecture.* **architectural** *(adj)*.

**arctic** 1 **the Arctic** *(n)* the frozen area around the North Pole. **Arctic** *(adj)*. 2 *(adj)* extremely cold and wintry.

**ardent** *(adj)* If you are **ardent** about something, you feel very strongly about it.

**arduous** *(**ard**-yoo-uss) (adj)* very difficult and demanding a lot of effort.

**area** 1 *(n)* the size of a surface. 2 *(n)* part of a place. *A poor area of the country.*

**arena** *(n)* a large area, used for sports or entertainment.

**argue** **arguing** **argued** 1 *(v)* to disagree with someone angrily. **argument** *(n)*, **argumentative** *(adj)*. 2 *(v)* to give your opinion about something. *Sean argued that whaling was cruel.* **argument** *(n)*.

**arid** *(adj)* Land that is **arid** is extremely dry because very little rain falls on it.

**arise** **arising** **arose** **arisen** 1 *(v)* If something, like a problem, **arises**, it comes into being. 2 *(v) (old fashioned)* to stand up. *Arise, Sir Francis!*

**aristocrat** *(n)* a member of the highest social rank, or nobility. **aristocracy** *(n)*, **aristocratic** *(adj)*.

**arithmetic** *(n)* calculations with numbers. Addition, subtraction, multiplication, and division are all types of arithmetic.

**arm** **arming** **armed** 1 *(n)* the part of your body between your shoulder and your hand. 2 *(v)* If a country **arms** itself, it gets ready for war. 3 **arms** *(plural n)* weapons.

**armadillo** *(n)* a mammal covered by hard, bony plates.

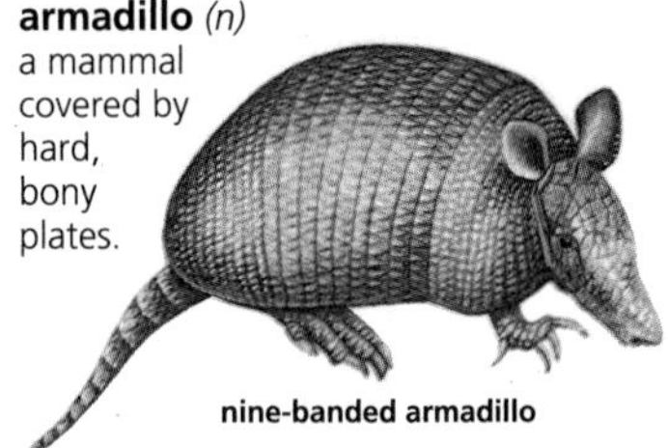

nine-banded armadillo

**armchair** *(n)* a comfortable chair with supports for your arms.

**armistice** *(n)* an agreement to stop fighting a war.

**armour** *(n)* metal covering worn by soldiers to protect them in battle.

**armpit** *(n)* the area under your arm where it joins your shoulder.

**army armies** *(n)* a large group of people trained to fight on land.

**aroma** *(n)* a pleasant smell.

**around 1** *(prep)* surrounding, or in a circle. *He tied a rope around the tree.* **2** *(adv)* in many different parts of a place. *We travelled around Spain.* **3** *(adv)* more or less. *There were around 30 of us.*

**arouse arousing aroused 1** *(v)* to wake someone. **2** *(v)* to stir up a feeling. *Tarquin's behaviour aroused my curiosity.*

**arrange arranging arranged 1** *(v)* to make plans for something to happen. **arrangement** *(n).* **2** *(v)* to place things so that they look attractive. **arrangement** *(n).* **3** *(n)* If someone has an **arranged marriage**, their parents choose a husband or wife for them.

**arrest arresting arrested** *(v)* to take someone prisoner. **arrest** *(n).*

**arrive arriving arrived 1** *(v)* to reach a place. *We arrived home early.* **arrival** *(n).* **2** *(v)* to come. *The great day arrived.*

**arrogant** *(adj)* conceited and proud. **arrogance** *(n),* **arrogantly** *(adv).*

**arrow 1** *(n)* a pointed stick, shot from a bow. **2** *(n)* a sign showing a direction.

**arson** *(n)* If someone commits **arson**, they deliberately and wrongly set fire to something. **arsonist** *(n).*

**art 1** *(n)* the skill of creating something beautiful by drawing, painting, or making things with your hands. **2** *(n)* something that requires a lot of skill. *The art of Chinese cookery.* **3 the arts** *(plural n)* forms of entertainment, such as music, theatre, and film.

**artery arteries** *(n)* one of the tubes that carry blood from your heart to all the other parts of your body. **arterial** *(adj).*

**arthritis** *(n)* a disease which makes people's joints swollen and painful.

**article 1** *(n)* an object, or a thing. **2** *(n)* a piece of writing published in a newspaper or magazine. **3** *(n)* a word, such as "a", "the", or "some", that goes in front of a noun.

**articulate** *(adj)* If you are **articulate**, you can express yourself clearly in words.

**artificial** *(adj)* false, not real, or not natural. *Artificial flowers.*

**artificial intelligence** *(n)* the use of computers to do things that previously needed human intelligence, such as understanding language.

**artist** *(n)* someone very skilled at painting, drawing, or making things. **artistic** *(adj),* **artistically** *(adv).*

**ascend** *(ass-end)* **ascending ascended** *(v)* to move upwards. **ascent** *(n).*

**ash ashes** *(n)* the powder that remains after something has been burnt.

**ashamed** *(adj)* If you are **ashamed**, you feel embarrassed and guilty.

**aside** *(adv)* to one side, or out of the way. *Sarah pushed her brothers aside.*

**ask asking asked 1** *(v)* to make a request or put a question to someone. **2** *(v)* to invite someone to do something.

**asleep** *(adj)* sleeping.

**aspect** *(n)* one feature or characteristic of something. *Robbie enjoys most aspects of school life.*

**aspiration** *(n)* a strong desire to do something great or important. *You need aspirations in order to succeed.* **aspire** *(v).*

**aspirin** *(n)* a drug that relieves pain and reduces fever.

**ass asses 1** *(n)* a donkey. **2** *(n) (informal)* a stupid person.

**assassinate assassinating assassinated** *(v)* to murder an important person. **assassin** *(n),* **assassination** *(n).*

**assault assaulting assaulted** *(v)* to attack someone or something violently. **assault** *(n).*

**assemble assembling assembled 1** *(v)* to gather together in one place. *All the school assembled in the hall.* **2** *(v)* to put all the parts of something together. *Fatima assembled the model.*

**assembly** *(n)* a meeting of lots of people.

**assent assenting assented** *(v)* to agree to something. **assent** *(n).*

**assertive** *(adj)* able to stand up for yourself and tell other people what you think or want. **assertiveness** *(n).*

**assess** assesses assessing assessed *(v)* to judge how good or bad something is. **assessment** *(n),* **assessor** *(n).*

**asset** *(n)* something or somebody who is helpful or useful. *Imran is a great asset to our team.*

**assignment** *(n)* a special job that is given to somebody. **assign** *(v).*

**assistant** *(n)* a person who helps someone else to do a task or job.

**association** 1 *(n)* an organization, club, or society. 2 *(n)* a connection that you make in your mind between different things. *Our holiday house has many happy associations for me.* **associate** *(v).*

**assonance** *(n)* repeated use of the same vowel sound in words that are close together, for example, "Fly by in the sky".

**assortment** *(n)* a mixture of different things. **assorted** *(adj).*

**assume** assuming assumed 1 *(v)* to suppose that something is true, without checking it. *I assume that you're right.* **assumption** *(n).* 2 *(v)* If you **assume** responsibility for something, you agree to look after it. 3 *(n)* An **assumed name** is a false name.

**assure** assuring assured 1 *(v)* to promise something, or say something positively. *Annie assured me of her support.* 2 *(v)* If you **assure** yourself about something, you make certain about it.

**asterisk** *(n)* a mark (*) used in printing and writing.

**asteroid** *(n)* a very small planet that travels round the Sun.

**asthma** *(ass-mer) (n)* If you have **asthma**, you sometimes wheeze and find it hard to breathe. **asthmatic** *(n),* **asthmatic** *(adj).*

**astonish** astonishes astonishing astonished *(v)* to make someone feel very surprised. **astonishment** *(n).*

**astray** 1 *(adv)* If something has gone **astray**, it has been lost. 2 If someone **leads you astray**, they encourage you to do something wrong.

**astride** *(prep)* If you sit **astride** something, like a horse or a bicycle, you sit with a leg on either side of it.

**astrology** *(n)* the study of stars and planets and the way they are supposed to affect people's lives. **astrologer** *(n).*

**astronaut** *(n)* someone who travels in space. *The picture shows an astronaut operating a manned manoeuvring unit (MMU), which is used for moving around outside the spaceship.*

**astronaut with manned manoeuvring unit**
(spacesuit cutaway)

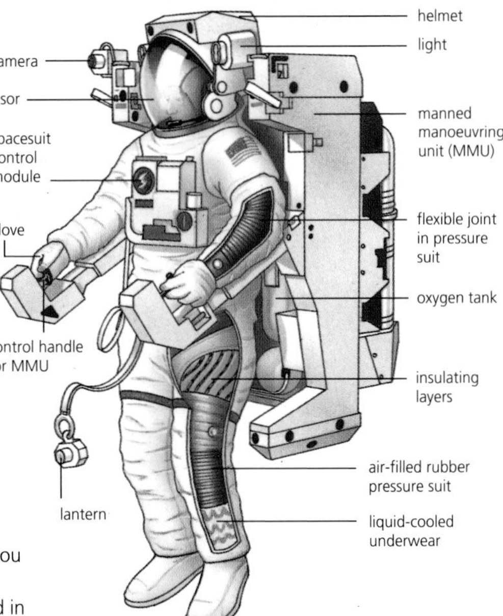


**astronomical** 1 *(adj)* to do with astronomy. 2 *(adj)* very large. *An astronomical amount of money.*

**astronomy** *(n)* the study of stars, planets and space. **astronomer** *(n).*

**asymmetrical** *(adj)* A shape that is **asymmetrical** cannot be divided into two equal halves.

**atheist** *(ay-thee-ist) (n)* someone who does not believe that there is a God. **atheism** *(n).*

**athlete** 1 *(n)* someone who takes part in sports such as running, jumping, and throwing. 2 *(n)* someone who is very good at sports. **athletic** *(adj).*

**athletics** *(n)* competitive sports that involve running, jumping, or throwing. **athletic** *(adj).*

**atlas** *(n)* a book of maps.

**atmosphere** *(at-muss-fear)* 1 *(n)* the mixture of gases that surrounds a planet. *The layers of the Earth's atmosphere are shown in this diagram.* 2 *(n)* the air in a particular place. *The atmosphere in some of our cities is very polluted.* **atmospheric** *(adj).* 3 *(n)* a mood or feeling created by a place or a work of art. *I didn't like the atmosphere in Uncle Merlin's house.* **atmospheric** *(adj).*

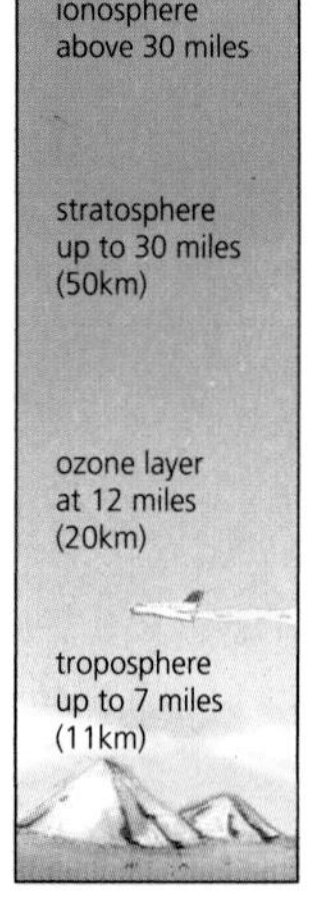


**layers of the atmosphere**

**atom** *(n)* the smallest part of a substance. Everything is made up of atoms.

**atomic** 1 *(adj)* to do with atoms. *Atomic structure.* 2 *(adj)* using the power created when atoms are split. *Atomic energy.*

**atone atoning atoned** *(v)* If you **atone** for something, you make up for it. *Kate atoned for her lateness by working hard.*

**atrocious** *(at-roh-shuss) (adj)* disgusting, or terrible. **atrociously** *(adv).*

**atrocity atrocities** *(n)* a very wicked or cruel act, often involving killing.

**attach attaches attaching attached** 1 *(v)* to join or fix one thing to another. **attachment** *(n).* 2 If you are **attached to** someone, you are very fond of them. **attachment** *(n).*

**attack attacking attacked** 1 *(v)* to try to hurt someone or something. **attack** *(n),* **attacker** *(n).* 2 *(v)* to criticize someone strongly. **attack** *(n).* 3 *(v)* to try to defeat an enemy or capture a place where the enemy is. *The troops attacked the castle.* **attack** *(n).* 4 *(n)* a sudden period of illness. *A bad attack of flu.*

**attainment** *(n)* an achievement. **attain** *(v),* **attainable** *(adj).*

**attempt attempting attempted** *(v)* to try to do something. **attempt** *(n).*

**attend attending attended** 1 *(v)* to be present in a place or at an event. *Thousands of people attended the concert.* **attendance** *(n).* 2 *(v)* If you **attend to** something, you deal with it.

**attendant** *(n)* someone who looks after an important person or place. *A museum attendant.*

**attention** 1 *(n)* concentration and careful thought. *Attention to detail.* 2 If you **pay attention**, you concentrate on something. 3 When soldiers **stand to attention**, they stand up straight, with their feet together and their arms down by their sides.

**attic** *(n)* a room in the roof of a building.

**attitude** 1 *(n)* your opinions and feelings about someone or something. *Aidan has a positive attitude towards his work.* 2 *(n)* the position in which you are standing or sitting.

**attract attracting attracted** 1 *(v)* If something **attracts** you, you are interested in it. **attraction** *(n).* 2 *(v)* If a person **attracts** you, you like them. **attraction** *(n).* 3 *(v)* If something **attracts** objects or people to itself, it pulls them towards itself. *Magnets attract iron and steel.* **attraction** *(n).*

**attractive** 1 *(adj)* pleasant, or pretty to look at. **attractiveness** *(n),* **attractively** *(adv).* 2 *(adj)* interesting, or exciting. *An attractive plan.* **attractiveness** *(n).*

**auburn** *(or-burn) (n)* a reddish-brown colour. **auburn** *(adj).*

**auction** *(n)* a sale where goods are sold to the person who offers the most money for them. **auctioneer** *(n).*

**audience** 1 *(n)* the people who watch or listen to a performance, speech, or show. 2 *(n)* a formal meeting with an important or powerful person. *An audience with the ambassador.*

**audio-visual** *(adj)* Audio-visual equipment uses sound and pictures, often to teach people something.

**audition** *(n)* a short performance by an actor, singer, etc. to see whether they are suitable for a part in a play, concert, etc. **audition** *(v)*.

**aunt** *(n)* the sister of your father or mother, or the wife of your uncle.

**au pair** *(oh-pair) (n)* a young person from another country who lives with a family and helps them, usually in order to learn a language.

**aural** *(or-al) (adj)* to do with listening. *My piano exam includes an aural test.*

**author** *(n)* the writer of a book, play, or poem. **authorship** *(n)*.

**authority** **authorities** 1 *(n)* the right to do something or to tell other people what to do. *The detectives have authority to search the house.* 2 *(n)* a group of people with power in a certain area. *A local health authority.* 3 *(n)* someone who knows a lot about a particular subject. *Sam is an authority on computers.*

**authorize** *or* **authorise** **authorizing** **authorized** *(v)* to give permission for something to happen. **authorization** *(n)*.

**autistic** *(adj)* Someone who is **autistic** has a mental illness which prevents them from communicating normally or from forming proper relationships with people.

**autobiography** **autobiographies** *(n)* a book that tells the story of the writer's life. **autobiographical** *(adj)*.

**autograph** *(n)* a famous person's signature.

**automatic** 1 *(adj)* An **automatic** machine can perform some actions without anyone operating it. 2 *(adj)* An **automatic** action happens without you thinking about it. **automatically** *(adv)*.

**autumn** *(n)* the season between summer and winter, when it gets colder and the leaves fall from the trees. **autumnal** *(adj)*.

**available** 1 *(adj)* ready to be used or bought. **availability** *(n)*. 2 *(adj)* not busy, and so free to see people. **availability** *(n)*.

**avalanche** *(av-er-larnsh) (n)* a large mass of snow and ice that suddenly moves down the side of a mountain.

**avenue** *(n)* a wide road in a town or city, often with trees on either side.

**average** 1 *(n)* In maths, you find an **average** by adding a group of figures together and then dividing the total by the number of figures you have added. *The average of 2, 4, and 6 is 4.* 2 *(adj)* usual, or ordinary. *An average day.*

**aviary** **aviaries** *(n)* a large cage for birds.

**aviation** *(n)* the science of building and flying aircraft. **aviator** *(n)*.

**avoid** **avoiding** **avoided** 1 *(v)* to keep away from a person or place. 2 *(v)* to try to prevent something from happening. *We must avoid making any mistakes.*

**await** **awaiting** **awaited** *(v)* to wait for or expect someone or something.

**awake** **awaking** **awoke** **awoken** 1 *(adj)* not asleep. *I'm wide awake.* 2 *(v)* to wake up. **awakening** *(n)*.

**award** **awarding** **awarded** *(v)* to give something to someone officially, often as a prize. **award** *(n)*.

**aware** *(adj)* If you are **aware** of something, you know that it exists. **awareness** *(n)*.

**away** 1 *(adv)* moving from a place, person, or thing. *Rosie ran away from me.* 2 *(adv)* distant from a place. *Three miles away.* 3 *(adv)* not at home, or not present. *Lizzie is away this week.*

**awe** *(n)* a feeling of admiration and respect, and a little fear. **awesome** *(adj)*.

**awful** 1 *(adj)* terrible, or horrible. 2 *(adj) (informal)* very great. *Lizzie spent an awful lot of money.* **awfully** *(adv)*.

**awkward** 1 *(adj)* causing difficulties. *An awkward catch.* **awkwardly** *(adv)*. 2 *(adj)* not able to relax and talk to people easily. **awkwardly** *(adv)*.

**axe** **axing** **axed** 1 *(n)* a tool with a sharp blade on the end of a long handle, used for chopping wood. 2 *(v)* to bring something to an end, usually in order to save money. *200 jobs will be axed.*

**axis** **axes** 1 *(n)* an imaginary line through the middle of an object, around which that object spins. *The Earth's axis.* 2 *(n)* a line at the side or the bottom of a graph.

**axle** *(n)* a rod in the centre of a wheel, around which the wheel turns.

# Bb

**babble** **babbling babbled** 1 *(v)* to talk in an excited way, without making any sense. 2 *(v)* to make sounds like a baby.

**baboon** *(n)* a large monkey that lives in Africa.

**olive baboons**

**baby** **babies** *(n)* a newly born or very young child or animal. **babyish** *(adj).*

**baby-sitter** *(n)* someone who is paid to stay in the house and look after children while their parents are out.

**bachelor** *(n)* a man who has never been married.

**back** **backing backed** 1 *(n)* the rear part of your body between your neck and your bottom. 2 *(n)* the opposite end or side from the front. **back** *(adj).* 3 *(adv)* to where someone or something was before. *Ed came back.* 4 *(v)* to support someone. 5 **back down** *(v)* to admit that you were wrong. 6 **back out** *(v)* to decide not to do something that you had agreed to do.

**backfire** **backfiring backfired** 1 *(v)* If a car **backfires**, there is a small explosion inside its exhaust pipe. 2 *(v)* If an action **backfires**, it does not work out as you had planned.

**background** 1 *(n)* the part of a picture that is behind the main subject. 2 *(n)* the facts or events that surround something and help to explain why it happened.

**backhand** *(n)* a stroke in tennis that you play with the back of your hand facing outwards and your arm across your body.

**backpack** 1 *(n)* a large bag that you carry on your back when you are walking or climbing. 2 *(n)* If you go **backpacking**, you go on a long walk or hike.

**backstroke** *(n)* a style of swimming in which you swim lying on your back.

**backwards** 1 **backwards or backward** *(adv)* in the direction that your back is facing. *Joe stepped backwards.* 2 *(adv)* in the opposite to the usual way. *Say the alphabet backwards.*

**bacteria** *(plural n)* microscopic living things which exist all around you and inside you. Many bacteria are useful, but some cause disease.

**bad** **worse worst** 1 *(adj)* not good. 2 *(adj)* serious. *A bad mistake.* 3 *(adj)* not fit to eat. *This fish has gone bad.*

**badge** *(n)* a small sign with a picture or message on it, that you pin to your clothes.

**badger** **badgering badgered** 1 *(n)* a mammal with a grey body and a black and white head. 2 *(v)* to keep asking someone to do something. *Fran badgered me to let her come with us.*

**badly** 1 *(adv)* not well, or not skilfully. 2 *(adv)* urgently. *I want it badly.*

**badminton** *(n)* a game like tennis, in which players use rackets to hit a shuttlecock over a high net.

**baffle** **baffling baffled** *(v)* to confuse or puzzle someone. **baffling** *(adj).*

**baggage** *(n)* suitcases and bags.

**baggy** **baggier baggiest** *(adj)* hanging in loose folds. *Baggy shorts.*

**bagpipes** *(plural n)* a musical instrument, played in Scotland and some other countries.

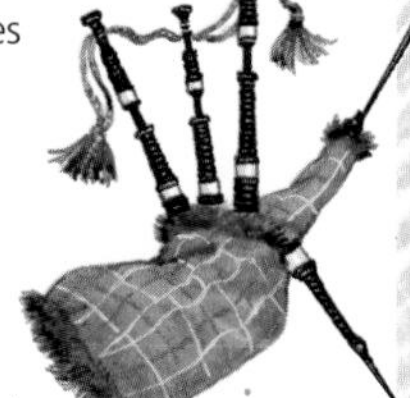

**Scottish bagpipes**

**bail** *(n)* a sum of money paid to a court to allow someone accused of a crime to be set free until their trial. *Jackson was released on bail.*

**bail out** *see* **bale out**.

**bait** *(n)* food used to attract a fish or an animal, so that you can catch them.

**bake** **baking baked** 1 *(v)* to cook food in an oven, especially bread or cakes. **baker** *(n),* **bakery** *(n).* 2 *(v)* to heat something in order to make it hard. *Bake the clay in a kiln before glazing it.*

**balaclava** *(n)* a woolly hat that covers your head and neck, like a helmet.

**balance** **balancing** **balanced** **1** *(v)* When two things **balance** in a pair of scales, they weigh the same and do not tip the scales either way. **2** *(n)* Your **balance** is your ability to keep steady and not fall over. **3** *(v)* If you **balance** something, you keep it steady and do not let it fall.

**balcony** **1** *(n)* a platform with railings on the outside of a building, usually on an upper level. **2** *(n)* the upstairs seating in a theatre.

**bald** *(borld)* **balder** **baldest** **1** *(adj)* Someone who is **bald** has very little or no hair on their head. **2** *(adj)* A **bald** fact or statement is stated simply, without any attempt to make it more pleasant.

**bale out** *or* **bail out** **baling out** **baled out** **1** *(v)* to jump out of an aircraft, using a parachute. **2** *(v)* If you **bale someone out**, you help them out of a difficult situation.

**ball** **1** *(n)* a round object, used in games. **2** *(n)* something made into a round shape. *A ball of wool.* **3** *(n)* a very formal party where people dance.

**ballad** *(n)* a song or poem that tells a story.

**ball bearings** *(n)* small metal balls used to help parts of machinery move more smoothly against each other.

**ballerina** *(n)* a leading woman ballet dancer.

**ballet** *(bal-ay)* **1** *(n)* a style of dance with set movements. **2** *(n)* a performance using dance and music, often to tell a story.

**balloon** **1** *(n)* a small bag made of thin rubber that is blown up and used as a decoration. **2** *See* **hot-air balloon**.

**ballot** *(n)* a secret way of voting for something.

**ballpoint** *(n)* a pen with a tiny ball at its tip that lets ink flow as you write.

**balsa** *(n)* a very light wood, used for making models.

**bamboo** *(n)* a tropical plant with a hard, hollow stem, often used for making furniture.

**ban** **banning** **banned** *(v)* to forbid something. **ban** *(n)*.

**banana** *(n)* a tropical fruit that is long, curved, and yellow.

**band** **banding** **banded** **1** *(n)* a narrow ring of rubber, paper, or other material, that is put around something to hold it together. **2** *(n)* a group of people who play music together. **3** *(v)* When people **band together**, they join together in a group in order to do something.

**bandage** *(n)* a long piece of cloth that is wrapped around an injured part of the body to protect it. **bandage** *(v)*.

**bandit** *(n)* an armed robber, usually one of a gang, who attacks travellers.

**bang** **banging** **banged** **1** *(n)* a sudden loud noise. **2** *(v)* to knock hard against something. **bang** *(n)*.

**banger** **1** *(n)* a firework that makes a loud noise. **2** *(n)* *(informal)* an old, battered car. **3** *(n)* *(slang)* a sausage.

**bangle** *(n)* a band of metal, plastic, etc. worn around the wrist.

**banish** **banishes** **banishing** **banished** *(v)* to send someone away from a place and order them not to return.

**banister** *or* **bannister** *(n)* a rail that runs along the side of a flight of stairs.

**bank** **banking** **banked** **1** *(n)* a place where people keep their money. **2** *(n)* the land along the side of a river or a canal. **3** *(n)* a place where something is stored and collected. *A bottle bank.* **4** **bank holiday** *(n)* a public holiday in Britain when the banks are closed. **5** *(v)* If you **bank on** something, you rely on it.

**banknote** *(n)* a piece of paper money.

**bankrupt** *(adj)* If a person or company is **bankrupt**, they cannot pay their debts.

**banner** *(n)* a long piece of material with writing on it, often carried in sports crowds and processions.

**bannister** *see* **banister**.

**banns** *(plural n)* an announcement of a wedding made in a church.

**banquet** *(n)* a formal meal for lots of people, usually on a special occasion.

**banter** **bantering** **bantered** *(v)* to tease someone in a friendly way. **banter** *(n)*.

**baptize** *or* **baptise** **baptizing** **baptized** *(v)* to pour water on someone's head, or to immerse someone in water, as a sign that they have become a Christian. **baptism** *(n)*.

**bar** 1 *(n)* a long stick of metal. *An iron bar.* 2 *(n)* a long, flat block of something hard. *A chocolate bar.* 3 *(n)* a place where drinks, especially alcoholic drinks, are sold.

**barbarian** *(n)* a member of a wild and uncivilized tribe that lived in the past.

**barbaric** *(adj)* very cruel.

**barbecue** 1 *(n)* a charcoal grill used for cooking meat and other food out of doors. 2 *(n)* an outdoor meal or party in which food is cooked using a barbecue.

**barbed wire** *(n)* wire with small spikes along it, used for fences.

**barber** *(n)* someone who cuts men's and boys' hair.

**bar code** *(n)* a band of thick and thin lines printed on goods sold in shops, which gives information about the goods.

**bare baring bared; barer barest** 1 *(adj)* wearing no clothes. 2 *(adj)* empty. *A bare room.* 3 *(v)* to uncover or reveal something. *The dog bared its teeth. Verity bared her secret thoughts.* 4 *(adj)* plain and simple. *Give me the bare facts.*

**bareback** *(adv)* If you ride a horse **bareback**, you do not use a saddle.

**barefaced** *(adj)* open and undisguised. *Barefaced cheek.*

**barely** *(adv)* only just. *Tarquin was so scared that he could barely speak.*

**bargain** 1 *(n)* something that you buy for less than the usual price. *This coat was a real bargain.* 2 *(n)* an agreement to do something in return for something else. **bargain** *(v).*

**barge barging barged** 1 *(n)* a long, flat-bottomed boat, used on canals. 2 *(v)* If you **barge** into someone, you knock against them roughly or push them out of the way.

**bark barking barked** 1 *(v)* When a dog **barks**, it makes a loud sound in its throat. **bark** *(n).* 2 *(n)* the hard covering on the outside of a tree. 3 *(v)* to shout at someone gruffly. *"Attention!" barked the sergeant.*

**bar mitzvah** *(n)* a celebration on a Jewish boy's 13th birthday, after which he can take part in his religion as an adult.

**barn** *(n)* a farm building where crops or animals are kept.

**barnacle** *(n)* a small shellfish that sticks itself firmly to rocks and other shellfish.

**barometer** *(n)* an instrument that measures changes in air pressure and shows how the weather will change.

**barracks barracks** *(n)* the buildings where soldiers live.

**barrage** 1 *(n)* a dam built across a river to control the level of the water. 2 *(n)* a large amount of something that all comes at the same time. *A barrage of letters.*

**barrel** 1 *(n)* a container for liquid, such as water or beer, which has curved sides and a flat top and bottom. 2 *(n)* the long part of a gun that looks like a tube.

**barren** *(adj)* If land is **barren**, farmers cannot grow crops on it.

**barricade barricading barricaded** 1 *(n)* a wall built in a hurry to stop people from getting past. 2 *(v)* If people **barricade** themselves into a place, they build walls to stop other people reaching them.

**barrier** 1 *(n)* a bar, fence, or wall that prevents people, traffic, water, etc. from going past it. 2 *(n)* something that stops you from communicating properly with someone else. *A language barrier.*

**barrow** 1 *(n)* a small cart used for carrying things. 2 *(n)* a mound of earth made to cover a grave in prehistoric times.

**barter bartering bartered** *(v)* to trade by exchanging food and other goods, rather than by using money. **barter** *(n).*

**base basing based** 1 *(n)* the lowest part of something, or the part that it stands on. 2 *(v)* to use something as the starting point for something else. *I based my story on a real event.* 3 *(n)* the place from which a business, army, etc. is controlled.

**baseball equipment**

**baseball** *(n)* an American game, played with a bat and ball and two teams of nine players. *The picture shows a baseball bat, ball, and glove.*

**basement** *(n)* an area or room in a building below ground level.

**bashful** *(adj)* shy. **bashfully** *(adv).*

**basic 1** *(adj)* simple and straightforward. **2 basics** *(plural n)* the most important things to know about a subject.

**basin 1** *(n)* a large bowl used for washing, usually fixed to a wall. **2** *(n)* a deep bowl, often used for mixing food.

**basis** *(n)* the idea or reason behind something. *The basis of a plan.*

**bask basking basked 1** *(v)* to lie or sit in the sunshine and enjoy it. **2** *(v)* If you **bask in** praise, you enjoy it.

**basket** *(n)* a container, usually with handles, made of cane, wire, etc.

**basketball** *(n)* a game played by two teams who try to score points by throwing a ball into a high net at the end of a court. *The picture shows a basketball player running, jumping, and shooting.*

**bat batting batted 1** *(n)* a small, flying mammal that comes out at night to feed. **2** *(n)* a piece of wood used for hitting the ball in games such as cricket, baseball, etc. *See* **baseball**. **3** *(v)* to take a turn at hitting the ball and scoring runs in games such as cricket and baseball. **batsman** *(n).*

**batch batches** *(n)* a group of things that arrive together or are made together.

**bath 1** *(n)* a large, open container for water in which you sit and wash your whole body. **2 baths** *(plural n)* a public swimming pool.

**bathe bathing bathed 1** *(v)* to go swimming in the sea or in a stream. **bather** *(n).* **2** *(v)* If you **bathe** part of your body that is sore, you wash it gently in water or antiseptic.

**bathroom** *(n)* a room that contains a bath, and often a shower and a toilet.

**batik** *(bat-**eek**)* *(n)* an Eastern method of printing designs on cloth. Parts of the cloth are covered with wax so that they are not coloured when the cloth is dyed.

**baton 1** *(n)* a short, thin stick used by a conductor to beat time for an orchestra. **2** *(n)* a short stick passed from one runner to another in a relay race.

**batter battering battered 1** *(n)* to hit someone or something many times. **battered** *(adj).* **2** *(v)* If someone **batters down** a door, they break through it by hitting it many times. **3** *(n)* a mixture of milk, eggs, and flour that can be cooked to make pancakes or used to coat food which you fry.

**battering ram** *(n)* a heavy, wooden beam, sometimes protected by a hut on wheels, that is rammed against an enemy's walls or gates.

**medieval battering ram**

**battery batteries** *(n)* a container full of chemicals which produce electrical power.

**battery farming** *(n)* a way of breeding and rearing poultry or cattle, or of producing eggs, in which a large number of animals are kept in small cages or pens.

**battle 1** *(n)* a fight between two armies. **2** *(n)* a struggle with someone.

**bawl bawling bawled 1** *(v)* to cry loudly like a baby. **2** *(v)* to shout loudly in a harsh voice. *"Get off my bike!" bawled Damian.*

**bay 1** *(n)* a part of the coast that curves inwards. **2** If you keep something or someone **at bay**, you fight them off. *Anna managed to keep her fears at bay.* **3 bay window** *(n)* a window that sticks out from the side of a house.

**bayonet** *(n)* a long knife that can be fitted to the end of a rifle.

**bazaar 1** *(n)* a street market, especially one held in Eastern countries. **2** *(n)* a sale held to raise money for charity.

**BC** the initials of the phrase "before Christ". BC is used to show that a date comes before the birth of Jesus Christ. *Julius Caesar died in 44BC.*

**beach** beaches *(n)* a strip of sand or pebbles where land meets water.

**beacon** *(n)* a light or fire used as a signal or warning.

**bead** *(n)* a small piece of glass, wood, or plastic with a hole through the middle, that can be threaded on to a string.

**beak** *(n)* the hard part of a bird's mouth.

**beaker** 1 *(n)* a tall drinking cup. 2 *(n)* a plastic or glass jar used in chemistry.

**beam** beaming beamed 1 *(n)* a thick ray of light from a torch, headlight, etc. 2 *(n)* a long, thick piece of wood, concrete, or metal that supports the roof or floors of a building. 3 *(v)* to smile widely. **beam** *(n)*.

**bean** 1 *(n)* **Beans** are large seeds that you can eat or that can be used to make a drink. *Baked beans. Coffee beans.* 2 *(informal)* If you are **full of beans**, you are very lively.

**bear** bearing bore borne 1 *(v)* to support or carry something. 2 *(v)* When a tree or plant **bears** fruit, flowers, or leaves, it produces them. 3 *(v)* to put up with something. 4 *(n)* a large, heavy mammal with thick fur. *The picture shows a young grizzly bear catching a salmon.*

grizzly bear

**beard** *(n)* the hair on a man's face.

**beast** 1 *(n) (old-fashioned)* a wild animal. 2 *(n) (informal)* a horrible or unkind person. **beastliness** *(n)*, **beastly** *(adj)*.

**beat** beating beat beaten 1 *(v)* to hit someone or something many times. **beating** *(n)*. 2 *(v)* to defeat someone in a game or contest. *Sue beat Cuthbert at chess.* 3 *(n)* the regular rhythm of a piece of music or of your heart. 4 *(v)* If you **beat** a mixture, you stir it up quickly with a whisk or fork.

**beautiful** *(adj)* very pleasant to look at or listen to. **beauty** *(n)*, **beautifully** *(adv)*.

**beaver** beavering beavered 1 *(n)* an animal with a wide, flat tail, that lives both on land and in water. 2 *(v)* If you **beaver away** at something, you work very hard at it.

**because** *(conj)* for the reason that. *I came because I wanted to see you.*

**beckon** beckoning beckoned *(v)* to make a sign to someone, asking them to come. *Jack beckoned us to follow him.*

**become** becoming became *(v)* to start to be. *When did you become suspicious?*

**bed** 1 *(n)* a piece of furniture that you sleep on. 2 *(n)* a place in a garden where flowers are planted. 3 *(n)* the bottom of an ocean or river.

**bedclothes** *(n)* sheets, duvets, blankets, etc.

**bedridden** *(adj)* If you are **bedridden**, you are too ill to get out of bed.

**bedsitter** *(n)* a rented room that someone lives and sleeps in.

**bee** *(n)* a flying insect, with yellow and black stripes, that makes honey.

**beehive** *(n)* a box used for keeping bees so that their honey can be collected.

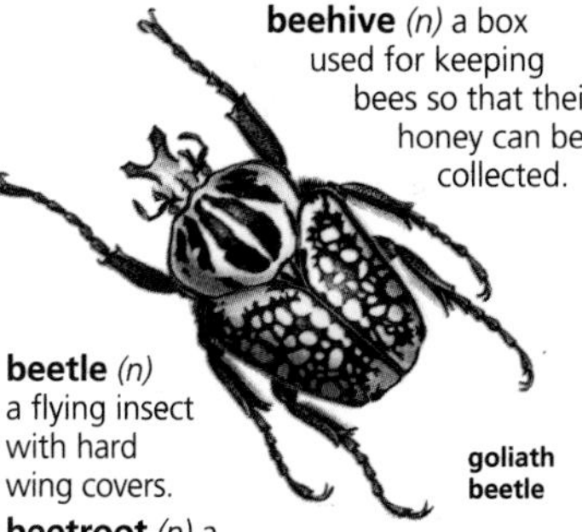
goliath beetle

**beetle** *(n)* a flying insect with hard wing covers.

**beetroot** *(n)* a purplish-red root vegetable.

**before** 1 *(prep)* sooner or earlier than. *The time before last.* 2 *(adv)* earlier. *I've been here before.*

**beg** begging begged 1 *(v)* to ask someone for help, especially for money or food. **beggar** *(n)*. 2 *(v)* to plead with someone to do something.

**begin** beginning began begun *(v)* to start. **beginner** *(n)*, **beginning** *(n)*.

**behalf** If you do something **on behalf** of someone else, you do it for them, or in their place. *On behalf of my family, I'd like to thank you all for coming.*

**behave** behaving behaved 1 *(v)* to do and say things in a particular way. *Matthew behaved very strangely.* **behaviour** *(n).* 2 *(v)* to act properly and avoid causing trouble.

**behind** 1 *(prep)* on the other side, or towards the back of something. *Look behind the curtain!* 2 *(prep)* further back, or in a lower position. *Joshua finished the race behind me.* 3 *(adv)* not making good progress. *I'm behind with my work.*

**beige** *(bayjh) (n)* a pale brown colour.

**belch** belches belching belched *(v)* to let out gases from your stomach through your mouth with a loud noise. **belch** *(n).*

**believe** believing believed 1 *(v)* to feel sure that something is true. **belief** *(n),* **believer** *(n).* 2 *(v)* to support someone or something. *I believe in rights for children.*

**bell** 1 *(n)* an instrument which makes a ringing sound. 2 *(informal)* If something **rings a bell**, you think you have heard it somewhere before.

**bellow** bellowing bellowed 1 *(v)* to shout or roar. **bellow** *(n).* 2 **bellows** *(plural n)* an instrument used for pumping air into something like an organ or a fire.

**belly** bellies *(n)* the stomach, or the part of a human's or animal's body that contains their stomach.

**belong** belonging belonged 1 *(v)* If something **belongs** to you, you own it. **belongings** *(plural n).* 2 *(v)* If you **belong** to a group, you are a member of it. 3 *(v)* If something **belongs** somewhere, that is its proper place.

**below** 1 *(prep)* lower than. 2 *(prep)* at or to a lower place. *We hid below the stairs.*

**belt** belting belted 1 *(n)* a strip of leather or other material that you wear around your waist. 2 *(n)* a moving band of rubber, used for transporting objects or for driving machinery. *Conveyor belt.* 3 *(v) (informal)* to hit someone hard. 4 *(v) (informal)* to travel very fast. 5 *(n)* an area, or strip. *Commuter belt. A belt of rain.*

**bench** benches 1 *(n)* a long, narrow seat for several people, usually made of wood. 2 *(n)* a table in a workshop or laboratory.

**bend** bending bent 1 *(v)* If you **bend**, **bend down**, or **bend over**, you lean forward from your waist. 2 *(v)* If something **bends**, it changes direction by turning to one side. *The road bends to the left.* **bend** *(n).* 3 *(v)* to change the shape of something so that it is not straight.

**beneath** 1 *(prep)* underneath. 2 *(prep)* lower than, or not worthy. *It's beneath my dignity to talk to her.*

**beneficial** *(adj)* Something that is **beneficial** is good for you.

**benefit** benefiting benefited 1 *(v)* If you **benefit** from something, you get an advantage from it or are helped by it. **benefit** *(n).* 2 *(n)* money paid by the government to people who need it, such as people who are poor, ill, disabled, or unemployed.

**bent** 1 *(adj)* crooked or curved. 2 *(adj) (slang)* dishonest.

**bereaved** *(adj)* A person is **bereaved** if a friend or relative of theirs has died.

**berry** berries *(n)* a small, often brightly coloured fruit, found on bushes or trees.

**berth** 1 *(n)* a bed in a ship, train, or caravan. 2 *(n)* a place in a harbour where a boat is tied up.

**beside** 1 *(prep)* next to. 2 If you are **beside yourself**, you are overcome with emotion. *Ann is beside herself with rage.*

**besides** 1 *(prep)* as well as, or apart from. *Who went to the match besides Jim?* 2 *(adv)* also, or in addition to this. *I hate boats and, besides, I can't swim.*

**besiege** besieging besieged *(v)* to surround a place to make it surrender.

**best** 1 *(adj)* better than everything else. 2 When you **do your best**, you try as hard as you can to do something. 3 **best man** *(n)* the friend of the bridegroom who helps him at his wedding.

**bet** betting bet 1 *(v)* to risk money on the result of something, such as a horse race. If you guess the result correctly, you win some money, if not, you lose money. **betting** *(n).* 2 *(v)* If you **bet** someone that they cannot do something, you dare them to do it. *I bet you can't climb that tree!* 3 *(v)* If you **bet** that someone does something, you predict that they will do it. *I bet Mona will trip over that cat.*

**betray** betraying betrayed 1 *(v)* If you betray someone, you deliberately let them down or do something to hurt them.

**betrayal** *(n).* 2 *(v)* If you **betray** your feelings, you cannot keep them hidden.

**better** 1 *(adj)* more suitable, or higher in quality. 2 *(adj)* no longer ill or hurting. 3 **better off** *(adj)* richer.

**between** 1 *(prep)* If something is **between** two things, it has them on either side of it. *Dan stood between two trees.* 2 *(prep)* from one to the other. *We threw the ball between us.* 3 *(prep)* somewhere within two limits. *Nadya left between three and four o'clock.*

**beverage** *(n)* a drink.

**biased** *(by-urst) (adj)* prejudiced, or favouring one person or point of view more than another. *Jonathan thinks that the referee is biased against our team.* **bias** *(n).*

**Bible** *(n)* the holy book of the Christian religion.

**bicycle** *(n)* a two-wheeled vehicle which you ride by steering with handlebars, and pushing the pedals. *The mountain bike shown below is a type of bicycle that has been specially developed for off-road cycling.*

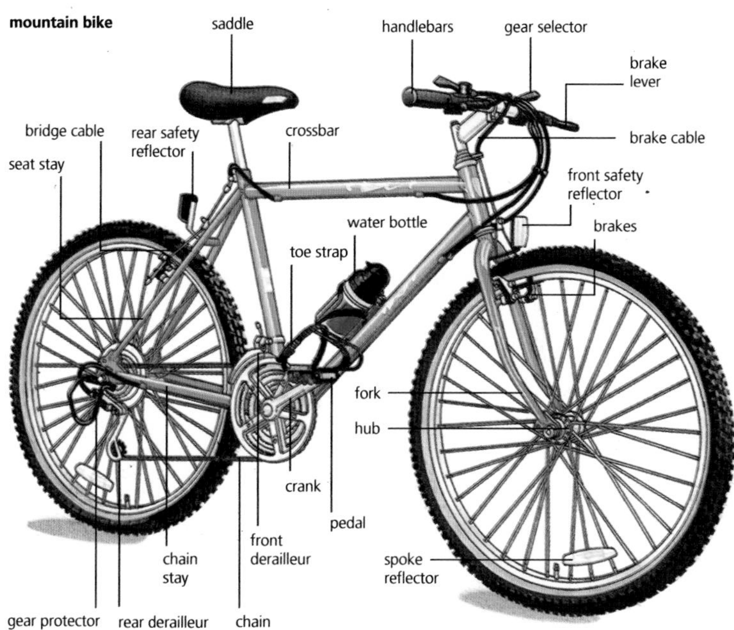


**beware** If a person or sign tells you to **beware of** something, they warn you to look out for something dangerous or harmful.

**bewilder bewildering bewildered** *(v)* to confuse or muddle someone. **bewilderment** *(n),* **bewildered** *(adj).*

**beyond** 1 *(prep)* on the far side of something. *We couldn't see beyond the bushes.* 2 *(prep)* If something is **beyond you**, you cannot understand it.

**bid bidding bid** 1 *(v)* to offer to buy something at an auction for a certain amount of money. **bid** *(n),* **bidder** *(n).* 2 *(v) (old-fashioned)* to order someone to do something. 3 *(n)* an attempt to do or win something. *A bid for fame.*

**bidet** *(bee-day) (n)* a low bowl in some bathrooms, in which you sit and wash yourself.

**big bigger biggest** *(adj)* large, or important.

**bigot** *(n)* someone who has a strong and unreasonable dislike of certain other people, especially people of a different race, nationality, or religion.

**bike** **biking** **biked** 1 *(n)* a bicycle, or a motorcycle. 2 *(v)* to ride a bicycle or motorcycle. **biker** *(n).*

**bikini** *(n)* a two-piece swimming costume worn by women and girls.

**bilingual** *(adj)* If someone is **bilingual**, they can speak two languages very well.

**bill** 1 *(n)* a piece of paper telling you how much money you owe for something that you have bought. 2 *(n)* a written plan for a new law, to be discussed in parliament. 3 *(n)* the American word for a banknote.

**billabong** *(n)* the Australian word for a pond that used to be part of a river.

**billiards** *(singular n)* a game like snooker, in which you use a stick, called a cue, to hit balls around a table and into pockets.

**billow** **billowing** **billowed** 1 *(v)* When a curtain, sail, sheet, etc. **billows**, it is pushed outwards by the wind. 2 *(v)* If smoke or fog **billows**, it rises up in large clouds. 3 *(n)* an ocean wave.

**binary** 1 *(adj)* made up of two parts or units. 2 *(adj)* **Binary** arithmetic uses only two digits, 1 and 0.

**bind** **binding** **bound** 1 *(v)* to tie something up. 2 *(v)* to wrap a piece of material tightly around something.

**bingo** *(n)* a game in which you cross out numbers on a card as they are called out.

**binoculars** *(plural n)* an instrument that you look through with both eyes to make distant things seem nearer.

**biodegradable** *(adj)* Something that is **biodegradable** can be destroyed naturally by bacteria. *Biodegradable packaging helps to reduce pollution.*

**biography** **biographies** *(n)* a book that tells someone's life story. **biographer** *(n),* **biographical** *(adj).*

**biology** *(n)* the scientific study of living things. **biologist** *(n),* **biological** *(adj).*

**biplane** *(n)* an aeroplane with two sets of wings, one above the other.

**bird** *(n)* a two-legged creature with wings, feathers, and a beak. All birds lay eggs, and most birds can fly.

**birth** 1 *(n)* the event of being born. 2 *(n)* the beginning of something. *The birth of talking films.* 3 When a woman **gives birth**, she has a baby.

**birthday** *(n)* a yearly celebration of the day that someone was born.

**biscuit** *(n)* a small, flat cake, which has been baked until it is hard.

**bisect** **bisecting** **bisected** *(v)* to divide a line, angle, or shape into two equal parts.

**bishop** 1 *(n)* a senior priest in the Christian church. 2 *(n)* a chesspiece that can move diagonally across the board. *The picture shows a bishop from a 12th-century Viking chess set. Also see* **chess**.

**bishop chesspiece**

**bit** 1 *(n)* a small piece or amount of something. 2 *(n)* the smallest unit of information in a computer's memory. 3 *(n)* the metal bar that goes in a horse's mouth and is attached to the reins.

**bitch** **bitches** **bitching** **bitched** 1 *(n)* a female dog. 2 *(v)* If you **bitch** about someone, you say unkind or untrue things about them.

**bite** **biting** **bit** **bitten** 1 *(v)* to close your teeth around something. *Lindsay bit into the apple.* **bite** *(n).* 2 *(v)* If an insect or snake **bites** you, it pricks your skin and injects poison into your body. **bite** *(n).*

**bitter** **bitterest** 1 *(adj)* tasting sharp and slightly sour, often in an unpleasant way. 2 *(adj)* upset and angry. 3 *(adj)* If the weather is **bitter**, it is very cold indeed.

**black** 1 *(n)* the colour of coal, or of the sky at night. **black** *(adj).* 2 *(adj)* **Black** people have naturally dark skin. **black** *(n).*

**blackberry** **blackberries** *(n)* a small, black fruit that grows on brambles. *See* **bramble**.

**black hole** *(n)* the area in space around a collapsed star that sucks in everything around it, even light.

**blackmail** *(n)* the crime of threatening to reveal a secret about someone unless they pay a sum of money. **blackmail** *(v).*

*Some words that begin with a "bi" sound are spelt "by".*

**blackout** *(n)* If someone has a **blackout**, they become unconscious for a short time. **black out** *(v)*.

**blacksmith** *(n)* someone who makes and fits horseshoes and mends things made of iron.

**bladder** *(n)* the organ in your body where waste liquid is stored before it leaves your body. *See* **organ**.

**blade 1** *(n)* a sharp edge on a knife, sword, dagger, etc. **2** *(n)* the long, thin part of an oar or propeller. **3** *(n)* a single piece of grass.

**blame blaming blamed** *(v)* If you **blame** someone for something, you say that it is their fault. **blame** *(n)*.

**bland blander blandest** *(adj)* mild and rather dull. *Bland food.*

**blank blanker blankest 1** *(adj)* If something is **blank** it has nothing on it. *A blank tape.* **2** *(n)* a cartridge for a gun that makes a noise but does not fire a bullet.

**blanket 1** *(n)* a thick cover for a bed. **2** *(n)* a thick covering of something, such as snow or flowers.

**blare blaring blared** *(v)* to make a very loud and unpleasant noise. *The radio has been blaring out all day.*

**blaspheme** *(blas-feem)* **blaspheming blasphemed** *(v)* to say offensive things about God or a religion. **blasphemy** *(n)*.

**blast blasting blasted 1** *(n)* a loud noise or explosion. **2** *(n)* a sudden rush of air. **3** *(v)* to fire a gun. **4** *(v)* When a rocket or spaceship **blasts off**, it leaves the ground.

**blatant** *(adj)* obvious and shameless. *Horace grinned as he told a blatant lie.*

**blaze blazing blazed 1** *(v)* to burn fiercely. **2** *(n)* a large fire.

**blazer** *(n)* a smart jacket, often worn as part of a school uniform.

**bleach bleaches bleaching bleached 1** *(n)* a chemical substance used to kill germs or to make cloth white. **2** *(v)* to make something white or very light. *The sun had bleached Jan's hair.*

**bleak bleaker bleakest 1** *(adj)* A **bleak** place is cold, empty, and depressing. **2** *(adj)* without hope. *A bleak future.*

**bleat** *(n)* the cry made by a sheep or goat. **bleat** *(v)*.

**bleed bleeding bled** *(v)* to lose blood. **bleeding** *(adj)*.

**blend blending blended** *(v)* to mix two or more things together. **blend** *(n)*.

**blender** *(n)* an electrical machine that chops and mixes food.

**bless blesses blessing blessed 1** *(v)* to ask God to look after someone or something. **blessing** *(n)*. **2** You say **bless you** when a person sneezes, or as a way of thanking someone.

**blind 1** *(adj)* Someone who is **blind** cannot see. **blindness** *(n)*. **2** *(adj)* A **blind** bend or corner is so sharp that drivers cannot see round it. **3** *(n)* a covering for a window that can be pulled over it.

**blink blinking blinked** *(v)* to move your eyelids up and down very quickly.

**blinkers** *(plural n)* leather flaps worn by racehorses on each side of their head, so that they can only see straight ahead.

**bliss** *(n)* great happiness. *It was bliss to be home.* **blissful** *(adj)*, **blissfully** *(adv)*.

**blister** *(n)* a sore bubble of skin, filled with liquid, that is caused by something burning your skin or rubbing against it.

**blitz 1** *(n)* a sudden attack in which bombs are dropped from the air. **2** *(n)* If you have a **blitz** on something, you tackle it energetically.

**blizzard** *(n)* a heavy snowstorm.

**bloated** *(adj)* fat and swollen, especially as a result of eating too much.

**block blocking blocked 1** *(n)* a large lump of something hard. **2** *(v)* to stop something from getting past or from happening. **3** *(n)* A **block** of flats is a tall building where a lot of people live. **4 block capitals** *(n)* capital letters.

**blood 1** *(n)* the red liquid that is pumped around your body by your heart. **2 blood donor** *(n)* a person who lets some blood be taken out of their body to be stored and given to someone else. **3 blood vessel** *(n)* one of the narrow tubes in your body through which your blood flows.

**bloodshed** *(n)* the killing that happens in a battle or war.

**bloodthirsty** *(adj)* Someone who is **bloodthirsty** really enjoys violence and killing. **bloodthirstiness** *(n)*.

**bloom** **blooming bloomed 1** *(n)* a flower on a plant. **2** *(v)* When a plant **blooms**, its flowers come out. **3** *(adj)* Someone who is **blooming** looks very healthy.

**blossom** **blossoming blossomed 1** *(n)* the small flowers that appear on trees in the spring. **2** *(v)* to grow or improve. *Gill has blossomed into a first-rate dancer.*

**blot** **blotting blotted 1** *(n)* a stain caused by spilled ink or paint. **2** *(v)* to dry ink on a page using a piece of soft paper.

**blotch** **blotches** *(n)* an area of reddened skin, or a stain. **blotchy** *(adj).*

**blouse** *(n)* a piece of clothing, like a loose shirt, worn by women and girls.

**blow** **blowing blew blown 1** *(v)* to force air out of your mouth. **2** *(v)* to move in the wind. *The leaves were blowing around.* **3** *(n)* a punch or hit on the body. **4** *(n)* a disappointment. **5 blow up** *(v)* to destroy something with an explosion.

**blubber** **blubbering blubbered 1** *(n)* the fat under the skin of a whale or seal. **2** *(v)* to cry noisily.

**blue** **bluer bluest 1** *(n)* the colour of the sky on a sunny day. **blue** *(adj).* **2** *(adj)* sad and depressed.

**bluff** **bluffing bluffed 1** *(v)* to pretend to be in a stronger position than you really are, or to know more about something than you really do. **bluff** *(n).* **2** If you **call someone's bluff**, you challenge them to do what they say they can do, because you think that they are bluffing.

**blunder** **blundering blundered 1** *(n)* a stupid mistake. **2** *(v)* to move in a clumsy and awkward way, usually because you cannot see where you are going.

**blunt** **blunter bluntest 1** *(adj)* not sharp. **2** *(adj)* direct and straightforward in what you say. **bluntness** *(n),* **bluntly** *(adv).*

**blur** **blurring blurred 1** *(v)* to make something smeared and unclear. **2** *(n)* a shape that is unclear because it has no outline or is moving fast. **blurred** *(adj).*

**blurt** **blurting blurted** *(v)* If you **blurt** something out, you say it suddenly, without thinking.

**blush** **blushes blushing blushed** *(v)* When you **blush**, your face turns red because you are embarrassed or ashamed.

**bluster** **blustering blustered** **1** *(v)* to blow in gusts. *The wind blustered round the chimney pots.* **blustery** *(adj).* **2** *(v)* to act or speak in an aggressive and over-confident way.

**boar** **1** *(n)* a male pig. **2** *(n)* a type of wild pig.

**board** **boarding boarded 1** *(n)* a flat piece of wood or stiff card. **2** *(v)* to get on to a train, an aeroplane, or a ship.

**boarder** *(n)* a student who lives at school during the term.

**boarding school** *(n)* a school which students live in during the term.

**boast** **boasting boasted 1** *(v)* to talk proudly about what you can do or what you own, in order to impress people. **boastful** *(adj).* **2** *(v)* If a place **boasts** something good, it possesses it. *Paris boasts many fine restaurants.*

**boat** **1** *(n)* a vehicle used for travelling on water. **2** If people are **in the same boat**, they are all in the same situation.

**bob** **bobbing bobbed 1** *(v)* to keep moving up and down on water. **2** *(n)* a short hairstyle in which the hair is all one length.

**body** **bodies. 1** *(n)* all the parts that a person or an animal is made of. *The human body.* **2** *(n)* the main part of something, especially a car or an aircraft. **3** *(n)* a dead person. *The detectives have found another body.*

**bodyguard** *(n)* someone who protects an important person from attacks.

**bog** *(n)* an area of wet, spongy land. **boggy** *(adj).*

**bogus** *(adj)* false. *A bogus policeman.*

**boil** **boiling boiled 1** *(v)* to heat a liquid until it starts to bubble and give off vapour. **boiling** *(adj).* **2** *(v)* to cook something in boiling water. **3** *(n)* an infected lump under the skin.

**boiler** *(n)* a tank that heats water for a house or other building.

**boiling point** *(n)* the temperature at which a liquid that has been heated turns to gas.

**boisterous** *(adj)* If you are **boisterous**, you behave in a rough and noisy way. **boisterousness** *(n),* **boisterously** *(adv).*

**bold** bolder boldest 1 *(adj)* Someone who is **bold** is very confident and shows no fear of danger. **boldness** *(n)*.
2 *(adj)* **Bold** colours stand out clearly.

**bollard** *(n)* a short post placed in a road to stop traffic from going in a particular direction.

**bolt** bolting bolted 1 *(n)* a metal bar that slides into place and locks something. **bolt** *(v)*. 2 *(n)* a strong metal pin, used with a metal nut to hold things together. 3 *(v)* to run away suddenly.

**bomb** bombing bombed 1 *(n)* a container filled with explosives, used in war or to blow up buildings, vehicles, etc. 2 *(v)* to attack a place with bombs.

**bombard** bombarding bombarded 1 *(v)* to attack a place with heavy gunfire. **bombardment** *(n)*. 2 *(v)* If you **bombard** someone with questions, you ask them lots of questions in a short time.

**bombshell** *(n)* something which makes you shocked and surprised.

**bond** bonding bonded 1 *(n)* a close friendship or connection with someone. *A bond developed between the boys.* 2 *(v)* If two things **bond**, they stick together. **bond** *(n)*. 3 **bonds** *(plural n)* ropes, chains, etc. used to tie someone up.

**bone** *(n)* one of the hard, white parts that make up the skeleton of a person or an animal.

**bonfire** *(n)* a large, outdoor fire, often used to burn garden rubbish.

**bonnet** 1 *(n)* the cover for a car's engine. 2 *(n)* a baby's or woman's hat, tied with strings under the chin.

**bonsai** *(bonz-eye)* **bonsai** *(n)* a tiny tree or shrub, grown in a pot for decoration.

**bonus** bonuses 1 *(n)* an extra reward that you get for doing something well. **bonus** *(adj)*. 2 *(n)* a good thing that is unexpected. *It's a bonus to have a cinema so close to our new house.*

**booby trap** *(n)* a hidden trap or trick which is set off when someone or something touches it.

**book** booking booked 1 *(n)* a set of pages that are bound together in a cover. 2 *(v)* to arrange for something to be kept for you to have or use later. *We've booked a holiday in Crete.*

**booklet** *(n)* a book with a paper cover and a small number of pages.

**bookworm** *(n)* someone who loves reading books.

**boom** booming boomed 1 *(n)* a very loud, deep sound, like an explosion. **boom** *(v)*. 2 *(v)* to speak in a loud, deep voice. 3 *(n)* a rapid increase in something. *A spending boom.*

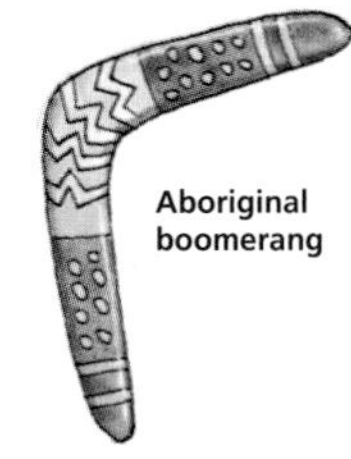
**Aboriginal boomerang**

**boomerang** *(n)* a curved stick that is thrown through the air and returns to the thrower if it misses its target.

**boost** boosting boosted 1 *(v)* to increase the power or amount of something. **boost** *(n)*. 2 *(n)* If something gives you a **boost**, it cheers you up.

**booster** 1 *(n)* a rocket that gives extra power to a spacecraft. *See* **space shuttle**. 2 *(n)* an injection of a drug, given to increase the effect of an earlier injection.

**boot** booting booted 1 *(n)* a heavy shoe that covers your ankle and sometimes part of your leg. 2 *(n)* the part of a car where luggage can be carried. 3 *(v)* When you **boot up** a computer, you turn it on and get it ready to work. 4 *(v)* *(informal)* to kick something hard.

**booty** *(singular n)* valuable objects that are taken away by pirates or an army after a battle.

**booze** *(n)* *(informal)* alcoholic drink. **boozer** *(n)*, **boozy** *(adj)*.

**border** bordering bordered 1 *(n)* the dividing line between one country or region and another. 2 *(v)* If one country **borders** another, their boundaries meet. 3 *(n)* a decorative strip around the edge of something. 4 *(n)* a long flowerbed.

**bore** boring bored 1 *(v)* If something or someone **bores** you, you find them very dull and uninteresting. **bore** *(n)*, **boredom** *(n)*. 2 *(v)* to make a hole in something with a drill. *This machine can bore into solid rock.*

**borrow** borrowing borrowed *(v)* to use someone else's belongings for a short time, with their permission.

**bosom** *(n)* a woman's breasts.

**boss** bosses bossing bossed
1 *(n)* someone in charge of a company or someone who people work for.
2 **boss about** *(v)* to keep telling somebody what to do. **bossy** *(adj)*.

**botany** *(singular n)* the study of plants. **botanist** *(n)*, **botanical** *(adj)*.

**bother** bothering bothered
1 *(v)* If something **bothers** you, it makes you feel uncomfortable. 2 *(v)* to interrupt someone who is busy. 3 *(v)* to make an effort to do something. *At least Kitty bothered to come to the meeting.*

**bottle** bottling bottled 1 *(n)* a glass or plastic container for liquids. 2 *(v)* to put things into bottles. 3 *(v)* If you **bottle up** your feelings, you keep them to yourself.

**bottleneck** *(n)* a narrow part of a road that causes traffic jams.

**bottom** 1 *(n)* the lowest part of something. **bottom** *(adj)*. 2 *(n)* the part of your body that you sit on.

**bough** *(rhymes with now) (n)* a thick branch on a tree.

**boulder** *(n)* a large rock.

**bounce** bouncing bounced
1 *(v)* to spring back after hitting something. **bounce** *(n)*, **bouncy** *(adj)*.
2 *(n)* If someone has lots of **bounce**, they are very cheerful. **bouncy** *(adj)*.

**bound** bounding bounded
1 *(v)* to move forward quickly with leaps and jumps. **bound** *(n)*. 2 *(v)* If something is **bound to** happen, it will definitely take place. 3 If a place is **out of bounds**, you are not allowed to go there.

**boundary** boundaries *(n)* the line that separates one area from another.

**bouquet** *(boh-**kay** or boo-**kay**) (n)* a bunch of flowers given as a present.

**bow** bowing bowed 1 *(rhymes with cow) (v)* to bend low, as a sign of respect or to accept applause. **bow** *(n)*. 2 *(rhymes with no) (n)* a knot with loops. 3 **bow** *or* **bows** *(rhymes with cow) (n)* the front of a ship. 4 *(rhymes with no) (n)* a piece of wood with strings stretched along it, used for playing stringed instruments.
5 *(rhymes with no) (n)* a curved piece of wood with a stretched string attached to it, used for shooting arrows.

**bowl** bowling bowled 1 *(n)* a deep dish. 2 *(v)* When you **bowl** in a game like cricket or baseball, you throw a ball for someone to hit with a bat. **bowler** *(n)*.

**bowls** *(n)* a game played with heavy, wooden balls called bowls.

**box** boxes boxing boxed 1 *(n)* a container, especially one with four flat sides. 2 *(v)* to fight with your fists as a sport. **boxer** *(n)*, **boxing** *(n)*.

**box office** *(n)* the place in a theatre or cinema where you buy tickets.

**boy** *(n)* a male child.

**boycott** boycotting boycotted *(v)* to refuse to take part in something or buy something as a way of making a protest.

**boyfriend** *(n)* the man or boy with whom a woman or girl is having a romantic relationship.

**bra** *(n)* a piece of underwear that supports a woman's breasts.

**brace** bracing braced 1 *(n)* an object that supports something or holds it in place. **brace** *(v)*. 2 *(n)* a wire device worn inside your mouth to straighten your teeth. 3 **braces** *(plural n)* two elastic straps worn over the shoulders to hold up a pair of trousers. 4 *(v)* If you **brace** yourself, you prepare yourself for a shock or for the force of something hitting you.

**bracelet** *(n)* a band worn around the wrist as a piece of jewellery.

**bracket** 1 *(n)* a support, made of metal or wood, used to hold up a shelf or cupboard. 2 *(plural n)* **Brackets** are a pair of curved lines, used to separate some words from the main writing.

**brag** bragging bragged *(v)* to talk in a boastful way.

**Braille** *(brayl) (n)* a system of printing for blind people, using raised dots that are read by feeling with the fingertips. *This picture shows what the word "Braille" looks like when it is printed in Braille.*

**B R A I L L E**

**brain** 1 *(n)* the organ inside your head that controls your body and allows you to think and have feelings. 2 *(n)* your mind or intelligence.

**brainstorm** **brainstorming** **brainstormed** 1 *(v)* When people **brainstorm**, they get together to share ideas on a topic or to solve a problem. **brainstorming** *(n)*. 2 *(n)* a sudden idea.

**brainwash** **brainwashes** **brainwashing** **brainwashed** *(v)* to make someone accept and believe something by saying it to them over and over again. **brainwashing** *(n)*.

**brainwave** *(n)* a sudden good idea.

**brainy** **brainier** **brainiest** *(adj)* *(informal)* clever, or intelligent.

**brake** **braking** **braked** 1 *(n)* You use **brakes** to slow down or stop a vehicle. 2 *(v)* to slow down or stop by using brakes.

**bramble** *(n)* a thorny bush that blackberries grow on.

**bramble**

**branch** **branches** **branching** **branched** 1 *(n)* a part of a tree that grows out of its trunk like an arm. 2 *(v)* When a road, river, etc. **branches**, it splits into two parts that go in different directions. 3 *(n)* A **branch** of a company or organization is one of its shops, offices, etc. in a particular area.

**brand** **branding** **branded** 1 *(n)* a particular make of a product. *A brand of toothpaste.* 2 *(v)* If someone **brands** an animal, they burn a mark on to its skin to show that it belongs to them. **brand** *(n)*.

**brass** 1 *(n)* a yellow metal made from copper and zinc. 2 *(adj)* The **brass** section in an orchestra contains musical instruments that are made of brass and usually have a funnel-shaped mouthpiece. *See* **horn**.

**brass rubbing** *(n)* a copy of a picture carved on a brass plate. Brass rubbings are made by rubbing with a wax crayon on a piece of paper placed over the plate.

**bravado** *(n)* If you are full of **bravado**, you pretend to be braver and more confident than you really are.

**brave** **braving** **braved**; **braver** **bravest** 1 *(adj)* If you are **brave**, you show courage and are willing to do difficult things. **bravery** *(n)*, **bravely** *(adv)*. 2 *(v)* If you **brave** something unpleasant and difficult, you face it deliberately. 3 *(n)* a Native American warrior.

**brawl** *(n)* a rough fight. **brawl** *(v)*.

**bray** **braying** **brayed** 1 *(v)* When a donkey **brays**, it makes a loud, harsh noise in its throat. 2 *(v)* When a person **brays**, they make a harsh noise like a donkey.

**brazen** 1 *(adj)* shameless. **brazenly** *(adv)*. 2 *(adj)* made of brass.

**brazier** *(bray-zee-er)* *(n)* a container for burning coals, used to keep people warm out of doors.

**bread** 1 *(n)* a baked food made from flour, water, and often yeast. 2 *(n)* *(slang)* money.

**breadline** *(n)* If people are on the **breadline**, they have only just enough money to live.

**breadth** 1 *(n)* the distance from one side of something to the other. 2 *(n)* a wide range. *Jack has a breadth of experience in caring for animals.*

**breadwinner** *(n)* someone who earns money for a family.

**break** **breaking** **broke** **broken** 1 *(v)* to damage something so that it is in pieces or so that it no longer works. **breakage** *(n)*, **breakable** *(adj)*. 2 *(n)* a rest from working or studying. *We had a ten minute break for coffee.* 3 *(v)* If someone **breaks** rules or the law, they do something that is not allowed. 4 **break in** *(v)* to get into a building by force. 5 **break out** *(v)* to begin suddenly. *Fighting broke out on the streets.*

**breakdown** 1 *(n)* If you have a **breakdown** while you are travelling, your car stops moving because its engine has stopped working. 2 *(n)* If someone has a **breakdown**, they are so worried or depressed that they become ill.

**breaker** *(n)* a big sea wave.

**breakfast** *(n)* the first meal of the day.

**breakthrough** *(n)* an important step towards achieving something. *A major breakthrough in medical research.*

**breakwater** 1 *(n)* a wall built in the sea to protect a harbour from the force of the waves. 2 *(n)* a barrier built on a beach to reduce the force of the waves.

**breast** 1 *(n)* A woman's **breasts** are the two round fleshy parts on her chest that can produce milk to feed a baby. 2 *(n) (old-fashioned)* a man's or a woman's chest.

**breaststroke** *(n)* a style of swimming on your front in which you move your arms forwards and out from your chest and kick your legs like a frog.

**breath** 1 *(n)* the air that you take into your lungs and breathe out again. 2 If you are **out of breath**, you have difficulty breathing. 3 If you say something **under your breath**, you say it very quietly.

**breathalyze** *or* **breathalyse** **breathalyzing breathalyzed** *(v)* When drivers are **breathalyzed**, they have to blow into a bag called a breathalyzer, which shows whether they have drunk too much alcohol to drive safely.

**breathe** **breathing breathed** *(v)* to take air in and out of your lungs.

**breathtaking** *(adj)* very beautiful or impressive. **breathtakingly** *(adv)*.

**breed** **breeding bred** 1 *(v)* to keep animals or plants so that you can produce more of them and control their quality. **breeder** *(n)*. 2 *(v)* When animals **breed**, they mate and produce babies. 3 *(n)* a particular type of animal. *A breed of dog.*

**breeze** *(n)* a gentle wind. **breezy** *(adj)*.

**brew** **brewing brewed** 1 *(v)* to make beer. 2 *(v)* to make tea or coffee. 3 *(v)* If something is **brewing**, it is about to start.

**bribe** **bribing bribed** 1 *(n)* money or a gift that you offer to someone to persuade them to do something for you, especially something wrong. 2 *(v)* to offer someone a bribe. **bribery** *(n)*.

**brick** *(n)* a block of hard, baked clay, used for building.

**bride** *(n)* a woman who is about to be married or has just been married.

**bridegroom** *(n)* a man who is about to be married or has just been married.

**bridesmaid** *(n)* a girl or woman who helps a bride on her wedding day.

**bridge** **bridging bridged** 1 *(n)* a structure built over a river, railway, etc. so that people or vehicles can get to the other side. 2 *(n)* a card game for four players. 3 *(n)* an upright piece of wood on a guitar, violin, etc. over which the strings are stretched. *See* **guitar**.

**bridges**

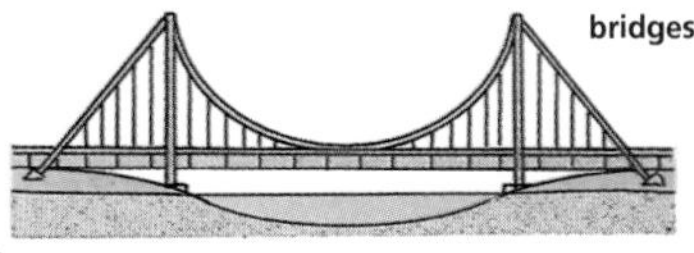
suspension bridge

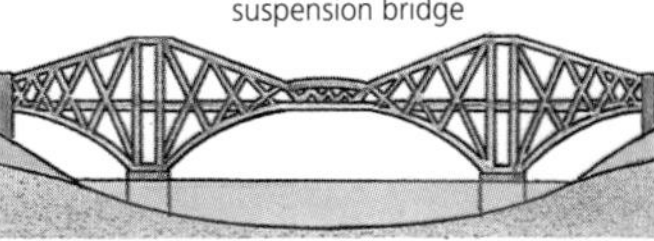
cantilever bridge

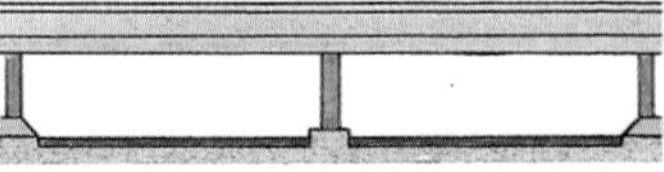
beam bridge

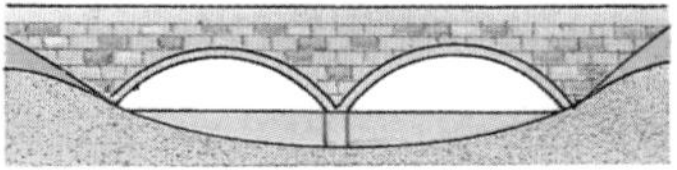
arch bridge

**bridle** *(n)* the straps that fit around a horse's head and mouth, and that are used to control it.

**bridle path** *(n)* a track or path for horse riders or walkers.

**brief** **briefer briefest** 1 *(adj)* lasting only a short time. *A brief visit.* **briefly** *(adv)*. 2 *(adj)* using only a few words. *Be as brief as you can.* **briefly** *(adv)*. 3 **briefs** *(plural n)* underpants.

**briefcase** *(n)* a bag with a handle, used for carrying papers.

**brigade** *(n)* an organized group of workers. *The fire brigade.*

**bright** **brighter brightest** 1 *(adj)* A **bright** light or colour is strong and can be seen clearly. **brightness** *(n)*, **brightly** *(adv)*. 2 *(adj)* cheerful. **brightly** *(adv)*. 3 *(adj) (informal)* clever.

**brilliant** 1 *(adj)* shining very brightly. **brilliance** *(n)*. 2 *(adj)* very clever. **brilliance** *(n)*. 3 *(adj)* very good.

**brine** *(n)* salty water.

**bring** **bringing brought** 1 *(v)* to take something or someone with you. *Bring a friend.* 2 *(v)* to make something happen or appear. *Hooligans bring trouble.* 3 *(v)* If a company **brings out** a product, it starts selling it. 4 **bring up** *(v)* to look after and guide a child as it grows up. 5 **bring in** *(v)* to introduce something. *The government is bringing in new employment laws.*

**brink** 1 *(n)* the edge of something, like a cliff or a river bank. 2 If you are **on the brink** of something, you are just about to do it. *Jake is on the brink of leaving.*

**brisk** **brisker briskest** *(adj)* quick and energetic. *A brisk walk.* **briskly** *(adv)*.

**bristle** 1 *(n)* one of the long, wiry hairs used to make brushes. **bristly** *(adj)*. 2 **bristles** *(plural n)* the short, stiff hairs that start to grow on a man's chin if he does not shave. **bristly** *(adj)*.

**brittle** *(adj)* easily snapped or broken.

**broad** **broader broadest** 1 *(adj)* wide. **broaden** *(v)*. 2 *(adj)* covering the most important points, but not the details. *A broad outline of the story.* **broadly** *(adv)*.

**broadcast** **broadcasting broadcast** *or* **broadcasted** 1 *(v)* to send out a programme on television or radio. 2 *(n)* a television or radio programme.

**broccoli** *(n)* a green vegetable with rounded heads on stalks.

**brochure** *(broh-shur)* *(n)* a booklet, usually with pictures, that gives information about a product or service.

**broke** *(adj)* *(informal)* If you are **broke**, you have no money.

**broken home** *(n)* A **broken home** is one where the family is not together because the parents have divorced.

**bronchitis** *(bron-ky-tiss)* *(n)* an illness of the throat and lungs that makes you cough a lot.

**bronze** 1 *(n)* a hard, reddish-brown metal that is a mixture of copper and tin. 2 *(n)* a reddish-brown colour.

**brooch** *(broach)* **brooches** *(n)* a piece of jewellery that you pin to your clothes.

**brood** **brooding brooded** 1 *(n)* a family of young birds. 2 *(v)* to keep worrying or thinking about something. *Hugh was brooding about his problems.*

**brook** *(n)* a small stream.

**broom** *(n)* a large brush with a long handle, used for sweeping floors.

**brother** *(n)* a boy or man who has the same parents as you. **brotherly** *(adj)*.

**brow** 1 *(n)* forehead. *A wrinkled brow.* 2 *(n)* the top of a hill.

**browbeat** **browbeating browbeat browbeaten** *(v)* If you **browbeat** someone, you bully them in an argument.

**browse** **browsing browsed** *(v)* to look casually at something. *Max browsed through the newspaper.*

**bruise** *(brewz)* *(n)* a dark mark that you get on your skin when you fall or are hit by something. **bruise** *(v)*, **bruised** *(adj)*.

**brush** **brushes brushing brushed** 1 *(n)* an object with bristles and a handle, used for sweeping, painting, or smoothing hair. 2 *(v)* to use a brush. 3 *(v)* to touch something lightly.

**brutal** *(adj)* cruel and violent. **brutality** *(n)*, **brutally** *(adv)*.

**brute** 1 *(n)* a rough and violent person. 2 *(n)* If you do something by **brute force**, you use a lot of strength instead of skill or intelligence.

**bubble** **bubbling bubbled** 1 *(n)* one of the tiny balls of gas in fizzy drinks, boiling water, etc. 2 *(v)* to make bubbles. *The water bubbled in the saucepan.*

**bubbly** 1 *(adj)* If a liquid is **bubbly**, it is full of balls of gas. 2 *(adj)* If a person is **bubbly**, they are very lively and talkative.

**buck** **bucking bucked** 1 *(n)* a male rabbit, kangaroo, etc. 2 *(v)* If a horse **bucks**, it jumps in the air with all four feet off the ground. 3 If you **pass the buck**, you pass the responsibility for something on to someone else. 4 *(n)* *(slang)* a dollar. 5 **buck up** *(v)* *(informal)* to hurry up.

**bucket** *(n)* a plastic or metal container with a handle, used for carrying liquids.

**buckle** **buckling buckled** 1 *(n)* a metal fastening on shoes, belts, or straps. **buckle** *(v)*. 2 *(v)* to crumple. *Hugh's legs buckled under him and he fell.*

**bud** *(n)* a small shoot on a plant that grows into a leaf or flower. *See* **flower**.

**Buddha 1** *(n)* the name given to Siddhartha Gautama, the teacher who founded the religion of Buddhism. **2** *(n)* a statue or picture of Buddha.

**Buddha**

**Buddhism** *(n)* a religion based on the teachings of Buddha and practised mainly in eastern and central Asia. Buddhists believe that you should not become too attached to material things and that you live many lives in different bodies. **Buddhist** *(n),* **Buddhist** *(adj).*

**budge budging budged** *(v)* If you cannot **budge** something, you are not able to move it.

**budgerigar** *(n)* a brightly coloured Australian bird, often kept as a pet.

**budget budgeting budgeted 1** *(n)* a plan for how money will be earned and spent. **2** *(v)* If you **budget** for something, you plan how to spend your money so that you can afford it.

**buff** *(n) (informal)* someone who knows a lot about a particular subject. *A film buff.*

**buffalo buffaloes** *(n)* a type of ox with heavy horns.

**buffet buffeting buffeted 1** *(buff-et) (v)* to strike and shake something or someone. *The wind buffeted the trees.* **2** *(boo-fay) (n)* a meal in which many cold dishes are laid on a table and people serve themselves. **3** *(boo-fay) (n)* a snack bar at a railway station, or on a train.

**bug bugging bugged 1** *(n)* an insect. **2** *(n) (informal)* a minor illness caused by germs. **3** *(n) (informal)* an error in a computer program or system that prevents it from working properly. **4** *(adj) (informal)* If a room is **bugged**, someone has hidden microphones there so that they can listen to what people are saying. **bug** *(n).* **5** *(v) (informal)* If someone or something **bugs** you, they annoy you.

**buggy buggies** *(n)* a chair on wheels, in which you push young children.

**build building built 1** *(v)* to make something by putting different parts together. **2** *(n)* the size and shape of a person's body. *Nick has quite a large build.* **3 build up** *(v)* to increase or make stronger. *The traffic has built up. You must build yourself up for the race.*

**building** *(n)* a structure with walls and a roof.

**bulb 1** *(n)* the onion-shaped root of some plants. **2** *(n)* the glass part of an electric light or torch that lights up when you switch it on. *When you switch on a light, an electric current travels along the connecting wires inside the bulb and makes the filament glow white hot.*

**bulb**

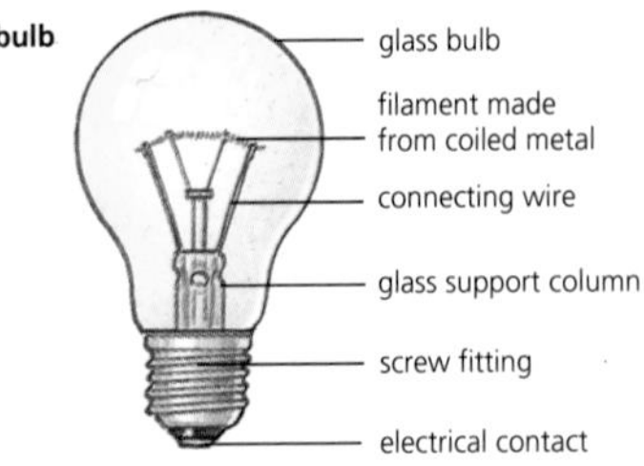


**bulge bulging bulged** *(v)* to swell out. *Sergei's bag bulged with gifts.* **bulge** *(n).*

**bulk 1** *(n)* The **bulk** of something is the main part of it. **2** When you buy **in bulk**, you buy in large quantities.

**bulky bulkier bulkiest 1** *(adj)* large and difficult to handle. **2** *(adj)* very filling. *Bulky food.*

**bull 1** *(n)* the male of the cattle family. **2** *(n)* a male elephant, seal, or whale.

**bulldozer** *(n)* a powerful tractor with a wide blade at the front, used for moving earth and rocks.

**bullet** *(n)* a small, pointed metal object fired from a gun.

**bulletin** *(n)* a short news report on television or radio.

**bulletproof** *(adj)* Something that is **bulletproof** is made to protect people from bullets. *Bulletproof glass.*

**bullion** *(n)* bars of gold or silver.

**bully bullies bullying bullied** *(v)* to frighten or hurt people who are smaller or weaker than you. **bully** *(n).*

**bump** **bumping** **bumped** **1** *(v)* to knock into something by accident. **bump** *(n).* **2** *(n)* the sound of one thing hitting something else. *I fell out of bed with a bump.* **3** *(n)* a round lump or swelling. **4** *(v) (informal)* If you **bump into** someone, you meet them by chance. **5** *(slang)* If someone has been **bumped off**, they have been killed.

**bumph** *(n) (slang)* a lot of printed papers.

**bumptious** *(adj)* loud and conceited.

**bumpy** **bumpier** **bumpiest** *(adj)* very uneven. *A bumpy road.*

**bun** **1** *(n)* a small, round cake or bread roll. **2** *(n)* hair fastened in a round shape at the back of the head.

**bunch** **bunches** *(n)* a group of people or things. **bunch** *(v).*

**bundle** **bundling** **bundled** **1** *(v)* to tie or wrap things together loosely. **bundle** *(n).* **2** *(v)* to handle someone quickly and carelessly. *We bundled Uncle Hector on to the train.*

**bung** **bunging** **bunged** **1** *(n)* a piece of cork, rubber, or wood used to close up the opening in a bottle or other container. **2** *(v) (slang)* to throw something roughly and carelessly. *Bung your bag in the car.*

**bungalow** *(n)* a house with one storey.

**bungee jumping** *(n)* a dangerous sport in which someone jumps from a high place and is stopped from hitting the ground by a long piece of elastic attached to their legs.

**bungle** **bungling** **bungled** *(v)* to do something badly or clumsily.

**bunk** **bunking** **bunked** **1** *(n)* a narrow bed. **2** **bunk beds** *(plural n)* two beds stacked one above the other. **3** **bunk off** *(v) (slang)* to miss something, like a lesson, on purpose.

**bunker** **1** *(n)* a place for storing coal. **2** *(n)* an underground shelter from bomb attacks and gunfire. **3** *(n)* a large, sand-filled hollow on a golf course.

**bunting** *(n)* small flags joined by a string and used for decoration.

**buoy** *(boy)* *(n)* a floating marker in the sea or in a river.

**buoyant** **1** *(adj)* able to keep afloat. **buoyancy** *(n).* **2** *(adj)* cheerful.

**burden** **burdening** **burdened** **1** *(n)* a heavy load that someone has to carry. **2** *(v)* to weigh someone down with heavy things. *We burdened Dad with our cases.*

**bureau** *(byoor-oh)* **bureaux** **1** *(n)* a writing desk with drawers. **2** *(n)* an office that provides information or some other service.

**burglar** *(n)* someone who breaks into a house and steals things. **burglary** *(n),* **burgle** *(v).*

**burn** **burning** **burnt** *or* **burned** **1** *(v)* to hurt or damage someone or something with heat or fire. **2** *(n)* a sore area of skin or a mark on something, caused by heat.

**burp** **burping** **burped** *(v)* to let out gases from your stomach through your mouth with a loud noise. **burp** *(n).*

**burrow** **burrowing** **burrowed** **1** *(n)* a tunnel or hole in the ground where a rabbit or other animal lives. **2** *(v)* to move along under the ground by digging.

**burst** **bursting** **burst** **1** *(v)* to explode or break apart suddenly. *The balloon burst.* **2** *(n)* a short, concentrated outbreak of something, such as speed, gunfire, or applause. **3** *(v)* to start doing something suddenly. *Kit burst into tears.*

**bury** **buries** **burying** **buried** **1** *(v)* to put a dead body into a grave. **burial** *(n).* **2** *(v)* to hide something in the ground or under a pile of things.

**bus** **buses** *(n)* a large vehicle, used for carrying passengers.

**bush** **bushes** **1** *(n)* a large plant with lots of branches. **2** **the bush** *(n)* the wild areas of Australia and Africa. **bushman** *(n).*

**bushy** **bushier** **bushiest** *(adj)* growing thickly. *Bushy eyebrows.*

**business** **businesses** **1** *(n)* the type of work that someone does. *Hank's in the music business.* **2** *(n)* the buying and selling of goods and services. *The company does a lot of business with Japan.* **3** *(n)* a company or shop that makes or sells things or provides a service. **4** If something is **none of your business**, it is nothing to do with you.

**businesslike** *(adj)* efficient and practical.

**busker** *(n)* someone who sings or plays music in the street, in order to earn money. **busking** *(n).*

marble bust

**bust** busting busted *or* **bust** 1 *(n)* a woman's breasts. **busty** *(adj)*. 2 *(n)* a statue of a person's head and shoulders. *This marble bust is of the Ancient Greek scientist, Galen.* 3 *(v)* *(informal)* to break something. **bust** *(adj)*.

**bustle** bustling bustled *(v)* to rush around being busy. **bustle** *(n)*.

**busy** busier busiest 1 *(adj)* If you are **busy**, you have a lot of things to do. **busily** *(adv)*. 2 *(adj)* A **busy** place has a lot of people in it and is full of activity.

**butcher** *(n)* someone who sells meat.

**butler** *(n)* the chief male servant in a house.

**butt** butting butted 1 *(n)* a large barrel for water. 2 *(v)* to hit with the head or horns. 3 *(n)* the handle of a gun.

**butter** *(n)* a yellow fat made from cream, used for cooking and spreading on bread.

**buttercup** *(n)* a small, yellow wild flower. *See* **plant**.

**butterfly** butterflies *(n)* a thin-bodied insect with large, brightly coloured wings.

peacock butterfly

**buttocks** *(plural n)* the two fleshy parts of your bottom.

**button** 1 *(n)* a round piece of plastic, metal, etc. that is sewn on to clothing and used as a fastener. **button** *(v)*. 2 *(n)* a small knob that you press to switch a machine on or off.

**buy** buying bought *(v)* to get something by paying money for it.

**buzz** buzzes buzzing buzzed *(v)* to make a noise like a bee. **buzz** *(n)*.

**bypass** bypasses bypassing bypassed 1 *(n)* a main road that goes around a town instead of through it. 2 *(v)* to avoid something by going around it. **bypass** *(adj)*.

**byte** *(n)* a unit of information that is contained in a computer's memory.

# Cc

**cabbage** *(n)* a large, leafy vegetable.

**cabin** 1 *(n)* the driver's area of a vehicle. 2 *(n)* a room for passengers on a ship or plane. 3 *(n)* a small, wooden house.

**cabinet** 1 *(n)* a cupboard with shelves or drawers. 2 *(n)* a group of top members of a government who advise the leader.

**cable** 1 *(n)* a thick wire or rope. 2 *(n)* a tight bundle of wires used for carrying electricity, television signals, etc.

**cactus** cacti *or* **cactuses** *(n)* a spiky plant that grows in hot, dry countries.

**café** *(kaf-ay)* *(n)* a small restaurant that serves snacks and hot drinks.

**cafeteria** *(n)* a self-service restaurant.

**caffeine** *(kaf-feen)* *(n)* a chemical found in tea and coffee which makes your brain and body more active.

**caftan** *(n)* a long, loose piece of clothing worn by men in Arab countries.

**cage** *(n)* a container made of wires or bars, in which animals or birds are kept.

**cajole** cajoling cajoled *(v)* to flatter someone into doing something.

**cake** *(n)* a sweet food made by baking flour, butter, eggs, and sugar together.

**calamity** calamities *(n)* a disaster.

**calcium** *(n)* a soft, white element found in teeth and bones.

**calculate** calculating calculated *(v)* to work something out, especially a sum. *Andy calculated that it would take about two hours to get there.* **calculation** *(n)*.

**calculator** *(n)* a small electronic machine, used for working out sums.

**calendar** *(n)* a chart showing all the days in a year.

**calf** calves 1 *(n)* a young cow, seal, elephant, etc. 2 *(n)* the fleshy part at the back of your leg, below your knee.

**call** calling called 1 *(v)* to shout out something, especially someone's name. 2 *(v)* to give someone or something a name. 3 *(v)* to telephone someone. 4 **call off** *(v)* If you **call something off**, you cancel it.

*Some words that begin with a "c" sound are spelt with a "k".*

**calligraphy** *(n)* the art of beautiful handwriting.

**callous** *(adj)* hard-hearted and cruel. **callously** *(adv).*

**calm** calming calmed; calmer calmest 1 *(adj)* peaceful and untroubled. **calmness** *(n),* **calmly** *(adv).* 2 *(v)* to soothe an animal or a person. 3 *(n)* peacefulness.

**calorie** *(n)* a measurement of the amount of energy that a food gives you.

**camcorder** *(n)* a video camera with a sound recorder, that is easy to carry.

**camel** *(n)* a mammal with one or two humps on its back that lives in the desert.

**camels**

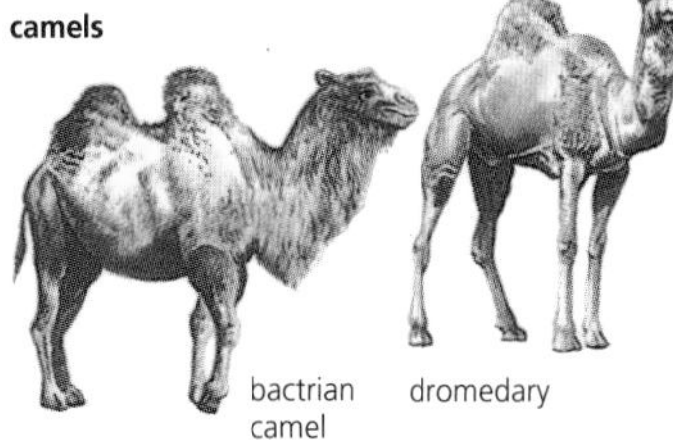


**cameo** *(kam-ee-oh)* 1 *(n)* a piece of coloured stone with a figure carved on it. 2 *(adj)* A **cameo** role is a small character part in a play or film, usually taken by a famous actor.

**cameo**

**camera** *(n)* a machine for taking photographs or making films.

**camouflage** *(kam-er-flarj)* *(n)* colouring or covering that makes animals, people, and objects look like their surroundings. *The praying mantis uses camouflage to hide from other creatures.*

**camp** camping camped *(v)* to have a holiday in a tent. **camping** *(n),* **camp** *(n).*

**campaign** *(n)* a series of actions organized over a period of time to achieve or win something. *An election campaign.*

**can** could 1 *(v)* to be able to do something. *Natalie can speak fluent French.* 2 *(v) (informal)* to be allowed to do something. *You can stay until dark.* 3 *(n)* a metal container.

**canal** *(n)* a man-made waterway, used by barges and narrow boats.

**cancel** cancelling cancelled *(v)* If someone **cancels** something, they say it is not going to happen. **cancellation** *(n).*

**cancer** *(n)* a serious disease in which some cells in the body produce harmful growths. **cancerous** *(adj).*

**candid** *(adj)* honest and open in what you are saying. **candidly** *(adv).*

**candidate** *(n)* someone taking an examination, applying for a job, or standing in an election. **candidacy** *(n).*

**candle** *(n)* a stick of wax with a string or wick running through it, which you burn to give light. **candlelight** *(n).*

**candy** candies *(n)* the American word for a sweet, or sweets.

**cane** caning caned 1 *(n)* the hollow stem of a plant like bamboo, used to make furniture. 2 *(n)* a stick, especially a walking stick or a stick used for beating someone. 3 *(v)* to beat someone with a cane as a punishment.

**canine** 1 *(adj)* to do with dogs. 2 *(n)* the pointed tooth on each side of your upper and lower jaw. *See* **teeth**.

**cannibal** *(n)* someone who eats human flesh. **cannibalism** *(n).*

**cannon** *(n)* a heavy gun which fires large metal balls.

**canoe** *(n)* a narrow boat that you move through the water by paddling.

**canteen** *(n)* an area in an office, school, etc. where you can eat meals.

**canter** cantering cantered *(v)* When a horse **canters**, it runs at a speed between a trot and a gallop. **canter** *(n).*

**canvas** *(n)* a type of coarse, strong cloth used for tents, sails, and clothing.

**canvass** canvasses canvassing canvassed *(v)* to ask people for their opinions or votes. **canvasser** *(n).*

**canyon** *(n)* a deep, narrow river valley.

**cap** 1 *(n)* a soft, flat hat. 2 *(n)* the top of a bottle, jar, or pen.

**capable** 1 *(adj)* able to do something. *Capable of learning*. **capability** *(n)*. 2 *(adj)* able to do something well and skilfully. *A capable tennis player.* **capably** *(adv)*.

**cape** *(n)* a sleeveless coat that you wear over your shoulders.

**capillary capillaries** *(n)* a small tube in your body which carries blood between arteries and veins.

**capital** 1 *(n)* the main city of a country, where the government is based. 2 *(n)* a large letter. *You begin a sentence with a capital.* 3 **capital punishment** *(n)* punishment by death.

**capitalism** *(n)* a way of organizing a country so that all the land, houses, factories, etc. belong to individuals rather than the state. **capitalist** *(n)*.

**capsize capsizing capsized** *(v)* If a boat **capsizes**, it turns over in the water.

**capsule** 1 *(n)* a small container of medicine that you can swallow. 2 *(n)* the part of a rocket or spacecraft in which the crew travel.

**captain** 1 *(n)* the person in charge of a ship or an aircraft. 2 *(n)* the leader of a sports team. 3 *(n)* an army officer.

**caption** *(n)* a short title or description printed under a cartoon, photograph, etc.

**captivate captivating captivated** *(v)* to delight someone.

**captive** *(n)* a person or animal who has been taken prisoner. **captivity** *(n)*.

**capture capturing captured** *(v)* to take a person or place by force.

**car** *(n)* a type of passenger motor vehicle.

**caramel** 1 *(n)* burnt sugar. 2 *(n)* a sweet made from burnt sugar, butter, and milk. 3 *(n)* a light brown colour.

**carat** *(n)* a unit for measuring the weight of precious metals.

**caravan** *(n)* a small home on wheels which can be towed by a car.

**carbohydrate** *(n)* one of the substances in foods such as bread and potatoes, that give you energy.

**carbon** 1 *(n)* an element found in coal and diamonds and in all plants and animals. 2 **carbon dioxide** *(n)* a gas that is breathed out by people and animals and is used to make drinks fizzy.

**carcass carcasses** *(n)* the body of a dead animal.

**card** 1 *(n)* stiff paper. 2 *(n)* a folded piece of card sent on birthdays and special occasions. 3 *(n)* one of a set of rectangular pieces of card, used in games.

**cardboard** *(n)* very thick card, used for making boxes.

**cardigan** *(n)* a knitted jacket which fastens down the front.

**care caring cared** 1 *(v)* If you **care** about someone or something, you are very concerned about what happens to them. 2 If you **take care** of someone, you look after them. 3 If you do something **with care**, you take trouble over it.

**career** *(n)* the series of jobs that a person has in their life, usually in the same profession. *A career in teaching.*

**carefree** *(adj)* Someone who is **carefree** has no worries.

**careful** *(adj)* Someone who is **careful** takes trouble over what they are doing and does not take risks. **carefully** *(adv)*.

**careless** *(adj)* not taking much trouble or care over things. **carelessness** *(n)*.

**caress caresses caressing caressed** *(v)* to touch gently. **caress** *(n)*.

**caretaker** *(n)* someone whose job is to look after a school or other building.

**cargo cargoes** *(n)* goods that are carried by ship or aircraft.

**caricature** *(n)* an exaggerated picture of someone.

**carnival** *(n)* a public celebration, when people wear colourful costumes, walk in processions, and dance in the streets.

**carol** *(n)* a religious song that people sing at Christmas. **carol** *(v)*.

**carpenter** *(n)* someone who makes or repairs wooden things. **carpentry** *(n)*.

**carpet** 1 *(n)* a thick floor covering. 2 *(n)* a thick layer of something.

**carriage** 1 *(n)* one of the parts of a train in which passengers travel. 2 *(n)* a vehicle with wheels that is pulled by horses.

**carrot** *(n)* an orange root vegetable.

**carry carries carrying carried** 1 *(v)* to hold on to something and take it somewhere. *Please carry this tray.* 2 *(v)* If a sound **carries**, it can be heard some distance away. **3** *(v)* If you **carry out** a plan or idea, you put it into practice.

**carton** *(n)* a cardboard or plastic box, usually containing food or drink.

**cartoon 1** *(n)* a short, animated film. **2** *(n)* a funny drawing or series of drawings. **cartoonist** *(n)*.

**cartridge 1** *(n)* a tube of ink used in a fountain pen. **2** *(n)* a container that holds a bullet or pellets and the explosive that fires them.

**cartwheel** *(n)* a circular, sideways handstand.

**carve carving carved 1** *(v)* to cut slices from a piece of meat. **2** *(v)* to cut a shape out of wood, stone, etc. **carving** *(n)*.

**case 1** *(n)* a container for carrying clothes when you travel. **2** *(n)* an example of something. *A case of extreme silliness.* **3** *(n)* a trial in a court of law. **4** *(n)* a crime that the police are investigating.

**cash cashes cashing cashed 1** *(n)* money in the form of notes and coins. **2** *(v)* If you **cash in** on something, you take advantage of it.

**cashier** *(n)* someone who takes or pays out money in a shop or bank.

**cashpoint** *(n)* a machine from which people can take out money from their bank accounts, using a plastic card.

**casino** *(n)* a place where people play gambling games such as roulette.

**casket** *(n) (poetic)* a jewellery box.

**casserole** *(n)* a stew that is cooked slowly in the oven.

**cassette** *(n)* a flat, plastic box that contains recording tape, used to record and play sound and pictures. *See* **tape**.

**cast 1** *(n)* the actors in a play or film. **2** *(n)* a hard plaster covering that supports a broken arm or leg.

**castaway** *(n)* someone left on a deserted island after a shipwreck.

**castle 1** *(n)* a large, strong building, often surrounded by a wall and a moat. **2** *(n)* a chesspiece, also known as a rook, that moves in straight lines. *See* **chess**.

**castrate castrating castrated** *(v)* to remove the sex organs of a male animal so that it cannot breed.

**casual 1** *(adj)* not planned. *A casual meeting.* **2** *(adj)* not formal. *Casual dress.*

**casualty casualties 1** *(n)* someone who is injured or killed in an accident, disaster, or war. **2** *(n)* the department in a hospital that handles accidents and emergencies.

**cat 1** *(n)* any member of the cat family, including lions, tigers, etc. **2** *(n)* a small furry mammal, often kept as a pet.

**catalogue 1** *(n)* a book listing things you can buy from a company, or works of art on show in an exhibition. **2** *(n)* a list of all the books in a library.

**catapult** *(n)* a simple, Y-shaped weapon, with elastic stretched over it, used for shooting small stones.

**catarrh** *(kat-arh) (n)* the thick liquid that blocks up your nose and throat when you have a cold.

**catastrophe** *(kat-ass-trof-ee) (n)* a sudden disaster.

**catch catches catching caught 1** *(v)* to grab hold of something moving through the air. **catch** *(n)*. **2** *(v)* to get someone whom you are chasing. *The police caught the thieves.* **3** *(v)* If you **catch** a bus or train, you get on it. **4** *(v)* If you **catch** someone doing something wrong, you see them doing it. **5** *(n)* a fastening on a door, box, etc.

**category categories** *(n)* a group of things that have something in common.

**cater catering catered 1** *(v)* to provide food for a lot of people. **catering** *(n)*. **2** *(v)* to provide people with the things that they need. *This shop caters for all tastes.*

**caterpillar** *(n)* a worm-like larva that changes into a butterfly or moth. *This picture shows a swallowtail caterpillar.*

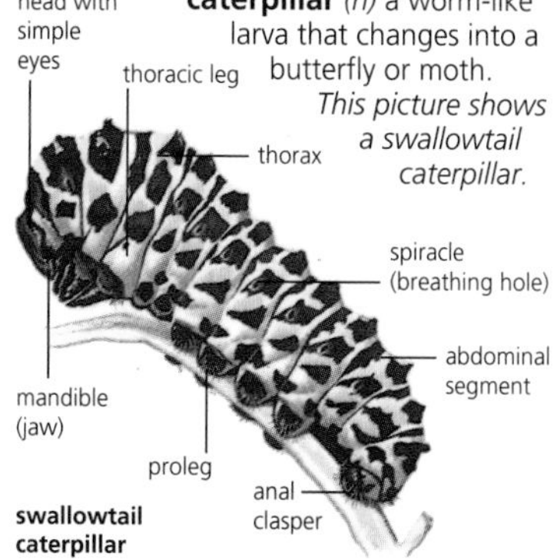


**swallowtail caterpillar**

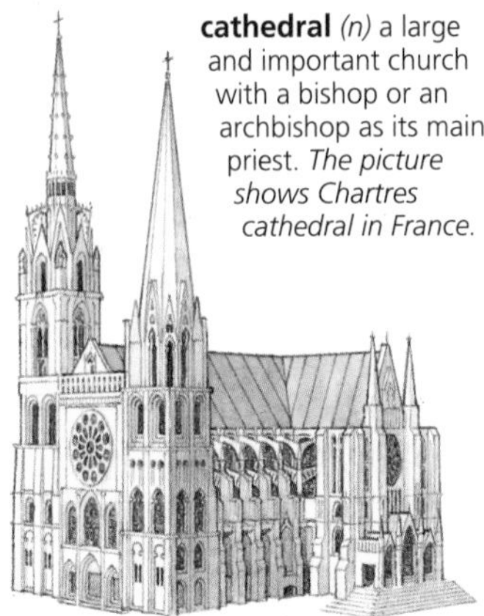

**cathedral** *(n)* a large and important church with a bishop or an archbishop as its main priest. *The picture shows Chartres cathedral in France.*

**Catholic** *(n)* a member of the Roman Catholic Church. **Catholic** *(adj).*

**cattle** *(plural n)* cows and bulls.

**cauldron** *(n)* a large, rounded cooking pot.

**cauliflower** *(n)* a vegetable with a large, white centre, surrounded by leaves.

**cause** causing caused 1 *(v)* to make something happen. 2 *(n)* the reason that something happens.

**cautious** *(adj)* If you are **cautious**, you try hard to avoid mistakes or danger. **caution** *(n),* **cautiously** *(adv).*

**cavalry** *(plural n)* soldiers who fight on horseback.

**cave** *(n)* a large hole underground or in the side of a hill or cliff.

**caveman** cavemen *(n)* someone who lived in caves in prehistoric times.

**cavern** *(n)* a large cave. **cavernous** *(adj).*

**caving** *(n)* If you go **caving**, you explore caves. **caver** *(n).*

**cavity** cavities *(n)* a hole or hollow space in something solid, such as a tooth.

**CD** *short for* **compact disc**.

**CD-ROM** *(n)* a disc used with a computer monitor or television screen which produces text and pictures. The initials stand for compact disc read only memory.

**cease** ceasing ceased *(v)* to stop.

**cease-fire** *(n)* a period during a war when both sides agree to stop fighting.

**ceaseless** *(adj)* never stopping.

**ceiling** *(n)* the upper surface inside a room.

**celebrate** celebrating celebrated *(v)* to do something enjoyable on a special occasion, such as having a party. **celebration** *(n),* **celebratory** *(adj).*

**celebrity** celebrities *(n)* a famous person, like an entertainer or a film star.

**celery** *(n)* a vegetable with white or green crisp stalks, often eaten in salads.

**celestial** *(adj)* to do with heaven.

**cell** 1 *(n)* a room in a prison or a police station where someone is locked up. 2 *(n)* a basic, microscopic part of a living thing.

**cellar** *(n)* a room below ground level in a house, often used for storage.

**Celsius** *or* **centigrade** *(adj)* measured on a temperature scale on which water boils at 100° and freezes at 0°.

**cement** *(n)* a grey powder, used in building, that becomes hard when you mix it with water and let it dry.

**cemetery** cemeteries *(n)* a place where people are buried.

**censor** censoring censored *(v)* to remove parts of a book, film, play, etc. that are thought to be harmful to people. **censor** *(n),* **censorship** *(n).*

**census** *(n)* an official count of all the people living in a country.

**centenary** centenaries *(n)* the hundredth anniversary of something.

**centigrade** *see* **Celsius**.

**centipede** *(n)* a very small creature with a very long body and lots of legs.

**central** 1 *(adj)* in the middle. **centrally** *(adv).* 2 *(adj)* most important. *The central problem.*

**centre** centring centred 1 *(n)* the middle of something. 2 *(n)* a place where people go to do a particular activity. *A sports centre.* 3 *(v)* to concentrate on something. *The story centres on China.*

**century** centuries *(n)* a period of 100 years.

**cereal** 1 *(n)* a grain crop grown for food, such as wheat, oats, or maize. 2 *(n)* a breakfast food usually made from grain and eaten with milk.

*Some words that begin with a "c" sound are spelt with a "k".*

**ceremony** ceremonies *(n)* formal actions, words, and often music, performed to mark an important occasion. *A wedding ceremony.*

**certain** 1 *(adj)* sure about something. *Alex was certain he had posted the letter.* 2 *(adj)* particular. *Will cannot eat certain foods.*

**certificate** *(n)* a piece of paper given to someone to prove that they have done something. *An examination certificate.*

**CFC** *short for* **chlorofluorocarbon**.

**chain** 1 *(n)* a line of metal rings, called links, joined together. 2 *(n)* a series of connected things. *A chain of events.* 3 **chain store** *(n)* one of a group of shops in different towns that are owned by the same company and sell similar goods.

**chair** 1 *(n)* a piece of furniture that you sit on, with four legs and a back. 2 *(n)* the person in charge of a meeting. **chair** *(v).*

**chair lift** *(n)* a line of chairs attached to a moving cable, used for carrying people up mountains.

**chalet** *(**shall**-ay)* *(n)* a small wooden house with a sloping roof.

**chalk** 1 *(n)* a soft, white rock. 2 *(n)* a stick of soft rock, used for writing on blackboards.

**challenge** challenging challenged 1 *(n)* something difficult that you try to do. 2 *(v)* to invite someone to fight you or to try to do something. **challenge** *(n).*

**chamber** 1 *(n)* a large room. 2 *(n)* a hollow place in something.

**chameleon** *(ker-**mee**-lee-un)* *(n)* a lizard that can change colour.

**chameleon**

**champagne** *(sham-**payn**)* *(n)* an expensive, sparkling white wine, drunk on special occasions.

**champion** *(n)* the winner of a contest.

**chance** 1 *(n)* the possibility of something happening. *We have a chance of winning the cup.* 2 *(n)* an opportunity to do something. 3 If you **take a chance**, you try something even though it is risky. 4 If something happens **by chance**, it happens accidentally.

**change** changing changed 1 *(v)* to become different or to make something different. **change** *(n).* 2 *(n)* If you pay more money than something costs, the money you get back is called **change**. 3 *(n)* coins rather than banknotes.

**channel** 1 *(n)* a narrow stretch of sea between two areas of land. 2 *(n)* a television or radio station.

**chant** chanting chanted *(v)* to say or sing a phrase over and over again.

**Chanukah** *see* **Hanukkah**.

**chaos** *(**kay**-oss)* *(n)* total confusion. **chaotic** *(adj),* **chaotically** *(adv).*

**chapel** 1 *(n)* a small church. 2 *(n)* a side section of a large church. 3 *(n)* a place in a school, prison, etc. where Christian services are held.

**chapter** *(n)* one of the parts into which a book is divided.

**character** 1 *(n)* Your **character** is what sort of person you are. 2 *(n)* one of the people in a story, book, film, or play.

**characteristic** 1 *(n)* a typical quality or feature. *Stubbornness is a characteristic of our family.* 2 *(adj)* typical. *Sophie worked with characteristic efficiency.*

**charcoal** *(n)* a form of carbon made from burnt wood.

**charge** charging charged 1 *(v)* to ask someone to pay a particular price for something. **charge** *(n).* 2 *(v)* to rush at someone in order to attack them. **charge** *(n).* 3 If someone is **in charge** of something, they have to deal with it or take control of it.

**chariot** *(n)* a small, horse-drawn vehicle, used in ancient times in battles or races. *The picture shows a Roman chariot.*

**Roman chariot**

*Some words that begin with a "c" sound are spelt with a "k".*

**charity** charities 1 *(singular n)* money or other help that is given to people in need. 2 *(n)* an organization which raises money to help people in need.

**charm** charming charmed *(v)* to please someone and make them like you. **charming** *(adj)*, **charm** *(n)*.

**chart** 1 *(n)* a drawing that shows information as a table or a picture. 2 *(n)* a map of the stars or the sea.

**charter** chartering chartered 1 *(n)* a formal document that states the rights or duties of a group of people. 2 *(v)* to hire a bus, coach, plane, etc. for private use.

**chase** chasing chased *(v)* to run after someone in order to catch them or make them go away. **chase** *(n)*.

**chasm** *(kaz-um)* *(n)* a deep crack in the surface of the Earth.

**chat** chatting chatted *(v)* to talk in a friendly and informal way. **chat** *(n)*.

**château** *(shat-oh)* châteaux *(n)* a castle or large country house in France.

*The picture shows the château of Azay-le Rideau in the Loire valley in France.*

**chatter** chattering chattered 1 *(v)* to talk about unimportant things. **chatter** *(n)*. 2 *(v)* When your teeth **chatter**, they knock together because you are cold.

**chauffeur** *(show-fur)* *(n)* someone whose job is to drive for somebody else.

**chauvinist** *(show-vin-ist)* 1 *(n)* a man who believes that women are inferior to men. 2 *(n)* someone who believes that no other country is as good or as important as their own.

**cheap** cheaper cheapest 1 *(adj)* not costing very much. 2 *(adj)* unkind and mean. *A cheap trick.*

**cheat** cheating cheated *(v)* to act dishonestly in order to win a game or get what you want. **cheat** *(n)*.

**check** checking checked 1 *(v)* to look at something in order to make sure that it is all right. **check** *(n)*. 2 *(v)* to stop something from moving or growing. 3 *(n)* a pattern of different coloured squares. **checked** *(adj)*.

**check out** *(n)* the place in the supermarket where you pay for your goods.

**checkup** *(n)* a medical examination to make sure that there is nothing wrong with you.

**cheek** 1 *(n)* the side of your face below your eyes. 2 *(n)* rude and disrespectful behaviour or speech. **cheeky** *(adj)*.

**cheer** cheering cheered 1 *(v)* to shout encouragement or approval. **cheer** *(n)*. 2 *(v)* If you **cheer up**, you become happier.

**cheerful** *(adj)* happy and lively. **cheerfulness** *(n)*, **cheerfully** *(adv)*.

**cheese** *(n)* a food made from the solid parts of milk after it has turned sour.

**cheetah** *(n)* a wild cat with a spotted coat that is found in Africa.

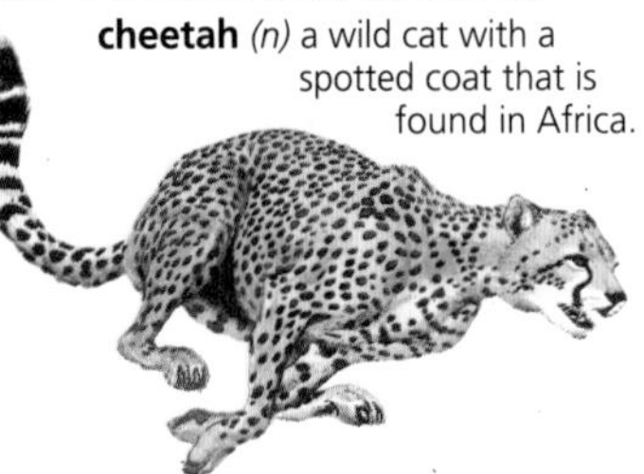

**chef** *(sheff)* *(n)* the chief cook in a restaurant.

**chemical** 1 *(n)* a substance used in chemistry. 2 *(adj)* to do with, or made by chemistry. *A chemical reaction. Chemical fertilizers.* **chemically** *(adv)*.

**chemist** 1 *(n)* a trained person who prepares and sells drugs and medicines. 2 *(n)* a shop that sells drugs and medicines.

**chemistry** *(n)* the scientific study of substances and the ways in which they react with each other.

**cheque** *(n)* a printed piece of paper on which someone writes to tell their bank to pay money from their account.

**cherish** cherishes cherishing cherished *(v)* to care for someone or something in a kind and loving way.

**cherry** cherries *(n)* a small red or black fruit with a stone at its centre.

**chess** *(n)* a game for two people with sixteen pieces each, played on a black and white board.

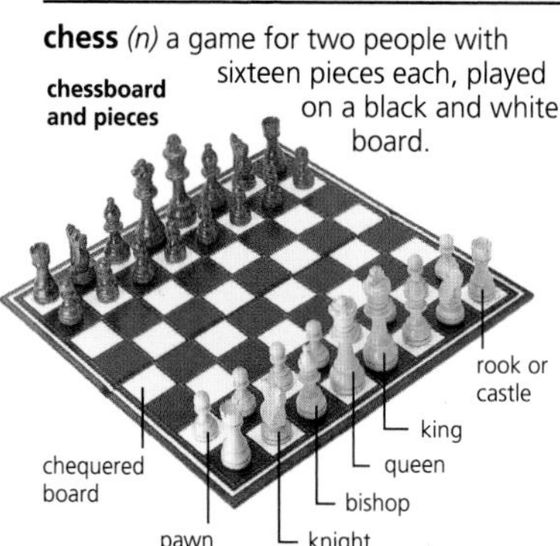


**chest** 1 *(n)* the front part of your body between your neck and waist. 2 *(n)* a large, strong box.

**chest of drawers** **chests of drawers** *(n)* a piece of furniture with drawers, used for storing clothes.

**chew** **chewing** **chewed** *(v)* to crush food in your teeth.

**chewing gum** *(n)* a kind of sweet that you chew, but do not swallow.

**chick** *(n)* a very young bird, especially a very young hen.

**chicken** 1 *(n)* a hen, usually a young one. 2 *(n)* the meat from a hen.

**chickenpox** *(n)* a common disease that gives you red, itchy spots on your skin.

**chief** 1 *(n)* the leader of a group of people. 2 *(adj)* main, or most important.

**child** **children** 1 *(n)* someone who is not yet grown up. 2 *(n)* a son or daughter.

**childhood** *(n)* the time when you are a child. *Marcus had a happy childhood.*

**childish** *(adj)* immature and stupid. **childishness** *(n)*, **childishly** *(adv)*.

**child minder** *(n)* someone who looks after children while their parents work.

**chill** **chilling** **chilled** 1 *(v)* to make something cold. 2 *(n)* a feeling of slight coldness. 3 *(n)* a cold. *Don't catch a chill.*

**chime** **chiming** **chimed** *(v)* When a bell or clock **chimes**, it makes a ringing sound.

**chimney** *(n)* a vertical pipe through which smoke escapes from a fire.

**chimpanzee** *(n)* a large ape with dark fur, that comes from Africa. *See* **ape**.

**chin** *(n)* the part of your face below your mouth.

**china** 1 *(n)* very thin, delicate pottery. 2 *(n)* cups, plates, and dishes made of china.

**chink** 1 *(n)* a narrow opening. 2 *(n)* a gentle jingling sound. *The chink of glasses.*

**chip** **chipping** **chipped** 1 *(v)* to break a small piece off something by accident. **chip** *(n)*. 2 *(n)* a long, thin piece of potato, cooked in oil. 3 *(n)* a tiny piece of silicon, with electronic circuits printed on it, used in computers and electronic equipment. *The silicon chip shown here is small enough to fit on your fingernail.*

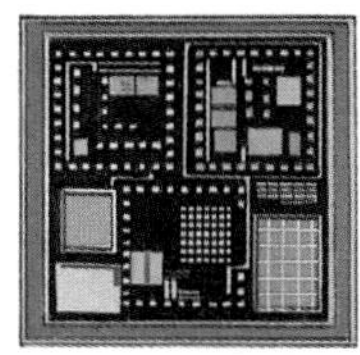
**silicon chip** (magnified)

**chlorine** *(klor-een)* *(n)* a strong-smelling gas which is added to water to kill harmful germs. **chlorinate** *(v)*.

**chlorofluorocarbon** *(klor-oh-flor-oh-kar-bon)* *(n)* a gas containing chlorine, that damages the Earth's ozone layer.

**chocolate** *(n)* a sweet food made from beans that grow on the cacao tree.

**choice** 1 *(n)* the thing or person that you have selected. *Jake was a good choice as team captain.* 2 *(n)* all the things that you can choose from. *This menu offers a very wide choice.* 3 *(adj)* of very good quality. *Choice fruit and vegetables.*

**choir** *(kwire)* *(n)* a group of people who sing together.

**choke** **choking** **choked** 1 *(v)* to struggle to breathe because something is blocking your breathing passages. 2 *(v)* to kill someone by squeezing their neck until they stop breathing.

**choose** **choosing** **chose** **chosen** 1 *(v)* to pick out one person or thing from several. 2 *(v)* to decide to do something.

**chop** **chopping** **chopped** *(v)* to cut something with a knife or an axe.

**choppy** **choppier** **choppiest** *(adj)* When the sea is **choppy**, it is quite rough.

**chopsticks** *(plural n)* narrow sticks for eating food, used by people in Far Eastern countries.

**choral** *(**kor**-al) (adj)* sung by a choir. *Choral music.*

**chord** *(kord) (n)* a combination of musical notes played at the same time.

**chore** *(chaw) (n)* a job that has to be done many times, such as washing dishes or cleaning.

**choreographer** *(kor-ee-**og**-raf-er) (n)* someone who arranges dance steps and movements for a ballet or show.

**chorus** *(**kor**-uss)* **choruses chorusing chorused 1** *(n)* the part of a song that is repeated after each verse. **2** *(v)* to say something all together.

**Christ** *(n)* the name given to Jesus, the man whom Christians believe is the son of God and the saviour. *This mosaic of Christ was made in the 12th century.*

**Christ**

**christening** *(n)* a ceremony in which a person is accepted into the Christian church and given a name. **christen** *(v).*

**Christianity** *(n)* the religion based on the life and teachings of Jesus Christ. Christians believe that Jesus is the son of God, and that they will live with God after they die, if they believe in him and follow his teachings. **Christian** *(n).*

**Christmas Christmases** *(n)* the festival which celebrates the birth of Jesus Christ.

**chronic 1** *(adj)* If something is **chronic**, it does not get better for a long time. *Chronic bronchitis.* **2** *(adj) (informal)* very bad.

**chronological** *(adj)* arranged in the order in which events happened. **chronology** *(n).*

**chrysalis** *(**kriss**-er-liss)* **chrysalises** *(n)* a moth or butterfly at the stage between a caterpillar and an adult.

**chubby chubbier chubbiest** *(adj)* slightly fat, or plump.

**chuck chucking chucked** *(v) (informal)* to throw something carelessly.

**chuckle chuckling chuckled** *(v)* to laugh quietly. **chuckle** *(n).*

**chunk** *(n)* a thick piece of something.

**church churches 1** *(n)* a building used by Christians for worship. **2** *(n)* a group of Christians.

**churn churning churned 1** *(n)* a large, metal container for milk. **2** *(v)* to move around roughly. *The tractor churned through the mud.*

**chutney** *(n)* a mixture of vegetables, fruit, and spices, eaten with other food.

**cigar** *(n)* a thick, brown roll of tobacco which people smoke.

**cigarette** *(n)* a thin roll of tobacco, covered with paper, which people smoke.

**cinder** *(n)* a small piece of wood or coal that has been partly burned.

**cinema** *(n)* a large building where people go to watch films.

**circa** *(prep)* the Latin word for about. You can also write circa as "c." *Geoffrey Chaucer was born circa 1340.*

**circle circling circled 1** *(n)* a flat, perfectly round shape. *The diagrams show parts of a circle.* **2** *(v)* to draw or make a circle around something. *The plane circled the airport.* **3** *(n)* a group of people who all know each other.

**parts of a circle**

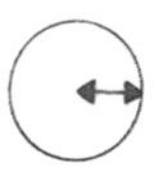

radius

circumference

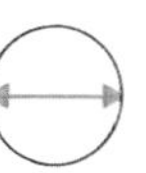

diameter

semicircle

**circuit** *(**sir**-kit)* **1** *(n)* a circular route. *A race circuit.* **2** *(n)* the complete path that an electrical current can flow around.

**circulation 1** *(n)* the number of copies of a newspaper, magazine, etc. that are bought each day, week, etc. **2** *(n)* the movement of blood around the body.

**circumcision** *(n)* the removal of the foreskin at the end of a boy's or a man's penis, usually for religious reasons.

**circumference 1** *(n)* the outer edge of a circle. *See* **circle**. **2** *(n)* the distance around the edge of a circle.

**circumstance** *(n)* The **circumstances** of an event are the things which affect the way it happens. *Laura took her exam under very difficult circumstances.*

*Some words that begin with a "c" sound are spelt with a "k".*
*Some words that begin with a "ci" sound are spelt "psy", "sci", "scy," or "si".*

**circus** circuses *(n)* a travelling show in which clowns and acrobats perform.

**citizen** 1 *(n)* a member of a particular country who has the right to live there. 2 *(n)* a person who lives in a particular town or city.

**citrus fruit** *(n)* a sharp-tasting, juicy fruit such as an orange, lemon, or grapefruit.

**city** cities *(n)* a very large or important town.

**civil** 1 *(adj)* polite. **civility** *(n)*. 2 **civil war** *(n)* a war between different groups of people within the same country.

**civilian** *(n)* someone who is not a member of the armed forces.

**civilization** 1 *(n)* a highly developed and organized society, especially one in the past. *The ancient civilization of Greece.* 2 *(n)* an advanced stage of human development, organization, and culture.

**claim** claiming claimed 1 *(v)* to say that something belongs to you, or that you have a right to have it. *My dad claims unemployment benefit.* **claim** *(n)*. 2 *(v)* to say that something is true. *Ned claims he can beat me.* **claim** *(n)*.

**clamber** clambering clambered *(v)* to climb up or over something with difficulty.

**clammy** clammier clammiest *(adj)* unpleasantly damp. *Clammy hands.*

**clamour** clamouring clamoured *(v)* to demand something noisily. *The children all clamoured for food.* **clamour** *(n)*.

**clamp** clamping clamped 1 *(n)* a tool for holding things firmly in place. 2 *(v)* When you **clamp down** on something, you control it more firmly.

**clan** *(n)* a large group of related families, especially in Scotland.

**clap** clapping clapped 1 *(v)* to hit your hands together to show that you have enjoyed something. 2 *(n)* a loud bang of thunder.

**clarify** clarifies clarifying clarified *(v)* to make something clear or easy to understand. **clarification** *(n)*.

**clarity** *(n)* clearness.

**clash** clashes clashing clashed 1 *(v)* to fight or argue violently. 2 *(v)* If colours **clash**, they look unpleasant together. 3 *(v)* to make a loud, crashing noise.

**clasp** clasping clasped 1 *(v)* to hold on to something firmly and tightly. 2 *(n)* a small fastener, for example, on a purse.

**class** classes 1 *(n)* a group of people who are taught together. 2 *(n)* a group of people in society. *The middle class.*

**classic** 1 *(adj)* of very good quality and likely to remain popular for a long time. *A classic film.* 2 *(adj)* typical. *A classic example of sixties style.*

**classical** 1 *(adj)* in the style of ancient Greece or Rome. *Classical architecture.* 2 **classical music** *(n)* serious music that does not become out of date.

**clatter** clattering clattered *(v)* When things **clatter**, they bang together noisily.

**claustrophobia** *(klos-trof-**oh**-bee-yuh)* *(n)* the fear of being in small, enclosed places. **claustrophobic** *(adj)*.

**claw** *(n)* a hard, curved nail on the foot of an animal or a bird.

**clay** *(n)* a kind of earth that is baked to make bricks or pottery.

**clean** cleaning cleaned; cleaner cleanest 1 *(adj)* not dirty, or not messy. 2 *(v)* to remove the dirt from something.

**cleanse** cleansing cleansed *(v)* to make something clean or pure.

**clear** clearing cleared; clearer clearest 1 *(adj)* easy to see through. 2 *(adj)* easy to understand. **clearly** *(adv)*. 3 *(v)* to remove things that are covering or blocking a place. *Clear the table.* **clear** *(adj)*.

**clench** clenches clenching clenched *(v)* to hold or squeeze something tightly.

**clergy** *(plural n)* priests in the Christian church.

**clever** cleverer cleverest 1 *(adj)* able to understand things or to do things quickly and easily. 2 *(adj)* intelligently and carefully thought out. *A clever plan.*

**cliché** *(**klee**-shay)* *(n)* a phrase that is used so often that it no longer has much meaning. *"Over the moon" is a cliché.*

**click** clicking clicked *(v)* to make a short, sharp sound. **click** *(n)*.

**client** *(n)* someone who uses the services of a professional person, such as a lawyer or an accountant.

**cliff** *(n)* a high, steep rock face on a coast.

*Some words that begin with a "c" sound are spelt with a "k".*

**cliffhanger** *(n)* a story, film, etc. that is exciting because you do not know what is going to happen next.

**climate** *(n)* the usual weather in a place. *A warm climate.* **climatic** *(adj).*

**climax** **climaxes** *(n)* the most exciting part of a story or an event, which usually happens near the end.

**climb** **climbing climbed** **1** *(v)* to move upwards. **climber** *(n).* **2** *(n)* an upwards movement or slope. **3** *(v)* to get on or off something, using your hands to support and help you.

**cling** **clinging clung** *(v)* to hold on to something or someone very tightly.

**clinic** *(n)* a room or building where people can go for specialist medical treatment or advice. *A health clinic.*

**clip** **clipping clipped** **1** *(v)* to trim something. *Clip the hedge.* **2** *(v)* to attach things together with a fastener. **3** *(n)* a small metal or plastic fastener. **4** *(n)* a short piece of a film shown by itself.

**clipboard** *(n)* a board with a clip at the top, for holding papers.

**cloak** **1** *(n)* a loose coat with no sleeves, that you wrap around your shoulders and do up at the neck. **2** **cloakroom** *(n)* a room where you can hang coats, or a room with toilets and basins.

**clock** *(n)* an instrument that tells the time.

**clockwise** *(adv)* in the direction that the hands of a clock move. **clockwise** *(adj).*

**clockwork** *(n)* a mechanism that works things like clocks and toys when they are wound up with a key. **clockwork** *(adj).*

**clod** *(n)* a lump of earth or clay.

**clog** **clogging clogged** **1** *(v)* to block something. *Some leaves had clogged the drain.* **2** *(n)* a heavy wooden shoe, often worn in the Netherlands.

**clone** **cloning cloned** *(v)* to grow a plant or animal from the cells of a parent plant or animal, so that it is identical to the parent. **clone** *(n).*

**close** **closing closed; closer closest** **1** *(cloze) (v)* to shut something. **2** *(cloze) (v)* to end something. *The judge closed the case.* **3** *(rhymes with dose) (adv)* near. *Stay close to me!* **close** *(adj).* **4** *(rhymes with dose) (adj)* careful. *Keep a close watch on the children.* **closely** *(adv).* **5** *(rhymes with dose) (adj)* When the weather is **close**, it is very hot and humid.

**closed-circuit television** *(n)* a television system that shows what happens nearby.

**close-up** *(n)* a very detailed view of something, especially a photograph taken from close to a person or thing.

**clot** **clotting clotted** *(v)* When a liquid, such as blood, **clots**, it becomes thicker and forms lumps. **clot** *(n).*

**cloth** **1** *(n)* material made from wool, cotton, etc. **2** *(n)* a small piece of material used for cleaning.

**clothes** *(plural n)* things that you wear, for example, shirts and trousers.

**cloud** **1** *(n)* a white or grey mass of water drops or ice crystals suspended in the air. **cloudy** *(adj).* **2** *(n)* a mass of smoke or dust. **cloudy** *(adj).*

**clown** **1** *(n)* an entertainer who wears funny clothes, has a painted face, and tries to make people laugh. **2** *(n)* someone who does silly or foolish things. **clown** *(v).*

**club** **1** *(n)* a group of people who meet regularly to enjoy a common interest. **2** *(n)* a stick with a metal or wooden head used in the game of golf. **3** *(n)* a thick, heavy stick used as a weapon. **4** **clubs** *(plural n)* one of the four suits in a pack of cards, with a black three-leafed symbol.

**clue** *(n)* something that helps you to find an answer to a question or a mystery.

**clump** **clumping clumped** **1** *(n)* a group of trees or other plants growing together. **2** *(v)* to walk slowly, with clumsy, noisy footsteps. *Edwin clumped up the stairs.*

**clumsy** **clumsier clumsiest** *(adj)* careless and awkward in the way that you move or behave. **clumsiness** *(n),* **clumsily** *(adv).*

**cluster** **clustering clustered** *(v)* to stand or grow close together. *The flowers clustered around the tree.* **cluster** *(n).*

**clutch** **clutches clutching clutched** *(v)* to hold on to something tightly.

**clutter** **cluttering cluttered** *(v)* to fill a place and make it messy. **clutter** *(n).*

**coach** **coaches** **1** *(n)* a bus used for long journeys. **2** *(n)* a teacher of a sport or skill. **3** *(n)* a carriage pulled by horses.

**coal** *(n)* a black rock which is burned as a fuel.

**coarse** **coarser coarsest** 1 *(adj)* If something is **coarse**, it has a rough texture or surface. **coarseness** *(n)*. 2 *(adj)* If a person is **coarse**, they are rude and have bad manners. **coarseness** *(n)*.

**coast** **coasting coasted** 1 *(n)* the land that is next to the sea. **coastal** *(adj)*. 2 *(v)* to move along in a car or other vehicle without using any power.

**coastguard** *(n)* someone who watches the sea for ships in danger and who looks out for smugglers.

**coat** 1 *(n)* a piece of clothing that you wear over other clothes to keep warm. 2 *(n)* an animal's fur or wool. 3 *(v)* to cover a surface with a thin layer of something.

**coax** *(kokes)* **coaxes coaxing coaxed** *(v)* to persuade someone gently and patiently to do something.

**cobbled** *(adj)* A **cobbled** road is paved with small, round stones, called cobbles.

**cobra** *(n)* a large, poisonous snake found in Africa and Asia.

**cobweb** *(n)* a very fine net of sticky threads, made by a spider to catch insects.

**cock** 1 *(n)* a fully-grown male chicken. 2 *(n)* a male bird.

**cockpit** *(n)* the area in the front of a plane where the pilot sits.

**cocktail** *(n)* a drink made by mixing several different kinds of drink together.

**cocoa** *(n)* a hot, milky drink made with the roasted and ground beans of the cacao tree.

**coconut** *(n)* a very large nut with a hard, hairy shell and sweet, white flesh.

**cocoon** *(n)* a covering made from threads or mucus, produced by some animals to protect themselves or their eggs.

**cod** **cod** *(n)* a fish which has white flesh that you can eat.

**code** 1 *(n)* a system of words, letters, or numbers, used instead of ordinary words to send secret messages, or to give information briefly. *Morse code.* 2 *(n)* a set of rules. *The highway code.*

**coeducation** *(n)* the system of teaching boys and girls together in the same school. **coeducational** *(adj)*.

**coerce** *(ko-erss)* **coercing coerced** *(v)* to force someone to do something.

**coffee** *(n)* a hot drink made with roasted and ground beans from the coffee shrub.

**coffin** *(n)* a box which contains the body or the ashes of a dead person.

**cog** *(n)* one of the teeth on the edge of a wheel that turns machinery. *See* **gear**.

**coherent** *(ko-**hear**-unt) (adj)* clear and logical. *A coherent argument.*

**coil** **coiling coiled** 1 *(v)* to wind something round and round into a series of loops. *The sailor coiled the rope neatly.* **coil** *(n)*. 2 *(v)* to form loops. *The snake coiled around Perdita's leg.*

**coin** *(n)* a piece of money in the form of a metal disc. **coinage** *(n)*.

**coincide** *(ko-in-**side**)* **coinciding coincided** *(v)* If two things **coincide**, they happen at the same time.

**coincidence** *(ko-**in**-sid-enss) (n)* a chance happening or meeting. **coincidental** *(adj)*.

**colander** *(n)* a bowl with holes in it, used for draining liquid off food.

**cold** **colder coldest** 1 *(adj)* having a low temperature. **cold** *(n)*. 2 *(adj)* unfriendly. **coldly** *(adv)*. 3 *(n)* a common, mild illness that causes sneezing and a sore throat.

**cold-blooded** 1 *(adj)* **Cold-blooded** animals have body temperatures that change according to the temperature of their surroundings. *Reptiles and fish are cold-blooded.* 2 *(adj)* A **cold-blooded** act is done deliberately and cruelly.

**collaborate** **collaborating collaborated** *(v)* to work with someone and help them to do something.

**collage** *(**kol**-arj) (n)* a picture made by sticking things on a surface, for example, sticking pieces of cloth on paper.

**collapse** **collapsing collapsed** *(v)* to fall down suddenly from weakness or illness.

**collar** 1 *(n)* the part of a shirt, blouse, coat, etc. which fits round your neck and is usually folded down. 2 *(n)* a thin band worn round the neck of a dog or cat.

**colleague** *(n)* someone who works with you.

**collect** **collecting collected** 1 *(v)* to gather things together. 2 *(v)* to fetch someone or something from a place.

**collection** 1 *(n)* a group of things gathered over a long time. *A shell collection.* 2 *(n)* If you hold a **collection** for something, you take money for it.

**college** *(n)* a place where students can continue to study after leaving school.

**collide** colliding collided *(v)* to crash into something violently, often at high speed. **collision** *(n).*

**colliery** collieries *(n)* a coal mine.

**colloquial** *(kol-oh-kwee-al) (adj)* **Colloquial** language is spoken, but not usually written down.

**colon** *(n)* the punctuation mark (:) used to introduce a list of things.

**colony** colonies 1 *(n)* a country that has been settled in by people from another country and is controlled by that country. 2 *(n)* a large group of insects that live together.

**colossal** *(adj)* extremely large.

**colour** colouring coloured 1 *(n)* When you say what **colour** something is, you say whether it is red, yellow, black, etc. 2 *(v)* to make something red, yellow, black, etc. 3 **colour blind** *(adj)* unable to see the difference between certain colours. *You may not be able to see the number in this pattern if you are colour blind.*

**colour blindness test**

**colt** *(n)* a young male horse.

**column** 1 *(n)* a tall, upright pillar that helps to support a building or statue. 2 *(n)* a row of figures or words running down a page.

**coma** *(n)* a state of deep unconsciousness from which it is very hard to wake up.

**comb** combing combed 1 *(n)* a flat piece of metal or plastic with a row of teeth, used for making your hair smooth and tidy. 2 *(v)* to use a comb to make your hair smooth and tidy.

**combat** combating combated 1 *(v)* to fight against something. *Regular brushing helps combat tooth decay.* 2 *(n)* fighting between people or armies.

**combine** combining combined *(v)* to join or mix two or more things together. **combination** *(n).*

**come** coming came come 1 *(v)* to move towards a place. *Louise came into the garden.* 2 *(v)* to arrive. *Barney waited for his friends to come.* 3 *(v)* If you **come from** a particular place, you were born in that place. 4 *(v)* If something **comes about**, it happens. 5 *(v)* If you **come across** something, you find it by chance.

**comedian** *(n)* an entertainer who tells jokes and funny stories.

**comedy** comedies 1 *(n)* a funny play or film. 2 *(n)* anything that makes people laugh. *Merlin's skating was a comedy.*

**comet** *(n)* an object that travels around the Sun, leaving a trail of light behind it.

**comfort** comforting comforted 1 *(v)* to make someone feel less worried or upset. *We comforted the lost child.* 2 *(n)* the feeling of being relaxed and free from pain or worries. **comfortable** *(adj).*

**comic** 1 *(n)* a magazine containing stories told with pictures. 2 *(n)* someone who tells jokes and funny stories. **comic** *(adj).* 3 *(adj)* funny or amusing.

**comma** *(n)* the punctuation mark (,) used for separating different parts of a sentence or different words in a list.

**command** commanding commanded 1 *(v)* to order someone to do something. 2 *(v)* to have control over a group of people in the armed forces.

**commemorate** commemorating commemorated *(v)* to do something special to remember an event or the life of an important person. **commemoration** *(n).*

**commence** commencing commenced *(v)* to begin something.

**commend** commending commended *(v)* to say that someone has done something very well. *The mayor commended our courage.*

**comment** commenting commented *(v)* to give an explanation or an opinion about something. **comment** *(n).*

**commentary** commentaries *(n)* a description of an event as it is happening, often broadcast on television or radio. *A race commentary.* **commentator** *(n).*

**commercial** 1 *(adj)* to do with buying and selling goods. *Commercial activities.* 2 *(adj)* having profit as a main aim. *A commercial scheme.* 3 *(n)* a television or radio advertisement.

**commiserate** commiserating commiserated *(v)* to share someone else's sadness or disappointment. *We commiserated with Aled over his bad luck.* commiserations *(plural n).*

**commit** committing committed 1 *(v)* to do something wrong or illegal. *To commit murder.* 2 *(v)* If you **commit** yourself to something, you promise that you will do it or support it. commitment *(n).*

**committee** *(n)* a group of people chosen to discuss things and make decisions for a larger group.

**common** commoner commonest 1 *(adj)* existing in large numbers. 2 *(adj)* happening often. *A common problem.* 3 *(adj)* ordinary and not special in any way. 3 *(adj)* shared by two or more people. *This feature is common to both cars.* 4 **common sense** *(n)* the ability to think and behave sensibly.

**commotion** *(n)* a lot of noisy, excited activity.

**communal** *(adj)* shared by several people. *A communal bathroom.*

**commune** *(n)* a group of people who live together and share things.

**communicate** communicating communicated *(v)* to share information, ideas, or feelings with another person by talking, writing, etc. communication *(n).*

**Communion** *(n)* a Christian service in which people eat bread and drink wine in memory of the death and resurrection of Jesus Christ.

**communism** *(n)* a way of organizing a country so that all the land, houses, factories, etc. belong to the state and the profits are shared among everyone. communist *(n),* communist *(adj).*

**community** communities *(n)* a group of people who live in the same area or who all have something in common.

**commuter** *(n)* someone who travels to work each day, usually by car or train.

**compact** *(adj)* cleverly designed to take up very little space. compactness *(n).*

**compact disc** *(n)* a disc with music or information stored on it.
*The picture inset below shows the thin metal layer inside the compact disc, with its pattern of pits and flats, which is read by a laser beam.*

**compact disc**
(magnified view from below)



**companion** *(n)* someone whom you spend time with, either through friendship or by chance.

**company** companies 1 *(n)* a group of people who work together to produce or sell something. 2 *(n)* a group of actors or dancers who work together. 3 *(n)* one or more guests. *We have company tonight.*

**comparative** 1 *(adj)* judged against other similar things. *This year's play was a comparative success.* 2 *(adj)* **Comparative** adjectives and adverbs are used when you compare two things or actions. *"Older" is the comparative of "old"; "more quickly" is the comparative of "quickly".*

**compare** comparing compared *(v)* to judge one thing against another and notice similarities and differences. comparison *(n).*

**compartment** 1 *(n)* one of the small areas into which a railway carriage is divided. 2 *(n)* a separate part of a container, used for keeping certain things.

**compass** compasses 1 *(n)* an instrument used for finding directions, with a magnetic needle that always points north. 2 **compasses** *(plural n)* an instrument used for drawing circles.

**compassion** *(n)* a feeling of sympathy for people who are suffering. compassionate *(adj).*

**compatible** *(adj)* If people or objects are **compatible**, they can live together or be used together without difficulty. compatibility *(n).*

**compel** compelling compelled *(v)* to make someone do something by giving them orders or by using force.

**compensate** compensating compensated *(v)* to make up for something. *Nothing can compensate for my suffering.* **compensation** *(n).*

**competent** *(adj)* If you are **competent** at something, you have the skill or ability to do it well. **competence** *(n).*

**competition** 1 *(n)* an event in which two or more people try to do something as well as they can, to see who is the best. **competitor** *(n),* **compete** *(v).* 2 *(n)* a situation in which two or more people are trying to get the same thing. *There was a lot of competition for places at the school.*

**competitive** 1 *(adj)* A **competitive** sport or game is one where the players try to win. 2 *(adj)* very eager to win.

**compile** compiling compiled *(v)* to write a book or a report by bringing together many different pieces of information. **compilation** *(n).*

**complain** complaining complained *(v)* to say you are unhappy about something.

**complaint** 1 *(n)* a statement saying that you are unhappy about something. 2 *(n)* an illness. *A heart complaint.*

**complete** completing completed 1 *(adj)* having all the parts that are needed or wanted. *A complete pack of cards.* 2 *(v)* to finish something. 3 *(adj)* in every way. *A complete surprise.*

**complex** complexes 1 *(adj)* very complicated. **complexity** *(n).* 2 *(n)* a group of buildings that are close together and are used for a particular purpose.

**complexion** *(n)* the colour and look of the skin on your face.

**complicated** *(adj)* Something that is **complicated** contains lots of different parts or ideas and so is difficult to use or understand. **complicate** *(v).*

**compliment** complimenting complimented *(v)* to tell someone that you admire them or think that they have done something well. **compliment** *(n).*

**complimentary** 1 *(adj)* If someone is **complimentary** about a person or thing, they praise it. 2 *(adj)* free, or without cost. *Complimentary tickets.*

**component** *(n)* a part of a machine or system.

**compose** composing composed *(v)* to write a piece of music, a poem, etc.

**compost** *(n)* a mixture of rotted plants that is added to soil to make it richer.

**comprehension** 1 *(n)* understanding. **comprehend** *(v).* 2 *(n)* a test in which you read or listen to a text and then answer questions about it, to show how well you have understood it.

**comprehensive** 1 *(n)* a secondary school where pupils of all abilities are taught together. 2 *(adj)* including everything that is necessary. *A comprehensive list.*

**compress** compresses compressing compressed *(v)* to press or squeeze something so that it will fit into a small space. **compression** *(n).*

**compromise** compromising compromised *(v)* to agree to accept something that is not exactly what you wanted. **compromise** *(n).*

**compulsory** *(adj)* If something is **compulsory**, there is a law or rule that says you must do it.

**computer** *(n)* a machine that can store large amounts of information and do very quick and complicated calculations. **computing** *(n).*

**conceal** concealing concealed *(v)* to hide something. **concealment** *(n).*

**conceited** *(adj)* too proud. **conceit** *(n).*

**conceive** conceiving conceived 1 *(v)* to form an idea in your mind. *Ian conceived a cunning plan.* 2 *(v)* to become pregnant.

**concentrate** concentrating concentrated *(v)* to focus your thoughts and attention on something. **concentration** *(n).*

**concentric** *(adj)* **Concentric** circles all have their centre at the same point.

**concept** *(n)* a general idea or understanding of something. *Leo has a very vague concept of history.*

**conception** 1 *(n)* a general idea that you have formed in your mind. *Do you have any conception of how big space is?* 2 *(n)* the act of becoming pregnant.

**concern** concerning concerned 1 *(v)* to involve you, or to be of interest to you.

*These plans concern you.* 2 *(v)* to be about a particular subject. *This project concerns local history.* **concerning** *(prep).*

**concerned** *(adj)* anxious and worried about something. **concern** *(n).*

**concert** *(n)* a performance by musicians or singers.

**concession** *(n)* a reduction in price for particular types of people. *The theatre offers concessions to students.*

**concise** *(adj)* saying a lot in a few words.

**conclude concluding concluded** 1 *(v)* to decide that something is true because of the facts that you have. **conclusion** *(n).* 2 *(v)* to finish or end something. **conclusion** *(n).*

**concoct concocting concocted** *(v)* to create something by mixing several different things together. **concoction** *(n).*

**concrete** 1 *(n)* a building material made from a mixture of sand, small stones, cement, and water. 2 *(adj)* real, or definite. *The detectives need concrete evidence.*

**concussion** *(n)* unconsciousness, dizziness, or sickness caused by a heavy blow to your head. **concussed** *(adj).*

**condemn condemning condemned** 1 *(v)* to say very strongly that you do not approve of something. *Mahatma Gandhi condemned violence.* **condemnation** *(n).* 2 *(v)* to force someone to suffer something unpleasant. *The judge condemned the murderer to death.*

**condense condensing condensed** *(v)* When a gas **condenses**, it turns into a liquid, usually as a result of cooling.

**condition** 1 *(n)* the general state of a person, an animal, or a thing. *My dog is in good condition. Terrible living conditions.* 2 *(n)* a medical problem that continues over a long time. *A heart condition.*

**conditional** *(adj)* depending on something else. *A conditional offer.*

**condom** *(n)* a rubber covering that a man wears on his penis as a contraceptive.

**conduct conducting conducted** 1 *(v)* to organize something and carry it out. *The police conducted an inquiry.* 2 *(v)* to stand in front of a group of musicians and direct their playing. 3 *(v)* If something **conducts** heat, electricity, or sound, it allows them to pass through it. **conduction** *(n).*

**conductor** 1 *(n)* someone who stands in front of a group of musicians and directs their playing. 2 *(n)* a substance that heat, electricity, or sound can travel through.

**cone** 1 *(n)* an object or shape with a round base and a point at the top. **conical** *(adj).* 2 *(n)* the hard, woody fruit of a pine or fir tree.

**confectionery** *(n)* sweets and chocolates. **confectioner** *(n).*

**conference** *(n)* a formal meeting for discussing ideas and opinions.

**confess confesses confessing confessed** *(v)* to admit that you have done something wrong. **confession** *(n).*

**confetti** *(plural n)* small pieces of coloured paper that are thrown over the bride and groom after a wedding.

**confide confiding confided** *(v)* If you **confide in** someone, you tell them a secret because you can trust them not to tell anyone else.

**confident** 1 *(adj)* having a strong belief in your own abilities. *Ella is a confident swimmer.* **confidence** *(n).* 2 *(adj)* certain that things will happen in the way you want. *I am confident that it will be sunny tomorrow.* **confidence** *(n).*

**confirm confirming confirmed** 1 *(v)* to say that something is definitely true or will definitely happen. **confirmation** *(n).* 2 *(v)* When someone is **confirmed**, they are accepted as a full member of the Christian church, in a ceremony. **confirmation** *(n).*

**confiscate confiscating confiscated** *(v)* to take something away from someone as a punishment or because that thing is not allowed. **confiscation** *(n).*

**conflict** 1 *(n)* a serious disagreement. 2 *(n)* a war, or a period of fighting.

**confront confronting confronted** *(v)* to meet or face someone in a threatening or accusing way. **confrontation** *(n).*

**confuse confusing confused** 1 *(v)* If someone or something **confuses** you, you do not understand them or know what to do. **confusion** *(n).* 2 *(v)* to mistake one thing for another. *I confused Alex with his brother.* **confusion** *(n).*

**congested** *(adj)* blocked-up and not allowing movement. *Congested roads. A congested nose.* **congestion** *(n).*

**congratulate** congratulating **congratulated** *(v)* to tell someone that you are pleased because they have done something well or something good has happened to them. **congratulations** *(plural n).*

**congregation** *(n)* a group of people gathered together for worship.

**conifer** *(n)* an evergreen tree that produces cones. **coniferous** *(adj).*

**conjunction** *(n)* a word that connects two parts of a sentence or phrase. *"And" and "but" are conjunctions.* *See* page 3.

**conjurer** *or* **conjuror** *(n)* someone who performs magic tricks to entertain people.

**conker** *(n)* a hard and shiny brown nut from the horse chestnut tree.

**connect** connecting connected *(v)* to join together two things, ideas, or places.

**connection** 1 *(n)* a link between objects or ideas. 2 *(n)* a train or bus arranged so that people getting off other trains or buses can use it to continue their journey.

**conquer** conquering conquered *(v)* to defeat an enemy and take control of them by force. **conqueror** *(n).*

**conscience** *(**kon**-shenss) (n)* your knowledge of what is right and wrong, that makes you feel guilty when you have done something wrong.

**conscientious** *(adj)* taking care to do things well. **conscientiously** *(adv).*

**conscious** 1 *(adj)* awake and able to see, hear, think, etc. **consciousness** *(n).* 2 *(adj)* aware of something. *I became conscious that everyone was looking at me.*

**consecutive** *(adj)* happening or following one after the other. *Marcia was away for four consecutive days.*

**consent** consenting consented *(v)* to agree to something. **consent** *(n).*

**consequence** *(n)* the result of an action.

**conservation** *(n)* the protection of nature, wildlife, and other valuable things, such as buildings and paintings.

**conservative** 1 *(adj)* moderate, cautious, and not extreme. *Marcus has conservative taste.* **conservatively** *(adv).*
2 **Conservative Party** *(n)* one of the main political parties in Britain, promoting private enterprise and competition.

**conservatory** conservatories *(n)* a glass room, used for growing plants.

**consider** considering considered 1 *(v)* to think about something carefully before deciding what to do. 2 *(v)* to believe that something is true. *Celia considers school a waste of time!* 3 *(v)* to take something into account. *Consider Danny's feelings.*

**considerable** *(adj)* fairly large. *A considerable amount of money.*

**considerate** *(adj)* If you are **considerate**, you think about other people's needs and feelings.

**consideration** 1 *(n)* careful thought that you give to something before making a decision. 2 If you show **consideration**, you care about other people's needs and feelings. **considerate** *(adj).*

**considering** *(conj)* taking into account certain things. *You got here very quickly, considering the weather.*

**consist** consisting consisted *(v)* If something **consists** of different things, it is made up of those things.

**consistent** *(adj)* always behaving in the same way or supporting the same ideas or principles. **consistency** *(n).*

**console** consoling consoled 1 *(kon-**sole**) (v)* to cheer up or comfort someone. **consolation** *(n).* 2 *(**kon**-sole) (n)* the control panel on a machine.

**consonant** *(n)* any of the letters in the alphabet except the five vowels.

**conspicuous** *(adj)* Something that is **conspicuous** stands out and can be seen easily. **conspicuously** *(adv).*

**conspiracy** conspiracies *(n)* a secret, illegal plan made by two or more people. **conspirator** *(n),* **conspire** *(v).*

**constable** *(n)* a British police officer of the lowest rank.

**constant** 1 *(adj)* happening all the time and never stopping. **constantly** *(adv).*
2 *(adj)* staying at the same rate or level all the time. *A constant speed.*

**constellation** *(n)* a group of stars that form a shape or pattern.

**constipated** *(adj)* If you are **constipated**, you find it hard to pass solids from your body frequently or easily. **constipation** *(n).*

**construct** constructing constructed *(v)* to build or make something. construction *(n)*.

**constructive** *(adj)* helpful and useful.

**consult** consulting consulted 1 *(v)* to go to a person for advice. 2 *(v)* to use a book or a map to find information.

**consultant** *(n)* a senior doctor who has specialist knowledge in one area of medicine.

**consume** consuming consumed 1 *(v)* to eat or drink something. 2 *(v)* to use something up. **consumption** *(n)*.

**consumer** *(n)* someone who buys goods, eats food, or uses services.

**contact** contacting contacted 1 When things are **in contact**, they touch each other. 2 If you are **in contact** with someone, you write or talk to them. 3 *(v)* to get in touch with someone.

**contact lens** contact lenses *(n)* a small plastic lens that fits closely over your eyeball to improve your eyesight.

**contagious** *(adj)* A **contagious** disease can be caught by touching someone or something already infected with it.

**contain** containing contained *(v)* When an object **contains** something, it holds that thing inside itself or that thing forms a part of it. *The chest contained the treasure. This book contains many stories.*

**contaminated** *(adj)* If something is **contaminated,** it has been made dirty or impure. **contamination** *(n)*.

**contemplate** contemplating contemplated 1 *(v)* to think seriously about something. *Matthew contemplated leaving college.* 2 *(v)* to look at something thoughtfully. **contemplation** *(n)*.

**contemporary** contemporaries 1 *(adj)* up-to-date, or modern. 2 *(adj)* If an event is **contemporary** with another event, they both happened at the same time. *A contemporary account of the war.* 3 *(n)* Your contemporaries are people of about the same age as you.

**contempt** *(n)* total lack of respect.

**contend** contending contended 1 *(v)* to compete. *Two teams contended for the cup.* 2 *(v)* to try to deal with a difficulty. *Lucy has a lot to contend with.*

**contented** *(adj)* happy and satisfied.

**contents** *(plural n)* the things that are inside something or form part of something.

**contest** *(n)* a competition. **contestant** *(n)*, **contest** *(v)*.

**continent** 1 *(n)* one of the seven large land masses of the Earth. **continental** *(adj)*. 2 **the Continent** *(n)* the mainland of Europe. **continental** *(adj)*.

**continents**

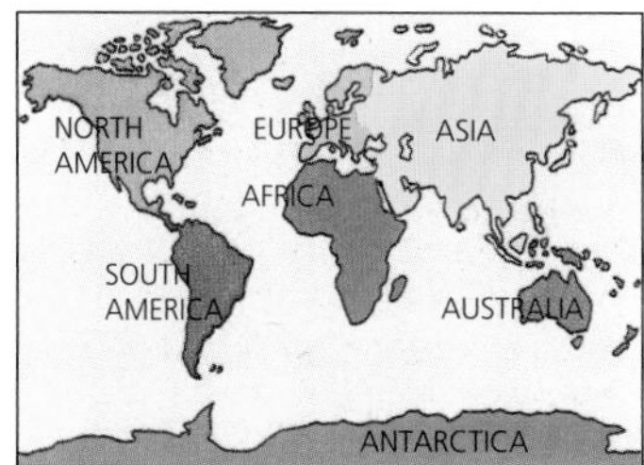


**continual** *(adj)* happening again and again. **continually** *(adv)*.

**continue** continuing continued *(v)* to go on doing something.

**continuous** *(adj)* If something is **continuous,** there are no gaps in it. *A continuous line.* **continuously** *(adv)*.

**contraceptive** *(n)* a device or drug that prevents a woman from becoming pregnant. **contraception** *(n)*.

**contract** contracting contracted *(v)* to become smaller. **contraction** *(n)*.

**contradict** contradicting contradicted *(v)* to say the opposite of what someone else has said. **contradiction** *(n)*.

**contraption** *(n)* a strange and complicated-looking machine.

**contrary** 1 *(kon-**trurry**)* *(adj)* opposite. 2 *(kon-**trair**-ee)* *(adj)* deliberately awkward and difficult.

**contrast** contrasting contrasted 1 *(kon-**trast**)* *(v)* to be very different from something else. *Claude's views contrast with mine.* **contrast** *(**kon**-trast)* *(n)*. 2 *(v)* *(kon-**trast**)* to identify the difference between things.

**contribute** contributing contributed *(v)* to give help or money to a person or an organization. **contribution** *(n)*.

**control** controlling controlled 1 *(v)* to make something or someone do what you want. **control** *(n)*. 2 *(plural n)* The **controls** of a machine are the levers and switches which make it work.

**controversial** *(adj)* causing a lot of argument. **controversy** *(n)*.

**convalescence** *(n)* the time during which someone recovers from an illness.

**convenient** *(adj)* useful, or easy to use. **convenience** *(n)*.

**convent** 1 *(n)* a building where nuns live and work. 2 *(n)* a school run by nuns.

**conventional** *(adj)* doing things in a traditional or accepted way.

**conversation** *(n)* If you hold a **conversation** with someone, you talk with them for a while. **converse** *(v)*.

**convert** converting converted *(v)* to make something into something else. *We've converted our loft into a bedroom.*

**conveyor belt** *(n)* a moving belt that carries objects in a factory.

**convict** convicting convicted 1 *(kon-**vikt**)* *(v)* to prove that someone is guilty of a crime. *Maria was convicted of stealing.* 2 *(**kon**-vikt)* *(n)* someone who is in prison because they have committed a crime.

**conviction** *(n)* a strong belief.

**convince** convincing convinced *(v)* to make someone believe you. *We convinced Hal that he should go on the stage.*

**convoy** *(n)* a group of trucks or other vehicles travelling together.

**cook** cooking cooked 1 *(v)* to prepare food for a meal. **cooking** *(n)*. 2 *(n)* someone whose job is to prepare food.

**cool** cooling cooled; cooler coolest 1 *(adj)* rather cold. **coolness** *(n)*. 2 *(v)* to lower the temperature of something. 3 *(adj)* unfriendly and distant. **coolly** *(adv)*.

**co-operate** co-operating co-operated *(v)* to work together. **co-operation** *(n)*.

**co-operative** *(adj)* If you are **co-operative,** you work well with other people. **co-operativeness** *(n)*.

**co-ordinate** co-ordinating co-ordinated *(v)* to organize activities or people so that they all work together. **co-ordination** *(n)*, **co-ordinator** *(n)*.

**co-ordinated** *(adj)* If you are **well co-ordinated**, you have good control over how you move your arms and legs.

**cope** coping coped *(v)* to deal with something successfully.

**copper** 1 *(n)* a reddish-brown metal. 2 *(n)* a reddish-brown colour. **coppery** *(adj)*.

**copy** copies copying copied 1 *(v)* to do the same as someone else. 2 *(n)* A **copy** is made to look or sound just like something else. 3 *(v)* to make a copy of something.

**coral** *(singular n)* sea creatures, closely related to sea anemones, whose skeletons remain after they die.

**cord** *(n)* a length of string or rope.

**cordial** 1 *(n)* a sweet, fruit drink. *Lime cordial.* 2 *(adj)* friendly. **cordially** *(adv)*.

**core** *(n)* the centre of something, such as an apple or the Earth. *See* **Earth**.

**cork** *(n)* soft bark used as a stopper in bottles or to make mats, tiles, etc.

**corkscrew** *(n)* a tool used for pulling corks out of bottles.

**corn** *(n)* the grain of crops such as wheat or barley.

**corner** cornering cornered 1 *(n)* the place where two sides of something meet. *A square has four corners.* 2 *(v)* to get a person or animal into a situation where they are trapped.

**coronary** coronaries 1 *(adj)* to do with the heart. 2 *(n)* a heart attack.

**coronation** *(n)* the ceremony in which a king or queen is crowned.

**corporal punishment** *(n)* physical punishment, such as beating.

**corporation** *(n)* a group of people who work together to run something.

**corpse** *(n)* a dead body.

**correct** correcting corrected 1 *(adj)* true, or right. **correctly** *(adv)*. 2 *(v)* to make something right. **correction** *(n)*.

**correspond** corresponding corresponded 1 *(v)* If two things **correspond**, they match in some way. 2 *(v)* When you **correspond** with someone, you write letters to each other. **correspondence** *(n)*.

**corridor** *(n)* a long passage in a building or train.

*Some words that begin with a "c" sound are spelt with a "k".*

**corrode** **corroding corroded** *(v)* to eat away at something. *Water corrodes metal and makes it rust.* **corrosive** *(adj).*

**corrugated** *(adj)* ridged, or rippled. *Corrugated iron.*

**corrupt** **corrupting corrupted** *(v)* to make someone bad or dishonest. **corrupt** *(adj).*

**cosmetic** **1 cosmetics** *(plural n)* beauty products such as lipstick or mascara. **2** *(adj)* changing the way that a person or a thing looks. *Cosmetic surgery.*

**cosmopolitan** *(adj)* feeling at home in more than one country.

**cosmos** *(n)* the universe. **cosmic** *(adj).*

**cost** **costing cost** *(v)* to have a certain price. *How much does this cost?* **cost** *(n).*

**costly** **costlier costliest** *(adj)* expensive. *Costly gifts.*

**costume** **1** *(n)* clothes worn by actors. **2** *(n)* clothes worn by people at a particular time in history.

**cosy** **cosier cosiest** *(adj)* comfortable, or snug.

**cottage** *(n)* a small house, usually in the country.

**cottage cheese** *(n)* cheese made from curdled skimmed milk.

**cotton plant**

raw cotton

**cotton** **1** *(n)* soft, thin material made from the cotton plant and used to make clothes. **cotton** *(adj).* **2** *(n)* sewing thread.

**cotton wool** *(n)* soft, raw cotton which you use to put cream on your skin.

**couch** **couches** *(n)* a long, soft seat with arms and a back, and room for two or more people.

**cough** *(coff)* **coughing coughed** *(v)* to make a sudden, harsh noise as you force air out of your lungs. **cough** *(n).*

**council** *(n)* a group of people chosen to look after the interests of a town, county, or organization.

**counsel** **counselling counselled** *(v)* to listen to people's problems and give advice. **counselling** *(n),* **counsellor** *(n).*

**count** **counting counted** **1** *(v)* to say numbers in order. **2** *(v)* to work out how many there are of something. *I counted the planes as they took off.* **3** *(v)* to rely on someone. *The team is counting on you.*

**counter** **1** *(n)* a small, flat, round playing piece used in some board games. **2** *(n)* a long, flat surface. *A shop counter.*

**counterfeit** *(n)* a fake that has been made to look like the real thing.

**countless** *(adj)* so many that you cannot count them.

**country** **countries** **1** *(n)* a part of the world with its own borders and government. **2** *(n)* undeveloped land away from towns or cities. **country** *(adj).*

**countryside** *(n)* undeveloped land away from towns or cities.

**county** **counties** *(n)* an area in some countries, such as Britain, with its own local government.

**couple** **1** *(n)* two of something. **2** *(n)* two people. *A married couple.*

**coupon** **1** *(n)* a small piece of paper which gives you a discount on something. **2** *(n)* a small form which you fill in to get information about something.

**courage** *(n)* bravery, or fearlessness. **courageous** *(adj),* **courageously** *(adv).*

**courgette** *(kor-**jhet**)* *(n)* a green, fleshy vegetable like a small marrow.

**course** **1** *(n)* a series of lessons. **2** *(n)* a part of a meal. **3** *(n)* a piece of ground where a sport is played. *A golf course.*

**court** **1** *(n)* a place where legal cases are heard. **2** *(n)* a place where games such as tennis or squash are played.

**courteous** *(**kur**-tee-us)* *(adj)* polite and respectful. **courtesy** *(n).*

**cousin** *(n)* Your **cousin** is the child of your uncle or aunt.

**cove** *(n)* a small bay.

**cover** **covering covered** **1** *(v)* to put something over something else. *Cover the table with a cloth.* **cover** *(n).* **2** *(v)* to teach or study something thoroughly. *Have you covered that topic?* **3** *(v)* to travel a certain distance. *We covered twenty miles today.*

**cow** **1** *(n)* an adult female farm animal that produces milk. **2** *(n)* an adult female seal or whale.

*Some words that begin with a "c" sound are spelt with a "k".*

**coward** *(n)* someone who is easily scared and keeps away from frightening situations. **cowardice** *(n)*, **cowardly** *(adj)*.

**crab** *(n)* a creature with a hard shell, eight legs, and two pincers.

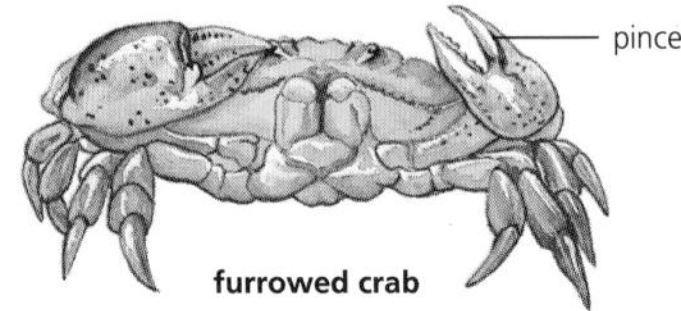

**furrowed crab**

**crack** cracking cracked 1 *(v)* to break or split, often with a loud, sharp noise. 2 *(n)* a thin split in something. 3 *(v)* to solve a problem. *The police cracked the crime.*

**cracker** 1 *(n)* a thin, plain biscuit, usually eaten with cheese. 2 *(n)* a paper-covered tube that contains presents, and bangs when you pull it apart.

**crackle** crackling crackled *(v)* to make a noise like lots of small bangs. *The dry leaves crackled.* **crackle** *(n)*.

**cradle** *(n)* a wooden bed for a young baby.

**craft** 1 *(n)* work or a hobby where you make things with your hands. 2 *(n)* a vehicle, such as a boat or plane.

**craftsman** craftsmen *(n)* someone skilled at making things with their hands. **craftmanship** *(n)*.

**crafty** craftier craftiest *(adj)* A **crafty** person is clever at tricking other people.

**crag** *(n)* a steep, sharp rock. **craggy** *(adj)*.

**cram** cramming crammed *(v)* to fit things into a small space. *I crammed all my clothes into a backpack.*

**cramp** *(n)* pain caused by a muscle tightening suddenly.

**cramped** *(adj)* If a place is **cramped**, there is not enough room in it for everyone or everything.

**crane** *(n)* a machine used for lifting heavy objects.

**crank** *(n)* *(informal)* someone with strange ideas. *A health food crank.*

**crash** crashes crashing crashed 1 *(v)* to make a loud noise like thunder. **crash** *(n)*. 2 *(n)* an accident in which a vehicle hits something at high speed. **crash** *(v)*. 3 *(v)* When a computer system or program **crashes**, it fails completely.

**crate** *(n)* a large, usually wooden box.

**crater** 1 *(n)* a large hole in the ground, caused by something, like a bomb or a meteorite, falling on it. 2 *(n)* the mouth of a volcano. *See* **volcano**.

**crave** craving craved *(v)* to want something desperately. **craving** *(n)*.

**crawl** crawling crawled 1 *(v)* to move on your hands and knees. 2 *(n)* a style of swimming on your front in which you use your arms in turn while kicking your legs.

**craze** *(n)* a fashion that does not last very long.

**crazy** crazier craziest 1 *(adj)* mad, or foolish. 2 *(adj)* *(informal)* very enthusiastic. *Josh is crazy about football.*

**creak** creaking creaked *(v)* to make a squeaky, grating noise. **creak** *(n)*.

**cream** 1 *(n)* a thick liquid taken from the top of the milk. *Strawberries and cream.* 2 *(n)* a thick, smooth substance like cream that you put on your skin. *Hand cream.*

**crease** creasing creased *(v)* to make lines or folds in something, especially material or paper. **crease** *(n)*.

**create** creating created *(v)* to make or design something. **creator** *(n)*.

**creation** *(n)* something that has been made.

**creative** *(adj)* If you are **creative**, you use your imagination and are good at thinking of new ideas. **creativity** *(n)*.

**creature** *(n)* an animal, bird, or insect.

**crèche** *(kresh)* *(n)* a place where babies and young children can be looked after safely while their parents are busy.

**credible** *(adj)* If something or someone is **credible**, you can believe in them or trust them. **credibility** *(n)*.

**credit** 1 *(n)* praise or acknowledgement. *No one gave me credit for my hard work.* 2 *(plural n)* The **credits** at the end of a film or television programme tell you who acted in it and made it.

**creek** 1 *(n)* a narrow inlet where the sea flows inland for a long way. 2 *(n)* a small stream.

**creep** creeping crept 1 *(v)* to move very slowly and quietly. 2 *(n)* *(slang)* an unpleasant person. 3 *(informal)* If something or someone **gives you the creeps**, they are unpleasant and frightening. **creepy** *(adj).*

**cremate** **cremating** **cremated** *(v)* to burn a dead body. **cremation** *(n).*

**crescent** 1 *(n)* a curved shape. 2 *(n)* a row of houses, built in a curve.

**crest** 1 *(n)* a comb or tuft of feathers on a bird's head. **crested** *(adj).* 2 *(n)* the top of something, such as a wave or a hill. 3 *(n)* a design that represents a noble family, a town, or an organization. *A school crest.*

**crevice** *(n)* a crack or split in a rock.

**crew** *(n)* a team of people who work together, especially on a ship.

**crib** **cribbing** **cribbed** 1 *(n)* a small baby's bed. 2 *(v) (informal)* to copy someone else's work and pretend it is your own.

**cricket** 1 *(n)* a game played by two teams of eleven players, with two bats, a ball, and two sets of stumps. **cricketer** *(n).* 2 *(n)* a jumping insect like a grasshopper.

**crime** *(n)* something that is against the law.

**criminal** 1 *(n)* someone who commits a crime. **criminally** *(adv).* 2 *(adj)* to do with crime. *A criminal investigation.*

**cripple** **crippling** **crippled** 1 *(n)* someone who is lame or disabled. **crippled** *(adj).* 2 *(v)* to stop someone or something from moving or working properly. *Strikes crippled the company.*

**crisis** **crises** *(n)* a time of danger and difficulty.

**crisp** **crisper** **crispest** 1 *(n)* a very thin slice of fried potato with salt or other flavours added. 2 *(adj)* hard and easily broken. *A crisp piece of toast.* **crispy** *(adj).* 3 *(adj)* fresh, dry and cool. *A crisp winter morning.* **crisply** *(adv).*

**critical** 1 *(adj)* If you are **critical** of someone or something, you find faults in them. 2 *(adj)* important, or serious. *A critical operation.*

**criticize** *or* **criticise** **criticizing** **criticized** 1 *(v)* to tell someone what they have done wrong. **criticism** *(n).* 2 *(v)* to point out the good and bad parts in a book, film, etc. **critic** *(n),* **criticism** *(n).*

**croak** **croaking** **croaked** 1 *(v)* When a frog **croaks**, it makes a deep, hoarse sound. **croak** *(n).* 2 *(v)* If you **croak**, you speak with a hoarse voice. **croaky** *(adj).*

**crochet** *(crow-shay)* **crocheting** **crocheted** *(v)* to make a kind of lace from cotton thread or wool, using a hooked needle. **crochet** *(n).*

**crockery** *(n)* pottery or china that you use at home, such as plates, cups, etc.

**crocodile** *(n)* a large, scaly reptile with short legs and strong jaws.

**crook** 1 *(n)* a dishonest person, or a criminal. 2 *(n)* a long stick with a hook at one end, used by shepherds.

**crooked** 1 *(adj)* bent. *A crooked path.* 2 *(adj) (informal)* dishonest. *A crooked deal.*

**crop** *(n)* a plant grown in large amounts, usually for food.

**cross** **crosses** **crossing** **crossed** 1 *(v)* to go from one side to the other. *Cross the road.* 2 *(adj)* angry, or not pleased. 3 *(n)* The shape x is a **cross**. So is +.

**cross-examine** **cross-examining** **cross-examined** *(v)* to question somebody very closely. **cross-examination** *(n).*

**crossroads** *(plural n)* a place where one road crosses another.

**cross-section** *(n)* a diagram which shows the inside of something, by cutting through it.

**crossword** *(n)* a puzzle in which you answer clues in order to fill blank spaces with words.

**crouch** **crouches** **crouching** **crouched** *(v)* When you **crouch**, you bend your legs and lower your body.

**crow** **crowing** **crowed** 1 *(v)* When a cockerel **crows**, it makes a loud, crying noise. 2 *(v)* to boast about something.

**crowd** *(n)* a lot of people packed together. **crowded** *(adj).*

**crown** 1 *(n)* a headdress worn by a king or queen. 2 *(n)* the top of something. *At last, we reached the crown of the hill.*

**crucial** *(adj)* extremely important, or vital.

**crucify** **crucifies** **crucifying** **crucified** *(v)* to put someone to death by fastening them to a cross and leaving them to die. **crucifixion** *(n).*

**crude** **cruder crudest 1** *(adj)* rough and poorly made. **crudely** *(adv).* **2** *(adj)* A **crude** joke is rude and not very funny.

**cruel** **crueller cruellest** *(adj)* A **cruel** person deliberately causes pain to others or is happy to see them suffer. **cruelty** *(n).*

**cruise** **cruising cruised 1** *(n)* If you go on a **cruise**, you take a holiday on a ship. **2** *(v)* to travel smoothly and easily. *We cruised along the motorway.*

**crumb** *(n)* a tiny piece of bread or cake.

**crumble** **crumbling crumbled** *(v)* to break into small pieces. **crumbly** *(adj).*

**crumple** **crumpling crumpled** *(v)* If you **crumple up** a piece of paper, you screw it into a ball.

**crunchy** **crunchier crunchiest** *(adj)* **Crunchy** food is hard and makes a loud noise when you chew it. **crunch** *(v).*

**crush** **crushes crushing crushed** *(v)* to squash something under a heavy weight.

**crust** **1** *(n)* the crisp, outer case of bread or pastry. **crusty** *(adj).* **2** *(n)* The Earth's **crust** is its thin, outer layer. *See* **Earth**.

**crutch** **crutches** *(n)* one of two long sticks with padded tops, used to help support someone with injured legs.

**cry** **cries crying cried 1** *(v)* to weep tears. **cry** *(n).* **2** *(v)* to shout out. **cry** *(n).*

**crystal** *(n)* a hard, glassy piece of rock with many sides.

**cub** *(n)* a young lion, wolf, bear, etc.

**cube** **cubing cubed 1** *(n)* a three-dimensional shape with six square faces, like a dice. **2** *(v)* to multiply a number by itself twice. *3 cubed is 3 x 3 x 3.*

**cubicle** *(n)* a small, private area in a changing room or public toilet.

**cucumber** *(n)* a long, green vegetable with a watery centre.

**cuddle** **cuddling cuddled** *(v)* to hold someone closely in your arms.

**cue** *(kyoo)* *(n)* a long stick used to hit the ball in games like snooker and pool.

**cuff** *(n)* the part of a shirt or blouse that goes round your wrist.

**cul-de-sac** *(n)* a road that is closed at one end.

**culprit** *(n)* someone who has done something wrong.

**cult** **1** *(n)* a religion with a small following. **2** *(n)* a strong, almost religious devotion to a person, an idea, or a way of life. *The hippie cult.*

**cultivate** **cultivating cultivated** *(v)* If you **cultivate** land, you grow crops on it. **cultivation** *(n).*

**culture** **1** *(n)* the arts, such as music, literature, painting, etc. **cultural** *(adj).* **2** *(n)* The **culture** of a group of people is their way of life, ideas, and traditions.

**cunning** *(adj)* A **cunning** person is clever at tricking people. **cunning** *(n).*

**cupboard** *(n)* a piece of furniture or a built-in space, used for storing things.

**curator** *(n)* the person in charge of a museum or art gallery.

**curb** **curbing curbed** *(v)* to control or hold back something. *I curbed my desire for another cake.*

**curdle** **curdling curdled** *(v)* When milk **curdles**, it goes sour and breaks up into curds and whey.

**curds** *(n)* the solid part of sour milk, often used to make cheese.

**cure** **curing cured** *(v)* to make someone better when they have been ill. **cure** *(n).*

**curious** **1** *(adj)* eager to find out. **curiosity** *(n).* **2** *(adj)* strange. *A curious creature.* **curiosity** *(n),* **curiously** *(adv).*

**curl** **curling curled 1** *(n)* a curved lock of hair. **2** *(v)* to bend into a spiral shape.

**currant** *(n)* a dried grape.

**currency** *(n)* the money used in a country.

**current** **1** *(adj)* happening now. **currently** *(adv).* **2** *(n)* the movement of water in a river or an ocean, or of electricity through a wire.

**curriculum** **curricula** *(n)* a programme of study for a school or college.

**curry** **curries** *(n)* a hot, spicy meal of meat or vegetables, served with rice.

**curse** **cursing cursed 1** *(n)* an evil spell meant to harm someone. **2** *(v)* to swear.

**cursor** *(n)* a small indicator which shows your position on a computer screen.

**curtains** *(plural n)* pieces of material that are pulled across a window or a stage to cover it.

**curtsy** *or* **curtsey curtsies curtsying curtsied** *(v)* to bend slightly at the knee to show respect or to accept applause.

**curve curving curved 1** *(v)* to bend or turn gently. **2** *(n)* a bend in something. **curved** *(adj).*

**cushion** *(n)* a type of pillow used to make chairs or sofas more comfortable.

**custard** *(n)* a sweet, yellow sauce.

**custody 1** *(n)* If someone has **custody** of a child, they have the legal right to look after that child. **2** If someone is **taken into custody**, the police arrest them.

**custom 1** *(n)* a tradition. **customary** *(adj).* **2 customs** *(n)* a checkpoint at country borders, ports, or airports where officials make sure that you are not carrying anything illegal.

**customer** *(n)* A shop's **customers** are the people who buy things from it.

**cut cutting cut 1** *(v)* to use a sharp instrument, such as scissors or a knife, to divide, shorten, or shape something. **2** *(n)* a skin wound. **3** *(v)* to reduce something. *The shop is cutting its prices.* **cut** *(n).* **4** *(v)* If you are **cut off** from other people, you cannot contact them.

**cute cuter cutest** *(adj)* charming and attractive.

**cutlery** *(singular n)* knives, forks, and spoons.

**cutting 1** *(n)* something cut off or cut out of something else. *A plant cutting. A newspaper cutting.* **2** *(adj)* A **cutting** remark is hurtful.

**cycle** *(sy-kul)* **cycling cycled 1** *(n)* a series of events which are repeated over and over again. *The cycle of the seasons.* **2** *(n)* a bicycle. *See* **bicycle**. **3** *(v)* to ride a bicycle. **cyclist** *(n).*

**cyclone** *(sy-klone) (n)* a very strong wind that blows in a spiral.

**cygnet** *(sig-net) (n)* a young swan. *See* **swan**.

**cylinder** *(sill-in-der) (n)* a shape with circular ends and straight sides. *Most drink cans are cylinders.* **cylindrical** *(adj).*

**cynical** *(sin-ik-al) (adj)* A **cynical** person always expects the worst to happen, and thinks that anything people do is for selfish reasons.

# Dd

**dab dabbing dabbed** *(v)* to touch a surface gently with something soft.

**dabble dabbling dabbled 1** *(v)* to dip something into water and splash it about. *Jim dabbled his fingers in the stream.* **2** *(v)* If you **dabble** in something, you do it, but not very seriously or very well.

**daffodil** *(n)* a spring plant with yellow, bell-like flowers.

**daft dafter daftest** *(adj) (informal)* silly, or foolish. *A daft idea.*

**dagger** *(n)* a short, pointed knife, used as a weapon.

**daily** *(adj)* produced or happening every day. *A daily newspaper.*

**dainty daintier daintiest** *(adj)* small and delicate. **daintiness** *(n),* **daintily** *(adj).*

**dairy dairies** *(n)* a place where milk is bottled and milk products, such as cheese and yogurt, are made.

**daisy daisies** *(n)* a wild flower with white petals and a yellow centre.

**dam** *(n)* a strong barrier built across a river to hold back water.

**damage damaging damaged 1** *(v)* to harm something. **2** *(n)* the harm that something does. *Flood damage.*

**damn** *(dam)* **damning damned 1** *(v)* to say that something or someone is very bad. *The critics damned the play.* **2** *(v)* to curse someone or something.

**damp damper dampest** *(adj)* slightly wet, or moist. **damp** *(n),* **dampen** *(v).*

**damsel** *(n) (old-fashioned)* a young woman.

**dance dancing danced 1** *(v)* to move in time to music. **dancer** *(n),* **dancing** *(n).* **2** *(n)* a ball, or a disco.

**dandruff** *(n)* small, white flakes of dead skin found in some people's hair.

**danger 1** *(n)* a situation that is not safe. *Are we in danger?* **2** *(n)* something or someone that is not safe. *George's bus is a danger on the road.* **dangerous** *(adj).* **3 danger!** *(interject)* a warning word.

*Some words that begin with a "cy" sound are spelt "ci", "psy", "scy", or "si".*

**dangle dangling dangled** *(v)* to swing or hang down. *Mo dangled from the tree.*

**dank danker dankest** *(adj)* unpleasantly wet or damp. *A cold, dank cellar.*

**dappled** *(adj)* marked with spots, or with light and dark patches. *A dappled pony.*

**dare daring dared 1** *(v)* to challenge someone to do something. **2** *(v)* to be brave enough to do something.

**dark darker darkest 1** *(adj)* without light. **darkness** *(n).* **2** *(adj)* containing more black than white. *Dark blue.*

**darkroom** *(n)* a room where you can develop photographs.

**darn darning darned** *(v)* to mend a hole in a piece of clothing by sewing across it.

**dart darting darted 1** *(n)* a pointed object that you throw at a board in the game of darts. **2** *(v)* to move forward suddenly. **3 darts** *(singular n)* a game in which players score points by throwing darts at a board with numbers on it.

**dash dashes dashing dashed 1** *(n)* a small line (-) used as a punctuation mark or in Morse code. **2** *(v)* to move quickly. *I dashed to the shop before it shut.*

**data** *(n)* information, or facts.

**database** *(n)* a store of information held on a computer.

**date dating dated 1** *(n)* a particular day, month, or year. **2** *(v)* If something **dates** from a certain time, it was made then.

**daughter** *(n)* Someone's **daughter** is their female child.

**dawdle dawdling dawdled 1** *(v)* to walk slowly. **2** *(v)* to do something slowly. *Gill dawdled over her breakfast.*

**dawn** *(n)* sunrise, or the beginning of the day. **dawn** *(v).*

**day 1** *(n)* a 24-hour period, from midnight to midnight. **2** *(n)* the light part of the day.

**daydream daydreaming daydreamed 1** *(n)* a dream you have while you are awake. **2** *(v)* to let your mind wander.

**daze** *(n)* If you are in a **daze**, you are stunned and unable to think clearly.

**dazzle dazzling dazzled 1** *(v)* to blind someone for a short time with a bright light. **dazzling** *(adj).* **2** *(v)* to amaze someone. **dazzling** *(adj).*

**dead** *(adj)* no longer alive.

**deadline** *(n)* a time by which a piece of work or a job must be finished.

**deadlock** *(n)* a situation where nothing can be agreed.

**deadly deadlier deadliest** *(adj)* capable of killing, or likely to kill.

**deaf deafer deafest** *(adj)* If someone is **deaf**, they cannot hear anything, or they can hear very little. **deafness** *(n).*

**deafening** *(adj)* very loud. *A deafening crash.* **deafeningly** *(adv).*

**deal dealing dealt 1** *(n)* a business agreement. **2** *(v)* When you **deal with** something, you sort it out. **3** *(v)* to give out cards to people playing a game.

**dear dearer dearest 1** *(adj)* highly valued, or much loved. *A dear friend.* **2** You use the word **Dear** when you write to someone. *Dear Sir.* **3** *(adj)* expensive.

**death** *(n)* the end of life.

**deathtrap** *(n)* a place or a vehicle that is very dangerous.

**debate debating debated** *(v)* to consider or discuss something. *The family debated where to go on holiday.*

**debris** *(deb-ree) (n)* the scattered remains of something.

**debt** *(det)* **1** *(n)* an amount of money that you owe. **2** If you are **in debt** to someone, you owe them money or a favour. **debtor** *(n).*

**debug debugging debugged** *(v)* to remove the faults in a computer program.

**debut** *(day-byoo) (n)* a first public appearance. *An acting debut.*

**decade** *(n)* a period of ten years.

**decaffeinated** *(adj)* If a drink, like coffee or tea, is **decaffeinated**, it has had most of its caffeine removed.

**decapitate decapitating decapitated** *(v)* to remove the head of a person or creature. **decapitation** *(n).*

**decay decaying decayed** *(v)* to rot, or to break up. **decay** *(n).*

**deceased** *(adj)* dead.

**deceive** **deceiving** **deceived** *(v)* to trick someone into believing something that is not true. **deceit** *(n),* **deceitful** *(adj).*

**decent** 1 *(adj)* good, or satisfactory. **decently** *(adv).* 2 *(adj)* respectable and proper. **decency** *(n),* **decently** *(adv).*

**deception** *(n)* a trick that makes people believe something that is not true.

**decide** **deciding** **decided** *(v)* to make up your mind about something.

**deciduous** *(adj)* Trees that are **deciduous** shed their leaves every year.

**decimal** 1 *(adj)* A **decimal** system uses units of tens, hundreds, thousands, etc. *Decimal currency.* 2 **decimal point** *(n)* a dot separating whole numbers from tenths, hundredths, thousandths, etc. *The number 4.624 uses a decimal point.* 3 *(n)* a fraction, or a whole number and a fraction, written with a decimal point. *0.5, 6.37, and 8.254 are all decimals.*

**decipher** **deciphering** **deciphered** *(v)* to work out something that is written in code or is hard to understand.

**decision** *(n)* If you make a **decision**, you make up your mind about something.

**decisive** *(adj)* If you are **decisive**, you make choices quickly and easily.

**deck** *(n)* the floor of a boat or ship.

**declare** **declaring** **declared** 1 *(v)* to say something firmly. *Al declared that he was going.* **declaration** *(n).* 2 *(v)* to announce something formally. *The King declared that the war was over.* **declaration** *(n).*

**decline** **declining** **declined** 1 *(v)* to refuse something politely. *I'm afraid we must decline your invitation.* 2 *(v)* to get worse, or to get smaller. **decline** *(n).*

**decode** **decoding** **decoded** *(v)* to turn something that is written in code into ordinary language.

**decompose** **decomposing** **decomposed** *(v)* to rot, or to decay.

**decongestant** *(n)* a drug that unblocks your nose, chest, etc. when you have a cold. **decongestion** *(n).*

**decorate** **decorating** **decorated** 1 *(v)* If you **decorate** something, you add things to it to make it prettier. 2 *(v)* If you **decorate** a room or a house, you paint it or put up wallpaper. **decorator** *(n).*

**decrease** **decreasing** **decreased** *(v)* to become less, smaller, or fewer. *Bud's enthusiasm for school has decreased.*

**decree** **decreeing** **decreed** *(v)* to give an order that must be obeyed.

**decrepit** *(adj)* old and feeble.

**dedicate** **dedicating** **dedicated** *(v)* If you **dedicate** yourself to something, you give lots of time and energy to it.

**deduce** **deducing** **deduced** *(v)* to work out something from clues, or from what you know already.

**deduct** **deducting** **deducted** *(v)* to take away or subtract something, especially money. **deductible** *(adj).*

**deduction** 1 *(n)* something that is worked out from clues. 2 *(n)* an amount that is taken away or subtracted from a larger amount.

**deed** *(n)* something that is done. *A good deed.*

**deep** **deeper** **deepest** 1 *(adj)* going a long way down. *A deep well.* **deepen** *(v).* 2 *(adj)* very intense and strong. *Deep sorrow.* **deepen** *(v),* **deeply** *(adv).*

**deer** **deer** *(n)* a fast-running wild animal. Male deer grow bony, branching antlers.

**deface** **defacing** **defaced** *(v)* to spoil the way something looks.

**defeat** **defeating** **defeated** 1 *(v)* to beat someone in a war or competition. 2 *(n)* If you suffer a **defeat**, you are beaten.

**defend** **defending** **defended** 1 *(v)* to protect something or someone from harm. **defence** *(n).* 2 *(v)* to support some idea or someone by arguing. **defence** *(n).*

**defensive** *(adj)* to do with defending yourself or others. *The players took defensive action.*

**defiant** *(adj)* If you are **defiant**, you stand up to someone or to some organization and refuse to obey them.

**deficient** *(adj)* lacking something. *My diet is deficient in protein.* **deficiency** *(n).*

**define** **defining** **defined** *(v)* to explain or describe something exactly.

**definite** 1 *(adj)* certain. *Do we have a definite date for the trip?* **definitely** *(adv).* 2 *(adj)* clear. *These drawings have a very definite outline.* 3 **definite article** *(n)* the grammatical term for "the".

**definition** *(n)* an explanation of the meaning of a word or an idea.

**deflate deflating deflated** *(v)* to let the air out of something like a tyre or a balloon. **deflation** *(n).*

**deflect deflecting deflected** *(v)* to make something go in a different direction. *His shield deflected the arrows.*

**deforestation** *(n)* the cutting down of forests.

**deformed** *(adj)* If someone or something is **deformed**, they are a strange shape.

**defraud defrauding defrauded** *(v)* to cheat someone out of something.

**defrost defrosting defrosted 1** *(v)* to allow frozen food to thaw out. **2** *(v)* to remove ice from a refrigerator or freezer.

**defuse defusing defused** *(v)* When someone **defuses** a bomb, they make it safe so it cannot explode.

**defy defies defying defied 1** *(v)* If you **defy** a person or a rule, you stand up to them and refuse to obey them. **2** *(v)* to challenge someone, or to dare them to do something. *I defy you to eat all that cake!*

**degenerate degenerating degenerated** *(v)* to become worse. *The lesson degenerated into a riot.*

**degrading** *(adj)* If something is **degrading**, it makes you feel worthless or disgraced. **degradation** *(n),* **degrade** *(v).*

**degree 1** *(n)* a unit for measuring temperature or angles. The symbol for a degree is °. *The temperature today reached 20° Celsius. A 90° angle.* **2** *(n)* a qualification given by a university or other institute of higher education.

**dehydrated** *(adj)* If you are **dehydrated**, you do not have enough water in your body. **dehydration** *(n),* **dehydrate** *(v).*

**deign** *(dane)* **deigning deigned** *(v)* to lower yourself to do something. *The lady deigned to give the beggar some money.*

**deity** *(day-it-ee)* **deities** *(n)* a god or goddess.

**dejected** *(adj)* sad and depressed.

**delay delaying delayed 1** *(v)* to be slow. *Don't delay or we'll miss the bus!* **2** *(v)* to make someone late. *The accident delayed me.* **3** *(v)* to put something off until later. *Sara delayed doing her homework.*

**delegate delegating delegated** *(v)* to give someone responsibility for doing a part of your job.

**delete deleting deleted** *(v)* to remove something from a piece of writing or computer text. **deletion** *(n).*

**deliberate deliberating deliberated 1** *(adj)* planned, or intended. **2** *(v)* to consider something carefully.

**delicate** *(adj)* finely made, or sensitive. *A delicate instrument.* **delicately** *(adv).*

**delicatessen** *(n)* a shop that sells unusual or foreign foods.

**delicious** *(adj)* very pleasing to taste or smell. **deliciously** *(adv).*

**delight delighting delighted 1** *(n)* great pleasure. **delightful** *(adj).* **2** *(v)* to please someone very much.

**delinquent** *(n)* a young person who is often in trouble with the police.

**delirious** *(adj)* If you are **delirious**, you cannot think straight because you have a fever or you are extremely happy.

**deliver delivering delivered 1** *(v)* to take something to someone. **delivery** *(n).* **2** *(v)* When someone **delivers** a baby, they help it to be born. **delivery** *(n).*

**deluge deluging deluged 1** *(n)* heavy rain, or a flood. **2** *(v)* If people **deluge** you with letters, presents, etc., they send you lots of them. **deluge** *(n).*

**demand demanding demanded** *(v)* to claim something, or to ask for something firmly. *We demand justice!*

**demanding** *(adj)* If somebody is **demanding**, they are always wanting things and are hard to please.

**demo** *(n) (informal)* a meeting or march to protest about something. Demo is short for demonstration.

**democracy democracies 1** *(n)* a way of governing a country, in which the people choose their leaders in elections. **2** *(n)* a country that has an elected government.

**democratic** *(adj)* A **democratic** system is one where all people have equal rights.

**demolish demolishes demolishing demolished** *(v)* to knock down something and break it up. *The builders demolished the house.* **demolition** *(n).*

**demon** *(n)* a devil, or an evil spirit.

**demonstrate** **demonstrating demonstrated** **1** *(v)* to show other people how to do something or how to use something. **demonstration** *(n)*. **2** *(v)* to join together with other people to protest against something. **demonstration** *(n)*. **3** *(v)* to show something clearly. *Alex demonstrated his anger by shouting.*

**den** *(n)* the home of a wild animal, such as a lion.

**denim** *(n)* strong, cotton material used for making jeans. **denim** *(adj)*.

**denominator** *(n)* In fractions, the **denominator** is the number under the line which shows how many equal parts the whole number can be divided into. *In the fraction 7/8, 8 is the denominator.*

**denounce** **denouncing denounced** *(v)* to say in public that someone has done something wrong.

**dense** **denser densest** *(adj)* thick, or closely packed. *Dense fog. Dense crowds.*

**density** *(n)* The **density** of an object is how heavy or light it is for its size.

**dent** **denting dented** *(v)* to damage something by making a hollow in it.

**dental** *(adj)* to do with teeth.

**dentist** *(n)* someone who is trained to check and treat teeth.

**dentures** *(plural n)* a set of false teeth.

**deny** **denies denying denied** **1** *(v)* to say that something is not true. **denial** *(n)*. **2** *(v)* to stop someone having something or going somewhere. *The guards denied us entry to the hall.*

**deodorant** *(n)* a substance used to hide the smell of sweat on your body.

**depart** **departing departed** *(v)* to leave, especially for a journey. **departure** *(n)*.

**department** *(n)* a part of a shop, hospital, university, etc.

**depend** **depending depended** **1** *(v)* If something **depends on** something else, it is related to it or influenced by it. **2** *(v)* to rely on someone or something.

**depict** **depicting depicted** *(v)* to show something in a picture, or by using words.

**deplorable** *(adj)* shockingly bad. *Louis has deplorable taste in music.*

**deport** **deporting deported** *(v)* to send someone back to their own country.

**depose** **deposing deposed** *(v)* If a king or queen is **deposed**, they have their power taken from them.

**deposit** *(n)* a sum of money given as the first part of a payment, or as a promise to pay for something. **deposit** *(v)*.

**depot** *(dep-oh)* *(n)* a warehouse, or a bus garage.

**depressed** *(adj)* sad and gloomy.

**depression** *(n)* sadness and gloominess.

**deprive** **depriving deprived** *(v)* to prevent someone from having something, or to take something away from someone. **deprived** *(adj)*.

**depth** **1** *(n)* deepness, or a measurement of deepness. **2** If you study something **in depth**, you study it thoroughly.

**deputy** **deputies** *(n)* someone who helps somebody else in their job and takes their place when they are ill or absent.

**deranged** *(adj)* insane.

**derelict** *(adj)* neglected and in ruins.

**derive** **deriving derived** *(v)* to take or receive something. *Eva derives a lot of pleasure from her work.*

**derv** *(n)* a fuel used in diesel engines.

**descant** *(n)* a tune that is played or sung above the main tune.

**descend** **descending descended** **1** *(v)* to climb down, or go down to a lower level. **2** *(v)* If you are **descended** from someone, you belong to a later generation of their family. **descendant** *(n)*.

**describe** **describing described** *(v)* to create a picture of something in words. **description** *(n)*, **descriptive** *(adj)*.

**desert** **deserting deserted** **1** *(dez-ut)* *(n)* a sandy or stony area where hardly any plants grow because there is so little rain. **desert** *(adj)*. **2** *(der-**zert**)* *(v)* to abandon someone, or to run away from the army.

**deserve** **deserving deserved** *(v)* to earn something because of the way you behave. *Uma deserves a reward.*

**design** *(n)* the shape and style of something. **design** *(v)*.

**desire** *(n)* a strong wish or need for something or someone. **desire** *(v)*.

**desk** *(n)* a table, often with drawers, used for working at or writing on.

**desolate** 1 *(adj)* deserted, or uninhabited. *A desolate village.* 2 *(adj)* sad and lonely. *After my friend left, I felt desolate.* **desolation** *(n).*

**despair** **despairing despaired** *(v)* to lose hope completely. **despair** *(n).*

**despatch** *see* **dispatch**.

**desperate** 1 *(adj)* If you are **desperate**, you will do anything to change your situation. **desperation** *(n).* 2 *(adj)* dangerous, or difficult. *A desperate shortage of medicine.* **desperately** *(adv).*

**despise** **despising despised** *(v)* to dislike someone and have no respect for them.

**despite** *(prep)* in spite of. *Rollo won the race, despite falling off his bike.*

**dessert** *(n)* the sweet course of a meal.

**destination** *(n)* the place that someone or something is travelling to.

**destiny** **destinies** *(n)* Your **destiny** is your fate or the future events in your life. *Cinderella's destiny was to marry a prince.*

**destitute** *(adj)* A **destitute** person has no money to live on.

**destroy** **destroying destroyed** *(v)* to ruin something or someone completely. **destruction** *(n).*

**destructive** *(adj)* causing lots of damage and unhappiness. **destructively** *(adv).*

**detach** **detaches detaching detached** *(v)* to separate one part of something from the rest of it. **detachable** *(adj).*

**detached** 1 *(adj)* A **detached** house stands by itself. 2 *(adj)* able to stand back from a situation and not get too involved.

**detail** 1 *(n)* a small part of something larger. 2 **details** *(plural n)* information about something.

**detective** *(n)* someone who investigates crimes, usually for the police.

**detention** *(n)* a punishment in which a pupil has to stay in school when other pupils are free.

**deter** **deterring deterred** *(v)* to prevent or discourage someone from doing something. **deterrent** *(n).*

**detergent** *(n)* liquid or powder used for cleaning things.

**deteriorate** **deteriorating deteriorated** *(v)* to get worse.

**determined** *(adj)* If you are **determined** to do something, you have made a firm decision to do it. **determination** *(n).*

**detest** **detesting detested** *(v)* to dislike something or someone very much.

**detonate** **detonating detonated** *(v)* to set off an explosion. **detonator** *(n).*

**detour** *(n)* a longer, alternative route to somewhere, usually avoiding an obstacle.

**detract** **detracting detracted** *(v)* to make something less enjoyable or valuable. *Rain detracts from a picnic.*

**deuce** *(jooss)* *(n)* In tennis, **deuce** is the score when both players have 40 points.

**devastated** 1 *(adj)* very badly damaged, or destroyed. **devastation** *(n),* **devastate** *(v).* 2 *(adj)* shocked and distressed.

**develop** **developing developed** 1 *(v)* to grow. *The girls' friendship developed slowly.* **development** *(n).* 2 *(v)* to build on something, or make something grow. *The farmer is developing the field as a camp site.* **developer** *(n),* **development** *(n).*

**deviate** **deviating deviated** *(v)* to do something different from what is normal or acceptable. *The cyclist deviated from his usual route.* **deviation** *(n).*

**device** 1 *(n)* a piece of equipment used for a certain job. 2 *(n)* If you are **left to your own devices**, you can do what you want.

**devil** 1 *(n)* In Christianity and Judaism, the **Devil** is the spirit of evil. 2 *(n)* If you call someone a **devil**, you mean that they are naughty or wicked.

**devious** *(adj)* 1 A **devious** person keeps their thoughts and actions secret, and cannot be trusted. **deviousness** *(n).* 2 *(adj)* complicated and indirect. *We took a devious route back home.*

**devise** **devising devised** *(v)* to think something up, or invent something.

**devoid** *(adj)* without something, or empty of something. *The house was devoid of furniture.*

**devoted** *(adj)* loyal and loving.

**devour** **devouring devoured** *(v)* to eat something quickly and greedily.

**devout** *(adj)* deeply religious.

**dew** *(n)* small drops of moisture which form overnight on cool surfaces outside.

**dexterity** *(n)* skill, especially in using your hands. **dexterous** *(adj).*

**diabetes** *(dye-a-**bee**-tees) (n)* a disease in which you have too much sugar in your blood. **diabetic** *(dye-a-**bet**-ik) (adj).*

**diabolical** 1 *(adj)* extremely wicked. *A diabolical villain.* 2 *(adj) (informal)* awful, or terrible. *A diabolical essay.*

**diagnose** diagnosing diagnosed *(v)* to work out what disease a patient has or what the cause of a problem is. diagnosis *(n).*

**diagonal** *(adj)* A **diagonal** line is a straight line joining opposite corners of a square or rectangle. **diagonally** *(adv).*

**diagram** *(n)* a drawing or plan that explains something simply.

**dial** dialling dialled 1 *(n)* the face on a clock, watch, or measuring instrument. 2 *(v)* to enter a number by pressing buttons or turning a dial on a telephone.

**dialect** *(n)* a way of speaking that belongs to a particular place.

**dialogue** *(n)* conversation, especially in a play, film, or book.

**diameter** *(n)* a straight line through the centre of a circle, from one side to another. *See* **circle**.

**diamond** 1 *(n)* a very hard, clear, precious stone. 2 *(n)* a shape with four equal sides, like a square standing on one of its corners. 3 **diamonds** *(plural n)* one of the four suits in a pack of cards.

**diarrhoea** *(dye-er-**ree**-a) (n)* a stomach illness which causes normally solid waste to become runny.

**diary** diaries *(n)* a book in which people write down things that happen each day, either to use as a record or to plan ahead.

**dice** *(plural n)* six-sided cubes with a different number of spots on each face, used in games. The singular of dice is die, although most people say dice.

**dictate** dictating dictated 1 *(v)* to talk aloud so that someone can write down what you say. **dictation** *(n).* 2 *(v)* to control something. *Our parents dictate the amount of pocket money we get.*

**dictator** *(n)* a person who has complete control of a country. **dictatorship** *(n).*

**dictionary** dictionaries *(n)* a book like this one that explains what words mean and shows you how to spell them.

**didgeridoo**

**didgeridoo** *or* **didjeridu** *(dij-er-ree-**doo**) (n)* a long, decorated tube, made from a hollowed-out branch or tree trunk, which is played as a musical instrument by Australian Aborigines.

**die** dying died 1 *(v)* to stop living, or to come to an end. 2 *(v)* If you are **dying** to do something, you really want to do it.

**diesel** *(dee-zull) (n)* a fuel used by trains and some motor vehicles.

**diet** dieting dieted 1 *(n)* Your **diet** is what you eat. **dietary** *(adj).* 2 *(v)* to choose what you eat in order to lose weight. 3 *(n)* a controlled eating plan.

**difference** 1 *(n)* the way in which things are not like each other. *What's the difference between margarine and butter?* **differ** *(v),* **different** *(adj).* 2 *(n)* the amount by which one number is less or more than another. *The difference between 5 and 2 is 3.*

**difficult** 1 *(adj)* not easy. *A difficult exam.* 2 *(adj)* A **difficult** person is not easy to get on with.

**difficulty** difficulties *(n)* a problem.

**dig** digging dug 1 *(v)* to use a spade to move earth. 2 *(n)* an unkind remark. 3 *(n)* an archaeological excavation.

**digestion** *(n)* the process of breaking down food in the stomach, so that it can be absorbed into the blood. **digest** *(v).*

**digit** *(dij-it)* 1 *(n)* a finger. 2 *(n)* a single figure. *625 is a three digit number.*

**digital** *(adj)* A **digital** display shows time, speed, etc. in numbers.

**dignified** *(adj)* calm, serious, and in control. **dignity** *(n).*

**dilapidated** *(adj)* shabby and falling to pieces. **dilapidation** *(n).*

**dilemma** *(n)* If you are **in a dilemma**, you have to choose between alternatives.

*Some words that begin with a "di" sound are spelt "dy".*

**diligent** *(adj)* hard-working.

**dilute diluting diluted** *(v)* to make a liquid weaker by adding water.

**dimension** *(n)* The **dimensions** of an object are its measurements or its size.

**diminish diminishes diminishing diminished** *(v)* If something **diminishes**, it becomes smaller or weaker.

**dinghy dinghies** *(n)* a small, open boat.

**dingy** *(din-jee)* **dingier dingiest** *(adj)* dull and shabby. *A dingy room.*

**dinner** *(n)* the main meal of the day, eaten at midday or in the evening.

**dinosaur** *(n)* the general name for the large, land-living reptiles that existed in prehistoric times.

**dinosaurs**

staurikosaurus

stegosaurus

triceratops

pachycephalosaurus

tyrannosaurus rex

spinosaurus

**dip dipping dipped 1** *(v)* to push something briefly into a liquid. *Dip your brush in the water.* **2** *(v)* to slope downwards. **3** *(n)* a short swim.

**diplomat** *(n)* a person who represents their country's government in a foreign country. **diplomacy** *(n).*

**diplomatic 1** *(adj)* If you are **diplomatic**, you are tactful and good at dealing with people. **diplomacy** *(n).* **2** *(adj)* to do with being a diplomat. *The diplomatic service.*

**dire direr direst** *(adj)* disastrous.

**direct directing directed 1** *(adj)* in a straight line, or by the shortest route. **2** *(v)* to supervise people, especially in a play or film. **3** *(v)* to tell someone the way to go.

**direction 1** *(n)* the way that someone or something is moving or pointing. *We travelled in a westerly direction.* **2 directions** *(plural n)* instructions.

**directory directories** *(n)* a book which gives addresses, phone numbers etc. in alphabetical order.

**dirty dirtier dirtiest 1** *(adj)* not clean. **dirt** *(n).* **2** *(adj)* unfair. *A dirty trick.*

**disabled** *(adj)* People who are **disabled** are restricted in what they can do, usually because of illness or injury. **disability** *(n).*

**disadvantage** *(n)* something which causes a problem or makes life difficult.

**disagree disagreeing disagreed** *(v)* to think differently from someone else.

**disappear disappearing disappeared** *(v)* to go out of sight. **disappearance** *(n).*

**disappoint disappointing disappointed** *(v)* to let someone down by failing to do what they expected.

**disapprove disapproving disapproved** *(v)* If you **disapprove** of something, you think it is bad or wrong. **disapproval** *(n).*

**disaster 1** *(n)* a very serious accident, earthquake, etc. in which many die. **disastrous** *(adj).* **2** *(n)* something that has gone completely wrong. **disastrous** *(adj).*

**disbelief** *(n)* refusal to believe something. *My story met with disbelief.*

**disc** *or* **disk 1** *(n)* a flat, circular shape. **2** *(n)* a piece of plastic, used for recording music or information. *Compact disc.*

*Some words that begin with a "di" sound are spelt "dy".*

**discard** discarding discarded *(v)* to throw something away.

**discipline** *(n)* control over the way you or other people behave. **discipline** *(v)*.

**disc jockey** *(n)* someone who introduces and plays pop music on the radio, at a disco, etc.

**disconnect** disconnecting disconnected 1 *(v)* to separate things that are joined together. 2 *(v)* to cut off something, like an electricity supply or a telephone line. **disconnected** *(adj)*.

**discontinue** discontinuing discontinued *(v)* to stop doing something that you have been doing regularly.

**discount** *(n)* a price cut.

**discourage** discouraging discouraged *(v)* If you **discourage** someone from doing something, you persuade them not to do it. **discouragement** *(n)*.

**discouraged** *(adj)* If you are **discouraged**, you lose your enthusiasm or confidence.

**discover** discovering discovered 1 *(v)* to find something. *We discovered the treasure.* **discovery** *(n)*. 2 *(v)* to find out about something. *I discovered that Abigail was lying.* **discovery** *(n)*.

**discreet** *(adj)* If you are **discreet**, you know the right thing to say, and can be trusted to keep a secret. **discretion** *(n)*.

**discriminate** discriminating discriminated *(v)* If you **discriminate** against someone, you are prejudiced against them and treat them unfairly. **discrimination** *(n)*.

**discus** *(disk-uss)* discuses *or* disci *(n)* a large, weighted disc that is thrown in athletics events. *This statue shows an ancient Greek athlete throwing the discus.*

**discus thrower**

**discuss** discusses discusssing discussed *(v)* to talk over something. **discussion** *(n)*.

**disease** 1 *(n)* an illness. 2 *(n)* sickness. *Disease spread throughout the city.*

**disgrace** disgracing disgraced 1 *(v)* If you **disgrace yourself**, you do something which other people disapprove of. 2 *(n)* If something is a **disgrace**, it is very bad indeed. **disgraceful** *(adj)*.

**disguise** disguising disguised 1 *(v)* to hide something. *Sebastian tried to disguise his boredom.* 2 *(n)* If you put on a **disguise**, you dress up to look like someone else.

**disgusting** *(adj)* very unpleasant and offensive to others. **disgustingly** *(adv)*.

**dish** dishes 1 *(n)* a bowl or plate, used for cooking or for serving food. 2 *(n)* one course of a meal. *A chicken dish.*

**dishonest** *(adj)* not truthful. **dishonesty** *(n)*.

**disillusion** disillusioning disillusioned *(v)* If you **disillusion** someone, you destroy their ideas about something.

**disinfectant** *(n)* a household chemical used to kill germs. **disinfect** *(v)*.

**disintegrate** disintegrating disintegrated 1 *(v)* to break into small pieces. **disintegration** *(n)*. 2 *(v)* to break up. *Mandy's family is disintegrating.*

**disk** 1 *(n)* a piece of plastic, used for recording computer data. 2 *See* **disc**.

**dislike** disliking disliked *(v)* If you **dislike** something or someone, you do not like them. **dislike** *(n)*.

**dislocate** dislocating dislocated *(v)* If you **dislocate** a bone, it comes out of its usual place. **dislocation** *(n)*.

**dismal** 1 *(adj)* gloomy and sad. 2 *(adj)* dreadful. *A dismal failure.*

**dismantle** dismantling dismantled *(v)* to take something to pieces.

**dismayed** *(adj)* If you are **dismayed**, you are upset and worried by something. **dismay** *(n)*.

**dismiss** dismisses dismissing dismissed 1 *(v)* to allow people to leave. *The teacher dismissed us early.* 2 *(v)* to put something out of your mind. *I've dismissed the idea of having a party.*

**disobedient** *(adj)* If you are **disobedient**, you do not do as you are told. **disobedience** *(n)*.

**disorganized** *or* **disorganised** *(adj)* muddled and not in order.

*Some words that begin with a "dis" sound are spelt "dys".*

**disown** **disowning disowned** *(v)* to act as though you do not know someone.

**dispatch** *or* **despatch** **dispatches dispatching dispatched** *(v)* to send something or somebody off.

**disperse** **dispersing dispersed** *(v)* to scatter. *The crowd dispersed.*

**displace** **displacing displaced** **1** *(v)* to take the place of something or somebody. *When you sit in a bath, you displace some water.* **2** *(v)* to move something or someone from their usual place.

**display** **displaying displayed** **1** *(v)* to show something. *Jo displayed no emotion.* **2** *(n)* a public show or exhibition. **3** *(n)* a screen or panel on electronic equipment, showing information.

**disposable** *(adj)* suitable for throwing away after use. **dispose** *(v).*

**disprove** **disproving disproved** *(v)* to show that something cannot be true.

**dispute** *(n)* a disagreement. **dispute** *(v).*

**disqualify** **disqualifies disqualifying disqualified** *(v)* to prevent someone from taking part in an activity, often because they have broken a rule.

**disregard** **disregarding disregarded** *(v)* to take no notice of someone or something. **disregard** *(n).*

**disrespect** *(n)* lack of respect, or rudeness. **disrespectful** *(adj).*

**disrupt** **disrupting disrupted** *(v)* to disturb or break up something which is happening. **disruption** *(n).*

**dissatisfied** *(adj)* If you are **dissatisfied**, you are unhappy or discontented. **dissatisfaction** *(n).*

**dissolve** **dissolving dissolved** *(v)* to mix with liquid. *Salt dissolves in water.*

**distance** **1** *(n)* the amount of space between two places. **2** If you see something **in the distance**, it is a long way off. **distant** *(adj).*

**distinct** **1** *(adj)* very clear. *Pascale has a distinct French accent.* **distinctly** *(adv).* **2** *(adj)* clearly different. **distinctive** *(adj).*

**distinction** *(n)* a clear difference.

**distinguish** **distinguishes distinguishing distinguished** *(v)* to tell the difference between things. *Can you distinguish between a frog and a toad?*

**distort** **distorting distorted** *(v)* to twist something out of shape. **distortion** *(n).*

**distract** **distracting distracted** *(v)* to put someone off what they are doing. *The television distracted me from my work.*

**distress** **1** *(n)* a feeling of great pain or sadness. **distressed** *(adj),* **distressing** *(adj).* **2** **distress signal** *(n)* a radio message, flare, etc. from a ship or aircraft to show that it is in trouble.

**distribute** **distributing distributed** **1** *(v)* to give things out. **2** *(v)* to deliver products to various places.

**district** *(n)* an area or region.

**distrust** *(n)* a feeling of not trusting someone. **distrust** *(v).*

**disturb** **disturbing disturbed** **1** *(v)* to interrupt somebody when they are doing something. **2** *(v)* to worry someone.

**disturbed** *(adj)* If someone is **disturbed**, they are unstable and have difficulty in controlling their behaviour.

**ditch** **ditches** *(n)* a long, narrow channel that drains water away.

**dive** **diving dived** **1** *(v)* to jump headfirst into water with your arms stretched out in front of you. **dive** *(n).* **2** *(v)* to drop down suddenly. *The kite dived to the ground.*

**diver** *(n)* someone who uses breathing apparatus to work or explore underwater. *See* **scuba diving**.

**diverse** *(adj)* varied, or assorted. *Hal has a diverse collection of friends.*

**diversion** **1** *(n)* When a road is closed, a **diversion** takes you on a different route. **divert** *(v).* **2** *(n)* something that takes your mind off other things. **divert** *(v).*

**divide** **dividing divided** **1** *(v)* to split into parts. **2** *(v)* In maths, if you **divide** a number by a second number, you work out how many times the second number will go into the first. *12 divided by 4 is 3, or* $12 \div 4 = 3$.

**divine** **1** *(adj)* to do with God, or like a god. **2** *(adj)* *(informal)* wonderful.

**division** **1** *(n)* the act of dividing one number by another. **2** *(n)* one of the parts into which something large has been divided. *Football League Division One.*

**divorce** *(n)* the ending of a marriage by a court of law. **divorce** *(v),* **divorced** *(adj).*

**Diwali** *(n)* a festival of light, celebrated by Hindus and Sikhs in the autumn. *At Diwali, Hindus decorate their doorsteps with rangoli patterns.*

**rangoli pattern**

**D.I.Y.** *(n)* home improvements, repairs, and decorations that you do yourself. DIY stands for do-it-yourself.

**dizzy** **dizzier dizziest** *(adj)* If you feel **dizzy**, you feel giddy and confused.

**do** **does doing did done** 1 *(v)* to perform an action. *What are you doing?* 2 *(v)* to deal with something. *I'm doing my hair.* 3 *(v)* to be acceptable. *Will this shirt do?* 4 *(v)* to make progress. *Tom is doing well at college.*

**dock** 1 *(n)* a place where ships load and unload. 2 *(n)* In a court of law, the **dock** is where the accused person stands.

**doctor** *(n)* someone trained to treat sick people.

**document** *(n)* a piece of paper containing important or useful information.

**documentary** **documentaries** *(n)* a film or television programme made about real situations and people.

**dodge** **dodging dodged** 1 *(v)* to avoid something or somebody by moving quickly. 2 *(v)* to avoid doing something.

**doe** *(n)* the female of animals such as rabbits, deer, or kangaroos.

**dog** *(n)* a four-legged mammal that is often kept as a pet.

**dole** *(n)* *(informal)* money paid by the government to people who have no jobs.

**bottlenose dolphin**

**dolphin** *(n)* an intelligent water mammal with a long snout. Dolphins live in warm seas and are very fast swimmers.

**dome** *(n)* a rounded roof.

**domestic** 1 *(adj)* to do with the home. *Domestic chores.* 2 *(adj)* **Domestic** animals are kept by people in their homes as pets.

**dominate** **dominating dominated** 1 *(v)* to control very powerfully. **domination** *(n)*. 2 *(v)* to be the main feature of a situation. *The castle dominates the view.*

**donate** **donating donated** *(v)* to give something as a present. *We donated our profits to charity.* **donation** *(n)*.

**donkey** *(n)* a long-eared mammal, related to the horse.

**donor** 1 *(n)* someone who gives something, usually to an organization or a charity. 2 *(n)* someone who gives part of their body, usually after they are dead, to help sick people. *A kidney donor.*

**doodle** **doodling doodled** *(v)* to draw absent-mindedly while you are thinking about something else. **doodle** *(n)*.

**doom** *(n)* a terrible fate, usually ending in death. **doomed** *(adj)*.

**door** 1 *(n)* a barrier at the entrance of a building, room, etc. 2 *(n)* a house, or a building. *My friend lives three doors away.*

**dormant** 1 *(adj)* A **dormant** animal shows no signs of action, as if it were asleep. 2 *(adj)* A **dormant** volcano is not active at present, but could still erupt. 3 *(adj)* When plants or seeds are **dormant**, they are alive, but not growing.

**dormitory** **dormitories** *(n)* a bedroom for several people, usually in a boarding school or youth hostel.

**DOS** *(n)* a system of commands that makes it possible to use a computer. DOS stands for disk operating system.

**dose** 1 *(n)* a measured amount of medicine. 2 *(n)* a brief experience of something unpleasant. *A dose of flu.*

**dot** *(n)* a small round point.

**dotty** **dottier dottiest** *(adj)* *(slang)* slightly crazy, or eccentric.

**double** **doubling doubled** *(v)* If you **double** something, you make it twice as big. **double** *(adj)*.

**doubt** *(dowt)* **doubting doubted** 1 *(v)* If you **doubt** something, you are uncertain about it. **doubtful** *(adj)*. 2 *(n)* uncertainty.

**dough** *(doh) (n)* a thick, sticky mixture of flour, water, etc., used to make bread.

**doughnut** *(doh-nut) (n)* a small cake made from dough and covered in sugar.

**dove** *(n)* a bird that makes a gentle, cooing sound.

**down 1** *(prep)* from a higher to a lower place. *Emma ran down the hill.* **downward** *(adj)*, **down** *(adv)*. **2** *(n)* the soft feathers of a bird. **3** *(adj)* sad, or depressed.

**dowry dowries** *(n)* the money or property that women in some cultures bring with them when they marry.

**doze dozing dozed** *(v)* to sleep lightly for a short time. **doze** *(n)*.

**dozen** *(n)* a group of twelve.

**drab** *(adj)* very dull and dreary.

**draft drafting drafted** *(v)* When you **draft** something, like a letter, you make a first rough copy of it. **draft** *(n)*.

**drag dragging dragged 1** *(v)* to pull something heavy along the ground. **2** *(v)* If something **drags**, it seems to go slowly.

**dragon** *(n)* a fire-breathing monster that appears in stories and legends. *In China, people make colourful dragons which dance in New Year processions.*

**Chinese dragon**

**drain draining drained 1** *(v)* to remove the liquid from something. **2** *(n)* a pipe or channel that takes away water or sewage.

**drama 1** *(n)* a play. **2** *(n)* If you study **drama**, you learn about acting and the theatre. **3** *(n)* something which affects people seriously.

**dramatic 1** *(adj)* to do with acting and the theatre. **2** *(adj)* very noticeable. *A dramatic change.* **dramatically** *(adv)*.

**dramatize** *or* **dramatise dramatizing dramatized 1** *(v)* to adapt a story into a play. **2** *(v)* to make something seem more exciting than it really is.

**drastic** *(adj)* If you do something **drastic**, you take action suddenly and violently.

**draught** *(draft) (n)* a flow of cold air.

**draughts** *(drafts) (plural n)* a game played by two people with black and white counters on a squared board.

**draw drawing drew drawn 1** *(v)* to make a picture with a pencil, pen, etc. **drawing** *(n)*. **2** *(v)* to pull something. *The carriage was drawn by horses.* **3** *(n)* If a competition ends in a **draw**, both sides are level.

**drawback** *(n)* a problem, or a disadvantage.

**drawer** *(n)* a sliding box in a piece of furniture, used for storing things.

**drawing pin** *(n)* a small pin with a flat, round head, used for fastening paper on noticeboards, walls, etc.

**dread dreading dreaded** *(v)* to be very afraid of something. **dread** *(n)*.

**dreadful 1** *(adj)* very unpleasant. *A dreadful accident.* **dreadfully** *(adv)*. **2** *(adj)* very bad. *A dreadful film.*

**dreadlocks** *(plural n)* a West Indian hairstyle, where the hair is grown long and twisted into strands.

**dream dreaming dreamed** *or* **dreamt 1** *(v)* to imagine events while you are asleep. **dream** *(n)*. **2** *(v)* If you **dream of** doing something, you really want to do it.

**dreary drearier dreariest** *(adj)* dull and miserable. **drearily** *(adv)*.

**drench drenches drenching drenched** *(v)* to make something completely wet.

**dress dresses dressing dressed 1** *(v)* to put clothes on. **2** *(n)* a piece of clothing, worn by women and girls, that covers the body from shoulders to legs. **3** *(n)* a general name for clothes. *Formal dress.*

**dresser** *(n)* a tall piece of kitchen furniture with shelves and cupboards.

**dressing 1** *(n)* a covering for a wound. **2** *(n)* a type of sauce for salads.

**dressing gown** *(n)* a loose robe, worn over your nightclothes.

**dress rehearsal** *(n)* the last rehearsal of a play, in full costume.

**dribble dribbling dribbled 1** *(v)* to let saliva trickle from your mouth. **2** *(v)* to run close to a ball, touching it often.

**drift** **drifting drifted 1** *(v)* When something **drifts**, it moves wherever the water or wind takes it. **2** *(n)* a pile of sand or snow, created by the wind. **3** *(v)* to move or act without any sense of purpose. *Ollie spent the whole day just drifting about.*

**drill 1** *(n)* a tool used for making holes. **drill** *(v)*. **2** *(n)* a way of doing something which is governed by strict rules. *Fire drill.*

**drink** **drinking drank drunk 1** *(n)* a liquid that you swallow. **2** *(v)* to swallow liquid. **3** *(n)* an alcoholic liquid.

**drip** **dripping dripped** *(v)* When a liquid **drips**, it falls slowly, drop by drop.

**drive** **driving drove driven 1** *(v)* to control a vehicle. **driver** *(n)*, **driving** *(n)*. **2** *(v)* to force someone into a desperate state. *Losing his passport drove Matt to despair.* **3** *(n)* a private road leading to a house. **4** *(n)* energy. *Jenny will succeed, because she has a lot of drive.*

**drivel** *(n)* If someone talks **drivel**, what they say is rubbish.

**drizzle** *(n)* light rain. **drizzle** *(v)*.

**drone** **droning droned 1** *(v)* to make a steady, dull sound. **2** *(v)* to talk in a dull, monotonous way. *Hector droned on about cricket.* **3** *(n)* a male bee that does not make honey and has no sting.

**drool** **drooling drooled 1** *(v)* to let saliva trickle from your mouth. **2** *(v)* If you **drool over** something, you really want it.

**droop** **drooping drooped 1** *(v)* to hang down, or to sag. **2** *(v)* When people **droop**, they run out of energy.

**drop** **dropping dropped 1** *(v)* to let something fall. **2** *(v)* to go downwards. *The acrobat dropped to the floor.* **3** *(n)* a small quantity of liquid. **4** *(v)* If you **drop out**, you stop doing something.

**drought** *(rhymes with shout)* *(n)* a long spell of very dry weather.

**drown** **drowning drowned** *(v)* When someone **drowns**, they die because their lungs fill with water.

**drowsy** **drowsier drowsiest** *(adj)* sleepy.

**drug 1** *(n)* a chemical substance used to treat illness. **2** *(n)* a chemical substance that people take because of its effect on them. Drugs are dangerous and usually cause addiction.

**drum** **drumming drummed 1** *(n)* a musical instrument with a hollow body covered with a stretched skin, that makes a loud noise when you hit it. **2** *(v)* to beat a drum or other surface with drumsticks or with your fingers. *Joe drummed his fingers on the table.* **drummer** *(n)*.

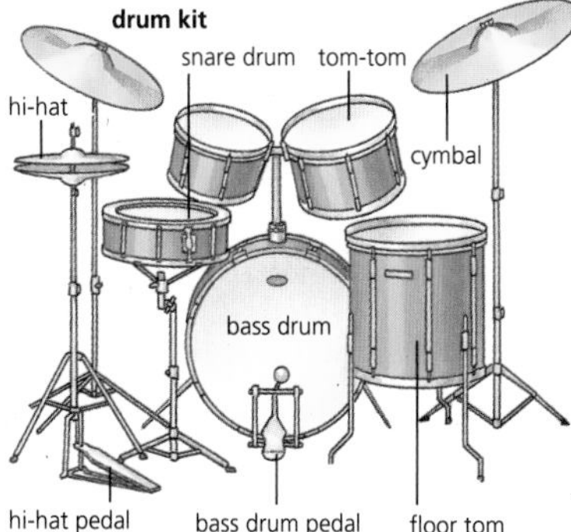


**drumstick 1** *(n)* a stick used to hit a drum. **2** *(n)* a leg of a chicken, turkey, etc.

**drunk 1** *(adj)* If a person is **drunk**, they have had too much alcohol to drink, and cannot control themselves. **2** *(n)* a person who often gets drunk. **drunkard** *(n)*.

**dry** **dries drying dried; drier driest** **1** *(v)* to take the moisture out of something. **2** *(adj)* not wet. **3** *(adj)* dull, or boring. *A dry speech.*

**dry-clean** **dry-cleaning dry-cleaned** *(v)* to clean clothes with special chemicals in order to remove stains. **dry-cleaner** *(n)*.

**dual 1** *(adj)* double. **2 dual carriageway** *(n)* a road with a dividing strip between traffic travelling in opposite directions.

**dubious** *(dyoo-bee-us)* *(adj)* not sure about something. **dubiously** *(adv)*.

**duck** **ducking ducked 1** *(n)* a water bird. **2** *(v)* to bend low to avoid something.

**due 1** *(adj)* expected to arrive or happen. **2** If something happens **due to** something else, it happens because of it.

**duel** *(n)* a sword or gun fight between two people, fought according to rules.

**duet** *(n)* a piece of music that is played, or a song that is sung, by two people.

**dull** **duller dullest 1** *(adj)* not bright. **2** *(adj)* not clever. **3** *(adj)* boring.

**dumb** *(adj)* not able to speak.

**dummy dummies 1** *(n)* a rubber teat given to a baby to suck. **2** *(n)* an imitation person or object.

**dump dumping dumped 1** *(v)* to leave something thoughtlessly or roughly. *Keith dumped his sports bag in the hall.* **2** *(n)* a place where unwanted things can be left. *A rubbish dump.*

**dune** *(n)* a sand hill made by the wind, near the sea, or in a desert.

**dung** *(n)* the solid waste products of large animals.

**dungeon** *(n)* a prison, usually underground.

**duplicate duplicating duplicated 1** *(v)* to make an exact copy of something. **duplication** *(n).* **2** *(n)* an exact copy.

**during** *(prep)* within a particular time. *Please call during the morning.*

**dusk** *(n)* the time of day after sunset when it is nearly dark.

**dust dusting dusted 1** *(n)* particles of dirt, fluff, etc. that gather on surfaces. **2** *(v)* to remove dust from surfaces with a cloth. **duster** *(n).*

**duty duties** *(n)* the things a person must do or ought to do.

**duvet** *(doo-vay)* *(n)* a thick, padded cover for a bed, filled with feathers or other light material.

**dwarf dwarves dwarfing dwarfed 1** *(n)* a very small person, animal, or plant. **dwarf** *(adj).* **2** *(v)* to make something else seem very small. *The skyscraper dwarfed all the buildings around it.*

**dwindle dwindling dwindled** *(v)* to become smaller or less. *The number of giant pandas is dwindling.*

**dye** *(n)* a substance used to change the colour of something. **dye** *(v).*

**dynamic** *(adj)* energetic and good at getting things done. **dynamism** *(n).*

**dynamite** *(n)* an explosive.

**dynamo** *(n)* a machine for converting the power of a turning wheel into electricity, sometimes used to power bicycle lights.

**dyslexia** *(dis-**lek**-see-er)* *(n)* If you have **dyslexia**, you find reading and spelling difficult because you confuse the order of letters. **dyslexic** *(adj).*

# Ee

**eager** *(adj)* keen and enthusiastic. **eagerness** *(n),* **eagerly** *(adv).*

**eagle** *(n)* a large bird of prey.

**Philippine eagle**

**ear** *(n)* the part of the body used for hearing.

**early earlier earliest 1** *(adj)* before the usual time. *An early start.* **earliness** *(n),* **early** *(adv).* **2** *(adj)* near the beginning of a period of time. *An early 20th-century house.*

**earn earning earned 1** *(v)* to work to receive money. **earnings** *(plural n).* **2** *(v)* to work to achieve a result. *You have earned your reward.*

**earnest** *(adj)* serious and keen. **earnestly** *(adv).*

**earth 1 Earth** *(n)* the planet on which we live. *The diagram shows the different layers of the Earth.* **earthly** *(adj).* **2** *(n)* soil.

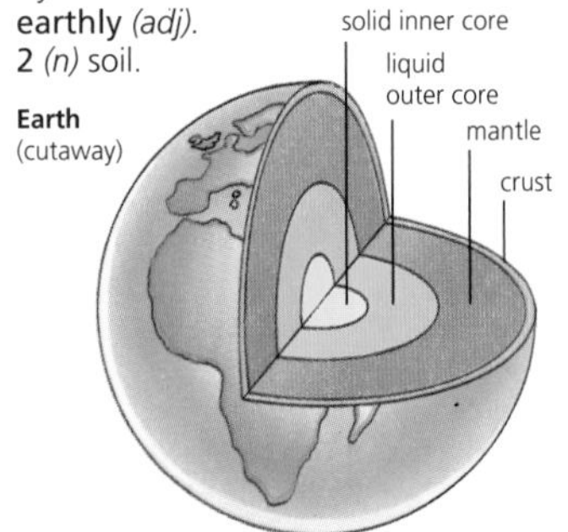

**Earth** (cutaway)

**earthquake** *(n)* a violent shaking of the Earth, caused by a movement of rock plates at the Earth's surface. *See* **fault**.

**easel** *(n)* a folding wooden stand for a painting.

**east 1** *(n)* one of the four main points of the compass, the direction from which the Sun rises. **2** *(adj)* An **east** wind blows from the east. **3** *(adj)* to do with, or existing in the east. *The east coast.* **eastern** *(adj).*

**Easter** *(n)* the festival in which Christians celebrate the resurrection of Jesus Christ.

**easy easier easiest** *(adj)* If something is **easy**, it does not require much effort or ability. **easiness** *(n),* **easily** *(adv).*

**eat eating ate eaten** *(v)* to take in food through your mouth.

**eavesdrop eavesdropping eavesdropped** *(v)* to listen in secret to someone's conversation.

**ebb ebbing ebbed** *(v)* When the tide **ebbs**, it goes out and the sea level goes down. **ebb** *(n).*

**eccentric** *(ek-sen-trick) (n)* someone with odd habits. **eccentric** *(adj).*

**echo echoes** *(n)* a sound that bounces back, usually in an empty place. **echo** *(v).*

**eclipse 1** *(n)* In an **eclipse of the Moon,** the Earth comes between the Sun and the Moon, so that all or part of the Moon's light is blocked out. **2** *(n)* In an **eclipse of the Sun**, the Moon comes between the Sun and the Earth, so that all or part of the Sun's light is blocked out.

**ecology 1** *(n)* the study of the relationship between plants, animals, and their environment. **2** *(n)* the study of how human activity affects the Earth.

**economical** *(adj)* not wasteful. *Our car is very economical on petrol.*

**economics** *(singular n)* the study of the way money is made and used in a society.

**economy economies** *(n)* the way a country runs its industry, trade, and finance.

**ecosystem** *(n)* a self-contained community of creatures, plants, and their environment.

**ecstasy ecstasies** *(n)* a feeling of great happiness. **ecstatic** *(adj).*

**eczema** *(ex-ma) (n)* a skin disease that makes the skin dry, rough, and itchy.

**edge edging edged 1** *(n)* a boundary. **2** *(v)* to move very slowly and carefully. *We edged along the ledge.* **3** If you are **on edge**, you are nervous or anxious.

**edgeways 1** *(adv)* sideways. **2** If you cannot get **a word in edgeways** in a discussion, other people do not give you a chance to speak.

**edible** *(adj)* able to be eaten. *Only pick the edible mushrooms!*

**edit editing edited** *(v)* to cut and put together pieces of film or video tape to make a film, television programme, etc.

**edition** *(n)* a version of a book or newspaper that is printed at a particular time. *A new paperback edition.*

**editor** *(n)* the person in charge of a newspaper or magazine.

**educate educating educated** *(v)* to give people knowledge or skill. **education** *(n).*

**eel** *(n)* a long, thin, snake-like fish.

**eerie eerier eeriest** *(adj)* strange and frightening. **eerily** *(adv).*

**effect** *(n)* the result or consequences of something.

**effective** *(adj)* If something or someone is **effective**, they do their job very well. **effectively** *(adv).*

**efficient** *(adj)* If someone or something is **efficient**, they work very well and do not waste time or energy. **efficiency** *(n).*

**effort** *(n)* If you make an **effort**, you try hard. **effortless** *(adj).*

**e.g.** the initials of the Latin phrase *exempli gratia*, meaning "for example".

**egg 1** *(n)* an oval or rounded object produced by female birds, reptiles, and fish, in which their young develop. **2** *(n)* a cell created within a woman's body which, when fertilized, grows into a baby.

**Eid ul-Adha** *(n)* a Muslim festival during the last month of the Islamic year when many Muslims make a pilgrimage to Mecca. Some Muslims celebrate the festival by sacrificing animals.

**Eid-ul-Fitr** *(n)* the Muslim festival to celebrate the end of the Ramadan period of fasting.

**either 1** *(conj)* **Either** can be used to indicate a choice. *You can either stay or go.* **2** *(pronoun)* one of two. *Take either of them.* **either** *(adj).* **3** *(adv)* also, or similarly. *If Ed's not going, I'm not either.*

**eject ejecting ejected** *(v)* to push something out. *Eject the tape.*

**elaborate** **elaborating** **elaborated** 1 *(el-**ab**-or-ut) (adj)* complicated and detailed. *An elaborate pattern.* **elaborately** *(adv).* 2 *(el-**ab**-or-ate) (v)* to give more details. *Please elaborate on your plans.*

**elapse** **elapsing** **elapsed** *(v)* When time **elapses**, it passes.

**elastic** *(n)* a rubbery material which stretches. **elasticity** *(n).*

**elated** *(adj)* very pleased and excited.

**elbow** *(n)* the joint that connects the upper and lower parts of your arm.

**elder** *(adj)* older. *My elder sister.*

**elderly** *(adj)* old.

**elect** **electing** **elected** *(v)* to choose someone by voting. **election** *(n).*

**electrician** *(n)* someone who installs electrical systems and mends electrical machines.

**electricity** *(n)* a form of energy that is used for lighting, heating, and making machines work. **electric** *(adj),* **electrical** *(adj).*

**electrocute** **electrocuting** **electrocuted** *(v)* to kill or injure someone with a severe electric shock. **electrocution** *(n).*

**electromagnet** *(n)* a magnet which works by electricity.

**electronic** *(adj)* **Electronic** machines are worked by minute amounts of electricity, and contain transistors, silicon chips, or valves which control an electric current. *Computers, televisions, and radios are all electronic.* **electronically** *(adv).*

**electronic mail** *(n)* messages sent by one computer to another.

**electronics** *(singular n)* the technology that makes electronic machines work.

**elegant** *(adj)* graceful and stylish. **elegance** *(n),* **elegantly** *(adv).*

**element** 1 *(n)* In chemistry, an **element** is a substance that cannot be split into a simpler substance. *Oxygen and copper are elements.* 2 *(n)* one of the simple, basic parts of something. *Claude taught me the elements of cooking.* 3 *(n)* a wire or coil in an electrical heater, toaster, etc. that heats up when electricity passes through it. 4 **the elements** *(plural n)* the weather.

**elementary** *(adj)* simple, or basic.

**elephant** *(n)* a large mammal with a long trunk and ivory tusks.

**elephants**

**elf** **elves** *(n)* a small, magical, mischievous person described in legends and fairy stories. **elfin** *(adj).*

**eligible** *(adj)* If you are **eligible** for something, like a job, you have the right qualifications for it. **eligibility** *(n).*

**eliminate** **eliminating** **eliminated** *(v)* to get rid of someone or something.

**elite** *(el-**eet**) (n)* a group of people who have special advantages and privileges.

**elocution** *(n)* the art of speaking clearly.

**elongate** **elongating** **elongated** *(v)* to make something longer or stretch it out.

**elope** **eloping** **eloped** *(v)* to run away from home to get married.

**eloquent** *(adj)* An **eloquent** person speaks easily and interestingly.

**else** 1 *(adv)* other, or different. *They have gone somewhere else.* 2 *(adv)* more. *Tell me if you need anything else.*

**elusive** *(adj)* very hard to find or catch.

**E-mail** *short for* **electronic mail**.

**embankment** 1 *(n)* a long, low, earth bank, built to carry a railway, road, etc. 2 *(n)* a high bank at the sides of a river, built to stop it from flooding.

**embark** **embarking** **embarked** *(v)* to go on board a ship or an aeroplane.

**embarrass** **embarrasses** **embarrassing** **embarrassed** *(v)* to make someone feel awkward and uncomfortable. *Ron is easily embarrasssed.* **embarrassment** *(n).*

**emblem** *(n)* a symbol, or a sign. *The emblem of our club is a spider.*

**embrace** embracing embraced *(v)* to hug someone. **embrace** *(n).*

**embroider** embroidering embroidered *(v)* to sew a picture or a design on to cloth. **embroidery** *(n).*

**embryo** *(em-bree-oh) (n)* an unborn baby in the very early stage of development in its mother's womb.

**emerald** 1 *(n)* a bright green precious stone. 2 *(n)* a bright green colour.

**emerge** emerging emerged 1 *(v)* If you **emerge** from somewhere, you come out into the open. **emergence** *(n).* 2 *(v)* to become known. *News is emerging of a serious road accident.*

**emergency** emergencies *(n)* a sudden and dangerous situation that must be dealt with quickly.

**emigrate** emigrating emigrated *(v)* to leave your own country in order to live in another one. **emigration** *(n).*

**eminent** *(v)* well-known and respected.

**emit** emitting emitted *(v)* to release or send out something, such as heat, light, or sound. *The spaceship emitted a strange beeping sound.*

**emotion** *(n)* a strong feeling, such as happiness, love, anger, or grief.

**emotional** 1 *(adj)* to do with your feelings. *Emotional problems.* 2 *(adj)* When someone becomes **emotional**, they show their feelings, especially by crying.

**emperor** *(n)* a male ruler of an empire.

**emphasize** *or* **emphasise** emphasizing emphasized *(v)* If you **emphasize** something, you make it stand out clearly because you think it is important. **emphasis** *(n),* **emphatic** *(adj).*

**empire** *(n)* a group of countries that all have the same ruler. *The Roman Empire.*

**employ** employing employed *(v)* to pay someone to work for you. **employer** *(n).*

**employee** *(n)* a person who works for someone or some organization and is paid by them. **employment** *(n).*

**empress** empresses *(n)* the female ruler of an empire, or the wife of an emperor.

**empty** empties emptying emptied; emptier emptiest 1 *(adj)* If something is **empty**, there is nothing inside it. 2 *(v)* to take the contents out of something.

**enable** enabling enabled *(v)* to make it possible for someone to do something.

**enchanted** *(adj)* A place or thing that is **enchanted** has been put under a magic spell or seems magical.

**enclose** enclosing enclosed *(v)* to put something in an envelope or package with a letter. **enclosure** *(n).*

**encore** *(on-kor) (n)* an extra item added to the end of a performance because the audience has been applauding so much.

**encounter** *(n)* an unexpected or difficult meeting. **encounter** *(v).*

**encourage** encouraging encouraged *(v)* to give someone confidence by praising or supporting them. **encouragement** *(n),* **encouraging** *(adj).*

**encyclopedia** *or* **encyclopaedia** *(en-sy-klo-pee-dee-a) (n)* a book or set of books with information about many different subjects. **encyclopedic** *(adj).*

**end** ending ended 1 *(n)* the last part of something. 2 *(n)* one of the two points furthest from the middle of an object. 3 *(v)* to finish something.

**endanger** endangering endangered *(v)* to be dangerous to someone or something. *Pollution endangers wildlife.*

**endangered species** *(n)* a type of animal that may soon become extinct.

**endless** *(adj)* Something **endless** has no end, or seems to have no end.

**endure** enduring endured 1 *(v)* If you **endure** something unpleasant or painful, you put up with it. **endurance** *(n).* 2 *(v)* If something **endures**, it lasts for a long time. **enduring** *(adj).*

**enemy** enemies 1 *(n)* someone who really hates you and wants to harm you. 2 *(n)* the country or army that you are fighting against in a war.

**energetic** *(adj)* strong and active.

**energy** energies 1 *(n)* the strength to do active things without getting tired. 2 *(n)* power which makes machines work and produces heat.

**engaged** 1 *(adj)* If two people are **engaged**, they have decided that they will get married. **engagement** *(n).* 2 *(adj)* If a telephone number or public toilet is **engaged**, it is in use.

**engine** 1 *(n)* a machine that changes an energy source, such as petrol, into movement. 2 *(n)* the front part of a train that pulls all the carriages.

**engineer** *(n)* someone who designs and builds machines, vehicles, bridges, etc.

**engrave** **engraving engraved** *(v)* to cut a design or letters into a metal or glass surface. **engraver** *(n)*, **engraving** *(n)*.

**engrossed** *(adj)* If you are **engrossed** in something, you give it all your attention.

**engulf** **engulfing engulfed** *(v)* to cover or swallow up someone or something. *A huge wave engulfed the swimmers.*

**enjoy** **enjoying enjoyed** *(v)* to get pleasure from doing something. **enjoyment** *(n)*, **enjoyable** *(adj)*.

**enlarge** **enlarging enlarged** *(v)* to make something bigger.

**enlist** **enlisting enlisted** *(v)* to join the army, navy, or air force.

**enormous** *(adj)* extremely large.

**enough** *(n)* as much as is needed.

**enquire** *see* **inquire**.

**enquiry** *see* **inquiry**.

**enrage** **enraging enraged** *(v)* to make someone angry.

**enrich** **enriches enriching enriched** *(v)* to improve the quality of something.

**enrol** **enrolling enrolled** *(v)* When you **enrol** in something, you put your name on a list because you want to join.

**ensure** **ensuring ensured** *(v)* to make certain that something happens. *Please ensure that you lock the door.*

**enter** **entering entered** 1 *(v)* to go into a place. 2 *(v)* to say that you want to take part in a competition, race, or exam. 3 *(v)* to type a small amount of information into a computer, or write it in a book.

**enterprising** *(adj)* An **enterprising** person has lots of good ideas and is ready to try things that are new and difficult.

**entertain** **entertaining entertained** *(v)* to amuse and interest someone. **entertainment** *(n)*, **entertaining** *(adj)*.

**enthusiastic** *(adj)* If you are **enthusiastic** about something, you are very keen to do it or like it very much. **enthusiasm** *(n)*, **enthusiast** *(n)*.

**entice** **enticing enticed** *(v)* to tempt someone to do something. **enticing** *(adj)*.

**entire** *(adj)* whole. **entirely** *(adv)*.

**entrance** **entrancing entranced** 1 *(**en**-trunss)* *(n)* the way into a place. 2 *(en-**transs**)* *(v)* to give someone a feeling of wonder and pleasure. **entrancing** *(adj)*.

**entrant** *(n)* someone who takes part in a competition, race, or exam.

**entrust** **entrusting entrusted** *(v)* If you **entrust** someone with something valuable or important, you give it to them to look after for you.

**entry** **entries** 1 *(n)* a way into a place. 2 *(n)* a picture, story, answer, etc. that you send into a competition. 3 *(n)* a piece of information in a diary, computer, etc.

**envelop** *(en-**vel**-erp)* **enveloping enveloped** *(v)* to cover or surround something completely. *The house was soon enveloped in flames.*

**envelope** *(**en**-ver-lope or **on**-ver-lope)* *(n)* a paper cover for a letter or card.

**enviable** *(adj)* If someone has something **enviable**, you would like to have it.

**envious** *(adj)* If you are **envious**, you wish that you could have something that someone else has. **enviously** *(adv)*.

**environment** 1 *(n)* the natural world of the land, sea, and air. **environmental** *(adj)*. 2 *(n)* all the things that influence your life, such as where you live, your family, and the things that happen to you.

**envy** **envies envying envied** *(v)* to wish that you could have something that someone else has. **envy** *(n)*.

**epic** 1 *(n)* a long story, poem, or film about heroic adventures and great battles. **epic** *(adj)*. 2 *(adj)* heroic, or impressive.

**epidemic** *(n)* When there is an **epidemic**, an infectious disease spreads quickly to many people.

**epilepsy** *(n)* a disease of the brain that causes a person to have sudden blackouts or fits. **epileptic** *(n)*, **epileptic** *(adj)*.

**epilogue** *(n)* a short speech or piece of writing at the end of a story, film, etc.

**episode** *(n)* one of the programmes in a television or radio serial.

**epitaph** *(n)* a short description of someone, written on their gravestone.

**equal** *(adj)* the same as something else in size, value, or amount. **equal** *(v)*.

**equality** *(n)* the same rights for everyone. *Racial equality.*

**equation** *(n)* a mathematical statement that one set of numbers or values is equal to another set of numbers or values, for example, 4 x 4 = 16 or 3x + 2y = 13.

**equator** *(n)* an imaginary line around the middle of the Earth, halfway between the North and South Poles. *The equator is marked by a red line on this picture.*

**equator**

**equilateral** *(adj)* An **equilateral** triangle has sides of equal length.

**equilibrium** *(n)* balance.

**equip** **equipping equipped** *(v)* to provide someone with all the things that they need.

**equipment** *(n)* the tools and machines that you need for a particular purpose.

**equivalent** *(adj)* If one thing is **equivalent** to another, it is the same as the other in amount, value, or importance. **equivalent** *(n)*.

**era** *(n)* a period of time in history. *The Jurassic era.*

**eradicate** **eradicating eradicated** *(v)* to get rid of something completely, especially something bad like disease, crime, or poverty.

**erase** **erasing erased 1** *(v)* to rub out something. **2** *(v)* to wipe out something stored in a computer or on a tape.

**eraser** *(n)* a small piece of rubber used for removing pencil mistakes.

**erect** **erecting erected 1** *(adj)* standing upright. **erection** *(n)*, **erectly** *(adv)*. **2** *(v)* to put up a structure. *This building was erected in 1982.* **erection** *(n)*.

**erode** **eroding eroded** *(v)* When something is **eroded**, it is gradually worn away by water or wind.

**erosion** *(n)* the gradual wearing away of a substance by water or wind.

**erotic** *(adj)* to do with sexual love.

**errand** *(n)* If someone sends you on an **errand**, they ask you to go somewhere nearby to take a message or to deliver or collect something.

**erratic** *(adj)* If something is **erratic**, it does not follow a regular pattern.

**error** *(n)* a mistake.

**erupt** **erupting erupted**. *(v)* When a volcano **erupts**, it throws out rocks, hot ash, and lava. **eruption** *(n)*.

**escalator** *(n)* a moving staircase.

**escape** **escaping escaped 1** *(v)* to break free from somewhere. **escape** *(n)*. **2** *(v)* to avoid something. *We escaped the rush.*

**escort** **escorting escorted** *(v)* to go somewhere with someone, especially to protect them. **escort** *(n)*.

**especially** *(adv)* specially, or mainly. *Crispin is especially good at singing. Alex loves sport, especially tennis.*

**espionage** *(n)* spying.

**essay** *(n)* a piece of writing about a particular subject.

**essential** *(adj)* vital and important.

**establish** **establishes establishing established 1** *(v)* to set up a business, society, or organization. **2** *(v)* to settle somewhere. *Bob is established in his flat.*

**estate 1** *(n)* a large area of land owned by one person. **2** *(n)* an area of land with houses, factories, or offices on it.

**estimate** **estimating estimated 1** *(v)* to work something out roughly. **2** *(ess-tim-ut)* *(n)* a rough guess or calculation.

**estuary** *(est-yur-ee)* **estuaries** *(n)* the wide part of a river where it joins the sea.

**etc.** an abbreviated form of the Latin phrase *et cetera*, which means "and the rest". Etc. is used at the end of lists.

**eternal** *(adj)* lasting for ever.

**ethnic** *(adj)* to do with different racial groups. **ethnically** *(adv)*.

**European** *(adj)* from Europe, or to do with Europe. **European** *(n)*.

**euthanasia** *(yoo-than-ay-zee-a)* *(n)* the painless killing of someone who is suffering from an incurable or painful disease, or who is very old. Euthanasia is against the law in Britain.

**evacuate** **evacuating** **evacuated** *(v)* to move away from an area because it is dangerous. *Evacuate the building!*

**evaluate** **evaluating** **evaluated** *(v)* to decide how good or how valuable something is, after thinking carefully.

**evaporate** **evaporating** **evaporated** *(v)* When a liquid **evaporates**, it changes into a vapour. **evaporation** *(n).*

**even** 1 *(adj)* An **even** number can be divided exactly by two. 2 *(adj)* equal. *An even score.* **evenly** *(adv).* 3 *(adj)* smooth and level. *An even surface.*

**evening** *(n)* the time of day between the late afternoon and the early part of the night.

**event** 1 *(n)* something that happens, especially something interesting or important. 2 *(n)* an activity, such as a race, that is held during a sports competition.

**eventually** *(adv)* finally, or at last.

**ever** 1 *(adv)* at any time. *Did you ever see a UFO?* 2 *(adv)* all the time. *Ever grateful.*

**evergreen** *(n)* a bush or tree which has green leaves all the year round.

**every** *(adj)* all the people or things in a group. *Every month of the year.*

**everyday** *(adj)* usual, or normal. *An everyday event.*

**evict** **evicting** **evicted** *(v)* to force someone to move out of their home.

**evidence** *(n)* information and facts that help to prove something or make you believe that something is true.

**evident** *(adj)* clear and obvious.

**evil** *(adj)* wicked and cruel. **evil** *(n).*

**evolution** 1 *(n)* the gradual development of animals and plants over thousands of years. **evolve** *(v).* 2 *(n)* gradual change into a different form. **evolve** *(v).*

**exact** *(adj)* perfectly correct and accurate.

**exaggerate** **exaggerating** **exaggerated** *(v)* to make something seem bigger, better, more important, etc. than it really is. **exaggeration** *(n).*

**exam** *(n)* an official test that you take to show how much you know about a subject. Exam is short for examination.

**examination** 1 *(n) See* **exam**. 2 *(n)* a careful check, or an inspection.

**examine** **examining** **examined** 1 *(v)* to look carefully at something. 2 *(v)* When doctors **examine** you, they check your body carefully to see what is wrong.

**example** 1 *(n)* something typical of a larger group of things. *The wallaby is an example of a marsupial.* 2 *(n)* a model for others to follow. *Felicity is an example to the rest of the class.*

**exasperate** **exasperating** **exasperated** *(v)* to make someone very annoyed.

**excavate** **excavating** **excavated** *(v)* to dig in the earth, either in order to put up a building or to discover ancient remains.

**exceed** **exceeding** **exceeded** 1 *(v)* to be greater or better than something else. *The party exceeded my hopes.* 2 *(v)* to do more than is allowed or expected. *Drivers who exceed the speed limit will be fined.*

**excellent** *(adj)* very good indeed.

**except** *(prep)* apart from. *Everyone except Hannah went home.* **except** *(conj).*

**exception** *(n)* something that is not included in a general rule or statement. *Tom hates girls, with just a few exceptions.*

**exceptional** *(adj)* outstanding, or rare.

**excerpt** *(n)* a short piece taken from a longer book, film, or piece of music.

**excess** **excesses** *(n)* too much of something. **excess** *(adj).*

**excessive** *(adj)* too much. *Augustus eats an excessive amount.* **excessively** *(adv).*

**exchange** **exchanging** **exchanged** *(v)* to give one thing and receive another. *We exchanged presents.* **exchange** *(n).*

**excite** **exciting** **excited** *(v)* to make someone eager and interested. **excitement** *(n),* **exciting** *(adj).*

**exclaim** **exclaiming** **exclaimed** *(v)* to say something loudly, especially because you are surprised or excited. **exclamation** *(n).*

**exclamation mark** *(n)* the punctuation mark (!) used after an expression of surprise, excitement, anger, etc.

**exclude** **excluding** **excluded** 1 *(v)* If you **exclude** something, you leave it out. *The list excludes prices.* 2 *(v)* to stop someone joining or taking part in something.

**excrete** **excreting** **excreted** *(v)* to pass solid waste matter out of your body.

**excruciating** *(adj)* extremely painful.

**excursion** *(n)* a short journey, often to a place of interest.

**excuse** **excusing excused 1** *(ex-**kuze**)* *(v)* to forgive someone for doing something. **2** *(ex-**kuse**)* *(n)* a reason you give to explain why you have done something wrong. **3** *(ex-**kuze**)* *(v)* to give someone permission not to do something. *The instructor excused Lydia from games.*

**execute** **executing executed** *(v)* to kill someone as a punishment. **execution** *(n).*

**exempt** *(adj)* If you are **exempt** from something, you do not have to take part in it. **exemption** *(n),* **exempt** *(v).*

**exercise 1** *(n)* physical activity that you do to keep fit and healthy. **exercise** *(v).* **2** *(n)* a piece of work that you do in order to practise a skill. *Piano exercises.*

**exhale** **exhaling exhaled** *(v)* to breathe out. **exhalation** *(n).*

**exhaust** **exhausting exhausted 1** *(v)* to make someone very tired. **exhaustion** *(n).* **2** *(v)* to use something up completely. *The explorers exhausted their food supplies.*

**exhibition** *(n)* a public display of works of art, historical objects, etc.

**exhilarating** *(adj)* very exciting and thrilling. **exhilaration** *(n).*

**exile** **exiling exiled** *(v)* to send someone away from their own country and order them not to return. **exile** *(n).*

**exist** **existing existed** *(v)* to live, or to be real. *Did King Arthur exist?* **existence** *(n).*

**exit** **exiting exited 1** *(v)* to leave, or to go out. **2** *(n)* the way out of a place.

**exotic 1** *(adj)* from a foreign, tropical country. *An exotic plant.* **2** *(adj)* strange and fascinating. *An exotic perfume.*

**expand** **expanding expanded** *(v)* to increase in size. **expansion** *(n).*

**expanse** *(n)* a very large area.

**expect** **expecting expected 1** *(v)* to think that something will happen. *I expect it will rain.* **2** *(v)* to wait for someone to arrive. *We're expecting visitors.* **3** *(v)* to think that something ought to happen. *Aunt Jane expects you to visit.* **4** *(informal)* If a woman is **expecting**, she is pregnant.

**expedition** *(n)* a long journey for a special purpose, such as exploring.

**expel** **expelling expelled** *(v)* If someone is **expelled** from a school, they have to leave as a punishment. **expulsion** *(n).*

**expense** *(n)* the spending of money, time, energy, etc. *Forget the expense!*

**expensive** *(adj)* costing a lot of money.

**experience 1** *(n)* something that happens to you. **experience** *(v).* **2** *(n)* the knowledge and skill that you gain by doing something. **experienced** *(adj).*

**experiment** *(n)* a scientific test to try out a theory or to see the effect of something. **experiment** *(v).*

**expert** *(n)* someone who is very skilled at something or knows a lot about a particular subject. **expertise** *(n).*

**explain** **explaining explained 1** *(v)* to make something clear so it is easier to understand. **explanation** *(n).* **2** *(v)* to give a reason for something. **explanation** *(n).*

**explode** **exploding exploded** *(v)* If something **explodes**, it blows apart with a loud bang and great force.

**exploit** **exploiting exploited** **1** *(ex-**ployt**)* *(v)* to treat someone unfairly. **exploitation** *(n).* **2** *(**ex**-ployt)* *(n)* a brave or daring deed.

**explore** **exploring explored** *(v)* to travel in order to discover what a place is like. **exploration** *(n),* **explorer** *(n).*

**explosion 1** *(n)* a sudden and noisy release of energy. **2** *(n)* a sudden increase or growth. *A population explosion.*

**explosive 1** *(n)* a substance that can blow up. **2** *(adj)* able or likely to explode.

**export** **exporting exported** *(v)* to send goods to another country to be sold there. **export** *(n).*

**expose** **exposing exposed 1** *(v)* to uncover something so that people can see it. **2** *(v)* to reveal the truth about someone or something.

**express** **expresses expressing expressed 1** *(v)* to show what you feel or think by saying, doing, or writing something. *Henry expressed his joy by dancing.* **2** *(adj)* very fast. *Express delivery.*

**expression 1** *(n)* the act of showing your feelings. **2** *(n)* the look on someone's face.

**exquisite** *(adj)* very beautiful and delicate. **exquisitely** *(adv).*

**extend** extending extended *(v)* to make something longer or bigger. *We are extending our house.* **extension** *(n).*

**extent** *(n)* the size, level, or scale of something. *What is the extent of the damage?*

**exterior** *(n)* the outside of something, especially a building. **exterior** *(adj).*

**exterminate** exterminating exterminated *(v)* to kill large numbers of people or animals. **extermination** *(n).*

**external** *(adj)* on the outside.

**extinct** *(adj)* If a type of animal or flower is **extinct**, it has died out. *Dodos became extinct over 200 years ago.* **extinction** *(n).*

**dodo**

**extinguish** extinguishes extinguishing extinguished *(v)* to put out a flame, fire, or light.

**extra** *(adj)* more than the usual amount. *An extra helping of chips.* **extra** *(adv).*

**extract** *(n)* a short section taken from a book, speech, piece of music, etc.

**extraordinary** *(adj)* very unusual, or remarkable. **extraordinarily** *(adv).*

**extraterrestrial** *(n)* a creature from outer space. **extraterrestrial** *(adj).*

**extravagant** *(adj)* An **extravagant** person spends too much money, or is wasteful in the way they use things. **extravagance** *(n),* **extravagantly** *(adv).*

**extreme** 1 *(adj)* very great. *Extreme happiness.* 2 *(adj)* furthest, or outermost. *I reached the extreme edge of the woods.*

**extrovert** *(n)* someone who enjoys being with other people and is talkative.

**eye** 1 *(n)* one of the two organs in your head that you use for seeing. 2 *(n)* the small hole in a needle.

**eyebrow** *(n)* the line of hair that grows above each of your eyes.

**eyelash** eyelashes *(n)* one of the short, curved hairs that grow on your eyelids.

**eyelid** *(n)* the upper or lower fold of skin that covers your eye when it is closed.

**eyewitness** eyewitnesses *(n)* someone who has seen something take place and can describe what happened.

# Ff

**fable** *(n)* a story that teaches a lesson. Fables are often about animals.

**fabric** *(n)* cloth, or material.

**fabulous** 1 *(adj)* wonderful, or marvellous. 2 *(adj)* existing only in stories and legends. *Fabulous creatures.*

**face** facing faced 1 *(n)* the front of your head, from your forehead to your chin. **facial** *(adj).* 2 *(n)* a side or surface of something. *A mountain face.* 3 *(v)* to look towards something. *Our flat faces the hill.*

**fact** 1 *(n)* a piece of information that is true. **factual** *(adj).* 2 **in fact** *(adv)* actually.

**factor** 1 *(n)* one of the things that helps to produce a result. 2 *(n)* a whole number that can be divided exactly into a larger number. *2 and 3 are factors of 6.*

**factory** factories *(n)* a building where things are made in large numbers.

**fad** *(n) (informal)* a temporary fashion or interest.

**fade** fading faded 1 *(v)* to become paler in colour. 2 *(v)* to become weaker. *Our hopes of rescue are fading.*

**faeces** *(fee-sees) (plural n)* the solid waste matter that people and animals pass out of their bodies.

**fail** failing failed 1 *(v)* If you **fail** an exam or test, you do not pass it. **fail** *(n).* 2 *(v)* If you **fail** to do something, you do not do it. **failure** *(n).*

**failing** *(n)* a fault or weakness in someone or something.

**faint** fainting fainted; fainter faintest 1 *(adj)* weak. *A faint sound.* **faintly** *(adv).* 2 *(v)* to become dizzy and lose consciousness for a short time.

**fair** fairer fairest 1 *(adj)* reasonable and equal. *Fair treatment.* **fairness** *(n),* **fairly** *(adv).* 2 *(adj)* **Fair** hair is light yellow. 3 *(n)* an outdoor entertainment with rides, amusements, and stalls. **fairground** *(n).*

**fairy** fairies 1 *(n)* a magical creature like a tiny person with wings, found in fairy stories. 2 **fairy story** *or* **fairy tale** *(n)* a children's story about magic, fairies, etc.

**faith** 1 *(n)* trust and confidence in someone or something. *Our coach has lots of faith in our team.* 2 *(n)* a religion.

**faithful** *(adj)* loyal and trustworthy.

**fake** **faking faked** 1 *(v)* to make a copy of something and pretend that it is genuine. *Mia faked her boss's signature.* 2 *(n)* a copy of something that is made to fool people. **fake** *(adj).*

**fall** **falling fell fallen** 1 *(v)* to drop down to the ground. **fall** *(n).* 2 *(v)* to decrease, or to become lower. *The temperature fell.* **fall** *(n).* 3 *(v)* to become. *Yves fell asleep.* 4 *(n)* the American word for autumn.

**false** 1 *(adj)* not true, or not correct. *False information.* **falsely** *(adv).* 2 *(adj)* not real. *False eyelashes.*

**fame** *(n)* being famous. *Terry longs for fame.* **famed** *(adj).*

**familiar** 1 *(adj)* well known, or easily recognized. *A familiar saying.* 2 *(adj)* If you are **familiar** with something, you know it well. **familiarity** *(n).*

**family** **families** 1 *(n)* a group of people related to each other, especially parents and their children. 2 *(n)* a group of related animals or plants. *The lion and the tiger belong to the cat family.* 3 **family tree** *(n)* a chart that shows how the members of a family are related over many generations.

**famine** *(n)* a serious shortage of food in a country.

**famous** *(adj)* If someone is **famous**, they are well known to many people.

**fan** 1 *(n)* an enthusiastic supporter of a sport, pop group, etc. 2 *(n)* a machine or an object that you use to blow or wave air on to you, in order to keep cool. **fan** *(v).*

**fanatic** *(n)* someone who is wildly enthusiastic about a belief, a cause, or an interest. *A football fanatic.* **fanatical** *(adj).*

**fancy** **fancies fancying fancied; fancier fanciest** 1 *(adj)* highly decorated, or elaborate. 2 *(v)* *(informal)* If you **fancy** something, you would like to do it or have it. *I fancy some lunch.*

**fang** *(n)* a long, pointed tooth.

**fantastic** 1 *(adj)* too strange to be believable. **fantastically** *(adv).* 2 *(adj)* extremely good. **fantastically** *(adv).*

**fantasy** **fantasies** *(n)* something that you imagine happening, but which is not likely to happen in real life. **fantasize** *(v).*

**far** **farther farthest** *or* **further furthest** 1 *(adv)* at or to a great distance. *Have you travelled far?* 2 *(adv)* very much. *I far prefer cycling to walking.* 3 *(adj)* opposite, or distant. *The far side of the river.*

**fare** *(n)* the cost of travelling on a bus, train, plane, etc.

**Far East** *(n)* the countries of eastern Asia, such as China and Japan.

**farewell** *(interject)* goodbye.

**farm** **farming farmed** 1 *(v)* to grow crops and rear animals. **farmer** *(n),* **farming** *(n).* 2 *(n)* land and buildings used for growing crops or rearing animals. *The picture shows a range of machinery used on a farm.* **farm** *(adj).*

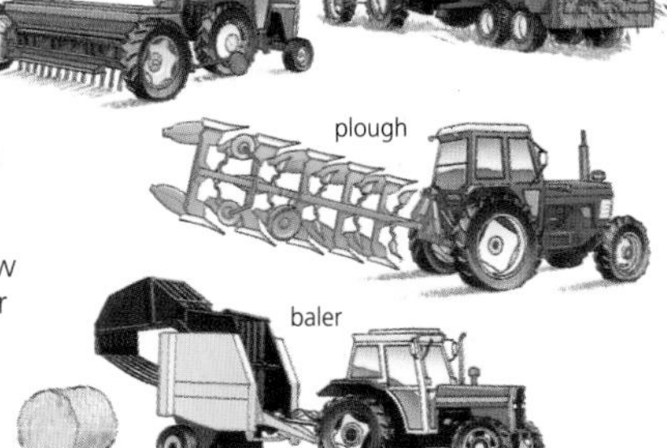


**fascinate** **fascinating fascinated** *(v)* If someone or something **fascinates** you, you are really interested and excited by them. **fascination** *(n).*

**fascism** *(fash-izm)* *(n)* a way of organizing a country according to extreme right-wing and nationalist principles, with a powerful dictator and only one political party. **fascist** *(n).*

**fashion** 1 *(n)* a style of clothing that is popular at a certain time. **fashionable** *(adj).* 2 *(n)* a way of doing things.

**fast** **fasting fasted; faster fastest** 1 *(adj)* quick. **fast** *(adv).* 2 *(v)* to give up eating food for a time. **fast** *(n).* 3 *(adv)* firmly, or tightly. *Kit's head was stuck fast.* 4 *(adj)* ahead of the right time. *Five minutes fast.*

**fasten** **fastening** **fastened** *(v)* to tie or join something firmly. **fastener** *(n)*.

**fat** **fatter** **fattest** 1 *(adj)* overweight, or plump. **fatness** *(n)*. 2 *(n)* the soft substance in the body of a person or animal that helps to keep them warm. 3 *(n)* a part of foods such as meat, milk, and cheese, that gives you energy and is stored in your body to keep you warm.

**fatal** 1 *(adj)* causing death. *A fatal accident.* **fatally** *(adv)*. 2 *(adj)* likely to have important, and usually bad, results. *A fatal decision.*

**fatality** **fatalities** *(n)* a death caused by an accident, a war, or another form of violence.

**fate** 1 *(n)* the force that some people believe controls events and decides what happens to people. 2 *(n)* Your **fate** is what will happen to you.

**fateful** *(adj)* important because it has a strong, usually unpleasant, effect on future events. *A fateful day.*

**father** *(n)* a male parent.

**fathom** **fathoming** **fathomed** 1 *(v)* If you cannot **fathom** something, you cannot understand it. 2 *(n)* a unit for measuring the depth of water. 1 fathom = 1.8 m or 6ft.

**fatigue** *(fat-eeg)* *(n)* great tiredness.

**fault** 1 *(n)* something wrong. *An electrical fault.* **faulty** *(adj)*. 2 *(n)* a weakness in someone's character. 3 *(n)* If something is your **fault**, you are to blame for it. 4 *(n)* a large crack in the Earth's surface that can cause earthquakes. *The picture shows a tear fault, where parts of the Earth's crust have pulled in opposite directions.*

**tear fault**

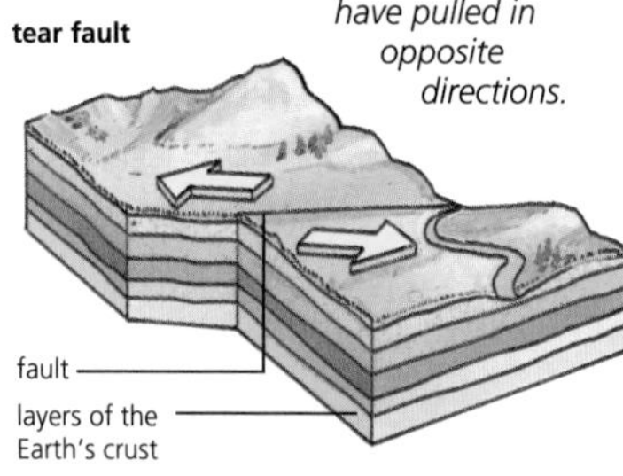


**fauna** *(n)* the animal life of a particular area. *Woodland fauna.*

**favour** **favouring** **favoured** 1 *(n)* something helpful or kind that you do for someone. 2 *(v)* to like one thing or person best. *Dad always favours Johnny!* 3 If you are **in favour of** something, you agree with it or support it.

**favourite** 1 *(n)* the person or thing that you like best. **favourite** *(adj)*. 2 *(n)* the person, team, or animal that is expected to win a race.

**favouritism** *(n)* unfair kindness shown to one person more than others.

**fawn** 1 *(n)* a young deer. 2 *(n)* a light brown colour.

**fear** **fearing** **feared** 1 *(n)* the feeling you have when you are in danger or you expect something bad to happen. **fearful** *(adj)*. 2 *(v)* to be afraid of something or someone. 3 *(v)* to be worried about something. *I fear we're going to be late.*

**fearsome** *(adj)* frightening. *A fearsome monster.*

**feasible** *(adj)* If something is **feasible**, it can be done. *A feasible plan.*

**feast** *(n)* a large meal for a lot of people on a special occasion. **feast** *(v)*.

**feat** *(n)* an amazing achievement.

**feather** *(n)* one of the light, fluffy parts that cover a bird's body. **feathered** *(adj)*.

jay
finch
curlew
sunbittern
**feathers**

**feature** 1 *(n)* Your **features** are the different parts of your face. 2 *(n)* an important part or quality of something.

**fed up** *(adj)* *(informal)* bored, or unhappy about something.

**fee** *(n)* the amount of money that someone charges for a service.

**feeble** **feebler** **feeblest** *(adj)* very weak.

**feed** **feeding** **fed** 1 *(v)* to give food to a person or an animal. 2 *(v)* When babies or animals **feed**, they eat. 3 *(n)* food for animals. 4 *(v)* to put something, for example, coins or information, into a machine. *Alicia fed all the data into her computer.*

**feedback** 1 *(n)* comments and reactions to something. *I'd like some feedback on these ideas.* 2 *(n)* the loud, piercing noise made when the sound produced by an amplifier goes back into it.

**feel feeling felt** 1 *(v)* to touch something with your fingers, or to experience something touching you. *Jess felt the sun on her face.* 2 *(v)* to have an emotion or sensation. *Maddy felt angry.* **feeling** *(n).* 3 *(v)* to think, or to have an opinion. *Barney felt that it was unfair.* **feeling** *(n).*

**feline** *(adj)* to do with cats.

**fell felling felled** *(v)* to cut something down or make something fall. *The gardener felled the tree.*

**fellow** 1 *(n) (old-fashioned)* a man or boy. 2 *(adj)* belonging to the same class or group. *I like my fellow students.*

**felt** 1 *(n)* a thick cloth made of wool or other fibres pressed together. 2 **felt-tip** *(n)* a colouring pen with a felt nib.

**female** *(n)* a person or animal of the sex that can give birth to young. **female** *(adj).*

**feminine** 1 *(adj)* to do with women. 2 *(adj)* having qualities that are supposed to be typical of women. **femininity** *(n).*

**feminist** *(n)* someone who believes strongly that women ought to have the same opportunities and rights that men have. **feminism** *(n),* **feminist** *(adj).*

**fen** *(n)* an area of flat, low, marshy land.

**fence fencing fenced** 1 *(n)* a wooden or wire barrier built to separate two areas of land. **fencing** *(n),* **fence** *(v).* 2 *(v)* to fight with long, thin swords called foils, as a sport. **fencer** *(n),* **fencing** *(n).*

**fencing**

**fend fending fended** 1 *(v)* If you **fend** for someone, you take care of them. 2 *(v)* If you **fend off** someone who is attacking you, you defend yourself.

**ferment fermenting fermented** *(v)* When a drink, such as beer or wine, **ferments**, a chemical change takes place which makes the sugar in it turn into alcohol. **fermentation** *(n).*

**fern** *(n)* a plant with feathery leaves, or fronds, and no flowers, that usually grows in damp places.

**ferocious** *(adj)* very fierce and savage.

**ferry ferries** *(n)* a boat or ship that regularly carries people across a stretch of water.

**fertile** 1 *(adj)* able to have babies. **fertility** *(n).* 2 *(adj)* **Fertile** land is good for growing crops and plants. **fertility** *(n).*

**fertilize** *or* **fertilise fertilizing fertilized** 1 *(v)* When an egg or a plant is **fertilized**, sperm joins with the egg, or pollen comes into contact with the reproductive part of the plant, so that reproduction begins. **fertilization** *(n).* 2 *(v)* to put a substance, such as manure, on land to make it richer and make crops grow better. **fertilizer** *(n).*

**fervent** *(adj)* If someone is **fervent** about something, they believe in it passionately.

**festival** 1 *(n)* a time when people celebrate something, such as a holy day. 2 *(n)* an organized set of artistic or musical events, often held at the same time each year. *An opera festival.*

**festive** *(adj)* cheerful and lively because there is something to celebrate.

**festoon festooning festooned** *(v)* to cover something with decorations.

**fetch fetches fetching fetched** *(v)* to go to get something or somebody.

**fête** *(fate) (n)* an outdoor event with games, stalls, and things for sale, usually held to raise money for charity.

**fetus** *or* **foetus** *(feet-uss)* **fetuses** *(n)* a baby or animal before it is born, at the stage when it is developing in its mother's womb. *See* **pregnant**.

**feud** *(rhymes with chewed) (n)* a bitter quarrel between two people or families that lasts for a long time. **feud** *(v).*

**fever** 1 *(n)* If someone has a **fever**, they have a high temperature. **feverish** *(adj).* 2 *(n)* great excitement or agitation.

**few fewer fewest** *(adj)* not many.

**fiancé** *(fee-on-say) (n)* If a man and woman are engaged to be married, he is her **fiancé**.

*Some words that begin with a "f" sound are spelt "ph".*

**fiancée** *(fee-on-say) (n)* If a man and woman are engaged to be married, she is his **fiancée**.

**fiasco** *(n)* a complete failure.

**fib fibbing fibbed** *(v)* to tell a small lie.

**fibre** 1 *(n)* a fine thread of cloth. 2 *(n)* a part of foods such as cereals and vegetables, which passes through the body, but is not digested.

**fickle** *(adj)* Someone who is **fickle** changes their mind very often.

**fiction** *(n)* stories that are made up.

**fiddle fiddling fiddled** 1 *(v)* to keep touching or playing about with something. 2 *(n) (informal)* a violin.

**fiddly** *(adj)* If something is **fiddly**, it is awkward to do because it is very small or very complicated.

**fidget fidgeting fidgeted** *(v)* to keep moving because you are bored or uneasy.

**field** *(n)* a piece of land, sometimes used for growing crops or playing sports.

**fielder** *(n)* someone who fetches or catches the ball in games like cricket and baseball. **fielding** *(n)*.

**field trip** *(n)* a visit that you go on with your school to study something in its natural environment.

**fiend** *(feend) (n)* a wicked person, or a devil. **fiendish** *(adj)*.

**fierce fiercer fiercest** *(adj)* violent, or aggressive. **fierceness** *(n)*, **fiercely** *(adv)*.

**fiery fierier fieriest** *(adj)* like fire, or to do with fire.

**fight fighting fought** 1 *(v)* to attack someone and try to hurt them. **fight** *(n)*. 2 *(v)* to have an argument. **fight** *(n)*.

**fighter** 1 *(n)* someone who fights, such as a boxer or soldier. 2 *(n)* an aeroplane used in a war.

**figure figuring figured** 1 *(n)* a written number. 2 *(n)* a person's shape. *Marilyn has a wonderful figure.* 3 *(n)* a person. *A well-known figure.*

**file filing filed** 1 *(n)* a box or folder for papers or documents. 2 *(v)* to put papers or documents away in a file. 3 *(n)* a tool used to make things smooth. **file** *(v)*. 4 **computer file** *(n)* a set of data held in a computer. 5 **single file** *(n)* a line of people one behind the other.

**fill filling filled** 1 *(v)* to make something full. 2 *(v)* If you **fill in** a form, you answer all the questions on it.

**fillet** *(n)* a piece of meat or fish with the bones taken out. **fillet** *(v)*.

**filling** 1 *(n)* a substance that a dentist puts into holes in your teeth to prevent more decay. 2 *(n)* the food inside a sandwich, pie, cake, etc.

**filling station** *(n)* a garage where you can buy petrol.

**filly fillies** *(n)* a young female horse.

**film filming filmed** 1 *(n)* a story shown on television or at the cinema. 2 *(n)* a roll of light-sensitive material, that you use in a camera to take photographs. 3 *(v)* to record something with a camera or a camcorder.

**filter** *(n)* a device that cleans liquids or gases as they pass through it. **filter** *(v)*.

**filth** 1 *(n)* dirt. **filthy** *(adj)*. 2 *(n)* rudeness.

**fin** 1 *(n)* a flap-like shape on the body of a fish, used for steering it through the water. 2 **fins** *(plural n)* long, flat attachments that you fit on your feet to help you swim. *See* **scuba diving**.

**finalize** *or* **finalise finalizing finalized** *(v)* to finish making arrangements. *Have you finalized the dates for your trip?*

**finance financing financed** 1 *(n)* money, or the management of money. *An expert in finance.* **financial** *(adj)*. 2 *(v)* to provide money for something.

**find finding found** 1 *(v)* to discover, or to come across something. 2 **find out** *(v)* to learn about something or someone.

**fine fining fined; finer finest** 1 *(adj)* very good, or excellent. 2 *(adj)* okay, or all right. 3 *(adj)* not rainy. *A fine day.* 4 *(adj)* thin, or delicate. 5 *(v)* to demand some money as a punishment. **fine** *(n)*.

**finger** 1 *(n)* one of the long parts of your hands that you can move. 2 *(n)* an object shaped like a finger. *A chocolate finger.*

**fingerprint** *(n)* the print made by the pattern of curved lines on your fingertips.

**finicky** *(adj)* fussy, especially about food.

**finish finishes finishing finished** 1 *(v)* to end or complete something. 2 *(n)* the end of something, such as a race.

**fiord** *see* **fjord**.

*Some words that begin with a "f" sound are spelt "ph".*

**fir** *(n)* a pointed, evergreen tree with needle-like leaves and cones.

**fire firing fired 1** *(n)* flames, heat, and light produced by burning. **2** *(v)* to shoot a gun or other weapon. **3** *(v)* to sack someone from their job.

**fire extinguisher** *(n)* a metal case containing chemicals and water, that you use to put out a fire.

**fireproof** *(adj)* made from materials that will not catch fire.

**firetrap** *(n)* a building that would be hard to escape from if it caught fire.

**firework** *(n)* a container, filled with gunpowder and other chemicals, that makes bangs and coloured sparks when it is lit.

**firm firmer firmest 1** *(adj)* strong and solid. *A firm bed.* **2** *(adj)* definite and not easily altered. *A firm decision.* **firmly** *(adv).* **3** *(n)* a business, or a company.

**first 1** *(n)* a person or a thing that acts or happens earliest. *Adam was the first to arrive.* **2** *(adj)* earliest in time. *The first bus.* **3** *(adv)* before something else. *Go home first, then come to our house.* **4** *(adj)* most important. *The first team.* **firstly** *(adv).*

**first aid** *(n)* medical help that is given to someone immediately after an accident.

**fish fish or fishes; fishes fishing fished 1** *(n)* an animal that lives in water and has scales, fins, and gills. **2** *(v)* to try to catch fish. **fishing** *(n).*

**fishy fishier fishiest 1** *(adj)* tasting or smelling of fish. **2** *(adj) (informal)* strange and suspicious. *A fishy story.*

**fist** *(n)* a tightly closed hand.

**fit fitting fitted; fitter fittest 1** *(adj)* healthy and strong. **fitness** *(n).* **2** *(v)* to be the right size or shape. **3** *(n)* a sudden, uncontrollable attack of something. *A fit of giggles.* **4** *(n)* If someone has an epileptic **fit**, they suddenly become unconscious and all their muscles tense.

**fix fixes fixing fixed 1** *(v)* to mend something. **2** *(v)* to decide on something. *I'll fix a date for the party.* **3** *(v)* to attach something to another thing. *Fix the picture to the wall.*

**fixture 1** *(n)* a sports match or event. **2** *(n)* an object that is fitted into a house, such as a bath or cupboard.

**fizz fizzes fizzing fizzed** *(v)* to bubble and hiss. **fizzy** *(adj).*

**fjord** *or* **fiord** *(fee-ord) (n)* a narrow channel of sea that runs inland between high cliffs, formed by a glacier.

**flabbergasted** *(adj) (informal)* stunned and surprised.

**flaccid** *(flass-id) (adj)* soft and limp.

**flag** *(n)* a piece of cloth with a pattern on it, that is a symbol of a country, organization, etc.

**international flags**

United Nations

Olympic Games

International Red Cross

Council of Europe

**flair** *(n)* natural skill or ability. *Raymond has a flair for cooking.*

**flake flaking flaked 1** *(n)* a small, thin piece of something. *Flakes of paint fell off the door.* **2** *(v)* If something **flakes**, small, thin pieces of it peel off. **flaky** *(adj).*

**flamboyant** *(adj)* bold, showy, and brightly coloured. **flamboyantly** *(adv).*

**flame** *(n)* a tongue of fire. **flaming** *(adj).*

**flamingo flamingos** *or* **flamingoes** *(n)* a pink, long-legged bird with webbed feet.

**flammable** *(adj)* likely to catch fire.

**flannel 1** *(n)* woven, woollen fabric. **2** *(n)* a square of cloth, used to wash your face.

**flap flapping flapped 1** *(v)* to move up and down. *The bird flapped its wings.* **2** *(v)* to swing loosely. *The sail flapped in the breeze.* **3** *(n)* something attached on one side only. *The flap of an envelope.*

**flare flaring flared 1** *(n)* a bright flame used as an emergency signal. **2** *(v)* If something **flares up**, it suddenly becomes stronger or more violent.

**flash flashes 1** *(n)* a short burst of light. **flash** *(v).* **2** *(n)* a short burst of something. *A flash of inspiration. A news flash.*

**flashback** *(n)* a part of a book or film that tells you what happened earlier.

**flashy flashier flashiest** *(adj)* showy and expensive. *Todd wears flashy clothes.*

**flask 1** *(n)* a narrow-necked bottle, used in a science laboratory. **2** *(n)* an insulated container that keeps liquids hot or cold.

**flat flatter flattest 1** *(adj)* level, or smooth. *A flat surface.* **2** *(adj)* not high. *Flat shoes.* **3** *(adj)* emptied of air. *A flat tyre.* **4** *(n)* a set of rooms for living in, usually on one floor of a building.

**flatter flattering flattered** *(v)* to praise someone, especially when you want a favour. **flattery** *(n).*

**flavour flavouring flavoured 1** *(n)* taste. **flavoured** *(adj).* **2** *(v)* to add taste to food. *Flavour the cake with vanilla.*

**flaw** *(n)* a fault, or a weakness.

**flea 1** *(n)* a small, jumping and biting insect that lives on the blood of people or animals. **2 flea market** *(n)* a street market selling old clothes and other second-hand items.

**flea** (magnified)

**fleck** *(n)* a spot, or a tiny patch of something. *A fleck of soot.*

**fledgling** *(n)* a young bird.

**flee fleeing fled** *(v)* to run away from danger.

**fleece** *(n)* a sheep's woolly coat.

**fleet** *(n)* a group of vehicles, such as ships or trucks.

**flesh 1** *(n)* the soft part of your body, made up of fat and muscle. **fleshy** *(adj).* **2** *(n)* the meat of an animal, or the part of a fruit or vegetable that you can eat.

**flex flexes flexing flexed 1** *(n)* the wire that joins a piece of electrical equipment to the plug. **2** *(v)* to bend or stretch something. *Tarzan flexed his muscles.*

**flexible** *(adj)* able to bend or change. *A flexible ruler.* **flexibility** *(n),* **flexibly** *(adv).*

**flick flicking flicked** *(v)* to move something with a quick, sudden movement. *Pete flicked a pea off the table.* **flick** *(n).*

**flicker flickering flickered** *(v)* to move unsteadily. *The fire flickered in the wind.*

**flight 1** *(n)* flying, or the ability to fly. **2** *(n)* a journey by aircraft. **3** If you **take flight**, you run away. **flight** *(n).*

**flimsy flimsier flimsiest** *(adj)* thin, or weak. *Flimsy material.* **flimsiness** *(n).*

**flinch flinches flinching flinched** *(v)* to make a quick movement away from a source of pain. *Di flinched as the nurse approached with a needle.*

**fling flinging flung** *(v)* to throw something violently.

**flint** *(n)* a hard, blackish-grey stone, used in prehistoric times for making tools and weapons.

**flip flipping flipped 1** *(v)* to toss or move something quickly. *Egon flipped the pancakes.* **2** *(v) (informal)* to become suddenly angry or excited.

**flippant** *(adj)* careless and not serious. *A flippant comment.* **flippancy** *(n).*

**flipper 1** *(n)* one of the broad, flat limbs of a sea creature, such as a seal or dolphin, that help it to swim. **2 flippers** *(plural n)* long, flat attachments that you fit on your feet to help you swim.

**flirt flirting flirted** *(v)* If you **flirt** with someone, you talk to them in a teasing, sexy way. **flirt** *(n),* **flirtatious** *(adj).*

**float floating floated 1** *(v)* to rest on water or air. **2** *(v)* to move lightly and easily. **3** *(n)* a decorated truck that forms part of a procession.

**flock flocking flocked 1** *(n)* a group of animals or birds. **2** *(v)* to gather in a crowd. *Fans flocked to see the band.*

**flog flogging flogged 1** *(v)* to beat someone with a whip or stick. **flogging** *(n).* **2** *(v) (slang)* to sell something.

**flood flooding flooded 1** *(v)* When something, like a river, **floods**, it overflows with liquid beyond its normal limits. **flood** *(n).* **2** *(v)* to overwhelm, or provide in large amounts. *Friends have flooded us with offers of help.*

**floodlight** *(n)* a strong light, used to light up buildings or sports grounds.

**floor 1** *(n)* the flat surface that you walk on inside a building. **2** *(n)* a storey in a building. *The skyscraper has 40 floors.*

**flop flopping flopped 1** *(v)* to fall limply. **floppy** *(adj).* **2** *(n) (informal)* a failure.

*Some words that begin with a "f" sound are spelt "ph".*

**floppy disk** *(n)* a flexible magnetic disk that stores computer data. Floppy disks are also called diskettes.

**flora** *(n)* the plant life of a particular area. *Woodland flora.*

**floral** *(adj)* flowery. *Floral curtains.*

**florist** *(n)* someone who sells flowers.

**flour** *(n)* powder made from ground wheat, corn, etc., that you use for cooking and baking. **floury** *(adj).*

**flourish flourishes flourishing flourished** *(v)* to grow and succeed. *Our new computer club is flourishing.*

**flout flouting flouted** *(v)* If you **flout** the rules, you break them deliberately.

**flow flowing flowed** *(v)* to move along smoothly like a river. **flow** *(n).*

**flower flowering flowered 1** *(n)* the coloured part of a plant which produces seeds or fruit. **2** *(v)* to blossom or produce flowers. **3** *(n)* a plant which has flowers.

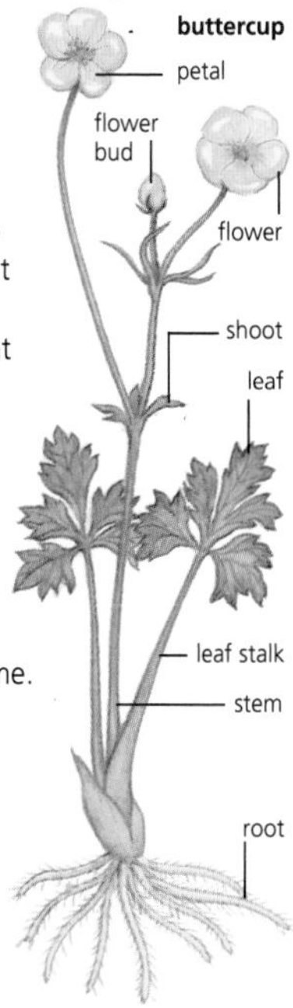

**flu** *(n)* an illness that gives you a high temperature and makes you feel weak. Flu is short for influenza.

**fluctuate fluctuating fluctuated** *(v)* to change all the time. *Petrol prices keep fluctuating.* **fluctuation** *(n).*

**fluent** *(adj)* able to speak smoothly and clearly, especially in another language. **fluently** *(adv).*

**fluff fluffing fluffed 1** *(n)* small, soft clumps of material that come off carpets, clothes, etc. **2** *(v)* When a bird **fluffs** its feathers, it shakes them out.

**fluid 1** *(n)* a flowing substance, either a liquid or gas. **2** *(adj)* flowing, or liquid.

**fluorescent 1** *(adj)* giving out a bright light. **2** *(adj)* A **fluorescent** colour is so bright that it seems to give out light when light shines on it.

**fluoride** *(n)* a chemical put in toothpaste and water to prevent tooth decay.

**flushed** *(adj)* If you are **flushed**, your face has become red. **flush** *(n).*

**fluster flustering flustered** *(v)* to confuse or rush someone.

**flutter fluttering fluttered** *(v)* to wave or flap rapidly. *Flags flutter in the breeze.*

**fly flies flying flew flown 1** *(v)* to travel through the air. **2** *(n)* an insect with wings. **3 flies** *(plural n)* a flap on trousers covering a zip or buttons. **4** *(v)* to move fast, or to do something fast. *Time just flew by.*

**flying saucer** *(n)* a saucer-shaped flying object, believed by some people to be a spacecraft from another planet.

**flyover** *(n)* a bridge that carries one road over another.

**foal** *(n)* a young horse.

**foam foaming foamed 1** *(n)* a mass of small bubbles. **2** *(v)* to make bubbles.

**focus focuses focusing focused** *(v)* to adjust your eyes or a camera lens so that you can see something clearly.

**fodder** *(n)* food for cows and horses.

**foe** *(n)* an enemy.

**foetus** *see* **fetus**.

**fog** *(n)* a very thick mist of water droplets in the air. **foggy** *(adj).*

**foghorn** *(n)* a loud siren used to warn ships in foggy weather.

**foil foiling foiled 1** *(n)* thin, silvery sheets of metal. **2** *(v)* to prevent someone from carrying out a plan. *The police foiled the robbers' plot.*

**fold folding folded 1** *(v)* to bend something over on itself. *Fold the sheets.* **2** *(n)* a small, fenced area for sheep.

**foliage** *(n)* leaves.

**folk folk** *or* **folks 1** *(n)* people, especially your family. **2** *(adj)* traditional, and belonging to ordinary people. *Folk music.*

**folklore** *(n)* the stories, customs, and knowledge of ordinary people, that are passed down to their children.

**follow** following followed 1 *(v)* to go behind someone. *The police car followed us.* 2 *(v)* to come after. *December follows November.* 3 *(v)* to be guided by someone or something. **follower** *(n)*.

**following** 1 *(prep)* next, or coming after something. *Following the dinner, there will be a dance.* 2 *(adj)* next, or after. *The following year.*

**folly** follies 1 *(n)* foolishness. 2 *(n)* a foolish act. 3 *(n)* a building with no real purpose. *The folly in the picture is on the Isle of Wight, England.*

folly

**fond** fonder fondest *(adj)* If you are **fond** of someone or something, you like them very much. **fondness** *(n)*.

**fondle** fondling fondled *(v)* to touch or stroke tenderly. *Claire fondled the kitten.*

**font** *(n)* a large, stone bowl used in a church to hold the water for baptisms.

**food** *(n)* substances that people, animals, and plants take in to stay alive and grow.

**food chain** *(n)* a group of animals and plants which are dependent on each other, since each one feeds on the one below them in the chain.

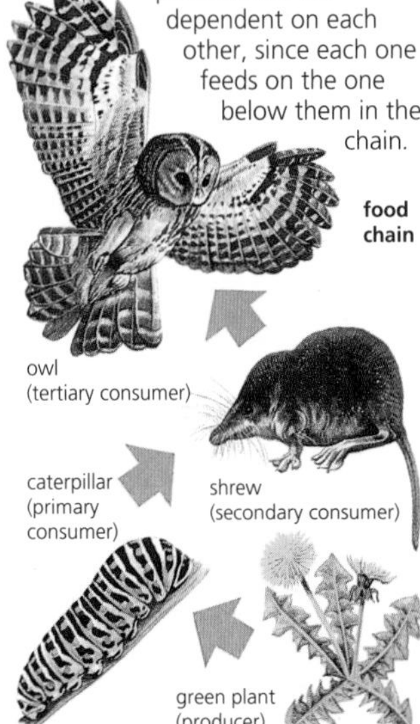

food chain

**food web** *(n)* the complex network of food chains in an ecosystem.

**fool** fooling fooled 1 *(n)* a silly person. **foolish** *(adj)*. 2 *(v)* to trick someone.

**foolproof** *(adj)* very simple to use, and unlikely to go wrong.

**foot** feet 1 *(n)* one of the two parts of your body that you walk on. 2 *(n)* the bottom, or the lower end of something. *The foot of the bed.*

**football** 1 *(n)* an outdoor ball game played by two teams who try to score goals. Soccer, rugby, and American football are types of football. **footballer** *(n)*. 2 *(n)* the ball used to play football.

**footnote** *(n)* a note at the bottom of a page.

**forbid** forbidding forbade forbidden *(v)* to tell someone not to do something. **forbidden** *(adj)*.

**forbidding** *(adj)* unfriendly, or off-putting. **forbiddingly** *(adv)*.

**force** forcing forced 1 *(v)* to make someone do something. 2 *(n)* strength, or power. 3 *(n)* an army, or other team of people. *The police force.*

**ford** *(n)* a shallow part of a stream or river that you can cross on foot or in a vehicle. **ford** *(v)*.

**forecast** forecasting forecast *or* forecasted *(v)* to say what you think will happen in the future. *The weatherman forecasts rain for tomorrow.* **forecast** *(n)*.

**foreground** *(n)* the part of a picture that is in front of the main subject. *This painting has a cottage in the foreground.*

**forehead** *(n)* the top part of your face between your hair and your eyes.

**foreign** *(adj)* to do with, or coming from another country. **foreigner** *(n)*.

**foresee** foreseeing foresaw foreseen *(v)* to expect or predict that something will happen. **foresight** *(n)*, **foreseeable** *(adj)*.

**forest** *(n)* a large area thickly covered with trees. **forested** *(adj)*.

**forever** *(adv)* always, or continually. *Matt is forever asking questions.*

**forfeit** forfeiting forfeited 1 *(n)* a penalty. *You have to pay a forfeit.* 2 *(v)* to lose the right to something. *Anyone who is late will forfeit their place in the team.*

**forge** forging forged 1 *(v)* to make illegal copies of paintings, money, etc. **forger** *(n)*, **forgery** *(n)*. 2 *(v)* If you **forge ahead**, you move forward or make progress. 3 *(n)* a blacksmith's shop.

**forget** forgetting forgot forgotten *(v)* If you **forget** something, you do not remember it. **forgetful** *(adj)*.

**forgive** forgiving forgave forgiven *(v)* to pardon someone, or to stop blaming them for something. **forgiveness** *(n)*.

**fork** 1 *(n)* an instrument with prongs, used for eating, or for working in a garden. 2 *(n)* a place where a road, river, tree, etc. branches in two or more directions. **fork** *(v)*, **forked** *(adj)*.

**forlorn** *(adj)* sad, or lonely.

**form** forming formed 1 *(n)* shape. *The monster took on a human form.* 2 *(n)* a type, or a kind. *Which form of travel do you prefer?* 3 *(v)* to make up or create something. *The lines formed a rectangle.* 4 *(n)* a class at school. 5 *(n)* a piece of paper with questions to be answered. 6 If you are in **good form**, you are fit and cheerful.

**formal** 1 *(adj)* official. *Formal permission.* **formally** *(adv)*. 2 *(adj)* proper and not casual. *Formal clothes.* **formally** *(adv)*.

**format** formatting formatted 1 *(v)* to prepare a computer disk to be used. 2 *(n)* the shape or style of something. *The new magazine has a larger format.*

**formation** 1 *(n)* the process of making something. *We are studying the formation of crystals.* 2 *(n)* a pattern, or a shape. *A cloud formation.*

**former** 1 *(n)* the first of two things that you have been talking about. *I like spiders and snakes, but I prefer the former.* 2 *(adj)* previous, or earlier. *Our former house.*

**formidable** *(adj)* difficult, or frightening. *A formidable enemy.* **formidably** *(adv)*.

**formula** formulas *or* formulae 1 *(n)* a rule in science or maths that is written with numbers and symbols. 2 *(n)* a suggested set of actions. *What's your formula for success?*

**fort** *(n)* a building like a castle, which is strongly built to survive attacks.

**forthcoming** *(adj)* coming soon. *Forthcoming attractions.*

**fortify** fortifies fortifying fortified *(v)* to make a place stronger against attack.

**fortnight** *(n)* a two-week period.

**fortress** fortresses *(n)* a castle or town that is strengthened against attack.

**fortunate** *(adj)* lucky. **fortunately** *(adv)*.

**fortune** 1 *(n)* chance, or good luck. 2 *(n)* a large amount of money. 3 *(n)* fate, or destiny.

**forward** 1 forward *or* forwards *(adv)* toward the front, or ahead. *We crept forward.* 2 *(adj)* toward the future. *I am looking forward to the holidays.* 3 *(n)* a player in football, hockey, etc. who has an attacking position and tries to score goals.

**fossil** *(n)* the remains or trace of an animal or a plant from millions of years ago, preserved as rock. *This picture shows examples of different types of fossils.*

**fossils**

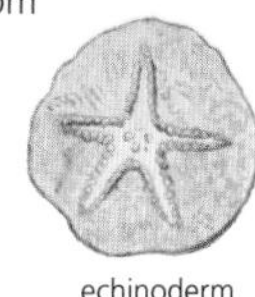

**foster** fostering fostered 1 *(v)* to encourage or develop something. *The new club fostered a sense of community.* 2 *(v)* to look after a child who is not your own, without becoming its legal parent.

**foul** fouler foulest 1 *(adj)* very dirty, or disgusting. 2 *(n)* a move in sport that is against the rules. **foul** *(v)*.

**found** founding founded *(v)* to set up or start something, such as a school.

**foundation** 1 *(n)* the base or basis of something. 2 **foundations** *(plural n)* a solid structure on which a building is built.

**fountain** *(n)* a shower of water, pumped up through an ornament into a pool.

**fountain pen** *(n)* a pen with a container inside it that supplies ink to the nib.

**fowl** fowl *or* fowls *(n)* a bird, such as a chicken or duck, that is kept for its eggs or meat.

**fox** foxes *(n)* a kind of wild dog, with large, pointed ears, and a bushy tail.

**foyer** *(foy-ay) (n)* the entrance hall of a cinema, theatre, or hotel.

**fraction** *(n)* a part of a whole number. *½, ¾, and ⅞ are all fractions.*

**fracture** fracturing fractured *(v)* to break or crack something, especially a bone. **fracture** *(n).*

**fragile** *(adj)* delicate, or easily broken.

**fragment** *(n)* a small piece of something.

**fragrant** *(adj)* sweet-smelling.

**frail** frailer frailest *(adj)* feeble and weak. **frailty** *(n).*

**frame** framing framed **1** *(n)* a border that surrounds something. *A picture frame.* **2** *(v)* to put something in a frame.

**framework** *(n)* the structure of a building or other object.

**frank** franker frankest *(adj)* open and honest. **frankness** *(n),* **frankly** *(adv).*

**frantic** *(adj)* wildly anxious, or wildly excited. **frantically** *(adv).*

**fraud** **1** *(n)* If you practise **fraud**, you gain money by tricking people. **2** *(n)* If someone is a **fraud**, they pretend to be something they are not.

**freak** **1** *(adj)* very unusual. *Freak weather conditions.* **2** *(n)* an unnatural or strange person or animal. **3** *(n) (informal)* someone who is very enthusiastic about something. *A health freak.*

**freckle** *(n)* a small, light brown spot on your skin, caused by the sun. **freckly** *(adj).*

**free** freeing freed; freer freest **1** *(adj)* If a person or animal is **free**, they can do what they like. **freely** *(adv).* **2** *(v)* If you **free** a person or animal, you let them go from a prison or cage. **3** *(adj)* not costing anything.

**freedom** *(n)* the right to do and say what you like.

**freeze** freezing froze frozen **1** *(v)* to become solid or icy at a very low temperature. *Water freezes at 0°C.* **freezing** *(adj).* **2** *(v)* to stop still.

**freezer** *(n)* a large refrigerator which is kept very cold so that you can store food in it for several months.

**freight** *(frate) (n)* goods or cargo carried by trains, ships, planes, etc.

**frenzy** frenzies *(n)* If you are in a frenzy, you are wildly excited or angry about something. **frenzied** *(adj).*

**frequency** frequencies **1** *(n)* how often something happens. *The frequency of road accidents has increased.* **2** *(n)* the number of radio waves per second of a radio signal. *High frequency radio signals.*

**frequent** *(adj)* common, or happening often. **frequently** *(adv).*

**fresco** frescos *or* frescoes *(n)* a painting made on a wall or ceiling while the plaster is still wet.

**fresh** fresher freshest **1** *(adj)* clean, or new. **freshly** *(adv).* **2** *(adj)* not frozen, or not tinned. *Fresh fruit.* **3** *(adj)* cool. *A fresh sea breeze.*

**freshwater** *(adj)* to do with, or living in water that does not contain salt.

**fret** fretting fretted **1** *(v)* to worry or get annoyed about something. **fretful** *(adj).* **2** *(n)* one of the bars on the fingerboard of a stringed musical instrument, such as a guitar. *See* **guitar**.

**friction** **1** *(n)* the force which slows objects down when they rub against each other. **2** *(n)* disagreement, or arguing.

**fridge** *short* for **refrigerator**.

**friend** *(n)* someone whom you enjoy being with and know well. **friendship** *(n).*

**friendly** friendlier friendliest *(adj)* kind and helpful. **friendliness** *(n).*

**frieze** *(freez) (n)* a decorated strip, usually along the top of a wall.

**fright** *(n)* a sudden feeling of fear.

**frighten** frightening frightened *(v)* to scare someone. **frightening** *(adj).*

**frightful** *(adj)* terrible, or shocking.

**frill** *(n)* a ruffled strip of material or paper, used as decoration. **frilly** *(adj).*

**fringe** *(n)* the hair that hangs over your forehead.

**frisk** frisking frisked **1** *(v)* to play in a lively way. **frisky** *(adj).* **2** *(v) (informal)* to search someone for weapons, drugs, etc.

*Some words that begin with a "f" sound are spelt "ph".*

**frivolous** *(adj)* silly and light-hearted.

**frog** *(n)* a small, greenish-brown amphibian with long back legs that it uses for jumping. *The pictures below show the life cycle of the common frog.*

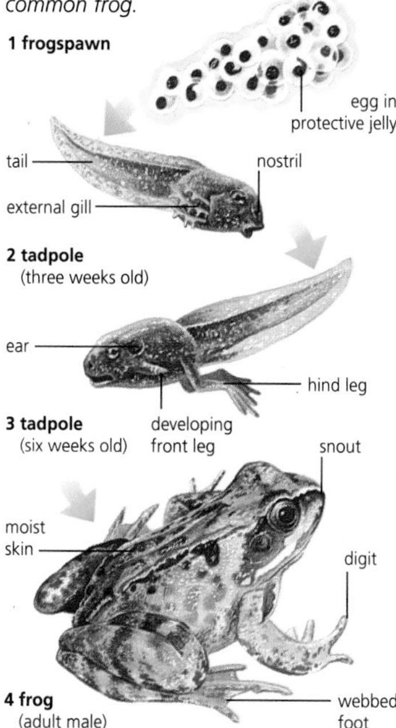


**frogman** frogmen *(n)* someone who swims underwater, using diving equipment, to investigate things.

**frolic** **frolicking frolicked** *(v)* to play happily. **frolic** *(n).*

**front** 1 *(n)* the part of something that faces forwards. **front** *(adj).* 2 *(n)* the place where armies are fighting.

**frontier** *(n)* the border between two countries.

**frost** *(n)* powdery ice that forms on things in freezing weather.

**frostbite** *(n)* If someone suffers from **frostbite**, parts of their body, such as their fingers, toes, or ears, are damaged by extreme cold. **frostbitten** *(adj).*

**frosty** **frostier frostiest** 1 *(adj)* covered with frost. 2 *(adj)* very cold, because there is a frost. 3 *(adj)* unfriendly. **frostily** *(adv).*

**froth** *(n)* lots of small bubbles on top of a liquid. **froth** *(v),* **frothy** *(adj).*

**frown** **frowning frowned** *(v)* to move your eyebrows together and wrinkle your forehead, often because you are annoyed.

**frozen** 1 *(adj)* If something, like food, is **frozen**, it has been made so cold that all the water in it has turned into ice. 2 *(adj)* extremely cold. *My hands are frozen.*

**frugal** *(adj)* very careful not to waste anything. **frugality** *(n),* **frugally** *(adv).*

**fruit** **fruit** *or* **fruits** *(n)* an edible part of a plant or tree, containing seeds.

**fruitful** *(adj)* successful, or useful.

**fruitless** *(adj)* unsuccessful, or useless.

**fruit machine** *(n)* a gambling machine that people operate to try to win money.

**frustrate** **frustrating frustrated** *(v)* to prevent someone from doing something. **frustration** *(n),* **frustrating** *(adj).*

**fry** **fries frying fried** *(v)* to cook food in hot oil. **frying pan** *(n).*

**fuel** *(n)* something that is used as a source of energy, such as coal, petrol, or gas. **fuel** *(v).*

**fugitive** *(n)* someone who is running away. **fugitive** *(adj).*

**fulcrum** **fulcrums** *or* **fulcra** *(n)* the point at which something balances or turns.

**fulfil** **fulfilling fulfilled** 1 *(v)* to do what is needed. *Toni fulfilled her promise by paying back all the money.* **fulfilment** *(n).* 2 *(v)* If you **fulfil** a need, a wish, or an ambition, you satisfy it. **fulfilment** *(n).*

**full** **fuller fullest** 1 *(adj)* If something is **full**, there is no room left inside it. 2 *(adj)* whole, or complete. *A full explanation.*

**full stop** *(n)* the punctuation mark (.) used to show that a sentence has ended or a word has been shortened.

**fumble** **fumbling fumbled** *(v)* to handle something uncertainly or clumsily.

**fume** **fuming fumed** 1 *(v)* to be very angry. 2 **fumes** *(plural n)* strong-smelling or poisonous gas, smoke, or vapour given off by something burning or by chemicals.

**functional** *(adj)* designed to work well rather than look beautiful.

**fund** *(n)* a store of money, or other things. *A fund of jokes.*

**fundamental** *(adj)* basic and necessary. *The fundamental principles of physics.*

**funeral** *(n)* the ceremony held after someone has died, at which the body is buried or cremated.

**funfair** *(n)* an outdoor entertainment with rides, amusements, and stalls.

**fungus** **fungi** *or* **funguses** *(n)* a type of plant that has no leaves, flowers, or roots. Mushrooms and toadstools are fungi.

**funnel** 1 *(n)* an open cone that narrows to a tube, used for pouring liquids and powders into narrow-necked containers. 2 *(n)* a chimney on a ship.

**funny** **funnier** **funniest** 1 *(adj)* amusing. **funnily** *(adv)*. 2 *(adj)* strange. *There's a funny smell in the kitchen.* **funnily** *(adv)*.

**fur** *(n)* the soft, hairy coat of an animal.

**furious** *(adj)* extremely angry.

**furnace** *(n)* an extremely hot oven, used to melt metal, glass, etc.

**furnish** **furnishes** **furnishing** **furnished** 1 *(v)* to equip a room or a house with carpets, curtains, and furniture. 2 *(v)* to supply something. *Can you furnish any proof of your age?*

**furniture** *(n)* large, movable things such as chairs, tables, and beds which are needed in a home.

**further education** *(n)* education for people who have left school but who are not at university.

**furthermore** *(adv)* in addition, or as well.

**furtive** *(adj)* sly and cautious. *A furtive glance.* **furtiveness** *(n)*.

**fury** **furies** *(n)* violent anger.

**fuse** 1 *(n)* a safety device in electrical equipment which cuts off the power in an emergency. 2 *(n)* a string or wick leading from a bomb, which is lit to make the bomb explode.

**fuss** **fusses** **fussing** **fussed** *(v)* to be unnecessarily worried or excited about something. **fuss** *(n)*.

**futile** *(adj)* If an action is **futile**, it is useless and a waste of time. **futility** *(n)*.

**future** *(n)* the time to come. **future** *(adj)*.

**fuzz** 1 *(n)* short, soft hair. **fuzzy** *(adj)*. 2 **the fuzz** *(slang)* the police.

# Gg

**gabble** **gabbling** **gabbled** *(v)* to talk too fast for people to understand you easily.

**gadget** *(n)* a small machine that does a particular job. *A gadget for slicing eggs.*

**gag** **gagging** **gagged** *(v)* to tie a piece of cloth around someone's mouth in order to stop them from talking. **gag** *(n)*.

**gain** **gaining** **gained** 1 *(v)* to get or win something. 2 *(n)* a profit, or an increase.

**gala** *(n)* a special event or entertainment. *A swimming gala.*

**galaxy** **galaxies** *(n)* a group of stars and planets. **galactic** *(adj)*.

**gale** *(n)* a very strong wind.

**galleon** *(n)* a sailing ship with three masts built in the 15th or 16th century.

**gallery** **galleries** *(n)* a place where exhibitions of paintings, sculpture, photographs, etc. are held.

**galley** 1 *(n)* the kitchen on a boat or aircraft. 2 *(n)* a long boat with oars, used in ancient times.

**gallop** **galloping** **galloped** *(v)* When a horse **gallops**, it runs as fast as it can.

**gallows** *(singular n)* a wooden frame used in the past for hanging criminals.

**galore** *(adv)* in large numbers. *There were rides galore at the fair.*

**gamble** **gambling** **gambled** *(v)* to bet money on a race, game, or something that might happen. **gambler** *(n)*.

**game** 1 *(n)* an activity with rules that can be played by one or more people. 2 *(n)* wild animals, including birds, that are hunted for sport and for food.

**gamekeeper** *(n)* someone whose job is to protect game.

**gang** **ganging** **ganged** 1 *(n)* a group of people, usually with a leader. 2 *(v)* If several people **gang up** on you, they all turn against you.

**gangplank** *(n)* a short bridge or piece of wood, used for getting on and off a boat.

**gangster** *(n)* a member of a criminal gang.

**gangway** 1 *(n)* a clear pathway between rows of seats, for people to walk down. 2 *(n)* a gangplank.

**gaol** *see* **jail**.

**gap** *(n)* a space between things.

**gape** **gaping gaped** 1 *(v)* to open your mouth wide, usually with surprise. 2 *(v)* to split or hang open.

**garage** 1 *(n)* a small building used for storing vehicles. 2 *(n)* a place where petrol is sold and vehicles are repaired.

**garbled** *(adj)* A **garbled** message is mixed up and does not make sense.

**garden** *(n)* a place where flowers, vegetables, shrubs, etc. are grown. **gardener** *(n)*, **gardening** *(n)*, **garden** *(v)*.

**gargle** **gargling gargled** *(v)* to move a liquid around your throat without swallowing it.

**gargoyle** *(n)* a grotesque stone head or figure, carved below the roof of old buildings, such as churches.

**gargoyle**

**garish** *(gair-ish)* *(adj)* brightly coloured and over-decorated. **garishly** *(adv)*.

**garland** *(n)* a ring of flowers, often worn around the neck or on the head.

**garlic** *(n)* a strong-smelling plant like an onion, used to add flavour to food.

**garment** *(n)* a piece of clothing.

**garnish** **garnishes garnishing garnished** *(v)* to decorate food with small amounts of other food or herbs.

**garter** *(n)* a piece of elastic that stops socks or stockings slipping down.

**gas** **gases** *or* **gasses** 1 *(n)* an air-like substance that will spread to fill any space. 2 *(n)* a gas that is used as a fuel.

**gash** **gashes** *(n)* a long, deep cut.

**gasp** **gasping gasped** *(v)* to take in breath suddenly because you are surprised or in pain. **gasp** *(n)*.

**gastric** *(adj)* to do with the stomach. *Gastric juices.*

**gate** *(n)* a frame or barrier that can be opened and closed.

**gateau** *(gat-oh)* **gateaux** *(n)* a rich cake, usually containing cream.

**gatecrash** **gatecrashes gatecrashing gatecrashed** *(v)* to go to a party when you are not invited. **gatecrasher** *(n)*.

**gather** **gathering gathered** 1 *(v)* to collect or pick things. *We gathered blackberries.* 2 *(v)* to come together in a group. *A crowd gathered.*

**gaudy** *(gor-dee)* **gaudier gaudiest** *(adj)* very brightly coloured and vulgar.

**gauge** *(rhymes with page)* *(n)* an instrument for measuring something. *A pressure gauge.*

**gaunt** *(adj)* unnaturally thin and bony.

**gauze** *(gorz)* *(n)* a very thin woven cloth, used as a bandage.

**gay** **gayer gayest** 1 *(adj)* homosexual. 2 *(adj)* *(old-fashioned)* happy and lively.

**gaze** **gazing gazed** *(v)* to stare at something steadily. **gaze** *(n)*.

**gear** 1 *(n)* equipment, or clothing. *Remember to bring your swimming gear.* 2 **gears** *(plural n)* a set of toothed wheels which fit together and pass on or change the movement of a machine. *This diagram shows how gears work. The arrows show the direction of movement.*

**gears**

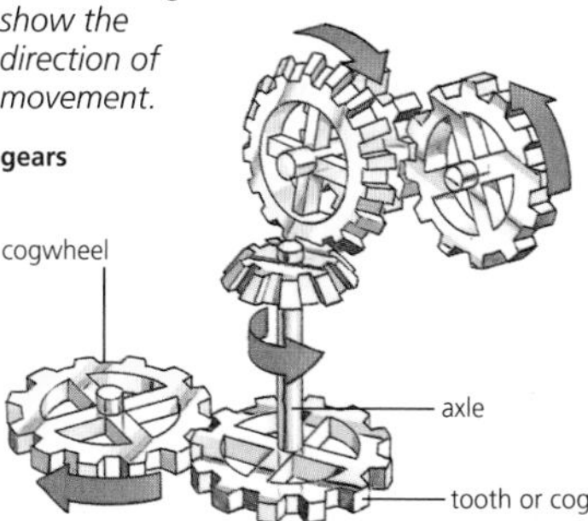


**gel** *(jel)* *(n)* a jelly-like substance. *Hair gel.*

**gem** *(n)* a precious stone, such as a diamond, ruby, or emerald.

**gender** *(n)* the sex of a person or creature.

**gene** *(jeen)* *(n)* one of the parts of the cells of all living things. Genes are passed from parents to children and control how you look. **genetic** *(adj)*.

**general** 1 *(adj)* to do with everybody or everything. *General knowledge.* **generally** *(adv)*. 2 *(adj)* not detailed, or not specialized.

**generation** *(n)* all the people born around the same time.

**generator** *(n)* a machine which produces electricity.

**generous** *(adj)* happy to use time and money to help others. **generosity** *(n).*

**genie** *(n)* In stories from the East, a **genie** is a spirit who grants people's wishes.

**genitals** *(plural n)* the sex organs on the outside of the body.

**genius** *(jee-nee-us)* **geniuses** *(n)* an unusually clever or talented person.

**gentle gentler gentlest 1** *(adj)* not rough. **gentleness** *(n).* **2** *(adj)* kind and sensitive. **gentleness** *(n).*

**gentleman gentlemen 1** *(n)* a polite name for a man. **2** *(n)* a man with good manners.

**genuine** *(jen-yoo-in) (adj)* real and not fake. *A genuine diamond.*

**geography** *(n)* the study of the Earth, including its people, resources, climate, and physical features. **geographer** *(n).*

**geology** *(n)* the study of the Earth's layers of soil and rock. **geologist** *(n).*

**geometric 1** *(adj)* to do with geometry. **2** *(adj)* A **geometric** shape is a regular shape, such as a circle, triangle, etc.

**geometry** *(n)* the branch of mathematics which is about lines, angles, shapes, etc.

**gerbil** *(n)* a small, furry rodent with long feet and a long, tufted tail.

**germ** *(n)* a very small living organism that can cause disease.

**germinate germinating germinated** *(v)* When seeds or beans **germinate**, they start to grow shoots and roots.

**gesticulate** *(jes-**tik**-yoo-late)* **gesticulating gesticulated** *(v)* to indicate something by waving your hands in an excited or angry way. **gesticulation** *(n).*

**gesture gesturing gestured 1** *(v)* to move your head or hands in order to communicate something. *The teacher gestured to Nikki to sit down.* **gesture** *(n).* **2** *(n)* an action which shows a feeling. *I sent her flowers as a gesture of sympathy.*

**get getting got 1** *(v)* to obtain something. *Please get me a paper.* **2** *(v)* to own something. *Have you got a pet?* **3** *(v)* to become. *The pond got bigger.* **4** *(v)* to arrive somewhere. *At last, we got home.* **5 get over** *(v)* to recover from something.

**getaway** *(n)* a fast escape from a situation, especially a crime.

**geyser** *(**gee**-zer) (n)* a hole in the ground through which hot water and steam shoot up in bursts. Geysers are found in volcanic areas.

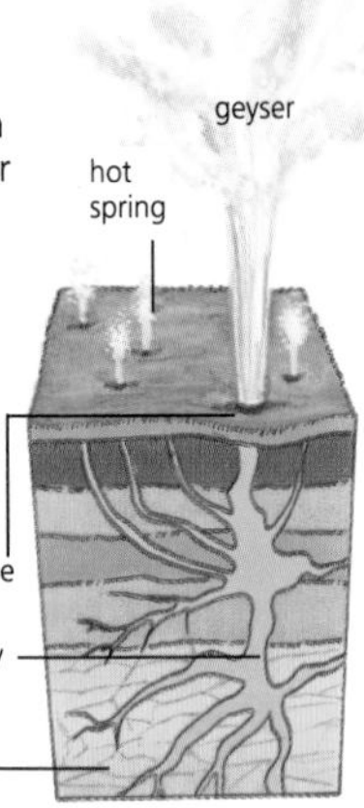

**geyser**

**ghastly ghastlier ghastliest** *(adj) (informal)* very bad, or unpleasant.

**ghetto ghettos** *or* **ghettoes** *(n)* an area of a city where a group of poor people of the same race or colour live together.

**ghost** *(n)* a spirit of a dead person, believed to haunt people or places.

**giant 1** *(n)* In stories, a **giant** is a very large, strong creature. **2** *(adj)* very large.

**giddy giddier giddiest** *(adj)* dizzy, light-headed, and unsteady. **giddiness** *(n).*

**gift 1** *(n)* a present. **2** *(n)* a special talent. *Pablo has a gift for painting.* **gifted** *(adj).*

**gig** *(n) (informal)* a booking for a musician or band to play in public.

**gigantic** *(jy-**gan**-tik) (adj)* huge, or enormous. **gigantically** *(adv).*

**giggle giggling giggled** *(v)* to laugh in a nervous, high-pitched way. **giggle** *(n).*

**gill** *(n)* one of the two organs on the sides of a fish, through which it breathes.

**gilt** *(adj)* decorated with a thin coating of gold leaf or gold paint. **gild** *(v).*

**gimmick** *(n)* something unusual, used to get people's attention. **gimmicky** *(adj).*

**gingerly** *(adv)* cautiously and carefully.

**gipsy** *see* **gypsy**.

**giraffe** *(n)* an African mammal with a very long neck and legs.

**girl** *(n)* a female child.

**girlfriend** *(n)* the girl or woman with whom a boy or man is having a romantic relationship.

**give giving gave given 1** *(v)* to hand over something to another person. *Give me that book!* **2** *(v)* to pay. *What will you give me for this?* **3 give in** *or* **give up** *(v)* to surrender, or stop trying.

**glacier** *(glass-ee-er) (n)* a huge mass of ice that flows down a mountain valley.

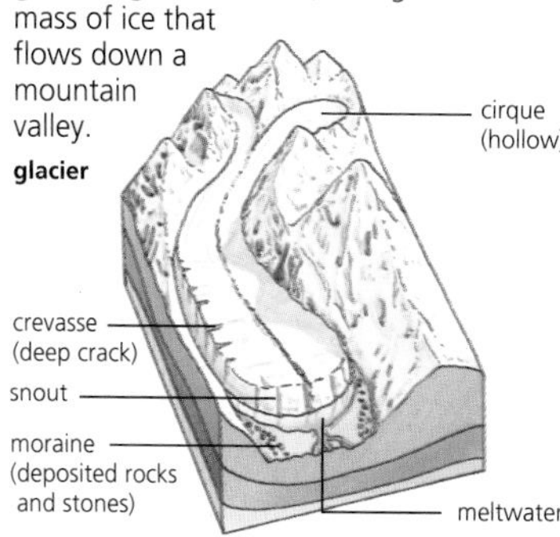


**glacier**

**glad gladder gladdest** *(adj)* pleased or happy. **gladness** *(n)*.

**gladiator** *(n)* an ancient Roman warrior who fought other gladiators or fierce animals in order to entertain the public.

**gladiators**

**glamorous** *(adj)* attractive and exciting.

**glance glancing glanced 1** *(v)* to look at something very briefly. **glance** *(n)*. **2** *(v)* to hit something and slide off at an angle. *The ball glanced off the goal post into the net.*

**gland** *(n)* an organ in the body which either produces natural chemicals or allows substances to leave the body. *Sweat glands.*

**glare glaring glared 1** *(v)* to look at someone in a very angry way. **glare** *(n)*. **2** *(n)* very bright light which dazzles.

**glaring** *(adj)* very obvious. *A glaring error.* **glaringly** *(adv)*.

**glass glasses 1** *(n)* a transparent material used in windows, bottles, etc. **2** *(n)* a container for drinking, made from glass.

**glasses** *(plural n)* lenses set in frames, worn to improve your eyesight.

**glaze glazing glazed 1** *(v)* to fit glass into a window. **glazier** *(n)*. **2** *(v)* If your eyes **glaze over**, they look fixed and glass-like because you are tired or bored.

**gleam gleaming gleamed** *(v)* to shine.

**glee** *(n)* enjoyment and delight.

**glide gliding glided** *(v)* to move smoothly and easily. *I glided over the ice.*

**glider** *(n)* a very light aircraft, which flies by floating and rising on air currents instead of by engine power.

**glimmer glimmering glimmered** *(v)* to shine faintly. **glimmer** *(n)*.

**glimpse glimpsing glimpsed** *(v)* to see something very briefly. **glimpse** *(n)*.

**glint glinting glinted** *(v)* to sparkle, or to flash. **glint** *(n)*.

**glisten glistening glistened** *(v)* to shine in a sparkling way.

**glitter glittering glittered** *(v)* to sparkle with many tiny lights or reflections.

**gloat gloating gloated** *(v)* to delight in your own good luck, or in someone else's bad luck.

**global warming** *(n)* a gradual rise in the temperature of the Earth's atmosphere, caused by an increase in the greenhouse effect. *See* **greenhouse effect**.

**globe 1** *(n)* a round model of the world. **2** *(n)* the world. **global** *(adj)*.

**glockenspiel** *(n)* a musical instrument with metal plates of different sizes, which are struck to give different notes.

**gloomy gloomier gloomiest 1** *(adj)* dull and dark. *A gloomy dungeon.* **gloom** *(n)*. **2** *(adj)* sad and pessimistic. **gloom** *(n)*.

**glory** glories 1 *(n)* fame and admiration. 2 *(n)* a beautiful and impressive sight.

**gloss** *(n)* a shine on a surface.

**glossary** glossaries *(n)* A **glossary** explains the meaning of technical words and phrases used in a book.

**glove** *(n)* a warm or protective hand covering.

**glow** glowing glowed *(v)* If something **glows**, it gives off a steady light, often because it is hot. **glow** *(n)*.

**glow-worm** *(n)* a small beetle whose tail gives off a green glow in the dark.

**glucose** *(n)* a natural sugar found in plants which gives energy to living things.

**glue** *(n)* a substance used to make one surface stick to another. **glue** *(v)*.

**glum** glummer glummest *(adj)* gloomy and miserable. **glumly** *(adv)*.

**glutton** *(n)* a very greedy person.

**gnarled** *(adj)* twisted and lumpy with age. *A gnarled oak tree.*

**gnash** gnashing gnashed *(v)* If you **gnash** your teeth, you grind them together in anger or grief.

**gnaw** gnawing gnawed *or* gnawn *(v)* to keep biting something. *The dog gnawed at the bone.*

**gnome** *(n)* In folk and fairy stories, **gnomes** are dwarf-like old men.

**go** goes going went gone 1 *(v)* to move away from or towards a place. *I'm going home.* 2 *(v)* to work properly. *The car won't go.* 3 *(v)* to become. *The class went quiet.* 4 *(v)* If you are **going** to do something, you will do it in the future. 5 *(n)* a turn. *It's my go.*

**goal** 1 *(n)* something that you aim for. *Shelagh's goal is to run for Ireland.* 2 *(n)* a frame with a net into which you aim a ball in sports such as soccer and netball.

**goat** *(n)* a farm animal with horns and a beard, reared mainly for its milk.

**gobble** gobbling gobbled *(v)* to eat food quickly and greedily.

**goblet** *(n)* an old-fashioned drinking container with a stem and a base, usually made from pottery or metal.

**goblin** *(n)* In fairy stories, **goblins** are small, unpleasant, ugly creatures.

**God** *(n)* In Christianity, Islam, and Judaism, **God** is the creator and ruler of the universe.

**god** *(n)* a supernatural being that is worshipped.

**goddess** goddesses *(n)* a female supernatural being that is worshipped.

**godparent** *(n)* someone who promises to help bring up a child as a Christian.

**goggles** *(plural n)* special glasses that fit tightly round your eyes to protect them.

**go-kart** *(n)* a very low, small, open vehicle, built for racing.

**gold** *(n)* a precious metal used in jewellery, and sometimes for money.

**goldfish** goldfish *or* goldfishes *(n)* an orange-coloured fish, often kept in ponds.

**golf** *(n)* a game in which players use clubs to hit a small, white ball round a course.

**gondola** *(n)* a light boat with high pointed ends, used in Venice.

**gondola**

**gong** *(n)* a metal disc that makes a loud sound when it is hit with a hammer.

**good** better best 1 *(adj)* of high quality, or deserving praise. 2 *(adj)* kind, or virtuous. *A good deed.* 3 *(adj)* suitable. 4 *(adj)* well-behaved. *A good child.* 5 *(adj)* fit and well. *I'm feeling good.*

**goodbye** *(interject)* a word said to someone who is leaving.

**goods** *(plural n)* a general name for things which are sold or things which someone owns. *Leather goods.*

**gooey** gooier gooiest *(adj) (informal)* sticky. **gooeyness** *(n)*.

**goose** geese *(n)* a large, long-necked bird with webbed feet.

**goose pimples** *(n)* tiny bumps on your skin which appear when you are cold or frightened.

**gorge** *(n)* a deep valley with steep, rocky sides. *See* **river**.

**gorgeous** *(adj)* beautiful or attractive.

**gorilla** *(n)* a very large, strong ape with dark fur, that comes from Africa.

**gorse** *(n)* a prickly, evergreen shrub with bright yellow flowers.

**gory gorier goriest** *(adj)* If something is gory, it involves a lot of blood. *A gory film.*

**gospel** *(n)* one of the first four books in the New Testament of the Bible, about the life and teachings of Jesus Christ.

**gossip gossiping gossiped** *(v)* to talk with enjoyment about other people's personal lives. **gossip** *(n),* **gossipy** *(adj).*

**govern governing governed** *(v)* to control a country, organization, etc. using laws or rules. **governor** *(n).*

**government** *(n)* the people who rule or govern a country or state.

**GP** *(n)* a family doctor, who treats common illnesses and refers patients to specialist doctors if necessary. GP is short for general practitioner.

**grab grabbing grabbed** *(v)* to take hold of something suddenly and roughly.

**grace** 1 *(n)* an elegant way of moving. **graceful** *(adj).* 2 *(n)* a short prayer of thanks before or after a meal.

**grade** *(n)* a mark given for work done in school, college, etc. *Grade B for maths.*

**gradient** *(n)* a slope, or the steepness of a slope.

**gradual** *(adj)* taking place slowly but steadily. *A gradual slope.* **gradually** *(adv).*

**graffiti** *(plural n)* things that people write or draw on the walls of public buildings.

**graft grafting grafted** 1 *(v)* to take skin from one part of the body to help repair an injury to another part. **graft** *(n).* 2 *(v)* *(informal)* to work hard. **graft** *(n).*

**grain** 1 *(n)* the seed of a cereal plant. 2 *(n)* a very small particle of salt, sand, etc.

**grammar** *(n)* the rules of writing or speaking a language. **grammatical** *(adj).*

**grand grander grandest** *(n)* large and impressive. **grandly** *(adv).*

**grandstand** *(n)* a covered structure at a sports ground with seats for spectators.

**grant granting granted** 1 *(v)* to give something or allow something. *We were granted permission to leave.* 2 If you take something **for granted**, you assume that you will get it, or you do not appreciate it.

**grape** *(n)* a small fruit that can be eaten as it is, dried to make currants, raisins etc., or crushed to make wine.

**grapefruit grapefruit** *or* **grapefruits** *(n)* a large, yellow citrus fruit.

**grapevine** 1 *(n)* a climbing plant on which grapes grow. 2 If you hear something **on the grapevine**, you hear news unofficially from other people.

**graph** *(n)* a diagram which shows how two sets of numbers are related.

**graphic** 1 *(adj)* very realistic. *A graphic report.* 2 *(adj)* to do with art and design.

**graphics** *(plural n)* the pictures in a computer game.

**grapple grappling grappled** *(v)* to wrestle with someone.

**grasp grasping grasped** 1 *(v)* to seize something and hold it tight. **grasp** *(n).* 2 *(v)* to understand something. **grasp** *(n).*

**grass grasses** *(n)* a green plant with long, thin leaves that grows wild and is used for lawns. **grassy** *(adj).*

**grasshopper** *(n)* a jumping insect with long back legs.

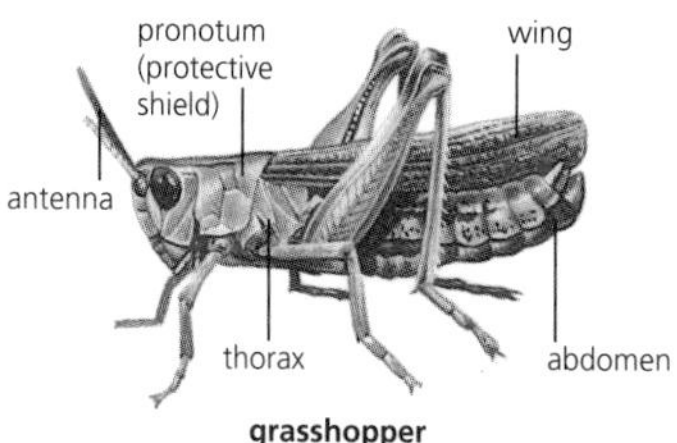


**grasshopper**

**grate grating grated** 1 *(v)* to shred food into small, thin pieces. *Grate the cheese.* 2 *(n)* a grid of metal bars in a fireplace.

**grateful** *(adj)* thankful for something. **gratefully** *(adv).*

**gratitude** *(n)* a feeling of being thankful.

**grave graver gravest** 1 *(n)* a place where a dead person is buried. 2 *(adj)* very serious. *Grave danger.* **gravely** *(adv).* 3 **gravestone** *(n)* a piece of carved stone that marks someone's grave.

**gravel** *(n)* small, loose stones used for paths and roads.

**gravity** *(n)* the force that pulls things towards the surface of the Earth and stops them from floating away into space.

**gravy** *(n)* a hot, savoury sauce, served with meat.

**graze grazing grazed** 1 *(v)* to scrape the surface off your skin. **graze** *(n)*. 2 *(v)* When animals **graze**, they eat grass that is growing in a field.

**grease** 1 *(n)* an oily substance found in animal fat, and in hair and skin. **greasy** *(adj)*. 2 *(n)* a thick, oily substance used on machines to help the parts move easily.

**great greater greatest** 1 *(adj)* very big or large. 2 *(adj)* very important or famous. *A great man.* **greatness** *(n)*. 3 *(adj)* very good, or wonderful. *We had a great time.*

**greedy greedier greediest** *(adj)* If you are **greedy**, you want more of something than you need. **greed** *(n)*, **greedily** *(adv)*.

**green greener greenest** 1 *(n)* the colour of grass or leaves. 2 *(adj)* concerned with protecting the environment. 3 *(n)* an area of ground used for an activity or sport. *A bowling green.*

**greenhouse** *(n)* a glass building used for growing plants.

**greenhouse effect** *(n)* the warming of the atmosphere around the Earth, caused by gases such as carbon dioxide, which collect in the atmosphere and prevent the Sun's heat from escaping.

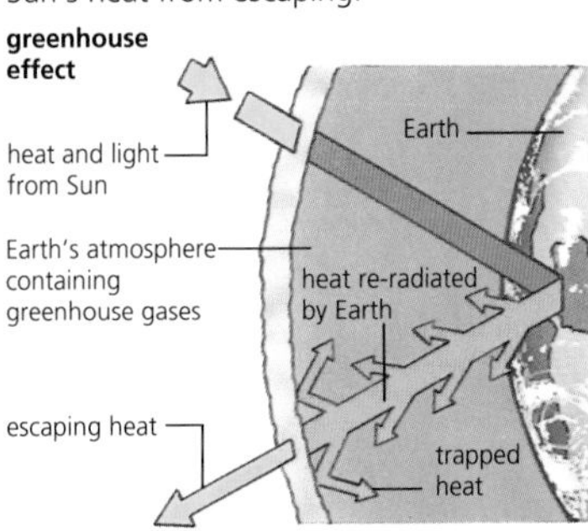


**greenhouse gases** *(plural n)* gases such as carbon dioxide, methane, and CFCs that are found in the Earth's atmosphere and help to hold heat in.

**greet greeting greeted** *(v)* to say something friendly or welcoming to someone when you meet them.

**grey** *(n)* the colour between black and white, like the colour of rain clouds.

**grid** *(n)* a set of straight lines that cross each other at right angles to form a regular pattern of squares.

**grief** *(n)* a feeling of great sadness.

**grievance** *(n)* If you have a **grievance**, you have a real or imagined reason to feel angry or annoyed about something.

**grieve grieving grieved** *(v)* to feel very sad, usually because someone whom you love has died.

**grill** *(n)* the part of a cooker that heats food from above. **grill** *(v)*.

**grim grimmer grimmest** *(adj)* gloomy, stern, and unpleasant. **grimly** *(adv)*.

**grime** *(n)* thick dirt. **grimy** *(adj)*.

**grin** *(n)* a large, cheerful smile. **grin** *(v)*.

**grind grinding ground** *(v)* to crush something into a powder.

**grip gripping gripped** *(v)* to hold something very tightly. **grip** *(n)*.

**gristle** *(n)* a tough substance, sometimes found in meat.

**grizzle grizzling grizzled** *(v)* to keep on whining and complaining.

**groan groaning groaned** *(v)* to make a long, low sound, showing that you are in pain or are unhappy. **groan** *(n)*.

**grocer** *(n)* someone who owns a shop selling food and household goods.

**groin** *(n)* the hollow between the top of your leg and your stomach.

**groom grooming groomed** 1 *(n)* someone who looks after horses. 2 *(v)* to brush and clean an animal, such as a horse. 3 *(n)* a man who is about to get married or has just been married.

**groove** *(n)* a long cut in the surface of something.

**grope groping groped** *(v)* to feel about for something that you cannot see.

**gross grosser grossest** 1 *(adj)* unpleasantly big and ugly. 2 *(adj)* very bad. *A gross error.*

**grotesque** *(grow-tesk)* *(adj)* unnatural and horrible. **grotesquely** *(adv)*.

**ground** 1 *(n)* the surface of the Earth. 2 *(n)* a piece of land used for playing a game or sport. *A football ground.*

**grounded** 1 *(adj)* If an aircraft is **grounded**, it cannot fly. 2 *(adj) (informal)* not allowed to go out, as a punishment.

**group** *(n)* a number of things that go together or are similar in some way.

**grovel grovelling grovelled** *(v)* to be unnaturally humble and polite to someone because you are afraid of them or think that they are very important.

**grow growing grew grown** 1 *(v)* to increase in size, length, or amount. 2 *(v)* to plant something and look after it so that it lives and gets bigger. 3 *(v)* to become. *Simon grew lazier and lazier.*

**growl growling growled** *(v)* When an animal **growls**, it makes a low, deep noise, usually because it is angry.

**grown-up** *(n)* an adult. **grown-up** *(adj).*

**growth** *(n)* the process of growing.

**grubby grubbier grubbiest** *(adj)* dirty.

**grudge** *(n)* a feeling of anger towards someone who has hurt or insulted you. *Jon bore a grudge against Ed for months.*

**gruelling** *(adj)* very demanding and tiring. *A gruelling job.*

**gruesome** *(adj)* disgusting and horrible.

**gruff gruffer gruffest** *(adj)* rough and bad-tempered. *A gruff voice.*

**grumble grumbling grumbled** *(v)* to complain about something in a bad-tempered way.

**grumpy grumpier grumpiest** *(adj)* bad-tempered. **grumpily** *(adv).*

**grunt grunting grunted** *(v)* to make a deep, gruff sound, like a pig. **grunt** *(n).*

**guarantee** 1 *(n)* a promise that if something breaks or goes wrong within a certain time, the makers will mend or replace it for you. **guarantee** *(v).* 2 *(n)* a promise that something will definitely happen. **guarantee** *(v).*

**guard guarding guarded** 1 *(v)* to protect a person or place from attack. **guard** *(n).* 2 *(v)* to watch a person carefully to prevent them from escaping. **guard** *(n).* 3 *(n)* a railway official who travels on a train.

**guardian** 1 *(n)* someone who has the legal responsibility to look after a child who is not their own. 2 *(n)* someone who guards or protects something.

**guess** *(gess)* **guesses guessing guessed** *(v)* to give an answer that may be right but which you cannot be sure about. *If you don't know the answer, try guessing.* **guess** *(n).*

**guest** 1 *(n)* someone who has been invited to visit you or to stay in your home. 2 *(n)* someone staying in a hotel.

**guide guiding guided** 1 *(v)* to help someone, usually by showing them around a place. **guide** *(n),* **guidebook** *(n).* 2 **guide dog** *(n)* a dog trained to lead a blind person.

**guillotine** *(gil-oh-teen) (n)* a machine with a sharp blade, used in the past to behead criminals.

**guilty guiltier guiltiest** 1 *(adj)* If you are **guilty**, you have committed a crime or done something wrong. **guilt** *(n).* 2 *(adj)* If you feel **guilty**, you feel bad because you have done something wrong or have failed to do something. **guilt** *(n).*

**guinea pig** *(gin-ee pig)* 1 *(n)* a small mammal with smooth fur, short ears, and a very short tail. 2 *(n)* a person who is used in an experiment.

**guitar** *(n)* a musical instrument with strings which you pluck or strum with your fingers or a plectrum.

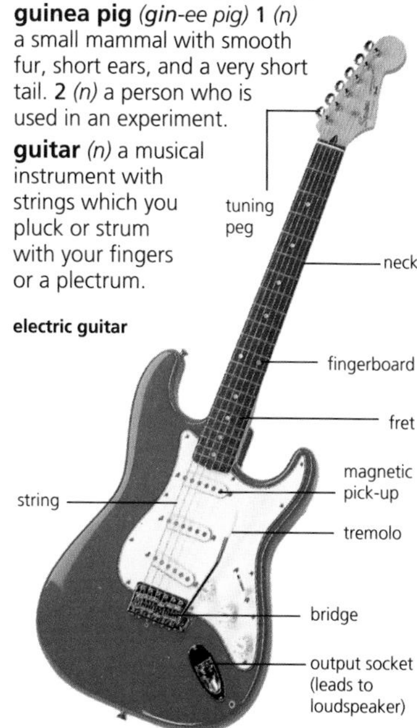

**electric guitar**

**gulf** *(n)* a large area of sea that is partly surrounded by land. *The Persian Gulf.*

**gull** *short for* **seagull**.

**gullible** *(adj)* ready to believe anything, and easy to trick.

**gully** **gullies** *(n)* a long, narrow valley or ditch.

**gulp** **gulping** **gulped** 1 *(v)* to swallow something quickly and noisily. 2 *(n)* a large mouthful of drink.

**gum** 1*(plural n)* Your **gums** are the areas of firm, pink flesh around the bottom of your teeth. 2 *(n)* glue. **gum** *(v)*.

**gun** *(n)* a weapon that fires bullets through a long metal tube.

**gunpowder** *(n)* a powder that explodes easily, used in fireworks and some guns.

**gurgle** **gurgling** **gurgled** 1 *(v)* When water **gurgles**, it makes a low, bubbling sound. **gurgle** *(n)*. 2 *(v)* to make a sound like gurgling water. *The baby gurgled.*

**gush** **gushes** **gushing** **gushed** *(v)* to flow fast in large amounts. **gush** *(n)*.

**gust** *(n)* a sudden, strong blast of wind.

**gut** **gutting** **gutted** 1 **guts** *(plural n)* the organs inside your body, especially your stomach and intestines. 2 *(v)* If a fire **guts** a building, it destroys the inside. 3 **guts** *(plural n) (informal)* courage.

**gutter** *(n)* a channel or length of tubing through which rain is drained away from a road or from the roof of a building.

**guzzle** **guzzling** **guzzled** *(v)* to eat or drink something quickly and noisily.

**gym** *(n)* a large room with special equipment for exercises and physical training. Gym is short for gymnasium.

**gymkhana** *(n)* a series of competitions for horses and their riders.

**gymnasium** *see* **gym**.

**gymnastics** *(singular n)* physical exercises, which involve difficult and carefully controlled body movements.

**gypsy** *or* **gipsy** *(jip-see)* **gypsies** *(n)* someone who usually lives in a caravan and travels from place to place.

**gyroscope** *(n)* a wheel which spins inside a frame and causes the frame to balance in any position.

**gyroscope**

# Hh

**habit** 1 *(n)* something that you do regularly, often without thinking about it. 2 *(n)* a piece of clothing, like a long loose dress, worn by monks and nuns.

**habitat** *(n)* the place and conditions in which a plant or animal lives naturally.

**habitually** *(adv)* usually, or normally. *Ted is habitually optimistic.* **habitual** *(adj)*.

**hack** **hacking** **hacked** 1 *(v)* to chop or cut something roughly. 2 *(v)* If you **hack** into a computer system, you manage to get information from it illegally. 3 *(n)* a long, steady ride on horseback.

**haemophilia** *or* **hemophilia** *(n)* *(hee-mer-fil-ee-a)* If people suffer from **haemophilia**, their blood does not clot, so they bleed severely when they cut themselves. **haemophiliac** *(n)*.

**haggard** *(adj)* Someone who is **haggard** looks thin, tired, and worried.

**haggle** **haggling** **haggled** *(v)* to argue, usually about the price of something.

**hail** **hailing** **hailed** *(v)* When it **hails**, small pieces of frozen rain fall from the sky. **hail** *(n)*.

**hair** *(n)* the mass of fine, soft strands that grow on your head or body, or on the body of an animal.

**haircut** *(n)* When you have a **haircut**, someone cuts and styles your hair.

**hairdresser** *(n)* someone who cuts and styles people's hair.

**hairgrip** *(n)* a piece of bent wire with sides that press together to hold your hair in place.

**hair-raising** *(adj)* very frightening.

**hairy** **hairier** **hairiest** 1 *(adj)* covered in hair. 2 *(adj) (slang)* dangerous and frightening.

**halal** *(n)* meat that has been produced and prepared according to the rules of the Muslim religion. **halal** *(adj)*.

**half** **halves** 1 *(n)* one of two equal parts of something. 2 *(adv)* partly, or not completely. *The meal was half cooked.*

**half-time** *(n)* a short break in the middle of a game, such as football or hockey.

**hall** 1 *(n)* an area of a house just inside the front door. 2 *(n)* a large room used for meetings or other public events.

**hallelujah** *(hal-ay-loo-ya) (interject)* a word used to express joy and thanks to God.

**Halloween** *or* **Hallowe'en** *(n)* the evening before All Saints Day, believed in the past to be the night when witches and ghosts were active.

**hallucinate** *(hal-oo-sin-ate)* **hallucinating hallucinated** *(v)* to see something in your mind that is not really there. **hallucination** *(n).*

**halo** *(hay-low)* **haloes** *(n)* a circle of light, around the heads of angels and holy people in paintings.

**halt halting halted** *(v)* to stop. **halt** *(n).*

**halve halving halved** 1 *(v)* to cut or divide something into two equal parts. 2 *(v)* to reduce something so that there is only half as much as there was. *We have halved the cast for our school play.*

**hamlet** *(n)* a very small village.

**hammer hammering hammered** 1 *(n)* a tool with a metal head on a handle, used for hitting things, such as nails. **hammer** *(v).* 2 *(v)* to hit something hard. *Elsa hammered on the door.*

**hammock** *(n)* a piece of strong cloth or net that is hung up by each end and used as a bed.

**hamper hampering hampered** 1 *(n)* a large box or basket used for carrying food, especially on a picnic. 2 *(v)* to make it difficult for someone to do something. *Bob's sandals hampered his running.*

**hamster** *(n)* a small animal like a mouse, with no tail, often kept as a pet.

**hand handing handed** 1 *(n)* the part of your body on the end of your arm that you use for picking things up, writing, eating, etc. 2 *(v)* to pass or give something to someone. *Hand me the salt.* 3 *(n)* a set of cards that you hold in your hand during a game of cards. 4 *(n)* one of the pointers on a clock. *The minute hand.* 5 If you **give someone a hand**, you help them.

**handbook** *(n)* a book that gives you information or advice.

**handcuffs** *(plural n)* metal rings joined by a chain, that are fixed around prisoners' wrists to prevent them from escaping. **handcuff** *(v).*

**handful** 1 *(n)* the amount of something that you can hold in your hand. 2 *(n)* a small number of people or things.

**handicap** 1 *(n)* If someone has a **handicap**, they are disabled in some way. **handicapped** *(adj).* 2 *(n)* something that makes it difficult for you to do something. *Laurie's platform shoes were a handicap in the race.*

**handkerchief** *(n)* a small square of cloth that you use for blowing your nose.

**handle handling handled** 1 *(n)* the part of an object you use to carry, move, or hold that object. *A door handle.* 2 *(v)* to pick something up and hold it in your hands. *Please handle with care.* 3 *(v)* to deal with someone or something.

**handlebars** *(plural n)* the bar at the front of a bicycle or motorcycle that you use to steer. *See* **bicycle**.

**handshake** *(n)* a way of greeting someone by taking their hand and shaking it.

**handsome** *(adj)* attractive, or good looking.

**handwriting** *(n)* the style you use for forming letters and words when you write. *Fred has very neat handwriting.*

**handy handier handiest** 1 *(adj)* useful and easy to use. 2 *(adj)* skilful. *Sasha is handy with a power drill.* 3 *(adj)* close by. *Is there a cloth handy?*

**hang hanging hung** *or* **hanged** 1 *(v)* to fix something somewhere by attaching the top of it and leaving the bottom free. *Hang your coat on this hook.* 2 *(v)* to kill someone by putting a rope around their neck and then taking the support from under their feet. The past tense and past participle of this sense of the verb is "hanged". 3 **hang up** *(v)* to end a telephone conversation by putting down the receiver.

**hangar** *(n)* a large building where aircraft are kept.

**hanger** *(n)* a piece of specially shaped wood, metal, or plastic used for hanging up clothes.

**hang-glider** *(n)* an aircraft like a giant kite, with a harness for a pilot hanging below it. **hang-gliding** *(n).*



**hang glider**

**harbour** *(n)* a place where ships shelter or unload their cargo.

**hangover** *(n)* a headache and a feeling of sickness that you get after drinking too much alcohol.

**hang-up** *(n) (informal)* If you have a **hang-up** about something, you worry about it all the time.

**hanker** **hankering** **hankered** *(v)* to wish or long for something. **hankering** *(n).*

**Hanukkah** *or* **Chanukah** *(hah-ner-ker) (n)* the Jewish festival of lights, when Jews remember the purification of the Temple. *At Hanukkah, Jews light candles on a menorah, or branched candlestick.*

**menorah**

**haphazard** *(adj)* disorganized. *The papers were scattered over the floor in a haphazard manner.* **haphazardly** *(adv).*

**happen** **happening** **happened** 1 *(v)* to take place, or to occur. 2 *(v)* If you **happen** to do something, you have the chance or luck to do it. *Ned happened to arrive just as the bus was leaving.*

**happy** **happier** **happiest** 1 *(adj)* pleased and contented. **happiness** *(n),* **happily** *(adv).* 2 *(n)* lucky, or fortunate. *Meeting Bob in town was a happy coincidence.*

**harangue** *(huh-rang)* **haranguing** **harangued** *(v)* to talk loudly or crossly to someone. **harangue** *(n).*

**harass** **harasses** **harassing** **harassed** *(v)* to pester or annoy someone.

**hard** **harder** **hardest** 1 *(adj)* firm and solid. *A hard bed.* **hardness** *(n).* 2 *(adj)* difficult. *A hard exam.* **hardness** *(n).*

**hard copy** *(n)* a printed version of a document created by a computer.

**hard disk** *(n)* a disk inside a computer, used for storing large amounts of data.

**harden** **hardening** **hardened** 1 *(v)* to become harder, or to make something harder. 2 *(v)* to become tough and unfeeling. **hardened** *(adj).*

**hardly** *(adv)* scarcely, or only just. *I could hardly wait to open my gifts.*

**hardship** *(n)* difficulty, or suffering.

**hardware** 1 *(n)* tools and other household equipment. 2 *(n)* computer equipment, such as a printer or VDU.

**hardy** **hardier** **hardiest** *(adj)* tough and able to survive in very difficult conditions.

**hare** *(n)* a mammal like a large rabbit, with long, strong back legs.

**harm** **harming** **harmed** *(v)* to injure or hurt someone or something. **harm** *(n),* **harmful** *(adj).*

**harmonica** *(n)* a small musical instrument, played by blowing out and drawing in your breath through it.

**harmony** **harmonies** 1 *(n)* agreement. *The team worked in harmony.* **harmonious** *(adj).* 2 *(n)* a pleasant-sounding set of musical notes played at the same time. **harmonious** *(adj).*

**harness** **harnesses** 1 *(n)* a set of leather straps on a horse, used to control it. 2 *(n)* an arrangement of straps, used to keep someone safe. *A climbing harness.*

**harp** *(n)* a large, triangular musical instrument with strings that you play by plucking. **harpist** *(n).*

harp

**harsh** **harsher** **harshest** 1 *(adj)* cruel, or unpleasant. *Harsh words.* 2 *(adj)* A **harsh** noise sounds rough and loud.

**harvest** **harvesting** **harvested** *(v)* to collect or gather up crops. **harvest** *(n).*

**hassle** **hassling** **hassled** 1 *(v) (informal)* to pester or annoy someone. 2 *(n) (informal)* a nuisance. *It was a hassle having to get up so early.*

**hasty** **hastier** **hastiest** *(adj)* quick, or hurried. *A hasty decision.* **haste** *(n).*

**hat** 1 *(n)* an item of clothing that you wear on your head. 2 **hat trick** *(n)* three successes in a row, such as three goals in a row in a football match.

**hatch** **hatches** **hatching** **hatched** 1 *(v)* When an egg **hatches**, a baby bird, reptile, or fish breaks out of it. 2 *(n)* a covered hole in a floor, door, wall, or ceiling. *A serving hatch.*

**hatchback** *(n)* a car with a rear door that opens upwards.

**hatchet** *(n)* a small axe.

**hate** **hating** **hated** *(v)* to dislike or detest someone or something. **hatred** *(n).*

**hateful** *(adj)* horrible. **hatefully** *(adv).*

**haul** **hauling** **hauled** *(v)* to pull something with difficulty.

**haunt** **haunting** **haunted** 1 *(v)* If a ghost **haunts** a place, it visits it often. **haunted** *(adj).* 2 *(v)* If something **haunts** you, you keep worrying about it. *Phil was haunted by his grandfather's words.* **haunting** *(adj).* 3 *(n)* a place you have visited often.

**have** **having** **had** 1 *(v)* to own or possess something. *I have a new bicycle.* 2 *(v)* to experience or enjoy something. *We had lunch.* 3 *(v)* to receive or get something. *Have you had your pocket money?*

**haven** 1 *(n)* a harbour. 2 *(n)* a safe place.

**havoc** *(n)* great damage and chaos.

**hawk** *(n)* a bird of prey, with a hooked beak and sharp claws.

**hay** *(n)* grass which is dried and fed to farm animals.

**hay fever** *(n)* an allergy to pollen or grass that makes you sneeze, makes your eyes water, and can make you wheeze.

**hazard** *(n)* a risk, or a danger. *A fire hazard.* **hazardous** *(adj).*

**hazel** 1 *(n)* a tree that produces hazelnuts. 2 *(n)* a greenish-brown colour.

**hazy** **hazier** **haziest** 1 *(adj)* misty. **hazily** *(adv).* 2 *(adj)* vague and unclear.

**head** **heading** **headed** 1 *(n)* the top part of your body where your brain, eyes, and mouth are. 2 *(n)* the person in charge. **head** *(adj).* 3 *(v)* to move towards something. *We headed for the exit.*

**headache** *(n)* a pain in your head.

**headdress** **headdresses** *(n)* a head covering.

**heading** *(n)* words written as a title above a section of writing.

**headlice** *(n)* tiny insects that live and breed in human hair.

**headline** 1 *(n)* the title of a newspaper article, printed in large type. 2 **headlines** *(plural n)* the most important items in a news broadcast.

**headquarters** **headquarters** *(n)* the place from which an organization is run.

**headway** *(n)* If you make **headway**, you go forwards or make progress.

**heal** **healing** **healed** *(v)* to cure someone, or make them healthy.

**health** *(n)* strength and fitness.

**health food** *(n)* food that is natural and good for you.

**healthy** **healthier** **healthiest** 1 *(adj)* if you are **healthy**, you are fit and well. **healthiness** *(n).* 2 *(adj)* Something that is **healthy** makes you fit. *A healthy diet.*

**heap** **heaping** **heaped** 1 *(n)* a pile. **heaped** *(adj).* 2 *(v)* to pile up.

**hear** **hearing** **heard** *(v)* to sense sounds through your ears. **hearing** *(n).*

**hearing aid** *(n)* a small piece of equipment that people wear in or behind their ears to help them hear.

**hearsay** *(n)* things you are told but have not actually seen or experienced.

**hearse** *(rhymes with curse) (n)* a car that carries a coffin to a funeral.

**heart** 1 *(n)* the organ in your chest that pumps blood around your body. 2 *(n)* courage, or enthusiasm. 3 *(n)* love and affection. *You have won my heart.* 4 If you learn something **off by heart**, you memorize it. 5 **hearts** *(plural n)* one of the four suits in a pack of cards, with a heart-shaped symbol.

**heart attack** *(n)* If someone has a **heart attack**, they collapse because their heart has started to beat irregularly.

**heartbroken** *(adj)* If you are **heartbroken**, you are extremely sad.

**hearth** *(n)* the area in front of a fireplace.

**heartless** *(adj)* cruel and unkind.

**hearty** **heartier heartiest** 1 *(adj)* cheerful and enthusiastic. **heartily** *(adv).* 2 *(adj)* A **hearty** meal is large and filling.

**heat** **heating heated** 1 *(n)* great warmth. 2 *(v)* to warm or cook something. 3 *(n)* passion. *In the heat of the argument, I lost my temper.* **heated** *(adj),* **heatedly** *(adv).* 4 *(n)* a stage in a competition. *The third heat.*

**heath** *(n)* a large, wild area of grasses, fern, and heather.

**heathen** *(n)* someone who does not believe in one of the main world religions.

**heather** *(n)* a small, spiky bush with pink, purple, or white flowers.

**heave** **heaving heaved** *(v)* to push, pull, lift, or throw something with great effort.

**heaven** 1 *(n)* a wonderful place where God is believed to live and where good people are believed to go after they die. 2 *(n)* a marvellous place, thing, or state. *It was heaven to be on holiday.* **heavenly** *(adj).* 3 **the heavens** *(plural n)* the sky.

**heavy** **heavier heaviest** 1 *(adj)* weighing a lot. **heaviness** *(n),* **heavily** *(adv).* 2 *(adj)* great in amount or force. *Heavy fighting. Heavy rain.* **heaviness** *(n),* **heavily** *(adv).*

**heckle** **heckling heckled** *(v)* to interrupt a speaker by making rude comments.

**hectic** *(adj)* very busy. **hectically** *(adv).*

**hedge** *(n)* a border made from bushes.

**hedgehog** *(n)* a small mammal, covered with prickles, that comes out at night.

**hedgerow** *(n)* a row of bushes.

**heel** 1 *(n)* the back part of your foot. 2 *(n)* something that supports the back part of your foot. *These shoes have high heels.*

**hefty** **heftier heftiest** *(adj) (informal)* large, or powerful. *A hefty lad.*

**heifer** *(hef-fer) (n)* a young cow that has not had a calf.

**height** *(n)* a measurement of how high something is.

**heighten** **heightening heightened** *(v)* to make something higher or stronger. *Try heightening the colours on your painting.*

**heir** *(air) (n)* someone who has been, or will be, left money, property, or a title. *The heir to the throne.*

**heiress** *(air-ess)* **heiresses** *(n)* a girl or woman who has been, or will be, left money, property, or a title.

**heirloom** *(air-loom) (n)* something precious that a family owns and hands down from one generation to the next.

**helicopter** *(n)* an aircraft with large, rotating blades on top, which can take off and land vertically.

**helicopter**

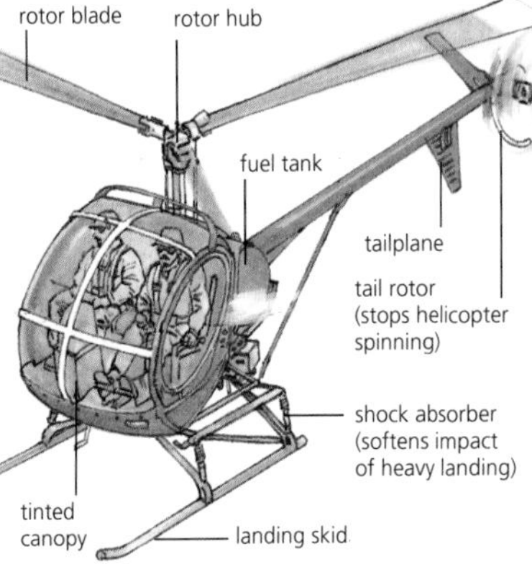


**hell** 1 *(n)* a place full of suffering and misery, where evil people are believed to go when they die. 2 *(n)* a very unpleasant place, thing, or state. **hellish** *(adj).*

**helm** *(n)* the wheel or handle used to steer a boat. **helmsman** *(n).*

**helmet** *(n)* a hard hat that protects your head.

**help** **helping** **helped** **1** *(v)* to assist. **2** *(n)* assistance. **helper** *(n).*

**helpful** *(adj)* friendly and willing to help. **helpfulness** *(n),* **helpfully** *(adv).*

**helping** *(n)* a portion of food.

**helpless** *(adj)* unable to look after yourself. **helplessness** *(n).*

**hem** **hemming** **hemmed** **1** *(v)* to fold over an edge of material and sew it down. **hem** *(n).* **2** *(v)* If you are **hemmed in**, you are surrounded and cannot get out.

**hemisphere** *(n)* one half of a sphere, especially of the Earth. *France is in the Earth's northern hemisphere.*

**hemophilia** *see* **haemophilia**.

**hen** **1** *(n)* a bird kept for its eggs and its meat. **2** *(n)* a female bird.

**herb** *(n)* a plant used in cooking or medicine. **herbal** *(adj).*

**herbs**

rosemary
mint
thyme
parsley
basil

**herd** **herding** **herded** **1** *(n)* a large group of animals. **2** *(v)* to make people or animals move together as a group. *We were all herded into a tiny room.*

**hereditary** *(adj)* passed from parent to child. *A hereditary disease.*

**heritage** *(n)* valuable or important traditions, buildings, etc. that belong to a country or family.

**hermit** *(n)* someone who has chosen to live totally alone.

**hero** **heroes** **1** *(n)* a brave or good person. **heroism** *(n),* **heroic** *(adj).* **2** *(n)* the main character in a book, play, etc.

**heroine** **1** *(n)* a brave or good girl or woman. **2** *(n)* the main female character in a book, play, etc.

**heron** *(n)* a long-legged bird, with a long, thin beak, that lives near water.

**hesitate** **hesitating** **hesitated** *(v)* to pause before you do something. **hesitation** *(n),* **hesitant** *(adj).*

**heyday** *(n)* Someone's **heyday** is the best or most successful period in their life.

**hibernate** **hibernating** **hibernated** *(v)* When animals **hibernate**, they spend the winter in a deep sleep in which their heartbeat, temperature, and breathing rate become very low. **hibernation** *(n).*

**hiccup** *or* **hiccough** **1** *(n)* a sudden sound in your throat, caused by a spasm in your chest. **2** *(n) (informal)* a small delay or problem.

**hide** **hiding** **hid** **hidden** **1** *(v)* to go where you cannot be seen. **2** *(v)* to keep something secret or concealed. **3** *(n)* an animal's skin that is used to make leather.

**hideous** *(adj)* ugly, or horrible.

**hiding** *(n) (informal)* a beating.

**hieroglyphics** *(hi-rer-**glif**-iks) (plural n)* writing used by ancient Egyptians, made up of pictures and symbols. *These hieroglyphics were used to represent both objects and letters or sounds.*

**hieroglyphics**

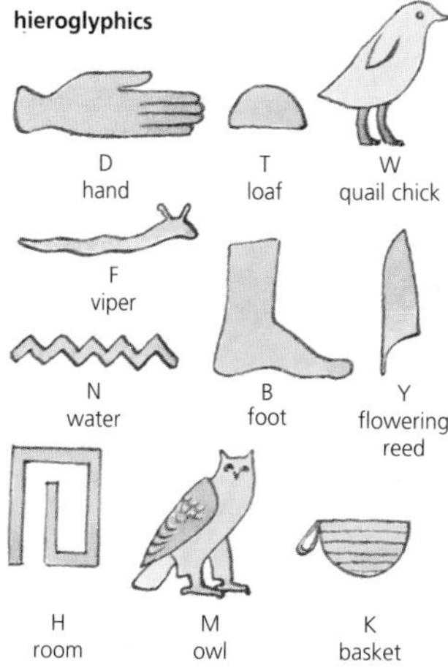


**high** **higher** **highest** **1** *(adj)* a long way from the ground. *A high hill.* **high** *(adv).* **2** *(adj)* measuring from top to bottom. *The tree was 30m high.* **3** *(adj)* more than the normal level or amount. *High prices.* **highly** *(adv).* **4** **high tide** *(n)* the time when the sea is furthest up the beach.

*Some words that begin with a "hi" sound are spelt "hy".*

**higher education** *(n)* education at college or university.

**highlands** *(plural n)* areas with mountains or hills. **highland** *(adj)*.

**highlight highlighting highlighted** 1 *(v)* to draw attention to something. 2 *(n)* the best or most interesting part of something. *Sports highlights.*

**hijack hijacking hijacked** *(v)* to take control of a plane or other vehicle and force its pilot or driver to go somewhere.

**hike** *(n)* a long walk in the country.

**hilarious** *(adj)* very funny. **hilarity** *(n)*.

**hill** *(n)* a raised area of land that is smaller than a mountain. **hilly** *(adj)*.

**hinder hindering hindered** *(v)* to make things difficult for someone.

**Hinduism** *(n)* the main religion of India. Hindus have lots of gods, and believe that they live many lives in different bodies. *This bronze statue represents Shiva, one of the main gods in Hinduism.* **Hindu** *(n)*.

Shiva

**hinge hinging hinged** 1 *(n)* a movable metal joint on a window or door. 2 *(v)* to depend on something. *My future hinges on your decision.*

**hint** 1 *(n)* a clue, or a helpful tip. **hint** *(v)*. 2 *(n)* a trace, or a tiny amount. *There's a hint of garlic in this soup.*

**hip** *(n)* the part of your body between the tops of your thighs and your waist.

**hippie** *or* **hippy** hippies *(n)* a name for someone who does not live or dress in a conventional way.

**hippopotamus** hippopotamuses *or* hippopotami *(n)* a large African mammal with thick skin, that lives near water.

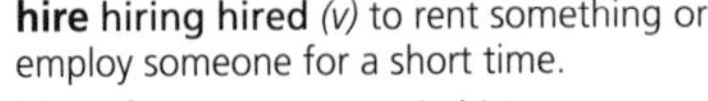

**hire hiring hired** *(v)* to rent something or employ someone for a short time.

**historic** *(adj)* important in history.

**history histories** 1 *(n)* the study of past events. **historian** *(n)*, **historical** *(adj)*. 2 *(n)* a description of past events.

**hit hitting hit** 1 *(v)* to smack or strike something with your hand, a bat, etc. **hit** *(n)*. 2 *(v)* to knock or bump into something. *The stone hit the window.* 3 *(n)* a successful song, play, etc.

**hitch hitches hitching hitched** 1 *(v)* to join something to a vehicle. *They hitched the trailer to the van.* 2 *(n)* a problem. *There's been a hitch in our plans.*

**hitchhike hitchhiking hitchhiked** *(v)* to travel by getting lifts in other people's vehicles. **hitchhiker** *(n)*.

**hi tech** *(adj)* very sophisticated and using the latest technology. Hi tech is short for high technology.

**HIV** 1 *(n)* a virus that can lead to AIDS. HIV stands for human immunodeficiency virus. 2 If someone is **HIV positive**, they have the HIV virus and may develop AIDS.

**hive** *(n)* a box for keeping bees so that their honey can be collected.

**hoard hoarding hoarded** *(v)* to collect and store things. **hoard** *(n)*, **hoarder** *(n)*.

**hoarding** *(n)* a high fence or board where posters are displayed.

**hoarse hoarser hoarsest** *(adj)* A **hoarse** voice is rough or croaky. **hoarseness** *(n)*.

**hoax** *(rhymes with pokes)* **hoaxes** *(n)* a trick, or a practical joke.

**hobble hobbling hobbled** *(v)* to walk with difficulty, because you are in pain or are injured.

**hobby hobbies** *(n)* something that you enjoy doing in your spare time.

**hockey** *(n)* a game played with sticks and a ball, by two teams trying to score goals.

**hoist hoisting hoisted** *(v)* to lift something heavy, usually with a piece of equipment. **hoist** *(n)*.

**hold holding held** 1 *(v)* to carry, support, or keep something. *Hold the cup carefully.* 2 *(v)* to contain something, or be able to contain it. *This mug holds a litre.* 3 *(v)* to organize or arrange something. *We are holding a party.*

---

*Some words that begin with a "hi" sound are spelt "hy".*

**hole** 1 *(n)* a hollow place, or a gap. 2 *(n)* an animal's burrow.

**holiday** *(n)* time away from school or work, especially a trip away from home.

**hollow** *(adj)* If something is **hollow**, it has an empty space inside it. **hollow** *(n)*.

**holly** *(n)* an evergreen tree or bush with prickly leaves and red berries.

**hologram** *(n)* an image made by laser beams that looks three-dimensional.

**holy** **holier holiest** *(adj)* to do with or belonging to God or a god.

**home** 1 *(n)* Your **home** is where you live or belong. 2 If you **feel at home** with something or someone, you feel comfortable with them.

**homesick** *(adj)* If you are **homesick**, you miss your home and family.

**homicide** *(n)* murder.

**homoeopathy** *(home-ee-**op**-ath-ee)* *(n)* a way of treating illness by giving people very small amounts of drugs that produce the same symptoms as the illness.

**homosexual** *(adj)* Someone who is **homosexual** has sexual feelings for a person of the same sex. **homosexual** *(n)*, **homosexuality** *(n)*.

**honest** *(adj)* An **honest** person is truthful and will not lie or steal. **honesty** *(n)*.

**honeycomb** *(n)* a wax structure made by bees and used to store honey.

**honeymoon** *(n)* a holiday that a husband and wife take together after their wedding.

**honour** **honouring honoured** 1 *(n)* Someone's **honour** is their good reputation and the respect that other people have for them. 2 *(v)* to give praise or an award. *The mayor honoured Kim for her bravery.*

**honourable** 1 *(adj)* An **honourable** action is good and deserves praise. 2 *(adj)* If someone is **honourable**, they keep their promises.

**hood** 1 *(n)* the part of a jacket or coat that goes over your head. 2 *(n)* the folding roof or cover of a car, pram, etc.

**hoof** **hooves** *or* **hoofs** *(n)* the hard covering on the foot of a horse, deer, etc.

**hook** *(n)* a curved piece of metal or plastic, used to catch or hold something.

**hooked** 1 *(adj)* curved. *A hooked nose.* 2 *(adj) (slang)* If you are **hooked**, you like something a lot, or are addicted to it.

**hooligan** *(n)* a noisy, violent person who makes trouble. **hooliganism** *(n)*.

**hop** **hopping hopped** *(v)* to jump, especially on one leg. **hop** *(n)*.

**hope** **hoping hoped** 1 *(v)* to wish for or expect something. 2 *(n)* a feeling of expectation or confidence. *Hope for the future.* **hopefulness** *(n)*, **hopeful** *(adj)*.

**hopeless** 1 *(adj)* without hope. **hopelessness** *(n)*. 2 *(adj)* bad, or lacking in skill.

**horde** *(n)* a large, noisy, moving crowd of people or animals.

**horizon** *(n)* the line where the sky and the earth or sea seem to meet.

**horizontal** *(adj)* flat and parallel to the ground. *A horizontal line.*

**hormone** *(n)* a chemical made in your body that affects the way that you grow and develop. **hormonal** *(adj)*.

**horn** 1 *(n)* a hard, bony growth on the head of some animals. **horned** *(adj)*. 2 *(n)* a musical instrument that you blow. *A French horn.* 3 *(n)* a machine that makes a hooting sound as a signal. *A car horn.*

**French horn**

**horoscope** *(n)* a prediction about your life, based on the position of the stars and planets when you were born.

**horrible** *(adj)* very unpleasant.

**horrid** *(adj)* nasty, or unkind.

**horrific** *(adj)* shocking. **horrifically** *(adv)*.

**horrify** **horrifies horrifying horrified** *(v)* to shock and disgust someone.

**horse** 1 *(n)* a large, strong animal with hooves, that people ride or use to pull coaches, ploughs, etc. 2 *(n)* a piece of gymnastics apparatus that you jump over.

**hose** *(n)* a long rubber or plastic tube through which liquids or gases travel.

*Some words that begin with a "h" sound are spelt "wh".*

**hospice** *(n)* a hospital that provides special care for people who are dying.

**hospitable** *(adj)* friendly and welcoming.

**hospital** *(n)* a place where you receive medical treatment and are looked after when you are ill.

**host** 1 *(n)* an organizer of an event. **host** *(v)*. 2 *(n)* a large number. *A host of angels.*

**hostage** *(n)* someone held prisoner and threatened by an enemy, as a way of demanding money or other conditions.

**hostel** *(n)* a building where people can stay, usually at low cost.

**hostess** **hostesses** *(n)* a female organizer of an event.

**hostile** *(adj)* unfriendly, or angry. *A hostile crowd.* **hostility** *(n)*.

**hot** **hotter** **hottest** 1 *(adj)* very warm. 2 *(adj)* very spicy and strong-tasting.

**hot-air balloon** *(n)* an aircraft lifted by an enormous bag filled with hot air or gas, with a basket for carrying passengers.

**hotel** *(n)* a place where you pay to stay overnight and have meals.

**hot-water bottle** *(n)* a rubber container for hot water, used to warm a bed.

**hound** **hounding** **hounded** 1 *(n)* a dog. 2 *(v)* to chase or pester somebody.

**hour** *(n)* a unit of time equal to 60 minutes. **hourly** *(adv)*.

**house** **housing** **housed** 1 *(n)* a building where people live. 2 If you **house** someone or something, you find a place for them to live or to be.

**houseboat** *(n)* a boat that people live on, with cooking and sleeping areas.

**household** 1 *(n)* all the people who live together in a house. 2 *(adj)* belonging to, or to do with a house or family.

**housework** *(n)* work done to keep a house clean and tidy.

**hovel** *(n)* a small, dirty house or hut.

**hover** **hovering** **hovered** 1 *(v)* to stay in one place in the air. 2 *(v)* to linger, or be uncertain. *Hal hovered in the doorway.*

**hovercraft** *(n)* a vehicle that can travel over land and water, supported by a cushion of air.

**however** 1 *(adv)* in whatever way, or to whatever extent. *You have to go, however much you hate it.* 2 *(adv)* on the other hand. *We can't come on Friday; however, we could manage Saturday.*

**howl** **howling** **howled** *(v)* to cry like a dog or wolf in pain. **howl** *(n)*.

**howler** *(n) (informal)* a silly and funny mistake with words.

**HQ** *short for* **headquarters**.

**hub** *(n)* the centre of a wheel. *See* **bicycle**.

**huddle** **huddling** **huddled** *(v)* to crowd together in a tight group. **huddle** *(n)*.

**huff** *(n)* a childish, sulky mood.

**hug** **hugging** **hugged** *(v)* to hold someone tightly in a loving or caring way.

**huge** **huger** **hugest** *(adj)* enormous, or gigantic. *A huge amount of money.*

**hulk** 1 *(n)* the remains of a wrecked ship. 2 *(n)* a large, clumsy person.

**hum** **humming** **hummed** 1 *(v)* to sing with your mouth closed. **hum** *(n)*. 2 *(v)* to make a steady, buzzing noise. **hum** *(n)*.

**human** 1 **human** *or* **human being** *(n)* a person. **human** *(adj)*. 2 *(adj)* natural and understandable. *It's only human to make mistakes sometimes.*

**humane** *(adj)* kind and merciful.

**humanities** *(plural n)* non-science subjects, such as literature, history, etc.

**humanity** 1 *(n)* all human beings. 2 *(n)* kindness and sympathy.

**humble** **humbler** **humblest** *(adj)* modest and not proud. **humbly** *(adv)*.

**humdrum** *(adj)* dull and routine.

**humid** *(adj)* warm and damp.

**humiliate** **humiliating** **humiliated** *(v)* to make someone look or feel totally foolish and undignified. **humiliation** *(n)*.

**humility** *(n)* If you show **humility**, you are not proud and you recognize your own faults.

**hummingbird** *(n)* a very small, brightly coloured tropical bird that hovers by flapping its wings rapidly.

**humour** 1 *(n)* a general name for things that make people laugh or smile. **humorous** *(adj)*. 2 *(n)* If you have a **sense of humour**, you are quick to appreciate the funny side of life. **humorous** *(adj)*.

**hump** *(n)* a small hill, or a large lump.

**hunch** hunches hunching hunched 1 *(v)* to lower your head into your shoulders and lean forward. 2 *(n)* an idea that is not backed by much reason or proof.

**hungry** hungrier hungriest *(adj)* wanting food. **hunger** *(n)*.

**hunk** *(n)* a large piece of something.

**hunt** hunting hunted 1 *(v)* to search for something. 2 *(v)* to chase foxes or other wild animals for sport. **hunting** *(n)*.

**hurdle** hurdling hurdled 1 *(n)* a small fence that you jump over in a race. *The sequence below shows a hurdler clearing a hurdle.* **hurdler** *(n)*, **hurdling** *(n)*. 2 *(v)* to jump over something. 3 *(n)* an obstacle.

**hurdling**

**hurl** hurling hurled *(v)* to throw something very strongly.

**hurricane** *(n)* a violent storm.

**hurry** hurries hurrying hurried *(v)* to do things as fast as possible. **hurried** *(adj)*.

**hurt** hurting hurt 1 *(v)* to cause pain. 2 *(v)* to be in pain. 3 *(v)* to upset somebody by being unkind. **hurtful** *(adj)*.

**husband** *(n)* the male partner in a marriage.

**hush** hushes hushing hushed 1 *(n)* a sudden period of quietness. 2 *(interject)* be quiet! 3 **hush up** *(v)* to keep something secret.

**husky** huskies; huskier huskiest 1 *(adj)* A **husky** voice sounds low and hoarse. **huskiness** *(n)*, **huskily** *(adv)*. 2 *(n)* a strong dog with a furry coat, bred to pull sledges in arctic conditions.

**hustle** hustling hustled *(v)* to push someone roughly in order to make them move. *Jill hustled us out of the room.*

**hut** 1 *(n)* a small, primitive house. 2 *(n)* a wooden shed.

**hutch** hutches *(n)* a wooden cage for rabbits or other small pets.

**hybrid** *(n)* a plant or an animal that has been bred from two different species.

**hydrant** *(n)* an outdoor water tap for use in emergencies.

**hydraulic** *(hi-**drol**-ik)* *(adj)* **Hydraulic** machines work by power that is created by liquid being forced through pipes.

**hydroelectricity** *(n)* electricity that is made from energy produced by running water. **hydroelectric** *(adj)*.

**hydrofoil** *(n)* a boat which rises out of the water when it is travelling fast.

**hydrogen** *(n)* a colourless gas that is lighter than air and catches fire easily.

**hyena** *(n)* a wild animal, like a dog, that eats the flesh of dead animals and has a shrieking howl.

**hygienic** *(hi-**jee**-nik)* *(adj)* clean and free enough from germs not to be a health risk. **hygiene** *(n)*, **hygienically** *(adv)*.

**hymn** *(him)* *(n)* a song of praise to God.

**hype** *(n)* extravagant claims made about something to promote it. **hype** *(v)*.

**hyperactive** *(adj)* If someone is **hyperactive**, they are abnormally restless and lively. **hyperactivity** *(n)*.

**hypermarket** *(n)* a very large self-service store, usually on the outskirts of a town.

**hyphen** *(**hi**-fern)* *(n)* the punctuation mark (-) used to separate the parts of a word made from two or more parts, for example, "easy-going" and "full-time".

**hypnotize** *or* **hypnotise** hypnotizing hypnotized *(v)* to put someone into a trance. **hypnotism** *(n)*, **hypnotist** *(n)*.

**hypochondriac** *(hi-per-**kon**-dree-ak)* *(n)* someone who continually thinks that they are ill or will become ill.

**hypocrite** *(**hip**-oh-krit)* *(n)* someone who pretends to believe or feel something that is different from their true beliefs or feelings. **hypocrisy** *(n)*, **hypocritical** *(adj)*.

**hypodermic** *(n)* a hollow needle used for giving injections.

**hypotenuse** *(n)* the side opposite the right angle of a right-angled triangle.

**hypothesis** hypotheses *(n)* an idea about the way that a scientific investigation or experiment will turn out.

**hysterical** *(adj)* If someone is **hysterical**, they are very emotional and out of control because they are very excited, frightened or angry. **hysteria** *(n)*, **hysterically** *(adv)*.

# Ii

**ice** **icing** **iced** **1** *(n)* frozen water. **icy** *(adj)*. **2** *(v)* If someone **ices** a cake, they cover it with a sweet coating. **icing** *(n)*.

**Ice age** *(n)* a period of time when a large part of the world was covered with ice.

**iceberg** *(n)* a huge mass of ice floating in the sea.

**ice cream** *(n)* a sweet, frozen food made from milk or cream.

**ice hockey** *(n)* a team game played with sticks, by skaters aiming to score goals.

**ice-rink** *(n)* a place where people skate on a prepared surface of ice.

**ice-skate** **ice-skating** **ice-skated** *(v)* to move around on ice, wearing high-sided boots with blades on the bottom.

**icicle** *(n)* a long, thin stem of ice, formed from dripping water which has frozen.

**icon** *or* **ikon** **1** *(n)* a picture of Jesus or a saint found in some Eastern churches such as the Greek and Russian Orthodox churches. **2** *(n)* one of several small pictures on a computer screen, representing programs or functions.

**icy** **icier** **iciest** **1** *(adj)* covered with ice, or very cold. **2** *(adj)* unfriendly. *An icy stare.*

**idea** *(n)* a thought, or a plan.

**ideal** **1** *(adj)* very suitable, or perfect. *Hamsters make ideal pets.* **2** *(n)* the situation you would most like to see. *My ideal is world peace.*

**identical** *(n)* exactly alike.

**identification** *(n)* something that proves who you are.

**identify** **identifies** **identifying** **identified** *(v)* to recognize something or somebody.

**identity** **identities** *(n)* Your **identity** is who you are.

**idiot** *(n)* a foolish person. **idiotic** *(adj)*.

**idle** **idler** **idlest** **1** *(adj)* lazy. **idleness** *(n)*, **idly** *(adv)*. **2** *(adj)* not active. *Idle hands.*

**idol** **1** *(n)* someone or something that is worshipped as a god. **2** *(n)* someone people love and admire. *A pop idol.*

**i.e.** an abbreviation of the Latin phrase *id est*, which means "that is", and is used to explain something. *It's the penultimate shop, i.e. the one before last.*

**igloo** *(n)* the traditional, dome-shaped house of the Inuit people, made of blocks of ice or hard snow.

**ignite** **igniting** **ignited** *(v)* to set fire to something.

**ignorant** *(adj)* not knowing about many things, or uneducated. **ignorance** *(n)*.

**ignore** **ignoring** **ignored** *(v)* to take no notice of something.

**ikon** *see* **icon**.

**ill** **worse** **worst** **1** *(adj)* sick. **illness** *(n)*. **2** *(adj)* bad. *Did you suffer any ill effects?*

**illegal** *(adj)* against the law.

**illegible** *(adj)* very difficult to read.

**illegitimate** *(adj)* An **illegitimate** child is born to parents who are not married.

**illiterate** *(adj)* not able to read and write.

**illogical** *(adj)* Something **illogical** is not reasonable and does not make sense.

**illuminate** **illuminating** **illuminated** **1** *(v)* to light up something, like a building. **2** *(v)* In the Middle Ages, manuscripts were **illuminated** by adding pictures and decoration to the text. *The letter "L", shown here, comes from a manuscript which was illuminated by monks.*

**illuminated letter**

**illusion** *(n)* something which appears to exist, but does not. **illusory** *(adj)*.

**illustration** *(n)* a picture in a magazine, book, etc. **illustrator** *(n)*, **illustrate** *(v)*.

**image** **1** *(n)* a picture in a book, on a television screen, etc. **2** *(n)* a picture that you have in your mind. **3** *(n)* Your **image** is the way that you appear to people.

**imagery** *(n)* descriptive language used by writers in poems, stories, etc. *Similes and metaphors are both types of imagery.*

**imagine** **imagining** **imagined** *(v)* to picture something in your mind. **imagination** *(n)*, **imaginary** *(adj)*.

**imitate** **imitating** **imitated** *(v)* to copy or mimic someone or something. **imitation** *(n)*.

**immature** 1 *(adj)* young and not fully developed. **immaturity** *(n)*. 2 *(adj)* silly and childish. **immaturity** *(n)*.

**immediately** *(adv)* now, or at once. **immediate** *(adj)*.

**immense** *(adj)* huge, or enormous.

**immerse** **immersing immersed** 1 *(v)* to cover something completely in a liquid. 2 *(v)* If you are **immersed** in something, you are completely involved in it.

**immigrant** *(n)* someone who comes from abroad to live permanently in a country. **immigration** *(n)*, **immigrate** *(v)*.

**imminent** *(adj)* about to happen.

**immobilize** *or* **immobilise** **immobilizing immobilized** *(v)* to prevent something or someone from moving.

**immoral** *(adj)* unfair, wrong, or wicked.

**immune** *(adj)* protected against a disease. **immunity** *(n)*, **immunize** *(v)*.

**impact** 1 *(n)* the action of one thing hitting another. 2 *(n)* the effect that something has on people.

**impartial** *(adj)* fair, or not favouring one person or point of view over another.

**impatient** *(adj)* in a hurry, or unable to wait. **impatience** *(n)*, **impatiently** *(adv)*.

**imperfect** 1 *(adj)* faulty, or not perfect. **imperfection** *(n)*. 2 *(adj)* The **imperfect** form of a verb is used to describe actions which continue, for example, "I was running, I am running, I will be running".

**imperial** 1 *(adj)* to do with an empire. 2 *(adj)* The **imperial** measurement system is the non-metric system. It uses units such as feet, pints, and ounces. *See* page 256.

**impersonal** *(adj)* lacking in warmth and feeling. *A cold, impersonal manner.*

**impersonate** **impersonating impersonated** *(v)* to pretend to be someone else, either seriously or for fun.

**impertinent** *(adj)* rude and cheeky. **impertinence** *(n)*.

**impetuous** *(adj)* Someone who is **impetuous** does things suddenly, without thinking first. **impetuously** *(adv)*.

**implement** *(n)* a tool or utensil.

**implication** *(n)* something suggested, but not actually said. *Dad didn't say "yes", but the implication is that we can go.*

**imply** **implies implying implied** *(v)* to suggest or mean something without actually saying it.

**impolite** *(adj)* If someone is **impolite**, they are rude and have bad manners.

**import** *(im-port)* **importing imported** *(v)* to bring foreign goods into your own country to be sold. **import** *(im-port)* *(n)*.

**important** 1 *(adj)* Something **important** is worth taking seriously and can have a great effect. *An important decision.* **importance** *(n)*, **importantly** *(adv)*. 2 *(adj)* An **important** person is powerful and holds a high position.

**impossible** *(adj)* If something is **impossible**, it cannot be done or cannot happen. **impossiblity** *(n)*.

**impostor** *(n)* someone who pretends to be someone that they are not.

**impractical** *(adj)* not sensible, or not useful. *An impractical plan.*

**impress** **impresses impressing impressed** *(v)* to make people think highly of you. **impressive** *(adj)*.

**impression** 1 *(n)* an idea, or a feeling. *I had the impression that Sid didn't like me.* 2 *(n)* an imitation of someone or something. *Do your impression of a seal.*

**impressionable** *(adj)* easily influenced by other people.

**imprison** **imprisoning imprisoned** *(v)* to put someone in prison or lock them up.

**improve** **improving improved** *(v)* to get better, or to make something better. **improvement** *(n)*.

**improvise** **improvising improvised** 1 *(v)* to do the best you can with what is available. *We improvised a shelter from old boxes.* 2 *(v)* When actors or musicians **improvise**, they make up words or music as they perform. **improvisation** *(adv)*.

**impudent** *(adj)* rude, cheeky, and outspoken. **impudence** *(n)*.

**impulse** *(n)* a sudden desire to do something. **impulsive** *(adj)*.

**inaccurate** *(adj)* not very precise, or not correct. **inaccuracy** *(n)*.

**inadequate** *(adj)* not enough, or not good enough. **inadequately** *(adv)*.

**inappropriate** *(adj)* unsuitable for the time, place, etc.

**inarticulate** *(adj)* not able to express yourself very clearly in words.

**inaudible** *(adj)* not loud enough to hear.

**inborn** *(adj)* If a skill or quality is **inborn**, you inherit it from your parents and it is natural to you.

**incapable** *(adj)* If you are **incapable** of doing something, you are unable to do it.

**incense** *(n)* a substance which is burnt to give off a sweet smell.

**incentive** *(n)* something that encourages you to make an effort. *The prospect of winning was an incentive to run fast.*

**incessant** *(adj)* nonstop, or continuous. *Incessant noise.* **incessantly** *(adv).*

**incident** *(n)* an event, or something which happens.

**incidentally** *(adv)* by the way.

**incite** **inciting** **incited** *(v)* to provoke or urge someone to do something.

**incline** **inclining** **inclined** 1 *(v)* to lean, or to slope. 2 If you are **inclined to** do something, you like to do it, or you tend to do it. *Roz is inclined to avoid exercise.*

**include** **including** **included** *(v)* to contain something or someone as part of something else. *We included Abigail in our plans.*

**inclusive** *(adj)* including and covering everything. *The rent is inclusive of bills.*

**incoherent** *(adj)* unclear, or not logical.

**income** *(n)* the money that someone earns or receives regularly.

**incompatible** *(adj)* If people or objects are **incompatible**, they cannot live together or be used together.

**incompetent** *(adj)* If you are **incompetent** at something, you cannot do it very well or effectively.

**incomplete** *(adj)* not finished, or not complete. **incompletely** *(adv).*

**incomprehensible** *(adj)* impossible to understand. **incomprehensibly** *(adv).*

**inconceivable** *(adj)* impossible to believe or imagine. **inconceivably** *(adv).*

**inconclusive** *(adj)* not clear, or not certain. *Inconclusive results.*

**inconsiderate** *(adj)* not thinking about other people's needs and feelings.

**inconspicuous** *(adj)* not easy to see.

**inconvenient** *(adj)* If something is **inconvenient**, it is awkward and causes difficulties. **inconvenience** *(n).*

**incorporate** **incorporating** **incorporated** *(v)* When you **incorporate** something into another thing, you make it a part of that thing. **incorporation** *(n).*

**incorrect** *(adj)* wrong. **incorrectly** *(adv).*

**increase** **increasing** **increased** *(v)* to grow in size or number. **increase** *(n).*

**incredible** *(adj)* unbelievable, or amazing. **incredibly** *(adv).*

**incriminate** **incriminating** **incriminated** *(v)* to show that someone is guilty of a crime or other wrong action.

**incubator** 1 *(n)* a container in which premature babies are kept safe and warm while they grow larger and stronger. 2 *(n)* a container in which eggs are kept warm until they hatch. **incubation** *(n).*

**incurable** *(adj)* A person with an **incurable** disease cannot be made better.

**indecent** *(adj)* rude, or shocking.

**indeed** *(adv)* certainly.

**indefinite** 1 *(adj)* not clear. 2 **indefinite article** *(n)* the grammatical term for "a", "an", or "some", used before a noun.

**independent** 1 *(adj)* free from the control of other people or things. **independence** *(n).* 2 *(adj)* not wanting or needing much help from other people. **independence** *(n).*

**indestructible** *(adj)* If something is **indestructible**, it cannot be destroyed.

**index** **indexes** *or* **indices** 1 *(n)* an alphabetical list that shows you where to find words or pictures. 2 *(n)* Your **index finger** is the one nearest to your thumb.

**indicate** **indicating** **indicated** 1 *(v)* to show, or to prove something. **indication** *(n).* 2 *(v)* to signal. *Drivers should always indicate before turning.* **indicator** *(n).*

**indifferent** *(adj)* not interested in something. *Amelia is indifferent to where we go.* **indifference** *(n).*

**indigestion** *(n)* If you have **indigestion**, your stomach hurts because you are having difficulty in digesting food.

**indignant** *(adj)* upset and annoyed because you feel that something is not fair. **indignation** *(n),* **indignantly** *(adv).*

**indirect** *(adj)* not straightforward. *An indirect route.* **indirectly** *(adv).*

**indispensable** *(adj)* essential and impossible to replace.

**indistinguishable** *(adj)* When two things are **indistinguishable**, you cannot tell them apart.

**individual** 1 *(adj)* single and separate. *The individual members of a group.* 2 *(n)* a person. *A strange individual.* 3 *(adj)* unusual, or different. *Rik has a very individual hairstyle.*

**indoors** *(adv)* inside a building.

**indulge** **indulging** **indulged** 1 *(v)* to let someone have their own way. 2 *(v)* If you **indulge in** something, you allow yourself to enjoy it.

**industrial** *(adj)* to do with businesses and factories. *The industrial area of the city.* **industrially** *(adv).*

**industry** **industries** *(n)* the business of making things or providing services in order to earn money.

**inefficient** *(adj)* If someone or something is **inefficient**, they do not work very well and they waste time and energy. **inefficiency** *(n).*

**inequality** **inequalities** *(n)* the treatment of people or things in an unequal or unfair way.

**inert** *(adj)* lifeless and unmoving.

**inevitable** *(adj)* certain to happen.

**inexpensive** *(adj)* cheap.

**inexperienced** *(adj)* An **inexperienced** person has had little practice in doing something.

**infamous** *(in-fer-muss) (adj)* Something or someone who is **infamous** has a very bad reputation.

**infant** 1 *(n)* a young child or baby. **infancy** *(n).* 2 *(n)* a schoolchild aged between four and seven.

**infatuated** *(adj)* If you are **infatuated** with someone, you like them so much that you stop thinking clearly and sensibly about your relationship. **infatuation** *(n).*

**infection** *(n)* an illness caused by germs.

**infectious** 1 *(adj)* An **infectious** disease is spread from one person to another by germs. 2 *(adj)* If a mood is **infectious**, it spreads easily. *Infectious laughter.*

**inferior** *(adj)* If something is **inferior** to something else, it is not as good.

**infertile** 1 *(adj)* unable to have babies. **infertility** *(n).* 2 *(adj)* **Infertile** land is useless for growing crops and plants.

**infested** *(adj)* full of animal or insect pests. **infestation** *(n),* **infest** *(v).*

**infiltrate** **infiltrating** **infiltrated** *(v)* to join an organization secretly, in order to spy on it or damage it in some way.

**infinite** *(in-fin-it) (adj)* endless. *Infinite possibilities.* **infinitely** *(adv).*

**infinitive** *(n)* the basic form of a verb, for example, "to run", "to be", "to write".

**infirmary** **infirmaries** *(n)* a hospital.

**inflammable** *(adj)* An **inflammable** substance can catch fire easily.

**inflatable** *(adj)* An **inflatable** object can be filled with air or blown up. *The picture shows an inflatable life raft.*

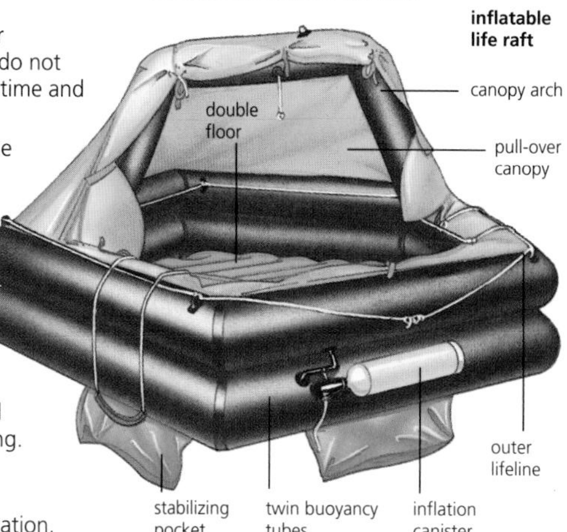


**inflate** **inflating** **inflated** *(v)* to make something expand by blowing air into it.

**inflation** *(n)* a widespread rise in prices.

**inflexible** *(adj)* not able to bend, or not able to change. **inflexibility** *(n).*

**inflict** **inflicting** **inflicted** *(v)* to cause suffering to somebody or something. *The bombing inflicted severe damage on the town.*

**influence** **influencing** **influenced** *(v)* to have an effect on someone or something. **influence** *(n).*

**influenza** *see* **flu**.

**inform** **informing** **informed** *(v)* to tell someone something.

**informal** *(adj)* relaxed, easy-going, and casual. *An informal party.* **informality** *(n).*

**information** *(n)* facts and knowledge.

**information technology** *(n)* the use of computers and other electronic equipment to produce, store, or communicate information.

**informative** *(adj)* Something that is **informative** provides useful information.

**infrequent** *(adj)* not happening very often. **infrequently** *(adv).*

**infuriate** **infuriating** **infuriated** *(v)* to make someone very angry.

**ingenious** *(in-jee-nee-us) (adj)* clever and original. *An ingenious plan.* **ingenuity** *(n).*

**ingredient** *(n)* one of the items that something is made from, especially an item of food in a recipe.

**inhabit** **inhabiting** **inhabited** *(v)* to live somewhere. **inhabitant** *(n).*

**inhale** **inhaling** **inhaled** *(v)* to breathe in. **inhalation** *(n).*

**inhaler** *(n)* a container from which you take medicine by breathing it in.

**inherit** **inheriting** **inherited** 1 *(v)* to receive money, property, or a title from someone who has died. **inheritance** *(n).* 2 *(v)* If you **inherit** a characteristic, it is passed down from one of your parents.

**initial** 1 *(adj)* first, or at the beginning. *My initial reaction was to scream.* **initially** *(adv).* 2 *(n)* the first letter of a name.

**initiative** *(in-ish-er-tiv) (n)* If you use your **initiative**, you do what is needed without other people telling you what to do.

**inject** **injecting** **injected** *(v)* to use a needle and syringe to put medicine into someone's body. **injection** *(n).*

**injure** **injuring** **injured** *(v)* to hurt or harm someone.

**injury** **injuries** *(n)* damage, or harm.

**injustice** 1 *(n)* unfairness. 2 *(n)* an unfair situation or action. *You did me an injustice when you called me a liar.*

**ink** *(n)* a coloured liquid used for writing and printing. **inky** *(adj).*

**inland** *(adj)* away from the sea. *The hotel is five miles inland.*

**inn** *(n)* a pub, or a small hotel.

**inner** 1 *(adj)* inside, or nearest the centre. *A bicycle tyre has an inner tube.* 2 *(adj)* private. *Nobody can know your inner thoughts.*

**innocent** *(adj)* not guilty. **innocence** *(n).*

**innovation** *(n)* a new idea, or an invention. **innovate** *(v),* **innovative** *(adj).*

**inoculate** **inoculating** **inoculated** *(v)* to inject a weak form of a disease into someone's body, so that they become protected against it. **inoculation** *(n).*

**inpatient** *(n)* someone who stays in hospital while being treated.

**input** 1 *(n)* something that is contributed or put into something else. *Sue's input has helped the team.* 2 *(n)* information fed into a computer. **input** *(v).*

**inquest** *(n)* an official investigation to find out why someone has died.

**inquire** *or* **enquire** **inquiring** **inquired** *(v)* to ask about somebody or something.

**inquiry** *or* **enquiry** *(n)* a study, or an investigation, especially an official one.

**inquisitive** *(adj)* questioning, or curious. **inquisitiveness** *(n),* **inquisitively** *(adv).*

**insane** *(adj)* mad. **insanity** *(n).*

**inscribe** **inscribing** **inscribed** 1 *(v)* to carve or engrave letters on a surface. 2 *(v)* to write a special message or dedication in a book.

**inscription** *(n)* a carved, engraved, or specially written message.

**insect** *(n)* a small creature, usually with three pairs of legs, two pairs of wings, and three sections to its body.

**insecticide** *(n)* a chemical used to kill insects.

**insecure** 1 *(adj)* unsafe, or not fastened properly. *This lock is insecure.* 2 *(adj)* anxious and not confident. **insecurity** *(n).*

**insensitive** *(adj)* thoughtless and unsympathetic to other people's feelings.

**insert** **inserting** **inserted** *(v)* to put something carefully inside something else. *Insert a coin in the slot.* **insertion** *(n).*

**inside** 1 *(n)* the interior or inner part of something. **inside** *(adj).* 2 *(prep)* in less than. *We were back home inside an hour.* 3 *(prep)* within. *Put it inside the bag.* 4 *(adv)* into. *He went inside the house.*

**insight** *(n)* If you have **insight** into something or somebody, you understand something about them that is not obvious.

**insignificant** *(adj)* not important. **insignificance** *(n),* **insignificantly** *(adv).*

**insincere** *(adj)* Someone who is **insincere** is not genuine, or not honest.

**insist** **insisting insisted** *(v)* If you **insist** on something, you demand it very firmly. **insistence** *(n),* **insistent** *(adj).*

**insolent** *(adj)* insulting and rude. **insolence** *(n),* **insolently** *(adv).*

**insoluble** 1 *(adj)* An **insoluble** substance will not dissolve. 2 *(adj)* An **insoluble** problem cannot be solved.

**insomnia** *(singular n)* If you have **insomnia**, you often find it very hard to sleep. **insomniac** *(n).*

**inspect** **inspecting inspected** *(v)* to look at something carefully. **inspection** *(n).*

**inspector** *(n)* someone who checks or examines things. *Ticket inspector.*

**inspire** **inspiring inspired** *(v)* to influence and encourage someone to do something. **inspiration** *(n).*

**install** **installing installed** *(v)* to put something in place, ready to be used. *Can you install this computer?* **installation** *(n).*

**instalment** 1 *(n)* If you pay for something by **instalments**, you pay for it in regular small amounts over a period of time. 2 *(n)* one part of a serialized story.

**instance** *(n)* an example. *Nancy gave me several instances of when I had been late.*

**instant** 1 *(n)* a moment. 2 *(adj)* happening straightaway. *Instant results.*

**instead** *(adv)* in place of. *Bill went to the party instead of Ben.*

**instep** *(n)* the top of your foot, between your toes and your ankle.

**instinct** 1 *(n)* behaviour that is natural rather than learnt. *Ducks swim by instinct.* 2 *(n)* If you have an **instinct** about something, you know or feel something without being told. **instinctive** *(adj).*

**institute** *(n)* an organization set up to promote or represent the interests of a particular cause or group of people.

**institution** 1 *(n)* a large organization where people live or work together, such as a hospital or college. **institutional** *(adj).* 2 *(n)* a well-established custom or tradition. *Marriage is an institution.*

**instruct** **instructing instructed** 1 *(v)* to give an order. *Instruct the crew to set sail.* **instruction** *(n).* 2 *(v)* to teach a subject or skill. *Tim instructed me in judo.* **instructor** *(n).*

**instrument** 1 *(n)* a tool used for delicate or scientific work. *Surgical instruments.* 2 *(n)* an object that you use to make music.

**insulate** **insulating insulated** *(v)* to cover something with material in order to stop heat or electricity escaping from it. **insulation** *(n),* **insulating** *(adj).*

**insult** **insulting insulted** *(v)* to say or do something rude and upsetting to somebody. **insult** *(n),* **insulting** *(adj).*

**insurance** *(n)* When you take out **insurance**, you pay money to a company which agrees to pay you in the case of sickness, fire, accident, etc. **insured** *(adj).*

**intact** *(adj)* unharmed, or complete. *Our books survived the flood intact.*

**intake** 1 *(n)* the amount of people or things that are taken in. *A high intake of music students.* 2 *(n)* the act of taking something in. *A sharp intake of breath.*

**integrity** *(n)* If someone has **integrity**, they are honest and stick to their principles.

**intellectual** 1 *(adj)* involving thought and reason. 2 *(n)* someone who spends most of their time thinking and studying.

**intelligent** *(adj)* clever and quick to understand, think, and learn. **intelligence** *(n),* **intelligently** *(adv).*

**intend** **intending intended** *(v)* to mean to do something. *I intend to go to France.*

**intense** *(adj)* very strong. *Intense heat.*

**intention** *(n)* the thing that you mean to do. *It's my intention to win this race.*

**interactive** *(adj)* An **interactive** computer program allows users to make choices in order to control and change it in some ways. **interact** *(v).*

**intercept** **intercepting** **intercepted** *(v)* to stop the movement of something or someone from one place to another. *Our goalkeeper intercepted the ball.*

**intercom** *(n)* a microphone and speaker system which allows you to listen and talk to someone in another room or building.

**interest** **interesting** **interested** *(v)* If something **interests** you, you want to know more about it. **interest** *(n).*

**interfere** **interfering** **interfered** *(v)* to involve yourself in a situation that has nothing to do with you. **interfering** *(adj).*

**interference** **1** *(n)* involvement in something that has nothing to do with you. **2** *(n)* interruptions in a television or radio signal, which mean that you cannot see or hear the programme properly.

**intergalactic** *(adj)* between galaxies. *Intergalactic space travel.*

**interior** *(n)* the inside of something, especially a building. **interior** *(adj).*

**interjection** *(n)* a word used as a greeting, or to express surprise, pain, or delight. *"Ah!", "oh!", and "hello!" are all interjections. See* page 3.

**intermediate** *(adj)* in between two things, or in the middle.

**internal** *(adj)* happening or existing inside someone or something.

**international** *(adj)* involving different countries. **internationally** *(adv).*

**interpret** **interpreting** **interpreted** **1** *(v)* to decide what something means. *I interpreted Jim's wave as a sign of friendship.* **2** *(v)* to translate for two people who each speak a different language. **interpreter** *(n).*

**interrogate** **interrogating** **interrogated** *(v)* to question someone thoroughly. **interrogation** *(n).*

**interrupt** **interrupting** **interrupted** **1** *(v)* to stop something happening for a short time. *Vicky interrupted our game.* **2** *(v)* to start talking before someone else has finished.

**interval** *(n)* a time between events or parts of a play, concert, show, etc.

**intervene** **intervening** **intervened** *(v)* to get involved in a situation to change what is happening. **intervention** *(n).*

**interview** *(n)* a meeting when someone is asked questions. *A job interview. A television interview.* **interview** *(v).*

**intestines** *(plural n)* the very long tube through which food passes when it is digested. **intestinal** *(adj). See* **organ**.

**intimate** *(adj)* Friends who are **intimate** are very close and tell each other how they feel. **intimacy** *(n),* **intimately** *(adv).*

**intimidate** **intimidating** **intimidated** *(v)* to frighten someone into doing something. **intimidation** *(n).*

**intolerable** *(adj)* unbearable.

**intolerant** *(adj)* People who are **intolerant** get unreasonably angry when other people think or behave in a different way from them. **intolerance** *(n).*

**intrepid** *(adj)* An **intrepid** person is courageous and bold.

**intricate** *(adj)* detailed and complicated. *An intricate pattern.* **intricacy** *(n).*

**intrigue** **intriguing** **intrigued** *(v)* to fascinate or puzzle someone.

**introduce** **introducing** **introduced** *(v)* to bring people together for the first time and tell each one the other's name.

**introduction** **1** *(n)* Your **introduction** to something is your first experience of it. **2** *(n)* the act of introducing one person to another. **3** *(n)* the opening words of a book, speech, etc. **introductory** *(adj).*

**introvert** *(n)* someone who keeps their thoughts and feelings to themselves and is quite shy. **introverted** *(adj).*

**intrude** **intruding** **intruded** *(v)* to force your way into a place or a situation where you are not wanted or invited.

**intuition** *(n)* a feeling about something that cannot be explained logically.

**Inuit** *(n)* a person or a race of people from the Arctic north of Canada, America, and Greenland. Inuits are also known as Eskimos. *This Inuit is fishing through a hole in the ice.* **Inuit** *(adj).*

**Inuit**

**inundate** **inundating** **inundated** **1** *(v)* to flood.

2 *(v)* to overwhelm someone with a large quantity of something. *My friends inundated me with presents.*

**invade** **invading** **invaded** *(v)* to send armed forces into another country in order to take it over. **invasion** *(n).*

**invalid** 1 *(in-va-lid) (n)* someone who is disabled, or who is seriously ill. 2 *(in-**val**-id) (adj)* If a ticket, library card, etc. is **invalid**, it cannot be used.

**invaluable** *(adj)* very useful indeed.

**invent** **inventing** **invented** 1 *(v)* to think of an orginal machine, device, idea, etc. **invention** *(n),* **inventor** *(n).* 2 *(v)* to make something up. *Leon invented a story to entertain his sister.* **invention** *(n).*

**inverted commas** *(n)* signs, (") or ('), used in writing to show that someone is speaking. Inverted commas are sometimes called speech marks or quotation marks.

**invest** **investing** **invested** *(v)* to give time or effort to something. *I've invested a lot of time in practising the trumpet.*

**investigate** **investigating** **investigated** *(v)* If you **investigate** something, like a crime, you find out as much as possible about it. **investigation** *(n).*

**invisible** *(adj)* Something that is **invisible** cannot be seen. **invisibility** *(n).*

**invite** **inviting** **invited** *(v)* to ask someone to do something, or to go somewhere. **invitation** *(n).*

**invoice** *(n)* a written request for payment for a job or something you have sold.

**involve** **involving** **involved** *(v)* to include something as a necessary part. *The project involves field work.*

**involved** *(adj)* taking part in something. *I was involved in the play.*

**inward** *or* **inwards** *(adv)* towards the inside.

**IQ** *(n)* a measure of a person's intelligence. The initials IQ stand for intelligence quotient.

**irate** *(adj)* angry, or very annoyed.

**iron** 1 *(n)* a strong, hard metal used to make things like gates and railings. Iron is also found in some foods and in your blood. 2 *(n)* a piece of electrical equipment, used to smooth creases out of clothing. **iron** *(v).*

**ironic** 1 *(adj)* If a situation is **ironic**, the opposite happens to what you would expect. *It was ironic that clumsy Rick should become a famous ballet dancer.* **irony** *(n).* 2 *(adj)* mildly sarcastic. *Rosa gave an ironic smile.* **irony** *(n).*

**irrational** 1 *(adj)* not sensible, or not logical. **irrationally** *(adv).* 2 *(adj)* insane, or unreasonable. **irrationally** *(adv).*

**irregular** *(adj)* not regular in shape, timing, size, etc. *An irregular bus service.*

**irrelevant** *(adj)* If something is **irrelevant**, it has nothing to do with a particular subject. *Irrelevant details.*

**irresponsible** *(adj)* reckless and not capable of taking responsibility.

**irrigate** **irrigating** **irrigated** *(v)* to supply water to crops by digging channels and laying pipes. **irrigation** *(n).*

**irritable** *(adj)* bad-tempered and grumpy.

**irritate** **irritating** **irritated** *(v)* to make someone feel annoyed. **irritation** *(n).*

**Islam** *(n)* the religion based on the teachings of Mohammed. Muslims believe that Allah is God and Mohammed is his prophet. Islam is based on prayer, fasting, charity, and pilgrimage. **Islamic** *(adj).*

**island** *(n)* land surrounded by water.

**isolate** **isolating** **isolated** *(v)* to keep someone or something separate, or on their own. **isolation** *(n).*

**isosceles** *(eye-**soss**-il-eez) (adj)* An **isosceles** triangle has two equal sides.

**issue** 1 *(n)* an edition of a newspaper or magazine. 2 *(n)* the main topic for debate or decision.

**IT** *short for* **information technology.**

**italic** *(n)* sloping print, used to emphasize certain words or to make them stand out. The word *italic* is printed in italic.

**itch** **itches** **itching** **itched** *(v)* If your skin **itches**, it is uncomfortable and you want to scratch it. **itch** *(n),* **itchy** *(adj).*

**item** *(n)* one of a number of things. *An item of clothing.*

**itinerary** **itineraries** *(n)* a detailed plan of a journey.

**ivy** **ivies** *(n)* an evergreen climbing or trailing plant, which has pointed leaves.

**ivy**

# Jj

**jab** **jabbing jabbed** 1 *(v)* to poke somebody with something sharp. *Katy jabbed her elbow into my ribs.* 2 *(n)* *(informal)* an injection. *A flu jab.*

**jabber** **jabbering jabbered** *(v)* to talk in a fast and excitable way that is hard to understand.

**jack** 1 *(n)* a tool used to raise a vehicle off the ground for repair. **jack** *(v).* 2 *(n)* a picture playing card with a value between that of a ten and a queen. The jack is sometimes called the knave.

**jackal** *(n)* a kind of wild dog that feeds off the dead bodies of other animals.

**jacket** *(n)* a piece of clothing worn on the top half of your body, with a front opening and long sleeves.

**jackknife** **jackknifing jackknifed** *(v)* When an articulated truck **jackknifes**, the trailer swings around at right angles to the direction of travel and the driver loses control.

**jacuzzi** *(n)* a large bath with underwater jets of water which massage your skin.

**jade** *(n)* a green, semiprecious stone, used for making ornaments and jewellery. *The picture shows a jade death mask made by the Mayas, an ancient civilization of Central America*

**jade death mask**

**jagged** *(jag-ed)* *(adj)* uneven and sharp. *A jagged edge.*

**jaguar** *(n)* a large wild cat, like a leopard, found in South and Central America.

**jaguar**

**jail** *or* **gaol** *(n)* a prison. **jailer** *(n).*

**jam** **jamming jammed** 1 *(n)* a sweet, sticky food, made from boiled fruit and sugar. 2 *(n)* a situation in which things cannot move. *A traffic jam.* 3 *(v)* to squeeze or wedge something into place. *Alvin jammed his bag into the locker.* 4 *(n)* *(informal)* a difficult situation. 5 *(v)* *(informal)* When musicians **jam**, they make up music as they play together.

**jangle** **jangling jangled** *(v)* to make a loud, unpleasant, ringing sound.

**jar** **jarring jarred** 1 *(n)* a small glass container with an airtight lid. 2 *(v)* to jolt or shake something or someone. *The fall jarred my knee.*

**jargon** *(n)* words used by people in a particular business or activity, that other people cannot easily understand.

**jaunt** *(n)* a short pleasure trip or outing.

**jaunty** **jauntier jauntiest** *(adj)* giving a carefree and self-confident impression. *Sophie wore a jaunty cap.* **jauntily** *(adv).*

**javelin** *(n)* a pointed, light, metal spear, thrown in an athletics event.

**jaw** 1 *(n)* one of the two bones between your nose and your chin that hold your teeth. *See* **skeleton**. 2 *(n)* the lower part of your face.

**jaywalk** **jaywalking jaywalked** *(v)* to cross a street carelessly, taking no notice of traffic or signals. **jaywalker** *(n).*

**jazz** *(n)* a lively, rhythmical type of music in which players often make up tunes.

**jazzy** **jazzier jazziest** *(adj)* *(informal)* Jazzy clothes are noticeable, and often have bright colours and a strong pattern.

**jealous** *(adj)* If you are **jealous** of someone, you want what they have. **jealousy** *(n),* **jealously** *(adv).*

**jeep** *(n)* an open vehicle, used for driving over rough country.

**jeer** **jeering jeered** *(v)* to make fun of someone in a loud, unpleasant way.

**Jehovah** *(n)* a name for God in the Old Testament.

**jellyfish** **jellyfish or jellyfishes** *(n)* a sea creature with a jelly-like body and trailing tentacles.

**jeopardy** *(jep-er-dee)* *(n)* If someone's job or life is in **jeopardy**, it is in danger or is threatened in some way.

**jerk** **jerking jerked** *(v)* to move suddenly, or to pull something suddenly and sharply. **jerky** *(adj).*

**jester** *(n)* an entertainer at a court in the Middle Ages.

**jet** 1 *(n)* a high-pressure stream of liquid or gas. 2 *(n)* an aircraft powered by jet engines.

**jet engine** *(n)* an engine that creates the forward thrust needed to move an aircraft, boat, etc. by sucking in air or water, and forcing it out at the rear.

**jet lag** *(n)* a feeling of tiredness and confusion after a long flight.

**jetty** jetties *(n)* a structure built out into the sea, where boats moor and unload.

**Jew** 1 *(n)* someone who belongs to the race of people descended from the ancient tribes of Israel. Jewish *(adj)*. 2 *(n)* someone who practises the religion of Judaism.

**jewel** *(n)* a precious stone such as a diamond, ruby, or emerald.

**jewellery** *(n)* ornaments that you wear, such as rings, bracelets, and necklaces, made of jewels, gold, etc.

**jigsaw** *(n)* a wooden or cardboard puzzle made up of pieces of a picture that have been cut up and have to be put back together.

**jinx** jinxes *(n)* something that is supposed to bring bad luck.

**job** 1 *(n)* a task. 2 *(n)* the work that someone does for a living.

**jockey** *(n)* someone who rides horses in races.

**jodhpurs** *(jod-pers) (plural n)* trousers that you wear for horse riding.

**jog** jogging jogged 1 *(v)* to run at a slow, steady pace. jogger *(n)*, jogging *(n)*. 2 *(v)* to knock something by accident.

**join** joining joined 1 *(v)* to fasten or tie two things together. join *(n)*. 2 *(v)* to come together with something or someone. *Please join us for supper.* 3 *(v)* to become a member of a club or group.

**joint** 1 *(adj)* done or shared by two or more people. *A joint effort.* 2 *(n)* a large piece of meat. 3 *(n)* a place where two bones meet, for example, your knee.

**joke** joking joked *(v)* to say funny things or play tricks on people in order to make them laugh. joke *(n)*.

**jolly** jollier jolliest 1 *(adj)* happy and cheerful. 2 *(adv)* very. *Jolly good!*

**jolt** jolting jolted 1 *(v)* to move roughly. *The cart jolted along the track.* jolt *(n)*. 2 *(v)* to bump into or knock someone or something. jolt *(n)*.

**jot** jotting jotted *(v)* to write something down quickly. *I jotted down some ideas.*

**joule** *(n)* a unit for measuring energy or work done.

**journal** 1 *(n)* a diary in which you write what you have done each day. 2 *(n)* a serious magazine.

**journalist** *(n)* someone who collects information and writes articles for newspapers and magazines. journalism *(n)*, journalistic *(adj)*.

**journey** *(n)* a trip from one place to another. journey *(v)*.

**joust** *(n)* a contest between two knights, riding horses and armed with lances. *The picture shows a medieval joust.*

jousting knights

**jovial** *(adj)* Someone who is **jovial** is cheerful and enjoys talking and laughing with other people. jovially *(adv)*.

**joy** 1 *(n)* a feeling of great happiness. 2 *(n) (informal)* good luck, or success. *I asked my dad for some money, but I didn't have any joy.*

**joyful** *(adj)* very happy. joyfulness *(n)*, joyfully *(adv)*.

**joyride** *(n)* a ride in a stolen car for the thrill of it. joyrider *(n)*, joyriding *(n)*.

**joystick** *(n)* a lever used to control movement in a computer game or in an aircraft.

**jubilant** *(adj)* very happy and delighted. *Josh was jubilant about winning the race.* jubilation *(n)*, jubilantly *(adv)*.

**jubilee** *(n)* a big celebration to mark the anniversary of a special event.

**Judaism** *(n)* the religion of the Jewish people, based on the law of Moses. Jews believe that they are God's chosen people. *The picture shows the symbol of Judaism, the six-pointed star of David.*

**judge** **judging judged** **1** *(v)* to hear cases in a law court and decide how a guilty person should be punished. **judge** *(n)*. **2** *(v)* to decide who is the winner of a competition. **judge** *(n)*.

**judgment** *or* **judgement** **1** *(n)* the ability to decide or judge something. **2** *(n)* a decision made by a judge.

**judo** *(n)* a sport in which two people fight each other using controlled movements, and each tries to throw the other to the ground. *This sequence shows a basic forward throw in judo, called Harai goshi.*

**judo** (forward throw)

**jug** *(n)* a container with a lip for pouring liquids.

**juggle** **juggling juggled** *(v)* to keep a set of balls, clubs, or other objects moving through the air by repeatedly throwing them up and catching them again, one after another. **juggler** *(n)*, **juggling** *(n)*.

**juggling equipment**

**juice** *(n)* liquid that comes out of fruit, vegetables, or meat. **juicy** *(adj)*.

**jukebox** **jukeboxes** *(n)* a machine that plays records when you put coins into it.

**jumble** **jumbling jumbled** **1** *(v)* to mix things up so that they are untidy and not well organized. **jumble** *(n)*. **2 jumble sale** *(n)* a sale of second-hand clothes and other objects, usually to raise money for charity or other good causes.

**jumbo** **1** *(adj)* very large. *A jumbo packet.* **2 jumbo jet** *(n) (informal)* a very large jet aircraft that can carry hundreds of passengers.

**jump** **jumping jumped** **1** *(v)* to leap, or to spring. **jump** *(n)*. **2** *(n)* an object that you jump over. *The horse fell at the last jump.* **3** *(v)* If you **jump at** something, you accept it eagerly.

**junction** *(n)* a place where roads or railway lines meet or join each other.

**jungle** *(n)* a thick, tropical forest.

**junior** **1** *(adj)* not very important in rank or position. *A junior manager.* **2** *(n)* someone who is younger than someone else. **3** *(adj)* for young children. *A junior encyclopedia.* **4** *(n)* a schoolchild aged between eight and eleven years.

**junk** **1** *(singular n)* things that are worthless or useless. *My room is full of junk!* **2 junk food** *(n)* food that is bad for you because it contains a lot of fat, sugar, and chemical additives. **3 junk mail** *(n)* advertising leaflets and letters that you receive without having asked for them.

**jury** **juries** *(n)* a group of people at a trial who decide whether the person accused of a crime is innocent or guilty.

**just** **1** *(adj)* fair and right. *A just decision.* **justly** *(adv)*. **2** *(adv)* exactly. *I'm sure I put the book just there.* **3** *(adv)* very recently. *I'm afraid that Humphrey has just left.*

**justice** **1** *(n)* fairness and rightness. **2** *(n)* the system of laws and punishments in a country.

**justify** **justifies justifying justified** *(v)* If you **justify** an action, you give a reason or explanation to show that it is necessary and acceptable. **justification** *(n)*.

**jut** **jutting jutted** *(v)* to stick out. *The cliff jutted into the sea.*

**juvenile** **1** *(n)* a young person who is not yet an adult, according to the law. **juvenile** *(adj)*. **2** *(adj)* childish. *Juvenile behaviour.* **3 juvenile delinquent** *(n)* a young person who breaks the law.

# Kk

**kaleidoscope** *(n)* a tube through which you see changing patterns made by mirrors and pieces of coloured glass.

**kangaroo** *(n)* a large Australian mammal that carries its young in a pouch.

**karaoke** *(ka-ree-**yoh**-kee) (n)* an entertainment in which people sing the words of popular songs while a machine plays the backing music.

**karate** *(ka-**rah**-tee) (n)* a sport in which two people fight using controlled movements, especially kicking with their feet and chopping with their hands.

**kayak** *(**ky**-ak) (n)* a covered, narrow boat in which you sit and move through the water by paddling with a double-bladed paddle.

**kayak**

**kebab** *(n)* small pieces of meat or vegetables, cooked on a skewer.

**keen keener keenest 1** *(adj)* enthusiastic and eager. *Kim is keen to join the team.* **2** If you are **keen on** someone or something, you like them very much.

**keep keeping kept 1** *(v)* to have something and not get rid of it. *Let's keep these books.* **2** *(v)* to stay the same. *Try to keep warm.* **3** *(v)* to continue doing something. *Debbie kept laughing at me.*

**keeper** *(n)* someone who looks after an animal, a park, or a museum collection.

**kennel 1** *(n)* a small hut for a dog to sleep in. **2 kennels** *(plural n)* a place where dogs are looked after while their owners are away.

**kerb** *(n)* the line of stones or concrete along the edge of a pavement.

**ketchup** *(n)* a thick tomato sauce.

**kettle** *(n)* a container with a handle and a spout, used for boiling water.

**key 1** *(n)* a shaped piece of metal used for opening a lock, starting a car, etc. **2** *(n)* one of the buttons on a computer or typewriter. **3** *(n)* one of the black and white bars that you press on a piano.

**keyboard 1** *(n)* the set of keys on a computer, typewriter, piano, etc. **2** *(n)* An **electronic keyboard** has keys like a piano, and controls to produce other sounds, and is worked by electricity.

**khaki** *(**kar**-kee) (n)* a yellowish-brown colour, often used for soldiers' uniforms.

**kibbutz** *(kib-**ootz**)* **kibbutzim** *(n)* a small community in Israel in which all the people live and work together.

**kick kicking kicked 1** *(v)* to hit something with your foot. **kick** *(n).* **2** *(n) (informal)* a feeling of excitement.

**kid kidding kidded 1** *(n)* a young goat. **2** *(n) (informal)* a child. **3** *(v) (informal)* to tell someone something untrue, as a joke.

**kidnap kidnapping kidnapped** *(v)* to capture someone and keep them until certain demands are met. **kidnapper** *(n).*

**kidney** *(n)* Your **kidneys** are the organs in your body that remove waste matter from your blood and make urine. *See* **organ**.

**kill killing killed** *(v)* to end the life of a person or an animal. **killer** *(n).*

**kiln** *(n)* a very hot oven, used to bake objects made of clay until they are hard and dry.

**kilt** *(n)* a pleated, tartan skirt worn by Scottish men as a traditional costume.

**kimono** *(n)* a long, loose dress with wide sleeves and a sash, worn by Japanese women.

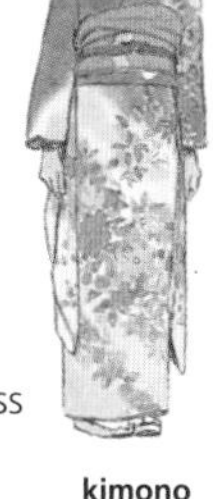
**kimono**

**kind kinder kindest 1** *(adj)* friendly, helpful, and generous. **2** *(n)* a type, or a sort.

**kindle kindling kindled 1** *(v)* to make something start to burn. *Claire kindled a fire.* **2** *(v)* to get something started. *The film kindled my interest in history.*

*Some words that begin with a "k" sound are spelt with a "c".*

**king** 1 *(n)* a man from a royal family who is the ruler of his country. 2 *(n)* a chesspiece that can move one square in any direction. *See* **chess**. 3 *(n)* a playing card with a picture of a king on it.

**kingdom** 1 *(n)* a country that has a king or queen as its ruler. 2 *(n)* a part of the natural world. *The animal kingdom.*

**kingfisher** *(n)* a small, brightly coloured bird that catches fish for food.

**kingfisher**

**kiosk** *(n)* a small stall from which sweets, newspapers, magazines, etc. are sold.

**kip** *(n)* *(slang)* a short sleep. **kip** *(v)*.

**kiss kisses kissing kissed** *(v)* to touch someone with your lips to greet them or show that you like or love them. **kiss** *(n)*.

**kit** 1 *(n)* the clothes and equipment that you need to play a sport. *Football kit.* 2 *(n)* a collection of parts that you fix together to make something. *A model plane kit.*

**kitchen** *(n)* a room in which food is prepared and cooked.

**kite** *(n)* a frame covered with paper or material which is flown in the wind, attached to a long piece of string. *The picture shows a stunt kite.*

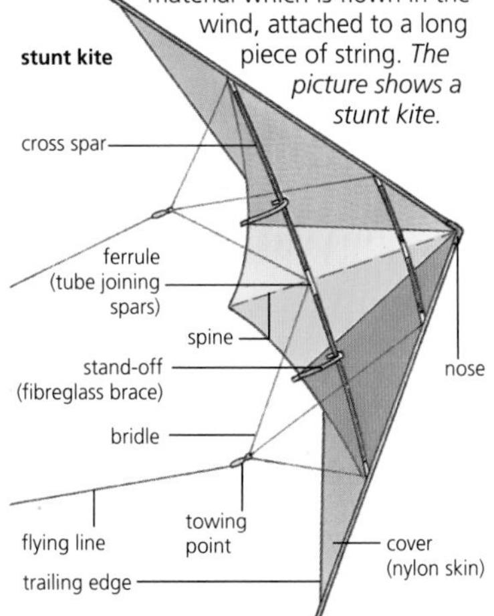


**kitten** *(n)* a young cat.

**kitty kitties** *(n)* an amount of money contributed by everyone in a group and then used to buy something.

**kiwi** 1 *(n)* a bird from New Zealand that cannot fly. 2 *(n)* *(informal)* a name for someone who comes from New Zealand.

**knack** *(n)* an ability to do something difficult or tricky.

**knave** *(n)* a picture playing card with a value between that of a ten and a queen. The knave is also called the jack.

**knead kneading kneaded** *(v)* When you **knead** dough, you punch and stretch dough to make it smooth.

**knee** *(n)* the joint between your upper and lower leg.

**kneel kneeling knelt** *(v)* to bend your legs and put your knees on the ground.

**knife knives** *(n)* a tool with a sharp blade, used for cutting things.

**knight** 1 *(n)* In medieval times, a **knight** was a warrior who fought on horseback. *See* **joust**. 2 *(n)* a chesspiece with a horse's head that always has to move three squares at a time. *See* **chess**.

**knit knitting knitted** 1 *(v)* to make things of wool, using two long, pointed needles. **knitting** *(n)*. 2 *(v)* When a bone **knits**, it heals after it has been broken.

**knob** 1 *(n)* a small, round handle on a drawer or door. 2 *(n)* a control button on a machine.

**knock knocking knocked** 1 *(v)* to bang or hit something. *Knock the nails into the wall with a hammer.* **knock** *(n)*. 2 **knock out** *(v)* to make someone unconscious.

**knocker** *(n)* a piece of metal attached to a door that you use to knock on the door.

**knot** *(n)* a fastening made by looping and twisting string or rope together. **knot** *(v)*.

**know knowing knew known** *(v)* to be familiar with a person, place, or piece of information.

**knowledge** *(singular n)* the things that someone or everyone knows.

**knuckle** *(n)* one of the joints where your fingers join your hand.

**koala** *(n)* an Australian mammal that looks like a small bear and lives in trees.

**Koran** *or* **Qur'an** *(n)* the holy book of Islam.

**kosher** *(adj)* **Kosher** food is food that has been prepared according to the laws of the Jewish religion.

*Some words that begin with a "k" sound are spelt with a "c".*

# Ll

**label** 1 *(n)* a piece of paper, cloth, plastic, etc. that is attached to something and gives information about it. **label** *(v)*. 2 *(n)* a word or phrase explaining something. *Picture labels.* **label** *(v)*.

**laboratory** laboratories *(n)* a room containing special equipment for people to use in scientific experiments.

**labour** labouring laboured 1 *(v)* to work hard. **labour** *(n)*. 2 *(n)* the work of giving birth to a baby. 3 **Labour Party** *(n)* one of the main political parties in Britain, which believes in social equality and the importance of the welfare state.

**lace** 1 *(n)* thin material made from cotton and silk, with a pattern of small holes and delicate stitches. **lacy** *(adj)*. 2 **laces** *(plural n)* long pieces of thin cord used to tie shoes. **lace** *(v)*.

**lack** lacking lacked *(v)* to be without something that you need. *The refugees lack food.* **lack** *(n)*.

**ladder** 1 *(n)* a metal, wooden, or rope structure that you use to climb up and down. Ladders are made from two long side pieces linked by a series of cross-pieces, called rungs. 2 *(n)* a long tear in a pair of tights or stockings. **ladder** *(v)*.

**laden** *(adj)* carrying a lot of things. *Matt arrived laden with presents.*

**ladle** *(n)* a large, deep spoon with a long handle, used for serving soup, casseroles, etc.

**lady** ladies *(n)* a polite name for a woman.

**lag** lagging lagged 1 *(v)* to cover water pipes with a thick material to stop them freezing in cold weather. **lagging** *(n)*. 2 *(v)* If you **lag behind** other people, you do not keep up with them.

**lagoon** *(n)* a large pool of seawater separated from the sea by a bank of sand.

**laid-back** *(adj) (informal)* very relaxed and calm.

**lair** *(n)* a place where a wild animal rests and sleeps.

**lake** *(n)* a large area of fresh water surrounded by land.

**lamb** 1 *(n)* a young sheep. 2 *(n)* meat from a young sheep.

**lame** lamer lamest 1 *(adj)* unable to walk properly, because of an injured leg. **lameness** *(n)*. 2 *(adj)* unconvincing, or weak. *A lame excuse.* **lamely** *(adv)*.

**lamp** *(n)* a light that uses gas, oil, or electricity.

**lance** *(n)* a long spear used in the past by soldiers riding horses.

**land** landing landed 1 *(n)* the part of the Earth's surface that is not covered by water. 2 *(v)* to come down from the air to the ground. *The plane landed safely.* 3 *(v) (informal)* to succeed in getting something. *I've landed a place in the team.*

**landfill** *(n)* rubbish and waste that is buried under the ground in large holes.

**landing** *(n)* an area of floor at the top of a staircase.

**landlady** landladies 1 *(n)* a woman who rents out a room, house, or flat. 2 *(n)* a woman who owns or runs a pub.

**landlord** 1 *(n)* a man who rents out a room, house, or flat. 2 *(n)* a man who owns or runs a pub.

**landmark** 1 *(n)* an object in a landscape that can be seen from a long way away. 2 *(n)* an important event in someone or something's development. *Leaving home was a landmark in Finn's life.*

**landscape** *(n)* a large area of land that you can view from one place.

**landslide** *(n)* a sudden fall of earth and rocks down the side of a mountain or hill.

**lane** 1 *(n)* a narrow road or street. 2 *(n)* one of the strips marked on a main road, that is wide enough for a single line of vehicles. 3 *(n)* one of the strips into which a race track or swimming pool is divided.

**language** 1 *(n)* the words that people use to talk and write to each other. 2 *(n)* a set of signs, symbols, or movements used to express meaning. *Sign language.*

**lanky** lankier lankiest *(adj)* Someone who is **lanky** is very tall and thin.

**lantern** *(n)* a candle with a protective frame around it.

**lap** **lapping lapped 1** *(n)* the flat area formed by the top part of your legs when you are sitting down. *Sit on my lap.* **2** *(n)* the distance around a running track. **3** *(v)* When water **laps** against something, it moves gently against it. **4** *(v)* When an animal **laps up** a drink, it flicks the liquid up into its mouth with its tongue.

**lapel** *(n)* part of the collar of a coat or jacket, that folds back over your chest.

**lapse 1** *(n)* a small mistake or failure. *Katy has been studying hard, with a slight lapse last week.* **lapse** *(v).* **2** *(n)* the passing of time. *After a lapse of two years, Jo-Jo returned.*

**laptop** *(n)* a portable computer that is so small and light you can use it on your lap.

**large** **larger largest 1** *(adj)* big. **largeness** *(n).* **2** If a person or an animal is **at large**, they are free.

**lark** *(n)* a small, brown bird that flies very high in the sky and has an attractive song.

**larva** **larvae** *(n)* an insect at the stage of development between an egg and a pupa.

**laryngitis** *(la-rin-**jy**-tuss) (n)* a swelling of the throat caused by an infection.

**larynx** *(**la**-rinx) (n)* the top of your windpipe, which holds your vocal cords.

**lasagne** *(laz-**an**-ya) (n)* an Italian dish made with layers of pasta and meat or vegetables, covered with a cheese sauce.

**laser 1** *(n)* a machine that makes a very narrow, powerful beam of light which can be used for light shows or for cutting things. **2 laser beam** *(n)* a concentrated beam of light, made by a laser.

**lash** **lashes lashing lashed 1** *(n)* a stroke with a whip. **2** *(v)* to tie things together very firmly using rope. **3** *(n)* one of the small hairs growing around your eyes.

**lasso** *(lass-**oo**)* **lassos** *or* **lassoes** *(n)* a length of rope with a large loop at one end, which can be thrown over an animal to catch it. **lasso** *(v).*

**last** **lasting lasted 1** *(adj)* coming at the end or after everything else. *Nelson's last words.* **lastly** *(adv).* **2** *(adj)* most recent. *Last week.* **3** *(v)* to go on for a certain length of time. *The trip will last ten days.*

**lasting** *(adj)* Something that is **lasting** keeps going for a long time.

**latch** **latches 1** *(n)* a lock or fastening for a door. **latch** *(v).* **2** If you leave a door **on the latch**, you close it, but do not lock it.

**late** **later latest 1** *(adj)* coming after the expected time. **lateness** *(n).* **2** *(adj)* near the end of a period of time. *The late 20th century.* **3** *(adj)* no longer alive. *The late Elvis Presley.*

**lately** *(adv)* recently.

**lateral 1** *(adj)* on or towards the side. **laterally** *(adv).* **2 lateral thinking** *(n)* the ability to think about problems in an unusual and not obvious way.

**lather** *(n)* a mass of white bubbles formed when soap is mixed with water.

**Latin** *(n)* the language of the Ancient Romans.

**latitude** *(n)* the position of a place, measured in degrees north or south of the equator.

**latter** *(n)* the second of two things just mentioned. *I like apples and pears, but I prefer the latter.*

**laugh** **laughing laughed** *(v)* to make a sound to show that you think something is funny. **laugh** *(n),* **laughter** *(n).*

**laughable** *(adj)* ridiculous and impossible to take seriously. *A laughable speech.*

**launch** **launches launching launched 1** *(v)* to put a large ship in the water for the first time. **launch** *(n).* **2** *(v)* to send a rocket into space. **launch** *(n).* **3** *(v)* to start or introduce something new. *The charity launched a fundraising campaign.* **launch** *(n).* **4 launch pad** *(n)* a place where rockets leave the ground to go into space.

**launderette** *(n)* a place where you pay to use washing machines and spin-dryers.

**laundry** **laundries 1** *(n)* clothes, towels, and sheets that are being washed or are about to be washed. **2** *(n)* a place where washing is done.

**lavatory** **lavatories** *(n)* a toilet.

**lavender** *(n)* a plant with pale purple flowers that has a pleasant smell.

**lavish** *(adj)* generous, or extravagant. *Lavish gifts.* **lavishly** *(adv).*

**law 1** *(n)* a rule made by the government that must be obeyed. **2** *(n)* a statement or principle in science, maths, etc. *The law of gravity.*

**law-abiding** *(adj)* If you are **law-abiding**, you obey the laws of a country.

**lawful** *(adj)* permitted by the law.

**lawn** *(n)* a piece of grass, usually next to a house.

**lawyer** *(n)* someone who advises people about the law and speaks for them in court.

**lax** *(adj)* relaxed, or not strict.

**laxative** *(n)* a medicine or food that you eat to help you empty your bowels.

**lay** **laying** **laid** **1** *(v)* to put, or to place. *Lay the clothes on the bed.* **2** *(v)* to produce an egg.

**lay-by** *(n)* a place by the side of the road where drivers can park.

**layer** *(n)* a thickness of something. *Layers of paint.* **layered** *(adj).*

**layout** *(n)* the pattern or design of something. *The layout of a book.*

**lazy** **lazier** **laziest** *(adj)* If you are **lazy**, you do not want to work or exercise. **laziness** *(n),* **laze** *(v),* **lazily** *(adv).*

**lead** **leading** **led** **1** *(leed) (v)* to show someone the way, usually by going in front of them. **leader** *(n).* **2** *(leed) (v)* to be in charge. **leader** *(n),* **leadership** *(n).* **3** *(led) (n)* a soft, grey metal. **4** *(leed) (n)* a suggestion, or a clue. *The police have several new leads.* **5** *(leed) (n)* a long strip attached to a collar, that you use to hold and control a dog.

**leaf** **leaves** *(n)* a flat and usually green part of a plant or tree, that grows out from a stem, twig, branch, etc. **leafy** *(adj).*

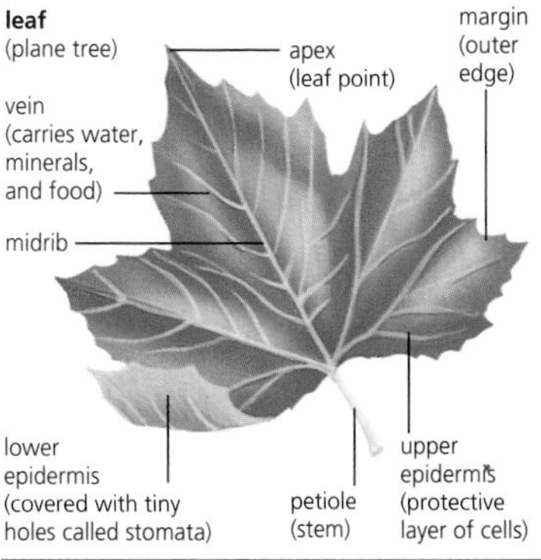


**leaflet** *(n)* a printed, and usually folded, piece of paper that gives information, or advertises something.

**league** *(leeg) (n)* a group of people, countries, or teams who have a shared interest or activity. *A football league.*

**leak** **leaking** **leaked** **1** *(v)* If a container **leaks**, it lets liquid or gas escape from it. **leak** *(n),* **leaky** *(adj).* **2** *(v)* If a liquid or gas **leaks**, it escapes through a hole or crack in a container. **leak** *(n).*

**lean** **leaning** **leant** *or* **leaned; leaner** **leanest** **1** *(v)* to bend towards or over something. *The mother leant over her baby.* **2** *(v)* to slope. *Look how that wall leans!* **3** *(v)* to rest your body against something for support. **4** *(adj)* slim and muscular. **5** *(adj)* If meat is **lean**, it has very little or no fat.

**leaning** *(n)* If you have a **leaning** towards something, you are interested in it or good at it.

**leap** **leaping** **leapt** *or* **leaped** *(v)* to jump over something, or to jump. **leap** *(n).*

**leap year** *(n)* a year that has 366 days, because there is an extra day in February. A leap year comes every fourth year.

**learn** **learning** **learnt** *or* **learned** **1** *(v)* to gain knowledge or a skill. **2** *(v)* to discover some news. *I learnt that Al was leaving.*

**leash** **leashes** *(n)* a long strip attached to a collar, that you use to hold and control a dog.

**least** **1** *(n)* the smallest amount. *Of all the children, Dan eats the least.* **least** *(adj).* **2** *(adv)* less than anything else. *Turnip is my least favourite vegetable.* **3** **at least** as a minimum. *I need at least three days off.*

**leather** *(n)* animal skin that is treated and used to make shoes, bags, and other goods. **leathery** *(adj).*

**leave** **leaving** **left** **1** *(v)* to go away. **2** *(v)* to let something stay or remain. *Leave the dishes, I'll do them later.* **3** *(n)* time away from work. **4** **leave behind** *(v)* If you **leave something behind**, you do not bring it. **5** **leave out** *(v)* If you **leave something out**, you do not include it.

**lecture** **1** *(n)* a talk given to a class or an audience in order to teach them something. **lecturer** *(n).* **2** *(n)* a telling-off that lasts a long time. **lecture** *(v).*

**ledge** *(n)* a narrow shelf. *A window ledge. A mountain ledge.*

**leek** *(n)* a long, white vegetable with green leaves at one end.

**left** 1 *(adj)* This page is on the **left** hand side of the book. **left** *(n),* **left** *(adv).* 2 In politics, people **on the left** support equal distribution of wealth and workers' rights.

**left-wing** *(adj)* believing in equal distribution of wealth and in workers' rights. **left wing** *(n),* **left-winger** *(n).*

**leg** 1 *(n)* the part of your body between your hip and your foot. 2 *(n)* one of the parts that support a chair, table, etc.

**legacy** **legacies** *(n)* money or property that has been left to someone in a will.

**legal** 1 *(adj)* to do with the law. *Legal documents.* 2 *(adj)* lawful, or allowed by law. **legally** *(adv).*

**legend** 1 *(n)* an old, well-known story. 2 *(n)* a very famous person. **legendary** *(adj).*

**legible** *(adj)* If handwriting or print is **legible**, it can be read easily.

**legislation** *(singular n)* laws. *Traffic legislation.* **legislate** *(v).*

**legitimate** 1 *(adj)* lawful, or acceptable. **legitimately** *(adv).* 2 *(adj)* A **legitimate** child is born to parents who are married.

**leisure** 1 *(n)* free time when you do not have to work. 2 **leisure centre** *(n)* a place where you can take part in activities such as swimming, badminton, etc.

**leisurely** *(adj)* unhurried. *We enjoyed a long, leisurely breakfast.*

**lemon** *(n)* a yellow citrus fruit with a thick skin.

**lemonade** *(n)* a sweet, fizzy drink that is sometimes lemon-flavoured.

**lend** **lending** **lent** *(v)* to let someone have something for a short time.

**length** 1 *(n)* the distance from one end of something to the other. 2 *(n)* the time from the start of something to the end.

**lengthen** **lengthening** **lengthened** *(v)* to make something longer.

**lengthways** *(adv)* in the direction of the longest side. *Fold the paper lengthways.*

**lenient** *(lee-nee-ent) (adj)* gentle and not strict. **leniently** *(adv).*

**lens** **lenses** 1 *(n)* the part of your eye that focuses light. 2 *(n)* a piece of curved glass or plastic in a pair of glasses or in a camera, telescope, etc. Lenses bend light to magnify or focus a picture. *The diagram shows how concave and convex lenses make light rays bend in different ways.*

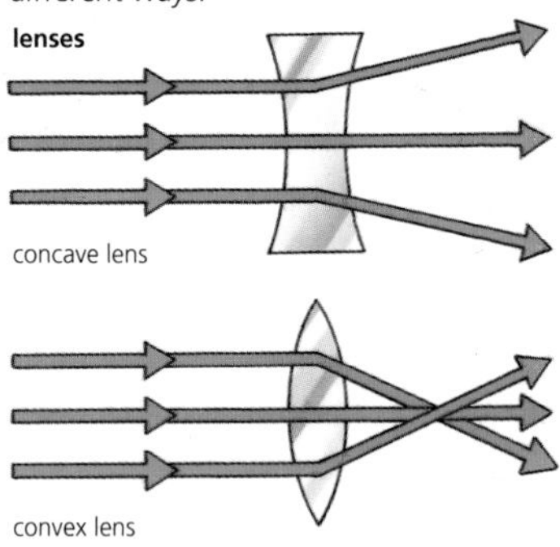


**lentil** *(n)* a small, dried seed that can be cooked and eaten.

**leopard** *(lep-erd) (n)* a large wild cat with a spotted coat.

**leotard** *(n)* a tight, one-piece garment worn for dancing or exercise.

**lesbian** *(adj)* Women who are **lesbian** have sexual feelings for other women.

**less** 1 *(adj)* smaller, or in smaller quantities. *My hamster eats less food than your cat.* **less** *(adv).* 2 *(prep)* minus. *You pay the ticket price, less ten per cent.*

**lessen** **lessening** **lessened** *(v)* to get smaller in size, strength, importance, etc. *Joe's fear lessened as he grew tired.*

**lesson** 1 *(n)* a set period in school when pupils are taught, or a session when a skill is taught. 2 *(n)* an experience that teaches you something.

**let** **letting** **let** 1 *(v)* to allow, or to permit something. 2 *(v)* to rent out a house, land, etc. 3 **let down** *(v)* If you **let someone down**, you disappoint them by not doing something that you promised.

**lethal** *(adj)* likely to kill. **lethally** *(adv).*

**letter** 1 *(n)* a sign that is part of an alphabet and is used in writing. *The letter A.* 2 *(n)* a message that you write to someone, or receive from someone.

**lettuce** *(n)* a green, leafy salad vegetable.

**leukaemia** *or* **leukemia** *(loo-**kee**-mee-a)* *(n)* a serious disease in which the blood makes too many white cells.

**level** 1 *(adj)* flat and smooth. **level** *(v).* 2 *(adj)* equal. *The scores are level.* 3 *(n)* a height. *Eye level. Sea level.* 4 *(n)* a grade, or a standard. *Advanced level study.*

**level crossing** *(n)* a place where a road and railway cross at the same level.

**lever** *(**lee**-ver)* 1 *(n)* a bar that you use to lift an object, by placing one end under the object and pushing down on the other end. **lever** *(v).* 2 *(n)* a handle that you use to make a machine work.

**liable** 1 *(adj)* likely. *Judy is liable to get angry.* 2 *(adj)* responsible by law for something you have done. **liability** *(n).*

**liar** *(n)* someone who tells lies.

**libel** *(n)* an untrue written statement about someone that is damaging.

**liberal** *(adj)* tolerant, especially of other people's ideas. **liberalism** *(n).*

**Liberal Democrats** *(n)* one of the main political parties in Britain, who follow a middle way between the policies of the Conservative and Labour parties.

**liberate** **liberating liberated** *(v)* to set someone free. **liberation** *(n).*

**liberated** *(adj)* Someone who is **liberated** has been set free, or feels free.

**liberty** **liberties** *(n)* freedom.

**library** **libraries** *(n)* a place where you can read or borrow books. **librarian** *(n).*

**lice** *(plural n)* small insects without wings, that live on animals or people.

**licence** *(n)* a document giving permission for you to do something or own something. *A driving licence.*

**licensed** *(adj)* If someone is **licensed** to do something, such as sell alcohol, they have official permission to do it.

**lichen** *(**ly**-ken or **lit**-chen )* *(n)* a moss-like plant that grows on stones, trees, etc.

**lick** **licking licked** *(v)* to pass your tongue over something. **lick** *(n).*

**lie** **lying lay lain** *or* **lying lied** 1 *(v)* to say something that is not true. The past tense of this sense of the verb is "lied". 2 *(n)* a statement that is untrue. 3 *(v)* to get into, or to be in, a flat, outstretched position. 4 *(v)* to be, or to be placed somewhere. *The village lies in a deep valley.*

**life** **lives** 1 *(n)* Your **life** is the time from your birth until your death. 2 *(n)* liveliness and cheerfulness. *I feel full of life today!*

**lifeguard** *(n)* someone who is trained to save swimmers in danger.

**life jacket** *(n)* a jacket that will keep you afloat if you fall into water.

**life jacket**

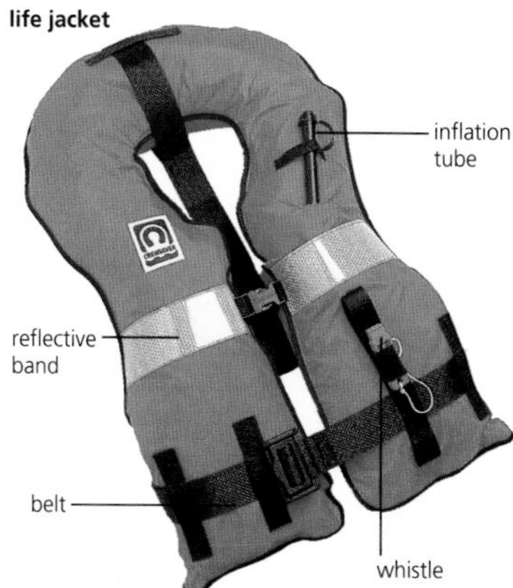


**lift** **lifting lifted** 1 *(v)* to raise something or someone. 2 *(n)* a machine that carries people or goods between floors of a building. 3 *(n)* a ride, especially in a car.

**light** **lighting lighted** *or* **lit; lighter lightest** 1 *(v)* to start something burning. 2 *(v)* to make something bright and visible. 3 *(n)* brightness, for example, from the Sun or a lamp. 4 *(adj)* not dark. *Light blue.* 5 *(n)* an object that gives out light, such as a torch or lamp. 6 *(adj)* weighing little. **lightness** *(n).* 7 *(adj)* gentle.

**lighthouse** *(n)* a tower, set in or near the sea, with a flashing light that guides ships or warns them of danger.

**lightning** *(n)* flashes of electricity in the sky, usually with thunder.

**lightweight** 1 *(adj)* not heavy. *A lightweight coat.* 2 *(adj)* not important, or not serious.

**light year** *(n)* a unit for measuring distance in space. A light year is the distance that light travels in one year.

**like** liking liked 1 *(v)* to enjoy or be pleased by something or someone. **liking** *(n).* 2 *(prep)* similar to. *I want a hat like yours.* 3 *(prep)* typical of. *It's just like Daisy to be late.*

**likely** likelier likeliest *(adj)* probable.

**likewise** *(adv)* also, or in the same way. *I'll dance if you do likewise.*

**limb** 1 *(n)* an arm or a leg. 2 *(n)* a branch of a tree.

**lime** *(n)* a green citrus fruit, shaped like a lemon.

**limelight** *(n)* If you are in the **limelight**, you are the centre of attention.

**limerick** *(n)* a nonsense verse made up of five lines that rhyme in a particular way.

**limit** limiting limited 1 *(n)* an edge, or a boundary. 2 *(v)* to keep within a certain area or amount. *I've limited myself to three cups of tea a day.* **limitation** *(n).*

**limited** 1 *(adj)* small and unable to increase. 2 *(n)* A **limited edition** of a book, picture, etc. may be valuable because it is one of only a small number.

**limp** limping limped; limper limpest 1 *(v)* to walk in an uneven way, usually because of an injury. **limp** *(n).* 2 *(adj)* floppy and not firm. *A limp handshake.*

**line** lining lined 1 *(n)* a long, narrow mark. 2 *(n)* a row of people or words. 3 *(n)* a piece of string, rope, etc. 4 *(v)* to make a lining for something.

**linger** lingering lingered *(v)* to stay, or to wait around. *The fans lingered outside the theatre.* **lingering** *(adj).*

**lining** *(n)* a piece of material sewn inside something. *This jacket has a silk lining.*

**link** linking linked 1 *(n)* one of the separate rings that make up a chain. 2 *(n)* a connection between things or people. 3 *(v)* to join objects, ideas, etc. together.

**lino** *(n)* a smooth, shiny material used as a floor covering. Lino is short for linoleum.

**linocut** *(n)* a print made from a block of lino with a pattern or picture cut into it.

**lion** *(n)* a large, wild cat with a mane, found in Africa and Asia.

**lip** 1 *(n)* Your **lips** are the pink edges of your mouth. 2 *(n)* the edge or rim of a cup or hole. 3 *(n) (slang)* cheek, or rude talk.

**lip-read** lip-reading lip-read *(v)* When deaf people **lip-read**, they watch someone's lips while they are talking in order to understand what they are saying.

**liquid** *(n)* a wet substance that you can pour. **liquid** *(adj).*

**liquidize** *or* **liquidise** liquidizing liquidized *(v)* to make solid food into a liquid. **liquidizer** *(n).*

**liquor** *(**lik**-er) (n)* a strong alcoholic drink, such as whisky, gin, or vodka.

**liquorice** *(**lik**-er-iss or **lik**-er-ish) (n)* a black substance that is made into sweets.

**lisp** *(n)* a way of talking in which you say 'th' instead of 's'. **lisp** *(v).*

**list** listing listed *(v)* to set down words, numbers, etc. in a line. **list** *(n).*

**listen** listening listened *(v)* to pay attention so that you can hear something.

**literacy** *(n)* the ability to read and write.

**literally** *(adv)* If you take someone **literally**, you believe their exact words.

**literature** *(n)* books, especially novels, plays, and poems. **literary** *(adj).*

**litmus** *(n)* a substance that turns red when touched by an acid, and blue when touched by an alkali.

**litter** 1 *(n)* rubbish that is left scattered around. **litter** *(v).* 2 *(n)* a group of kittens, piglets, puppies, etc. born at the same time to one mother.

**little** littler littlest 1 *(adj)* small in size. 2 *(n)* a small amount of something. *I'll have a little.* 3 *(adj)* not much. *We have little time.*

**live** living lived 1 *(liv) (v)* to be alive. 2 *(live) (adj)* alive or living. *You can buy live chickens here.* 3 *(liv) (v)* to have your home somewhere. *Josie lives in Chicago.* 4 *(live) (adj)* broadcast as it is happening.

**lively** livelier liveliest *(adj)* active and full of life. **liveliness** *(n).*

**liver** *(n)* the organ in your body that cleans your blood. *See* **organ**.

**livestock** *(n)* animals kept on a farm, such as horses, sheep, and cows.

**living** 1 *(adj)* alive now. 2 *(n)* money to live. *Joe earns his living by painting.*

**living room** *(n)* a lounge, or a sitting room.

*Some words that begin with a "li" sound are spelt "ly".*

**lizard** *(n)* a small reptile with a long body and a tail. *The picture shows four kinds of lizard.*

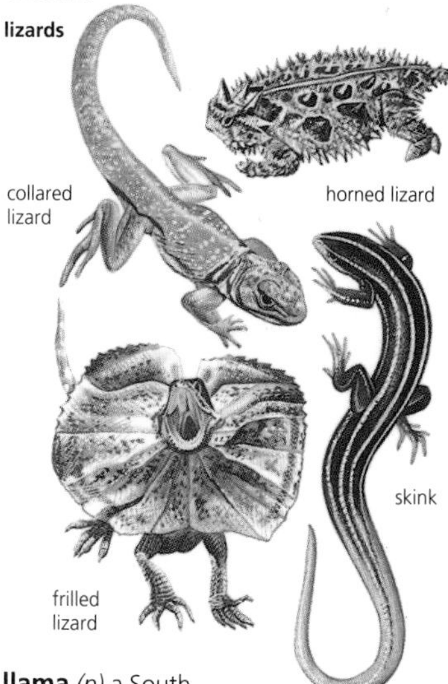


**llama** *(n)* a South American mammal, kept for its wool and meat.

**load** loading loaded 1 *(n)* something that is carried, especially something heavy. 2 *(v)* to put things on to or into something. *Bill loaded the car with boxes.* 3 *(v)* to put a bullet into a gun, a film into a camera, or a program into a computer.

**loaf** loaves 1 *(n)* bread baked in a shape. 2 *(n)* food that has been cooked in a loaf-shaped tin. *Meat loaf.*

**loan** loaning loaned 1 *(v)* to lend something to someone. 2 *(n)* an amount of money that you borrow.

**loathe** loathing loathed *(v)* to hate or dislike someone or something.

**lob** lobbing lobbed *(v)* to throw or hit a ball high into the air.

**lobster** *(n)* a sea creature with a shell, ten legs, and a long body. Lobsters can be eaten.

**lobster**

**local** *(adj)* near your house, or to do with the area where you live. **locally** *(adv).*

**locate** locating located *(v)* to find out where something is.

**location** 1 *(n)* the place or position where someone or something is. 2 If a film or television programme is made **on location**, it is filmed out of the studio.

**lock** locking locked 1 *(n)* a part of a door, box, etc. that you can open and shut with a key. 2 *(v)* to fasten something with a key. 3 **locks** *(plural n) (poetic)* hair.

**locker** *(n)* a small cupboard with a lock, where you can leave your belongings.

**locket** *(n)* a piece of jewellery, worn on a chain around the neck, which often contains a photograph.

**locomotive** *(n)* a railway engine.

**locust** *(n)* an insect like a grasshopper, which eats and destroys crops.

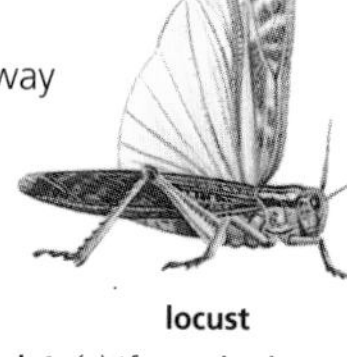


**lodge** lodging lodged 1 *(v)* If you **lodge** with someone, you stay in their house and usually pay them money. 2 *(v)* to get stuck somewhere. *The pea lodged in Tim's ear.*

**lodger** *(n)* somebody who pays to live in a room in someone else's house.

**loft** *(n)* a room in the roof of a building.

**lofty** loftier loftiest 1 *(adj)* very high and imposing. *A lofty mansion.* 2 *(adj)* distant and haughty. **loftily** *(adv).*

**log** logging logged 1 *(n)* a part of a tree that has been chopped up. 2 *(n)* a record kept by the captain of a ship. 3 *(v)* If you **log on** or **log in** to a computer, you start using it by entering a name or password.

**logic** *(n)* careful and correct reasoning. **logical** *(adj),* **logically** *(adv).*

**logo** *(loh-go) (n)* a symbol that represents a particular company or organization.

**loiter** *(loy-ter)* loitering loitered *(v)* to stand around, usually because you have nothing to do.

**loll** lolling lolled 1 *(v)* to sit or stand in a lazy, sloppy way. *Wayne lolled on the sofa.* 2 *(v)* to hang loosely. *The wolf's tongue lolled out of its mouth.*

**lonely** **lonelier loneliest** 1 *(adj)* If you are **lonely**, you are sad because you are by yourself. **loneliness** *(n)*. 2 *(adj)* far from other people or things. *A lonely farmhouse.*

**long** **longing longed; longer longest** 1 *(adj)* more than the average length, distance, time, etc. *A long walk.* **long** *(adv)*. 2 *(adj)* from one end to the other. *The footpath was about two miles long.* 3 *(adj)* taking a lot of time. *Is the film very long?* 4 *(v)* If you **long for** something, you want it very much. **longing** *(n)*.

**longitude** *(n)* the position of a place, measured in degrees east or west of a line that runs through the Greenwich Observatory in London, England.

**long-sighted** *(adj)* If you are **long-sighted**, you are able to see things more clearly when they are far away.

**long-winded** *(adj)* unnecessarily long and boring.

**look** **looking looked** 1 *(v)* to use your eyes to see things. 2 *(v)* to seem or appear. *You look happy.* 3 *(n)* a glance or expression on someone's face. *An angry look.* 4 *(v)* If you **look after** someone or something, you take care of them. 5 *(v)* If you **look forward** to something, you wait for it eagerly.

**loom** **looming loomed** 1 *(v)* to appear in a sudden or frightening way. *A tall figure loomed out of the shadows.* 2 *(n)* a machine used for weaving cloth.

**loop** *(n)* a curve or circle in a piece of string, rope, etc. **loop** *(v)*.

**loose** **looser loosest** 1 *(adj)* not fitting tightly. *Loose trousers.* **loosely** *(adv)*. 2 *(adj)* not firm. *A loose tooth.*

**loosen** **loosening loosened** *(v)* to make something less tight.

**loot** **looting looted** 1 *(v)* to steal from shops or houses in a riot or war. **looter** *(n)*. 2 *(n)* stolen money or valuables.

**lopsided** *(adj)* unbalanced, or with one side heavier than the other.

**lorry** **lorries** *(n)* a large motor vehicle used for carrying goods by road.

**lose** **losing lost** 1 *(v)* If you **lose** something, you do not have it any more. 2 *(v)* to be beaten or defeated in a game, argument, etc.

**loss** **losses** 1 *(n)* the losing of something. *Loss of life.* 2 *(n)* something that is lost.

**lot** 1 *(n)* a large number or amount. 2 *(n)* a group of objects that are sold together at an auction.

**lotion** *(n)* a cream that you put on your skin or hair.

**lottery** **lotteries** *(n)* a competition in which you buy tickets with the aim of winning a prize.

**loud** **louder loudest** 1 *(adj)* noisy, or producing a lot of sound. **loudly** *(adv)*. 2 *(adj)* very bright and colourful.

**loudspeaker** *(n)* a machine that turns electrical signals into sounds.

**lounge** **lounging lounged** 1 *(v)* to sit around lazily. 2 *(n)* a comfortable room for sitting in.

**love** **loving loved** 1 *(v)* to like someone or something very much. **love** *(n)*. 2 If you are **in love** with someone, you are passionately fond of them. 3 If you **make love**, you have sexual intercourse with someone. **lover** *(n)*. 4 *(n)* in tennis, a score of no points.

**lovely** **lovelier loveliest** 1 *(adj)* If someone is **lovely**, they are beautiful to look at, or have a very attractive personality. **loveliness** *(n)*. 2 *(adj)* enjoyable. *We had a lovely day.*

**low** **lower lowest** 1 *(adj)* not high. *A low table.* 2 *(adj)* A **low** sound is quiet and soft, or deep in pitch. 3 *(adj)* depressed or ill. 4 **low tide** *(n)* the time when the sea is furthest down the beach.

**lower** **lowering lowered** 1 *(v)* to move something down. 2 *(adj)* not as high as something else.

**loyal** *(adj)* Someone who is **loyal** supports their friends and does not betray or desert them. **loyalty** *(n)*, **loyally** *(adv)*.

**luck** 1 *(n)* something that happens by chance. 2 *(n)* good fortune, or good things that happen to you that have not been planned. *Wish me luck!*

**lucky** **luckier luckiest** 1 *(adj)* Someone who is **lucky** is fortunate and good things seem to happen to them. 2 *(adj)* Something that is **lucky** happens by chance and is fortunate. **luckily** *(adv)*

**ludicrous** *(loo-dik-russ)* *(adj)* ridiculous or foolish. **ludicrously** *(adv)*.

**lug** **lugging** **lugged** *(v)* to move something heavy.

**luggage** *(n)* cases and bags that you take with you when you travel.

**lukewarm** 1 *(adj)* slightly warm. 2 *(adj)* not keen, or not enthusiastic.

**lull** **lulling** **lulled** 1 *(n)* a short pause or break during a period of fighting or activity. 2 *(v)* to make someone feel peaceful, safe, or sleepy. *The sound of the waves on the shore lulled Fay to sleep.*

**lullaby** **lullabies** *(n)* a gentle song sung to send a baby to sleep.

**lumber** **lumbering** **lumbered** 1 *(v)* to move around heavily and clumsily. *The elephants lumbered into view.* 2 If you are **lumbered** with an unpleasant job or duty, you have been left to deal with it.

**luminous** *(adj)* shining, or glowing in the dark. **luminously** *(adv).*

**lump** 1 *(n)* a mass of solid matter. *A lump of pastry.* 2 *(n)* a swelling. *Look at this lump on my head!*

**lunar** *(adj)* to do with the Moon.

**lunatic** 1 *(n) (informal)* a foolish and annoying person. **lunacy** *(n),* **lunatic** *(adj).* 2 *(n)* an insane person.

**lunch** **lunches** *(n)* the meal that you eat in the middle of the day.

**lung** *(n)* Your **lungs** are the two organs inside your chest that you use to breathe. *See* **organ**.

**lunge** **lunging** **lunged** *(v)* to move forward quickly and suddenly. **lunge** *(n).*

**lurch** **lurches** **lurching** **lurched** *(v)* to move in an unsteady, jerky way. *The train lurched to a halt.*

**lure** **luring** **lured** *(v)* to attract someone or some creature and perhaps lead them into a trap. **lure** *(n).*

**lurid** 1 *(adj)* vivid and glowing. *A lurid yellow.* 2 *(adj)* sensational and shocking. *Lurid newspaper stories.*

**lurk** **lurking** **lurked** *(v)* to wait around secretly. *The robbers lurked in the garden.*

**luxury** **luxuries** *(n)* something expensive which you do not really need, but which is enjoyable to have. **luxury** *(adj).*

**lyric** 1 *(n)* a short poem that expresses strong feelings, especially love. 2 **lyrics** *(plural n)* the words of a song.

# Mm

**macabre** *(mak-**ar**-brer) (adj)* gruesome and frightening.

**machine** *(n)* a piece of equipment made of moving parts, that is used to do a job.

**machinery** *(singular n)* a group of machines, or the parts of a machine.

**macho** *(adj) (slang)* If men or boys are **macho**, they act in an exaggeratedly masculine way.

**mad** **madder** **maddest** 1 *(adj)* insane. **madness** *(n).* 2 *(adj)* very foolish.

**madam** *(n)* a formal name for a woman, used in speech and writing. *Dear Madam.*

**magazine** *(n)* a thin book that is published regularly, and contains articles, photographs, advertisements, etc.

**maggot** *(n)* the larva of certain flies, such as the bluebottle and the housefly.

**magic** 1 *(n)* In stories, **magic** is the power to make impossible things happen. **magical** *(adj).* 2 *(n)* clever tricks done to entertain people. **magician** *(n).*

**magnet** *(n)* a piece of metal that attracts iron or steel. **magnetic** *(adj).*

**magnificent** *(adj)* very impressive or beautiful. **magnificently** *(adv).*

**magnify** **magnifies** **magnifying** **magnified** 1 *(v)* to make something appear larger so that it can be seen more easily. 2 **magnifying glass** *(n)* a glass lens that makes things look bigger.

**magnitude** *(n)* the size or importance of something. *The magnitude of a task.*

**mahogany** *(n)* a hard, dark, reddish-brown wood.

**maid** 1 *(n)* a female servant, especially in a hotel. 2 *(n) (poetic)* a young, unmarried woman.

**maiden** 1 *(n) (poetic)* a young, unmarried woman. 2 *(n)* A woman's **maiden name** is the surname she has before she marries.

**mail** 1 *(n)* letters and parcels sent by post. **mail** *(v).* 2 *(n)* If you buy something by **mail order**, you order it and pay for it, and then the item is posted to you.

**maim** **maiming** **maimed** *(v)* to injure someone so badly that part of their body is damaged for life.

**main** **1** *(adj)* largest, or most important. **2 mains** *(plural n)* the large pipes or wires that supply water, gas, or electricity to a building.

**mainframe** *(n)* a large and very powerful computer to which other smaller computers are connected.

**mainly** **1** *(adv)* most importantly. *I mainly like swimming.* **2** *(adv)* almost completely. *The film was mainly rubbish.* **3** *(adv)* usually. *I mainly go on holiday abroad.*

**maintain** **maintaining** **maintained** *(v)* to keep a machine or building in good condition. **maintenance** *(n).*

**maize** *(n)* a crop plant that produces sweetcorn.

**majesty** **majesties** **1** *(n)* dignity and grandeur. **majestic** *(adj),* **majestically** *(adv).* **2** *(n)* The formal title for a king or a queen is **His Majesty** or **Her Majesty**.

**major** *(adj)* important, or serious.

**majority** **majorities** **1** *(n)* more than half of a group of people or things. **2** *(n)* the number of votes by which someone wins an election.

**make** **making** **made** **1** *(v)* to build or produce something. *Mum makes great cakes.* **2** *(v)* to do something. *Wallis made two phone calls.* **3** *(v)* to cause something to happen. *The view made Jules feel dizzy.* **4** *(v)* to add up to. *Four and two make six.*

**makeshift** *(adj)* A **makeshift** object is made from whatever is available and is only meant to be used for a short time.

**make-up** *(n)* the coloured powders and creams that women and actors put on their faces.

**male** *(n)* a person or animal of the sex that fertilizes the female. **male** *(adj).*

**malicious** *(mal-ish-uss) (adj)* hurting other people deliberately. **malice** *(n).*

**mall** *(mawl) (n)* a large shopping centre.

**malnutrition** *(n)* illness caused by not having enough food or by eating the wrong kind of food.

**malt** *(n)* dried grain, usually barley, used for making whisky and milky drinks.

**mammal** *(n)* an animal that feeds its young on its own milk. *Human beings, cats, mice, and dolphins are all mammals.*

**mammoth** **1** *(n)* an extinct animal, like a large elephant, with long, curved tusks. **2** *(adj)* very large. *This is a mammoth task!*

**man** **men** **1** *(n)* an adult, male human being. **2** *(n)* the human race.

**manage** **managing** **managed** **1** *(v)* to be in charge of a shop, business, etc. **management** *(n).* **2** *(v)* to be able to do something that is difficult or awkward.

**manager** *(n)* someone in charge of a shop, business, group of people, etc.

**mane** *(n)* the long, thick hair on the head and neck of a lion or horse.

**manger** *(n)* a container from which cattle and horses eat.

**mangle** **mangling** **mangled** *(v)* to crush and twist something. **mangled** *(adj).*

**manhole** *(n)* a covered hole in the ground, leading to sewers or underground pipes.

**maniac** *(may-nee-ak) (n)* someone who is mad, or acts in a wild or violent way.

**manicure** *(n)* a treatment for your hands and fingernails.

**manipulate** **manipulating** **manipulated** **1** *(v)* to use your hands in a skilful way. *Karen manipulated the plane's controls.* **2** *(v)* to influence people so that they do what you want them to do.

**mankind** *(n)* the human race.

**manner** **1** *(n)* the way in which you do something. **2** *(n)* the way that someone behaves. *Giles has a very gentle manner.* **3 manners** *(n)* polite behaviour.

**manoeuvre** *(man-oo-ver) (n)* a difficult movement that needs skill. *The pilots performed breathtaking manoeuvres.*

**manor** *(n)* a large, old country house surrounded by land.

**mantelpiece** *(n)* a wooden or stone shelf above a fireplace.

**manual** **1** *(adj)* worked by hand. *A manual typewriter.* **2** *(n)* an instruction book. **3 manual work** *(n)* physical work.

**manufacture** **manufacturing** **manufactured** *(v)* to make something with machines in a factory.

**manure** *(n)* animal waste put on land to improve the quality of the soil and to make crops grow better.

**manuscript** 1 *(n)* the original handwritten or typed pages of a book, poem, piece of music, etc., before it is printed. 2 *(n)* a handwritten document.

**many** more most 1 *(adj)* great in number. **many** *(pronoun)*. 2 **how many?** what number?

**Maori** *(mauw-ree)* **Maori** *or* **Maoris** *(n)* one of the native people of New Zealand who lived there before the Europeans arrived. **Maori** *(adj)*.

**map** *(n)* a detailed plan of an area, showing features such as towns, roads, rivers, mountains, etc. **map** *(v)*.

**maple** *(n)* a tree with large, five-pointed leaves. Maple sap is used to make syrup.

**marathon** *(n)* a running race of roughly 26 miles (42km), that is run along roads.

**marble** 1 *(n)* a hard stone with coloured patterns in it, used for building and making sculptures. 2 **marbles** *(singular n)* a children's game, played with small glass balls, called marbles, on the ground.

**march** marches marching marched 1 *(v)* When soldiers **march**, they walk together with regular steps. 2 *(v)* to walk quickly and in a determined way. *Camilla marched up to the door.*

**mare** *(n)* an adult, female horse.

**margarine** *(n)* a yellow fat, similar to butter, often made from vegetable oil.

**margin** *(n)* the long blank space that runs down the edge of a page.

**marine** *(adj)* to do with the sea.

**mark** marking marked 1 *(n)* a scratch or stain on something. 2 *(n)* a number or letter on a piece of work that shows how good it is. **mark** *(v)*.

**market** *(n)* a group of stalls, usually in the open air, where things are sold.

**marmalade** *(n)* a jam made from oranges or other citrus fruit and usually eaten on toast for breakfast.

**maroon** marooning marooned 1 *(v)* If someone is **marooned** somewhere, they are stuck there and cannot leave. 2 *(n)* a dark reddish-brown colour. **maroon** *(adj)*.

**marquee** *(mar-kee)* *(n)* a large tent used for parties and fêtes.

**marriage** *(n)* the relationship between a husband and wife.

**married** *(adj)* Someone who is **married** has a husband or wife.

**marrow** 1 *(n)* the soft substance found inside bones. 2 *(n)* a large, long green vegetable.

**marry** marries marrying married 1 *(v)* When people **marry**, they go through a ceremony in which they promise to spend their lives together. 2 *(v)* to perform a marriage ceremony.

**marsh** *(n)* an area of wet, low-lying land.

**marsupial** *(mar-soo-pee-ul)* *(n)* a kind of mammal. Female marsupials carry their young in their pouches.

**martial** *(mar-shall)* 1 *(adj)* to do with war or soldiers. 2 **martial arts** *(n)* styles of fighting or self-defence that come from the Far East, for example, judo and karate.

**martyr** *(mar-ter)* *(n)* someone who is killed or made to suffer, because of their beliefs. **martyrdom** *(n)*.

**marvel** marvelling marvelled *(v)* If you **marvel** at something, you are filled with surprise and wonder.

**marvellous** *(adj)* very good indeed.

**mascara** *(n)* a substance put on eyelashes to make them look thicker.

**mascot** *(n)* something that is supposed to bring luck, such as an animal or a toy.

**masculine** 1 *(adj)* to do with men. 2 *(adj)* having qualities that are supposed to be typical of men. **masculinity** *(n)*.

**mask** *(n)* a covering worn over the face to hide, protect, or disguise it.

**masonry** *(n)* stone used in a building.

**mass** masses 1 *(n)* a large number of people or things together. 2 *(adj)* **Mass-produced** things are made in large quantities, usually by machine.

**massacre** *(mass-er-ker)* *(n)* the killing of a very large number of people.

**massage** *(mass-arj)* massaging massaged *(v)* to rub someone's body with your fingers in order to help them relax, or loosen their muscles. **massage** *(n)*.

**massive** *(adj)* huge and bulky.

**mass media** *(plural n)* a general word for forms of communication that reach a large number of people, such as television, radio, and newspapers.

**mast** *(n)* a tall pole that stands on the deck of a boat and supports its sails.

**master mastering mastered** 1 *(v)* If you **master** a subject or skill, you become very good at it. 2 *(n)* a name for a male teacher in some secondary schools.

**mastermind masterminding masterminded** *(v)* to plan and control the way something is carried out.

**masterpiece** *(n)* a brilliant piece of art, literature, music, etc.

**mat** *(n)* a thick pad of material used for covering a floor, protecting a table, etc.

**match matches matching matched** 1 *(n)* a sports game. 2 *(v)* If two things **match**, they go well together. 3 *(n)* a small, thin stick of wood with a chemical tip which is struck to produce a flame.

**mate mating mated** 1 *(v)* When male and female animals **mate**, they have sexual intercourse in order to reproduce. **mating** *(n)*. 2 *(n)* the male or female partner of a couple or pair.

**material** 1 *(n)* the substances from which something is made. *What materials is a house made of?* 2 *(n)* cloth, or fabric.

**materialistic** *(adj)* People who are **materialistic** are only concerned with money and possessions. **materialism** *(n)*.

**maternal** *(adj)* to do with being a mother. *Maternal feelings.*

**maternity** 1 *(n)* motherhood. 2 **maternity ward** *(n)* a large room in a hospital for women who have just had or are about to have a baby.

**mathematics** *(n)* the study of numbers, quantities, and shapes. **mathematical** *(adj)*.

**matinée** *(mat-in-ay)* *(n)* an afternoon performance of a play or film.

**matt** *(adj)* not shiny. *Matt paint.*

**matter mattering mattered** 1 *(n)* something that needs to be dealt with. 2 *(v)* If something **matters**, it is important.

**mattress mattresses** *(n)* a soft, thick pad, usually containing springs, that you put on the base of a bed to sleep on.

**mature maturer maturest** 1 *(adj)* adult, or fully grown. 2 *(adj)* behaving in a sensible, adult way. **maturity** *(n)*. 3 *(adj)* ripe. *A mature cheese.*

**maul mauling mauled** *(v)* to handle someone or something in a rough and possibly damaging way.

**maximum** *(n)* the greatest possible amount, or the upper limit. *Two hours is the maximum allowed.* **maximum** *(adj)*.

**maybe** *(adv)* perhaps.

**mayhem** *(n)* a situation of confusion or violent destruction.

**mayonnaise** *(n)* a creamy sauce made from egg yolks, oil, and vinegar.

**mayor** *(n)* the leader of a town, city, or district council.

**maze** *(n)* a complicated network of paths or lines, made as a puzzle to find your way through.

**meadow** *(n)* a field of grass, often used for animals to graze in.

**meal** *(n)* food which is served and eaten, usually at a particular time of day. Breakfast, lunch, and tea are meals.

**mean meaning meant; meaner meanest** 1 *(v)* to intend to do something. *I mean to go skating.* 2 *(v)* to try to convey a message. *What does this word mean?* 3 *(adj)* not generous, or unkind.

**meaning** 1 *(n)* the idea behind something spoken or written. 2 *(n)* the importance or significance of something. *What is the meaning of life?*

**meantime** *(n)* the time in between. *We leave early tomorrow morning. In the meantime, let's get some rest!*

**meanwhile** *(adv)* at the same time. *George went to explore. Meanwhile, Hattie ate the picnic.*

**measles** *(n)* a infectious disease causing fever and a rash.

**measly measlier measliest** *(adj)* *(informal)* inadequate, or not very generous.

**measure measuring measured** *(v)* to find out the size, weight, etc. of something. **measurement** *(n)*.

**meat** *(n)* the edible flesh of an animal.

**mechanic** *(n)* someone who is skilled at operating or mending machinery.

**mechanical** *(adj)* operated by machinery. *A mechanical toy.* **mechanically** *(adv).*

**mechanism** *(n)* the system of moving parts inside a machine.

**medal** *(n)* a piece of metal, shaped like a coin, star, or cross, which is given to someone for being brave, or for service to their country, or as a prize for sporting achievement.

**media** *(plural n)* a general name for different forms of communication, such as television, radio, and newspapers.

**mediaeval** *see* **medieval**.

**medical** 1 *(adj)* to do with health treatment. *Medical advice.* 2 *(n) (informal)* an examination by a doctor.

**medicine** 1 *(n)* a substance, usually liquid, used in treating illness. **medicinal** *(adj).* 2 *(singular n)* the treatment of illness. *Doctors must study medicine.*

**medieval** *or* **mediaeval** *(adj)* to do with the Middle Ages, the period between approximately AD1000 and AD1450.

**mediocre** *(mee-dee-**oh**-ker) (adj)* of average or less than average quality.

**meditate** **meditating meditated** *(v)* to think very deeply about something.

**medium** 1 *(adj)* average, or middle. *Medium height.* 2 *(n)* **Mediums** claim to make contact with the spirits of the dead.

**meek** **meeker meekest** *(adj)* quiet, humble, and obedient. **meekly** *(adv).*

**meet** **meeting met** 1 *(v)* to come face to face with someone or something. 2 *(v)* to come together. *The two paths met at the summit of the mountain.*

**meeting** *(n)* an arranged event in which people come together, often to discuss something.

**megabyte** *(n)* a unit used to measure the capacity of a computer's memory.

**mellow** **mellowing mellowed** *(v)* to become gentler and more relaxed.

**melody** **melodies** *(n)* a tune.

**melon** *(n)* a large, rounded, juicy fruit.

**melt** **melting melted** *(v)* When a substance **melts**, it changes from a solid to a liquid because it has become hotter.

**member** *(n)* someone who belongs to a club, group, family, etc. **membership** *(n).*

**Member of Parliament** *or* **MP** *(n)* someone elected by the people of a district to represent them in parliament.

**memorable** *(adj)* easily remembered, or worth remembering. **memorably** *(adv).*

**memorize** *or* **memorise** **memorizing memorized** *(v)* to learn something by heart.

**memory** **memories** 1 *(n)* the power to remember things. 2 *(n)* something that you remember from the past. *Happy memories.* 3 *(n)* the part of a computer in which information is stored.

**menace** 1 *(n)* a threat, or a danger. 2 *(n) (informal)* a nuisance.

**mend** **mending mended** *(v)* to repair something which is broken.

**menstruate** **menstruating menstruated** *(v)* When a woman or girl **menstruates**, blood comes from her womb, about once a month.

**mental** *(adj)* to do with the mind.

**mention** **mentioning mentioned** *(v)* to speak briefly about something. *Polly mentioned that she would be away.*

**menu** 1 *(n)* a list of foods served in a café, restaurant, etc. 2 *(n)* a list of choices shown on a computer screen.

**merchant** *(n)* someone who sells goods for profit, especially someone who trades with foreign countries.

**mercury** *(n)* a poisonous, silvery, liquid metal. Mercury is used in thermometers.

**mercy** **mercies** *(n)* If you show **mercy** to someone, you are kind to them and do not punish them. **merciful** *(adj).*

**merely** *(adv)* only, or simply.

**merit** *(n)* If something has **merit**, it is good. **merit** *(v).*

**mermaid** *(n)* In stories, a **mermaid** is a sea creature with the upper body of a girl and the tail of a fish.

**merry** **merrier merriest** 1 *(adj)* cheerful, or joyful. 2 *(adj) (informal)* slightly drunk.

**mess** 1 *(n)* a dirty or untidy state or thing. *My room is a mess!* **messy** *(adj),* **messily** *(adv).* 2 *(n)* a confused and disorganized state or thing. *My life is a mess!*

**message** 1 *(n)* information sent to someone else. 2 *(n)* the meaning of something, like a book or film.

**messenger** *(n)* someone who carries a message.

**metal** *(n)* a chemical substance, such as iron, copper, or silver, which is usually hard and shiny, and is a good conductor of heat and electricity. **metallic** *(adj).*

**metaphor** *(n)* a way of describing something as though it were something else, for example, "The princess is a jewel, and her father is a raging bull."

**meter** *(n)* an instrument for measuring the quantity of something, especially the amount of something that has been used.

**method** *(n)* a way of doing something.

**methodical** *(adj)* careful, logical, and well-organized. **methodically** *(adv).*

**meticulous** *(adj)* very careful and precise.

**metric** *(adj)* The **metric** system of measurement is based on units of ten. Metres, litres, and kilograms are all metric measurements. *See* page 256.

**microbe** *(n)* a living thing that is too small to be seen without a microscope.

**microchip** *(n)* a minute piece of silicon with electronic circuits printed on it, used in computers and other electronic equipment. *See* **chip**.

**microlight** *(n)* a very light aircraft with large, fabric-covered wings.

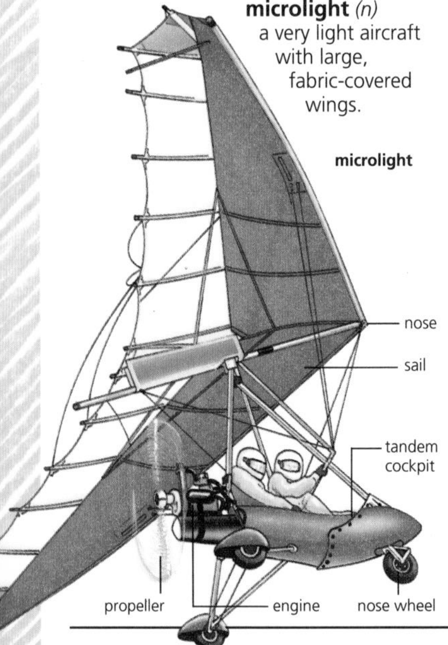


**microorganism** *(n)* a living thing that is too small to be seen without a microscope.

**microphone** *(n)* an instrument that changes sound into an electric current, to make the sound louder, record it, or transmit it to radio or television stations.

**microscope** *(n)* a instrument that magnifies very small things so that they look large enough to be seen and studied.

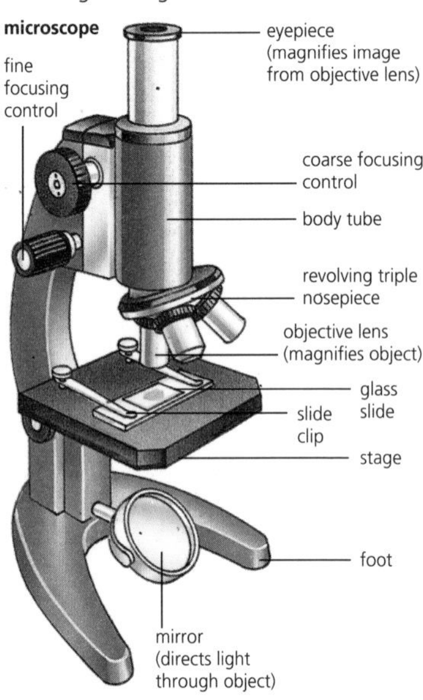


**microscopic** *(adj)* too small to be seen without a microscope.

**microwave oven** *(n)* an oven which cooks food very quickly by beaming high frequency waves into it.

**midday** *(n)* noon, or 12 o'clock in the middle of the day. **midday** *(adj).*

**middle** *(adj)* central, or half-way between two extremes. **middle** *(n).*

**middle-aged** *(adj)* A **middle-aged** person is between 40 and 60 years old.

**Middle Ages** *(n)* the period between approximately AD1000 and AD1450.

**Middle East** *(n)* the hot countries of Western Asia between the eastern end of the Mediterranean Sea and India. Israel, Iraq, and Iran are all in the Middle East.

**midnight** *(n)* 12 o'clock in the middle of the night. **midnight** *(adj).*

**midwife** **midwives** *(n)* a nurse trained to help when a baby is being born.

**might** *(n)* strength, or force.

**migraine** *(n)* a very bad headache which makes you feel sick.

**migrate** **migrating** **migrated** *(v)* When birds **migrate**, they fly at a particular time of year to live in another region. **migration** *(n),* **migratory** *(adj).*

**mild** **milder** **mildest** **1** *(adj)* gentle and not aggressive. **2** *(adj)* moderate and not too harsh. *Mild weather.*

**militant** *(adj)* prepared to fight or to be very aggressive in support of a cause.

**military** *(adj)* to do with soldiers and the armed forces. *A military hospital.*

**milk** **milking** **milked** **1** *(n)* the white liquid produced by female mammals to feed their young. **milky** *(adj).* **2** *(v)* to take milk from a cow or other animal. **3 milk tooth** *(n)* one of your first teeth, that falls out and is replaced by a permanent tooth.

**mill** **1** *(n)* a building containing machinery for grinding grain into flour. **mill** *(v).* **2** *(n)* a large factory that processes textiles, wood, paper, etc. *A cotton mill.*

**millennium** **milleniums** *or* **millenia** *(n)* a period of a thousand years.

**millet** *(n)* a cereal crop with tiny seeds, grown especially in India.

**million** *(n)* a thousand thousands (1,000,000).

**millionaire** *(n)* someone whose money and property is worth at least a million pounds or dollars.

**milometer** *(n)* an instrument that counts how many miles a vehicle has travelled.

**mime** *(n)* a form of acting without words.

**mimic** **mimicking** **mimicked** *(v)* to imitate someone else's speech or actions.

**minaret** *(n)* the tall tower of a mosque, from which Muslims are called to prayer.

**mince** **mincing** **minced** **1** *(v)* to cut or chop meat or similar substances into very small pieces. **2** *(n)* finely chopped meat.

**mincemeat** *(n)* a sweet mixture of finely chopped dried fruit, spices, etc. used in pies and tarts.

**mind** **minding** **minded** **1** *(n)* the part of you that thinks, remembers, dreams, etc. **2** *(v)* to care, or to be bothered about something. **3** *(v)* to watch out for something. *Mind the step!*

**mine** **mining** **mined** **1** *(adj)* belonging to me. **2** *(v)* to dig up minerals from below the ground. **mine** *(n),* **miner** *(n).*

**mineral** **1** *(n)* a substance found in the earth, that can be obtained by mining. **2 mineral water** *(n)* water that has mineral salts and gases dissolved in it.

**mingle** **mingling** **mingled** *(v)* to mix together. *The guests mingled happily.*

**miniature** *(min-it-cher) (adj)* If something is **miniature**, it is a small version of something bigger.

**minibeast** *(n)* an insect or other small creature.

**minibus** **minibuses** *(n)* a small bus that can usually carry between eight and sixteen passengers.

**minimize** *or* **minimise** **minimizing** **minimized** **1** *(v)* to make something as small as possible. *Colin's map minimized our chance of getting lost.* **2** *(v)* to make something seem as unimportant or insignificant as possible. *When we told Mum what had happened, we minimized the danger.*

**minimum** *(n)* the smallest possible amount, or the lowest limit. *We need a minimum of six people.* **minimum** *(adj).*

**minister** **1** *(n)* a clergyman. **ministry** *(n).* **2** *(n)* someone in charge of a government department. *The Health Minister.*

**minor** *(adj)* less important, or less serious. *This is a minor issue.*

**minority** **minorities** **1** *(n)* a small number or part within a bigger group. **2** *(n)* a group of people of a particular race or religion living among a larger group of a different race or religion.

**mint** **1** *(n)* a strongly-scented plant with leaves that are used for flavouring. **2** *(n)* a peppermint-flavoured sweet.

**minus** *(prep)* In maths, a **minus** sign (-) is used in a subtraction sum. *6 minus 4 equals two, or 6 - 4 = 2.*

**minute** **minuter** **minutest** **1** *(min-it) (n)* a unit of time equal to 60 seconds. **2** *(my-**newt**) (adj)* very small indeed.

**miracle** *(mir-ak-ul) (n)* a remarkable and unexpected event. **miraculous** *(adj).*

**mirage** *(mir-arj) (n)* something that you think you see in the distance, such as water, which is not really there.

**mirror** *(n)* a metal or glass surface which reflects the image of whatever is in front of it.

**misbehave** misbehaving misbehaved *(v)* to behave badly.

**miscarriage** *(n)* When a pregnant woman has a **miscarriage**, the baby dies in her womb, usually early in the pregnancy. **miscarry** *(v).*

**miscellaneous** *(miss-el-ay-nee-uss) (adj)* assorted, or of different types.

**mischief** *(n)* playful, mildly naughty behaviour that may cause annoyance to others. **mischievous** *(adj).*

**miser** *(my-zer) (n)* a very mean person who spends as little as possible in order to hoard money. **miserly** *(adj).*

**miserable** *(adj)* sad, unhappy, or dejected. **misery** *(n),* **miserably** *(adv).*

**misfit** *(n)* someone not suited to the people or situation around them.

**misfortune** 1 *(n)* an unlucky event. 2 *(n)* bad luck.

**misguided** *(adj)* If you are **misguided**, you have the wrong idea about something. **misguidedly** *(adv).*

**mishap** *(n)* an unfortunate accident.

**mislay** mislaying mislaid *(v)* to lose something for a short while, because you have put it in a place where you cannot find it.

**mislead** misleading misled *(v)* to give someone the wrong idea about something. **misleading** *(adj).*

**misprint** *(n)* a mistake in a book, newspaper, etc. where the letters have been printed wrongly.

**miss** misses missing missed 1 *(v)* to fail to hit something. 2 *(v)* to fail to catch, see, do, etc. 3 *(v)* to be unhappy because someone or something is not with you. *I missed Gurdit when he went away.*

**missile** *(n)* a weapon which is thrown or shot at a target. *An atomic missile.*

**mist** *(n)* a cloud of water droplets in the air. **misty** *(adj).*

**mistake** mistaking mistook mistaken 1 *(n)* an error, or a misunderstanding. 2 *(v)* to believe that someone is somebody different. *I mistook Tracey for her sister.*

**mistletoe** *(n)* an evergreen plant that grows as a parasite on trees. Mistletoe has white berries and is often used as a Christmas decoration.

**mistletoe**

**mistreat** mistreating mistreated *(v)* to treat something roughly or badly.

**mistress** mistresses *(n)* a name for a female teacher in some schools.

**mistrust** mistrusting mistrusted *(v)* to be suspicious of someone. **mistrust** *(n).*

**misunderstanding** 1 *(n)* a failure to understand. **misunderstand** *(v).* 2 *(n)* a disagreement between two people.

**misuse** *(mis-yooze)* misusing misused *(v)* to use something in the wrong way.

**mix** mixes mixing mixed *(v)* to combine or blend different things. **mixture** *(n).*

**moan** moaning moaned 1 *(v)* to complain in a dreary way. 2 *(v)* to make a low, sad sound, usually because you are in pain or are unhappy. **moan** *(n).*

**mob** *(n)* a large, dangerous crowd.

**mobile** *(adj)* able to move or be moved. *A mobile crane.*

**mock** mocking mocked 1 *(v)* to make fun of someone in an unpleasant way. **mockery** *(n).* 2 *(adj)* false, or imitation. *A mock battle.* 3 *(n)* a practice examination.

**model** 1 *(n)* a small version of a real-life object, made to scale. 2 *(n)* someone who poses for an artist or a photographer.

**modem** *(n)* a piece of electronic equipment used to send information between computers by telephone.

**moderate** *(adj)* not extreme.

**modern** *(adj)* up-to-date, or new in style.

**modernize** *or* **modernise** modernizing modernized *(v)* to make something more modern or up to date.

**modest** *(adj)* not boastful about your abilities or achievements. **modesty** *(n).*

**modify** modifies modifying modified *(v)* to alter something slightly.

*Some words that begin with a "mi" sound are spelt "my".*

**Mohammed** *or* **Muhammad** *(n)* the founder of the Islamic religion. Muslims believe that Mohammed is God's main prophet.

**moist** *(adj)* damp and slightly wet.

**mole** 1 *(n)* a small, furry mammal that digs tunnels and lives underground. 2 *(n)* a small growth on the skin.

mole

**molecule** *(n)* the smallest particle of a substance that can exist on its own, usually made of two or more atoms bonded together. **molecular** *(adj).*

**molest** **molesting molested** 1 *(v)* to disturb, annoy, or interfere with someone. 2 *(v)* to abuse or attack someone sexually.

**molten** *(adj)* **Molten** metal is so hot that is has melted to become a liquid.

**moment** 1 *(n)* a very brief period of time. 2 If something is happening **at the moment**, it is happening now.

**monarch** *(n)* a ruler, such as a king or queen, who has usually inherited his or her position. **monarchy** *(n).*

**monastery** **monasteries** *(n)* a group of buildings where monks live and work.

**money** **monies** *(n)* the coins and notes which people use to buy things.

**mongrel** *(n)* a dog of mixed breed.

**monitor** **monitoring monitored** 1 *(v)* to keep a check on something over a period of time. 2 *(n)* the visual display unit of a computer.

**monk** *(n)* a man who lives in a religious community and has promised to devote his life to God.

**monkey** *(n)* an animal like a small ape, usually with a tail.

**monologue** *(mon-oh-log) (n)* a long speech by one person.

**monotonous** *(adj)* going on and on in a dull and boring way. **monotony** *(n).*

**monsoon** *(n)* a season of torrential rain and strong winds in Asian countries.

**monster** 1 *(n)* In stories, a **monster** is a large, fierce, or horrible creature. 2 *(n)* a very wicked person.

**monstrous** 1 *(adj)* extremely large, terrible, or strange. *A monstrous creature.* **monstrosity** *(n).* 2 *(adj)* wrong and wicked. *Monstrous behaviour.*

**month** *(n)* a four-week period. **monthly** *(adj),* **monthly** *(adv).*

**monument** 1 *(n)* an old, important statue, building, etc. 2 *(n)* a statue, building, etc. that is meant to remind people of an event or a person.

**mood** 1 *(n)* Your **mood** is the way that you are feeling. 2 If you are **in a mood**, you feel sulky or bad-tempered.

**moody** **moodier moodiest** 1 *(adj)* cross, or unhappy. **moodily** *(adv).* 2 *(adj)* having frequent changes of mood or feelings.

**moon** 1 *(n)* a satellite of a planet. *Mars has two moons.* 2 **Moon** *(n)* the satellite that moves around the Earth once each month and reflects light from the Sun. *The first diagram below shows how the Moon moves around the Earth, while the second identifies the different phases of the Moon as they are seen from the Earth during the course of a month.*

**The Moon's motion**

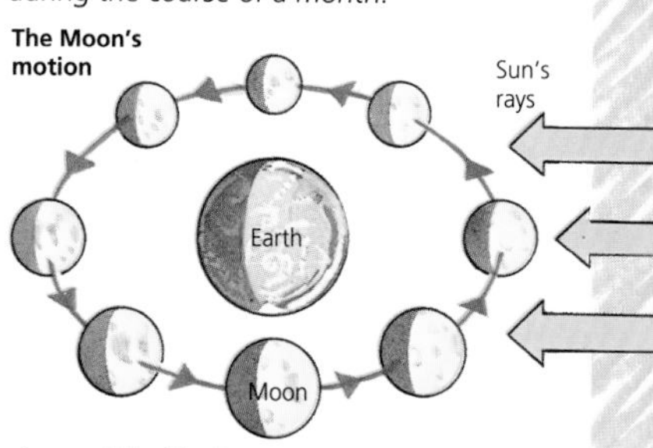


**phases of the Moon**

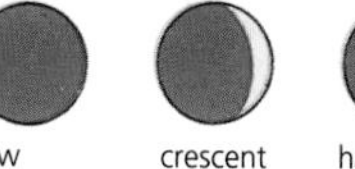

new Moon (invisible)

crescent Moon (waxing)

half-Moon (first quarter)

gibbous Moon (waxing)

full Moon

gibbous Moon (waning)

half-Moon (last quarter)

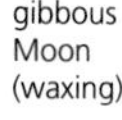

crescent Moon (old Moon)

**moonlight** *(n)* the light of the Earth's moon that you can see at night.

**moor mooring moored 1** *(n)* an open, grassy area, often covered with heather. **moorland** *(n)*. 2 *(v)* If you **moor** a boat, you tie it up or anchor it. **moorings** *(n)*.

**mop** *(n)* a long stick with a sponge or bundle of cloth or string at one end, used to clean floors. **mop** *(v)*.

**mope moping moped** *(v)* to be miserable and depressed.

**moral 1** *(adj)* to do with right and wrong. *A moral dilemma.* **morality** *(n)*. 2 *(plural n)* Your **morals** are your standards of behaviour. **3** *(n)* the lesson taught by a story.

**morale** *(mor-**ahl**)* *(n)* hope, or confidence. *We have to keep up morale.*

**morbid** *(adj)* very interested in death and gruesome things. **morbidly** *(adv)*.

**more most 1** *(adj)* greater in number, size, etc. **more** *(n)*, **more** *(adv)*. **2 more or less** roughly, or nearly.

**Morse code** *(n)* a way of sending messages that uses long and short bursts of light or sound to represent letters.

**morsel** *(n)* a small piece of food.

**mortal 1** *(adj)* unable to live forever. **2** *(n)* a human being. **3** *(adj)* deadly, or causing death. *A mortal wound.* **mortally** *(adv)*.

**mortar** *(n)* a mixture of sand, water, and cement that is used for building.

**mortgage** *(n)* a loan from a building society or bank to buy a house.

**mosaic** *(moh-**zay**-ik)* *(n)* a pattern or picture made up of small pieces of coloured stone or glass.

**Moslem** *see* **Muslim**.

**mosque** *(mosk)* *(n)* a building used by Muslims for worship.

**mosquito** *(moss-**kee**-toe)* **mosquitoes** *or* **mosquitos** *(n)* a small insect which sucks blood from animals and humans.

**moss mosses** *(n)* a small, furry, green plant that grows on wet soil or stone.

**moth** *(n)* an insect like a butterfly, that usually flies at night.

**emperor moth** (male)

**motion** *(n)* movement.

**motivate motivating motivated** *(n)* to encourage someone to do something. *The coach tried to motivate his team to win.*

**motive** *(n)* a reason for doing something.

**motor 1** *(n)* a machine that changes electricity into mechanical energy to produce movement. **2** *(adj)* to do with cars or engines. *Motor mechanics.*

**motorbike** *(n)* *(informal)* a motorcycle.

**motorcycle** *(n)* a two-wheeled vehicle with an engine. *The picture shows a Yamaha TDM850 motorcycle.*

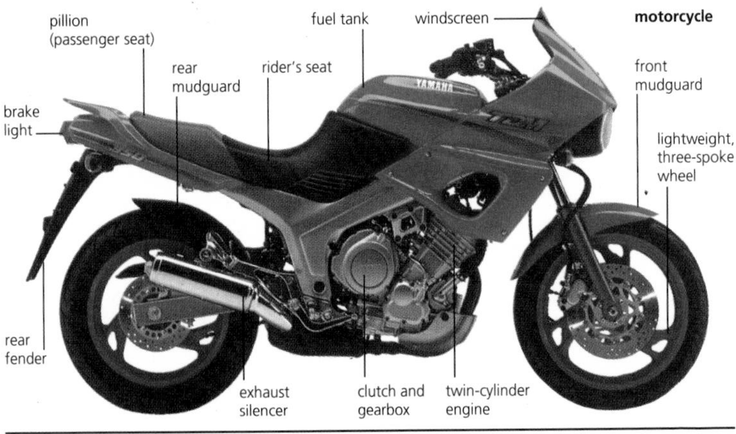

**motorcycle**

**motorist** *(n)* a car driver.

**motorway** *(n)* a wide road with several lanes for fast, long-distance traffic.

**mottled** *(adj)* covered with patches of different colours.

**motto** **mottos** *or* **mottoes** *(n)* a short sentence that is meant to guide your behaviour.

**mould** **moulding moulded** 1 *(v)* to model or shape something. *Mould the clay into a cat shape.* **mould** *(n).* 2 *(n)* a furry fungus that grows on old food or damp walls. **mouldy** *(adj).*

**moult** **moulting moulted** *(v)* When a bird or animal **moults**, its outer covering of fur, feathers, or skin comes off so that a new one can grow.

**mound** *(n)* a hill, or a pile.

**mount** **mounting mounted** 1 *(v)* to get on, or to climb up. *Mount the horse.* **mount** *(n).* 2 *(n)* a mountain.

**mountain** 1 *(n)* a very high piece of land, higher than a hill. 2 *(n)* a large amount of something. *A mountain of work.*

**mountain bike** *(n)* a strong bicycle with many gears that can be ridden on rough or hilly ground. *See* **bicycle**.

**mountaineer** *(n)* someone who climbs mountains. **mountaineering** *(n).*

**mourn** **mourning mourned** *(v)* to be very sad and grieve for someone who has died. **mourner** *(n),* **mourning** *(n).*

**mournful** *(adj)* sad and miserable.

**mouse** **mice** 1 *(n)* a small, furry animal with a long tail. 2 *(n)* a small control box that you use to move the cursor on your computer screen.

**harvest mouse**

**mousse** *(moose)* 1 *(n)* a cold food made with beaten egg whites, that tastes light and fluffy. *Chocolate mousse.* 2 *(n)* a substance that you use to style your hair.

**moustache** *(n)* the hair on a man's top lip.

**mouth** 1 *(n)* the part of your face that you use for eating and talking. 2 *(n)* the entrance to a cave or river.

**mouth organ** *(n)* a small musical instrument that you play by blowing out and drawing in your breath through it.

**move** **moving moved** 1 *(v)* to change place or position. 2 *(n)* a step, or a movement.

**movement** 1 *(n)* a change from one place to another. 2 *(n)* a group of people who have joined together to support a cause. *The peace movement.*

**mow** **mowing mowed mown** *(v)* to cut grass, corn, etc. **mower** *(n).*

**MP** *see* **Member of Parliament**.

**mph** The initials **mph** stand for miles per hour. *This car's top speed is 130mph.*

**much** 1 *(adv)* greatly. *It's much too expensive.* **much** *(adj).* 2 *(n)* a large amount of something. *I don't eat much.*

**muck** **mucking mucked** 1 *(n)* dirt, or mess. **mucky** *(adj).* 2 **muck about** *(v)* *(slang)* to act in a silly way.

**mucus** *(mew-kuss)* *(n)* a slimy substance made in some parts of your body, such as your nose.

**mud** *(n)* wet, sticky earth. **muddy** *(adj).*

**muddle** **muddling muddled** 1 *(v)* to mix things up, or to confuse them. **muddled** *(adj).* 2 *(n)* a mess, or a confusion.

**muesli** *(myooz-lee)* *(n)* a breakfast cereal made with grain, dried fruit, and nuts.

**muffle** **muffling muffled** *(v)* to make a sound quieter or duller. *Hannah tried to muffle her laughter with a handkerchief.*

**mug** **mugging mugged** 1 *(n)* a large cup with a handle. 2 *(v)* *(informal)* to attack someone and try to steal their money.

**muggy** **muggier muggiest** *(adj)* If the weather is **muggy**, it is warm and damp.

**Muhammad** *see* **Mohammed**.

**multicultural** *(adj)* involving or made up of people from different races or religions. *A multicultural community.*

**multilingual** *(adj)* using several different languages. *A multilingual guidebook.*

**multimedia** *(adj)* combining different media, such as sound, pictures, and text. *A multimedia computer game.*

**multiple** 1 *(adj)* made up of many parts or things. *Theresa suffered multiple injuries.* 2 *(n)* a number into which a smaller number can go an exact number of times. *10 and 15 are multiples of 5.*

**multiply multiplies multiplying multiplied** 1 *(v)* to grow in number or amount. *The weeds keep multiplying.* 2 *(v)* to add the same number to itself several times. *If you multiply 3 by 4, you get 12.* **multiplication** *(n).*

**multiracial** *(adj)* involving people of different races. *A multiracial school.*

**multistorey** *(adj)* having several floors.

**multitude** 1 *(n)* a crowd of people. 2 *(n)* a large number of things.

**mummy mummies** *(n)* a dead body that has been preserved and wrapped in cloth to make it last for a very long time.

**mumps** *(n)* an infectious illness that makes the glands in your neck swell up.

**munch munches munching munched** *(v)* to chew or crunch food.

**mural** *(n)* a wall painting.

**murder murdering murdered** *(v)* to kill someone. **murder** *(n),* **murderer** *(n).*

**murky murkier murkiest** *(adj)* dark, dirty, and gloomy.

**murmur murmuring murmured** 1 *(v)* to talk very quietly. **murmur** *(n).* 2 *(v)* to make a quiet, low, continuous sound. *The wind murmured in the trees.* **murmur** *(n).*

**muscle** *(n)* Your **muscles** pull on your bones to make them move. *The diagram shows the muscles that move your arm.*

**upper arm muscles**
biceps
triceps
tendons (attach muscle to bone)

**museum** *(n)* a place where interesting objects are displayed for people to look at.

**mushroom** *(n)* a type of plant that has no leaves, flowers, or roots. Many mushrooms can be eaten.

**music** 1 *(n)* a pleasant arrangement of sounds, played on instruments or sung. 2 *(n)* printed or written signs or notes that represent musical sounds. *Can you read music?*

**musical** 1 *(adj)* If you are **musical**, you are very interested in music, or able to play an instrument well. 2 *(adj)* to do with music. *Musical instruments.* 3 *(n)* a play or film which includes singing and dancing.

**musician** *(n)* someone who plays or composes music.

**Muslim** *or* **Moslem** *(n)* someone who follows the religion of Islam. **Muslim** *(adj).*

**mussel** *(n)* a type of shellfish that you can eat.

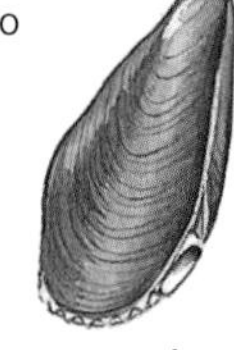
**mussel**

**must** 1 *(v)* to have to do something. *I must go now.* 2 *(v)* to be definitely doing something. *He must be lying.*

**mustard** *(n)* a hot and spicy food flavouring, usually eaten with meat.

**musty mustier mustiest** *(adj)* smelling of damp or mould. **mustiness** *(n).*

**mutant** *(n)* a living thing that has developed different characteristics because of a change in its parents' genes.

**mutilate** *(myoo-til-ate)* **mutilating mutilated** *(v)* to injure or damage someone or something. **mutilation** *(n).*

**mutiny mutinies** *(n)* a revolt against someone in charge, especially in the army or navy. **mutineer** *(n),* **mutiny** *(v).*

**mutter muttering muttered** *(v)* to say something quietly so that people cannot hear you properly.

**mutual** *(adj)* shared, or joint. *A mutual friend.* **mutually** *(adv).*

**muzzle** 1 *(n)* an animal's nose and mouth. 2 *(n)* a cover for an animal's mouth which stops it biting. **muzzle** *(v).*

**mysterious** *(adj)* puzzling and intriguing. *A mysterious stranger.*

**mystery mysteries** *(n)* something that is puzzling or hard to understand.

**mystify mystifies mystifying mystified** *(v)* to puzzle or confuse someone.

**myth** 1 *(n)* an old story or legend, especially one about gods and heroes. **mythical** *(adj).* 2 *(n)* a false idea that many people believe.

**mythology mythologies** *(n)* a set of stories about subjects like the ancient gods and heroes. **mythological** *(adj).*

# Nn

**nag** **nagging nagged** *(v)* to try to persuade someone to do something by speaking about it constantly. **nag** *(n).*

**nail** 1 *(n)* the hard covering at the end of your fingers and toes. 2 *(n)* a small piece of pointed metal that you hammer into something. **nail** *(v).*

**naked** *(adj)* bare, or uncovered. **nakedness** *(n),* **nakedly** *(adv).*

**name** 1 *(n)* what a person or thing is called. **name** *(v).* 2 *(n)* a reputation. *Wayne made his name as a singer.*

**nanny** **nannies** 1 *(n)* someone trained to look after young children in their home. 2 **nanny goat** *(n)* a female goat.

**nap** **napping napped** *(v)* to sleep for a short time. **nap** *(n).*

**napkin** *(n)* a square piece of cloth that you use to protect your clothes at meals.

**narrate** **narrating narrated** *(v)* to tell a story. **narration** *(n),* **narrator** *(n).*

**narrative** 1 *(n)* a story, or an account of something that has happened. 2 *(adj)* telling a story. *Narrative verse.*

**narrow** **narrower narrowest** *(adj)* thin, or not wide. **narrowness** *(n).*

**nasal** *(adj)* to do with your nose.

**nasty** **nastier nastiest** 1 *(adj)* disgusting, or unpleasant. 2 *(adj)* cruel, or unkind.

**nation** *(n)* a large group of people who live in the same part of the world and often share the same language, customs, etc. **national** *(adj),* **nationally** *(adv).*

**nationalist** *(n)* someone who is proud of their country, or who fights for its independence. **nationalism** *(n).*

**nationality** **nationalities** *(n)* Your **nationality** is the nation or country to which you belong. *American nationality.*

**nationalize** *or* **nationalise** **nationalizing nationalized** *(v)* If an industry is **nationalized**, its ownership is transferred from a private company to the government. **nationalization** *(n).*

**native** 1 *(n)* someone born in a particular place. *Barry is a native of Australia.* **native** *(adj).* 2 **native country** *(n)* the country where you were born.

**Nativity** 1 *(n)* the birth of Jesus Christ. 2 **nativity play** *(n)* a play telling the story of the birth of Jesus Christ.

**natural** 1 *(adj)* found in nature, or to do with nature. 2 *(adj)* normal, or usual. *It's only natural to need a rest after a run.*

**natural history** *(n)* the study of animals and plants.

**naturalist** *(n)* someone who studies animals and plants.

**nature** 1 *(n)* everything in the world that is not made by people, such as plants, animals, the weather, etc. 2 *(n)* Your **nature** is your character.

**naughty** **naughtier naughtiest** *(adj)* badly-behaved, or disobedient. **naughtiness** *(n),* **naughtily** *(adv).*

**nausea** *(nor-zee-er) (n)* a feeling of sickness. **nauseous** *(adj).*

**nautical** *(adj)* to do with ships and sailing.

**naval** *(adj)* to do with a navy or warships.

**navel** *(n)* the small, round hollow in your stomach, where your umbilical cord was attached when you were born.

**navigate** **navigating navigated** *(v)* to travel in a ship, plane, or other vehicle, using maps, compasses, etc. to guide you. **navigation** *(n),* **navigator** *(n).*

**navy** **navies** 1 *(n)* the ships and sailors that defend a country at sea. 2 **navy blue** *(n)* a very dark blue colour.

**nb** the initials of the the Latin phrase *nota bene* which means "note well". The initials nb are used to make people take notice of something important.

**near** **nearing neared** 1 *(prep)* close to. *Alex lives near me.* 2 *(v)* to come close to something. *The train neared the station.*

**neat** **neater neatest** 1 *(adj)* tidy and orderly. **neatly** *(adv).* 2 *(adj)* simple and pleasing. *A neat solution.* **neatly** *(adv).*

**necessary** *(adj)* If something is **necessary**, you have to do it or have it. **necessity** *(n),* **necessarily** *(adv).*

**neck** *(n)* the part of your body that joins your head to your shoulders.

**necklace** *(n)* a piece of jewellery worn around your neck.

*Some words that begin with a "na" sound are spelt "gna" or "kna".*

**nectar** *(n)* a sweet liquid that bees collect from flowers and turn into honey.

**need** **needing needed** 1 *(v)* to want something urgently. *The refugees need food and shelter.* 2 *(v)* to have to do something. *I need to revise for my exams.*

**needle** 1 *(n)* a thin, pointed piece of metal, with a hole for thread at one end, used for sewing. 2 *(n)* a long, thin, pointed rod, used for knitting. 3 *(n)* a thin, hollow tube with a sharp end that doctors use for giving injections or taking blood.

**negative** 1 *(adj)* giving the answer "no". 2 *(n)* a photographic film, used to make prints, which shows light areas as dark, and dark areas as light. 3 *(adj)* A **negative** number is less than zero.

**neglect** **neglecting neglected** *(v)* to fail to look after someone or something. **neglect** *(n),* **neglectful** *(adj).*

**negotiate** **negotiating negotiated** *(v)* to bargain or discuss something, in order to come to an agreement. **negotiation** *(n).*

**neighbour** *(n)* someone who lives next door or near to you.

**neighbourhood** *(n)* the local area around your house.

**neither** *(adj)* not either. *Neither of my brothers likes custard.* **neither** *(pronoun).*

**nephew** *(n)* Someone's **nephew** is their brother's or sister's son.

**nerve** 1 *(n)* Your **nerves** are the thin fibres that send messages between your brain and other parts of your body, so that you can move and feel. 2 *(n)* courage and calmness. *You need lots of nerve to be a lion tamer.* 3 *(n) (informal)* cheek, or rudeness. *Harry's got a nerve!*

**nervous** 1 *(adj)* easily upset or frightened. **nervousness** *(n).* 2 *(adj)* to do with the nerves. *The nervous system.* 3 *(n)* If someone has a **nervous breakdown**, they are so worried or depressed about something that they become ill.

**nest** *(n)* a place built by birds and many other animals to lay their eggs and bring up their young. **nest** *(v).*

**nestle** **nestling nestled** *(v)* to settle into a comfortable position. *The baby nestled against her mother's shoulder.*

**net** 1 *(n)* material made from fine threads or ropes that are knotted together with holes between them. 2 *(n)* a bag made from net material and attached to a pole, that you use to catch fish, butterflies, etc.

**netball** *(n)* a game played by two teams, in which goals are scored by throwing a ball through a high net.

**nettle** *(n)* a weed that stings you if you touch it.

**network** **networking networked** 1 *(n)* a system of things that are connected to each other. *A rail network.* 2 *(v)* to connect computers so that they can work together.

**neuter** **neutering neutered** 1 *(adj)* neither masculine nor feminine. 2 *(v)* If you **neuter** an animal, you remove its sex organs so that it cannot reproduce.

**neutral** *(adj)* In chemistry, a **neutral** substance is neither an acid nor an alkali.

**neutralize** *or* **neutralise** **neutralizing neutralized** *(v)* to stop something from working or from having an effect.

**nevertheless** *(adv)* in spite of that, or yet. *Titus was cold and hungry. Nevertheless, he kept on walking.*

**new** **newer newest** 1 *(adj)* just made, or just begun. 2 *(adj)* different or strange.

**newsagent** *(n)* a person or shop that sells newspapers, magazines, etc.

**newspaper** *(n)* sheets of folded paper containing news reports, articles, etc.

**newt** *(n)* a small creature that lives on land but lays its eggs in water.

**marbled newt**

**next** 1 *(adj)* immediately following. *We'll catch the next train.* **next** *(adv).* 2 *(adj)* nearest. *Bruno's desk is next to mine.* **next** *(adv).* 3 **next door** in or at the nearest house, building, etc.

**nib** *(n)* the part of a pen through which ink flows.

*Some words that begin with a "n" sound are spelt "kn" or "pn".*

**nibble** **nibbling nibbled** *(v)* to bite something gently, or to take small bites of something. **nibble** *(n).*

**nice** **nicer nicest** *(adj)* pleasant, or good.

**nickname** *(n)* a name that you give to a friend. **nickname** *(v).*

**niece** *(n)* Someone's **niece** is their brother's or sister's daughter.

**night** *(n)* the time between sunset and sunrise, when it is dark.

**nightie** *(n) (informal)* a loose dress that girls or women wear in bed.

**nightly** *(adv)* happening every night. *The doctor visits nightly.* **nightly** *(adj).*

**nightmare** *(n)* a frightening or unpleasant dream or situation.

**nil** *(n)* nothing, or zero.

**nimble** **nimbler nimblest** *(adj)* moving quickly and lightly. **nimbly** *(adv).*

**nipple** *(n)* one of the two small, raised parts on a person's chest.

**nits** *(plural n)* eggs laid by lice.

**no** **1** *(interject)* a word used to refuse something. **2** *(adj)* not any. *Have no fear.*

**no.** *short for* **number**.

**noble** **nobler noblest** **1** *(adj)* A **noble** family is aristocratic and of high rank. **nobility** *(n).* **2** *(adj)* good and unselfish.

**nobody** *(pronoun)* not a single person.

**nocturnal** *(adj)* A **nocturnal** animal is active at night. *Owls are nocturnal.*

**noise** *(n)* a sound, especially a loud or unpleasant one. **noisy** *(adj),* **noisiness** *(n).*

**nomad** *(n)* a member of a tribe that wanders around, instead of living in one place. **nomadic** *(adj).*

**nominate** **nominating nominated** *(v)* to suggest that someone would be the right person to do a job. *I nominate George as leader.* **nomination** *(n).*

**nonetheless** *(adv)* in spite of that. *Henry fell over. Nonetheless, he won the race.*

**nonfiction** *(n)* writing that gives information about real things, people, and events, rather than made-up stories.

**nonsense** *(n)* If something is **nonsense**, it is silly or has no meaning.

**nonstop** *(adj)* without any stops or breaks. *A nonstop flight.* **nonstop** *(adv).*

**no one** *or* **no-one** *(pronoun)* not a single person. *There is no one in the park.*

**noose** *(n)* a loop at the end of a rope, which closes up as the rope is pulled.

**normal** *(adj)* usual and ordinary. **normality** *(n),* **normally** *(adv).*

**north** **1** *(n)* one of the four main points of the compass, the direction on your right when you face the setting Sun in the northern hemisphere. **2** *(adj)* A **north** wind blows from the north. **3** **North Pole** *(n)* the very cold part of the Earth in the far north.

**nose** *(n)* the part of your face that you use when you smell and breathe.

**nostalgic** *(adj)* People who are **nostalgic** like to think about the past and are sad that things have changed since then.

**nostril** *(n)* Your **nostrils** are the two holes in your nose through which you breathe and smell.

**nosy** **nosier nosiest** *(adj) (informal)* A **nosy** person is too interested in things that do not concern them. **nosily** *(adv).*

**note** **1** *(n)* a short letter or message. **2** *(n)* a piece of paper money. **3** *(n)* a musical sound or the symbol that represents it.

**nothing** **1** *(pronoun)* not anything at all. *There was nothing in the cupboard.* **2** *(pronoun)* not anything important. *I did nothing today.*

**notice** **noticing noticed** **1** *(v)* to see or become aware of something. **2** *(n)* a written message put in a public place to tell people about something.

**notify** **notifies notifying notified** *(v)* to tell someone about something officially or formally. **notification** *(n).*

**notorious** *(adj)* well known for something bad. *The school is notorious for bullying.*

**nought** *(nort) (n)* the number 0, or zero.

**noun** *(n)* a word that refers to a person or thing. *"Dog", "happiness", and "France" are all nouns. See* page 3.

**nourish** *(nuh-rish)* **nourishes nourishing nourished** *(v)* to give a person, animal, or plant enough food to keep them strong and healthy.

**novel** **1** *(n)* a book that tells a story. **2** *(adj)* new and interesting. *A novel idea.*

*Some words that begin with a "n" sound are spelt "gn" or "kn".*
*Some words that begin with a "ni" sound are spelt "ny".*

**novelty** **novelties** *(n)* something new, interesting, and unusual. **novelty** *(adj)*.

**novice** *(n)* a beginner, or someone who is not very experienced.

**nowhere** *(adv)* not any place. *There was nowhere to hide.*

**nuclear** *(new-klee-ur)* **1** *(adj)* to do with the splitting of atoms. *Nuclear physics.* **2 nuclear power** *(n)* power created by the splitting of atoms.

**nude** *(adj)* naked. **nudist** *(n)*, **nudity** *(n)*.

**nudge** **nudging nudged** *(v)* to give someone or something a small push, often with your elbow. **nudge** *(n)*.

**nuisance** *(new-sunss)* *(n)* someone or something that annoys you and causes problems for you.

**numb** *(num)* *(adj)* unable to feel anything. **numbness** *(n)*, **numb** *(v)*.

**number** *(n)* a word or sign used for counting and doing sums.

**numeral** *(n)* a written sign that represents a number. *Roman numerals.*

**numerate** *(adj)* able to understand basic arithmetic. **numeracy** *(n)*.

**numerator** *(n)* In fractions, the **numerator** is the number above the line, which shows how many parts of the denominator are taken.

**numerical** *(adj)* to do with numbers. *Numerical order.* **numerically** *(adv)*.

**nun** *(n)* a woman who lives in a Christian religious community and has promised to devote her life to God.

**nurse** *(n)* someone who looks after people who are ill, usually in a hospital.

**nursery** **nurseries** **1** *(n)* a place where babies and very young children are looked after while their parents are at work. **2 nursery school** *(n)* a school for children aged three to five.

**nut** **1** *(n)* a fruit with a hard shell that grows on trees. **2** *(n)* a small piece of metal with a hole in the middle that screws onto a bolt and holds it in place.

**nutritious** *(nyoo-**trish**-uss)* *(adj)* Food that is **nutritious** contains substances that your body can use to help you stay healthy and strong.

**nylon** *(n)* a light, man-made fibre, used to make tights, fishing line, etc.

# Oo

**oaf** *(n)* a clumsy and rude person.

**OAP** *(n)* an old person who receives a pension. The initials OAP stand for old age pensioner.

**oar** *(n)* a wooden pole with a flat blade at one end, used for rowing a boat.

**oasis** *(oh-**ay**-siss)* **oases** *(n)* a place in a desert where there is water, and where plants and trees grow.

**oath** **1** *(n)* a serious, formal promise. **2** *(n)* a swear word.

**obedient** *(adj)* doing what you are told to do. **obedience** *(n)*, **obediently** *(adv)*.

**obey** **obeying obeyed** *(v)* to do the things that someone tells you to do.

**object** **objecting objected** **1** *(**ob**-jekt)* *(n)* something that you can see and touch, but is not alive. **2** *(**ob**-jekt)* *(n)* the thing that you are trying to achieve. **3** *(ob-**jekt**)* *(v)* If you **object** to something, you dislike it or disagree with it. **objection** *(n)*.

**objective** **1** *(adj)* based on facts, not on feelings or opinions. *An objective report.* **objectivity** *(n)*, **objectively** *(adv)*. **2** *(n)* an aim that you are working towards. *Our objective is to make a pollution-free car.*

**obligation** *(n)* something that it is your duty to do. **obligatory** *(adj)*.

**oblige** **obliging obliged** *(v)* If you are **obliged** to do something, you have to do it. **obligatory** *(adj)*.

**oblong** *(n)* a shape with four straight sides and four right angles, that is longer than it is wide.

**obnoxious** *(adj)* very unpleasant.

**obscene** **obscener obscenest** *(adj)* indecent and shocking. **obscenity** *(n)*.

**obscure** **obscuring obscured; obscurer obscurest** **1** *(adj)* not well known. **2** *(v)* to make it difficult to see something. *The pillar obscured our view of the stage.*

**observant** *(adj)* good at noticing things.

**observatory** **observatories** *(n)* a building containing telescopes and other scientific instruments for studying the sky and the stars.

**observe** observing observed 1 *(v)* to watch someone or something carefully. **observation** *(n)*. 2 *(v)* to notice something by looking or watching. *I observed that Helen was pale.* 3 *(v)* to make a remark. *Jonathan observed that the train was late again.*

**obsess** obsesses obsessing obsessed *(v)* If something **obsesses** you, you think about it all the time. **obsession** *(n)*.

**obstacle** *(n)* something that gets in your way or prevents you from doing something.

**obstinate** *(adj)* stubborn and unwilling to change your mind. **obstinacy** *(n)*.

**occasional** *(adj)* happening sometimes. *Occasional visits.* **occasionally** *(adv)*.

**occupation** 1 *(n)* a job. 2 *(n)* something that you enjoy doing in your free time.

**occupy** occupies occupying occupied 1 *(v)* to live in a building, room, etc. *Who occupies this house?* 2 *(v)* to keep someone busy and happy. *The computer occupied the boys for hours.*

**occur** occurring occurred 1 *(v)* to happen. 2 *(v)* If something **occurs to you**, you suddenly think of it.

**ocean** *(oh-shun)* *(n)* one of the large areas of water on the Earth. *This map shows the five main oceans of the world.*

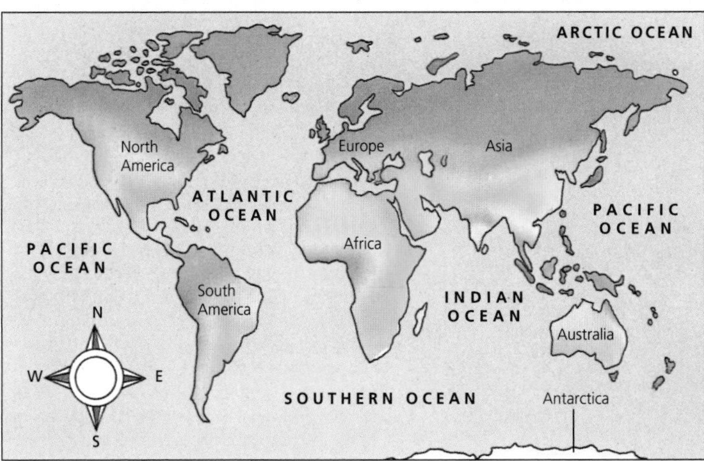


**obstruct** obstructing obstructed 1 *(v)* to block a road or path. *Fallen trees obstructed the road.* **obstruction** *(n)*. 2 *(v)* to prevent something happening, or to make something difficult. *Max obstructed all attempts to make him tidy his room.* **obstructive** *(adj)*.

**obtain** obtaining obtained *(v)* to get, or to be given something.

**obtuse** 1 *(adj)* slow to understand things. 2 *(adj)* An **obtuse** angle is an angle of between 90° and 180°.

**obvious** *(adj)* easy to see or understand.

**occasion** 1 *(n)* a time when something happens. *Zucas had been to London on several occasions.* 2 *(n)* a special or important event.

**o'clock** *(adv)* a word you use when saying what the time is. O'clock is short for "of the clock". *It's 3 o'clock.*

**octave** *(n)* the eight note gap in a musical scale between a note and the note of the same name above or below it.

**octopus** octopuses *(n)* a sea creature with a soft body and eight long tentacles.

**odd odder oddest 1** *(adj)* strange and difficult to explain or understand. **2** *(adj)* An **odd** number cannot be divided exactly by two. *1, 47, and 895 are odd numbers.* **3** *(adj)* not matching. *Odd socks.*

**odds** *(plural n)* the probability of something happening.

**odour** *(oh-der) (n)* a smell.

**off 1** *(prep)* away from a place. *Take that off the table.* **2** *(adv)* not switched on. *The light's off.* **3** If food has gone **off**, it has gone bad and can no longer be eaten.

**offence 1** *(n)* a crime. **2** If you **cause offence**, you upset someone. **3** If you **take offence**, you feel upset by something.

**offend offending offended 1** *(v)* to upset someone. **2** *(v)* to commit a crime.

**offensive** *(adj)* unpleasant and upsetting. **offensively** *(adv).*

**offer offering offered 1** *(v)* to ask someone if they would like something. *Offer Sam some cake.* **offer** *(n).* **2** *(v)* to say you are willing to do something for someone. *I offered to take the message.*

**offhand 1** *(adj)* abrupt, or casual. **2** *(adj)* without preparation. *I don't know the answer offhand.*

**office** *(n)* a room or building in which people work, usually sitting at desks.

**officer** *(n)* someone who is in charge of other people, especially in the armed forces or the police.

**official 1** *(adj)* approved by someone in authority. *An official enquiry.* **2** *(n)* someone in an important position.

**off-licence** *(n)* a shop which sells alcoholic drinks.

**off-peak** *(adj)* happening when there is less activity or demand. *Off-peak travel.*

**off-putting** *(adj) (informal)* discouraging or disturbing.

**offspring** *(plural n)* an animal's young, or a human's children.

**often** *(adv)* many times.

**ogre** *(oh-ger) (n)* a fierce, cruel giant in fairy stories.

**oil oiling oiled 1** *(n)* a thick, smooth liquid. Different types of oil are used for heating buildings, for cooking, and for making machines run smoothly. **oily** *(adj).* **2** *(v)* to cover something with oil. *You should oil your bicycle chain regularly.*

**oil rig** *(n)* a large platform used as a base for drilling for oil under the sea or under the ground.

**old older oldest 1** *(adj)* Someone who is **old** has lived for a long time. **2** *(adj)* Something that is **old** has existed or been used for a long time. **3** *(adj)* from an earlier time. *My old French teacher.*

**old-fashioned** *(adj)* no longer fashionable or popular.

**ominous** *(adj)* If something is **ominous**, it makes you feel that something bad is going to happen. *An ominous silence.*

**omit omitting omitted 1** *(v)* to leave something out. *Hans omitted a line from the song.* **2** *(v)* If you **omit** to do something, you do not do it. *Rupert omitted to eat his breakfast.*

**omnibus omnibuses** *(n)* a collection of stories or television programmes, that were first published or shown separately.

**once 1** *(adv)* one time. *I've been to Paris once.* **2** *(adv)* in the past. *Once this country was covered with ice.* **3** *(conj)* after something has happened. *I'll tell you all about it once we get home.* **4 at once** immediately. *Stop that at once!*

**one-way 1** *(adj)* Traffic can only travel in one direction down a **one-way** street. **2** *(adj)* A **one-way** ticket allows you to travel to a place but not back again.

**onion** *(n)* a round vegetable with a strong smell and taste.

**on-line** *(adj)* **On-line** information is stored on computer disks and can be searched and read by computer.

**only 1** *(adv)* not more than, or just. *Fred only has two friends.* **2** *(adj)* with nothing or no one else. *Maria was the only person there.* **3** *(conj)* but. *We would have been on time, only the car broke down.* **4** *(n)* An **only child** has no brothers or sisters.

**onomatopoeia** *(on-oh-mat-er-pee-er) (n)* a word that sounds like the thing it describes. *"Pop" and "sizzle" are examples of onomatopoeia.*

**onward** *or* **onwards** *(adv)* forward. *We lived there from 1987 onward.*

**ooze oozing oozed** *(v)* to flow out slowly. *Mud oozed from my shoes.*

**opaque** *(oh-pake) (adj)* not clear enough to see through. *Opaque glass.*

**open** 1 *(adj)* not shut. **open** *(v).* 2 *(adj)* not covered, or not enclosed. *Open land. Open air.* 3 *(adj)* If you are **open** about something, you are honest about it. **openly** *(adv).* 4 *(v)* to start, or to begin. *The story opens in a wild wood.*

**opening** 1 *(n)* a hole or a space in something. 2 *(adj)* coming at the beginning. *The opening lines of a play.*

**opera** *(n)* a play in which the words are sung. **operatic** *(adj).*

**operation** *(n)* the cutting open of someone's body in order to repair a damaged part or remove a diseased part. **operate** *(v).*

**opinion** *(n)* the ideas and beliefs that you have about something.

**opponent** *(n)* someone who is against you in a fight or a game.

**opportunity** **opportunities** *(n)* a chance to do something. *An opportunity to learn.*

**opposite** 1 *(prep)* facing. *I sat opposite Tim.* **opposite** *(adj).* 2 *(adj)* completely different. *Sue ran in the opposite direction.* **opposite** *(n).*

**opposition** 1 *(n)* When there is **opposition** to something, people are against it. 2 **the Opposition** *(n)* the main political party that is not in power.

**oppress** **oppresses** **oppressing** **oppressed** *(v)* to treat people in a cruel, unjust, and hard way. **oppression** *(n).*

**opt** **opting** **opted** 1 *(v)* to choose to have or do something. *Lydia opted to learn German.* 2 **opt out** *(v)* to choose not to take part in something.

**optical** 1 *(adj)* to do with eyesight or eyes. 2 **optical illusion** *(n)* something you think you see which is not really there.

**optician** *(n)* someone who tests eyesight and supplies glasses and contact lenses.

**optimistic** *(adj)* People who are **optimistic** always believe that things will turn out well and successfully.

**option** *(n)* something that you can choose to do.

**optional** *(adj)* If something is **optional**, you can choose whether or not to have it or do it.

**oral** 1 *(adj)* to do with your mouth. *Oral hygiene.* **orally** *(adv).* 2 *(n)* a spoken exam or test. *A French oral.*

**orange** 1 *(n)* the colour of carrots, or a mixture of red and yellow. **orange** *(adj).* 2 *(n)* a round fruit with a thick, orange skin and sweet, juicy flesh.

**orbit** *(n)* the invisible path followed by an object circling a planet or star. **orbit** *(v).*

**orchard** *(n)* a field or farm where fruit trees are grown.

**orchestra** *(n)* a large group of musicians who play their instruments together.

**orchid** *(or-kid) (n)* a plant with colourful and often unusually shaped flowers.

**ordeal** *(n)* a very difficult and testing experience.

**order** **ordering** **ordered** 1 *(v)* to tell someone that they have to do something. **order** *(n).* 2 *(v)* to ask for something in a restaurant. **order** *(n).*

**ordinary** *(adj)* normal, or usual.

**organ** 1 *(n)* a large musical instrument with one or more keyboards and pipes of different lengths. **organist** *(n).* 2 *(n)* a part of the body that does a particular job. *The diagram shows the main human organs used for breathing, and for digesting and excreting food. The kidneys are shown separately because they are positioned behind the intestines.*

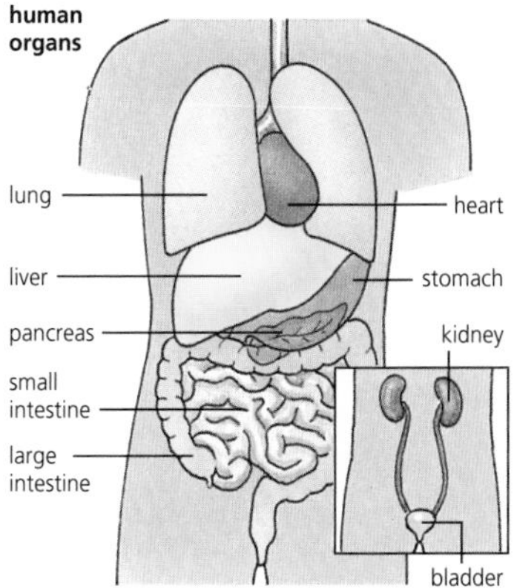


**organic** *(adj)* using only natural products and no chemicals, pesticides, etc. *Organic farming.*

*Some words that begin with an "or" sound are spelt "au" or "aw".*

**organism** *(n)* a living plant or animal.

**organization** *or* **organisation** 1 *(n)* a large company, charity, or other group. 2 *(n)* the task of planning and running something. *We left the organization of the party to Geoffrey.*

**organize** *or* **organise** organizing organized 1 *(v)* to plan and run an event. 2 *(v)* to arrange things neatly and in order.

**oriental** *(adj)* belonging to, or coming from the countries of the Far East, especially Japan and China. **Orient** *(n).*

**orienteering** *(n)* a sport in which people find their way across rough country as fast as they can, using a map and compass.

**origami** *(n)* the Japanese art of paper folding.

**origin** *(n)* the point where something began. *What was the origin of the name?*

**original** 1 *(adj)* first, or earliest. *Who were the original Australians?* **originally** *(adv).* 2 *(adj)* new and imaginative. *An original idea.* **originality** *(n).* 3 *(n)* a work of art that is not a copy. **original** *(adj).*

**ornament** *(n)* a small, attractive object that you use to decorate a room.

**ornithology** *(n)* the study of birds.

**orphan** *(n)* a child whose parents are both dead. **orphaned** *(adj).*

**orphanage** *(n)* a place where orphans live and are looked after.

**orthodontist** *(n)* someone who straightens uneven teeth.

**ostrich** ostriches *(n)* a large African bird that cannot fly.

**otherwise** 1 *(conj)* or if not. *Catch a bus. Otherwise, take a taxi.* 2 *(adv)* apart from that. *I'm tired, but otherwise I'm fine.*

**otter** *(n)* a furry mammal that lives near water and eats fish.

**ought** *(ort) (v)* If you **ought** to do something, you should do it.

**out** 1 *(adv)* not in. *I called round but you were out.* 2 *(adv)* no longer burning, or no longer alight. *The fire went out.* 3 *(adv)* no longer taking part in a game. *You will be out if you get a question wrong.* 4 *(adv)* aloud. *Pat called out to me.*

**outback** *(n)* the remote areas of Australia, away from the cities.

**outbreak** *(n)* a sudden start of something, such as a disease or war.

**outburst** *(n)* a sudden pouring out of strong emotion. *An outburst of anger.*

**outcast** *(n)* someone who is not accepted by other people.

**outcome** *(n)* the result of something.

**outcry** outcries *(n)* a loud complaint about something by a lot of people.

**outdo** outdoes outdoing outdid outdone *(v)* If you **outdo** someone, you do something better than they do.

**outdoors** *(adv)* outside, or in the open air. **outdoor** *(adj).*

**outer** *(adj)* on the outside, or furthest from the middle. *The outer edge.*

**outfit** *(n)* a set of clothes.

**outgoing** *(adj)* very sociable and friendly.

**outgrow** outgrowing outgrew outgrown *(v)* to grow too big or too old for something.

**outing** *(n)* a short trip somewhere for pleasure.

**outlaw** outlawing outlawed 1 *(n)* *(old-fashioned)* a criminal, usually in the Wild West. 2 *(v)* to forbid something by law.

**outlet** 1 *(n)* a pipe or hole that lets out liquid or gas. 2 *(n)* a shop where a company's products can be bought.

**outline** 1 *(n)* the line which shows the edge of something. 2 *(n)* the basic points or ideas about something. *A plot outline.*

**outlook** *(n)* your general attitude to things. *Yasmin has a very positive outlook.*

**outnumber** outnumbering outnumbered *(v)* to be larger in number than another group. *Girls outnumber boys on this course by four to one.*

**outpatient** *(n)* someone who is treated at a hospital, but does not stay there.

**outpost** *(n)* a remote fort or settlement.

**output** 1 *(n)* the amount produced by a person, machine, or business. 2 *(n)* information produced by a computer.

**outrageous** *(adj)* very shocking, or offensive. **outrageously** *(adv).*

**outright** 1 *(adj)* totally, or completely. *The outright winner.* 2 *(adv)* instantly. *Kirk was dismissed outright for stealing.*

*Some words that begin with an "or" sound are spelt "au" or "aw".*

**outside** 1 *(adv)* out of a building, or in the open air. **outside** *(prep)*. 2 *(n)* the surface of something or the part that surrounds the rest of it. *The outside of the box was painted pink.* **outside** *(adj)*.

**outskirts** *(plural n)* the outer edges of a town.

**outspoken** *(adj)* expressing your views strongly and clearly, especially when you are criticizing someone.

**outstanding** *(adj)* extremely good. *An outstanding performance.*

**outward** 1 *(adj)* appearing on the surface. *Philip's outward appearance was calm.* **outwardly** *(adv)*. 2 **outwards** *(adv)* towards the outside. *Facing outwards.*

**outwit** **outwitting outwitted** *(v)* to gain an advantage over someone by being cleverer than them.

**oval** *(n)* a shape like an egg. **oval** *(adj)*.

**ovary** **ovaries** *(n)* the female organ that produces eggs.

**oven** *(n)* a closed space where you cook food.

**over** 1 *(prep)* above, or on top of something. *The shelf over the bed.* 2 *(prep)* across. *Rachel stepped over the line.* 3 *(prep)* more than. *Over 12 years old.* 4 *(adv)* finished. *The party's over.* 5 *(v)* If you **get over** an illness or an experience, you recover from it.

**overall** *(adv)* generally, or considering everything. *Overall, the day was a success.*

**overalls** *(plural n)* a piece of clothing worn over your clothes when you are doing a dirty job.

**overarm** *(adv)* throwing or hitting with your arm above your shoulder. *Rex served overarm.* **overarm** *(adj)*.

**overbearing** *(adj)* very dominating or bossy.

**overboard** *(adv)* over the side of a boat. *The pirate fell overboard.*

**overcast** *(adj)* An **overcast** sky has dark clouds.

**overcome** **overcoming overcame overcome** *(v)* to defeat or deal with something, such as a feeling or problem. *I must overcome my fear of spiders.*

**overdue** *(adj)* late. *My library books are overdue.*

**overflow** **overflowing overflowed** 1 *(v)* to flow over the edges of something. *The bath overflowed.* 2 *(n)* a pipe or hole through which water can flow out of a bath, sink, etc. when it becomes too full.

**overgrown** *(adj)* An **overgrown** garden is covered with weeds because it has not been looked after.

**overhaul** **overhauling overhauled** *(v)* to examine carefully all the parts of a piece of equipment and make any repairs that are needed. **overhaul** *(n)*.

**overhear** **overhearing overheard** *(v)* to hear what someone else is saying when they do not know that you are listening.

**overjoyed** *(adj)* extremely happy.

**overlap** **overlapping overlapped** *(v)* to cover part of something else. *Arrange the roof tiles so that they overlap.*

**overleaf** *(adv)* on the next page.

**overload** **overloading overloaded** *(v)* to give something or someone too much to carry or too much work to do.

**overlook** **overlooking overlooked** 1 *(v)* to be able to look down on something from a window or room. *Our room overlooked the beach.* 2 *(v)* to choose to ignore something wrong that someone has done. *I overlooked Jude's rudeness.*

**overnight** 1 *(adv)* during the night. *We stayed overnight.* **overnight** *(adj)*. 2 *(adv)* suddenly. *Toby changed overnight.*

**overpower** **overpowering overpowered** 1 *(v)* to defeat someone, because you are stronger than they are. 2 *(v)* to affect someone very strongly. *The foul smell overpowered me.*

**overrated** *(adj)* If something is **overrated**, it is not as good as many people say.

**overrule** **overruling overruled** *(v)* If someone in authority **overrules** a decision, they say that the decision was wrong and has to be changed.

**overrun** **overrunning overran overrun** 1 *(v)* to spread all over a place in large numbers. *Rats are overrunning the town.* 2 *(v)* If something **overruns**, it goes on for longer than it was meant to.

**overseas** *(adj)* to or from other countries. *Overseas visitors.*

**oversleep** oversleeping overslept *(v)* to sleep for longer than you intended.

**overtake** overtaking overtook overtaken *(v)* to go past another moving vehicle in order to get in front of it.

**overthrow** overthrowing overthrew overthrown *(v)* to defeat a leader or ruler and remove them from power by force.

**overtime** *(n)* time spent working beyond normal working hours.

**overturn** overturning overturned 1 *(v)* to turn something over so that it is upside down, or on its side. 2 *(v)* to reverse a decision that someone else has made.

**overwhelm** overwhelming overwhelmed 1 *(v)* to defeat someone completely. 2 *(v)* to have a very strong effect. *The applause overwhelmed me.*

**overwork** overworking overworked *(v)* to work too hard.

**ovulation** *(n)* the production of eggs by the ovaries.

**owe** owing owed 1 *(v)* to have to pay money to someone, especially money that you have borrowed. 2 *(v)* to have a duty to do something for someone, in return for something they have done for you. *I owe you a favour.* 3 *(v)* to be grateful to someone for giving you something. *My sister owes her life to the brave fireman.* 4 **owing to** because of. *The bus was late owing to roadworks.*

**owl** *(n)* a bird with large eyes, that hunts at night.

**own** owning owned 1 *(adj)* belonging to you. *My own pen.* 2 *(v)* to possess, or to have something. **owner** *(n)*. 3 *(v)* If you **own up** to something, you confess that you have done something wrong. 4 **on your own** alone and by yourself.

**ox** oxen *(n)* a large, horned mammal, often used for carrying or pulling things.

**oxygen** *(n)* a colourless gas found in air, that humans and animals need to live.

**oyster** *(n)* a flat, edible shellfish that occasionally contains a pearl. *See* **pearl**.

**ozone** 1 *(n)* a form of oxygen that can be poisonous in large quantities. 2 **ozone layer** *(n)* a layer of ozone high above the Earth's surface that blocks out some of the Sun's harmful rays. *See* **atmosphere**.

# Pp

**pace** pacing paced 1 *(n)* a step, or a stride. 2 *(n)* a rate of speed. *A rapid pace.* 3 *(v)* to walk backwards and forwards. *Archie paced up and down the hall.*

**pacifist** *(n)* someone who strongly believes that war and violence are wrong, and who will not fight. **pacifism** *(n)*.

**pacify** pacifies pacifying pacified *(v)* to make someone feel calmer.

**pack** packing packed 1 *(v)* to put objects into a box, case, bag, etc. 2 *(v)* to fill a space tightly. *A crowd packed the stadium.* 3 *(n)* a collection of objects. *A pack of cards.* 4 *(n)* a group of wild animals. *A pack of wolves.* 5 *(n)* a bundle, or a load.

**package** 1 *(n)* a parcel. 2 *(n)* a computer program that can do several related things. *A desktop publishing package.* 3 **package holiday** *(n)* a holiday where the travel, hotel, etc. are included in the price and are arranged for you.

**packaging** *(n)* the wrapping on things that you buy.

**packet** *(n)* a small container or package. *A packet of seeds.*

**pact** *(n)* an agreement, often between two countries.

**pad** padding padded 1 *(n)* a wad of soft material, used to absorb liquid, give protection, etc. 2 *(v)* to cover something with soft material. 3 *(v)* to walk softly. *Barney padded along the corridor.* 4 *(n)* sheets of paper fastened together.

**padding** *(n)* stuffing.

**paddle** paddling paddled 1 *(v)* to walk in shallow water. 2 *(n)* a short, wide oar, used to propel some boats. **paddle** *(v)*.

**paddock** *(n)* a small field where horses can be kept.

**paddy field** *(n)* a wet field where rice is grown.

**padlock** *(n)* a lock with a curved metal bar that you can fix on to things.

**paediatrician** *(pee-dee-at-rish-un)* *(n)* a doctor who is trained to treat children.

**page** 1 *(n)* a sheet of paper in a book, newspaper, etc. 2 *(n)* In the past, **pages** were young, boy servants. Nowadays, a page is a boy attendant at a wedding.

**pageant** *(n)* a public show where people walk in processions or act out historical scenes. **pageantry** *(n)*.

**pain** *(n)* a feeling of physical hurt or of great unhappiness.

**painful** *(adj)* If something is **painful**, it hurts you physically or makes you very unhappy. **painfully** *(adv)*.

**painkiller** *(n)* a pill or medicine that you take to stop pain.

**painstaking** *(adj)* careful and thorough.

**paint** painting painted 1 *(n)* a liquid that you use to colour surfaces. 2 *(v)* to use paint to make a picture or cover a surface. **painter** *(n)*, **painting** *(n)*.

**pair** *(n)* two things that match or go together. **pair** *(v)*.

**palace** *(n)* a large, splendid building.

**pale** paler palest *(adj)* light or whitish in colour. **paleness** *(n)*.

**palette** *(n)* a flat board that you mix paints on, with a hole for your thumb.

**palindrome** *(n)* a word or sentence that reads the same backwards as forwards. *The names Hannah, Bob, and Otto are palindromes.*

**palm** 1 *(n)* the flat surface on the inside of your hand. 2 *(n)* a tall, tropical tree with large leaves at the top.

**pampas** 1 *(n)* a huge, treeless plain in South America. 2 **pampas grass** *(n)* a type of tall, feathery grass.

**pamper** pampering pampered *(v)* to spoil yourself or someone else with food, kindness, etc.

**pamphlet** *(n)* a small, thin booklet.

**pan** panning panned 1 *(n)* a round, metal container, used for cooking. 2 *(v)* to look for gold by washing earth in a pan or sieve. 3 *(v)* to move a camera, in order to follow an action. *The cameraman panned across the landscape.*

**pancake** *(n)* a thin, flat cake, made from batter and fried in a pan.

**pancreas** *(n)* a gland near your stomach which makes a fluid that helps you to digest food.

**panda** *(n)* an animal like a bear that lives in China.

giant panda

**pane** *(n)* a sheet of glass in a window or door.

**panel** 1 *(n)* a flat piece of wood or other material. **panelling** *(n)*. 2 *(n)* a board with controls or instruments on it. 3 *(n)* a group of people chosen to do something, such as judge a competition. **panellist** *(n)*.

**pang** *(n)* a brief pain or feeling of emotion. *A pang of regret.*

**panic** 1 *(n)* a feeling of terror or fright. **panic** *(v)*. 2 *(adj)* If you are **panic-stricken**, you are struck with a sudden fear.

**pannier** 1 *(n)* a basket hung on an animal, such as a donkey. 2 *(n)* a bag hung beside the rear wheel of a bicycle.

**panorama** *(n)* a wide view of an area.

**pansy** pansies *(n)* a small garden flower, usually coloured purple, yellow, or white.

**pant** panting panted *(v)* to breathe quickly and loudly because you are out of breath.

**panther** *(n)* a leopard, especially the black leopard.

**pantomime** *(n)* a Christmas play, based on a fairy tale, with songs and jokes.

**pantry** pantries *(n)* a small room where food or crockery is kept.

**pants** *(plural n)* underwear that covers your bottom.

**paper** 1 *(n)* thin material usually made from wood-pulp. 2 *(n)* a newspaper. 3 *(n)* part of an exam. 4 *(v)* to put wallpaper up, or cover something with paper.

**paperback** *(n)* a book with a paper cover.

**paperweight** *(n)* a heavy, often decorative object, used for holding down papers.

**papier mâché** *(pap-ee-ay-mash-ay) (n)* the art of making models, pots, etc. out of pieces of paper soaked in glue.

**papyrus** *(pa-pye-rus)* **papyri** *(n)* paper made from the papyrus plant, which grew in ancient Egypt.

**parable** *(n)* a fable or story that has a moral or religious lesson.

**parachute** *(pa-ra-shoot) (n)* a large piece of cloth fastened to thin ropes, that is used to drop people or loads safely from aeroplanes. **parachutist** *(n)*.

**parcel** *(n)* a package, or something wrapped up in paper. **parcel** *(v)*.

**pardon** **pardoning pardoned** 1 *(v)* to forgive or excuse someone, or to release them from punishment. 2 *(interject)* You say **pardon** as a polite way of asking someone to repeat what they have said. 3 *(interject)* You say **pardon** after you have done something rude, to say sorry.

**parachute**

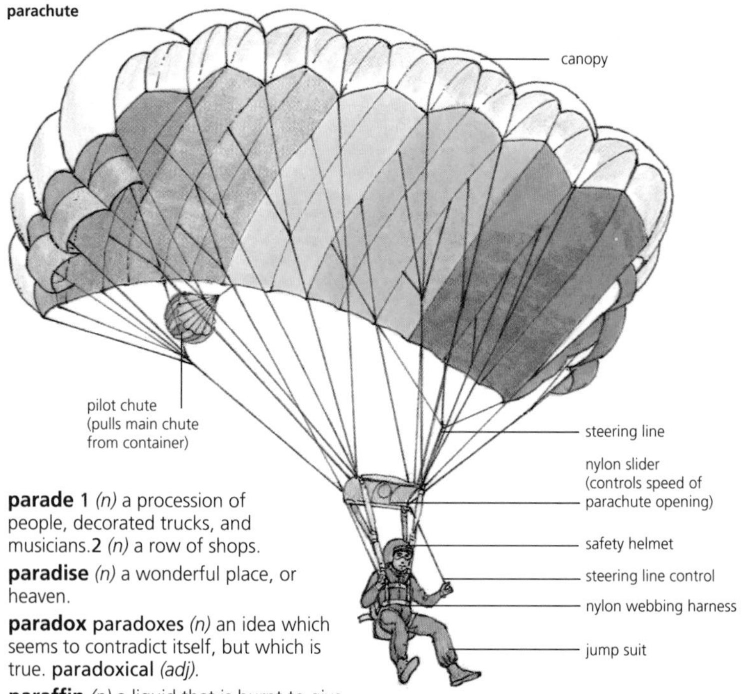


**parade** 1 *(n)* a procession of people, decorated trucks, and musicians.2 *(n)* a row of shops.

**paradise** *(n)* a wonderful place, or heaven.

**paradox** **paradoxes** *(n)* an idea which seems to contradict itself, but which is true. **paradoxical** *(adj)*.

**paraffin** *(n)* a liquid that is burnt to give light or heat in a lamp or stove.

**paragraph** *(n)* a short passage in a piece of writing, which begins on a new line.

**parallel** *(adj)* **Parallel** lines stay the same distance from each other.

**paralyse** **paralysing paralysed** *(v)* to make someone or something lose power, feeling, or movement. **paralysis** *(n)*.

**parasite** *(n)* an animal or plant that gets its food by living on or inside another animal or plant. **parasitic** *(adj)*.

**parasol** *(n)* a type of umbrella that shades you from the sun.

**parent** *(n)* a mother or father. **parenthood** *(n)*, **parental** *(adj)*.

**parish** **parishes** *(n)* an area that has its own church.

**parishioner** *(n)* someone who lives in a parish.

**park** **parking parked** 1 *(n)* a large garden, or a piece of ground for public use. 2 *(v)* to leave a car in a parking place or on the side of a street.

**parking meter** *(n)* a machine that you put money into, in order to pay for parking on the street.

**parliament** *(n)* the group of people who have been elected to make the laws of a country. **parliamentary** *(adj)*.

**parody** **parodies** *(n)* a funny imitation of a song, speech, etc. **parody** *(v)*.

**parole** *(n)* the early release of a prisoner on condition that they behave well.

**parrot** *(n)* a tropical bird that has a curved beak and brightly coloured feathers. *This parrot comes from South America.*

scarlet macaw

**parsnip** *(n)* a pale yellow root vegetable.

**parson** *(n)* a priest, or a vicar.

**part** **parting** **parted** **1** *(n)* a portion, or a piece. **2** *(n)* a character or role in a play or film. *Nat played the part of Hamlet.* **3** *(v)* to separate, or to divide. *We parted at the crossroads.* **4** *(v)* If you **part with** something, you give it away.

**partial** *(par-shal)* *(adj)* not complete. *A partial success.* **partially** *(adv)*.

**participate** **participating** **participated** *(v)* to join in or share in an activity or event. **participant** *(n)*, **participation** *(n)*.

**participle** *(n)* a form of a verb. The English language has two participles, the present, for example, "playing", and the past, for example, "played". Participles can be used as adjectives, for example, "shining", "crumpled", "swollen".

**particle** *(n)* an extremely small thing or part of something.

**particular** **1** *(adj)* individual, or special. *I want this particular painting.* **2** *(adj)* very fussy about small things. **3** *(n)* a fact, or a detail. *Please send me some particulars about the course.* **4** **in particular** especially. *All the rides are fun, but you must try one in particular.*

**parting** **1** *(n)* a line in your hair where it is combed in two directions. **2** *(n)* a separation. *An emotional parting.*

**partly** *(adv)* not completely.

**partner** **1** *(n)* one of two or more people who do something together. *Business partners.* **partnership** *(n)*. **2** *(n)* a husband, wife, or permanent companion.

**part of speech** **parts of speech** *(n)* a term, such as noun, verb, adjective, etc., that describes a word's type and function. *See* page 3.

**part-time** *(adj)* If you have a **part-time** job, you work for a few hours or a few days each week. **part time** *(adv)*.

**party** **parties** **1** *(n)* an organized occasion with music, games, refreshments, etc. when people enjoy themselves in a group. **2** *(n)* a group of people working together. *A search party.* **3** *(n)* an organized group of people with similar political beliefs, who try to win elections.

**pass** **passes** **passing** **passed** **1** *(v)* to go past someone or something. *Pass the park and then turn left.* **2** *(v)* to give something to somebody. *Pass the salt.* **3** *(v)* to kick, throw, or hit a ball to someone in your team in a sport or game. **pass** *(n)*. **4** *(v)* to succeed in a test or exam. **pass** *(n)*. **5** **pass away** *(v)* to die. **6** **pass out** *(v)* to faint.

**passage** **1** *(n)* a corridor. **2** *(n)* a short section in a book or piece of music.

**passenger** *(n)* someone who travels in a car or other vehicle and is not the driver.

**passer-by** **passers-by** *(n)* someone who happens to be going past.

**passion** *(n)* a very strong feeling of anger, love, hatred, etc.

**passionate** *(adj)* If you are **passionate** about something or someone, you have strong feelings about them.

**passive** *(adj)* If you are **passive**, you let things happen to you and do not react when you are attacked. **passively** *(adv)*.

**Passover** *(n)* a Jewish festival in the spring, in memory of how God rescued the Israelites from slavery in Egypt.

**passport** *(n)* an official booklet which proves who you are, and allows you to travel abroad.

**password** *(n)* a secret word that you need to know to get into a building or computer system.

**past** **1** *(n)* the period of time before the present. **past** *(adj)*. **2** *(adj)* finished, or ended. **3** *(adj)* previous. *I've had past experience of this type of work.* **4** *(prep)* by, after, or beyond. **past** *(adv)*.

**pasta** *(n)* a food made from flour, eggs, and water, that is made into shapes.

**paste** pasting pasted 1 *(n)* a soft, sticky mixture that you can spread. *Wallpaper paste. Fish paste.* 2 *(v)* to stick with glue.

**pastel** 1 *(n)* a chalky crayon. 2 *(adj)* soft and light in colour.

**pasteurized** *or* **pasteurised** *(adj)* Milk that is **pasteurized** has been boiled to kill bacteria. **pasteurize** *(v).*

**pastoral** *(adj)* to do with the countryside.

**pastry** pastries 1 *(n)* a dough that is rolled out and used for pies. 2 *(n)* a small cake made from pastry.

**pasture** *(n)* grazing land for animals.

**pasty** pasties *(n)* a small pie, usually filled with meat and vegetables.

**pat** patting patted *(v)* to tap or stroke something gently with your hand. *James patted the dog.* **pat** *(n).*

**patch** patches patching patched 1 *(v)* to put a piece of material on something in order to mend it. **patch** *(n).* 2 *(n)* a small, odd-shaped part of something, such as an area of white fur on a black dog. 3 *(n)* a piece of ground. *A vegetable patch.*

**patchwork** *(n)* patterned fabric, made by sewing small patches of different material together.

**patchy** patchier patchiest *(adj)* uneven. *Patchy fog made the road dangerous.*

**pâté** *(pat-ay)* *(n)* a soft paste, usually made of meat or fish, that is spread on toast, crackers, etc.

**patent** patenting patented 1 *(v)* If you invent something, you can **patent** it to stop other people copying your idea. 2 *(adj)* obvious, or open. *A patent lie.*

**paternal** *(adj)* to do with being a father.

**path** *(n)* a track, or a route. **pathway** *(n).*

**pathetic** *(adj)* feeble, or useless.

**patience** 1 *(n)* the ability to put up with difficult things and to wait calmly. 2 *(n)* a card game for one player.

**patient** 1 *(adj)* good at putting up with things and waiting calmly. 2 *(n)* someone who is receiving medical treatment.

**patio** *(n)* a paved area next to a house, used for sitting outside.

**patriot** *(n)* someone who loves their country and is prepared to fight for it. **patriotism** *(n),* **patriotic** *(adj).*

**patrol** patrolling patrolled *(v)* to walk or travel around an area to protect it or to keep watch on people. *Police are patrolling the neighbourhood.* **patrol** *(n).*

**patron** *(pay-tron)* 1 *(n)* a customer of a shop, or someone who supports a theatre, artist, writer, etc. 2 **patron saint** *(n)* a saint who is believed to look after a particular country or group of people.

**patronize** *or* **patronise** patronizing patronized 1 *(v)* to talk down to someone or act as though you are better than them. 2 *(v)* If you **patronize** a shop, restaurant, etc. you go there regularly.

**patter** pattering pattered 1 *(v)* to make light, quick, patting sounds. *The rain pattered on my umbrella.* **patter** *(n).* 2 *(n)* fast talk. *A magician's patter.*

**pattern** 1 *(n)* an arrangement of colours, shapes, etc. on paper or material. 2 *(n)* a model that you can copy from. *A dress pattern.*

**pause** pausing paused *(v)* to stop for a short time. **pause** *(n).*

**pavement** *(n)* a raised path beside a street.

**pavilion** *(n)* a building at a sports ground where players can get changed, rest, etc.

**paw** *(n)* the foot of an animal, such as a dog or cat.

**pawn** pawning pawned 1 *(v)* to leave a valuable item at a shop called a pawnbroker's, in return for a loan. 2 *(n)* the smallest chess piece. *See* **chess**.

**pay** paying paid 1 *(v)* to give money for something. **payment** *(n).* 2 *(v)* to be worthwhile, or to be advantageous. *It pays to be polite.* 3 *(v)* to suffer. *Ed paid for his mistake.* 4 *(n)* wages, or salary.

**PC** 1 *(n)* the initials for personal computer. 2 *(n)* the initials for police constable. 3 *(adj) (informal)* Someone who is **PC** makes a great effort not to offend minority groups, women, etc. The initials PC stand for politically correct.

**PE** *(n)* a lesson at school in which you do sports, gymnastics, etc. The initials PE stand for physical education.

**pea** *(n)* a small, round, green vegetable which grows in a pod.

**peace** 1 *(n)* calm and quiet. **peaceful** *(adj).* 2 *(n)* a period without war.

**peach** peaches *(n)* a soft fruit with a furry skin and a stone at its centre.

**peacock** *(n)* a large, blue and green bird with long tail-feathers.

**peak** 1 *(n)* the top of something, such as a mountain. 2 *(n)* the highest or best point. *The peak of Jess's career.* **peak** *(v)*. 3 *(n)* the curved, front part of a cap.

**peal** pealing pealed *(v)* When bells **peal**, they ring.

**pear** *(n)* a juicy fruit that gets narrower towards its stalk.

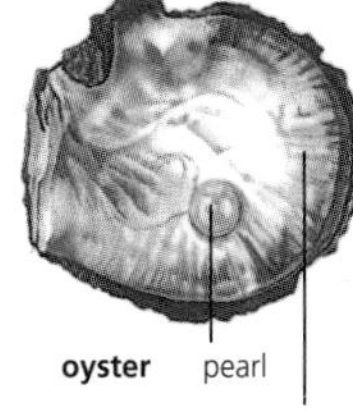


**oyster**

**pearl** *(n)* a small, round, whitish object that grows inside oysters and other shellfish and is used to make jewellery.

**peasant** 1 *(n)* someone who works on a small piece of land. 2 *(n)* In medieval times, **peasants** were agricultural labourers who worked for their local lord.

**peat** *(n)* dark brown, partly decayed vegetable matter used as fuel or compost.

**pebble** *(n)* a small, round stone.

**peck** pecking pecked 1 *(v)* When a bird **pecks** at something, it strikes it or picks it up with its beak. 2 *(n) (informal)* a quick kiss. *Mum gave me a peck on the cheek.*

**peculiar** 1 *(adj)* strange, or odd. 2 **peculiar to** belonging to, or exclusive to. *Koalas are peculiar to Australia.*

**pedal** *(n)* a lever on a bicycle, piano, etc. that you push with your foot. **pedal** *(v)*.

**peddle** peddling peddled *(v)* to travel around selling things, especially drugs.

**pedestrian** 1 *(n)* someone who travels on foot. 2 **pedestrian crossing** *(n)* a place for people to cross the road safely.

**peel** peeling peeled 1 *(n)* the tough outer skin of a fruit. 2 *(v)* to remove the peel of a fruit. 3 *(v)* to come off. *I got so sunburnt that the skin on my back peeled.*

**peep** peeping peeped *(v)* to glance or look secretly at something. **peep** *(n)*.

**peer** peering peered 1 *(v)* to look hard at something which is difficult to see. 2 *(plural n)* Your **peers** are people of similar age and type to you.

**peg** *(n)* a thin piece of wood, metal, or plastic, used to hold things down or hang things up. **peg** *(v)*.

**pelican** *(n)* a large water bird with a pouch below its beak where it holds the fish that it catches.

**pelican**

**pen** 1 *(n)* an instrument used for writing with ink. 2 *(n)* a small fenced area that contains sheep, cattle, etc.

**penalize** *or* **penalise** penalizing penalized *(v)* to make someone suffer a punishment.

**penalty** 1 *(n)* a punishment. 2 *(n)* an advantage won in a game when the opposing side breaks a rule.

**pence** *(n)* **Pence** is a plural of penny. *This costs 50 pence.*

**pencil** *(n)* an instrument used for drawing and writing, made from a stick of graphite in a wood casing.

**pendulum** *(n)* a weight in some clocks which moves from side to side and helps to keep the clock ticking regularly.

**penetrate** penetrating penetrated *(v)* to go inside or through something. *The nail penetrated Nick's shoe.* **penetration** *(n)*.

**pen friend** *(n)* someone, usually from abroad, who exchanges letters with you.

**penguin** *(n)* a seabird of the Antarctic region that cannot fly.

**emperor penguin**

**peninsula** *(n)* a piece of land that sticks out into the sea, and is surrounded on three sides by water. **peninsular** *(adj)*.

**penis** penises *(n)* the male organ used for urinating and sexual intercourse.

**penknife** penknives *(n)* a small knife with blades that fold into a case.

**pen name** *(n)* a public name used by a writer.

**penniless** *(adj)* If you are **penniless**, you have absolutely no money.

**penny** **pennies** *or* **pence** *(n)* the smallest unit of money in Britain.

**pension** *(n)* an amount of money paid regularly to someone who has retired from work. **pensioner** *(n)*.

**penultimate** *(adj)* next to last. *"This" is the penultimate word in this sentence.*

**people** *(plural n)* human beings.

**pepper** **1** *(n)* a spicy powder used to flavour food. **2** *(n)* a hollow vegetable, usually red, green, or yellow.

**per** **1** *(prep)* in each, or for each. *There's enough for three sweets per person.* **2** **per annum** *(adv)* each year. **3** **per cent** *(n)* one in every hundred. *Ten per cent of a hundred is ten.*

**perceive** **perceiving perceived** *(v)* to notice something, or to understand a situation.

**percentage** *(n)* a fraction or proportion of something, expressed as a number out of a hundred. The symbol for percentage is %.

**perceptive** *(adj)* If you are **perceptive**, you are quick to notice things or understand situations.

**perch** **perches perching perched** **1** *(n)* a place where a bird stands. **2** *(v)* to sit or stand on the edge of something.

**percussion** *(n)* musical instruments which are played by being hit or shaken.

**perfect** **perfecting perfected** **1** *(adj)* without any faults. **perfection** *(n)*. **2** *(v)* to succeed, with effort, in making something work well. *After much practice, Callum perfected his juggling act.*

**perform** **performing performed** **1** *(v)* to do something, or to carry something out. **2** *(v)* to give a show in public.

**performance** *(n)* the public acting of a play, showing of a film, etc.

**perfume** *(n)* a liquid put on your skin to make you smell pleasant.

**perimeter** **1** *(n)* the outside edge of an area. **2** *(n)* the distance around the edge of a shape or an area.

**period** **1** *(n)* a length of time. *A period of history.* **2** *(n)* the monthly flow of blood from the womb of a girl or woman.

**periodical** **1** *(adj)* happening at intervals. **periodically** *(adv)*. **2** *(n)* a journal or magazine that is published regularly.

**periscope** *(n)* a vertical tube, often used in submarines, that allows you to see something from a position a long way below it.

**perish** **perishes perishing perished** **1** *(v)* to die. **2** *(v)* If a substance, such as food or rubber, **perishes**, it becomes rotten.

**perk** **perking perked** **1** *(n)* *(informal)* an extra advantage that comes from doing a particular job. *A perk of working in this café is the free food.* **2** *(v)* If you **perk up**, you become more cheerful. **perky** *(adj)*.

**permanent** *(adj)* lasting for a long time or for ever. **permanence** *(n)*.

**permissible** *(adj)* If something is **permissible**, it is allowed.

**permission** *(n)* If you give **permission** for something, you say that it can happen.

**permissive** *(adj)* Someone who is **permissive** is very tolerant and allows freedom where others would not.

**permit** **permitting permitted** *(v)* to allow something.

**perpendicular** *(n)* a line at right angles to another line, or vertical to the ground.

**perpetual** *(adj)* never-ending, or unchanging. **perpetually** *(adv)*.

**perplex** **perplexes perplexing perplexed** *(v)* to make someone puzzled and slightly worried. **perplexity** *(n)*.

**persecute** **persecuting persecuted** *(v)* to treat someone cruelly and unfairly because you are prejudiced against them. **persecution** *(n)*.

**persevere** **persevering persevered** *(v)* If you **persevere** at something, you keep on trying and do not give up.

**persist** **persisting persisted** *(v)* to keep on doing something. **persistent** *(adj)*.

**person** *(n)* an individual human being.

**personal** *(adj)* to do with one person only. *This letter is personal and private.*

**personal computer** *(n)* a small computer that can stand on a desk or table and can be used at home.

**personality** **personalities** **1** *(n)* the type of character someone has. *An outgoing personality.* **2** *(n)* a famous person.

**personal stereo** *(n)* a small cassette or disc player with headphones, that you can carry around.

**perspective** 1 *(n)* a particular way of looking at a situation. *I enjoyed the trip, but from Guy's perspective, it was a disaster.* 2 If a picture is **in perspective**, distant objects are drawn smaller than nearer ones so that the view looks exactly as someone would see it.

**perspire** perspiring perspired *(v)* to sweat. **perspiration** *(n).*

**persuade** persuading persuaded *(v)* to make someone do something, by telling them reasons why they should do it. **persuasion** *(n),* **persuasive** *(adj).*

**perturb** perturbing perturbed *(v)* to worry or confuse somebody. *Harry's questions perturbed me.*

**perverse** *(adj)* deliberately unreasonable and stubborn. **perversity** *(n).*

**pervert** *(per-vert) (n)* someone who behaves in an unacceptable, disgusting, or harmful way, particularly in sexual matters. **perverted** *(per-ver-ted) (adj).*

**pessimistic** *(adj)* People who are **pessimistic** are gloomy and always think that the worst will happen. **pessimism** *(n),* **pessimist** *(n).*

**pest** 1 *(n)* an insect that destroys or damages flowers, fruit, or vegetables. 2 *(n)* a persistently annoying person.

**pester** pestering pestered *(v)* to keep annoying other people, often by asking or telling them something again and again.

**pesticide** *(n)* a chemical used to kill pests, usually insects.

**pet** 1 *(n)* a tame animal kept for company or pleasure. 2 *(n)* somebody's favourite person or thing. *Teacher's pet.*

**petal** *(n)* one of the coloured, outer parts of a flower head. *See* **flower**.

**petition** *(n)* a letter, signed by many people, asking those in power to change their policy or actions. **petition** *(v).*

**petrified** *(adj)* unable to move because you are so frightened.

**petrol** *(n)* a liquid fuel used in many vehicles.

**petty** pettier pettiest *(adj)* trivial and unimportant. *Petty criticisms.*

**pH** *(n)* a measure of how acidic or alkaline a substance is.

**phantom** *(n)* a ghost.

**Pharaoh** *(fair-oh) (n)* one of the kings of ancient Egypt.

**pharmacist** *(n)* a trained person who prepares and sells drugs and medicines.

**phase** phasing phased 1 *(n)* a stage in someone or something's growth or development. 2 **phase in** *(v)* to start something gradually. 3 **phase out** *(v)* to stop something gradually.

**pheasant** *(fez-ant) (n)* a large bird with a long tail that is shot for sport and food.

**phenomenon** *(fin-om-in-on)* phenomena *(n)* something very unusual and remarkable. **phenomenal** *(adj).*

**philosophical** *(fil-oss-off-ik-al)* 1 *(adj)* to do with philosophy. 2 *(adj)* If you are **philosophical**, you accept difficulties and problems calmly.

**philosophy** *(fil-oss-off-ee)* 1 *(n)* the study of ideas about human life. 2 *(n)* A person's **philosophy** is their set of ideas and beliefs on how life should be lived.

**phlegm** *(flem) (n)* the thick substance that you cough up when you have a cold.

**phobia** *(n)* an overpowering fear of something. **phobic** *(adj).*

**phone** *short for* **telephone**.

**photo** *short for* **photograph**.

**photocopy** photocopies *(n)* a copy of a document made by a photocopier. **photocopy** *(v).*

**photo finish** photo finishes *(n)* a very close end to a race, where a photograph has to be studied to decide who has won.

**photofit** *(n)* a portrait put together by the police to trace someone suspected of a crime.

**photogenic** *(foh-toh-jen-ik) (adj)* If someone is **photogenic**, they look very good in photographs.

**photograph** *(n)* a picture taken by a camera on film and developed on paper.

**photography** *(n)* the creation of a picture by exposing a film inside a camera to light. **photographer** *(n).*

**phrase** *(n)* a group of words that have a meaning, but do not form a sentence.

**physical** 1 *(adj)* to do with the body. *Physical education.* **physically** *(adv).* 2 *(adj)* to do with the shape and appearance of things. *Physical geography.* **physically** *(adv).*

**physics** *(singular n)* the scientific study of energy, movement, heat, sound, light, etc. **physicist** *(n).*

**physiotherapy** *(n)* treatment for damaged muscles and joints, using exercise and massage.

**piano** *(n)* a large keyboard instrument with strings inside it. **pianist** *(n).*

**grand piano and pianist**

**pick** picking picked 1 *(v)* to choose, or to select. *Pick a number.* 2 *(v)* to collect, or to gather. *Have you picked all the strawberries?* 3 *(v)* If someone **picks on** you, they keep criticizing you.

**picket** picketing picketed *(v)* to stand outside a place of work making a protest and sometimes trying to prevent people from entering. **picket** *(n).*

**pickle** pickling pickled 1 *(v)* to preserve food in vinegar or in salt water. 2 *(n)* a mixture of chopped, cooked vegetables and spices, often eaten with cold meals.

**pickpocket** *(n)* someone who steals from people's pockets or bags.

**pick-up** *(n)* a small truck with an open back.

**picky** pickier pickiest *(adj) (informal)* fussy, or choosy. *A picky eater.*

**picnic** picnicking picnicked 1 *(n)* a packed meal taken away from home to be eaten out-of-doors. 2 *(v)* to eat a picnic. **picnicker** *(n).*

**picture** *(n)* an image of something, for example, a painting or a photograph.

**picturesque** *(pik-chur-esk) (adj)* If a place or a view is **picturesque**, it is beautiful to look at.

**pie** *(n)* a pastry case filled with meat, fruit, etc. and baked in an oven.

**piece** 1 *(n)* a bit or section of something. 2 *(n)* something written or made. *A piece of embroidery.*

**pier** *(n)* a platform of metal and wood extending into the sea.

**pierce** piercing pierced *(v)* to make a hole in something. *Pierce the potatoes with a skewer.*

**piercing** *(adj)* very loud and shrill. *A piercing scream.*

**pig** 1 *(n)* a farm animal with a blunt snout, which is kept for its meat. 2 *(n) (informal)* a greedy and disgusting person.

**pigeon** *(n)* a common bird, sometimes used for racing or for carrying messages.

**piggy-back** *(n)* If someone gives you a **piggy-back**, they carry you on their shoulders or on their back.

**pigment** *(n)* a substance that gives colour to something. There is pigment in paints and in your skin.

**pigsty** pigsties 1 *(n)* a shelter and yard where pigs are kept. 2 *(n)* a very untidy and often dirty place. *My room is a pigsty!*

**pile** 1 *(n)* a heap or mound of something. **pile** *(v).* 2 **pile-up** *(n) (informal)* a serious road crash involving several vehicles.

**pilfer** pilfering pilfered *(v)* to steal small things. **pilferer** *(n).*

**pilgrimage** *(n)* a journey to worship at a holy place. **pilgrim** *(n).*

**pill** 1 *(n)* a small, solid tablet of medicine. 2 **the pill** *(n) (informal)* a pill that women take daily as a contraceptive.

**pillar** *(n)* a column which supports part of a building.

**pillow** *(n)* a large, soft cushion on which you rest your head when you are lying in bed.

**pillowcase** *(n)* a fabric cover that you put over a pillow to keep it clean.

**pilot** piloting piloted 1 *(n)* someone who flies an aircraft. **pilot** *(v).* 2 *(n)* someone who steers a ship in and out of port. 3 *(adj)* done as an experiment. *A pilot television programme.* **pilot** *(n).* 4 *(v)* to control or guide something.

**pimple** *(n)* a small, raised spot on the skin. **pimply** *(adj).*

**pin** pinning pinned 1 *(n)* a thin, pointed piece of metal, usually used to join material together. **pin** *(v).* 2 *(v)* to hold something or someone firmly in position. *Sophia pinned me against the wall.*

*Some words that begin with a "pi" sound are spelt "py".*

**pinball** *(n)* a game in which you shoot small balls around obstacles on a table.

**pincer** *(pin-ser) (n)* the pinching claw of a shellfish, such as a crab.

**pinch** **pinches pinching pinched 1** *(v)* to squeeze someone's skin painfully between your thumb and index finger. **pinch** *(n).* **2** *(n)* a small amount of something. *A pinch of salt.* **3** *(v) (informal)* to steal something. *Someone's pinched my bike!*

**pine** *(n)* a tall, straight, evergreen tree with cones and needles.

**pineapple** *(n)* a large, tropical fruit with yellow flesh and a tough skin.

**ping pong** *see* **table tennis**.

**pins and needles** *(singular n) (informal)* a pricking, tingling feeling that you get when some of the blood supply to part of your body has been cut off.

**pioneer 1** *(n)* someone who explores unknown territory and settles there. **2** *(n)* one of the first people to work in a new and unknown area. *Pioneers of flight.*

**pious** *(py-uss) (adj)* Someone who is **pious** practises their religion faithfully and seriously. **piety** *(n).*

**pip** *(n)* the small, hard seed of a fruit.

**pipe** **piping piped 1** *(n)* a tube, usually used to carry liquids. **2** *(v)* to send something along pipes, tubes, or wires. **3** *(n)* a tube with a bowl on the end of it, used for smoking tobacco. **4** *(n)* a tube with holes in it, used as a musical instrument or as part of an instrument.

**pipeline 1** *(n)* a large pipe that carries water, gas, oil, etc. over long distances. **2** If something is **in the pipeline**, it is being planned.

**piping 1** *(n)* a system of pipes. **2** *(adj)* very high or shrill. *A piping voice.* **3** If food is **piping hot**, it is very hot indeed.

**pirate** **pirating pirated 1** *(n)* someone who attacks and steals from ships at sea. **piracy** *(n).* **2** *(v)* If someone **pirates** a tape, computer game, etc. they make illegal copies and sell them. **pirated** *(adj).*

**pistol** *(n)* a small handgun.

**pit 1** *(n)* a hole in the ground. **2** *(n)* a small dip. **3** *(n)* a coal mine. **4 the pits** *(n)* the place where racing cars pull in for fuel and repairs during a race.

**pitch** **pitches pitching pitched 1** *(n)* an area of grass on which a sport is played. **2** *(v)* When you **pitch** a tent, you put it up.

**pitcher** *(n)* an open-topped water container like a large jug.

**pitfall** *(n)* a hidden danger or difficulty.

**pitiful 1** *(adj)* causing or deserving pity. *The lost children were in a pitiful state.* **2** *(adj)* useless, or worthless. *A pitiful piece of work.*

**pitiless** *(adj)* showing no pity or mercy.

**pity** **pities pitying pitied** *(v)* If you **pity** someone, you feel sorry for them.

**pivot** *(n)* a central point on which something turns or balances. **pivot** *(v).*

**pizza** *(n)* a flat, round base of dough, with toppings of cheese, tomatoes, etc.

**placard** *(n)* a poster or notice.

**placate** **placating placated** *(v)* to make someone calm or happy, often by giving them something that they want.

**place** **placing placed 1** *(n)* a particular area or position. **2** *(v)* to put something somewhere, deliberately and carefully. *Place the vase on the shelf.* **3** If something is **in place**, it is in its proper position.

**placid** *(plass-id) (adj)* Someone who is **placid** is calm and even-tempered. **placidly** *(adv).*

**plague** *(playg)* **plaguing plagued 1** *(n)* a serious disease which spreads quickly to many people. **2** *(v)* If something **plagues** you, you are troubled and annoyed by it. *The explorers were plagued by flies.*

**plain** **plainer plainest 1** *(adj)* ordinary in appearance, and not fancy or beautiful. **2** *(n)* a large, level area of land. **3** *(adj)* simple and straightforward. *Plain facts.*

**plaintive** *(adj)* sad and mournful. *A plaintive cry.* **plaintively** *(adv).*

**plait** *(plat) (n)* a length of hair that has been divided into three and twisted together. **plait** *(v),* **plaited** *(adj).*

**plan** **planning planned 1** *(v)* to work out how you will do something. **plan** *(n).* **2** *(v)* If you **plan** to do something, you intend to do it. **3** *(n)* a map of a room, building, or small area.

**plane** *(n)* a machine with wings and an engine that flies through the air. Plane is short for aeroplane.

**planet** *(n)* one of the nine round objects circling the Sun. *This picture shows the planets of the solar system, in their correct order, but not drawn to scale.*

**plateau** *(plat-oh)* **plateaus** *or* **plateaux** *(n)* an area of high, flat land.

**platform** *(n)* a flat, raised structure on which people or things can stand.

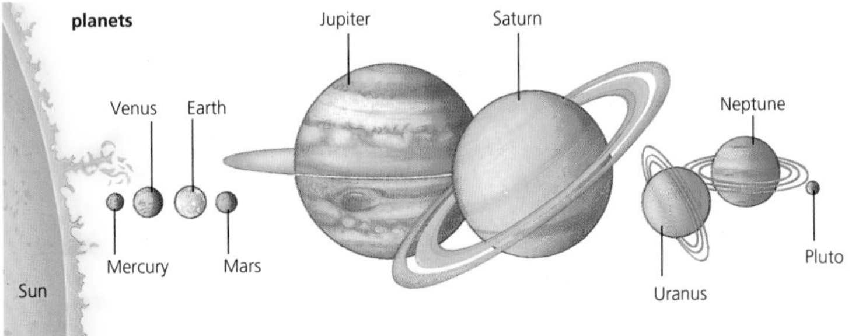


**plank** *(n)* a long, flat strip of wood used, for example, for floorboards.

**plankton** *(n)* a general name for minute animals and plants which live in water.

**plant planting planted 1** *(n)* a living organism that is often green, with stems, roots, and leaves. **2** *(v)* to put plants or seeds in the ground so that they can grow. **3** *(v)* to put something in a secret place. *Terrorists planted a bomb in the store.* **4** *(n)* a factory, laboratory, or power station. *A chemical plant.* **5** *(n)* large industrial machinery or buildings.

**plantation 1** *(n)* a farm in a hot country where coffee, tea, rubber, etc. are grown. **2** *(n)* a place where a large number of trees or bushes have been planted.

**plaque** *(plak or plahk)* **1** *(n)* a plate with words inscribed on it, usually on a wall in a public place. **2** *(n)* the coating made from food, bacteria, and saliva that forms on your teeth and can cause tooth decay.

**plaster 1** *(n)* a substance made of lime, sand, and water, used by builders to put a smooth finish on walls. **2** *(n)* a sticky bandage that you put on a skin wound.

**plastic** *(n)* a man-made substance that is light and strong and can be moulded into different shapes.

**plastic surgery** *(n)* operations on skin and body tissue to repair damage or to improve someone's appearance.

**plate 1** *(n)* a flat dish for food. **2** *(n)* an illustration in a book.

**platypus platypuses** *(n)* an Australian mammal with a broad bill.

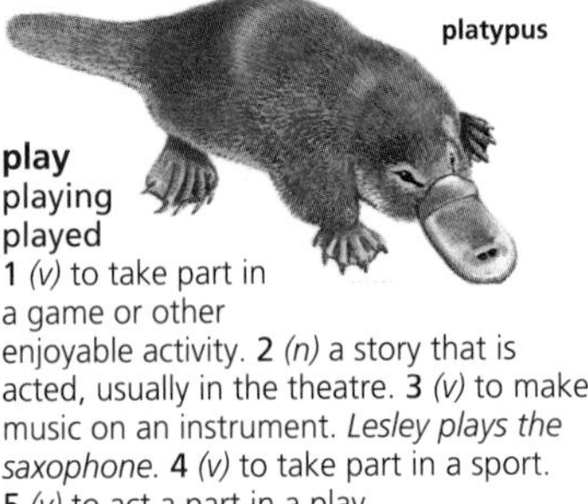


**play playing played 1** *(v)* to take part in a game or other enjoyable activity. **2** *(n)* a story that is acted, usually in the theatre. **3** *(v)* to make music on an instrument. *Lesley plays the saxophone.* **4** *(v)* to take part in a sport. **5** *(v)* to act a part in a play.

**plea** *(n)* a strongly felt, emotional request. *A plea for mercy.*

**plead pleading pleaded 1** *(v)* If you **plead** with someone, you beg them to do something. **2** *(v)* to say whether you are guilty or not guilty, in a court. *I plead guilty.*

**pleasant** *(adj)* enjoyable and likeable.

**please pleasing pleased 1** *(v)* to satisfy, or to give pleasure. *Your present pleased me greatly.* **2** *(interject)* You say **please** when you ask for something politely.

**pleasure** *(n)* a feeling of enjoyment or satisfaction. **pleasurable** *(adj).*

**pleat** *(n)* one of a series of parallel folds in a piece of clothing, such as a skirt. **pleated** *(adj).*

**pledge pledging pledged** *(v)* to make a firm promise. **pledge** *(n).*

**plentiful** *(adj)* existing in large amounts. *Food was plentiful at the feast.*

**plenty** *(n)* a great number, or a large amount. *There's plenty of space.*

**pliable** *(ply-ab-ul)* **1** *(adj)* If an object or material is **pliable**, it can be bent easily. **2** *(adj)* If a person is **pliable**, they can be influenced easily.

**plight** *(n)* a situation of great danger or hardship. *The plight of the refugees.*

**plimsoll** *or* **plimsole** *(n)* a soft, canvas shoe, often worn for sports or PE.

**plod** **plodding plodded** *(v)* to walk or work in a slow and deliberate way.

**plot** **1** *(n)* a secret plan. **plot** *(v)*. **2** *(n)* a small area of land. *A building plot.* **3** *(n)* the story of a novel, film, play, etc.

**plough** *(rhymes with cow)* **ploughing ploughed** **1** *(n)* a piece of farm equipment used to turn over soil before seeds are sown. **plough** *(v)*. *See* **farm**. **2** *(v)* If you **plough through** something, you work hard to get through it.

**pluck** **plucking plucked** **1** *(v)* to pick fruit or flowers. **2** *(v)* to play notes on a stringed instrument, by pulling on the strings. **3** *(v)* to pull feathers out of a bird. **4** *(n)* courage and bravery. **plucky** *(adj)*.

**plug** **1** *(n)* an object pushed into a hole to block it. *A bath plug.* **plug** *(v)*. **2** *(n)* an electrical connector.

**plum** *(n)* a small, soft fruit with a purple, yellow, or red skin.

**plumage** *(plew-mij)* *(n)* a bird's feathers.

**plumber** *(plum-er)* *(n)* someone who installs and repairs water and heating systems.

**plumbing** *(plum-ing)* *(n)* the system of water pipes in a building.

**plump** **plumper plumpest** *(adj)* slightly fat, or rounded in shape.

**plunder** **plundering plundered** *(v)* to use violence in order to steal things, usually during a battle. **plunder** *(n)*.

**plunge** **plunging plunged** **1** *(v)* to dive into water. **plunge** *(n)*. **2** *(v)* to push something into water. **3** *(v)* to slope steeply. *The cliffs plunged to the sea.*

**plural** *(n)* the form of a word that is used for two or more of something. *The plural of child is children.*

**p.m.** the initials of the Latin phrase *post meridiem* which means "after midday". *School finishes at 4 p.m.*

**pneumatic** *(new-mat-ik)* **1** *(adj)* filled with air. *Pneumatic tyres.* **2** *(adj)* operated by compressed air. *A pneumatic drill.*

**pneumonia** *(new-moan-ee-a)* *(n)* a serious lung disease.

**poach** **poaches poaching poached** *(v)* to catch fish or animals illegally on someone else's land. **poacher** *(n)*.

**pocket** *(n)* a pouch sewn on to or into clothing and used for carrying things.

**pod** *(n)* a long case that holds the seeds of certain plants. *A pea pod.*

**podgy** **podgier podgiest** *(adj)* slightly fat.

**poem** *(n)* a piece of writing set out in short lines, often with a noticeable rhythm and some words that rhyme.

**poetry** *(n)* a general word for poems. *Do you write poetry?* **poet** *(n)*.

**point** **pointing pointed** **1** *(v)* to show where something is, especially using your index finger. **2** *(n)* the sharp end of something. *A pencil point.* **3** *(n)* the main purpose behind something that is said or done. *The point of the presentation was to get people thinking.* **4** *(n)* a specific place or stage. *Don't go beyond this point.* **5** *(n)* a unit for scoring in a game. **6** *(v)* If you **point out** something, you draw attention to it or explain it.

**pointless** *(adj)* If something is **pointless**, it has no realistic purpose. *It's pointless to take your bikini on an Arctic expedition.*

**poise** **poising poised** *(v)* to be balanced. *The cat was poised on the window ledge.*

**poison** *(n)* a substance that can kill or harm someone if it is swallowed or breathed in. **poison** *(v)*, **poisonous** *(adj)*.

**poke** **poking poked** *(v)* to prod sharply with a finger or pointed object. **poke** *(n)*.

**poky** *or* **pokey** **pokier pokiest** *(adj)* *(informal)* very small and cramped.

**pole** **1** *(n)* a long, smooth piece of wood, metal, plastic, etc. **2** *(n)* one of the two points on the Earth's surface that are furthest away from the equator.

**pole vault** *(n)* a jump over a high bar, using a flexible pole. **pole-vault** *(v)*.

**police** *(plural n)* the people whose job is to make sure that the law is obeyed. **policeman** *(n),* **policewoman** *(n).*

**policy** **policies** *(n)* a general plan of action. *A traffic policy.*

**polish** **polishes** *(n)* a cleaning substance used to make things shine. **polish** *(v).*

**polished** *(adj)* well-rehearsed and confident. *A polished performance.*

**polite** **politer** **politest** *(adj)* well-behaved and courteous to other people.

**politician** *(n)* someone involved in the government of a country, such as an MP.

**politics** *(n)* the debate and activity involved in governing a country. **political** *(adj),* **politically** *(adv).*

**poll** 1 *(n)* a counting of votes in an election. 2 *(n)* a survey of people's opinions or beliefs.

**pollen** *(singular n)* fine grains found inside flowers, containing fertilizing cells.

**pollinate** **pollinating** **pollinated** *(v)* to transfer pollen from one flower to another in order to fertilize the flower.

**polling station** *(n)* a building where people go to vote in elections.

**pollution** *(n)* damage to the environment caused by human activities. **pollute** *(v).*

**polo** *(n)* a game played on horseback by two teams who try to hit a small ball through goal posts, using long mallets.

**polygamy** *(n)* the state of being married to several people at once.

**polygon** *(n)* a flat shape with many sides.

**polystyrene** *(n)* a light, stiff plastic often used to make disposable cups and packing materials.

**polythene** *(n)* a light, flexible plastic used to make bags.

**pompous** *(adj)* full of self-importance.

**pond** *(n)* a small, enclosed pool of fresh water.

**ponder** **pondering** **pondered** *(v)* to think about things carefully.

**pony** **ponies** *(n)* a small horse.

**pony trekking** *(n)* If you go **pony trekking**, you ride ponies across the countryside for pleasure.

**pool** **pooling** **pooled** 1 *(n)* a small area of still water. 2 *(n)* a swimming pool. 3 *(n)* a game in which you use a stick, called a cue, to hit coloured balls into pockets on a table. 4 *(v)* If people **pool** money, ideas, etc. they put them together to be shared.

**pools** *(n)* a competition in which people win money if they guess the results of certain football matches correctly.

**poor** **poorer** **poorest** 1 *(adj)* If you are **poor**, you do not have much money. 2 *(adj)* low in quality or standard. *Poor eyesight.* 3 *(adj)* unfortunate and provoking sympathy. *Poor Alex!*

**poorly** 1 *(adv)* badly. *The room was poorly lit.* 2 *(adj)* ill. *Sadie is poorly today.*

**pop** **popping** **popped** 1 *(v)* to make a small bang or bursting sound. **pop** *(n).* 2 **pop music** *(n)* modern, popular music with a strong, and often fast, beat. 3 *(v)* to go somewhere quickly. *Gary has just popped out.*

**Pope** *(n)* the head of the Roman Catholic Church.

**poppy** **poppies** *(n)* a flower with large, colourful petals.

**popular** *(adj)* liked or enjoyed by many people. **popularity** *(n),* **popularly** *(adv).*

**populated** *(adj)* If a place is **populated**, it has people living there.

**population** 1 *(n)* the people who live in a place. 2 *(n)* the number of people who live in a place.

**porcelain** *(pore-ser-lin)* *(n)* very fine china, often used to make ornaments or cups and saucers.

**porch** **porches** *(n)* a covered area around a doorway.

**Malaysian porcupine**

**porcupine** *(n)* a rodent covered with long, sharp spines.

**pore** *(n)* one of the tiny holes in your skin through which you sweat.

**porous** *(adj)* Something that is **porous** lets liquid or gas through it.

**porridge** *(n)* a breakfast food made by boiling oats in milk or water.

**port** 1 *(n)* a town with a harbour. 2 *(n)* the left side of a ship or aircraft.

**portable** *(adj)* able to be carried easily.

**porter** *(n)* someone who carries luggage for people at a railway station or hotel.

**portion** *(n)* a part, or a piece.

**portrait** 1 *(n)* a drawing, painting, or photograph of a person. 2 *(n)* a description of something.

**portray** **portraying portrayed** 1 *(v)* to show or describe someone or something in a certain way. *The author portrays Hattie as an eccentric.* **portrayal** *(n).* 2 *(v)* to act a part in a play or a film.

**pose** **posing posed** 1 *(v)* to keep your body in a particular position so that you can be photographed, painted, or drawn. **pose** *(n).* 2 *(v)* to pretend to be someone else in order to deceive people. *The thieves posed as policemen.*

**posh** **posher poshest** 1 *(adj) (informal)* upper-class. *A posh accent.* 2 *(adj) (informal)* very smart and expensive.

**position** **positioning positioned** 1 *(n)* the place where something is. 2 *(v)* to put something in a particular place. *Position the pictures carefully.* 3 *(n)* the way in which someone is standing, sitting, etc. 4 *(n)* your place in a race or competition.

**positive** 1 *(adj)* sure, or certain. 2 *(adj)* hopeful and optimistic. *A positive outlook.*

**possession** 1 *(n)* something that you own. **possess** *(v).* 2 If something is **in your possession**, you own it or have it.

**possessive** 1 *(adj)* wanting to keep something or someone for yourself and not to share them with other people. 2 *(n)* the form of a noun or pronoun that shows that something belongs to it. *In "This ball is mine" and "Tom's bat", "mine" and "Tom's" are possessives.*

**possible** *(adj)* If something is **possible**, it might happen or might be true. **possibility** *(n),* **possibly** *(adv).*

**post** **posting posted** 1 *(n)* a long, thick piece of wood, concrete, or metal that is fixed in the ground. 2 *(n)* a particular job. 3 *(v)* to send a letter or parcel from one place to another. 4 *(singular n)* the letters and parcels that you send or receive.

**postage** *(n)* the cost of sending a letter or parcel by post.

**postcard** *(n)* a card that you send by post, usually with a picture on one side.

**postcode** *(n)* the set of numbers and letters at the end of an address, used to help sort letters, parcels, etc. quickly.

**poster** *(n)* a large, printed picture or notice that can be put up on a wall.

**postmark** *(n)* an official mark on a letter to show when and where it was posted.

**postpone** **postponing postponed** *(v)* to put something off until later. *We had to postpone the match because of rain.*

**postscript** *(n)* a short message, beginning "ps", which is added to the end of a letter, after your signature.

**posture** *(n)* the position of your body when you stand, sit, or walk.

**posy** **posies** *(n)* a small bunch of flowers.

**pot** **potting potted** 1 *(n)* a round container used for cooking or storing food. 2 *(n)* a container used for growing plants. 3 *(v)* to hit a ball into a pocket in snooker, pool, or billiards.

**potato** **potatoes** *(n)* a round, root vegetable.

**potent** *(adj)* powerful, or strong. *A potent drug.* **potency** *(n).*

**potential** 1 *(n)* Your **potential** is what you are capable of achieving in the future. 2 *(n)* If an idea, place, etc. has **potential**, you think that you can develop it into something better.

**potholing** *(n)* the sport of exploring underground caves. **potholer** *(n).*

**potter** 1 *(n)* someone who makes objects out of clay, such as bowls, plates, vases, etc. 2 *(v)* to be occupied in a leisurely way. *Pandora pottered around the house.*

**pottery** **potteries** 1 *(n)* objects made of baked clay, such as bowls, plates, etc. 2 *(n)* a place where clay objects are made.

**potty** **potties; pottier pottiest** 1 *(n)* a type of bowl that very young children use instead of a toilet. 2 *(adj) (informal)* slightly mad.

**pouch** **pouches** 1 *(n)* a small leather or fabric bag. 2 *(n)* a flap of skin in which kangaroos and other marsupials carry their young.

**poultry** *(plural n)* farmyard birds kept for their eggs and meat.

**pounce** **pouncing pounced** *(v)* to jump on something suddenly and grab it.

**pound** **pounding** **pounded** **1** *(n)* the main unit of money in Britain. **2** *(n)* a unit of weight, equal to 0.454kgs. *See* page 256. **3** *(v)* to keep hitting something noisily and with force. *The rain pounded on the roof.*

**pour** **pouring** **poured** **1** *(v)* to make liquid flow out of a jug, bottle, etc. **2** *(v)* to rain heavily.

**pout** **pouting** **pouted** *(v)* to push out your lips because you are cross or disappointed about something. **pout** *(n).*

**poverty** *(n)* the state of being poor.

**powder** *(n)* tiny grains of a solid substance. **powdery** *(adj).*

**power** **1** *(n)* control over other people or things. **powerful** *(adj).* **2** *(n)* great force, or great strength. **powerful** *(adj).* **3** *(n)* electricity or other forms of energy. **4** **power cut** *(n)* a temporary stoppage in the electricity supply.

**practical** **1** *(adj)* to do with experience or action rather than with theory and ideas. *A practical approach.* **2** *(adj)* good at making and doing things with your hands. **3** *(adj)* sensible and useful. *Brown is a practical colour for a carpet.*

**practical joke** *(n)* a humorous trick played on someone.

**practically** **1** *(adv)* almost. *It's practically impossible.* **2** *(adv)* in a sensible way. *Abby tackled the job very practically.*

**practice** **1** *(n)* the regular repetition of an action in order to improve it. *Piano practice.* **2** *(n)* a custom or habit. *The practice of sending birthday cards.* **3** **in practice** *(adv)* what really happens when you do something rather than what is meant to happen.

**practise** **practising** **practised** **1** *(v)* to do something over and over again so that you improve. **2** *(v)* If someone **practises** a religion, they follow its teachings and attend its services or ceremonies. **3** *(v)* to work as a doctor or lawyer.

**prairie** *(n)* a large area of grassland in North America.

**praise** **praising** **praised** **1** *(v)* to say good things about someone because you admire them or think that they have done something well. **praise** *(n).* **2** *(v)* to thank and worship God. **praise** *(n).*

**prance** **prancing** **pranced** **1** *(v)* to leap in a lively way. **2** *(v)* When horses **prance**, they walk quickly with high steps.

**prank** *(n)* a trick played on someone.

**prawn** *(n)* a small shellfish that you can cook and eat.

**pray** **praying** **prayed** **1** *(v)* to talk to God, either out loud or silently. **prayer** *(n).* **2** *(v)* to hope very much that something happens. *I am praying for rain.*

**preach** **preaches** **preaching** **preached** **1** *(v)* to give a religious talk to people, especially during a church service. **preacher** *(n).* **2** *(v)* to tell other people what they should do. *Don't preach at me!*

**precarious** *(adj)* unsafe and risky. *Our position on the ledge was precarious.*

**precaution** *(n)* something that you do in order to prevent something dangerous or unpleasant from happening. *Let's take a first aid kit as a precaution.*

**precede** *(pree-**seed**)* **preceding** **preceded** *(v)* If one thing **precedes** something else, it comes before it.

**precinct** *(**pree**-sinkt)* *(n)* a shopping area in a town, where traffic is not allowed.

**precious** *(**presh**-uss)* **1** *(adj)* rare and valuable. **2** *(adj)* very special to you.

**precipice** *(n)* a steep cliff face.

**precise** *(adj)* exact, accurate, and neat.

**precocious** *(prek-**oh**-shuss)* *(adj)* **Precocious** children are very advanced for their age.

**predator** *(n)* an animal that hunts and kills other animals. **predatory** *(adj).*

**predicament** *(n)* an awkward or difficult situation.

**predict** **predicting** **predicted** *(v)* to say what you think will happen in the future. **prediction** *(n).*

**preen** **preening** **preened** *(v)* When birds **preen** themselves, they clean and arrange their feathers with their beaks.

**preface** *(**pref**-uss)* *(n)* an introduction at the front of a book.

**prefect** *(n)* a school pupil who has special duties and responsibilities.

**prefer** **preferring** **preferred** *(v)* to like one thing better than another. *I prefer oranges to apples.* **preference** *(n).*

**pregnant** *(adj)* A woman who is **pregnant** has a baby growing in her womb. *This diagram of a pregnant woman's womb shows a baby ready to be born.* **pregnancy** *(n).*

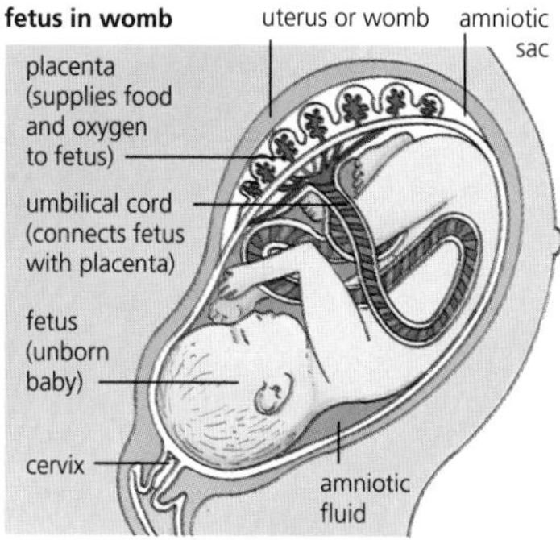


**prehistoric** *(adj)* belonging to a time very long ago before history was written.

**prejudice** 1 *(n)* a fixed and unreasonable opinion. **prejudiced** *(adj).* 2 *(n)* unfair behaviour that results from having fixed opinions. *Racial prejudice.*

**preliminary** *(adj)* preparing the way for what comes later. *A preliminary talk.*

**premature** *(adj)* happening or coming too early. *A premature baby.*

**premier** *(prem-ee-er)* 1 *(adj)* leading, top, or principal. *America's premier rock group.* 2 *(n)* the leader of a government.

**première** *(prem-ee-air)* *(n)* the first public performance of a film or play.

**premises** *(plural n)* a building and the land that belongs to it.

**preoccupied** *(adj)* If you are **preoccupied,** your thoughts are completely taken up with something.

**prep** 1 *(n)* *(informal)* homework. Prep is short for preparation. 2 **prep school** *(n)* a private school for pupils up to the age of thirteen. Prep school is short for preparatory school.

**prepare** **preparing prepared** *(v)* to get ready. **preparation** *(n).*

**preposition** *(n)* a word showing the position of things or people in relation to each other. *"On", "beside", and "with" are prepositions. See* page 3.

**preposterous** *(adj)* ridiculous and absurd. **preposterously** *(adv).*

**preschool** *(adj)* to do with children who are too young to go to school.

**prescribe** **prescribing prescribed** *(v)* When doctors **prescribe** medicine for a patient, they decide what drugs they should take and write an order, or prescription, to a chemist.

**prescription** *(n)* an order for drugs written by a doctor to a chemist.

**present** **presenting presented**
1 *(prez-ent)* *(adj)* If someone is **present** in a place, they are there. 2 *(prez-ent)* *(n)* the time now. 3 *(priz-ent)* *(v)* to give someone a gift or prize in a formal way. 4 *(prez-ent)* *(n)* something that you buy or make to give to somebody.

**presentation** 1 *(n)* the formal giving of a prize or present. *We had a presentation for our teacher.* 2 *(n)* the way something is produced and the way it looks.

**presently** *(adv)* soon, or shortly.

**preserve** **preserving preserved** 1 *(v)* to protect something so that it stays in its original state. **preservation** *(n).* 2 *(v)* to treat food so that it does not go bad. **preservative** *(n).* 3 *(n)* jam. *Plum preserve.*

**president** 1 *(n)* the elected head of state of a republic. **presidency** *(n).* 2 *(n)* the head of a society or organization.

**press** **presses pressing pressed** 1 *(v)* to push firmly. *Press the button.* **pressure** *(n).* 2 *(v)* to persuade strongly. *We pressed Eddie to join in.* 3 *(v)* to smooth out the creases in clothes with an iron. **4 the press** *(n)* a general name for newspapers and the people who produce them.

**press-up** *or* **push-up** *(n)* an exercise in which you lie on the floor and raise your body off it by pushing with your arms.

**pressure** 1 *(n)* the force with which you press on something. *Apply pressure here.* 2 *(n)* the force with which a liquid or gas pushes against something. *Air pressure.*

**prestige** *(press-teej)* *(n)* the good reputation and high status that come from being successful, powerful, rich, etc.

**presumably** *(adv)* probably.

**presume** **presuming presumed** *(v)* to think that something is true without being certain. *I presume you like chocolate.*

**pretend** **pretending pretended** *(v)* to try to make people believe that things are different from the way they really are.

**pretext** *(n)* a false reason. *Joe went to the pub on the pretext of walking the dog.*

**pretty** **prettier prettiest** 1 *(adj)* pleasing to look at and attractive. **prettiness** *(n).* 2 *(adv) (informal)* quite. *A pretty bad film.*

**prevail** **prevailing prevailed** *(v)* to succeed despite difficulties.

**prevent** **preventing prevented** *(v)* to stop something from happening.

**preview** *(n)* a showing of a play or film before it is released for public viewing.

**previous** *(adj)* former, or happening before. *I like this school more than my previous one.* **previously** *(adv).*

**prey** *(pray)* **prey; preying preyed** 1 *(n)* a creature that is hunted and eaten by other animals. 2 *(v)* When an animal **preys on** another animal, it hunts it and eats it.

**price** *(n)* the amount that you have to pay for something.

**priceless** *(adj)* If something is **priceless**, it is too valuable for anyone to say how much it is worth.

**prick** **pricking pricked** *(v)* to make a small hole in something with a sharp point. **prick** *(n).*

**prickle** *(n)* a sharp point, for example, on a rose bush. **prickly** *(adj).*

**pride** 1 *(n)* a feeling of satisfaction in something that you do. *Zara takes pride in her work.* 2 *(n)* a too high opinion of your own importance and cleverness.

**priest** *(n)* a religious leader who takes services in a church, temple, etc.

**prim** **primmer primmest** *(adj)* Someone who is **prim** is very formal and hates anything rough or rude.

**prima donna** 1 *(n)* a female opera star. 2 *(n) (informal)* someone who is demanding and often bad-tempered.

**primary** 1 *(adj)* most important, chief, or main. 2 *(adj)* first, or earliest. *Primary education.*

**primary colours** *(n)* In painting, the **primary colours** are red, yellow, and blue, which can be mixed to make all the other colours.

**primary school** *(n)* a school for children aged from five to eleven, or five to nine.

**primate** *(n)* any member of the group of intelligent mammals that includes humans, apes, and monkeys.

**prime** *(adj)* of first importance or quality. *Prime Minister. Prime beef.*

**Prime Minister** *(n)* the leader of a government in some countries.

**prime number** *(n)* a number that can be divided only by itself or by 1. *7, 13, and 29 are all prime numbers.*

**primitive** 1 *(adj)* simple, and not highly developed or civilized. *A primitive tribe.* 2 *(adj)* uncivilized, basic, and crude. *Primitive conditions.*

**prince** *(n)* the son of a king or queen.

**princess** **princesses** *(n)* the daughter of a king or queen, or the wife of a prince.

**principal** *(adj)* most important, chief, or main. **principally** *(adv).*

**principle** 1 *(n)* a scientific rule or truth. 2 *(n)* a basic rule which governs your behaviour. *It's against Rollo's principles to eat meat.*

**print** **printing printed** 1 *(v)* to produce words or pictures on a page with a machine that uses ink. **printer** *(n).* 2 *(v)* to write using letters that do not join up.

**print-out** *(n)* a printed copy of information stored in a computer.

**prior** *(adj)* earlier. *A prior engagement.*

**priority** **priorities** *(n)* something that is more important than other things.

**prise** **prising prised** *(v)* to force something open, using a lever.

**prism** *(n)* a clear glass or plastic shape that bends light or breaks it up into the colours of the spectrum. *See* **spectrum**.

**prison** *(n)* a building where people are forced to stay, usually as a punishment for a crime.

**private** 1 *(adj)* concerning or belonging to one person, organization, etc. and no one else. *Private possessions.* **privacy** *(n).* 2 *(adj)* secret. *Private thoughts.*

**privatize** *or* **privatise** **privatizing privatized** *(v)* to sell or hand over a government-funded public industry or organization to private individuals or companies. **privatization** *(n).*

**privilege** *(n)* a special advantage given to a person or a group of people.

**prize** **prizing prized** 1 *(n)* a reward for winning a game or a competition. 2 *(v)* to value something very much. *I prize my freedom.* **prized** *(adj).*

**probable** *(adj)* likely, or expected to happen. *It is probable that Yves will win.* **probability** *(n),* **probably** *(adv).*

**probation** 1 *(n)* If someone is **on probation** at work, they are having a trial period. 2 *(n)* If an offender is put **on probation**, they are supervised for a certain time by a probation officer.

**probe** **probing probed** *(v)* to examine or explore something very carefully.

**problem** 1 *(n)* a difficult situation that needs to be sorted out or overcome. 2 *(n)* a puzzle or question to be solved. *A maths problem.*

**proceed** **proceeding proceeded** 1 *(v)* to move forward, or to carry on. 2 **proceeds** *(plural n)* the money an event raises.

**process** **processes processing processed** 1 *(pro-sess) (n)* an organized series of actions that produce a result. *We studied the process of making rubber.* 2 *(pro-sess) (v)* to take part in a procession.

**procession** *(n)* a number of people walking or driving along a route as part of a public festival, religious service, etc.

**proclaim** **proclaiming proclaimed** *(v)* to announce something publicly.

**prod** **prodding prodded** *(v)* to poke something or someone. **prod** *(n).*

**prodigy** *(prod-ij-ee)* **prodigies** *(n)* Child **prodigies** are extraordinarily clever or talented for their age.

**produce** **producing produced** 1 *(prod-yuce) (v)* to make something. 2 *(prod-yuce) (n)* things that are produced or grown for eating. *Dairy produce.* 3 *(prod-yuce) (v)* to bring something out for people to see. *Ginger produced a mouse from his pocket.*

**product** 1 *(n)* something that is manufactured or made by a natural process. 2 *(n)* the result you get when you multiply two numbers. *15 is the product of 3 and 5.*

**production** 1 *(n)* the process of manufacturing or growing something. 2 *(n)* a play, opera, show, etc.

**productive** *(adj)* making a lot of products, or producing good results.

**profession** *(n)* a job for which you need special training or study.

**professional** 1 *(n)* a member of a profession, for example, a doctor, teacher, or lawyer. 2 *(adj)* paid to do something that people do for a hobby. *Professional actors.* **professional** *(n).*

**professor** *(n)* the head and principal teacher of a university department.

**proficient** *(prof-ish-ent) (adj)* If you are **proficient** at doing something, you are able to do it properly and skilfully.

**profile** 1 *(n)* the outline of someone's face, seen from the side. 2 *(n)* a brief account of someone's life or progress.

**profit** *(n)* the money made by selling something, after the cost of making it or buying it has been taken away. **profit** *(v).*

**profound** *(adj)* very deeply felt or thought. *Profound sadness.*

**program** *(n)* a series of instructions written in a special code that controls the way that a computer works. **program** *(v).*

**programme** 1 *(n)* a television or radio show. 2 *(n)* a pamphlet that gives you information about an event.

**programmer** *(n)* someone whose job is to program a computer.

**progress** **progresses progressing progressed** 1 *(v)* to move forward, or to improve slowly. *How are you progressing with your French?* **progress** *(n).* 2 If something is **in progress**, it is happening.

**prohibit** **prohibiting prohibited** *(v)* to stop or ban something officially.

**project** **projecting projected** 1 *(proj-ekt) (n)* a scheme, or a plan. 2 *(n) (proj-ekt)* a study of something, worked on over a period of time. *A project on the Romans.* 3 *(pro-jekt) (v)* to stick out. 4 *(pro-jekt) (v)* to show an image on a screen.

**projection** 1 *(n)* something that sticks out. 2 *(n)* a forecast, or a prediction.

**projector** *(n)* a piece of equipment which shows slides or film on a screen.

**prologue** *(pro-log) (n)* a short speech or piece of writing which introduces a play, story, or poem.

**prolong prolonging prolonged** *(v)* to make something last longer.

**promenade** *(n)* a paved road or path beside the beach at a seaside resort.

**prominent** 1 *(adj)* very easily seen. *The windmill is a prominent landmark.* 2 *(adj)* famous, or important. *A prominent politician.*

**promise promising promised** 1 *(v)* to say definitely that you will do something. **promise** *(n)*. 2 *(n)* Someone who shows **promise** seems likely to do well in the future. **promising** *(adj)*.

**promote promoting promoted** 1 *(v)* to move someone to a more important job. **promotion** *(n)*. 2 *(v)* If a sports team is **promoted**, it moves to a higher league. **promotion** *(n)*. 3 *(v)* to make the public aware of something or someone. *Merlin is busy promoting his book.* **promotion** *(n)*.

**prompt prompting prompted; prompter promptest** 1 *(adj)* very quick and without delay. *A prompt answer.* **promptly** *(adv)*. 2 *(v)* to remind actors of their lines when they have forgotten them during a play. **prompt** *(n)*.

**prone** *(adj)* vulnerable, or easily affected by something harmful. *Dakita is prone to colds in the winter.*

**pronoun** *(n)* a word that is used in place of a noun. "I", "me", "her" and "it" are all pronouns. *See* page 3.

**pronounce pronouncing pronounced** 1 *(v)* to say words in a particular way. *How do you pronounce "psychic"?* 2 *(v)* to make a formal announcement. *The mayor pronounced the fair open.*

**pronunciation** *(pro-nun-see-**ay**-shun) (n)* the way a word is pronounced.

**proof** *(n)* evidence that something is true. *Do you have proof of your age?*

**prop propping propped** *(v)* to support something that would otherwise fall down. *Prop the ladder against the wall.*

**propaganda** *(singular n)* biased information, used to present a certain viewpoint.

**propel propelling propelled** *(v)* to drive or push something forward.

**propeller** *(n)* a set of rotating blades which provide force to move a vehicle.

**proper** 1 *(adj)* accepted, or right. *Is this the proper way to sit?* **properly** *(adv)*. 2 *(adj)* real. *A proper explanation.* 3 *(adj)* correct in behaviour. *Prim and proper.*

**proper noun** *(n)* the name of a particular person, place, time, etc. such as "Jane", "New York", "Wednesday".

**property properties** *(n)* the things that you own. *Whose property is this pen?*

**prophecy** *(**prof**-ess-ee)* **prophecies** *(n)* a prediction of what will happen in the future. **prophesy** *(**prof**-ess-eye) (v)*.

**prophet** *(**prof**-it) (n)* someone who predicts what will happen in the future.

**proportion** 1 *(n)* a part of something. *A large proportion of the class.* 2 *(n)* the amount of something in relation to other things. *The proportion of boys to girls in the school is growing.* 3 If something is **in proportion** to something else, it is the right size in relation to it. *My large nose is in proportion to my eyes.*

**propose proposing proposed** 1 *(v)* to suggest a plan or an idea. 2 *(v)* to ask someone to marry you.

**prose** *(n)* writing that is in ordinary lines, not in verse.

**prosecute prosecuting prosecuted** *(v)* to accuse someone in a court of law.

**prospect** *(n)* something in the future that you look forward to or dread.

**prosper prospering prospered** *(v)* to be successful, or to thrive. **prosperous** *(adj)*.

**protect protecting protected** *(v)* to guard or shelter something.

**protein** *(pro-teen) (n)* a substance found in foods such as meat, cheese, and lentils.

**protest protesting protested** *(pro-**test**) (v)* to object to something strongly and publicly. **protest** *(**pro**-test) (n)*.

**Protestant** *(**prot**-iss-tant) (n)* a Christian who does not belong to the Roman Catholic or Orthodox church.

**prototype** *(n)* the first version of a new invention. **prototype** *(adj)*.

**protractor** *(n)* a semicircular instrument, used for measuring angles.

**protrude protruding protruded** *(v)* to stick out, or to jut out.

**proud** prouder proudest 1 *(adj)* pleased with what you or someone else has achieved. 2 *(adj)* thinking too highly of your own importance or abilities.

**prove** proving proved *(v)* to show that something is true.

**proverb** *(n)* a wise, old saying.

**provide** providing provided 1 *(v)* to supply the things that someone needs. 2 provided *(conj)* on condition that, or as long as. *I will go, provided you go too.*

**province** *(n)* a district, or a region of a country.

**provisions** *(plural n)* groceries and other household goods.

**provisional** *(adj)* temporary, or not yet definite. *A provisional driving licence.*

**provoke** provoking provoked *(v)* to annoy someone and make them angry.

**prowl** prowling prowled *(v)* to move around quietly and secretly, like an animal looking for food.

**prudent** *(adj)* If you are prudent, you are cautious and think carefully before you do something. prudence *(n)*.

**prune** pruning pruned 1 *(n)* a dried plum. 2 *(v)* to cut branches off a tree or bush, to make it grow more strongly.

**pry** pries prying pried *(v)* to look into other people's business in a nosy way.

**ps** *short for* **postscript**.

**psalm** *(sahm)* *(n)* a sacred song or poem, especially one from the Bible.

**psychiatrist** *(sy-ky-a-trist)* *(n)* a doctor who is trained to treat mental illness.

**psychic** *(sy-kik)* *(adj)* Someone who is psychic can use their mind in an unusual way, for example, to tell what people are thinking or to predict the future.

**psychologist** *(sy-kol-oj-ist)* *(n)* someone who studies people's minds and the ways that people behave. psychology *(n)*.

**pto** The letters pto at the bottom of a page stand for please turn over.

**pub** *(n)* a place where adults can go to drink alcohol. Pub is short for public house.

**puberty** *(pew-ber-tee)* *(n)* the time when your body changes from a child's to an adult's.

**public** 1 *(adj)* to do with people. *Public opinion.* 2 *(adj)* belonging to, or for everybody. *Public transport.* publicly *(adj)*. 3 the public *(n)* people in general.

**publication** 1 *(n)* The publication of a book or magazine is the production and distribution of it, so that people can buy it. 2 *(n)* a book, or a magazine.

**publicity** *(n)* information that tells you about a person or an event. *The film got a lot of publicity in the newspapers.*

**publicize** *or* **publicise** publicizing publicized *(v)* to make something known to as many people as possible.

**publish** publishes publishing published *(v)* to produce and distribute a book, magazine, etc. so people can buy it.

**pudding** 1 *(n)* a sweet food served at the end of a meal. 2 *(n)* a sponge or suet mixture cooked with fruit or meat.

**puddle** *(n)* a small pool of rainwater or other liquid.

**puff** puffing puffed 1 *(v)* to blow or breathe out something, such as smoke or steam. puff *(n)*. 2 puff up *(v)* to swell up.

**puffin** *(n)* a black and white sea bird whose beak becomes brightly coloured in the mating season.

**pugnacious** *(adj)* fond of fighting or quarrelling. pugnaciously *(adv)*.

**pull** pulling pulled 1 *(v)* to move something towards you. pull *(n)*. 2 *(v)* If you pull out of something, you stop doing it. *Adam pulled out of the team.* 3 pull up *(v)* to stop a vehicle.

**pulley** *(n)* a wheel with a grooved rim in which a rope or chain can run, used to lift loads more easily.

**pulp** *(n)* a soft, crushed mass of something, such as fruit, vegetables, or wood. pulp *(v)*.

**pulpit** *(n)* a raised, enclosed platform in a church where a priest stands to preach.

**pulse** *(n)* a steady beat or throb, especially the pumping of blood through your body.

**pummel** pummelling pummelled *(v)* to punch someone or something repeatedly.

**pump** *(n)* a machine that forces liquids or gases from one container into another. *A bicycle pump. A water pump.* pump *(v)*.

**pumpkin** *(n)* a very big, round, orange fruit that grows on the ground.

**pun** *(n)* a joke based on a word that has two meanings. **pun** *(v).*

**punch** punches punching punched 1 *(v)* to hit something or someone with your fist. **punch** *(n).* 2 *(n)* a drink made from fruit juice, spices, and usually alcohol. 3 *(n)* a metal tool used for making holes.

**punctual** *(adj)* If you are **punctual**, you arrive at the right time.

**punctuation** *(n)* marks that you use in writing to divide up sentences, to show that someone is speaking, or to show questions, etc. **punctuate** *(v).*

**puncture** *(n)* a hole in a ball, tyre, etc., made by a sharp object. **puncture** *(v).*

**punish** punishes punishing punished *(v)* If you **punish** someone, you make them suffer for committing a crime, or for behaving badly. **punishment** *(n).*

**puny** punier puniest *(adj)* small and feeble. **puniness** *(n),* **punily** *(adv).*

**pupa** pupae *or* pupas *(n)* an insect at the stage of development between larva and adult.

**pupil** 1 *(n)* someone who is being taught, especially a schoolchild. 2 *(n)* the round, black part of your eye.

**puppet** *(n)* a toy that you control by pulling strings that are attached to it or by moving your hand inside it.

**puppy** puppies *(n)* a young dog.

**purchase** purchasing purchased 1 *(v)* to buy something. **purchaser** *(n).* 2 *(n)* something that has been bought.

**pure** purer purest *(adj)* clean and not mixed with anything else. *Pure gold.*

**purée** *(pyoor-ay) (n)* liquidized or sieved food. **purée** *(v).*

**purpose** 1 *(n)* a reason, or an intention. 2 **on purpose** deliberately.

**purr** purring purred 1 *(v)* When a cat **purrs**, it makes a low sound in its throat to show pleasure. **purr** *(n).* 2 *(v)* to make a low sound like a cat.

**purse** *(n)* a small container in which people keep their money.

**pursue** *(per-syoo)* pursuing pursued *(v)* to follow or chase something.

**pursuit** *(per-syoot)* 1 *(n)* an activity, or an occupation. 2 *(n)* If you are in **pursuit** of someone, you are trying to catch them.

**pus** *(n)* a thick, yellowish liquid that comes out of an infected wound.

**push** pushes pushing pushed 1 *(v)* to move something away from you. **push** *(n).* 2 *(v)* to press yourself forward. *We pushed through the crowd.*

**push-up** *see* **press-up**.

**put** putting put 1 *(v)* to place, lay, or move something. 2 *(v)* to express in words. *How can I put this?* 3 **put down** *(v)* to kill an animal because it is very ill. 4 **put off** *(v)* If you **put something off**, you delay doing it.

**putty** putties *(n)* a paste that sets hard, used to fix windows into frames.

**puzzle** 1 *(n)* a game or activity for which you have to think hard in order to solve problems. *A crossword puzzle.* **puzzle** *(v).* 2 *(n)* something or someone that is hard to understand. **puzzle** *(v).*

**pyjamas** *(plural n)* a shirt and trousers that you wear in bed.

**pylon** *(n)* a tall, metal tower that supports electricity cables.

**pyramid** 1 *(n)* a solid shape with triangular sides that meet at the top. 2 *(n)* an ancient Egyptian stone monument where Pharaohs and their treasure were buried. *The picture shows a cutaway view of the Great Pyramid in Egypt.*

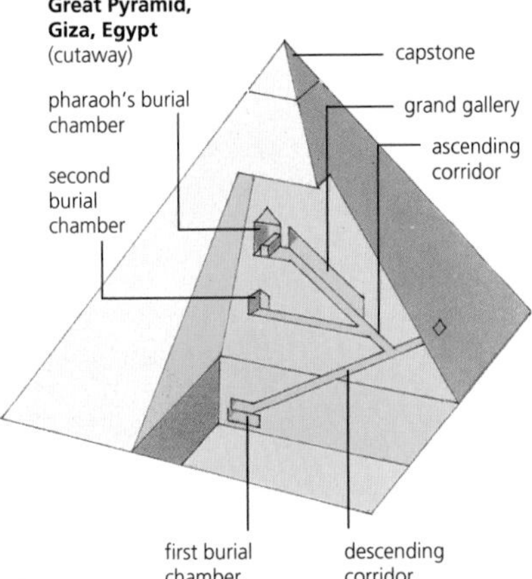

# Qq

**quack** **quacking quacked** *(v)* When ducks **quack**, they make a sharp, loud sound. **quack** *(n)*.

**quadrilateral** *(n)* a flat shape with four straight sides. **quadrilateral** *(adj)*.

**quadruped** *(n)* a four-footed animal.

**quadruple** *(adj)* four times as big, or four times as many. **quadruple** *(v)*.

**quaint** **quainter quaintest** *(adj)* charming and old-fashioned. *A quaint little fishing village.*

**quake** **quaking quaked** *(v)* to shake and tremble with fear.

**qualification** *(n)* a skill or ability that makes you able to do something.

**qualify** **qualifies qualifying qualified** *(v)* to reach a level or standard that allows you to do something. *Winning the match qualified us to play in the final.*

**quality** *(n)* The **quality** of something is how good or bad it is. *Poor quality.*

**qualm** *(rhymes with arm) (n)* a feeling of worry or uneasiness.

**quantity** **quantities** *(n)* an amount or number.

**quarantine** *(n)* When an animal is put in **quarantine**, it is kept away from other animals in case it has a disease.

**quarrel** **quarrelling quarrelled** **1** *(v)* to argue, or to disagree. **2** *(n)* an argument.

**quarry** **quarries** *(n)* a place where stone, slate, etc. is dug from the ground.

**quarter** *(n)* one of four equal parts.

**quaver** **quavering quavered** *(v)* to shake, or to tremble. *Jo's voice quavered.*

**quay** *(key) (n)* a place where boats can stop to load or unload.

**queasy** **queasier queasiest** *(adj)* feeling sick and uneasy. **queasiness** *(n)*.

**queen** **1** *(n)* a woman from a royal family, who is the ruler of her country. **2** *(n)* the wife of a king. **3** *(n)* a playing card with a picture of a queen on it. **4** *(n)* the most powerful chesspiece, that can move in any direction. *See* **chess**.

**queer** **queerer queerest** *(adj)* odd, or strange. **queerly** *(adv)*.

**quench** **quenches quenching quenched** **1** *(v)* If you **quench** a fire, you put it out. **2** *(v)* If you **quench** your thirst, you drink until you are no longer thirsty.

**query** *(kweer-ee)* **queries** *(n)* a question or doubt about something. **query** *(v)*.

**quest** *(n)* a long search.

**question** **1** *(n)* a sentence that asks something. **2** *(n)* a problem, or something to be discussed. *The question of bullying.*

**question mark** *(n)* the punctuation mark (?), used to indicate a question.

**questionnaire** *(n)* a list of questions that are asked to find out your opinions.

**queue** *(kyoo) (n)* a line of people waiting for something. **queue** *(v)*.

**quibble** **quibbling quibbled** *(v)* to argue about unimportant things.

**quick** **quicker quickest** **1** *(adj)* fast. **quickly** *(adv)*. **2** *(adj)* clever and lively.

**quicksand** *(n)* loose, wet sand that you can sink into.

**quiet** **quieter quietest** **1** *(adj)* not loud. *A quiet voice.* **quietly** *(adv)*. **2** *(adj)* calm and peaceful. *A quiet day.* **quietly** *(adv)*.

**quilt** *(n)* a warm, usually padded covering for a bed.

**quilted** *(adj)* If material is **quilted**, it is padded and sewn in lines.

**quip** *(n)* a witty or clever remark.

**quit** **quitting quit** *or* **quitted** *(v)* to stop doing something. *Dad has quit smoking.*

**quite** **1** *(adv)* rather, or fairly. *Quite good.* **2** *(adv)* completely. *Has he quite finished?*

**quiver** **quivering quivered** *(v)* to tremble or vibrate. **quiver** *(n)*.

**quiz** **quizzes** *(n)* a test or game where you have to answer questions. **quiz** *(v)*.

**quotation** *(n)* a sentence or short passage from a book, play, speech etc. which is repeated by someone else.

**quotation mark** *(n)* a punctuation mark (") or (') used to show where speech begins and ends or to highlight words.

**quote** **quoting quoted** *(v)* to repeat words that were spoken or written by someone else. **quote** *(n)*.

**Qur'an** *see* **Koran**.

# Rr

**rabbi** *(rab-eye) (n)* a Jewish religious leader.

**rabbit** *(n)* a small, long-eared, furry mammal that lives in a burrow.

**rabble** *(n)* a noisy crowd of people.

**rabies** *(ray-beez) (n)* a fatal disease that makes dogs and other animals go mad.

**race racing raced 1** *(n)* a test of speed. *A running race.* **race** *(v).* **2** *(n)* one of the major groups into which human beings can be divided. People of the same race share physical characteristics, such as skin colour. **3** *(v)* to run or move very fast.

**racial 1** *(adj)* to do with a person's race. *What is your racial origin?* **2** *(adj)* to do with different races. *Racial harmony.*

**racist** *(adj)* Someone who is **racist** thinks that some races are better than others, and treats people of other races unfairly or cruelly. **racism** *(n),* **racist** *(n).*

**rack racking racked 1** *(n)* a framework for holding things or for hanging things from. *A plate rack. A clothes rack.* **2** *(n)* an instrument of torture, used to stretch the body of a victim. **3** *(v)* If you **rack your brains**, you think very hard. *I racked my brains to remember his name.*

**racket 1 racket** *or* **racquet** *(n)* a stringed bat that you use in tennis, squash, and badminton. **2** *(n)* a very loud noise. **3** *(n)* a dishonest activity. *A drugs racket.*

**racquet** *see* **racket**.

**radar** *(n)* Planes and ships use **radar** to find solid objects by reflecting radio waves off them. Radar stands for radio detecting and ranging.

**radiant 1** *(adj)* bright and shining. **2** *(adj)* Someone who is **radiant** looks very healthy and happy.

**radiate radiating radiated 1** *(v)* to spread out from the centre. **2** *(v)* to send out something strongly. *Mario radiates confidence.*

**radiation 1** *(n)* the sending out of rays of light, heat, etc. **2** *(n)* particles that are sent out from a radioactive substance.

**radiator** *(n)* a metal container through which hot water or steam circulates, sending out heat into a room.

**radical** *(adj)* If a change is **radical**, it is thorough and has important and far-reaching effects. **radically** *(adv).*

**radio** *(n)* a piece of equipment that you use to listen to sounds sent by electrical waves. **radio** *(adj).*

**radioactive** *(adj)* giving off strong, usually harmful rays. **radioactivity** *(n).*

**radiography** *(n)* the process of taking X-ray photographs of people's bones, organs, etc. **radiographer** *(n).*

**radish radishes** *(n)* a small red and white vegetable that you eat in salads.

**radius** *(ray-dee-uss)* **radiuses** *or* **radii** *(n)* a straight line drawn from the centre of a circle to its outer edge. *See* **circle**.

**raffle** *(n)* a way of raising money, by selling tickets and then giving prizes to people with winning tickets. **raffle** *(v).*

**raft 1** *(n)* a floating platform, often made from logs tied together. **2** *(n)* an inflatable craft with a flat bottom. **rafting** *(n).*

**rag 1** *(n)* a piece of old cloth. **2 rags** *(plural n)* very old, torn clothing.

**rage raging raged 1** If you are **in a rage**, you are very angry. **2** *(v)* to be violent or noisy. *The wind raged outside.*

**ragged** *(rag-ed) (adj)* old, torn, and scruffy. **raggedly** *(adv).*

**raid** *(n)* a sudden attack on a place.

**rail 1** *(n)* a fixed bar or metal track. **2** *(n)* the railway. *We travelled by rail.* **rail** *(adj).*

**railway 1** *(n)* a train track. **2** *(n)* a system of transport using trains.

**rain raining rained** *(n)* water that falls from clouds. **rain** *(v),* **rainy** *(adj).*

**rainbow** *(n)* the arch of different colours caused by sunlight shining through raindrops. *See* **spectrum**.

**rainfall** *(n)* the amount of rain that falls in one place in a certain time.

**rainforest** *(n)* a thick, tropical forest where a lot of rain falls. **rainforest** *(adj).*

**raise raising raised 1** *(v)* to lift something up. *Raise your glasses.* **2** *(v)* If you **raise** money, you collect it for a particular cause or charity.

**raisin** *(n)* a dried grape.

**rake** *(n)* a garden tool with metal teeth, used to level soil or to collect leaves, grass cuttings, etc. **rake** *(v).*

**rally rallies** *(n)* a large meeting. *A political rally.*

**ram ramming rammed 1** *(n)* a male sheep. **2** *(v)* to crash into something deliberately. **3** *(v)* to push something into a space. *Kit rammed clothes into the bag.*

**RAM** *(n)* the part of a computer's memory which is lost when you switch the computer off. The initials RAM stand for random access memory.

**Ramadan** *(n)* the ninth month of the Islamic year when Muslims must not eat between sunrise and sunset.

**ramble rambling rambled 1** *(v)* to go on a long country walk for pleasure. **ramble** *(n).* **2** *(v)* to speak for a long time in a way that is hard to follow.

**rambling** *(adj)* badly planned, or out of control. *A rambling house.*

**ramp 1** *(n)* a man-made slope linking one level with another. **2** *(n)* a ridge across a road, designed to slow vehicles down.

**rampage** *(n)* If you go **on the rampage**, you rush about in a noisy and destructive way. **rampage** *(v).*

**rampant** *(adj)* wild and unrestrained.

**ramshackle** *(adj)* rickety, or likely to fall apart. *A ramshackle cottage.*

**ranch ranches** *(n)* a large farm for cattle, usually in North America. **rancher** *(n).*

**rancid** *(adj)* **Rancid** food tastes sour because it has gone bad.

**random 1** *(adj)* without any fixed plan or order. *A random selection.* **randomly** *(adv).* **2** If you do something **at random**, you do it without any plan or purpose.

**range ranging ranged 1** *(n)* a collection or number of things. **2** *(v)* to vary between one extreme and the other. *My relatives' ages range from 6 to 97.* **range** *(n).* **3** *(n)* the distance that a bullet or rocket can travel. **4** *(n)* a long chain of mountains. **5** *(v)* to wander over a large area. *Cattle range over the land.* **6** *(n)* a cooking stove.

**rank 1** *(n)* an official position or job level. *The rank of colonel.* **2** *(n)* a line of people or things. *A taxi rank.*

**ransack ransacking ransacked** *(v)* to search a place wildly, usually looking for things to steal.

**ransom** *(n)* money that is demanded before someone can be set free.

**rant ranting ranted** *(v)* to talk or shout in a loud and angry manner.

**rap rapping rapped 1** *(v)* to hit something sharply and quickly. **rap** *(n).* **2** *(n)* a type of music where words are spoken in a rhythmical way with a musical backing. **rap** *(v).*

**rape raping raped** *(v)* to force someone to have sexual intercourse. **rapist** *(n).*

**rapid** *(adj)* quick and speedy. **rapidity** *(n),* **rapidly** *(adv).*

**rapier** *(n)* a long, double-edged sword, used in the 16th and 17th centuries.

**rare rarer rarest 1** *(adj)* not often seen, or unusual. **rarity** *(n),* **rarely** *(adv).* **2** *(adj)* **Rare** meat is very lightly cooked.

**rascal** *(n)* a usually friendly name for someone who is very mischievous.

**rash rashes; rasher rashest 1** *(n)* spots or red patches on your skin, caused by an allergy or illness. **2** *(adj)* acting quickly without thinking first. **rashly** *(adv).*

**rasher** *(n)* a thin slice of bacon.

**raspberry raspberries** *(n)* a small, red, soft fruit.

**rat 1** *(n)* a long-tailed rodent like a large mouse. **2** *(n) (informal)* a disloyal or treacherous person. **3 rat race** *(n)* very stressful competition for success at work.

**rate rating rated 1** *(n)* the speed at which something happens. *Rhonda spends money at an alarming rate.* **2** *(n)* a charge, or a fee. *Maurice charges very high rates for his work.* **3** *(n)* standard, or quality. *A first-rate performance.* **4** *(v)* to value someone or something. *Dillon's fellow runners rate him highly.* **rating** *(n).*

**rather 1** *(adv)* fairly, or quite. *It's rather a long way to walk.* **2** *(adv)* more willingly. *I'd rather be at the seaside than at school.*

**ratio** *(ray-shee-oh) (n)* the proportion of one thing to another, expressed in its simplest terms. *In a group of 15 girls and 5 boys, the ratio of girls to boys is 3 to 1.*

**ration** *(n)* a limited amount, or a share. *You've had your ration of sweets!*

**rational** 1 *(adj)* sensible and logical. *A rational decision.* **rationally** *(adv).* 2 *(adj)* calm, reasonable, and sane. *Rational behaviour.* **rationally** *(adv).*

**rattle** **rattling rattled** 1 *(v)* to make a rapid series of short, sharp noises. **rattle** *(n).* 2 *(n)* a baby's toy.

**rattlesnake** *(n)* a poisonous snake with a tail that rattles as it vibrates.

**raucous** *(raw-kus) (adj)* harsh, or loud. **raucously** *(adv).*

**rave** **raving raved** 1 *(v)* to speak in a wild, uncontrolled way. 2 *(v) (informal)* to be very enthusiastic about something. *Gary raves about football.*

**ravenous** *(adj)* very hungry.

**raw** **rawer rawest** 1 *(adj)* Food that is **raw** has not been cooked or processed. 2 **raw materials** *(n)* the basic things used to make something.

**ray** 1 *(n)* a strong line of light, radiation, etc. 2 *(n)* a type of fish with a flat body, large wing-like fins, and a long tail.

**giant devil ray**

open mouth

**razor** *(n)* an instrument with a blade, used to shave hair from the skin.

**reach** **reaches reaching reached** 1 *(v)* to stretch out to something with your hand. *Can you reach the top shelf?* 2 *(v)* to extend, or to go as far as. *Our garden reaches down to the river.* 3 *(v)* to arrive somewhere. *We reached the summit.*

**react** **reacting reacted** *(v)* to respond to something that happens. *The firemen reacted quickly to the alarm.* **reaction** *(n).*

**reactor** *(n)* a large machine in which nuclear energy is produced.

**read** **reading read** *(v)* to look at written or printed words and understand what they mean.

**readily** *(adv)* easily, or willingly. *James readily volunteered to help out.*

**ready** **readier readiest** *(adj)* If you are **ready**, you are prepared, or you are in a position to start.

**real** 1 *(adj)* true and not imaginary. *The real story.* **reality** *(n).* 2 *(adj)* genuine and not artificial. *A real diamond.*

**realistic** 1 *(adj)* very like the real thing. *A realistic model.* 2 *(adj)* sensible, practical, or correct. *A realistic price.* 3 *(adj)* viewing things as they really are. *Frannie is realistic about her problems.* **realistically** *(adv).*

**reality** **realities** 1 *(n)* truth, or the actual situation. *Being a model looks glamorous, but the reality is not much fun.* 2 *(n)* a fact of life that must be faced. *After a holiday, we must return to the reality of work.*

**realize** *or* **realise** **realizing realized** *(v)* to become aware that something is true. *I realized how late it was.* **realization** *(n).*

**really** 1 *(adv)* actually, or in reality. *Is it really true?* 2 *(adv)* very. *I'm really happy.*

**reap** **reaping reaped** 1 *(v)* to cut a crop for harvest. 2 *(v)* If you **reap the reward** for something you have done, you experience the results of it.

**reappear** **reappearing reappeared** *(v)* to come into sight again. *The Sun reappeared from behind the clouds.* **reappearance** *(n).*

**rear** **rearing reared** 1 *(v)* to breed and bring up young animals. 2 *(v)* to care for and educate children. 3 *(n)* the back of something. **rear** *(adj).*

**rearrange** **rearranging rearranged** *(v)* to arrange things differently.

**reason** *(n)* the cause of something, or the motive behind someone's action.

**reasonable** 1 *(adj)* fair. *Your offer seems reasonable.* 2 *(adj)* sensible. *Hal always remains reasonable in arguments.* 3 *(adj)* moderate, or quite good.

**reassure** **reassuring reassured** *(v)* to calm someone and give them confidence. **reassurance** *(n).*

**rebel** *(**reb**-ul) (n)* someone who fights against a government or people in authority. **rebel** *(rib-**ell**) (v),* **rebellious** *(rib-**ell**-ee-uss) (adj).*

**rebellion** *(n)* armed resistance against a government.

**rebuke** **rebuking rebuked** *(v)* to tell someone off. **rebuke** *(n).*

**recall** **recalling recalled** *(v)* to remember something. *I can recall the day we met.*

**recap** recapping recapped *(v) (informal)* to repeat the main points of what has been said. **recap** *(n).*

**receipt** *(re-seet) (n)* a piece of paper acknowledging that money or goods have been received.

**receive** receiving received *(v)* to get or to accept something.

**receiver** *(n)* the part of a telephone that you hold in your hand.

**recent** *(adj)* happening, made, or done a short time ago. **recently** *(adv).*

**reception** 1 *(n)* the way in which something or someone is received. *The reception on our television is very bad.* 2 *(n)* a formal party.

**recession** *(n)* a time when a country produces fewer goods and more people become unemployed.

**recipe** *(ress-ip-ee) (n)* a set of instructions for preparing and cooking food.

**recipient** *(n)* a person who receives something. *The recipient of the first prize.*

**recite** reciting recited *(v)* to say aloud something that you have learnt by heart. **recitation** *(n).*

**reckless** *(n)* careless about your own and other people's safety. *Reckless driving.*

**reckon** reckoning reckoned 1 *(v)* to calculate or count up. 2 *(v)* to think, or to have an opinion. *I reckon we will win.*

**reclaim** reclaiming reclaimed *(v)* to get back something that is yours. *Maud reclaimed her jewels from the safe.*

**recline** reclining reclined *(v)* to lean or lie back.

**recognize** *or* **recognise** recognizing recognized *(v)* to see someone and know who they are. **recognition** *(n).*

**recollect** recollecting recollected *(v)* to remember, or to recall. **recollection** *(n).*

**recommend** recommending recommended *(v)* to suggest something or someone because you think that they are good. **recommendation** *(n).*

**reconcile** reconciling reconciled 1 *(v)* to bring back together people who have fallen out with each other. **reconciliation** *(n).* 2 *(v)* to decide to put up with something. *I reconciled myself to working over the holidays.*

**reconsider** reconsidering reconsidered *(v)* to think again about a decision.

**reconstruction** 1 *(n)* the rebuilding of something that has been destroyed. **reconstruct** *(v).* 2 *(n)* the careful piecing together of past events. **reconstruct** *(v).*

**record** recording recorded 1 *(v)* to write down information so that it can be kept. **record** *(n).* 2 *(v)* to put music or other sounds on to a tape or disc. **recording** *(n).* 3 *(n)* If you set a **record** in something like a sport, you do it better than anyone has ever done before.

**recorder** 1 *(n)* a machine for recording sounds on magnetic tape. 2 *(n)* a woodwind musical instrument.

**recover** recovering recovered 1 *(v)* to get better after an illness or difficulty. **recovery** *(n).* 2 *(v)* to get back something that has been lost or stolen. **recovery** *(n).*

**recreation** *(rek-ree-**ay**-shun) (singular n)* the games, sports, hobbies, etc. that people do for pleasure in their spare time. **recreational** *(adj).*

**recruit** *(re-**kroot**) (n)* someone who has recently joined a business, or an organization such as the armed forces.

**rectangle** *(n)* a four-sided shape with two pairs of equal, parallel sides and four right angles. **rectangular** *(adj).*

**recur** recurring recurred *(v)* to happen again. *This problem recurs every week.* **recurrence** *(n),* **recurrent** *(adj).*

**recycle** recycling recycled *(v)* to process used items, such as glass bottles, newspapers, and aluminium cans, so that they can be used to make new products.

**redeem** redeeming redeemed 1 *(v)* to save, or to rescue. *Glen redeemed our reputation by scoring three goals.* **redemption** *(n).* 2 *(v)* to claim back or exchange something. *Caroline redeemed her tokens for a set of glasses.*

**red herring** *(n)* something that diverts people unnecessarily from what they should be doing.

**red tape** *(n)* rules, regulations, and paperwork that make it difficult to get things done.

**reduce** reducing reduced *(v)* to make something smaller or less. *Todd is trying to reduce his weight.* **reduction** *(n).*

*Some words that begin with a "r" sound are spelt "wr".*

**redundant** *(adj)* no longer needed, especially for a job. *When the pit closed, the miners were made redundant.*

**reed** 1 *(n)* a plant with long, thin, hollow stems that grows in or near water. 2 *(n)* a piece of thin cane or metal in the mouthpiece of some musical instruments, such as a clarinet, oboe, or saxophone.

**reef** 1 *(n)* a line of rocks or coral close to the surface of the sea. 2 **reef knot** *(n)* a strong double knot.

**reek** **reeking reeked** *(v)* to smell strongly of something unpleasant. *I reek of smoke.*

**reel** **reeling reeled** 1 *(n)* a cylinder on which thread, film, etc. is wound. 2 *(v)* to stagger around unsteadily. *The drunk reeled into a lamppost.* 3 *(v)* If you **reel off** something, you say it very fast.

**ref** *short for* **referee**.

**refectory** **refectories** *(n)* a communal dining hall. *A school refectory.*

**refer** **referring referred** 1 *(v)* If you **refer** to a book, you look in it for information. 2 *(v)* If you **refer** to something while talking or writing, you mention it.

**referee** *(n)* someone who supervises a sports match or game and makes sure that the players obey the rules.

**reference** *(n)* a mention of someone or something. *There was a reference to you in the speech.*

**reference book** *(n)* a book that you use to find information. *Encyclopedias and dictionaries are reference books.*

**referendum** **referendums** *or* **referenda** *(n)* a vote by the people of a country on a very important question.

**refill** **refilling refilled** *(v)* to fill something again. **refill** *(n).*

**refined** *(adj)* A **refined** person is very polite, with elegant manners and tastes.

**refinery** **refineries** *(n)* a factory where raw materials are purified. **refine** *(v).*

**reflect** **reflecting reflected** 1 *(v)* to show an image of something on a shiny surface. **reflection** *(n).* 2 *(v)* to think carefully. *Arthur reflected on the meaning of life.* **reflection** *(n).*

**reflective** 1 *(adj)* acting like a mirror. 2 *(adj)* thoughtful. **reflectively** *(adv).*

**reflex** **reflexes** 1 *(n)* an automatic and instinctive action. *Blinking is a reflex.* **reflex** *(adj).* 2 *(adj)* A **reflex** angle is an angle between 180° and 360°.

**reform** **reforming reformed** *(v)* to improve something that is unsatisfactory. *Buster is trying to reform his behaviour.*

**refrain** **refraining refrained** 1 *(v)* to stop yourself from doing something. *Please refrain from standing on the seats.* 2 *(n)* a regularly repeated chorus or song.

**refresh** **refreshes refreshing refreshed** *(v)* to make someone feel fresh and strong again. **refreshing** *(adj).*

**refreshments** *(plural n)* drink and small amounts of food.

**refrigerator** *(n)* a very cold cabinet used for storing food and drink.

**refuel** **refuelling refuelled** *(v)* to take on more fuel.

**refuge** *(n)* a place of shelter and safety.

**refugee** *(n)* a person who has been forced to leave their home because of war, persecution, or natural disaster.

**refund** **refunding refunded** *(v)* to give money back to the person who paid it. **refund** *(n).*

**refuse** **refusing refused** 1 *(rif-**yooz**)* *(v)* to say you will not do something or accept something. **refusal** *(n).* 2 *(**ref**-yuce)* *(n)* rubbish, or waste.

**regal** *(adj)* to do with or fit for a king or queen. **regally** *(adv).*

**regard** **regarding regarded** 1 *(v)* to have an opinion about something. *Doug regards politicians with contempt.* **regard** *(n).* 2 *(plural n)* If someone sends you their **regards**, they send you their best wishes.

**regarding** *(prep)* about, or concerning.

**regardless** *(adj)* without considering anything or anyone else. *Nina drove very fast, regardless of the other drivers.*

**reggae** *(**reg**-ay)* *(n)* a type of pop music which came from the West Indies.

**region** *(n)* a large area or district. **regional** *(adj),* **regionally** *(adv).*

**register** 1 *(n)* a book in which names or official records are kept. *A class register.* **registration** *(n).* 2 *(v)* to enter something on an official list. *All cars must be registered.* **registration** *(n).*

**register office** *or* **registry office** *(n)* a place where people can get married, and where births and deaths are recorded.

**regret** regretting regretted *(v)* to be sad or sorry about something. **regret** *(n)*.

**regular** 1 *(adj)* usual, or normal. *This is my regular route home.* 2 *(adj)* happening at predictable times. *Regular meals.* 3 *(adj)* even, or steady. *A regular heartbeat.*

**regulation** 1 *(n)* an official rule. 2 *(n)* the act of controlling or adjusting something.

**regurgitate** *(re-**gurj**-it-ate)* **regurgitating regurgitated** *(v)* to bring food from the stomach back into the mouth.

**rehearse** *(re-**herss**)* **rehearsing rehearsed** *(v)* to practise for a public performance. **rehearsal** *(n)*.

**reign** *(rain)* **reigning reigned** *(v)* to rule as a king or queen. **reign** *(n)*.

**reimburse** *(re-im-**burss**)* **reimbursing reimbursed** *(v)* to pay someone back the money they have had to spend on your behalf. *The company will reimburse your train fare.* **reimbursement** *(n)*.

**reindeer** **reindeer** *(n)* a deer that lives in Arctic areas.

**reinforce** **reinforcing reinforced** *(v)* to strengthen something.

**reject** **rejecting rejected** 1 *(re-**jekt**)* *(v)* to refuse to accept something. *Julius rejected all offers of help.* **rejection** *(n)*. 2 *(**ree**-jekt)* *(n)* something or someone that is not wanted or accepted.

**rejoice** **rejoicing rejoiced** *(v)* to be very happy about something.

**relate** **relating related** 1 *(v)* If things **relate** to each other, there is a connection between them. 2 *(v)* If people **relate** to each other, they get on well together. 3 *(v)* to tell a story.

**related** *(adj)* If you are **related** to someone, you are part of their family.

**relation** 1 *(n)* a connection between things. 2 *(n)* a member of your family.

**relationship** 1 *(n)* the way in which two people get on together. 2 *(n)* the way in which things are connected.

**relative** 1 *(n)* a member of your family. 2 *(adj)* compared with others. *We live in relative luxury.*

**relatively** *(adv)* compared with others. *A 50 year old seems relatively young in a room full of pensioners.*

**relax** **relaxes relaxing relaxed** 1 *(v)* to rest and take things easy. **relaxation** *(n)*. 2 *(v)* to become less tense and anxious. **relaxation** *(n)*.

**relay** 1 *(**ree**-lay)* *(n)* a team race in which members of the team take it in turn to run, passing a baton from one runner to the next. 2 *(re-**lay**)* *(v)* to pass a message on to someone else.

**release** **releasing released** 1 *(v)* to free something or someone. **release** *(n)*. 2 *(v)* If a record, film, etc. is **released**, it is issued for the first time. **release** *(n)*.

**relent** **relenting relented** *(v)* to become less strict or more merciful. *I was meant to stay in all day, but Mum relented.*

**relentless** *(adj)* unceasing and determined. *Relentless activity.*

**relevant** *(adj)* If something is **relevant**, it is directly concerned with what is being discussed or dealt with. **relevance** *(n)*.

**reliable** *(adj)* trustworthy, or dependable. **reliability** *(n)*, **reliably** *(adv)*.

**relic** *(n)* something that has survived from the distant past.

**relief** 1 *(n)* a feeling of freedom from pain or worry. 2 *(n)* aid given to people in special need. *Famine relief.* 3 **relief map** *(n)* a map which shows the areas of high and low ground by shades of colour.

**relieve** **relieving relieved** 1 *(v)* to ease someone's trouble or pain. 2 *(v)* If you **relieve** someone, you take over a duty from them.

**religion** 1 *(n)* belief in God or gods. **religious** *(adj)*. 2 *(n)* the practice of your belief through worship, obedience, and prayer. **religious** *(adj)*.

**relish** **relishes relishing relished** 1 *(v)* to enjoy something greatly. 2 *(n)* a sauce.

**reluctant** *(adj)* not wanting to do something. **reluctance** *(n)*.

**rely** **relies relying relied** *(v)* If you **rely on** somebody or something, you need and trust them. *I had to rely on my friends to help me.* **reliant** *(adj)*.

**remain** **remaining remained** *(v)* to be left behind or left over.

**remainder** *(n)* the amount left over.

**remains** 1 *(plural n)* things left over. *The remains of my lunch.* 2 *(plural n)* a body after death. 3 *(plural n)* the ruins of ancient buildings. *Roman remains.*

**remark** **remarking remarked** *(v)* to make a comment about something. **remark** *(n).*

**remarkable** *(adj)* unusual and worth noticing. **remarkably** *(adv).*

**remedial** *(adj)* intended to help someone with a learning problem or physical difficulty. *Remedial maths.*

**remedy** **remedies** 1 *(n)* a cure for an illness. 2 *(n)* the answer to a problem.

**remember** **remembering remembered** 1 *(v)* to keep something in your mind. *I'll always remember Marco.* 2 *(v)* to bring something to mind. *Try to remember the answer.*

**remind** **reminding reminded** *(v)* to make someone remember something.

**reminisce** *(rem-in-iss)* **reminiscing reminisced** *(v)* to think or talk about the past and things that you remember.

**remnant** *(n)* a piece or part of something that is left over. *A remnant of material.*

**remorse** *(n)* a strong feeling of guilt and regret about something you have done.

**remote** **remoter remotest** *(adj)* far away, isolated, or distant.

**remote control** *(n)* a sytem by which machines can be operated from a distance, usually by radio signals or by an infra-red beam. **remote-controlled** *(adj).*

**remove** **removing removed** *(v)* to take something away. **removal** *(n).*

**rendezvous** *(ron-day-voo)* **rendezvous** *(n)* an arranged place and time for a meeting. **rendezvous** *(v).*

**renew** **renewing renewed** 1 *(v)* to replace something old with something new. **renewal** *(n).* 2 *(v)* to extend the period of a library loan, club membership, etc. **renewal** *(n).*

**renewable energy** *(n)* power from sources, such as wind, waves, and the Sun, that can never be used up.

**renovate** **renovating renovated** *(v)* to restore something to good condition, or to make it more modern. **renovation** *(n).*

**renowned** *(adj)* famous, or well-known.

**rent** *(n)* money paid by a tenant to the owner of a house, flat, etc. in return for living in it. **rent** *(v).*

**rental** *(n)* the hiring of equipment, such as televisions, cars, or machinery.

**repair** **repairing repaired** *(v)* to make something work again, or to mend something that is broken. **repair** *(n).*

**repay** **repaying repaid** *(v)* to pay back money or something else. *I repayed her visit.* **repayment** *(n).*

**repeat** **repeating repeated** *(v)* to say or do something again. **repetition** *(n).*

**repel** **repelling repelled** 1 *(v)* to drive away. *The army repelled the enemy forces.* 2 *(v)* to disgust someone.

**repellent** 1 *(adj)* disgusting. *A repellent smell.* 2 *(n)* a chemical that keeps insects and other pests away.

**repent** **repenting repented** *(v)* to be deeply sorry for the bad things that you have done. **repentant** *(adj).*

**repetition** *(n)* the repeating of words or actions. **repetitive** *(adj).*

**replace** **replacing replaced** 1 *(v)* to put one thing or person in place of another. **replacement** *(n).* 2 *(v)* to put something back where it was.

**replay** 1 *(n)* a second match between two teams or players, when the first match has ended in a draw. 2 *(v)* a second playing of a tape so that people can see or hear something again.

**replica** *(n)* an exact copy of something.

**reply** **replies replying replied** *(v)* to give an answer or a response. **reply** *(n).*

**report** **reporting reported** *(v)* to give a written or a spoken account of things that have happened. **report** *(n).*

**reporter** *(n)* someone who reports the news for radio, television, or a newspaper.

**represent** **representing represented** 1 *(v)* to act on behalf of someone else. 2 *(v)* to stand for something. *On a map, the colour blue represents water.* **representation** *(n).*

**repress** **represses repressing repressed** 1 *(v)* If you **repress** an emotion, like anger, you keep it under control and do not show it. **repressed** *(adj).* 2 *(v)* to keep people under very strict control. *The King repressed his people.* **repression** *(n).*

**reprieve** *(rip-reeve)* **reprieving reprieved** *(v)* to postpone or cancel a punishment, especially a death sentence.

**reprimand reprimanding reprimanded** *(v)* to tell someone off formally. **reprimand** *(n).*

**reproach reproaches reproaching reproached** *(v)* to blame someone, or show that you disapprove of them. *Annie reproached me for forgetting her birthday.* **reproach** *(n).*

**reproduce reproducing reproduced** 1 *(v)* to make a copy of something. **reproduction** *(n).* 2 *(v)* When animals **reproduce,** they breed and produce babies. **reproduction** *(n).*

**reptile** *(n)* a cold-blooded animal with a scaly skin, that lays eggs. *Lizards, snakes, and tortoises are all reptiles.*

**republic** *(n)* a country or state that elects its government and does not have a king or queen. **republican** *(adj).*

**repugnant** *(adj)* very unpleasant and disgusting. *A repugnant smell.*

**repulse repulsing repulsed** *(v)* to drive, or to force back. *The crew repulsed the aliens' attack.*

**repulsive** *(adj)* very ugly, or disgusting. *A repulsive monster.* **repulsively** *(adv).*

**reputable** *(adj)* reliable and trustworthy. *A reputable dealer.* **reputably** *(adv).*

**reputation** *(n)* the opinion that other people have of you. *Abdul has a reputation for hard work.*

**reputed** *(adj)* supposed to be, or thought to be. *Dominic is reputed to be very good at chess.* **reputedly** *(adv).*

**request requesting requested** 1 *(v)* to ask for something politely. *Visitors are requested not to take photographs.* 2 *(n)* something that you ask for. *That's a very strange request!*

**require requiring required** 1 *(v)* to need something. *Do you require anything to eat?* 2 *(v)* If someone **requires** you to do something, you must do it.

**requirement** *(n)* something that you need to do or have. *The ability to swim 50m is a requirement of this sailing club.*

**reread rereading reread** *(v)* to read something again.

**rescue rescuing rescued** *(v)* to save someone who is in danger or is trapped somewhere. **rescue** *(n),* **rescuer** *(n).*

**research researches researching researched** *(v)* to study and find out about a subject, usually by reading a lot of books about it, or by doing experiments. **research** *(n).*

**resemble resembling resembled** *(v)* to be or look like somebody or something. *Lucy resembles her dad.* **resemblance** *(n).*

**resent resenting resented** *(v)* to feel hurt or angry about something that has been done or said to you. *I resent being treated as an idiot.* **resentment** *(n),* **resentful** *(adj).*

**reservation** 1 *(n)* an area of land set aside for native people. 2 *(n)* a booking. *We have a reservation for this flight.* 3 *(plural n)* If you have **reservations** about something, you feel doubtful about it.

**reserve reserving reserved** 1 *(v)* to arrange for something to be kept for you. *Harvey reserved a seat on the train.* 2 *(n)* an extra member of a team who plays if one of the team is injured or cannot play. 3 *(n)* a protected place where animals can live and breed safely. *A nature reserve.*

**reserved** 1 *(adj)* If a seat, table, or room is **reserved**, it is kept for someone to use later. 2 *(adj)* Someone who is **reserved** behaves in a quiet, shy way and does not show their feelings much.

**reservoir** *(**rez**-er-vwar)* *(n)* a natural or artificial lake used for storing a large amount of water.

**resident** *(n)* someone who lives in a particular place. *The village residents.*

**resign** *(riz-**ine**)* **resigning resigned** 1 *(v)* to give up a job. **resignation** *(rez-ig-**nay**-shun)* *(n).* 2 *(v)* If you **resign yourself** to something, you accept it without complaining or worrying about it. **resignation** *(n),* **resigned** *(adj).*

**resist resisting resisted** 1 *(v)* to refuse to accept something. *Jessie resisted all offers of help.* 2 *(v)* to fight back. *The villagers resisted the advancing army.* 3 *(v)* to stop yourself doing something that you would like to do. *I resisted tickling Theo's feet.*

**resistance** *(n)* fighting back. *Resistance is useless in this situation.*

**resolution** *(n)* a promise to yourself that you will try hard to do something. *New Year resolutions.*

**resolve resolving resolved 1** *(v)* to decide that you will try hard to do something. *Shane resolved to find a part-time job.* **resolve** *(n).* **2** *(v)* to deal with a problem or difficulty successfully. *We need to resolve this dispute.*

**resort resorting resorted 1** *(n)* a place where people go on holiday. *A skiing resort.* **2** *(v)* If you **resort to** something, you turn to it because you do not have any other choices. **3** If you do something **as a last resort**, you do it because everything else has failed to work.

**resource** *(n)* something valuable or useful to a place or person. *North Sea oil is one of Britain's most valuable resources.*

**respect respecting respected 1** *(v)* to admire and have a high opinion of someone. **respect** *(n).* **2** *(n)* a detail or particular part of something. *I liked Guy's plan in many respects.*

**respectable 1** *(adj)* behaving in a decent way that does not offend anyone. **2** *(adj)* reasonably good. *A respectable score.*

**respiration** *(n)* breathing, or the process of taking in oxygen and sending out carbon dioxide.

**respond responding responded 1** *(v)* to reply. **response** *(n).* **2** *(v)* to react to something. *Don't respond to teasing.*

**responsibility responsibilities 1** *(n)* a duty. *It's my responsibility to provide tea.* **2** *(n)* If you **take responsibility** for something bad that has happened, you agree that you are to blame for it.

**responsible 1** *(adj)* If someone is **responsible** for something, they have to do it and it is their fault if it goes wrong. **2** *(adj)* If a person is **responsible,** they are sensible and can be trusted.

**rest resting rested 1** *(v)* to relax, or to sleep. **rest** *(n).* **2** *(v)* the others, or the remaining part of something. *I came first and beat all the rest.* **3** *(v)* to lean on something. *Rest your rackets against the wall.* **4** *(v)* to stop and stay in one place. *The spotlight rested on his face.*

**restaurant** *(n)* a place where people pay to eat meals.

**restless** *(adj)* If someone is **restless,** they find it hard to keep still or to concentrate on anything. **restlessness** *(n).*

**restore restoring restored 1** *(v)* to repair something that has been damaged. **2** *(v)* to give or bring something back. *Please restore the pen to its owner.*

**restrain restraining restrained** *(v)* to prevent someone from doing something. *We managed to restrain Harry from eating another ice cream.* **restraint** *(n).*

**restrained** *(adj)* A **restrained** person is very quiet and controlled.

**restrict restricting restricted** *(v)* to keep something within limits. *Please restrict yourself to one cake.* **restriction** *(n).*

**result resulting resulted 1** *(n)* something that happens because of something else. *The result of our efforts was a delicious meal.* **2** *(v)* If one thing **results in** something else, it causes it. **3** *(n)* a final score or mark. *Football results.*

**Resurrection** *(n)* In the Christian religion, the **Resurrection** is Christ's coming back to life after his death.

**resuscitate** *(re-suss-it-ate)* **resuscitating resuscitated** *(v)* to make someone conscious again after they have stopped breathing. **resuscitation** *(n).*

**retail retailing retailed** *(v)* to sell goods to the public. **retailer** *(n).*

**retain retaining retained** *(v)* to keep something. *Please retain your receipt.*

**retaliate retaliating retaliated** *(v)* to do something unpleasant to someone because they have done something unpleasant to you. **retaliation** *(n).*

**retard retarding retarded** *(v)* to slow down. *The children's poor diet retarded their growth.* **retarded** *(adj).*

**retch** *(retch or reach)* **retches retching retched** *(v)* When you **retch,** you feel your throat and stomach move as if you are going to be sick. **retch** *(n).*

**retire retiring retired 1** *(v)* to give up work, usually because of your age. **retirement** *(n).* **2** *(v)* to go to a quieter place. *The jury has retired to consider its verdict.* **3** *(v) (old-fashioned)* to go to bed.

**retort** **retorting retorted** *(v)* to answer someone quickly and sharply. **retort** *(n).*

**retrace** **retracing retraced** *(v)* to go back over something. *I retraced my steps.*

**retreat** **retreating retreated 1** *(v)* to move back or withdraw from a difficult situation. **retreat** *(n).* **2** *(n)* a quiet place where you can go to think or be alone.

**retrieve** **retrieving retrieved** *(v)* to get or bring something back. *Franny retrieved her umbrella from the lost property office.*

**return** **returning returned 1** *(v)* to go back. **2** *(v)* to give or send something back. **3 in return** in exchange for something, or as a payment for something. **4 return ticket** *(n)* a ticket that allows you to travel to a place and back again.

**reunion** *(n)* a meeting between people who have not met for a long time.

**reusable** *(adj)* If something is **reusable**, it can be used again rather than being thrown away.

**rev** **revving revved** *(v) (informal)* to make an engine run quickly and noisily.

**reveal** **revealing revealed** *(v)* to allow something to be seen or known. *Carmen would not reveal her secret hiding place.*

**revel** **revelling revelled** *(v)* If you **revel in** something, you enjoy it very much.

**revelation** *(n)* a very surprising fact that is made known to people.

**revenge** *(n)* action that you take to pay someone back for harm that they have done to you or to your friends.

**reverberate** **reverberating reverberated** *(v)* to echo loudly and repeatedly. **reverberation** *(n).*

**reverence** *(n)* great respect and admiration. **reverent** *(adj).*

**reverse** **reversing reversed 1** *(n)* the opposite. *This looks fun, but it's quite the reverse.* **2** *(v)* to turn something round or inside out. *You can reverse this jacket.* **3** *(v)* to move a vehicle backwards.

**revert** **reverting reverted** *(v)* to go back to the way things were. *Gina soon reverted to her old habits.* **reversion** *(n).*

**review** *(n)* a piece of writing that gives an opinion about a new book, play, film, etc. **reviewer** *(n),* **review** *(v).*

**revise** **revising revised 1** *(v)* to look at your school work and try to learn it before an exam. **revision** *(n).* **2** *(v)* to change and correct something, usually in order to bring it up to date. *We need to revise our plan of the school.* **revision** *(n).*

**revive** **reviving revived 1** *(v)* to bring someone back to consciousness after they have been unconscious. **2** *(v)* to bring something back into use. *We've revived a play from the 1950s.* **revival** *(n).*

**revolt** **revolting revolted 1** *(v)* to fight against authority. **revolt** *(n).* **2** *(v)* If something **revolts** you, you find it horrible and disgusting.

**revolution 1** *(n)* a violent uprising by the people of a country, intended to change its political system. **2** *(n)* a very large, important change.

**revolutionize** *or* **revolutionise** **revolutionizing revolutionized** *(v)* to change something totally. *The CD-ROM will revolutionize computer use.*

**revolve** **revolving revolved 1** *(v)* to turn round and round in a circle. **2** *(v)* If something **revolves around** a person or thing, that person or thing is the most important part of it. *Hester's life revolves around television.*

**revolver** *(n)* a small handgun that can fire several shots before it needs to be reloaded.

**reward** *(n)* something that you receive as a present for doing something good or useful. **reward** *(v).*

**rewarding** *(adj)* If something is **rewarding**, it gives you pleasure and satisfaction. *A rewarding job.*

**rhinoceros** **rhinoceroses** *or* **rhinoceros** *(n)* a large, heavy mammal that comes from Africa and Asia and has one or two large horns on its nose.

**rhinoceros**

**rhubarb** *(roo-barb) (n)* a plant with long red or green stems that can be cooked and eaten.

**rhyme** *(rime)* **rhyming rhymed 1** *(v)* If words **rhyme**, they end with the same sound. *Seat rhymes with beat and feet.* **rhyme** *(n).* **2** *(n)* a short poem.

**rhythm** *(rith-um) (n)* a regular beat in music, poetry, or dance. **rhythmic** *(adj).*

**rib** *(n)* one of the curved bones which protect your lungs. *See* **skeleton**.

**rice** *(n)* a kind of tall grass that is grown in flooded fields and whose seeds can be cooked and eaten.

**rich riches; richer richest 1** *(adj)* having a lot of money and possessions. **2** *(adj)* If something is **rich** in a particular thing, it contains a lot of it. *Milk is rich in calcium.* **3** *(adj)* Food that is **rich** contains a lot of fat or sugar and makes you feel full very quickly. **4 riches** *(plural n)* great wealth.

**rickety** *(adj)* old, weak, and likely to break. *A rickety chair.*

**ricochet** *(rick-oh-shay)* **ricocheting ricocheted** *(v)* If a stone or a bullet **ricochets**, it hits a hard surface and flies off in a different direction.

**rid ridding rid 1** *(v)* to remove something that is unwanted. **2** If you **get rid of** something, you throw it away.

**riddle** *(n)* a question that seems to make no sense, but which has a clever answer.

**ride riding rode ridden** *(v)* to sit on a horse, bicycle, or motorcycle and travel along on it. **rider** *(n),* **ride** *(n).*

**ridge 1** *(n)* a narrow, raised piece of land. **2** *(n)* a narrow, raised strip on something.

**ridicule ridiculing ridiculed** *(v)* to make fun of someone or something.

**ridiculous** *(adj)* extremely silly or foolish.

**rifle** *(n)* a long-barrelled gun that you hold against your shoulder as you fire it.

**rig rigging rigged 1** *(n)* a large structure on the land or in the sea, used to drill for oil or gas under the ground. **2** *(v)* to control something dishonestly. *Natalie rigged the competition so that she won.*

**rigging** *(n)* the ropes on a boat or ship which support and control the sails.

**right 1** *(adj)* This page faces the **right** hand side of the book. **right** *(n),* **right** *(adv).* **2** *(adj)* correct. *I got the answers right.* **3** *(adj)* good, fair, and acceptable. *It's not right to be cruel to animals.* **4** *(adv)* exactly. *We parked right outside the cinema.* **5** *(n)* something that the law allows you to have or do. *The right to vote.* **6** In politics, people **on the right** support capitalism, free enterprise, and firm law and order.

**right angle** *(n)* an angle of 90°, like one of the angles of a square.

**righteous** *(rite-yus) (adj)* Someone who is **righteous** does not do anything that is bad or against the law.

**right-wing** *(adj)* If you are **right-wing**, you believe in capitalism, free enterprise, and firm law and order.

**rigid** *(rij-id)* **1** *(adj)* stiff and difficult to bend. **rigidity** *(n).* **2** *(adj)* very strict and difficult to change. *A rigid rule.*

**rim** *(n)* the outside or top edge of something. *The jug has a blue rim.*

**rind** *(n)* the outer layer on cheese, bacon, and some fruits. *Lemon rind.*

**ring ringing rang rung 1** *(n)* a circle. *Put a ring around the correct answer.* **ring** *(v).* **2** *(n)* a thin band worn on your finger as a piece of jewellery. **3** *(v)* When a bell **rings**, it makes a musical sound. **4** *(v)* to telephone someone. **ring** *(n).*

**ringleader** *(n)* the leader of a group of people who commit crimes or do things that are wrong.

**rink** *(n)* an indoor area with a specially prepared surface that is used for ice-skating or roller-skating.

**rinse rinsing rinsed** *(v)* to wash something in clean water without using any soap. **rinse** *(n).*

**riot rioting rioted** *(v)* If people **riot**, they behave in a noisy, violent, and usually uncontrollable way. **riot** *(n),* **riotous** *(adj).*

**rip ripping ripped 1** *(v)* to tear something. **rip** *(n).* **2 rip off** *(v) (slang)* If someone **rips you off**, they sell you a faulty product or charge an unfair amount of money for something. **rip-off** *(n).*

**ripe riper ripest** *(adj)* ready to be harvested, picked, or eaten. *Ripe fruit.*

**ripple 1** *(n)* a very small wave on the surface of a lake, pond, etc. **2** *(n)* a small wave of sound. *A ripple of laughter.*

*Some words that begin with a "r" sound are spelt "wr".*

**rise** **rising rose risen 1** *(v)* to go or move upwards. *The balloon rose into the air.* **2** *(v)* to stand up. **3** *(v)* to increase. *Prices rose dramatically last year.* **rise** *(n).*

**risk** **risking risked** *(v)* to do something that might cause something unpleasant to happen. *Joel risked falling to rescue the kitten.* **risk** *(n),* **risky** *(adj).*

**ritual** *(n)* a set of actions that are always performed in the same way as part of a religious ceremony or a social custom.

**rival** **rivalling rivalled 1** *(n)* someone whom you are competing against. **2** *(v)* to be as good as something or someone else. *No team can rival us at ice hockey.*

**river** *(n)* a large stream of fresh water that flows into a lake or sea. *The picture shows how a river develops and changes as it flows from its source to its mouth.*

**river**

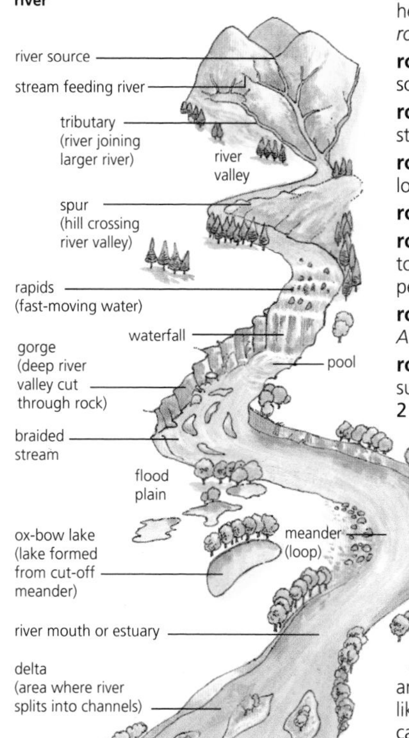


**rivet** **riveting riveted 1** *(n)* a strong metal bolt that is used to fasten pieces of metal together. **rivet** *(v).* **2** *(v)* If you are **riveted** by something, you find it so interesting that you cannot stop watching it or listening to it. **riveting** *(adj).*

**road** *(n)* a wide path with a smooth surface on which vehicles travel.

**roadworks** *(plural n)* repair work being done to a road.

**roam** **roaming roamed** *(v)* to wander around without any particular purpose. *I roamed the streets until dark.* **roam** *(n).*

**roar** **roaring roared** *(v)* to make a loud, deep noise. *The lion roared.* **roar** *(n).*

**roaring** *(adj)* If you do a **roaring** trade, you sell a lot of things.

**roast** **roasting roasted 1** *(v)* to cook meat or vegetables in a hot oven. **2** *(n)* a joint of meat that has been cooked in a hot oven. **3** *(v)* to be very hot. *I was roasted by the sun.* **roasting** *(adj).*

**rob** **robbing robbed** *(v)* to steal something from somebody. **robber** *(n).*

**robbery** **robberies** *(n)* the crime of stealing money or goods.

**robe** *(n)* a piece of clothing like a long, loose coat.

**robin** *(n)* a bird with a red breast.

**robot** *(n)* a machine that is programmed to do jobs that are usually performed by a person. **robotic** *(adj),* **robotics** *(n).*

**robust** *(adj)* strong. *A robust bicycle. A robust child.* **robustly** *(adv).*

**rock** **rocking rocked 1** *(n)* the very hard substance of which the Earth is made. **2** *(n)* a large stone. **3** *(v)* to move gently backwards and forwards or from side to side. **4** *(n)* a hard sweet, shaped like a long stick, usually sold at the seaside. **5** **rock music** *(n)* pop music with a very strong beat and a simple tune.

**rocket** **rocketing rocketed** **1** *(v)* to increase very quickly. *The price of oil has rocketed.* **2** *(n)* a firework that shoots high into the air and then explodes. **3** *(n)* a vehicle shaped like a long tube with a pointed end, that can travel very fast through the air. *See* **space shuttle**.

*Some words that begin with a "r" sound are spelt "wr".*

**rodent** *(n)* a mammal with large, sharp front teeth that it uses for gnawing things. *Rats and squirrels are rodents.*

**rodeo** *(n)* an entertainment in which cowboys show off their skills.

**rogue** *(rohg) (n)* a dishonest person.

**role** 1 *(n)* the job or purpose of a person or thing. *Gavin's role is to supervise the workers.* 2 *(n)* the part that a person acts in a play. *Julian played the role of Hamlet.*

**roll rolling rolled** 1 *(v)* to move along by turning over and over. *The ball rolled down the hill.* 2 *(v)* to make something into the shape of a ball or tube. **roll** *(n).* 3 *(v)* to flatten something by pushing a rounded object over it. *Roll the pastry.* 4 *(n)* a small round loaf of bread to be eaten by one person. 5 *(n)* a continuous, deep, vibrating sound. *A roll of thunder.*

**roller** 1 *(n)* an object shaped like a tube, that can turn round and round and is used in machines. *An ink roller.* 2 *(n)* a small plastic tube that you wind hair around to make it curl.

**roller coaster** *(n)* a fairground ride consisting of a train of carriages that travels fast over a track that rises, falls, and curves.

**roller-skating** *(n)* the sport of moving about on shoes or boots with wheels attached to them. **roller-skate** *(v).*

**ROM** *(n)* permanent computer memory that can be read but not changed. The initials ROM stand for read-only memory.

**romance** 1 *(n)* a love affair. 2 *(n)* an exciting story, usually about love. 3 *(n)* mystery and excitement. *The romance of the East.*

**Roman numerals** *(n)* letters used by the Ancient Romans to represent figures. Roman numerals are sometimes used today, for example, on some clocks.

**Roman numerals**

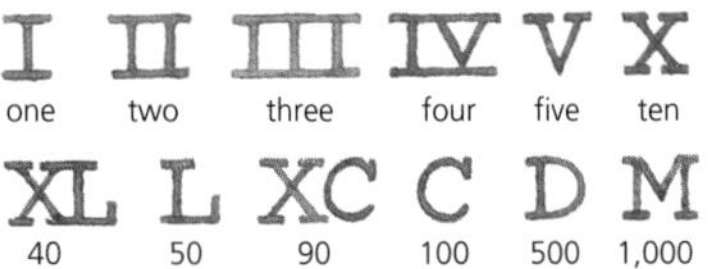


**romantic** 1 *(adj)* like a love story. *How romantic of Igor to send you roses!* 2 *(adj)* like a fairy story. *A romantic castle.*

**romp romping romped** *(v)* to play in a noisy and energetic way. **romp** *(n).*

**roof** 1 *(n)* the covering on the top of a building. 2 *(n)* the top part of something. *The roof of your mouth. The roof of a car.*

**roof rack** *(n)* a frame placed on top of a car, for carrying luggage.

**rook** 1 *(n)* a large, black bird like a crow, that lives in a big group called a rookery. 2 *(n)* a chesspiece, also known as a castle, that can move in straight lines across the board but not diagonally. *See* **chess**.

**room** 1 *(n)* one of the separate parts of a house or building, with its own door and walls. 2 *(n)* enough space for something. *Is there room for us all to go in your car?*

**roost roosting roosted** 1 *(n)* a place where birds rest or build their nests. 2 *(v)* When birds **roost**, they settle somewhere for the night.

**root rooting rooted** 1 *(n)* the part of a plant that grows under the ground. 2 *(v)* to form roots. *I took some plant cuttings, but they didn't root.* 3 *(plural n)* Your **roots** are where your family comes from, where you grew up, and where you feel that you belong.

**rope** *(n)* a strong, thick cord, made from twisted fibres.

**rose** 1 *(n)* a garden flower that usually has a sweet smell and grows on bushes with thorns. 2 *(n)* a light pink colour.

**rosette** *(n)* a large, round badge with ribbons attached to it, worn to show that you have won something, or that you support a particular person, team, or political party.

**Rosh Hashanah** *or* **Rosh Hashana** *(n)* the Jewish New Year.

**rosy rosier rosiest** 1 *(adj)* pink. *Rosy cheeks.* 2 *(adj)* hopeful. *A rosy future.*

**rot rotting rotted** *(v)* When something **rots**, it becomes weak and starts to break up because it is old or damp. **rot** *(n).*

**rota** *(n)* a list of people who take it in turns to do a job.

**rotary** *(adj)* turning round and round, or rotating. *This mowing machine has a rotary action.*

**rotate rotating rotated** 1 *(v)* to turn round and round like a wheel. 2 *(v)* to do things or use things in a fixed order, one after the other. **rotation** *(n).*

**rotten** 1 *(adj)* Food that is **rotten** has gone bad and cannot be eaten. 2 *(adj)* If floorboards, furniture, etc. are **rotten**, they have become weak and have started to break up. 3 *(adj) (informal)* very bad, or unpleasant. *A rotten trick.*

**rough** *(ruff)* **rougher roughest** 1 *(adj)* A **rough** surface is not smooth, but has dents or bumps in it. 2 *(adj)* Someone who is **rough** is not gentle or polite and may fight with people. **roughly** *(adv).* 3 *(adj) (informal)* difficult and unpleasant. *Moira had a rough time in her last job.* 4 *(adj)* vague, or not exact. *A rough idea.* **roughly** *(adv).* 5 *(adj)* **Rough** work is work that you do as preparation for the final version.

**roughage** *(ruff-ij) (n)* the fibre found in foods such as cereals and vegetables, which passes through the body but is not digested.

**round** rounder roundest 1 *(adj)* shaped like a circle or a ball. 2 *(prep)* on all sides of something. *We have a fence round our garden.* 3 *(prep)* going in a circle. *We walked round the tree.* 4 *(adj)* returning to a place. *A round trip from London to New York.* 5 *(n)* a series of visits made by a postman, milkman, doctor, etc. 6 *(n)* a set of matches or games in a competition. 7 *(n)* a simple song in which people start singing one after another, so that they are singing different parts of the song at the same time.

**roundabout** 1 *(n)* a road junction where vehicles must go round in a circle to join the road that they want. 2 *(n)* a round, revolving platform in a playground, that children can ride on.

**rounders** *(singular n)* a ball game in which players score points by hitting a ball and then running round four posts called bases.

**rouse** rousing roused 1 *(v)* to wake someone up. 2 *(v)* to make someone feel interested or excited. **rousing** *(adj).*

**route** *(root) (n)* the set of roads or paths that you follow to get from one place to another.

**routine** *(root-een)* 1 *(n)* a regular way of doing things. 2 *(adj)* Something that is **routine** is normal and not at all difficult or unusual.

**row** rowing rowed 1 *(rhymes with low) (n)* a line of people or things, side by side. 2 *(rhymes with low) (v)* to use oars in order to to move a boat through water. **row** *(n).* 3 *(rhymes with cow) (n)* an angry argument or quarrel. **row** *(v).* 4 *(rhymes with cow) (n)* a dreadful noise.

**rowdy** rowdier rowdiest *(adj)* wild and noisy. *Rowdy games.* **rowdiness** *(n).*

**royal** *(adj)* to do with a king or queen, or a member of their family. **royalty** *(n).*

**RSVP** the initials of the French phrase *Répondez s'il vous plaît*, which means "please reply". RSVP is often written at the bottom of an invitation.

**rub** rubbing rubbed 1 *(v)* to press one thing against another and move them backwards and forwards. *Finnigan rubbed his chin thoughtfully.* 2 *(v)* If you **rub out** pencil marks, you use a rubber to remove them from the paper. 3 *(v) (informal)* If you **rub it in**, you keep telling someone about their mistakes.

**rubber** 1 *(n)* a substance made from the juice of a rubber tree, or produced artificially. Rubber is strong, elastic, and waterproof and is used for making things like tyres, balls, and boots. 2 *(n)* a small piece of rubber used for rubbing out pencil marks.

**rubbish** 1 *(n)* things that you throw away because they are not useful or valuable. 2 *(n)* nonsense. *Don't talk rubbish!*

**rubble** *(n)* broken bricks and stones. *All that was left of their house was a pile of rubble.*

**ruby** rubies *(n)* a dark red precious stone.

**rucksack** *(n)* a large bag that you carry on your back.

**rudder** *(n)* a hinged plate, attached to the back of a boat or aeroplane, and used for steering.

**rude** ruder rudest *(adj)* not polite. **rudeness** *(n),* **rudely** *(adv).*

**ruffle** ruffling ruffled 1 *(v)* to disturb something that was smooth so that it becomes uneven or messy. *She ruffled his hair.* 2 *(v)* to make someone feel annoyed or worried. *Zack's questioning ruffled me.*

**rug** 1 *(n)* a thick mat, made from wool or other fibres. 2 *(n)* a small blanket.

**rugby** *or* **rugger** *(n)* a game played by two teams with an oval-shaped ball which they can kick, pass, or carry.

**rugged** *(rug-id)* 1 *(adj)* wild and rocky. *Rugged countryside.* 2 *(adj)* tough and strong. *I have always admired Kirk's rugged good looks.*

**rugger** *see* **rugby**.

**ruin** **ruining** **ruined** 1 *(v)* to spoil something completely. **ruin** *(n)*. 2 *(n)* a building that has been destroyed or very badly damaged. 3 *(v)* to make someone lose all their money. *The costs of the case nearly ruined Geoffrey.*

**rule** **ruling** **ruled** 1 *(n)* an official instruction that tells you what you must or must not do. 2 *(v)* to govern a country, or have power over it. 3 *(n)* the time during which a person rules a country. 4 *(v)* to make an official decision or judgement. *The judge ruled that the father should be allowed to see his children.* **ruling** *(n)*. 5 If you do something **as a rule**, you usually do it. 6 **rule out** *(v)* If you **rule something out**, you decide that it is not possible.

**ruler** 1 *(n)* a long, flat piece of wood, plastic, or metal that you use for measuring and drawing straight lines. 2 *(n)* someone who rules a country.

**rumble** **rumbling** **rumbled** *(v)* to make a low, rolling noise like the sound of thunder. **rumble** *(n)*.

**rummage** *(rum-ij)* **rummaging** **rummaged** *(v)* to look for something by moving things around in an untidy or careless way. *Ned rummaged in his backpack for a toffee.*

**rumour** *(n)* something that lots of people are saying although it may not be true.

**rump** *(n)* the back part of an animal, above its hind legs.

**run** **running** **ran** **run** 1 *(v)* to move quickly, using your legs. **run** *(n)*. 2 *(v)* to take someone somewhere in a car. *Shall I run you home?* 3 *(v)* to function, or to work. *Most lorries run on diesel.* 4 *(v)* to be in charge of something. *Octavia runs a small business.* 5 *(n)* a point in a game of cricket. 6 *(n)* a small enclosure for animals. *A chicken run.* 7 *(v)* If you **run away**, you escape from a place or leave it secretly. 8 *(v)* If you have **run out of** something, you have used it all and have none left. 9 If someone is **run over**, they are hit by a car or other vehicle.

**runaway** 1 *(n)* a child who has run away from home. 2 *(adj)* out of control. *A runaway train.* 3 *(adj)* very easy. *A runaway victory.*

**rung** *(n)* one of the horizontal bars on a ladder.

**runner** 1 *(n)* someone who runs in a race. 2 *(n)* a rod or bar on which something slides.

**runner-up** **runners-up** *(n)* the person or team that comes second in a race or competition.

**runny** **runnier** **runniest** 1 *(adj)* If something is **runny**, it flows, or moves like a liquid. *Runny paint.* 2 *(adj)* If you have a **runny** nose, mucus is dripping from it.

**runway** *(n)* a strip of land that aircraft use for taking off and landing.

**rural** *(adj)* to do with the countryside or farming.

**rush** **rushes** **rushing** **rushed** 1 *(v)* to go somewhere quickly, or to do something quickly. *Ed rushed to the shop before it shut.* **rush** *(n)*. 2 **rushes** *(plural n)* tall plants with rounded stems that grow in damp places.

**rust** **rusting** **rusted** 1 *(n)* the reddish-brown substance that can form on iron and steel when they get wet. **rusty** *(adj)*. 2 *(v)* to become covered with rust. *The door hinges have rusted.*

**rustle** **rustling** **rustled** 1 *(v)* When leaves, papers, etc. **rustle**, they make a soft, crackling sound as they move together gently. 2 *(v)* to steal horses or cattle. **rustler** *(n)*, **rustling** *(n)*. 3 *(v)* *(informal)* If you **rustle up** something, you provide it quickly. *Russell rustled up some supper.*

**rut** 1 *(n)* a deep, narrow track made in the ground by wheels. 2 *(n)* If someone is **in a rut**, they do the same sort of thing all the time.

**ruthless** *(adj)* Someone who is **ruthless** is cruel and has no pity. **ruthlessness** *(n)*.

# Ss

**Sabbath** *(n)* the weekly day of rest in some religions. The Jewish Sabbath is Saturday, while the Christian Sabbath is Sunday.

**sabotage** *(sab-er-tahj) (n)* deliberate damage intended to cause difficulties for an enemy, employer, etc. **sabotage** *(v)*.

**sack sacking sacked** 1 *(n)* a large bag made of strong cloth, used for carrying coal, potatoes, flour, etc. 2 *(v)* If an employer **sacks** someone, the employer tells them that they no longer have a job and must leave. **sack** *(n)*.

**sacred** *(say-krid) (adj)* holy, or connected with religion. *Sacred music.*

**sacrifice sacrificing sacrificed** 1 *(n)* the killing of an animal or person as an offering to a god. **sacrifice** *(v)*, **sacrificial** *(adj)*. 2 *(v)* to give up something important or enjoyable for a good reason. *I sacrificed my supper to go to the play.* **sacrifice** *(n)*.

**sad sadder saddest** 1 *(adj)* unhappy. **sadness** *(n)*, **sadden** *(v)*, **sadly** *(adv)*. 2 *(adj)* Something which is **sad** makes you feel unhappy. *Sad news.*

**saddle** 1 *(n)* a leather seat on the back of a horse, on which a rider sits. 2 *(n)* a seat for a bicycle.

**safari** *(n)* an expedition to see or to hunt large wild animals.

**safe safer safest** 1 *(adj)* not in danger of being harmed or stolen. **safety** *(n)*. 2 *(adj)* not dangerous, or not risky. *Is this ladder safe?* 3 *(n)* a strong box in which you can lock away money or valuables.

**safeguard safeguarding safeguarded** *(v)* to protect something. **safeguard** *(n)*.

**sag sagging sagged** *(v)* to hang down or sink down. *The bed sagged in the middle.*

**sage** 1 *(n)* a herb whose leaves are often used in cooking. 2 *(n)* a wise person.

**sail sailing sailed** 1 *(n)* a large sheet of strong cloth, such as canvas, that makes a boat or ship move when it catches the wind. 2 *(v)* to travel in a boat or ship. 3 *(n)* an arm of a windmill.

**sailboard** *(n)* a flat board with a mast and sail fixed to it, used for windsurfing. *See* **windsurfing**.

**sailor** *(n)* someone who works on a ship as a member of the crew.

**saint** *(n)* a man or woman honoured by the Christian church, because of their very holy life. The short form of Saint is St.

**Saint Peter**

**sake** *(n)* If you do something for someone else's **sake**, you do it in order to help or please them.

**salad** 1 *(n)* a mixture of raw vegetables. 2 *(n)* a mixture of cold foods. *Rice salad.*

**salary salaries** *(n)* the money someone is paid for their work.

**sale** 1 *(n)* a time when goods are sold at cheaper prices than usual. 2 **for sale** available for people to buy. 3 **on sale** available in the shops.

**saliva** *(n)* the liquid in your mouth that keeps it moist and helps you to swallow and begin to digest food.

**salmon salmon** *(n)* a large fish with a silvery skin and pink flesh.

**salt** 1 *(n)* a common, white substance, found in sea water and under the ground, and used for adding flavour to food. 2 If you take something with **a pinch of salt**, you do not believe that it is really true.

**salute saluting saluted** *(v)* When soldiers **salute**, they raise their hand to their forehead as a sign of respect.

**salvage salvaging salvaged** *(v)* to rescue something from a shipwreck, fire, etc. **salvage** *(n)*.

**salvation** *(n)* the state of being saved from evil, harm, or destruction.

**sample** *(n)* a small amount of something that shows what the whole of it is like. *A blood sample.*

**samurai** *(sam-yoo-rye)* **samurai** *(n)* a Japanese warrior.

**sanctuary sanctuaries** 1 *(n)* a holy place. 2 *(n)* a place where someone who is being hunted can be safe. 3 *(n)* a place where birds or animals are protected.

**sand** *(n)* tiny grains of rock which make up beaches and deserts. **sandy** *(adj).*

**sandal** *(n)* a light, open shoe with straps that go over your foot.

**sandpaper** *(n)* paper with grains of sand stuck to it that you rub over surfaces to make them smooth.

**sandwich** **sandwiches** *(n)* two pieces of bread around a filling of cheese, meat, or some other food.

**sane** **saner** **sanest** *(adj)* Someone who is sane has a healthy mind. **sanity** *(n).*

**sanitary** **1** *(adj)* clean and free from germs. **2** **sanitary towel** *(n)* a pad of soft material that some women and girls wear during their periods.

**sanitation** *(n)* a system to protect people from dirt and disease, for example, by a clean water supply and sewage disposal.

**sap** *(n)* the liquid in the stems of plants.

**sapling** *(n)* a young tree.

**sapphire** *(saf-fire)* *(n)* a bright blue precious stone.

**sarcastic** *(adj)* If you are **sarcastic**, you say the opposite of what you really mean as a way of criticizing or mocking someone. **sarcasm** *(n),* **sarcastically** *(adv).*

**sardine** *(n)* a small sea fish, often sold in tins as food.

**sari** *(sah-ree)* *(n)* a long piece of light material, worn draped around the body. Saris are worn mainly by Indian women and girls.

**sari**

**sash** **sashes** *(n)* a strip of material worn around the waist or across the chest.

**satchel** *(n)* a leather bag for school books carried over the shoulder or on the back.

**satellite** **1** *(n)* a machine that is sent into orbit around the Earth. **2** *(n)* a moon or other natural object that moves in orbit around a planet.

**satellite dish** **satellite dishes** *(n)* a dish-shaped receiver for satellite television.

**satellite television** *(n)* television programmes that are transmitted by satellite and received by a satellite dish.

**satire** *(n)* a type of clever, mocking humour that points out the faults in certain people or ideas. **satirical** *(adj).*

**satisfaction** *(n)* a feeling of contentment, because you have done something that you wanted to do or have done something well.

**satisfactory** *(adj)* good enough.

**satisfy** **satisfies** **satisfying** **satisfied** *(v)* to please someone by doing enough or giving them enough. **satisfied** *(adj).*

**saturate** **saturating** **saturated** *(v)* to make something very wet.

**sauce** *(n)* a thick liquid served with food.

**saucepan** *(n)* a metal cooking pot with a handle and, sometimes, a lid.

**saucer** *(n)* a small, curved plate that is placed under a cup.

**sauna** *(sor-nah)* *(n)* a room filled with steam where people sit and sweat a lot.

**sausage** *(n)* minced meat, bread, herbs, etc. in a tube of thin skin.

**savage** **1** *(adj)* wild and vicious. *A savage dog.* **2** *(n)* an uncivilized person.

**save** **saving** **saved** **1** *(v)* to rescue someone or something from danger. **2** *(v)* If something **saves** time, space, energy, etc., it does not waste it. **3** *(v)* to keep money to use in the future rather than spending it now. **4** *(v)* to stop a ball from going into a goal. **save** *(n).*

**savings** *(n)* money that you have saved.

**savoury** *(adj)* salty or spicy, and not sweet.

**saw** *(n)* a tool with a toothed blade, used for cutting wood. **saw** *(v).*

**sawdust** *(n)* the powder that you get when you saw wood.

**say** **saying** **said** **1** *(v)* to speak. *What did you say?* **2** *(v)* to mean something. *What does that sign say?*

**saying** *(n)* a well-known phrase that gives advice.

**scab** *(n)* the hard covering that forms over a wound when it is healing.

**scaffolding** *(n)* the structure of metal poles and wooden planks that workmen stand on when they are working on a building.

**scald** **scalding** **scalded** *(v)* to burn yourself with very hot liquid. **scald** *(n).*

**scale** 1 *(n)* one of the small, hard pieces of skin that cover the body of a fish, snake, or other reptile. **scaly** *(adj).* 2 *(n)* a series of musical notes going up or down in order. 3 *(n)* the relationship between measurements on a map or model and the actual measurements. 4 **scales** *(plural n)* an instrument used for weighing things.

**scallop** *(n)* a shellfish with two hinged shells or valves.

**scalp** *(n)* the skin on the top of your head where your hair grows.

**scalpel** *(n)* a small, sharp knife used by surgeons.

**scamper scampering scampered** *(v)* to run somewhere with short, quick steps.

**scan scanning scanned** 1 *(v)* to look through a book or piece of writing because you are searching for something. 2 *(v)* to look carefully along something. *We scanned the horizon for ships.*

**scandal** *(n)* gossip about someone's dishonest or immoral behaviour.

**scanty scantier scantiest** *(adj)* not enough, or not big enough. *Scanty food.*

**scapegoat** *(n)* someone who is made to take all the blame for something.

**scar** *(n)* a mark left on your skin by an old cut or wound. **scar** *(v).*

**scarce** *(adj)* Something that is **scarce** is hard to find because there is so little of it.

**scarcely** *(adv)* hardly. *I've scarcely seen Susie today.*

**scare scaring scared** *(v)* to frighten a person or an animal. **scare** *(n),* **scary** *(adj).*

**scarecrow** *(n)* a model of a person, put in a field to frighten birds away.

**scarf scarfs** *or* **scarves** *(n)* a strip of material worn round your neck or head.

**scatter scattering scattered** *(v)* to throw things over a wide area. *Scatter the seed.*

**scatterbrained** *(adj)* If you are **scatterbrained**, you are always forgetting things.

**scavenge scavenging scavenged** *(v)* to search among rubbish for food or something useful. **scavenger** *(n).*

**scene** 1 *(n)* a view, or a picture. *Fleur paints country scenes.* 2 *(n)* a part of a play or film where the events all happen in the same place. 3 *(n)* the place where something happens. *The scene of the accident.* 4 If you **make a scene**, you get very angry with someone in public.

**scenery** 1 *(n)* the natural countryside of an area, such as trees, hills, mountains, and lakes. 2 *(n)* the painted boards and curtains that are used on stage as the background to a play, opera, or ballet.

**scent** 1 *(n)* a pleasant smell. *The scent of roses.* **scented** *(adj).* 2 *(n)* a liquid that you can put on your skin to make you smell pleasant. 3 *(n)* an animal's smell.

**sceptical** *(adj)* If you are **sceptical** about something, you doubt whether it is really true. **sceptic** *(n),* **scepticism** *(n).*

**schedule** *(shed-yool)* **scheduling scheduled** 1 *(n)* a plan, programme, or timetable. 2 *(v)* If you **schedule** an event, you plan it for a particular time.

**scheme** *(skeem)* *(n)* a plan, or an arrangement.

**scholarship** *(n)* a prize that pays for you to go to a school or college, and that you win by doing well in an exam. **scholar** *(n).*

**school** 1 *(n)* a place where children go to be taught. 2 *(n)* a group of fish or other sea creatures. *A school of porpoises.*

**science** *(n)* the study of nature and the physical world by testing, experimenting, and measuring. **scientist** *(n),* **scientific** *(adj),* **scientifically** *(adv).*

**science fiction** *(n)* stories about life in the future, or life on other planets.

**scissors** *(plural n)* a sharp tool with two blades, used for cutting paper, fabric, etc.

**scoff scoffing scoffed** 1 *(v)* to be scornful and mocking about someone or something. *Nat scoffed at the idea of ballet lessons.* 2 *(v)* *(informal)* to eat very fast and greedily. *Lisa scoffed her lunch.*

**scold scolding scolded** *(v)* to tell someone off.

**scoop scooping scooped** 1 *(v)* to lift or pick up something. *Jasper scooped up a handful of snow.* 2 *(n)* a spoon, especially a serving spoon.

**scooter** 1 *(n)* a type of child's bicycle, with two wheels and a flat board which you stand on with one foot, while pushing on the ground with the other foot. 2 *(n)* a small motorcycle.

**scope** *(n)* the range of opportunity that something gives. *There's plenty of scope for improving this garden.*

**scorch** scorches scorching scorched 1 *(v)* to burn something slightly, usually with an iron. **scorch** *(n)*. 2 *(adj)* If the weather is **scorching**, it is extremely hot.

**score** scoring scored 1 *(v)* to get a goal or win a point in a game. 2 *(n)* the number of points or goals that each team wins in a game. 3 *(n)* twenty. *Seth lived for four score years.* 4 **scores** *(plural n)* a large number. *Richard receives scores of letters.*

**scorn** *(n)* a strong feeling of contempt and superiority. *Gwen poured scorn on my idea of being a doctor.* **scornful** *(adj)*.

**scorpion** *(n)* a creature like a long spider, with a deadly sting in its tail. Scorpions live in deserts and warm countries.

Sahara scorpion

**scoundrel** *(n)* a person who cheats and lies.

**scour** scouring scoured 1 *(v)* to clean something by rubbing it hard. 2 *(v)* to search an area thoroughly. *Police scoured the building for clues.*

**scowl** scowling scowled *(v)* to make an angry face. **scowl** *(n)*.

**scrabble** scrabbling scrabbled *(v)* to dig or scratch in the ground with your hands or feet, usually in order to find something.

**scramble** scrambling scrambled 1 *(v)* to climb over rocks or hills. 2 *(v)* to rush or struggle to get somewhere.

**scrap** scrapping scrapped 1 *(n)* a small piece of paper, food, etc. 2 *(n)* metal from old cars or machines. 3 *(v)* to get rid of something. *We decided to scrap our plan because of the weather.*

**scrapbook** *(n)* a book in which you stick pictures, newspaper cuttings, etc.

**scrape** scraping scraped 1 *(v)* to clean, peel, or scratch something with a sharp object. **scrape** *(n)*. 2 *(n) (informal)* an awkward situation. 3 *(v)* If you **scrape through** an exam, you only just pass it.

**scratch** scratches scratching scratched 1 *(v)* to make a mark or a cut. **scratch** *(n)*. 2 *(v)* to rub a part of you that itches. **scratch** *(n)*. 3 *(informal)* If you do something **from scratch**, you start from the beginning.

**scrawl** scrawling scrawled *(v)* to write in a quick, careless way. **scrawl** *(n)*.

**scream** screaming screamed *(v)* to cry out loudly, or to shriek. **scream** *(n)*.

**screech** screeches *(n)* a high, unpleasant sound. **screech** *(v)*.

**screen** 1 *(n)* a wall, or a barrier. **screen** *(v)*. 2 *(n)* the front of a television set or computer monitor, or the white surface that films are shown on.

**screw** screwing screwed 1 *(n)* a metal fastener, like a nail, with a groove in its head and a spiral thread. 2 *(v)* to fasten something with screws. 3 *(v)* If you **screw on** a lid, you turn or twist it. 4 *(v)* If you **screw up** paper or material, you make it into a ball, ready to be thrown away.

**screwdriver** *(n)* a tool with a flat tip that fits into the head of a screw, in order to turn it.

**scribble** scribbling scribbled 1 *(v)* to write carelessly or quickly. **scribble** *(n)*. 2 *(v)* to make meaningless marks with a pencil, pen, or crayon. **scribble** *(n)*.

**scribe** *(n)* someone who copied books by hand, before printing was invented.

**script** *(n)* the written version of what an actor or broadcaster says.

**scripture** *(n)* religious writing, especially the Bible.

**scroll** scrolling scrolled 1 *(n)* a rolled-up piece of paper or parchment with writing on it. *The picture shows a Hebrew scroll made of parchment.* 2 *(v)* to move the text on a computer screen up and down so that you can see it.

scroll

**scrounge** scrounging scrounged *(v) (informal)* to get things free from people by asking for them.

**scrub** scrubbing scrubbed 1 *(v)* to clean something by rubbing it hard with a brush. 2 *(n)* low bushes or short trees.

**scruffy** scruffier scruffiest *(adj)* shabby and untidy. **scruffily** *(adv)*.

**scrupulous** *(screw-pyoo-luss) (adj)* careful and exact. *Tobia is scrupulous about money.*

**scrutinize** *or* **scrutinise** scrutinizing **scrutinized** *(v)* to examine something closely. **scrutiny** *(n).*

**scuba diving** *(n)* underwater swimming, with an air tank on your back that is connected to your mouth by a hose. Scuba stands for self-contained underwater breathing apparatus. **scuba diver** *(n).*

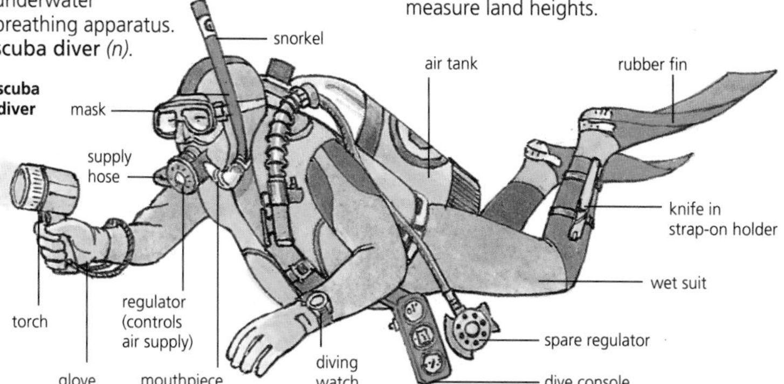

**scuba diver**

**seagull** *(n)* a large grey or white bird that is commonly seen near the sea.

**sea horse** *(n)* a fish with a head shaped like a horse's head and a long, curling tail.

**seal** sealing sealed 1 *(n)* a sea mammal with small flippers that breeds on land. 2 *(v)* to close something up. *We've sealed up the old well.* **seal** *(n).*

**sea level** *(n)* the average level of the surface of the sea, which is used to measure land heights.

**scuffle** *(n)* a small fight. **scuffle** *(v).*

**sculpture** 1 *(n)* something carved or shaped out of wood, stone, metal, etc. *This sculpture by Henry Moore is called "Recumbent Figure".* 2 *(n)* the art or work of making sculpture. **sculptor** *(n),* **sculpt** *(v).*

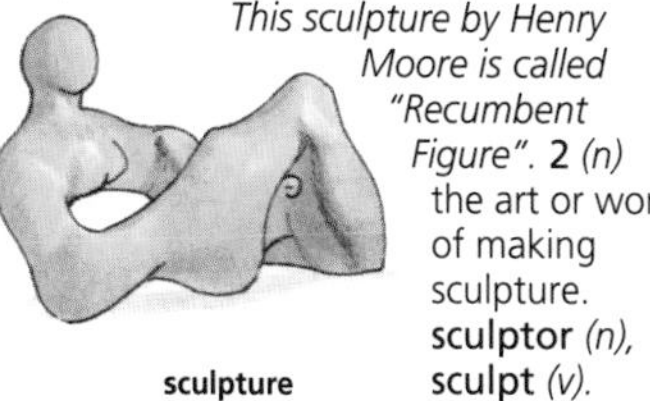
**sculpture**

**scum** *(n)* a layer of dirty froth on top of a liquid.

**scurry** scurries scurrying scurried *(v)* to hurry, or to run with short, quick steps.

**scuttle** scuttling scuttled *(v)* to dash.

**scythe** *(sythe) (n)* a tool with a large, curved blade, used for cutting grass or crops.

**sea** *(n)* a large area of salt water.

**seafarer** *(n)* a sailor, or someone who travels by sea. **seafaring** *(adj).*

**seafood** *(n)* fish or shellfish that are eaten as food.

**sea lion** *(n)* a sea mammal, like a seal, with sticking-out ears and large flippers.

**seam** 1 *(n)* a line of sewing that joins two pieces of material. 2 *(n)* a band of a different kind of rock between layers of other rocks. *A coal seam.*

**seaplane** *(n)* an aircraft that can take off and land on water.

**search** searches searching searched *(v)* to explore or examine something closely. **search** *(n).*

**searching** *(adj)* deep and thorough. *Searching questions.*

**searchlight** *(n)* a large, powerful light that can be turned in a particular direction.

**seasick** *(adj)* If you are **seasick**, you feel ill because of the rolling movement of a boat or ship.

**season** seasoning seasoned 1 *(n)* a time of the year. The four seasons are spring, summer, autumn, and winter. **seasonal** *(adj).* 2 *(v)* to add flavour to food with salt, spices, etc. **seasoning** *(n).* 3 If a food is **in season**, it is fresh and easily available.

**seat** **seating seated 1** *(n)* a place where you can sit. **2** *(v)* to sit. *Jack seated himself on the arm of the sofa.* **3** *(v)* to have room for people to sit down. *This table seats six.*

**seat belt** *(n)* a belt that you wear across your lap and chest in a car or plane in order to make you safer.

**secluded** *(adj)* quiet and private. *A secluded valley.* **seclusion** *(n).*

**second 1** *(adj)* next, or after the first. **second** *(adv),* **secondly** *(adv).* **2** *(n)* a sixtieth of a minute.

**secondary** *(adj)* to do with the second stage of something. *Secondary education.*

**secondary school** *(n)* a school for pupils aged 11 or 13 upwards.

**second-hand** *(adj)* If something is **second-hand**, it has belonged to another person first.

**second-rate** *(adj)* not very good.

**secret 1** *(n)* a mystery, or something that only a few people know. **2** *(adj)* not known by many people. **secrecy** *(n),* **secretly** *(adv).* **3 in secret** privately.

**secret agent** *(n)* a spy, or someone who obtains secret information.

**secretary** **secretaries** *(n)* someone whose job is to type letters, answer the telephone, keep records, and do other office work. **secretarial** *(adj).*

**secrete** **secreting secreted 1** *(v)* to produce a liquid. *Some snakes secrete poison.* **secretion** *(n).* **2** *(v)* to hide. *The spy secreted the message in his shoe.*

**section 1** *(n)* a part or division of something. **2** *(n)* a drawing or plan that shows a slice through an object.

**secure 1** *(adj)* If you feel **secure**, you feel safe and sure of yourself. **security** *(n).* **2** *(adj)* safe, firmly closed, or well-protected. **security** *(n),* **secure** *(v).*

**sedate** *(adj)* calm and unhurried. *A sedate walk.* **sedately** *(v).*

**sediment** *(n)* solid pieces that settle at the bottom of a liquid.

**seduce** **seducing seduced** *(v)* If you **seduce** someone, you tempt or persuade them to do something, especially to have sex. **seduction** *(n),* **seductive** *(adj).*

**see** **seeing saw seen 1** *(v)* to use your eyes, to look at, or to notice something or someone. **2** *(v)* to understand, or to recognize. *I see what you mean.* **3** *(v)* If you **see about** something, you deal with it or think it over. **4** *(v)* If you **see through** someone or something, you are not deceived or tricked by them.

**seed** *(n)* a small, hard object that grows into a plant.

**seedling** *(n)* a young plant that has been grown from a seed.

**seek** **seeking sought** *(v)* to look for something, or search for something.

**seem** **seeming seemed** *(v)* to appear to be, or to give the impression of being.

**seep** **seeping seeped** *(v)* to flow or trickle slowly. *Water seeped into the boat.*

**seethe** **seething seethed 1** *(v)* to bubble and boil. **2** *(v)* to be very angry or excited.

**segment** *(n)* a piece of something. *Lucy divided the orange into segments.*

**seize** *(seez)* **seizing seized 1** *(v)* to take something quickly or by force. *Molly seized a rolling pin.* **2** *(v)* If something **seizes up**, it jams or stops working.

**seldom** *(adv)* rarely. *We seldom see Tim.*

**select** **selecting selected** *(v)* to pick or choose.

**selective** *(adj)* If you are **selective**, you choose carefully.

**self** **selves** *(n)* your individual nature or personality.

**self-catering** *(adj)* If you go on a **self-catering** holiday, you do your own cooking.

**self-centred** *(adj)* thinking only about yourself.

**self-confident** *(adj)* If you are **self-confident**, you know that you are all right, and that you can do things well. **self-confidence** *(n).*

**self-conscious** *(adj)* If you are **self-conscious**, you think that people are looking at you, and you worry about what they are thinking. **self-consciously** *(adv).*

**self-control** *(n)* control of yourself and your feelings. **self-controlled** *(adj).*

**self-defence** *(n)* the act of protecting yourself against an attacker.

**self-explanatory** *(adj)* If something is **self-explanatory**, it does not need any further explanation.

**selfish** *(adj)* putting your own feelings and needs first. **selfishness** *(n).*

**self-respect** *(n)* reasonable pride in yourself and your abilities.

**self-service** *(adj)* If a shop or garage is **self-service**, you help yourself to what you want, and pay for it at the checkout.

**self-sufficient** *(adj)* If a family or community is **self-sufficient**, they grow or make everything that they need. **self-sufficiency** *(n).*

**sell selling sold** *(v)* to give something in exchange for money.

**semaphore** *(n)* a way of sending a message by signalling with your arms or with flags. *The picture shows the message SOS in semaphore.*

**semaphore**

**semen** *(see-men)* *(n)* the liquid produced by males, that carries sperm to fertilize the female's egg.

**semicircle** *(n)* half a circle. **semicircular** *(adj).*

**semicolon** *(n)* the punctuation mark (;) used to separate parts of a sentence.

**semidetached** *(adj)* A **semidetached** house is joined to another house on one side.

**semifinal** *(n)* a match to decide who will play in the final. **semifinalist** *(n).*

**send sending sent 1** *(v)* to make someone or something go somewhere. *Send Tamara to the shop.* **2** *(v)* If you **send for** something or someone, you make them come to you. *I'll send for tea.*

**send off sending off sent off 1** *(v)* to make a player leave the sports field as a punishment. **2** *(v)* to write to ask for something. *We sent off for a catalogue.*

**senile** *(adj)* weak in mind and body because of old age. **senility** *(n).*

**senior** *(adj)* Someone who is **senior** to you is older or more important than you.

**senior citizen** *(n)* an old person, especially a pensioner.

**sensation 1** *(n)* a feeling. *Moira had no sensation in her toes.* **2** *(n)* something that causes a lot of excitement and interest.

**sense 1** *(n)* good judgement, or understanding. *Topsy has no sense.* **2** *(n)* the ability to feel or be aware of something. *A sense of direction.* **3** *(n)* Your five **senses** are sight, hearing, touch, taste, and smell. **4** *(n)* meaning. *I can't make sense of this story.*

**senseless 1** *(adj)* pointless, or without meaning. *A senseless attack.* **senselessly** *(adv).* **2** *(adj)* unconscious.

**sensible** *(adj)* If you are **sensible**, you think carefully and do not do stupid or dangerous things. **sensibly** *(adv).*

**sensitive 1** *(adj)* easily offended, or easily hurt. **sensitivity** *(n).* **2** *(adj)* aware of other people's feelings. **sensitivity** *(n).*

**sensor** *(n)* an instrument that can detect changes in heat, sound, pressure, etc.

**sentence 1** *(n)* a group of words that make sense. A sentence starts with a capital letter and ends with a full stop. **2** *(n)* a punishment given to a criminal in court. *A prison sentence.* **sentence** *(v).*

**sentimental** *(adj)* to do with emotion, romance, or feelings. *Sentimental value.*

**sentry sentries** *(n)* a soldier who stands guard.

**separate separating separated 1** *(sep-er-ate)* *(v)* to part or divide something or some people. **separation** *(n).* **2** *(sep-er-rut)* *(adj)* different, individual, or not together. *The children have separate bedrooms.* **separately** *(adv).* **3** *(sep-er-ate)* *(v)* If a husband and wife **separate**, they stop living together. **separation** *(n).*

**septic** *(adj)* infected with bacteria.

**sequel** *(see-kwell)* *(n)* a book or film that continues the story from another.

**sequence** *(see-kwence)* *(n)* a series of things that follow in order. *My life is a sequence of disasters.*

**serene** *(adj)* calm and peaceful. **serenity** *(n),* **serenely** *(adv).*

**serial** *(n)* a story that is told in several instalments. *A television serial.*

**series** series 1 *(n)* a group of related things, that follow in order. *A series of lessons.* 2 *(n)* a number of television or radio programmes that are linked in some way. *A detective series.*

**serious** 1 *(adj)* solemn and thoughtful. *A serious boy.* 2 *(adj)* sincere, or not joking. *Jo is serious about leaving school.* 3 *(adj)* very bad, or worrying. *A serious illness.*

**sermon** *(n)* a religious talk given during a church service.

**servant** *(n)* someone who works in somebody else's house, doing housework, cooking, etc.

**serve** **serving served** 1 *(v)* to work for someone. 2 *(v)* to give someone food or help them in a shop. 3 *(v)* to begin play in games like tennis, by hitting the ball.

**service** 1 *(n)* The **service** in a restaurant, shop, etc. is the way that you are looked after. 2 *(n)* a business or organization that provides you with something. *The police service.* 3 *(n)* a religious ceremony or meeting. 4 **services** *(plural n)* an area next to a motorway where you can eat, rest, and fill up your vehicle with fuel.

**serviette** *(n)* a square piece of cloth that you use to protect your clothes at meals.

**session** *(n)* a period of time used for an activity. *A training sesssion.*

**set** **setting set** 1 *(n)* a group of things that go together. *A chess set.* 2 *(n)* the scenery for a play or film. 3 *(adj)* ready. *Are we all set to leave?* 4 *(adj)* fixed. *A set time.* 5 *(v)* to put, fix, or arrange. *Set the alarm for 6 a.m.* 6 *(v)* If a liquid **sets**, it becomes hard or solid.

**setback** *(n)* something that delays you or stops you making progress.

**settee** *(n)* a long, soft seat with arms and a back, and room for two or more people.

**settle** **settling settled** 1 *(v)* to sort out, decide, or agree on something. *We settled the argument.* 2 *(v)* to make yourself comfortable. *Phillip settled down with a book.* 3 *(v)* If you **settle in**, you get used to your new house, school, etc.

**set up** **setting up set up** *(v)* to get something ready for use, or arrange it.

**sever** **severing severed** *(v)* to cut or break something. *The two countries have severed all ties.*

**several** *(adj)* a small number of people, things, etc. **several** *(pronoun).*

**severe** **severer severest** *(adj)* strict, harsh, or demanding. **severity** *(n).*

**sew** *(so)* **sewing sewed sewn** *(v)* to stitch using a needle and thread.

**sewage** *(n)* liquid and solid waste that is carried away in sewers and drains.

**sewer** *(n)* an underground pipe that carries liquid and solid waste away.

male

female

**sex** **sexes** 1 *(n)* A person's **sex** is their identity as male or female. *The symbols used for the male and female sexes are shown here.* 2 *(n)* the instinct which causes two people to be physically attracted to each other. **sexual** *(adj).* 3 *(n)* the act of sexual intercourse.

**sexist** *(adj)* Someone who is **sexist** discriminates against members of one or the other sex. *It is sexist to assume that girls can't play football.* **sexism** *(n),* **sexist** *(n).*

**sexual intercourse** *(n)* an intimate physical act between a man and a woman, in which a man's penis enters a woman's vagina.

**sexy** **sexier sexiest** *(adj)* attractive in a sexual way. **sexily** *(adv).*

**shabby** **shabbier shabbiest** *(adj)* worn, neglected, or in need of repair. *Shabby clothes.* **shabbiness** *(n).*

**shack** *(n)* a small, roughly built hut or house.

**shade** **shading shaded** 1 *(v)* to shelter something from the light. *The hat shaded Imogen's face.* **shade** *(n).* 2 *(n)* an area that is sheltered from the light. *Come and sit in the shade.* **shady** *(adj).* 3 *(n)* a level of colour or meaning. 4 *(v)* to make part of a drawing darker than the rest. **shading** *(n).*

**shadow** *(n)* a dark shape made by something blocking out light.

**shaft** 1 *(n)* the long, narrow bar of a spear, arrow, or paddle. 2 *(n)* a thin beam of light. 3 *(n)* the entrance to a mine.

**shake** **shaking shook shaken** 1 *(v)* to tremble, or to quiver. 2 *(v)* to take hold of something and move it quickly up and down. *Shake the bottle.*

**shaky** shakier shakiest 1 *(adj)* unsteady and wobbly. *Shaky legs.* 2 *(adj)* not very good, or not very strong. *Shaky spelling.*

**shallow** shallower shallowest *(adj)* not deep. *Shallow water.*

**sham** *(n)* something that is not what it seems to be. **sham** *(adj).*

**shambles** *(singular n)* If something is a **shambles**, it is chaotic and very badly organized. *The play was a shambles.*

**shame** 1 *(n)* a feeling of guilt and sadness about something you have done. 2 *(n)* a pity, or a sad thing to have happened. *It's a shame Pat can't come.*

**shampoo** *(n)* a soapy liquid used for washing hair, carpets, etc. **shampoo** *(v).*

**shamrock** *(n)* a small, green plant whose leaves are divided into three parts. The shamrock is the national emblem of Ireland.

**shanty** shanties *(n)* a rhythmic song that was sung by sailors as they worked.

**shantytown** *(n)* an area of very poor temporary housing.

**shape** *(n)* the form or outline of something.

**share** sharing shared 1 *(v)* to divide what you have between two or more people. 2 *(n)* the portion of something that you receive.

**shark** *(n)* a large and often fierce sea fish with very sharp teeth.

**tiger shark**

**sharp** sharper sharpest 1 *(adj)* A **sharp** edge is fine or pointed, and is likely to prick or cut. 2 *(adj)* quick-witted, or clever. 3 *(adj)* sudden and dramatic. *A sharp turn.* 4 *(adj)* slightly sour. *Lemon juice tastes sharp.* 5 *(adj)* clearly outlined. *A sharp picture.* 6 *(adv)* exactly. *Be here at three o'clock sharp.* 7 *(adj)* cross and abrupt.

**shatter** shattering shattered *(v)* to break into tiny pieces.

**shattered** 1 *(adj)* tired and exhausted. 2 *(adj)* shocked and upset.

**shave** shaving shaved *(v)* to remove hair with a razor.

**shawl** *(n)* a piece of soft material, sometimes wrapped around a baby or worn by women over their shoulders.

**shear** shearing sheared shorn 1 *(v)* to cut the fleece off a sheep. 2 **shears** *(plural n)* a cutting tool with two blades, used for trimming hedges, grass, etc.

**shed** shedding shed 1 *(n)* a small hut used for storing things. 2 *(v)* to let something fall or drop off. *Some trees shed their leaves.*

**sheep** sheep *(n)* a farm animal kept for its wool and meat.

**sheepish** *(adj)* embarrassed or ashamed, often because you have done something foolish. **sheepishly** *(adv).*

**sheer** sheerer sheerest 1 *(adj)* extremely steep. *A sheer cliff.* 2 *(adj)* total and complete. *Sheer bliss.*

**sheet** 1 *(n)* a large, rectangular piece of cloth used to cover a bed. 2 *(n)* a thin, flat piece of paper, glass, metal, etc.

**sheik** *or* **sheikh** *(shake) (n)* the head of an Arab tribe, village, or family.

**shelf** shelves *(n)* a horizontal board on a wall or in a cupboard, used for storing things.

**shell** 1 *(n)* a protective outer case. Nuts, shellfish, and eggs all have shells. 2 *(n)* a type of bomb that is fired from a gun.

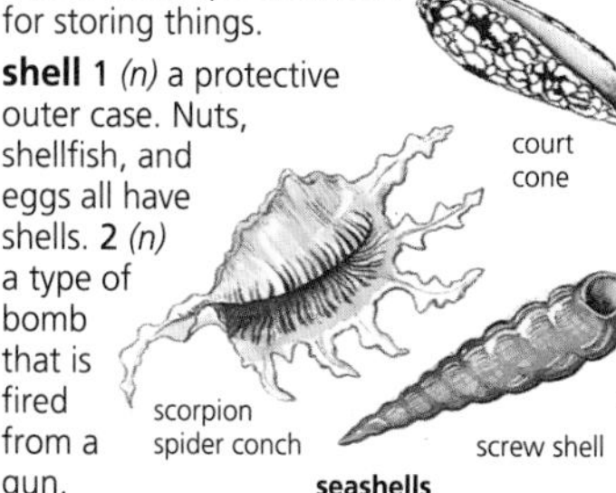


**seashells**

**shellfish** shellfish *(n)* a sea creature with a shell, such as a crab, lobster, or mussel.

**shelter** *(n)* a place where you can keep dry in wet weather, or stay safe from danger. **shelter** *(v).*

**shelve** shelving shelved *(v)* to put something on a shelf or shelves.

**shepherd** *(n)* someone whose job is to look after sheep.

**shield** *(n)* a piece of armour, carried to protect your body from attack.

**shift** **shifting shifted 1** *(v)* to move something heavy. **2** *(n)* a set period of continuous work. *A night shift.*

**shimmer** **shimmering shimmered** *(v)* to shine with a flickering light.

**shin** *(n)* the front part of your leg between your knee and ankle.

**shine** **shining shone** *(v)* to give off a bright light.

**shingle** *(n)* small, rounded pebbles.

**ship** *(n)* a large boat used for sea travel.

**shipshape** *(adj)* clean, tidy, and in good order.

**shipwreck** *(n)* the remains of a wrecked ship.

**shipyard** *(n)* a place where ships are built or repaired.

**shirk** **shirking shirked** *(v)* to avoid doing much work. **shirker** *(n).*

**shirt** *(n)* a piece of clothing that you wear on the top half of your body. Shirts usually have a collar, sleeves, and buttons.

**shiver** **shivering shivered** *(v)* to shake with cold or fear. **shiver** *(n),* **shivery** *(adj).*

**shoal** *(n)* a large group of fish swimming together.

**shock** **shocking shocked 1** *(n)* a sudden, violent fright. **2** *(v)* to give someone a fright. **3** *(v)* to horrify and disgust someone. *The news shocked us all.* **4** *(n)* the violent effect of an electric current passing through someone's body.

**shoddy** **shoddier shoddiest** *(adj)* carelessly produced and of poor quality.

**shoe** *(n)* an outer covering for the foot, often made of leather.

**shoehorn** *(n)* a narrow piece of plastic or metal that you use to help your heel slip easily into a shoe.

**shoot** **shooting shot 1** *(v)* to fire a gun. **shot** *(n).* **2** *(v)* to make a film or video. **3** *(v)* to move very fast. **4** *(n)* a young plant that has just appeared above the surface, or a new part of a plant that is just beginning to grow. *See* **flower**.

**shooting star** *(n)* a piece of rock from space, which burns up as it enters the Earth's atmosphere.

**shop** **shopping shopped 1** *(n)* a place where goods are displayed and sold. **2** *(v)* to go to the shops in order to buy goods. **shopper** *(n),* **shopping** *(n).*

**shoplifter** *(n)* someone who steals goods from a shop. **shoplifting** *(n).*

**shore** *(n)* the edge of the land where it meets a sea, river, or lake.

**short** **shorter shortest 1** *(adj)* less than the average length, distance, time, etc. *A short book.* **short** *(adv).* **2** If you are **short of** something, you have less of it than you need. *Henry is very short of money.*

**shortage** *(n)* When there is a **shortage** of something, there is not enough of it. *A food shortage.*

**shortcoming** *(n)* a failing, or a weak point in someone or something.

**shorthand** *(n)* a system of writing symbols instead of words, used for very quick note-taking.

**short-handed** *(adj)* If you are **short-handed**, you do not have enough people to do a job.

**shortly** *(adv)* soon, or presently.

**short-sighted 1** *(adj)* unable to see things clearly when they are far away. **2** *(adj)* not aware of future consequences. *A short-sighted decision.*

**short-tempered** *(adj)* Someone who is **short-tempered** becomes angry very quickly and easily.

**shot 1** *(n)* the firing of a gun. **2** *(n)* a photograph. **3** *(n) (informal)* an injection.

**shoulder** *(n)* the part of your body between your neck and your arm.

**shout** **shouting shouted** *(v)* to call out loudly. **shout** *(n).*

**shove** *(shuv)* **shoving shoved** *(v)* to push roughly. **shove** *(n).*

**shovel** *(n)* a type of spade with raised sides. **shovel** *(v).*

**show** **showing showed 1** *(v)* to let something be seen. *Show me the picture!* **2** *(v)* to explain, or to demonstrate. *Show me how!* **3** *(v)* to guide or lead someone. *Let me show you to your seat.* **4** *(v)* to be visible. *That stain won't show.* **5** *(n)* a public performance, or an exhibition.

**show business** *(n)* the world of theatre, films, television, and entertainment.

**shower** showering showered 1 *(n)* a brief fall of rain. 2 *(n)* a piece of equipment that produces a fine spray of water for washing your body. 3 *(v)* to fall in large numbers. *Leaves showered from the tree.*

**showjumping** *(n)* a sport in which horses and riders jump over fences.

**show-off** *(n)* someone who behaves in a boastful way in order to impress people.

**shrapnel** *(n)* small pieces of metal scattered by an exploding shell or bomb.

**shred** *(n)* a long, thin strip of cloth or paper that has been torn off something.

**shrew** *(n)* a small, insect-eating mammal with a long nose and small eyes.

**shrewd** shrewder shrewdest *(adj)* clever, experienced, and cunning in dealing with practical situations.

**shriek** *(n)* a shrill, piercing cry. **shriek** *(v)*.

**shrill** shriller shrillest *(adj)* harsh, high-pitched, and piercing. *We heard a shrill scream.*

**shrimp** *(n)* a small, edible shellfish.

**shrine** *(n)* a holy building that often contains sacred relics.

**shrink** shrinking shrank shrunk 1 *(v)* If something **shrinks**, it becomes smaller, often after being wet. *My shirt has shrunk.* 2 *(v)* to move away because you are frightened. *The children shrank closer to the wall as the creature approached.*

**shrivel** shrivelling shrivelled *(v)* If something **shrivels**, it becomes smaller, often after drying in heat. **shrivelled** *(adj)*.

**shrub** *(n)* a small plant or bush with woody stems.

**shrubbery** shrubberies *(n)* an area where shrubs are planted.

**shrug** shrugging shrugged *(v)* to raise your shoulders in order to show doubt or lack of interest.

**shudder** shuddering shuddered *(v)* to shake violently from cold or fear.

**shuffle** shuffling shuffled 1 *(v)* to walk slowly, hardly raising your feet from the floor. 2 *(v)* to mix together playing cards, papers, etc.

**shun** shunning shunned *(v)* to avoid someone or something. *Mo shunned any contact with the outside world.*

**shunt** shunting shunted *(v)* to move things from one place to another. *The engine shunted the carriages into a siding.*

**shut** shutting shut 1 *(v)* to block an opening, or close something with a door, lid, cover, etc. *Shut the door behind you.* **shut** *(adj)*. 2 **shut down** *(v)* to stop, or to close down. *The local factory has shut down.*

**shutter** *(n)* a cover to protect the outside of a window and keep out the light.

**shuttle** 1 *(n)* a bus or other form of transport that travels frequently between two places. 2 *See* **space shuttle**.

**shy** shier shiest *(adj)* If someone is **shy**, they are timid and do not enjoy meeting new people. **shyness** *(n)*, **shyly** *(adj)*.

**sibling** *(n)* a brother, or a sister.

**sick** sicker sickest 1 *(adj)* unwell. **sickness** *(n)*. 2 If you are **sick**, you vomit. 3 *(adj) (informal)* If you are **sick of** something, you have had too much of it.

**sicken** sickening sickened *(v)* to make someone feel shocked and disgusted.

**sickly** sicklier sickliest 1 *(adj)* If food is **sickly**, it makes you feel sick. 2 *(adj)* weak and often ill.

**side** 1 *(n)* a surface of a shape or object. 2 *(n)* an outer part of something that is not the front or the back. 3 *(n)* a team.

**sideboard** *(n)* a piece of furniture with a large, flat surface and drawers or cupboards below.

**sideburns** *(plural n)* the hair that grows down the sides of a man's face.

**side effect** *(n)* an effect of taking a medicine besides the intended effect.

**sideshow** *(n)* a small entertainment at a fair.

**sidetrack** sidetracking sidetracked *(v)* to distract someone from what they are doing or saying.

**sidewalk** *(n)* the American word for a pavement.

**siding** *(n)* a section of railway track used for storing or shunting carriages.

**siege** *(seej)* *(n)* the military action of surrounding a place, like a castle or city, and waiting for its defenders to surrender.

**siesta** *(see-***est***-a)* *(n)* an afternoon rest, taken in hot countries.

*Some words that begin with a "si" are spelt "cy", "psy", or "sci".*

**sieve** *(siv)* *(n)* a container with lots of very small holes in it, used for separating large from small pieces, or liquids from solids.

**sift sifting sifted 1** *(v)* to put substances through a sieve to get rid of lumps. **2** *(v)* to examine something carefully. *Police sifted the evidence for clues.*

**sigh** *(rhymes with lie)* **sighing sighed** *(v)* to breathe out deeply, often to express sadness or relief. **sigh** *(n).*

**sight 1** *(n)* the ability to see. **2** *(n)* a view, or a scene. *A marvellous sight.*

**sightseer** *(n)* someone who travels to see interesting places for pleasure.

**sign signing signed 1** *(n)* a symbol that stands for something. *A minus sign.* **2** *(n)* a public notice giving information. *A road sign.* **3** *(v)* to write your name in your own way. **4 sign language** *(n)* a way of communicating that uses the hands rather than speech and is used especially by deaf people.

**signal 1** *(n)* a form of communication that does not use speech. *A railway signal.* **signal** *(v).* **2** *(n)* Television and radio **signals** are pictures and sounds sent through the air by electrical pulses.

**signature** *(n)* the individual way that you write your name.

**signature tune** *(n)* the music that is always played at the beginning and end of a television or radio series.

**significant** *(adj)* important, or meaning a great deal. **significance** *(n).*

**Sikh** *(seek)* *(n)* a member of an Indian religious sect that believes in a single god. **Sikhism** *(n).*

**silage** *(n)* cut grass or hay that is stored and used as animal feed.

**silencer** *(n)* an attachment that reduces noise from a vehicle exhaust or gun.

**silent** *(adj)* absolutely quiet. **silence** *(n).*

**silhouette** *(sil-oo-**ett**)* *(n)* a dark outline seen against a light background.

**silk** *(n)* a soft, smooth fabric made from fibres produced by a silkworm. **silky** *(adj).*

**silly sillier silliest** *(adj)* foolish, or not sensible. **silliness** *(n).*

**silo 1** *(n)* a tower or pit for storing grain, grass for silage, etc. **2** *(n)* an underground shelter for a guided missile.

**silver 1** *(n)* a precious, shiny, grey metal used in jewellery and coins. **2** *(n)* coins made from silver or silver-coloured metal. **3** *(n)* the colour of silver. **silver** *(adj),* **silvery** *(adj).*

**similar** *(adj)* alike, or of the same type.

**simile** *(**sim**-ill-ee)* *(n)* a way of describing something by comparing it with something else, for example, "Her eyes are like stars and her lips are like roses".

**simmer simmering simmered** *(v)* to boil very gently.

**simple simpler simplest 1** *(adj)* easy, or not hard to understand or do. **simplicity** *(n),* **simply** *(adv).* **2** *(adj)* plain and not fussy. *A simple meal.* **simplicity** *(n).*

**simplify simplifies simplifying simplified** *(v)* to make something easier or less complicated. **simplification** *(n).*

**simply 1** *(adv)* in a simple way. **2** *(adv)* absolutely. *Simply marvellous.*

**simultaneous** *(adj)* happening at the same time. **simultaneously** *(adv).*

**sin** *(n)* bad behaviour that goes against moral and religious laws. **sinful** *(adj).*

**since 1** *(prep)* from the time that. *I've lived here since I was three.* **2** *(conj)* as, or because. *Since you've been so helpful, we'll give you a treat.*

**sincere** *(sin-**seer**)* **sincerer sincerest** *(adj)* If you are **sincere**, you are honest and truthful in what you say and do. **sincerity** *(n),* **sincerely** *(adv).*

**sing singing sang sung** *(v)* to make a musical noise with your voice. **singer** *(n).*

**singe singeing singed** *(v)* to scorch or burn something at the tip or the surface.

**single 1** *(adj)* individual, or only one. **2** *(adj)* unmarried. **3** *(adj)* one-way. *A single ticket.* **4** *(n)* a tape or CD with one main song on it.

**singular** *(adj)* to do with one thing or one person.

**sinister** *(adj)* Something that is **sinister** seems evil and threatening.

**sink sinking sank sunk 1** *(v)* a basin with taps and a plughole, used for washing. **2** *(v)* to go down slowly. *Sophie sank to her knees.* **3** *(v)* to make a ship sink.

**sip sipping sipped** *(v)* to drink slowly in small amounts. **sip** *(n).*

*Some words that begin with a "si" sound are spelt "ci" or "cy".*

**sit** **sitting** **sat** 1 *(v)* to rest on your buttocks. 2 *(v)* If you **sit** an exam, you try to answer the questions in it.

**site** *(n)* the place where something is or happens. *The site of the battle.*

**situation** *(n)* the circumstances which exist at a particular time.

**size** *(n)* the measurement of how large or small something is.

**sizzle** **sizzling** **sizzled** *(v)* to make a hissing noise, like sausages frying.

**skate** **skating** **skated** 1 *(n)* a boot with a blade on the bottom, used for moving across ice. 2 *(v)* to move smoothly across ice, wearing skates.

**skateboard** *(n)* a small board with wheels, that you stand on and ride.

**skeleton** *(n)* the framework of bones in a body.

**skeleton**

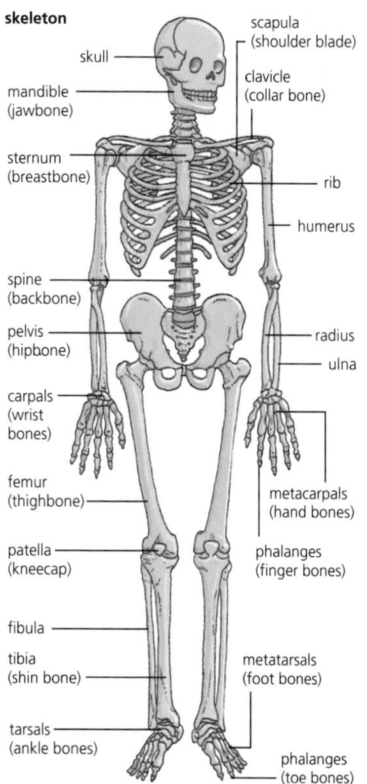


**sketch** **sketches** *(n)* a quick, rough drawing of something. **sketch** *(v).*

**skewer** *(n)* a long pin for holding meat or vegetables while they are cooking.

**ski** *(n)* one of a pair of long, narrow runners which you fasten to boots, and use for travelling over snow. **skiing** *(n).*

**skid** **skidding** **skidded** *(v)* to slide on a slippery surface.

**skill** *(n)* an ability to do something well.

**skim** **skimming** **skimmed** 1 *(v)* to take something off the top of a liquid. 2 *(v)* to glide across a surface.

**skin** 1 *(n)* the outer covering of tissue on the bodies of humans and animals. 2 *(n)* the outer layer of a fruit or vegetable.

**skip** **skipping** **skipped** 1 *(v)* to jump over a turning rope. 2 *(v)* to move along in a bouncy way, hopping on each foot in turn. 3 *(v) (informal)* to leave something out deliberately. *I skipped the gory scenes in my book.*

**skirt** *(n)* a piece of clothing worn by women and girls, that hangs from the waist.

**skive** **skiving** **skived** *(v) (informal)* to avoid doing any work. **skiver** *(n).*

**skull** *(n)* the bony framework of your head. *See* **skeleton**.

**sky** **skies** *(n)* the upper atmosphere as seen from the Earth.

**skyscraper** *(n)* a very tall building with many storeys.

**slab** *(n)* a large, flat block of stone, wood, or other heavy material.

**slack** **slacker** **slackest** 1 *(adj)* loose, or not tight. 2 *(adj)* not busy. *Trade is slack for many shops.*

**slalom** *(slar-lum)* *(n)* an event in which competitors ski downhill, between poles.

**slalom skier**

**slam** slamming slammed *(v)* to close something heavily and loudly. *Jessica slammed the book shut.*

**slander** *(n)* an untrue, spoken statement that damages someone's name or reputation. **slander** *(v).*

**slang** *(n)* words and expressions used by particular groups of people, but not in formal speech or writing.

**slant** slanting slanted *(v)* to slope, or be at an angle. *My handwriting slants to the left.*

**slap** slapping slapped *(v)* to hit someone or something with the palm of your hand. **slap** *(n).*

**slapdash** *(adj)* **Slapdash** work is done carelessly and hurriedly.

**slapstick** *(n)* rough and noisy comedy, often performed by clowns.

**slash** slashes slashing slashed 1 *(v)* to make a sharp, sweeping cut in something with a knife or blade. 2 *(v)* to reduce something dramatically. *The shop has slashed all its prices.*

**slate** 1 *(n)* a blue-grey rock that can be split into thin pieces, and is often used for roofing. 2 *(n)* a tile made from slate.

**slaughter** *(slaw-ter)* slaughtering slaughtered 1 *(v)* to kill animals for their meat. 2 *(n)* the brutal killing of large numbers of people.

**slave** *(n)* someone who is forced to work for someone else, without being paid. **slavery** *(n).*

**slay** slaying slayed slew slain *(v) (poetic)* to kill someone in a violent way. *The knight slew the dragon.*

**sled** *or* **sledge** *(n)* a vehicle with wooden or metal runners, used for travelling over snow and ice.

**sledgehammer** *(n)* a heavy hammer.

**sleek** sleeker sleekest *(adj)* smooth and shiny.

**sleep** sleeping slept *(v)* to rest in an unconscious state. **sleep** *(n).*

**sleepy** sleepier sleepiest *(adj)* tired, or drowsy. **sleepiness** *(n).*

**sleet** *(n)* partly melted falling snow, or partly frozen rain.

**sleeve** *(n)* the part of a garment that covers your arm.

**sleigh** *(slay)* *(n)* a sled, usually pulled by horses or other animals. *The picture shows a reindeer pulling a sleigh.*

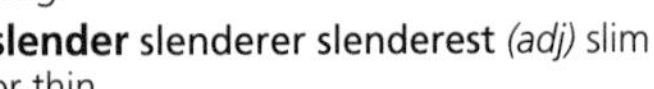

**slender** slenderer slenderest *(adj)* slim or thin.

**slice** *(n)* a thin piece or a wedge of food cut from a larger piece. **slice** *(v).*

**slick** slicker slickest 1 *(adj)* very fast, efficient and professional. *A slick performance.* 2 *(n)* a pool of oil covering an area of water or road.

**slide** sliding slid 1 *(v)* to move smoothly over a surface. *Amy slid across the floor.* 2 *(n)* a transparency inside a frame, that you view on a projector screen.

**slight** slightest *(adj)* small, or not very important. *A slight delay.* **slightly** *(adv).*

**slim** slimmer slimmest 1 *(adj)* thin and graceful. 2 *(adj)* very small. *A slim chance.*

**slime** *(n)* a slippery substance, such as mud. **slimy** *(adj).*

**sling** *(n)* a piece of cloth used to support an injured arm.

**slip** slipping slipped 1 *(v)* to lose your balance on a slippery surface. 2 *(v)* to move quickly and easily. *George slipped away silently.* 3 *(n)* a small mistake. 4 *(n)* a light garment worn under a skirt or dress.

**slipper** *(n)* a soft, light shoe that you wear indoors.

**slippery** *(adj)* smooth, oily, or wet, and very hard to grip on to.

**slit** slitting slit *(v)* to make a long, narrow cut in something. **slit** *(n).*

**slither** slithering slithered *(v)* to slip and slide along like a snake.

**slog** slogging slogged 1 *(v)* to work hard. **slog** *(n).* 2 *(n)* a long, hard walk.

**slogan** *(n)* an easily-remembered word or phrase used in advertising.

**slop** slopping slopped *(v)* to splash or spill liquid.

**slope** sloping sloped *(v)* to be at an angle. *The wall slopes to the left.*

**sloppy** **sloppier sloppiest 1** *(adj)* wet, or slushy. **2** *(adj) (informal)* careless and untidy. *Sloppy work.* **3** *(adj) (informal)* very sentimental. *Sloppy love songs.*

**slot 1** *(n)* a small, narrow space or groove in which something is fitted. **2 slot machine** *(n)* a machine that gives out a product or provides amusement when a coin is put in its slot.

**sloth** *(slowth)* **1** *(n)* a very slow-moving South American mammal. **2** *(n)* laziness.

**slouch** **slouches slouching slouched** *(v)* to sit, stand, or walk in a lazy way, with your shoulders and head drooping.

**slovenly** *(adj)* careless, untidy, and dirty.

**slow** **slower slowest 1** *(adj)* not fast. **slowness** *(n)*. **2** *(adj)* behind the right time. *My watch is five minutes slow.*

**sludge** *(n)* soft, thick mud.

**slug** *(n)* a soft, slimy creature that is similar to a snail, but has no shell.

**sluggish** *(adj)* slow-moving and lacking in energy. **sluggishness** *(n)*.

**slum** *(n)* an overcrowded, poor, and neglected area of housing.

**slump** **slumping slumped** *(v)* to fall in a heavy or uncontrolled way. *Maurice slumped to the ground.*

**slur** **slurring slurred** *(v)* to pronounce words unclearly by running different sounds into one another.

**slush** *(singular n)* snow that has partly melted. **slushy** *(adj)*.

**sly** **slier sliest** *(adj)* crafty, cunning, and secretive. **slyly** *(adv)*.

**smack** **smacking smacked** *(v)* to hit someone with the palm of your hand as a punishment. **smack** *(n)*.

**small** **smaller smallest** *(adj)* little, or tiny.

**smart** **smarting smarted; smarter smartest 1** *(adj)* well-dressed, tidy, and clean. **smartness** *(n)*. **2** *(adj)* clever, or quick-thinking. **3** *(v)* to sting, or to hurt.

**smash** **smashes smashing smashed 1** *(v)* to break something into many pieces by hitting or dropping it. **2** *(n)* a car crash.

**smear** **smearing smeared** *(v)* to rub something sticky or greasy over a surface.

**smell** **smelling smelled** *or* **smelt 1** *(v)* to sense through your nose. *I can smell food.* **2** *(n)* an odour, or a scent. **3** *(v)* to give off a smell, especially an unpleasant one. *Your socks smell horrible!*

**smelt** **smelting smelted** *(v)* to heat rock containing metal so that the metal melts and can be removed.

**smile** **smiling smiled** *(v)* When you **smile,** your mouth widens and turns up at the corners to show that you are happy or amused. **smile** *(n)*.

**smirk** **smirking smirked** *(v)* to smile in an unpleasant way. **smirk** *(n)*.

**smog** *(n)* a mixture of fog and smoke that sometimes hangs in the air over cities and industrial areas.

**smoke** **smoking smoked 1** *(n)* the mixture of gas and tiny particles that is given off when something burns. **smoky** *(adj)*, **smoke** *(v)*. **2** *(v)* to hold a cigarette or cigar in your mouth and breathe in its smoke. **smoker** *(n)*, **smoking** *(n)*.

**smooth** **smoother smoothest 1** *(adj)* even and flat, or not rough and bumpy. **smoothness** *(n)*. **2** *(adj)* happening easily, with no problems or difficulties.

**smother** *(smuth-er)* **smothering smothered 1** *(v)* to cover someone's nose and mouth so that they cannot breathe. **2** *(v)* to cover something completely. *Kirsten smothered her strawberries with cream.* **3** *(v)* to protect someone too closely.

**smoulder** **smouldering smouldered** *(v)* to burn slowly, with no flames.

**smudge** **smudging smudged** *(v)* to make a messy mark by rubbing ink, paint, etc. **smudge** *(n)*.

**smug** **smugger smuggest** *(adj)* If you are **smug,** you are too pleased with yourself. **smugly** *(adv)*.

**smuggle** **smuggling smuggled 1** *(v)* to take goods into a country illegally. **smuggler** *(n)*. **2** *(v)* to take something into or out of a place secretly. *We smuggled Jim's present into the house.*

**snack** *(n)* a small, light meal.

**snag** *(n)* a small problem or difficulty.

**snail** *(n)* a small creature with no legs, a soft, slimy body, and a shell on its back.

**garden snail**

**snake** *(n)* a long, thin reptile that has no legs and slithers along the ground.

corn snake

**snap** snapping snapped 1 *(v)* to break with a sudden, loud, cracking sound. 2 *(v)* to try to bite someone. *The dog snapped at me.* 3 *(v)* to speak sharply and angrily to someone. **snappy** *(adj).* 4 *(n)* a card game. 5 *(n) (informal)* a photograph.

**snapshot** *(n)* a photograph taken with a simple camera.

**snare** *(n)* a trap for birds or animals.

**snarl** snarling snarled 1 *(v)* If an animal **snarls**, it shows its teeth and growls. 2 *(v)* to say something angrily.

**snatch** snatches snatching snatched 1 *(v)* to take or grab something roughly. 2 *(n)* a small part. *I overheard snatches of their conversation.*

**sneak** sneaking sneaked *(v)* to move quietly and secretly. *Melissa sneaked up on me from behind.*

**sneer** sneering sneered *(v)* to smile in an unpleasant, mocking way. **sneer** *(n).*

**sneeze** sneezing sneezed *(v)* to push out air through your nose and mouth suddenly, often because you have a cold. **sneeze** *(n).*

**sniff** sniffing sniffed 1 *(v)* to breathe in strongly and often noisily through your nose. **sniff** *(n).* 2 *(v)* to smell something.

**sniffle** sniffling sniffled *(v) (informal)* to breathe noisily through your nose, usually because you have a cold.

**snigger** sniggering sniggered *(v)* to laugh quietly or secretly.

**snip** snipping snipped *(v)* to cut something using small, quick scissor cuts.

**snivel** snivelling snivelled *(v)* to cry or complain in a noisy, whining way.

**snob** *(n)* someone who looks down on people who are not rich and powerful.

**snooker** *(n)* a game in which players use long cues to knock coloured balls across a table and into pockets.

**snoop** snooping snooped *(v) (informal)* to look around somewhere secretly.

**snooze** snoozing snoozed *(v) (informal)* to sleep lightly for a short time, usually during the day. **snooze** *(n).*

**snore** snoring snored *(v)* to breathe noisily through your mouth while you are asleep. **snore** *(n).*

**snorkel** *(n)* a tube that you use to breathe through when you are swimming underwater. See **scuba diving**.

**snort** snorting snorted *(v)* to breathe the air out noisily through your nose. **snort** *(n).*

**snout** *(n)* the nose and mouth of a pig or similar animal.

**snow** *(n)* light flakes of ice that fall from the sky when it is very cold. **snow** *(v).*

**snowflake** (magnified)

**snowplough** *(n)* a vehicle used to push snow off a road or railway line.

**snub** snubbing snubbed *(v)* to behave in a rude, unfriendly way towards someone. **snub** *(n).*

**snuffle** snuffling snuffled *(v)* to breathe noisily and with difficulty.

**snug** snugger snuggest *(adj)* warm, cosy, and comfortable. *The cottage was warm and snug.*

**snuggle** snuggling snuggled *(v)* to sit or lie close to someone or something so that you are warm and comfortable.

**soak** soaking soaked 1 *(v)* to put something in water and leave it there. 2 *(v)* When something **soaks up** liquid, it absorbs it or takes it in.

**soap** *(n)* a substance that you rub on your skin when you wash. **soapy** *(adj).*

**soap opera** *(n)* a television series about the everyday lives of a group of people.

**soar** soaring soared *(v)* to fly very high in the air.

**sob** sobbing sobbed *(v)* to breathe in short bursts because you are crying.

**sober** 1 *(adj)* not drunk. 2 *(adj)* careful and serious. *A sober warning.*

**sob story** sob stories *(n)* a sad tale about yourself, intended to make people feel sorry for you.

**soccer** *(n)* a game played by two teams of eleven players who try to score goals.

**sociable** *(adj)* Someone who is **sociable** enjoys talking to people and spending time with them. **sociability** *(n)*.

**social 1** *(adj)* to do with the way that people live together. *Social problems.* **2** *(adj)* to do with activities that you take part in with other people in your spare time. *An exciting social life.*

**socialism** *(n)* a way of organizing a country, with the main industries owned by the government so that everyone can benefit from the money made by them. **socialist** *(n)*, **socialist** *(adj)*.

**social security** *(n)* money paid by the government to people who are ill, disabled, unemployed or poor.

**social services** *(plural n)* services provided by the government for people who have problems with health, childcare, housing, etc.

**society** **societies 1** *(n)* all the people who live in the same country or area and share the same laws and customs. **2** *(n)* an organization for people who share the same interests. *A music society.*

**sock** *(n)* a piece of clothing that you wear on your foot.

**socket** *(n)* a hole or set of holes into which an electrical plug or bulb fits.

**sodden** *(adj)* extremely wet.

**sofa** *(n)* a long, soft seat with arms and a back, and room for two or more people.

**soft** **softer softest 1** *(adj)* not stiff or hard, and easy to press or bend into a different shape. **2** *(adj)* smooth and gentle to touch. *Soft skin.* **3** *(adj)* pleasantly quiet and gentle. *Soft music.* **4 soft drink** *(n)* a cold drink that does not contain alcohol.

**softhearted** *(adj)* very kind, sympathetic, and generous to others.

**software** *(n)* a general name for computer programs.

**soggy** **soggier soggiest** *(adj)* very wet and heavy.

**soil** *(n)* ground or earth in which plants grow.

**solar** *(adj)* to do with the Sun.

**solar energy** *(n)* energy from the Sun that can be used for heating, lighting, etc.

**solar system** *(n)* the Sun and the planets that move around it. *See* **planet**.

**solder** **soldering soldered** *(v)* to join pieces of metal together, using hot, liquid metal to stick them.

**soldier** *(n)* someone who is in the army.

**sole 1** *(n)* the underneath part of the foot. **2** *(adj)* only. *I was the sole survivor.*

**solemn** *(adj)* very serious. **solemnity** *(n)*.

**solid 1** *(adj)* hard and firm. *The water had frozen solid.* **2** *(adj)* not hollow. *A solid chocolate egg.*

**solidly 1** *(adv)* firmly and strongly. *This house is very solidly built.* **2** *(adv)* without interruption. *Alma worked solidly for two hours.*

**solitary 1** *(adj)* If someone is **solitary**, they spend a lot of time alone. **2** *(adj)* single. *Not one solitary person.*

**solo** *(n)* a piece of music that is played or sung by one person. **soloist** *(n)*.

**soluble** *(adj)* A substance that is **soluble** can be dissolved in liquid.

**solution 1** *(n)* the answer to a problem or difficulty. **2** *(n)* a liquid that has something dissolved in it.

**solve** **solving solved** *(v)* to find the answer to a problem.

**solvent** *(n)* a liquid that makes other substances dissolve.

**sombre** *(som-bur)* *(adj)* dark and gloomy.

**some 1** *(adj)* a number of things, or an amount of something. *There were some children in the park. Would you like some cake?* **2** *(pronoun)* a certain number of people or things. *Some of us are going abroad.*

**somersault** *(n)* When you do a **somersault**, you tuck your head into your chest and roll over forwards on the ground or in the air. **somersault** *(v)*.

**son** *(n)* Someone's **son** is their male child.

**sonar** *(n)* a piece of equipment that is used on ships to calculate how deep the water is, or where underwater objects are, by bouncing sound off things.

**song 1** *(n)* a piece of music with words for singing. **2** *(n)* the musical sounds made by a bird.

**sonic** *(adj)* to do with sound waves.

**soon** **sooner soonest** *(adv)* in a short time. *I'll visit you soon.*

**soot** *(n)* black powder that is produced when something is burnt. **sooty** *(adj).*

**soothe soothing soothed 1** *(v)* to make someone less angry or upset. **2** *(v)* to make something less painful.

**sophisticated** *(sof-iss-tik-ate-id)* **1** *(adj)* **Sophisticated** people have a lot of knowledge and experience of fashion, culture, etc. **sophistication** *(n).* **2** *(adj)* cleverly designed to do difficult or complicated things. **sophistication** *(n).*

**sorbet** *(sor-bay) (n)* a frozen dessert, rather like ice cream, made with fruit, sugar, and sometimes beaten egg whites.

**sorcerer** *(n)* someone who performs magic by calling up evil spirits. **sorcery** *(n).*

**sordid 1** *(adj)* dishonest and shameful. **2** *(adj)* dirty and messy.

**sore sorer sorest 1** *(adj)* painful. **2** *(n)* an area of infected, painful skin. *A cold sore.*

**sorrow** *(n)* great sadness. **sorrowful** *(adj),* **sorrowfully** *(adv).*

**sorry sorrier sorriest 1** *(interject)* a word that you say when you feel unhappy or upset because you have done something wrong or because someone is suffering. **2** *(adj)* If you feel **sorry** for someone, you have sympathy and compassion for them.

**sort sorting sorted 1** *(n)* a type, or a kind. **2** *(v)* to arrange things into groups. **3** *(v)* If you **sort out** a problem, you deal with it and solve it.

**SOS** *(n)* a signal sent out by a ship or plane to say that it needs urgent help. The initials SOS stand for save our souls.

**soul** *(n)* your spirit, which many people believe lives on after you have died.

**sound sounding sounded 1** *(n)* something that you hear. **2** *(v)* If a horn or bell **sounds**, it makes a noise. **3** *(v)* to give an impression. *Australia sounds great.*

**sound effects** *(plural n)* noises that make a play or film more realistic.

**soundproof** *(adj)* A **soundproof** room does not let any sound in or out of it.

**soundtrack** *(n)* the recorded sound for a film.

**soup** *(n)* a liquid food made with vegetables or meat. *Tomato soup.*

**sour 1** *(adj)* having a bitter taste. **2** *(adj)* bad-tempered. *A sour expression.*

**source 1** *(n)* the place, person, or thing from which something comes. *The source of the problem.* **2** *(n)* the place where a stream or river starts.

**south 1** *(n)* one of the four main points of the compass, the direction to your left when you face the setting Sun in the northern hemisphere. **2** *(adj)* A **south wind** blows from the south. **3 South Pole** *(n)* the very cold part of the Earth in the far south.

**souvenir** *(soo-ven-ear) (n)* an object you keep to remind you of a place, event, etc.

**sovereign** *(sov-rin) (n)* a king or queen.

**sow sowing sowed sown** *or* **sowed 1** *(so) (v)* to put seeds in the soil to grow. **2** *(rhymes with how) (n)* a female pig.

**soya** *(n)* a kind of bean that can be cooked and eaten, or made into milk, oil, or flour to be used in cooking.

**space 1** *(n)* an empty or available area. *We need lots of space.* **2** *(n)* the universe beyond the Earth's atmosphere.

**spacecraft** *(n)* a vehicle that travels in space.

**space shuttle** *(n)* a spacecraft made up of four parts (the orbiter, the external fuel tank, and two booster rockets), which separate after the launch. *This picture shows how the parts of a space shuttle separate.*

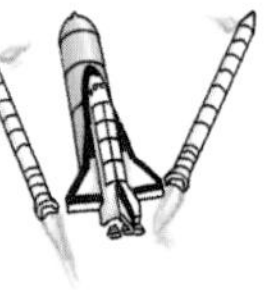

**spacesuit** *(n)* the protective clothing that an astronaut wears in space. *See* **astronaut**.

**spade 1** *(n)* a tool with a flat blade and a long handle, used for digging. **2 spades** *(plural n)* one of the four suits in a pack of cards, with a black symbol like a heart with a stalk.

**spaghetti** *(n)* long, thin strings of pasta.

**span 1** *(n)* Your **span** is the distance between your little finger and thumb when your hand is outstretched. **2** *(n)* the span of something is its length from one end to the other.

**spank** **spanking spanked** *(v)* to smack someone as a punishment.

**spanner** *(n)* a tool used for tightening and loosening nuts.

**spare** *(adj)* free for extra use. *Spare time.*

**spark** *(n)* a red-hot speck caused by fire, electricity, or friction. **spark** *(v).*

**sparkle** **sparkling sparkled** *(v)* to shine with lots of flashing points of light.

**sparrow** *(n)* a small, brown bird.

**spawn** *(n)* the eggs produced by fish and amphibians.

**speak** **speaking spoke spoken** *(v)* to talk, or to say words.

**speaker** 1 *(n)* somebody who gives a speech in public. 2 *(n)* a piece of equipment that turns electrical signals into sound. Speaker is short for loudspeaker.

**spear** *(n)* a long, pointed weapon that used to be thrown in battle.

**special** 1 *(adj)* extraordinary and important. *A special day.* 2 *(adj)* particular. *There's a special key for this door.*

**specialist** *(n)* an expert at one particular job. **specialism** *(n).*

**speciality** **specialities** *(n)* the thing that you are particularly good at.

**specialize** *or* **specialise** **specializing specialized** *(v)* to concentrate on one thing that you are good at or interested in. *Alice specializes in medieval art.*

**species** *(spee-sheez)* **species** *(n)* one of the groups into which animals and plants are divided, according to characteristics. *The domestic dog is a species of mammal.*

**specific** *(adj)* particular, definite, or individually named. *A specific type of tea.*

**specify** **specifies specifying specified** *(v)* to mention something in an exact way. *Please specify your nationality.*

**specimen** *(n)* a sample, or an example. *A specimen of your blood.*

**speck** *(n)* a minute piece of something, like dust or dirt.

**speckled** *(adj)* covered with small, irregular marks. *A speckled egg.*

**spectacle** *(n)* a remarkable and dramatic sight. *The display was quite a spectacle.*

**spectacles** *(plural n)* lenses set in frames which are worn to improve your eyesight.

**spectacular** *(adj)* remarkable and dramatic to look at. *A spectacular waterfall.*

**spectator** *(n)* someone who watches an event. **spectate** *(v).*

**spectre** *(spek-tur)* *(n)* a ghost.

**spectrum** **spectra** *(n)* the range of colours that is revealed when light shines through a prism or through water drops.

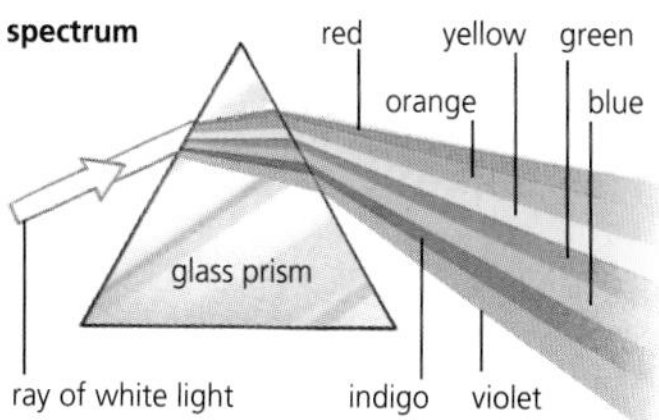

**spectrum**

**speech** **speeches** 1 *(n)* the ability to speak. 2 *(n)* a talk given to a group of people.

**speechless** *(adj)* unable to speak. *Dad was speechless with rage.*

**speed** **speeding sped** *or* **speeded** 1 *(n)* the rate at which something moves. 2 *(v)* to travel very fast, or to travel faster than is allowed. 3 *(n)* quickness of movement.

**speedometer** *(n)* an instrument in a vehicle that shows how fast it is moving.

**spell** **spelling spelt** *or* **spelled** 1 *(v)* to write or say the letters of a word in their correct order. 2 *(n)* a short period of time. *A spell of silence.* 3 *(n)* words that are supposed to have magical powers.

**spend** **spending spent** 1 *(v)* to use money to buy things. 2 *(v)* If you **spend** time or energy, you use it.

**sperm** *(n)* one of the reproductive cells from a male that is capable of fertilizing eggs in a female.

**sphere** *(sfear)* *(n)* a ball or globe shape. **spherical** *(sfe-rik-al)* *(adj).*

**sphinx** *(sfinks)* **sphinxes** *(n)* a mythical monster with a woman's head and a lion's body. *The picture shows the statue of the sphinx at Giza, in Egypt.*

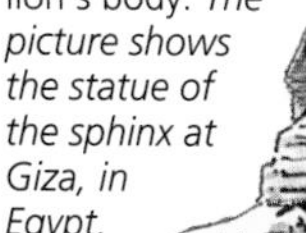

**sphinx**

**spice** *(n)* a substance with a distinctive smell or taste, used to flavour foods.

**spider** *(n)* an eight-legged creature that weaves a web to trap flies for food.

**orange-kneed tarantula**

**spike** *(n)* a sharp point. **spiky** *(adj)*.

**spill** **spilling spilt** *or* **spilled** *(v)* If you **spill** something, you let the contents of a container fall out accidentally.

**spin** **spinning spun** *(v)* to turn round fast on the spot.

**spindly** **spindlier spindliest** *(adj)* long, thin, and rather weak.

**spine** *(n)* the backbone. *See* **skeleton**.

**spinster** *(n)* a woman who has never been married.

**spiral** *(adj)* A **spiral** pattern winds around in circles like a spring. **spiral** *(n)*, **spiral** *(v)*.

**spire** *(n)* the pointed cone on top of a church tower. *See* **cathedral**.

**spirit** 1 *(n)* the part of a person that is not physical and is expressed in their deepest thoughts and feelings. 2 *(n)* a ghost, or a being with no physical form.

**spiritual** *(adj)* to do with beliefs, feelings, and thoughts, and not physical things.

**spit** **spitting spat** *or* **spit** *(v)* to force saliva out of your mouth.

**spite** 1 *(n)* deliberate nastiness. **spiteful** *(adj)*. 2 **in spite of** without taking notice of. *Ingrid went out in spite of the rain.*

**splash** **splashes splashing splashed** *(v)* to scatter liquid. **splash** *(n)*.

**splendid** *(adj)* impressive, excellent, or very good. **splendidly** *(adv)*.

**splint** *(n)* a piece of wood, plastic, or metal, used to support a broken or damaged limb.

**splinter** *(n)* a thin, sharp piece of wood, glass, metal, etc. **splinter** *(v)*.

**split** **splitting split** 1 *(v)* to break something into separate pieces. 2 *(n)* a crack. 3 *(v)* If a couple **splits up**, they stop going out together or living together.

**splutter** **spluttering spluttered** 1 *(v)* to speak with difficulty, usually because you are upset. 2 *(v)* to make choking and spitting noises.

**spoil** **spoiling spoilt** *or* **spoiled** 1 *(v)* to ruin or wreck something. 2 *(adj)* If children are **spoilt**, their parents have let them have their own way too often.

**sponge** 1 *(n)* soft material, filled with holes, used for washing and cleaning. **spongy** *(adj)*. 2 *(n)* a light cake.

**sponsor** **sponsoring sponsored** *(v)* to give money to people who are doing something worthwhile, often for charity.

**spontaneous** *(adj)* without previous thought or planning. **spontaneity** *(n)*.

**spool** *(n)* a reel on which film, tape, thread, etc. is wound.

**spoon** *(n)* a piece of cutlery, used for eating desserts, soups, etc.

**sport** *(n)* a general name for games involving physical activity.

**spot** **spotting spotted** 1 *(n)* a small mark that is usually round. **spotted** *(adj)*. 2 *(n)* a sore, red place on the skin. **spotty** *(adj)*. 3 *(n)* a place, or a location. *A good spot for a picnic.* 4 *(v)* to notice something.

**spotless** *(adj)* absolutely clean.

**spotlight** *(n)* a powerful light used to light up a small area.

**spouse** *(n)* a husband, or a wife.

**spout** *(n)* a tube through which liquid is poured. *The spout of a kettle.*

**sprain** **spraining sprained** *(v)* to injure a joint by twisting it. *Liz sprained her ankle.*

**sprawl** **sprawling sprawled** 1 *(v)* to sit or lie with your arms and legs spread out carelessly. 2 *(v)* to spread out in all directions. *The city sprawled for miles.*

**spray** **spraying sprayed** *(v)* to scatter liquid in very fine drops. **spray** *(n)*.

**spread** **spreading spread** 1 *(v)* to unfold something, or to stretch something out. *Joel spread his arms wide.* 2 *(v)* to cover a surface with something. *Spread butter on the bread.* 3 *(v)* to scatter, or to make known. *Spread the news.*

**sprightly** **sprightlier sprighliest** *(adj)* lively and energetic.

**spring** **springing sprang sprung** 1 *(n)* the season between winter and summer, when it becomes warmer and leaves grow on the trees. 2 *(v)* to jump suddenly. *The lion sprang at the antelope.* 3 *(n)* a coil of metal which moves back to its original shape after being compressed or pushed down. 4 *(n)* a place where water rises up from underground and becomes a stream.

**springboard** *(n)* a flexible board that people jump on in order to increase their height or force in diving or gymnastics.

**spring-clean** spring-cleaning spring-cleaned *(v)* to clean a house thoroughly, concentrating on the places that do not get cleaned often.

**sprinkle** sprinkling sprinkled *(v)* to scatter liquid or powder in small amounts. *Sprinkle the dish with grated cheese.*

**sprint** sprinting sprinted 1 *(v)* to run fast. 2 *(n)* a very fast race run over a short distance. **sprinter** *(n).*

**sprint start**

**sprout** sprouting sprouted 1 *(v)* When a plant **sprouts**, it starts to grow and produce shoots or buds. 2 *(n)* a round, green vegetable.

**spurt** spurting spurted 1 *(v)* When liquid **spurts**, it flows or gushes suddenly. **spurt** *(n).* 2 *(n)* a sudden burst of energy, growth, or speed.

**spy** spies spying spied 1 *(v)* to watch something closely from a hidden place. 2 *(n)* someone who secretly collects information about an enemy. **spy** *(v).*

**squabble** *(n)* a childish argument.

**squad** *(n)* a small group of people involved in the same activity, such as soldiers or football players.

**squalid** *(adj)* dirty and unpleasant.

**squander** squandering squandered *(v)* to spend money wastefully.

**square** squaring squared 1 *(n)* a shape with four equal sides and four right angles. 2 *(v)* to multiply a number by itself. *4 squared is 16.* 3 **square root** *(n)* the number that, when multiplied by itself, gives a particular number. *5 is the square root of 25.*

**squash** squashes squashing squashed 1 *(v)* to crush or flatten something. 2 *(n)* a concentrated fruit drink.

**squat** squatting squatted 1 *(v)* to crouch with your knees bent. 2 *(v)* to live, without permission, in an empty house that does not belong to you. **squatter** *(n).*

**squawk** squawking squawked *(v)* to make a loud, harsh cry like the noise of a parrot. **squawk** *(n).*

**squeak** squeaking squeaked *(v)* to make a short, high-pitched sound like the noise of a mouse. **squeak** *(n).*

**squeal** squealing squealed *(v)* to make a shrill, high-pitched sound, usually because you are frightened or in pain. **squeal** *(n).*

**squeamish** *(adj)* easily sickened or shocked. **squeamishly** *(adv).*

**squeeze** squeezing squeezed 1 *(v)* to press something firmly together from opposite sides. **squeeze** *(n).* 2 *(v)* to force something into or through a space. *We squeezed into the bus.* **squeeze** *(n).*

**squid** *(n)* a sea creature with a long, soft body and ten tentacles. Squids swim by squirting water out of their bodies with great force.

**squid**

**squint** squinting squinted *(v)* If you **squint** at something, you nearly close your eyes in order to see it more clearly.

**squirm** squirming squirmed *(v)* to wriggle about uncomfortably.

**squirrel** *(n)* a red or grey tree-climbing rodent with a thick, bushy tail.

**grey squirrel**

**squirt** **squirting squirted** *(v)* to send out a stream of liquid. **squirt** *(n).*

**stab** **stabbing stabbed** *(v)* to wound someone by piercing their skin with a knife or other sharp instrument. **stab** *(n).*

**stable** 1 *(n)* a building or a part of a building where a horse is kept. 2 *(adj)* firm and steady. *Before you climb the ladder, check that it is stable.* 3 *(adj)* safe and secure. *A stable upbringing.*

**stack** **stacking stacked** *(v)* to pile things up, one on top of another. **stack** *(n).*

**stadium** **stadiums** *or* **stadia** *(n)* a sports ground surrounded by rows of seats.

**staff** 1 *(plural n)* the people who work in an organization. *The school staff.* 2 *(n) (old-fashioned)* a thick, wooden stick.

**stag** *(n)* an adult male deer.

**stage** 1 *(n)* a period of development. *Our plans are at an early stage.* 2 *(n)* a level of progress. *You have done so well that you can move to the next stage.* 3 *(n)* an area where plays and concerts are performed. 4 If you **go on the stage**, you become an actor.

**stage-struck** *(adj)* Someone who is **stage-struck** thinks that the theatre is very glamorous, and wants to be an actor.

**stagger** **staggering staggered** 1 *(v)* to walk or stand unsteadily. 2 *(v)* to astonish and amaze someone. 3 *(v)* When you **stagger** events, you time them so that they do not happen at the same time.

**staggering** *(adj)* amazing, or astonishing. *A staggering sum of money.*

**stagnant** *(adj)* If water is **stagnant**, it is an odd colour, stale and often smelly.

**staid** *(adj)* If someone is **staid**, they are not lively and do not like change.

**stain** *(n)* a mark on something that is hard to remove. **stain** *(v).*

**stained glass** *(n)* coloured pieces of glass, held together by lead strips.

**stainless steel** *(n)* a type of steel that does not rust or tarnish.

**stairs** *(plural n)* steps that lead from one level of a building to another.

**stake** 1 *(n)* a thick, pointed post that can be driven into the ground. 2 *(n)* If you have a **stake** in something, you are involved in it or you have put money into it. 3 If something is **at stake**, it is at risk.

**stalactite** *(n)* a thin piece of rock, shaped like an icicle, which hangs from the roof of a cave. *The picture below shows stalactites in a cave.*

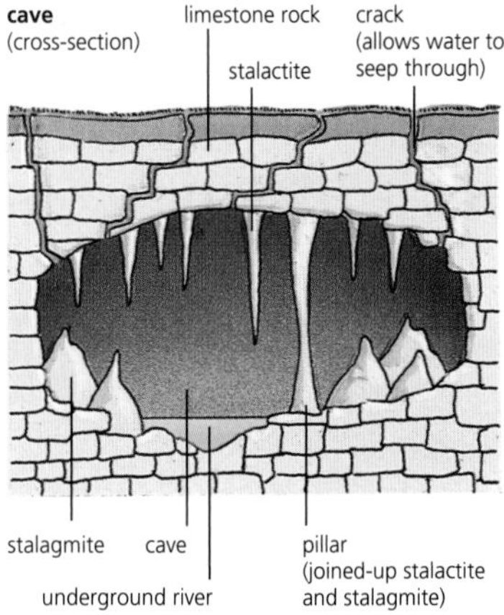


**stalagmite** *(n)* a piece of rock which sticks up from the floor of a cave. *The picture above shows stalagmites in a cave.*

**stale** **staler stalest** *(adj)* no longer fresh.

**stalemate** *(n)* a situation in an argument or game of chess, in which neither side can win.

**stalk** *(stork)* **stalking stalked** 1 *(n)* the long, main part of a plant from which the leaves, flowers, and fruit grow. 2 *(v)* to follow slowly and quietly. *The lion stalked its prey.* 3 *(v)* to walk in a proud, stiff way. *Harvey stalked out.*

**stall** **stalling stalled** 1 *(v)* When a car **stalls**, its engine stops suddenly. 2 *(n)* a table from which things are sold in a market or jumble sale. 3 *(v)* to delay doing something. 4 *(plural n)* In a theatre, the **stalls** are the seats on the ground floor.

**stallion** *(n)* a male horse.

**stamina** *(n)* the energy to keep doing something for a long while. *You need stamina for long-distance running.*

**stammer** **stammering stammered** *(v)* If you **stammer** when you speak, you repeat the first sound of a word before you manage to say the whole word.

**stamp** stamping stamped 1 *(n)* a small piece of paper that you stick on a letter or parcel to show that you have paid to send it. **stamp** *(v)*.2 *(n)* an object used to print a mark on paper. You press the stamp first on to an ink pad and then on to paper. **stamp** *(v)*. 3 *(v)* to bang your foot down. *Viola stamped her feet in rage.*

**stampede** stampeding stampeded *(v)* When people or animals **stampede**, they rush somewhere wildly. **stampede** *(n)*.

**stand** standing stood 1 *(v)* to be on your feet with your body upright. 2 *(v)* to put something somewhere. *Stand the vase on the table.* 3 *(n)* a covered area for spectators at a sports ground. 4 **stand for** *(v)* to represent. *US stands for United States.* 5 *(v)* If you **cannot stand** something, you are unable to bear it.

**standard** 1 *(adj)* usual, or average. 2 *(n)* a way of judging or measuring how good something is. *Standards of grammar.*

**stand-in** *(n)* someone who takes the place of another person when that person cannot be there. **stand in** *(v)*.

**standstill** *(n)* If something comes to a **standstill**, it stops completely.

**stanza** *(n)* one of the groups of lines into which a poem is divided. Another name for stanza is verse.

**staple** *(n)* a small piece of wire which is punched through sheets of paper to hold them together. **stapler** *(n)*, **staple** *(v)*.

**star** starring starred 1 *(n)* a ball of burning gases in space, seen from the Earth as a tiny point of light in the sky at night. **starry** *(adj)*. 2 *(n)* a shape with several points, usually five or six. 3 *(n)* a well-known actor or entertainer. 4 *(v)* to take the main part in a film or play.

**starboard** *(n)* the right-hand side of a ship or aircraft. **starboard** *(adj)*.

**starch** starches 1 *(n)* a substance found in foods such as potatoes, bread, and rice. Starch gives you energy. 2 *(n)* a substance used for making cloth stiff.

**stare** staring stared *(v)* to look at someone or something for a long time without moving your eyes. **stare** *(n)*.

**stark** starker starkest 1 *(adj)* bare and plain. *A stark landscape.* 2 *(adj)* totally, or completely. *The emperor was stark naked.*

**start** starting started 1 *(v)* to set something in motion, or to be set in motion. 2 *(v)* the beginning of something. 3 *(v)* to jump in surprise.

**startle** startling startled *(v)* to surprise someone and make them jump.

**starve** starving starved *(v)* to suffer or die from hunger. **starvation** *(n)*.

**starving** 1 *(adj)* suffering or dying from hunger. 2 *(adj) (informal)* very hungry.

**state** stating stated 1 *(v)* to say something clearly. *Please state your name.* 2 *(n)* the way that something is, or the condition that something or someone is in. *Your room is in a terrible state.*

**statement** 1 *(n)* something that is said formally. 2 *(n)* a list of all the amounts paid into and out of a bank account.

**static** 1 *(adj)* not moving, or not changing. *A static situation.* 2 *(n)* electricity that is produced by friction.

**station** 1 *(n)* a place where trains and buses stop. *A bus station.* 2 *(n)* a building used as the base for a police force, ambulance service, or fire brigade. 3 *(n)* a radio or television channel.

**stationary** *(adj)* at rest, or not moving.

**stationery** *(n)* writing materials, such as paper, envelopes, and pens.

**statistic** *(n)* a fact or piece of information, expressed as a number or percentage. **statistically** *(adj)*.

**statue** *(n)* a model of a person or animal made from metal, stone, etc.

**status** statuses *(n)* a person's rank or position in society.

**statute** *(n)* a rule, or a law.

**stave** *(n)* the set of five lines on which music is written.

**stay** **staying stayed** **1** *(v)* to remain where you are. **2** *(v)* to spend time somewhere. *We didn't stay long at the party.* **3** *(n)* a period of time spent somewhere as a visitor. *Have you had an enjoyable stay?*

**steady** **steadier steadiest** **1** *(adj)* continuous and not changing much. *Steady progress.* **2** *(adj)* not shaking, or not moving about. *A steady hand.*

**steal** **stealing stole stolen** **1** *(v)* to take and keep something that does not belong to you. **2** **steal away** *(v)* to leave quietly.

**stealthy** *(stelthy)* **stealthier stealthiest** *(adj)* secret and quiet. *We made a stealthy exit.*

**steam** **steaming steamed** **1** *(n)* the vapour formed when water boils. **2** *(v)* When glass **steams up**, it gets covered with condensation. **3** *(informal)* If you **let off steam**, you release your stored-up energy or feelings.

**steam-engine** *(n)* an engine powered by steam pushing pistons.

**steamroller** *(n)* a steam-driven vehicle used to flatten road surfaces.

**steel** **1** *(n)* a hard, strong metal made mainly from iron. **2** **steel band** *(n)* a group that plays music on drums made from oil barrels.

**steep** **steeper steepest** **1** *(adj)* sharply sloping up or down. *A steep hill.* **2** *(adj)* sharp, or rapid. *A steep drop in numbers.*

**steeple** *(n)* a church tower with a spire.

**steer** **steering steered** *(v)* to make a vehicle go in a particular direction.

**stem** *(n)* the long, main part of a plant, from which the leaves, flowers, and fruit grow. *See* **flower**.

**stench** **stenches** *(n)* a strong, unpleasant smell.

**stencil** *(n)* a piece of card, plastic, or metal with a design cut out of it, which can be painted over to transfer the design on to a surface. **stencil** *(v)*.

**step** **stepping stepped** **1** *(v)* to move your foot forward and put it down. **step** *(n)*. **2** *(n)* the sound of someone walking. *I can hear steps.* **3** *(n)* one of the flat surfaces on a staircase. **4** *(informal)* If someone tells you to **watch your step**, they are telling you to be careful.

**stepfamily** **stepfamilies** *(n)* the family of your stepfather or stepmother.

**stepfather** *(n)* the man who is married to your mother, but is not your father.

**stepmother** *(n)* the woman who is married to your father, but is not your mother.

**stereo** **1** *(n)* sound that comes from two different directions at the same time. **2** *(n)* a CD player, cassette player, or radio with stereo speakers.

**stereotype** *(n)* a simplified idea of a person or thing. *People in advertisements are always stereotypes.* **stereotypical** *(adj)*.

**sterile** **1** *(adj)* free from germs. **2** *(adj)* unable to have babies.

**sterilize** *or* **sterilise** **sterilizing sterilized** *(v)* to clean something and make it free from germs. **sterilization** *(n)*.

**sterling** *(n)* the currency of Great Britain.

**stern** **sterner sternest** **1** *(adj)* serious and severe. *Paula gave me a stern look.* **2** *(n)* the back end of a ship.

**stethoscope** *(n)* a Y-shaped tube joined to two earpieces, used by a doctor to listen to your heartbeat or breathing.

stethoscope

**stew** *(n)* meat or vegetables, cooked slowly in liquid. **stew** *(v)*.

**steward** **1** *(n)* a man who looks after passengers on an aeroplane or ship. **2** *(n)* someone who helps to direct people at a public event, such as a race or concert.

**stewardess** *(n)* a woman who looks after passengers on an aeroplane or ship.

**stick** **sticking stuck** **1** *(n)* a long, thin piece of wood. **2** *(n)* a long, thin piece of something. *A stick of chalk.* **3** *(v)* to glue or fasten one thing to another. **4** *(v)* to push something pointed into something else. *Fran stuck a needle into her finger.*

**sticker** *(n)* a sticky paper or plastic badge that you can attach to things.

**stiff** **stiffer stiffest** **1** *(adj)* difficult to bend or turn. **2** *(adj)* If you feel **stiff**, your muscles hurt. **3** *(adj)* difficult, or severe. *A stiff exam.* **4** *(adj)* formal and distant.

**stifle** **stifling stifled** *(v)* If you **stifle** a cough, sneeze, or yawn, you close your mouth to prevent if from being noticed.

**stile** *(n)* a step used to climb over a wall or fence.

**still** 1 *(adj)* not moving. *Stand still!* 2 *(adv)* even now. *Are you still here?* 3 *(adj)* not fizzy. *Still orange drink.* 4 *(adv)* however.

**stimulate** **stimulating stimulated** 1 *(v)* to fill someone with exciting new ideas. 2 *(v)* to encourage something to grow or develop.

**sting** **stinging stung** 1 *(n)* the sharp part of an insect, animal, or plant that can pierce your skin and leave some poison in it. **sting** *(v)*. 2 *(v)* to hurt with a sharp or throbbing pain. *My eyes are stinging.*

**stingy** *(stin-jee)* **stingier stingiest** *(adj)* very mean. **stingily** *(adv)*.

**stink** **stinking stank stunk** *(v)* to have an unpleasant smell. **stink** *(n)*.

**stir** **stirring stirred** 1 *(v)* to mix a liquid by moving a spoon or stick round and round in it. 2 *(v)* to move slightly.

**stitch** **stitches stitching stitched** 1 *(v)* to make loops of thread or wool in sewing or knitting. **stitch** *(n)*. 2 *(n)* a sharp pain in your side, caused by exercise.

**stock** **stocking stocked** 1 *(v)* If a shop **stocks** a product, it keeps a supply of it to sell. **stock** *(n)*. 2 *(n)* a liquid used in cooking, made from the juices of meat or vegetables.

**stockist** *(n)* a shop that keeps a supply of a particular product.

**stocks** *(plural n)* a heavy, wooden frame with holes in it, used in the past to hold criminals by their ankles.

**medieval stocks**

**stocky** **stockier stockiest** *(adj)* A **stocky** person is short, broad, and strong.

**stodgy** **stodgier stodgiest** *(adj)* **Stodgy** food is very heavy and filling.

**stoke** **stoking stoked** *(v)* to put more fuel on a fire in order to keep it burning.

**stomach** 1 *(n)* the organ which digests your food. *See* **organ**. 2 *(n)* the front part of your body, just below your waist.

**stone** 1 *(n)* a small piece of rock, usually found on the ground. **stony** *(adj)*. 2 *(n)* a hard material used for building, making sculptures, etc. 3 *(n)* a hard seed found in the middle of a fruit such as a peach.

**stool** *(n)* a small seat with no back.

**stoop** **stooping stooped** 1 *(v)* to bend down low. 2 *(v)* to move with your head and shoulders bent forwards. **stoop** *(n)*.

**stop** **stopping stopped** 1 *(v)* When something **stops**, it comes to an end. 2 *(v)* If you **stop** something, you put an end to it or do not do it any more. 3 *(v)* to be no longer moving or working. *My watch has stopped.* 4 *(n)* one of the places where a bus or train picks up passengers.

**stopper** *(n)* a piece of cork or plastic that fits into the top of a test tube, jar, or bottle, in order to close it.

**stopwatch** *(n)* a watch that you can start and stop, used for timing races.

**storage** *(n)* If you put something in **storage**, you put it in a place where it can be kept until it is needed. **storage** *(adj)*.

**store** **storing stored** 1 *(v)* to put things away until they are needed. **store** *(n)*. 2 *(n)* a large shop with many departments.

**storey** **storeys** *or* **stories** *(n)* one layer or floor of a building.

**storm** **storming stormed** 1 *(n)* a period of bad weather with strong wind and rain, and sometimes thunder and lightning. **stormy** *(adj)*. 2 *(v)* If you **storm out**, you rush out of a place angrily.

**story** **stories** 1 *(n)* an account of someone's life or adventures, especially one that has been made up. 2 *(n)* a lie.

**stout** **stouter stoutest** 1 *(adj)* quite fat. 2 *(adj)* strong and thick. *Stout shoes.*

**stove** *(n)* a piece of equipment used for cooking or for heating a room.

**stowaway** *(n)* someone who hides in a plane, ship, etc. because they want to escape secretly or cannot afford a ticket.

**straggle** **straggling straggled** *(v)* to follow slowly behind a group of people.

**straight** straighter straightest 1 *(adj)* not bent, or not curved. *A straight line.* 2 *(adj)* level, or neat. *Put your hat straight.* 3 *(adj)* honest, or correct. *A straight answer.*

**straightaway** *(adv)* at once.

**straightforward** 1 *(adj)* simple and uncomplicated. *A straightforward operation.* 2 *(adj)* honest, or to the point. *A straightforward answer.*

**strain** straining strained 1 *(n)* stress, or tension. 2 *(v)* If you **strain** a muscle in your body, you damage it by pulling it or overusing it. 3 *(v)* If you **strain** a mixture, you pour it through a sieve or colander, to separate the solids from the liquid.

**strait** *(n)* a narrow strip of water between two seas or two countries.

**strand** 1 *(n)* one of the threads or wires that are twisted together to form a rope. 2 *(n)* a single hair.

**stranded** *(adj)* If you are **stranded** somewhere, you are stuck there and cannot get away.

**strange** stranger strangest *(adj)* odd, unusual, or unfamiliar. **strangeness** *(n).*

**stranger** 1 *(n)* someone you do not know. 2 *(n)* someone in a place where they have not been before.

**strangle** strangling strangled *(v)* to kill someone by squeezing their throat so that they cannot breathe. **strangulation** *(n).*

**strap** *(n)* a strip of leather or material, used to fasten things together. **strap** *(v).*

**strategy** strategies *(n)* a clever plan for winning or achieving something.

**straw** 1 *(n)* dried stalks of corn, wheat, etc. 2 *(n)* a thin, hollow tube through which you can drink.

**strawberry** strawberries *(n)* a soft, red fruit.

**stray** straying strayed 1 *(v)* to wander away, or get lost. 2 *(n)* a lost cat or dog.

**streak** streaking streaked 1 *(n)* a stripe of colour. 2 *(v)* to move very fast.

**stream** 1 *(n)* a small river. 2 *(n)* a large line of moving people, cars, etc. 3 *(n)* a class of schoolchildren who are at the same level in their work.

**streamer** *(n)* a long, thin strip of coloured paper, used as a decoration.

**streamlined** *(adj)* A **streamlined** vehicle is designed to cut through air or water very quickly and easily.

**street** *(n)* a road with houses or other buildings along it.

**streetwise** *(adj)* If you are **streetwise**, you know how to survive in towns or cities without getting into trouble.

**strength** 1 *(n)* If you have **strength**, you are physically strong. **strengthen** *(v).* 2 *(n)* Someone's **strengths** are their good points, or the things they can do well.

**strenuous** *(stren-yoo-uss) (adj)* Something that is **strenuous** needs a lot of energy or effort. **strenuously** *(adv).*

**stress** stresses stressing stressed 1 *(n)* worry, strain, or pressure. **stressful** *(adj).* 2 *(v)* If you **stress** something, you show that it is important. **stress** *(n).*

**stretch** stretches stretching stretched 1 *(v)* to make something bigger, longer, or greater. 2 *(v)* to reach out with your arms. **stretch** *(n).* 3 *(v)* to extend, or to spread out. *The forest stretches for miles.*

**stretcher** *(n)* a bed made of a piece of canvas stretched between two poles, and used for carrying an injured person.

**strict** stricter strictest 1 *(adj)* If someone is **strict**, they make you obey the rules and behave properly. **strictness** *(n).* 2 *(adj)* complete, or total. *Strict concentration.*

**stride** striding strode striden *(v)* to walk with long steps. **stride** *(n).*

**strike** striking struck 1 *(v)* to hit or attack someone or something. **strike** *(n).* 2 *(v)* When a clock **strikes**, it chimes. 3 *(v)* If you **strike** a match, you light it. 4 *(v)* When people **strike**, they refuse to work because of an argument or disagreement with their employer. **strike** *(n),* **striker** *(n).*

**string** stringing strung 1 *(n)* a thin cord or rope. 2 *(n)* a thin wire on a musical instrument such as a guitar. 3 *(v)* to put a row of objects on a piece of string or wire. *Natasha was stringing beads.*

**strings** *(plural n)* the section of an orchestra that is made up of instruments with strings, such as violins and cellos.

**strip** stripping stripped 1 *(v)* to take something off. *Jo stripped the wallpaper off the wall.* 2 *(v)* to undress. 3 *(n)* a narrow piece of paper, material, etc.

**stripe** *(n)* a band of colour. **stripy** *(adj).*

**strive** **striving strove striven** *(v)* to make a great effort to do something. *Strive to do your best.*

**stroke** **stroking stroked** 1 *(n)* a hit. *A stroke of lightning.* 2 *(v)* to pass your hand gently over something. *Sam stroked the cat.* 3 *(n)* a way of moving in swimming.

**stroll** *(n)* a short, relaxed walk. **stroll** *(v).*

**strong** **stronger strongest** 1 *(adj)* powerful, or having great force. *A strong wind.* 2 *(adj)* hard to break. 3 *(adj)* full of taste, spices, alcohol, etc. *A strong curry.*

**stronghold** *(n)* a fortress, or a place that is well defended.

**stroppy** **stroppier stroppiest** *(adj) (informal)* quarrelsome and unhelpful.

**structure** *(n)* a building, or something that has been put together.

**struggle** **struggling struggled** 1 *(v)* If you **struggle** with someone, you fight or wrestle with them. **struggle** *(n).* 2 *(v)* If you **struggle** with something, you find it difficult to do. **struggle** *(n).*

**strum** **strumming strummed** *(v)* to play a guitar, banjo, etc. by brushing your fingers over the strings.

**strut** **strutting strutted** *(v)* to walk stiffly and proudly with your chest pushed out.

**stub** **stubbing stubbed** 1 *(n)* a short end of something, such as a pencil or cigarette. 2 *(v)* to hurt your toe by banging it against something. 3 **stub out** *(v)* to put a cigarette out.

**stubble** 1 *(n)* short, spiky pieces of corn or wheat, left in a field after harvesting. 2 *(n)* the short hair that grows on a man's face if he does not shave. **stubbly** *(adj).*

**stubborn** *(adj)* obstinate, or determined not to give way. **stubbornness** *(n).*

**stuck-up** *(adj) (informal)* conceited and snobbish.

**stud** 1 *(n)* a small, round piece of metal, such as a fastener or an earring. 2 *(n)* one of the short pegs on the bottom of football or hockey boots.

**student** *(n)* someone who is studying, especially in a college or university.

**studio** 1 *(n)* a room in which an artist or a photographer works. 2 *(n)* a place where films, tapes, CDs, etc. are made.

**studious** *(adj)* If you are **studious**, you like to study, and work carefully.

**study** **studies studying studying** 1 *(n)* an office or room where someone works. 2 *(v)* to spend time learning a subject or skill. 3 *(v)* to examine something carefully.

**stuff** **stuffing stuffed** 1 *(n)* a substance, or a material. 2 *(v)* to fill something tightly. *James stuffed his pockets with sweets.* 3 If you are **stuffed up**, you cannot breathe through your nose.

**stuffy** **stuffier stuffiest** 1 *(adj)* A **stuffy** room has stale air in it. **stuffiness** *(n).* 2 *(adj)* prim and easily shocked.

**stumble** **stumbling stumbled** 1 *(v)* to trip up, or to walk in an unsteady way. 2 *(v)* to make mistakes when you are talking or reading aloud.

**stump** *(n)* the part that is left when a tree is cut down.

**stun** **stunning stunned** *(v)* If you **stun** someone, you shock them or knock them out.

**stunning** *(adj)* beautiful, or amazing.

**stunt** 1 *(n)* a dangerous trick or act. 2 **publicity stunt** *(n)* a trick to get public attention for a company, organization, event, etc. 3 *(n)* A **stunt man** takes the place of an actor to perform the dangerous actions in a film.

**stupendous** *(adj)* very good, or very big.

**stupid** **stupider stupidest** *(adj)* silly, or unintelligent. **stupidity** *(n).*

**sturdy** **sturdier sturdiest** *(adj)* strong and firm. *A sturdy tree.*

**stutter** **stuttering stuttered** *(v)* If you **stutter** when you speak, you repeat the first sound of a word before you manage to say the whole word.

**sty** **sties** 1 *(n)* a pen in which pigs live. 2 **sty** *or* **stye** *(n)* a red, painful swelling on your eyelid.

**style** 1 *(n)* a way of doing something, such as writing, dressing, building, etc. 2 *(n)* smartness or elegance. **stylish** *(adj).*

**subconscious** *(n)* part of your mind that influences you without your being aware of it. **subconsciously** *(adv).*

**subdued** 1 *(adj)* unusually quiet and restrained. 2 *(adj)* not bright. *Subdued lighting.*

**subject** 1 *(n)* the topic of a book, newspaper article, conversation, etc. 2 *(n)* an area of study, such as geography or mathematics. 3 If you are **subject to** something, you are likely to be affected by it. *Laura is subject to colds.*

**subjective** *(adj)* to do with opinions rather than facts. *A subjective report.*

**submarine** *(n)* a ship that can travel under the water for long periods.

**submerge** submerging submerged *(v)* to put something under water.

**submit** submitting submitted 1 *(v)* to hand in, or put something forward. *Can I submit a plan?* 2 *(v)* to agree to obey something. *I submitted to their decision.*

**subscribe** subscribing subscribed *(v)* to pay money regularly for a paper or magazine. **subscription** *(n).*

**subsequent** *(adj)* coming after, or following. *Al lost the first game, but won the subsequent ones.* **subsequently** *(adv).*

**subside** subsiding subsided *(v)* to become less. *The noise subsided.*

**substance** *(n)* a material. Objects, powders, and liquids are all substances.

**substantial** *(adj)* solid, large, or important. **substantially** *(adv).*

**substitute** *(n)* something or someone used instead of another, such as a footballer who plays when another player is injured. **substitution** *(n),* **substitute** *(v).*

**subtitle** 1 *(n)* the second, less important title of a book, film, etc. 2 **subtitles** *(plural n)* the translated words that appear on the screen during a foreign film.

**subtle** *(sut-ul)* subtler subtlest 1 *(adj)* delicate, or not easy to notice. *A subtle flavour.* 2 *(adj)* using clever or disguised methods. *A subtle plan.* **subtlety** *(n).*

**subtract** subtracting subtracted *(v)* to take one number away from another. *Subtract three from six.* **subtraction** *(n).*

**suburb** *(n)* an area of housing at the edge of a large town or a city.

**subway** *(n)* a covered path for pedestrians under a road or railway.

**succeed** succeeding succeeded 1 *(v)* to manage to do something. *Bill succeeded in fixing the car.* 2 *(v)* to do well or get what you want. **successful** *(adj).*

**suck** sucking sucked 1 *(v)* to draw something into your mouth, using your tongue and lips. *George still sucks his thumb.* **suck** *(n).* 2 *(v)* to pull strongly. *The vacuum cleaner sucked up my ring.*

**sudden** *(adj)* quick, or unexpected.

**suede** *(swayd)* *(n)* soft leather with a smooth, velvet-like surface.

**suffer** suffering suffered 1 *(v)* to experience something bad, such as unhappiness or pain. **sufferer** *(n),* **suffering** *(n).* 2 *(v)* If you **suffer** from an illness, you get it often, or have it for a long time. *Jacob suffers from hay fever.*

**sufficient** *(suf-ish-unt)* *(adj)* enough or adequate. *We left sufficient food for the cats while we were away.*

**suffocate** suffocating suffocated 1 *(v)* to die because you cannot breathe. **suffocation** *(n).* 2 *(v)* to stop someone breathing, so that they die.

**sugar** *(n)* a sweet substance that comes from plants and is used in foods and drinks. **sugary** *(adj).*

**suggest** suggesting suggested *(v)* to put something forward as an idea or a possibility. *I suggested going to China for our next holiday.* **suggestion** *(n).*

**suicide** *(soo-iss-ide)* *(n)* If someone commits **suicide**, they kill themselves.

**suit** suiting suited 1 *(n)* a set of smart, matching clothes, usually a man's jacket and trousers. 2 *(n)* one of the four types of playing card in a pack of cards. The four suits are clubs, diamonds, hearts, and spades. 3 *(v)* If a hairstyle or an outfit **suits** you, it makes you look good.

**suitable** *(adj)* right for a particular purpose. **suitability** *(n),* **suitably** *(adv).*

**suitcase** *(n)* a container used for carrying clothes when you travel.

**suite** *(sweet)* 1 *(n)* a set of matching furniture. 2 *(n)* a set of rooms in a hotel.

**sulk** sulking sulked *(v)* If you **sulk**, you are angry and silent. **sulk** *(n),* **sulky** *(adj).*

**sullen** *(adj)* gloomy, silent, and bad-tempered. **sullenly** *(adv).*

**sultan** *(n)* an emperor or ruler of a Muslim country.

**sultana** *(n)* a small, brown, dried fruit, made from grapes.

**sultry** sultrier sultriest 1 *(adj)* If the weather is **sultry**, it is hot and humid. 2 *(adj)* passionate or sexy.

**sum** 1 *(n)* an amount of money. 2 *(n)* an arithmetic problem.

**summary** summaries *(n)* a short statement of the main points of something. **summarize** *(v)*.

**summit** 1 *(n)* the top of a mountain. 2 *(n)* a meeting of leaders from different countries.

**summon** summoning summoned *(v)* to call or request someone to come. *Summon the next witness.*

**sun** 1 **Sun** *(n)* the star that the Earth moves around, and that gives us light and warmth. 2 *(n)* light and warmth from the Sun.

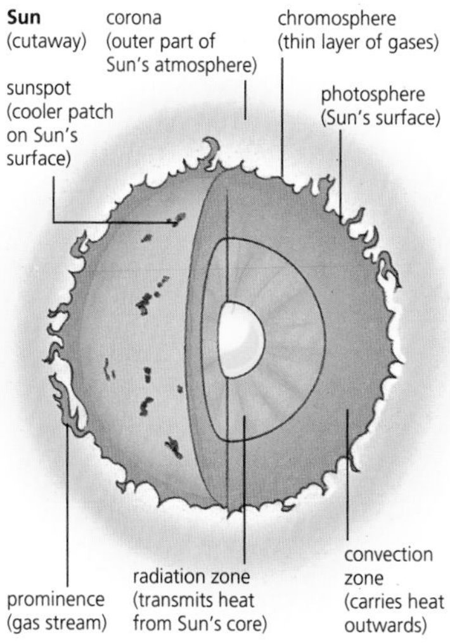


**sunbathe** sunbathing sunbathed *(v)* to sit or lie in sunlight in order to make your body suntanned.

**sunburn** *(n)* sore, red skin caused by staying in sunlight too long.

**sundial** *(n)* an instrument that shows the time by using the Sun's light. A pointer casts a shadow that moves slowly around a flat, marked dial.

**sundial**

**sunstroke** *(n)* an illness, caused by staying in hot sunlight for too long, that gives you a fever and a headache.

**suntan** *(n)* If you have a **suntan**, your skin is brown because you have been in hot sunlight. **suntanned** *(adj)*.

**super** *(adj)* very good.

**superb** *(adj)* excellent, or magnificent.

**superficial** 1 *(adj)* on the surface. *A superficial cut.* 2 *(adj)* not deep, or not thorough. *A superficial interest in music.*

**superfluous** *(adj)* more than is needed or wanted. *A superfluous remark.*

**superior** 1 *(adj)* better. *Dad thinks butter is superior to margarine.* 2 *(adj)* If you act in a **superior** way, you behave as if you are better than other people.

**superlative** *(soo-per-la-tiv)* 1 *(adj)* **Superlative** adjectives and adverbs are used to describe the greatest or highest degree of things or actions. "Biggest" is the superlative of "big" and "most quickly" is the superlative of "quickly". **superlative** *(n)*. 2 *(adj)* very good.

**supermarket** *(n)* a large shop that sells food and other household items.

**supernatural** *(adj)* involving things that natural laws cannot explain, such as ghosts. **supernaturally** *(adv)*.

**supersonic** *(adj)* faster than the speed of sound. *The picture shows Concorde, which flies at supersonic speeds.*

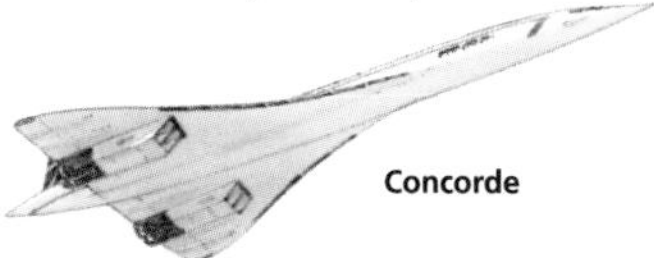
**Concorde**

**superstitious** *(adj)* People who are **superstitious** are afraid that something bad will happen if they do not follow certain rules. **superstition** *(n)*.

**supervise** supervising supervised *(v)* to watch over, and be in charge of someone while they do something.

**supple** suppler supplest *(adj)* able to move or bend your body easily.

**supplement** *(n)* an additional piece. *This newspaper has a colour supplement.*

**supplies** *(plural n)* food and equipment taken on an expedition.

**supply** supplies supplying supplied *(v)* to provide someone with what they want or need. *Ali supplies me with magazines.*

**support** supporting supported 1 *(v)* to hold something up in order to keep it from falling. 2 *(n)* to help and encourage someone. *We supported Cal when he was in trouble.* 3 *(v)* to believe in someone or something. *I support the Green Party.*

**suppose** supposing supposed *(v)* to think that something is true, or to expect something. *I suppose you're right. I suppose that Justin will be late.*

**suppress** suppresses suppressing suppressed 1 *(v)* to stop something happening. *The king suppressed a revolt.* **suppression** *(n)*. 2 *(v)* to hide or control something. *Carly suppressed her giggles.*

**sure** surer surest *(adj)* certain and definite. *Are you sure that he's here?*

**surf** surfing surfed *(v)* to ride on breaking waves, using a surfboard. **surfer** *(n)*, **surfing** *(n)*.

**surfing**

**surface** *(n)* the outer face or top of something.

**surge** surging surged *(v)* to rush forward or upward. *The crowd surged forward as the gate opened.* **surge** *(n)*.

**surgeon** *(sur-jun)* *(n)* a doctor who performs operations.

**surgery** *(sur-jer-ee)* surgeries 1 *(n)* a place where you go to see a doctor, dentist, vet, etc. 2 *(n)* medical treatment that involves cutting the patient open to repair, remove, or replace body parts.

**surname** *(n)* a person's last name or family name.

**surplus** *(adj)* spare, or more than what is needed. *Surplus clothes.*

**surprise** surprising surprised *(v)* to do or say something unexpected. *Alvin's outburst surprised us all.* **surprise** *(n)*.

**surrender** surrendering surrendered *(v)* to give up, or to admit that you are beaten in a fight or battle. **surrender** *(n)*.

**surround** surrounding surrounded *(v)* to be on every side of something. *The soldiers surrounded the castle.*

**surroundings** *(plural n)* the things around something or someone.

**survey** surveying surveyed 1 *(**sur**-vay)* *(n)* a report on what people think about something. *A survey of reactions to the plan.* 2 *(sur-**vay**)* *(v)* to look at the whole of a scene or situation. *Mum surveyed the mess with horror.*

**survive** surviving survived *(v)* to stay alive, especially after some dangerous event. *Only one passenger survived the car crash.* **survival** *(n)*, **survivor** *(n)*.

**suspect** suspecting suspected 1 *(suss-**pekt**)* *(v)* to think that someone should not be trusted. **suspicion** *(n)*. 2 *(suss-**pekt**)* *(v)* to think that something is wrong with a situation. **suspicion** *(n)*. 3 *(**suss**-pekt)* *(n)* someone thought to be responsible for a crime.

**suspend** suspending suspended 1 *(v)* to hang something downwards. *Suspend a banner from the window.* 2 *(v)* to punish someone by stopping them taking part in an activity for a short while. *The headteacher suspended Sophie from school.* **suspension** *(n)*. 3 *(v)* to stop something for a short time.

**suspense** *(n)* an anxious and uncertain feeling, caused by having to wait to see what happens.

**suspicious** 1 *(adj)* If you feel **suspicious**, you think that something is wrong. **suspicion** *(n)*. 2 *(adj)* If something is **suspicious**, it makes people think that something is wrong.

**sustain** sustaining sustained 1 *(v)* If something **sustains** you, it gives you energy. *The soup sustained the walkers.* 2 *(v)* to suffer something. *Tracey sustained some nasty bruises.*

**barn swallow**

**swallow** swallowing swallowed 1 *(v)* to make food or drink pass down your throat. 2 *(n)* a migrating bird with a forked tail and long wings.

**swamp** *(n)* an area of wet, marshy ground.

**swan** *(n)* a water bird with white feathers, webbed feet, and a long neck.

swan and cygnets

**swank** swanking swanked *(v) (informal)* to show off. swanky *(adj)*.

**swap** *or* **swop** swapping swapped *(v)* to exchange one thing for another.

**swarm** swarming swarmed 1 *(v)* When bees **swarm**, they fly together in a thick mass. 2 *(adj)* If a place is **swarming** with people, it is very crowded.

**swarthy** swarthier swarthiest *(adj)* A **swarthy** person has dark skin.

**swat** swatting swatted *(v)* to kill a fly with a quick blow.

**sway** swaying swayed *(v)* to move or swing from side to side. *The corn swayed in the wind.*

**swear** swearing swore sworn 1 *(v)* to use rude words. 2 *(v)* to make a formal, solemn promise. *I swear to tell the truth.*

**sweat** sweating sweated *(v)* When you **sweat**, you let out moisture through the pores in your skin, because you are hot or anxious. sweat *(n)*.

**sweater** *(n)* a knitted piece of clothing that you wear on the top half of your body.

**sweatshirt** *(n)* a collarless, casual top with long sleeves.

**sweep** sweeping swept 1 *(v)* to clean up somewhere, using a brush. 2 *(v)* to move rapidly and forcefully. *The duchess swept into the room.* 3 *(n)* someone whose job is to sweep chimneys.

**sweeping** *(adj)* Something that is **sweeping** affects many things or people. *Sweeping changes in the firm have resulted in many job losses.*

**sweet** sweeter sweetest 1 *(n)* a small piece of food, made with sugar or chocolate. 2 *(adj)* Food that is **sweet** has a sugary flavour, not a savoury one. 3 *(adj)* pleasant, or cute. sweetly *(adv)*.

**swell** swelling swelled swollen *(v)* to grow fatter. *Jake's knee swelled where he had knocked it.* swollen *(adj)*.

**sweltering** *(adj)* When the weather is **sweltering**, it is very hot indeed.

**swerve** swerving swerved *(v)* to change direction quickly, usually to avoid something.

**swift** swifter swiftest *(adj)* fast, or rapid. swiftness *(n)*, swiftly *(adv)*.

**swig** swigging swigged *(v)* to drink in large gulps from a bottle, flask, etc.

**swim** swimming swam swum *(v)* to propel yourself through water, using your arms and legs. swimmer *(n)*.

**swindle** swindling swindled *(v)* to cheat someone out of something, especially money. swindler *(n)*.

**swine** swine 1 *(n) (old-fashioned)* a pig. 2 *(n)* a very unpleasant person.

**swing** swinging swung 1 *(v)* to move from side to side. 2 *(n)* a piece of play equipment that you sit on and move backwards and forwards. swing *(v)*.

**swipe** swiping swiped 1 *(v) (informal)* to hit something or somebody hard. swipe *(n)*. 2 *(v) (slang)* to steal something. *Max swiped my chocolate!*

**swirl** swirling swirled *(v)* to move in circles. *Water swirled into the plughole.*

**switch** switches switching switched 1 *(v)* to exchange one thing for another. 2 *(v)* to change from one thing to another. *Miles switched courses.* 3 *(v)* to turn on a piece of electrical equipment. switch *(n)*.

**swivel** swivelling swivelled *(v)* to turn or rotate on the spot.

**swoop** swooping swooped *(v)* When a bird **swoops**, it pounces on another creature by flying downwards suddenly.

**swop** *see* **swap**.

**sword** *(sord) (n)* a weapon with a handle and a long, sharp blade.

**swot** swotting swotted 1 *(v) (informal)* to study very hard, often for an exam. 2 *(n) (informal)* a name that other people give to someone who studies very hard.

**syllable** *(n)* one of the sounds in a word. *The word America has four syllables; A-me-ri-ca.*

**syllabus** **syllabuses** *or* **syllabi** *(n)* a programme of work that must be covered for a particular subject or exam.

**symbol** *(n)* a design or object that represents something else. *A dove is a symbol of peace.* **symbolic** *(adj).*

**symmetrical** *(adj)* One half of a **symmetrical** shape exactly mirrors the other. **symmetry** *(n).*

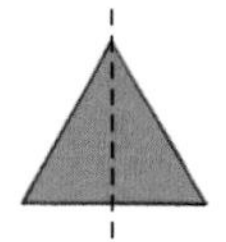

**symmetrical shapes**

**sympathy** **sympathies** 1 *(n)* the sharing and understanding of other people's troubles. *After her accident, Polly's friends gave her lots of sympathy.* **sympathetic** *(adj).* 2 If you are **in sympathy** with somebody's aims or actions, you agree with them and support them.

**symphony** **symphonies** *(n)* a long piece of music for an orchestra.

**symptom** *(n)* something that shows that you have an illness. *A rash is one of the symptoms of measles.*

**synagogue** *(n) (sin-a-gog)* a building used by Jews for worship.

**synchronize** *or* **synchronise** *(sin-kron-ize)* **synchronizing synchronized** *(v)* to make things happen at exactly the same time. **synchronization** *(n).*

**synonym** *(sin-oh-nim) (n)* a word that means the same, or nearly the same, as another word. *Large is a synonym of big.*

**synopsis** **synopses** *(n)* a brief summary of a longer piece of writing.

**synthetic** *(adj)* Something that is **synthetic** is man-made or artificial.

**syringe** *(n)* a tube with a plunger and a hollow needle, used for giving injections and taking blood samples.

**syrup** *(n)* a sweet, sticky, substance made from sugar. **syrupy** *(adj).*

**system** 1 *(n)* a group of things which exist or work together in an organized way. *A heating system.* 2 *(n)* a way of organizing or arranging things. *The education system.*

# Tt

**tab** 1 *(n)* a small piece of paper, metal, etc. that you can hold or pull. 2 *(informal)* If you **keep tabs on** someone, you watch them closely to see what they are doing.

**tabby** **tabbies** *(n)* a cat with a grey or brownish-yellow striped coat.

**table** 1 *(n)* a piece of furniture with a flat top resting on legs. 2 *(n)* a chart showing figures or information. 3 **tables** *(plural n)* lists of numbers multiplied by other numbers.

**tablespoon** *(n)* a large spoon used as a measure in cooking, or to serve food.

**tablet** 1 *(n)* a small, solid piece of medicine that you swallow. 2 *(n)* a piece of stone with writing carved on it.

**table tennis** *(n)* a game for two or four players, who hit a small, light ball over a low net on a table, using round bats.

**tabloid** *(n)* a newspaper printed on small pages, with lots of pictures. **tabloid** *(adj).*

**taboo** *(adj)* If a subject is **taboo**, you may upset or offend people if you talk about it. *Death is a taboo subject in some societies.* **taboo** *(n).*

**taciturn** *(adj)* Someone who is **taciturn** is quiet and shy and does not talk much.

**tack** **tacking tacked** 1 *(n)* a small, sharp nail. 2 *(v)* to attach or fix something using tacks. *I tacked a poster to the wall.* 3 *(v)* If you **tack** material, you sew it loosely before doing it neatly. **tack** *(n).* 4 *(n)* equipment that you need to ride a horse, such as a saddle and bridle.

**tackle** **tackling tackled** 1 *(v)* If you **tackle** someone in a ball game, you try to get the ball away from them. **tackle** *(n).* 2 *(v)* to deal with a problem or difficulty.

**tact** *(n)* If you handle a person or situation with **tact**, you are sensitive and do not upset anyone. **tactful** *(adj).*

**tactics** *(plural n)* plans or methods to win a game or battle. **tactical** *(adj).*

**tag** **tagging tagged** 1 *(n)* a label. 2 *(v)* If you **tag along** with someone, you go with them.

**tail** **tailing tailed** **1** *(n)* the long part at the end of an animal's body. **2** *(n)* something that is like a tail. *We joined the tail of the procession.* **3** *(v)* If you **tail** someone, you follow them closely. **4** *(v)* If something **tails off**, it gets less or weakens. *Misha's enthusiasm for the project has tailed off.*

**tailor** **1** *(n)* someone who makes or alters clothes, especially men's suits. **tailor** *(v).* **2** *(adj)* If something is **tailor-made**, it fits or suits you perfectly. **tailor** *(v).*

**take** **taking took taken** **1** *(v)* to move or carry something. *Take your plate into the kitchen.* **2** *(v)* to get, seize, or capture something. **3** *(v)* to accept something. *Do you take credit cards?* **4** *(v)* to use something. *This camera takes most types of film.* **5** *(v)* If you **take after** someone in your family, you look like them or have the same characteristics as them.

**takeaway** **1** *(n)* a restaurant selling meals that you take and eat somewhere else. **2** *(n)* a meal that you buy from a takeaway restaurant. *An Indian takeaway.*

**takeoff** *(n)* the beginning of a flight, when the aircraft leaves the ground.

**takings** *(plural n)* money received from customers in a shop, cinema, etc.

**talcum** *(n)* a fine, white powder that you can use to dry your body or to make it smell nice.

**tale** **1** *(n) (old-fashioned)* a story. **2** *(n)* a lie, or a complaint about someone.

**talent** *(n)* an ability, or a skill.

**talk** **talking talked** **1** *(v)* to speak. **2** *(n)* a conversation. **3** *(n)* a speech, or a lecture.

**talkative** *(adj)* If you are **talkative**, you talk a lot.

**tall** **taller tallest** *(adj)* high, or higher than usual. *A tall tower. A tall woman.*

**tally** **tallies tallying tallied** **1** *(n)* a count, or a record. *Keep a tally of what I owe you.* **2** *(v)* to add up or match. *These figures don't quite tally.*

**Talmud** *(singular n)* the books containing the laws of the Jewish religion.

**tame** **tamer tamest** **1** *(adj)* A **tame** animal is not wild, and can live with people. **tame** *(v).* **2** *(adj)* not very exciting.

**tamper** **tampering tampered** *(v)* to interfere with something, so that it becomes damaged or broken.

**tampon** *(n)* a plug of soft material that some women and girls wear inside their vagina to absorb the flow of blood during their periods.

**tan** **1** *(n)* a light, yellow-brown colour. **2** *(n)* If you have a **tan**, your skin has become darker because you have been out in the sun a lot. **tan** *(v),* **tanned** *(adj).*

**tandem** *(n)* a bicycle for two people.

**tandoori** *(n)* an Indian method of cooking meat, bread, etc. by baking it in a clay oven.

**tangent** *(n)* a straight line that touches the edge of a curve in one place.

**tangle** **tangling tangled** *(n)* to make things twisted and muddled. **tangle** *(n).*

**tank** **1** *(n)* a large container for liquid or gas. **2** *(n)* an armoured vehicle used by soldiers.

**tanker** *(n)* a ship or lorry that carries gas or liquid.

**tantrum** *(n)* a fit of temper.

**tap** **tapping tapped** **1** *(n)* a piece of equipment used to control the flow of a liquid. **2** *(v)* to hit or knock something gently. **tap** *(n).* **3** **tap-dancing** *(n)* dancing with shoes that have metal plates on their soles and make a clicking noise.

**tape** **taping taped** **1** *(n)* a thin piece of material, paper, plastic, etc. *A name tape.* **2** *(v)* to record sound or pictures on audio or video tape. **3** *(n)* a long piece of magnetic ribbon used for recording sound or pictures, usually contained in a plastic case, or cassette. *The picture shows an audio tape.*

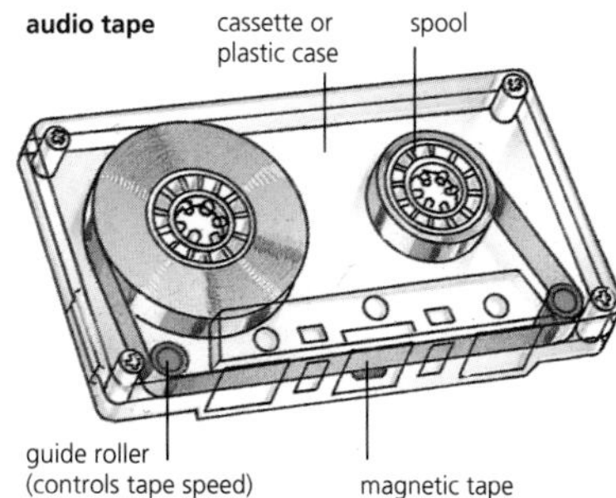

**tape measure** *(n)* a long, thin strip of ribbon or steel, marked in centimetres or inches so you can measure things with it.

**taper tapering tapered 1** *(v)* to become narrower at one end. **2** *(n)* a wooden strip or thin candle used for carrying a flame. *We lit the candles with a taper.*

**tape recorder** *(n)* an electrical machine that you use to play or record music or sound. **tape-record** *(v).*

**tapestry tapestries** *(n)* a piece of cloth with pictures or patterns woven into it.

**tar** *(n)* a thick, black, sticky substance, used for making roads.

**target targeting targeted 1** *(n)* something that you aim at or attack. **target** *(v).* **2** *(n)* a round object marked with circles, which an archer aims his arrows at. **3** *(v)* If you **target** something, you concentrate on it. *The publicity campaign is targeting a young audience.*

**tarmac** *(n)* a mixture of tar and small stones that is used on road surfaces.

**tarnish tarnishes tarnishing tarnished** *(v)* If something **tarnishes**, it becomes duller or less bright.

**tart tarter tartest 1** *(n)* an open fruit pie or pastry. **2** *(adj)* tasting sour or sharp.

**tartan** *(n)* woollen cloth patterned with squares of different colours.

**task** *(n)* a job, or a duty.

**tassel** *(n)* a bunch of threads tied at one end, used as a decoration on clothing, furniture, etc. **tasselled** *(adj).*

**taste tasting tasted 1** *(n)* Your sense of **taste** tells you what food you are eating. **2** *(n)* The **taste** of a food is whether it is sweet, sour, bitter, salty, etc. *This diagram of a human tongue shows the areas where different tastes are detected most strongly.* **taste** *(v),* **tasty** *(adj).* **3** *(n)* If you have good **taste**, you make good choices of furnishings, clothes, etc. **4** *(v)* to try a bit of food or drink to see if you like it. **taste** *(n).*

**areas of taste**
(human tongue)

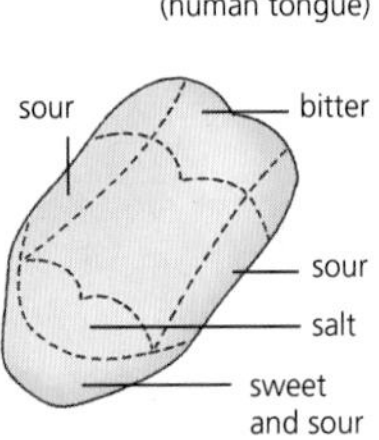


**tattered** *(adj)* old and torn, or scruffy.

**tattoo** *(n)* a picture or words that have been permanently printed on somebody's skin, using ink and needles. **tattoo** *(v).*

**tatty tattier tattiest** *(adj)* shabby and worn out. **tattily** *(adv).*

**taunt taunting taunted** *(v)* to try to make someone angry or upset by teasing them. *Jim taunted George about his size.*

**taut** *(adj)* stretched tight. *A taut rope.*

**tavern** *(n) (old-fashioned)* a pub, or an inn.

**tawny** *(n)* a light, sandy-brown colour. **tawny** *(adj).*

**tax taxes** *(n)* money that has to be paid to the government for public services. **taxation** *(n),* **tax** *(v).*

**taxi taxiing taxied 1** *(n)* a car with a driver who you pay to take you where you want to go. **2** *(v)* When planes **taxi**, they move along the ground.

**taxing** *(adj)* If something is **taxing**, it is demanding and puts a strain on you. *A taxing job.*

**tea 1** *(n)* a drink made from the leaves of a tea plant. **2** *(n)* a light afternoon meal. **3** *(n)* an evening meal, or supper.

**teach teaches teaching taught** *(v)* to give a lesson, or show someone how to do something. *Joel taught me to swim.* **teacher** *(n),* **teaching** *(n).*

**team teaming teamed 1** *(n)* a group of people who work together or play a sport together. **2** *(v)* If two people **team up**, they join together to do something.

**tear tearing tore torn 1** *(teer) (n)* a drop of liquid that comes from your eye. **2** *(tare) (n)* a rip in a piece of paper or material. **3** *(tare) (v)* to pull one part of something away from the rest. *Ben has torn his trousers.* **4** *(tare) (v)* to move very fast. *Louise tore down the street.*

**tease teasing teased** *(v)* to mock someone by saying unkind things to them.

**teaspoon** *(n)* a small spoon used for stirring drinks, or as a measure in cooking.

**teat 1** *(n)* a nipple of an animal, from which its babies can suck milk. **2** *(n)* a rubber top for a baby's bottle, with a small hole in the top of it.

**technical** 1 *(adj)* to do with science, machines, industry, etc. 2 *(adj)* using words that only experts understand. *Once we started to talk about computers, the conversation became very technical.*

**technician** *(n)* someone who looks after scientific equipment, or does practical laboratory work.

**technique** *(tek-**neek**)* *(n)* a skilful way of doing something.

**technology** **technologies** *(n)* the use of science to do practical things. **technological** *(adj).*

**tedious** *(**tee**-dee-us)* *(adj)* long and boring. *A tedious book.* **tediously** *(adv).*

**teenage** *(adj)* to do with people aged from 13 to 19. **teenager** *(n).*

**teens** *(plural n)* the years between 13 and 19. *Tanya is in her teens.*

**teepee** *see* **tepee**.

**teeth** *(plural n)* the white, bone-like structures in your mouth that you use for biting and chewing food. *The diagram shows a lower set of adult teeth.*

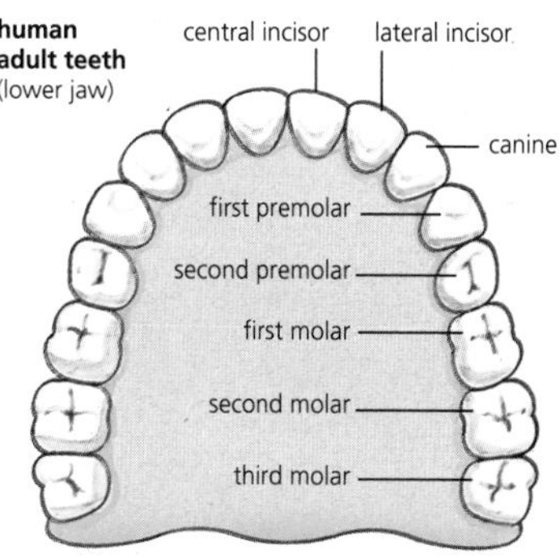


**teething** 1 *(adj)* If a baby is **teething**, new teeth are coming through its gums. 2 **teething troubles** *(plural n)* temporary problems that you may experience when you start a new job or activity.

**teetotal** *(adj)* If a person is **teetotal**, they never drink alcohol. **teetotaller** *(n).*

**telecommunications** *(plural n)* the science and technology of sending messages by telephone, satellite, radio, television, etc.

**telegram** *(n)* a message that is written down and sent by radio or electrical signals. Telegrams usually give urgent news or congratulations.

**telepathy** *(n)* If you use **telepathy**, you send your thoughts to someone else without speaking, writing, or making signs. **telepathic** *(adj).*

**telephone** *(n)* a machine that uses electrical wires and radio waves to enable you to speak to someone far away.

**telephoto lens** *(n)* a camera lens that makes things that are far away look closer and larger.

**telescope** *(n)* a tube-shaped instrument which makes small things look closer and larger, used especially for looking at stars.

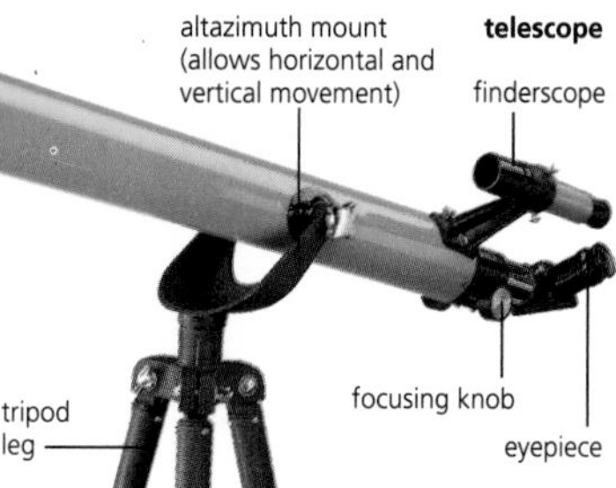


**television** 1 *(n)* a piece of equipment with a screen, that receives and broadcasts moving pictures and sound. 2 *(n)* the sending of sounds and moving pictures along radio waves to be picked up by a television set.

**tell** **telling** **told** 1 *(v)* to speak to someone. 2 *(v)* to show something. *The red light tells you to stop.* 3 *(v)* to recognize or be certain. *It was hard to tell who it was.* 4 **tell off** *(v)* If you **tell someone off**, you scold them because they have done something wrong.

**temper** *(n)* an angry or impatient mood.

**temperament** *(n)* your nature, or your personality. *A calm temperament.*

**temperamental** 1 *(adj)* excitable, unpredictable, or moody. *A temperamental artist.* 2 *(adj)* caused by your temperament.

**temperate** *(adj)* If an area has a **temperate** climate, it has neither very high nor very low temperatures.

**temperature** 1 *(n)* a measure of how cold or hot something is. 2 *(n)* If you have a **temperature**, your body is hotter than normal because you are ill.

**tempest** *(n) (poetic)* a violent storm.

**template** *(n)* a shape or pattern that you draw or cut around to make the same shape in paper, metal, material, etc.

**temple** *(n)* a building used for worship.

**tempo** *(n)* the speed or timing of a piece of music.

**temporary** *(adj)* If something is **temporary** it lasts for only a short time.

**tempt tempting tempted** 1 *(v)* If you **tempt** someone, you make them want something by telling them how good it is. **tempting** *(adj).* 2 *(v)* If you are **tempted,** you are attracted to doing something bad.

**temptation** 1 *(n)* the act of being tempted. *Try to resist temptation.* 2 *(n)* something that you want to have or do, although you know it is wrong.

**tenant** *(n)* someone who rents a room, house, office, etc.

**tend tending tended** 1 *(v)* If something **tends** to happen, it often or usually happens. 2 *(v)* If you **tend** a person, animal, or plant, you take care of it.

**tendency tendencies** *(n)* If you have a **tendency** to do something, you often or usually do it.

**tender** 1 *(adj)* sore, or sensitive. *Sal's bruises felt tender.* **tenderness** *(n).* 2 *(adj)* soft. *A tender steak.* 3 *(adj)* gentle and kind. *A tender kiss.* **tenderness** *(n).*

**tendon** *(n)* a strong, thick cord that joins a muscle to a bone. *See* **muscle**.

**tennis** *(n)* a game played on a court by two or four players using rackets to hit a ball over a net.

**tense tenser tensest** 1 *(adj)* nervous or worried. *Miriam is always tense before an exam.* 2 *(adj)* stretched tight and stiff. *Tense muscles.* **tense** *(v).* 3 *(n)* a form of a verb that shows whether an action happened in the past, is happening in the present, or will happen in the future.

**tension** 1 *(n)* the tightness or stiffness of a rope, wire, etc. *You can feel the tension in our dog's lead when he pulls.* 2 *(n)* a feeling of worry, nervousness, or suspense. *Tension mounted as the boxers entered the ring.* 3 *(n)* If there is **tension** between two people, there is difficulty or strain in their relationship.

**tent** *(n)* a shelter made of nylon or cloth, supported by poles and ropes.

**ridge tent**

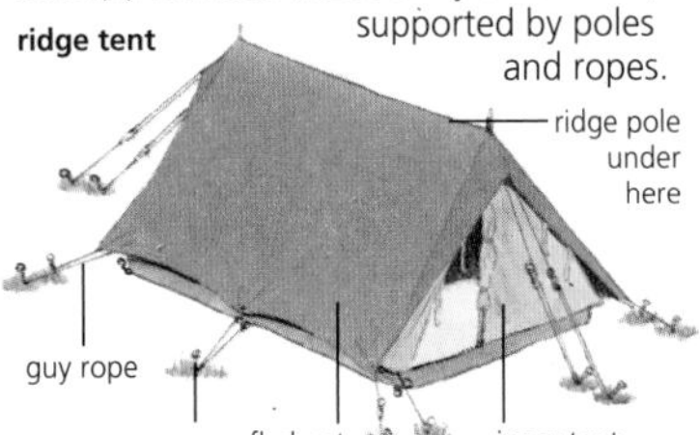

ridge pole under here

guy rope

peg

flysheet

inner tent

**tentacle** *(n)* one of the long, flexible limbs of some animals, such as octopuses or squids. *See* **squid**.

**tentative** *(adj)* hesitant, or unsure. *Giles made a tentative attempt to join in.*

**tenterhooks** If you are **on tenterhooks**, you are in suspense, waiting for something to happen.

**tenuous** *(ten-yoo-uss) (adj)* not very important, or not very significant.

**tepee** *or* **teepee** *(n)* a round tent made from animal skins or canvas, used by Native Americans.

**tepee**

**tepid** *(adj)* slightly warm.

**term** 1 *(n)* a part of the school year. 2 *(n)* a length of time. *The job is for a term of six months.* 3 *(n)* a word. *Musical terms.*

**terminal** 1 *(n)* a building where passengers arrive and leave. *An airport terminal.* 2 *(n)* a computer keyboard and screen linked to a network. 3 *(adj)* If someone has a **terminal** illness, they cannot be cured and will die.

**terminate terminating terminated** *(v)* to stop, or to end.

**terrace** 1 *(n)* a row of houses joined together. **terraced** *(adj).* 2 *(n)* a flat area next to a house, café, etc. where you can sit.

**terrain** *(n)* ground, or land.

**terrapin** *(n)* a water reptile with webbed feet and a shell.

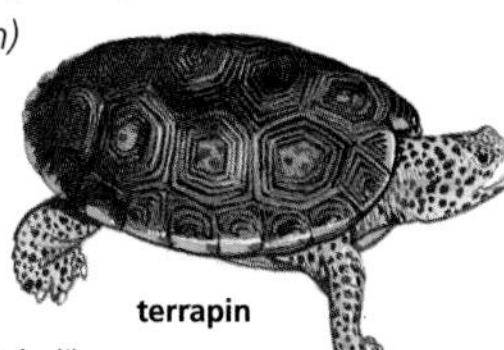
terrapin

**terrestrial** *(adj)* to do with the Earth, or living on the Earth.

**terrible** *(adj)* very bad, shocking, or awful. **terribly** *(adv).*

**terrific** 1 *(adj)* very good, or enjoyable. 2 *(adj)* very great. *Rod set off at a terrific speed.* **terrifically** *(adv).*

**terrify** terrifies terrifying terrified *(v)* to frighten someone very much.

**territory** territories *(n)* an area of land, especially land that belongs to someone.

**terror** *(n)* great fear.

**terrorist** *(n)* someone who uses violence, for example, bombing or hijacking, for political reasons. **terrorism** *(n).*

**terrorize** *or* **terrorise** terrorizing terrorized *(v)* to frighten someone very much.

**terse** terser tersest *(adj)* brief and abrupt. *When I asked Aunt Agatha her age, she gave a terse reply.*

**tessellate** tessellating tessellated *(v)* When shapes **tessellate**, they fit together exactly, without leaving gaps. *The picture shows how hexagons tessellate.*

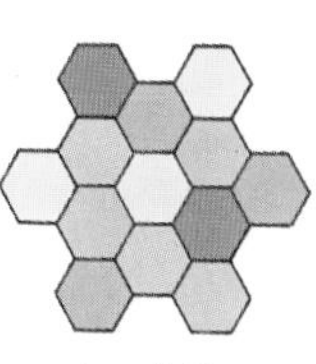
tessellating shapes

**test** testing tested 1 *(n)* a set of questions or actions used to check your knowledge or skill. *A driving test.* **test** *(v).* 2 *(n)* a medical examination or check-up. *A blood test.* 3 *(v)* to try something out. *Esther tested the new recipe.* **test** *(n).*

**testicle** *(n)* one of the two glands behind a man's penis that produce sperm.

**testify** testifies testifying testified *(v)* to state the truth, or to give evidence in a court of law.

**test match** test matches *(n)* a cricket or rugby match played between teams from different countries.

**test tube** 1 *(n)* a small, thin, glass tube used in a science laboratory. 2 **test tube baby** *(n)* a baby that develops from an egg which has been fertilized outside the mother's body, but which then grows normally inside her womb.

**tetanus** *(n)* a serious disease caused by bacteria getting into a cut or wound.

**tether** tethering tethered 1 *(v)* to tie up an animal so that it cannot move far. 2 If you are **at the end of your tether**, you have run out of patience or energy.

**text** *(n)* the main section of writing in a book, rather than the pictures or index.

**textbook** *(n)* a book that you use at school or college as part of your course.

**textile** *(n)* a fabric or cloth.

**texture** *(n)* the feel of something, especially its roughness or smoothness.

**thank** thanking thanked 1 *(v)* to tell someone that you are grateful for what they have done. 2 **thanks** *(plural n)* spoken or written words showing that you are grateful.

**thankful** *(adj)* glad, or grateful. *Helena was thankful for a decent meal.*

**thatch** thatches *(n)* reeds or straw used for making roofs. **thatched** *(adj).*

**thaw** thawing thawed 1 *(v)* to become soft or liquid after being frozen. *Leave the turkey to thaw overnight.* 2 *(n)* a time when snow and ice melt because the weather has become warmer.

**theatre** 1 *(n)* a place where you go to watch plays, shows, etc. 2 *(n)* a part of a hospital where surgeons operate.

**theatrical** 1 *(adj)* to do with the theatre. *Theatrical costumes.* 2 *(adj)* intended to create a dramatic effect.

**theft** *(n)* the crime of stealing.

**their** *(pronoun)* belonging to them. *Have the girls brought their books?* **theirs** *(pronoun).*

**theme** *(theem)* 1 *(n)* the subject of a speech, book, film, etc. 2 *(n)* a melody, or a tune. 3 **theme park** *(n)* a park with rides and attractions, based on a subject such as the Wild West.

**then** 1 *(adv)* at that time. *I didn't know Pandora then.* 2 *(adv)* afterwards. *Eat first, then talk.* 3 *(adv)* as a result. *If you stay up late, then you'll be tired tomorrow.*

**theorem** *(n)* a statement, especially in maths, that can be proved to be true. *Pythagoras' theorem.*

**theory** *(theery)* **theories** 1 *(n)* an idea that is intended to explain something. 2 *(n)* the rules and principles of a subject, rather than its practice. **theoretical** *(adj).* 3 If something should happen **in theory,** you expect it to happen, but it may not.

**therapy** **therapies** *(n)* a treatment for illness, such as physiotherapy, art therapy, or speech therapy. **therapist** *(n).*

**there** 1 *(adv)* to, in, or at that place. *Let's not go there again!* 2 *(pronoun)* The word **there** is often used as a subject in sentences. *There is a man outside. There has been some mistake.*

**therefore** *(adv)* as a result. *Stanley is ill, therefore Joe must take his place.*

**thermal** *(adj)* to do with heat, or holding in heat. *Thermal underwear.*

**thermometer** *(n)* an instrument used to measure temperature.

**thermostat** *(n)* a device connected to a radiator, iron, etc. that switches off the heat when the temperature gets too high.

**thesaurus** *(thi-saw-russ)* **thesauruses** *or* **thesauri** *(n)* a book containing lists of words with similar or related meanings.

**thick** **thicker thickest** 1 *(adj)* wide, fat, and dense. *Thick walls. Thick soup.* **thickness** *(n).* 2 *(adj) (informal)* stupid.

**thicket** *(n)* a thick growth of plants, bushes, or small trees.

**thief** **thieves** *(n)* someone who steals things. **thieve** *(v),* **thieving** *(adj).*

**thigh** *(n)* the top part of your leg, between your knee and your hip.

**thin** **thinner thinnest** *(adj)* not fat, not thick, or not dense. *A thin cat. A thin sauce.* **thinness** *(n).*

**thing** 1 *(n)* an object, idea, or event. 2 **things** *(plural n)* belongings.

**think** **thinking thought** 1 *(v)* to use your mind. *Try to think of the answer.* **thinker** *(n).* 2 *(v)* to have an idea or opinion. *Will thinks girls are silly.*

**third** 1 *(n)* one of three equal parts. 2 *(adj)* If you come **third** in a race, you finish behind two other people.

**Third World** *(n)* the poorer, developing countries of the world.

**thirst** 1 *(n)* a need for liquid. **thirst** *(v).* 2 *(n)* a longing for something. *Jesse has a great thirst for adventure.* **thirst** *(v).*

**thirsty** **thirstier thirstiest** *(adj)* wanting to drink something. **thirstily** *(adv).*

**thistle** *(n)* a wild plant with prickly leaves and purple flowers.

**spear thistle**

**thorn** *(n)* a sharp point on the stem of a plant, such as a rose.

**thorny** **thornier thorniest** 1 *(adj)* covered with thorns. 2 *(adj)* difficult. *A thorny problem.*

**thorough** *(adj)* doing a job carefully and completely. **thoroughness** *(n).*

**though** 1 *(conj)* even if, or despite the fact that. *I'm still hungry, though I've just had lunch.* 2 *(adv)* nevertheless. *He's quite friendly; I don't like him, though.*

**thought** 1 *(n)* an idea. 2 If you are **deep in thought**, you are thinking hard about something.

**thoughtful** 1 *(adj)* serious, or involving a lot of thought. *A thoughtful essay.* 2 *(adj)* A **thoughtful** person considers other people's feelings and needs. *A thoughtful gesture.*

**thoughtless** *(adj)* A **thoughtless** person does not consider other people's feelings and needs.

**thrash** **thrashes thrashing thrashed** 1 *(v)* to beat an animal or person with a stick or whip. 2 *(v)* to beat someone thoroughly in a game. **thrashing** *(n).*

**thread** **threading threaded** 1 *(n)* a strand of cotton, silk, etc. used for sewing. 2 *(v)* to pass a thread through something, like the eye of a needle or a set of beads. 3 *(n)* the raised, spiral ridge around a screw.

**threadbare** *(adj)* If your clothes are **threadbare,** they are old and worn out.

**threaten** threatening threatened *(v)* If someone or something **threatens** you, they frighten you or put you in danger.

**three-dimensional** *or* **3-D** *(adj)* solid, or not flat. *Cubes and spheres are three-dimensional shapes.*

**thresh** threshes threshing threshed *(v)* to separate the grain of a crop, like wheat, from the chaff and straw.

**threshold** 1 *(n)* the base of a doorway. 2 *(n)* the beginning of something. *We are on the threshold of a great adventure!*

**thrifty** thriftier thriftiest *(n)* not wasting money, food, supplies, etc.

**thrill** *(n)* a feeling of excitement and pleasure. **thrill** *(v)*, **thrilling** *(adj)*.

**thriller** *(n)* an exciting story about mystery, danger, or crime.

**thrive** thriving thrived *(v)* to do well and flourish. *Roses thrive in our garden. Yasmin is thriving at her new school.*

**throat** 1 *(n)* the front of your neck. 2 *(n)* the passage that runs from your mouth into your stomach or lungs.

**throb** throbbing throbbed *(v)* to beat in a regular way. *The drumbeat throbbed in my ears.* **throb** *(n)*.

**throne** *(n)* an elaborate chair for a king or queen.

**throne**

**throttle** throttling throttled *(v)* If you **throttle** someone, you squeeze their throat so that they cannot breathe.

**through** 1 *(prep)* from one end or side to the other. *Lily squeezed through the crowd.* **through** *(adv)*. 2 *(prep)* by way of, or because of. *Elsa got the job through a friend.* 3 *(adv)* completely. *Jacques was wet through.* **through** *(adj)*.

**throughout** *(prep)* all the way through. *Chickenpox spread throughout the school.* **throughout** *(adv)*.

**throw** throwing threw thrown 1 *(v)* to make something move, especially through the air. *Throw the ball.* 2 **throw away** *(v)* to get rid of something. 3 **throw up** *(v)* *(informal)* to vomit.

**thrush** thrushes *(n)* a garden bird with a brown back and a spotted breast.

**song thrush**

**thrust** thrusting thrust 1 *(v)* to push something suddenly and hard. 2 *(n)* The **thrust** of an argument is its main point.

**thud** *(n)* a noise like the sound of a heavy object falling on the ground. **thud** *(v)*.

**thug** *(n)* a violent person.

**thumb** thumbing thumbed 1 *(n)* the short, thick digit that you have on each hand. 2 *(v)* to turn over the pages of a book. 3 *(v)* *(informal)* If you **thumb a lift**, you hitchhike.

**thump** thumping thumped 1 *(v)* to hit someone or something with your fist. **thump** *(n)*. 2 *(n)* a dull sound.

**thunder** thundering thundered 1 *(n)* the loud, rumbling sound that you hear during a storm. 2 *(v)* to make a loud noise like thunder. *The trucks thundered past.*

**thwart** thwarting thwarted *(v)* If you **thwart** somebody's plans, you prevent them from happening.

**tick** 1 *(n)* the sound that a clock or watch makes. **tick** *(v)*. 2 *(n)* a mark that someone makes to show that an answer is correct or that something has been done. **tick** *(v)*.

**ticket** *(n)* a printed piece of paper or card that proves you have paid to do something. *A train ticket.*

**tickle** tickling tickled *(v)* to keep touching or poking someone gently, often making them laugh or feel irritated.

**tide** *(n)* the constant change in sea level, caused by the pull of the Sun and the Moon. **tidal** *(adj)*.

**tidings** *(plural n)* *(poetic)* news.

**tidy** tidier tidiest *(adj)* neat, or in proper order. **tidiness** *(n)*, **tidy** *(v)*.

**tie** ties tying tied 1 *(v)* to join two pieces of string, cord, etc. together with a knot. 2 *(n)* a long piece of fabric which is worn knotted around the collar of a shirt. 3 *(n)* a situation in which two people finish level in a competition. *There was a tie for second place.* **tie** *(v)*.

**tie-break** *or* **tiebreaker** *(n)* a special game played to decide the result of a match or competition when the players have won the same number of points.

**tier** *(teer) (n)* one of several levels, placed one above the other, for example, a row of seats in a theatre or a layer of a wedding cake. **tiered** *(adj).*

**tiger** *(n)* a large, striped wild cat found in Asia.

**tiger and cubs**

**tight** **tighter tightest 1** *(adj)* fitting closely, or fastened closely. *Tight jeans.* **2** *(adj)* fully stretched. *Is the rope tight?* **3** *(adj) (informal)* mean with money.

**tights** *(plural n)* a close-fitting garment that covers your hips, legs, and feet.

**tile** *(n)* a small, flat piece of baked clay, cork, slate, etc., often used for covering floors, roofs, or walls. **tile** *(v).*

**Dutch tile**

**till 1** *(prep)* until. *Wait there till I call for you.* **2** *(n)* a drawer or box in a shop, used to hold money, and often part of a cash register.

**tilt** **tilting tilted** *(v)* to lean to one side.

**timber** *(n)* cut wood used for building, furniture making, etc.

**time** **timing timed 1** *(n)* the passing of seconds, minutes, hours, etc. **2** *(n)* a particular moment shown on a clock or watch. *What is the time?* **3** *(n)* a particular period. *A time of happiness.* **4** *(v)* to measure how long something takes. *I'll time you while you run.* **5** *(v)* to choose the moment for something. *Harry timed his entrance perfectly.*

**timetable** *(n)* a printed chart of the times when events, lessons, travel departures, etc. are planned to happen.

**timid** *(adj)* shy and easily frightened. **timidly** *(adv).*

**tin 1** *(n)* a silvery metal used to make alloys and food cans. **2** *(n)* a food can.

**tinge** *(tinj)* **1** *(n)* a very small amount of added colour. *White with a tinge of pink.* **2** *(n)* a slight feeling. *Indra's smile had a tinge of sadness to it.*

**tingle** **tingling tingled** *(v)* to sting, prick, or tickle. **tingle** *(n).*

**tinker** **tinkering tinkered** *(v)* to work at or fiddle with something, with the aim of repairing it or improving it.

**tint** *(n)* a small amount of added colour.

**tiny** **tinier tiniest** *(adj)* very small, or minute.

**tip** **tipping tipped 1** *(v)* to make something lean or fall over. **2** *(v)* to lean, or to fall over. **3** *(n)* the thin end of something. *The tip of a snooker cue.* **4** *(n)* a useful hint. **5** *(n)* extra money given to a waitress, taxi driver, etc. as thanks for their services. **6** *(n)* a rubbish dump.

**tiptoe** **tiptoeing tiptoed** *(v)* to walk quietly, without putting your heels down.

**tire** **tiring tired 1** *(v)* to make someone tired, or to become tired and weak. **2** *(v)* to become bored. *I tired of Terry's chatter.*

**tiresome** *(adj)* boring, irritating, or annoying. **tiresomely** *(adv).*

**tissue** *(n)* soft, thin paper used for wiping, wrapping, etc.

**title 1** *(n)* the name of a book, film, painting, etc. **2** *(n)* the very first part of a person's name, for example, Miss, Mrs, Mr. **3** *(n)* a special name, showing a high position in society, for example, Sir, Dame, Lord, Lady. **titled** *(adj).*

**toad** *(n)* an amphibian like a frog, but with a rougher skin.

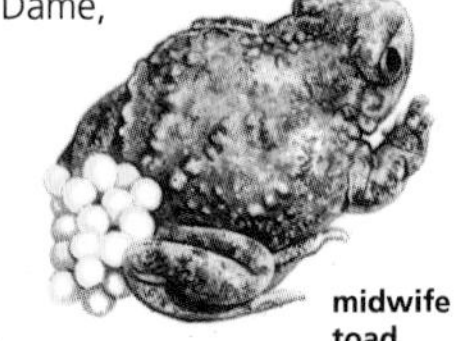
**midwife toad**

**toadstool** *(n)* a usually poisonous fungus with a rounded top on a stalk.

**toast** **toasting toasted 1** *(n)* grilled bread. **toast** *(v).* **2** *(v)* to drink in honour of someone. *Let's toast the bride and groom.* **toast** *(n).*

---

*Some words that begin with a "ti" sound are spelt "ty".*

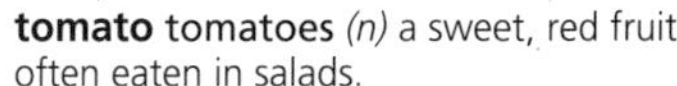

**tobacco** *(n)* the chopped, dried leaves of the tobacco plant, smoked in pipes, cigars, and cigarettes.

**toboggan tobogganing tobogganed** 1 *(n)* a small sledge. 2 (v) to travel by toboggan, especially downhill.

**today** 1 *(n)* on this day. *I'm going out today.* 2 *(n)* nowadays, or at the present time. *Today, most adults in the western world can read and write.*

**toddler** *(n)* a young child who has just learned to walk.

**toe** *(n)* one of the five digits at the end of your foot.

**toffee** *(n)* a chewy sweet made from boiled sugar and butter.

**toga** *(n)* a piece of clothing worn by ancient Romans. It was wrapped around the body and over the left shoulder.

**toga**

**together** *(adv)* with another person or thing. *The boys arrived at the party together.*

**toil toiling toiled** *(v)* to work very hard and continuously. *The labourers toiled in the fields.* **toil** *(n).*

**toilet** 1 *(n)* a large bowl with flushing water, used for disposing of urine and faeces. 2 *(n)* a room or building containing toilets.

**token** 1 *(n)* a small, physical object, used to represent something larger or to show someone's feelings. *Rodney gave Lisa a ring as a token of his love.* 2 *(n)* a card or piece of paper that can be exchanged for goods or services. *A book token.*

**tolerate tolerating tolerated** *(v)* If you **tolerate** something, you put up with it or endure it. *It is difficult to tolerate rude people.* **tolerance** *(n),* **tolerant** *(adj).*

**toll tolling tolled** 1 *(v)* to ring a bell, usually in a slow, solemn way. 2 *(n)* a charge for using a private road or bridge. 3 If something has **taken its toll**, it results in serious damage or suffering.

**tomahawk** (n) a war axe used by Native Americans. *This decorated tomahawk was used by the Shawnee people.*

**tomahawk**

**tomato tomatoes** *(n)* a sweet, red fruit, often eaten in salads.

**tomb** *(n)* a grave, usually for an important person.

**tomboy** *(n)* a girl who enjoys activities usually associated with boys, such as climbing trees or playing football.

**tomorrow** *(n)* the day after today.

**tone** 1 *(n)* the way that something sounds. 2 *(n)* the general atmosphere of a place or situation. *The tone of our conversation was cheerful.* 3 *(n)* a shade of a colour. *A pink tone.*

**tongs** *(plural n)* a tool with two arms, used for picking up things.

**tongue** *(tung) (n)* a flap of muscle in your mouth, used for tasting, eating, and talking. *See* **taste**.

**tonic** *(n)* something that makes you feel better. *Our seaside trip was a real tonic.*

**tonight** *(n)* this evening or night.

**tonsillitis** *(n)* a disease that makes your tonsils infected and painful.

**tonsils** *(plural n)* two flaps of soft tissue in your throat at the back of your mouth.

**too** 1 *(adv)* as well, or in addition. *Is Janey coming too?* 2 *(adv)* very, extremely, or more than enough. *The heavy metal band was too noisy for Granny.*

**tool** *(n)* a piece of equipment that you use to do a particular job.

**tooth teeth** 1 *(n)* one of the white, bone-like structures in your mouth, used for biting and chewing food. *Also see* **teeth**. 2 *(n)* one of a row of sticking out parts on a saw, comb, cogwheel, etc.

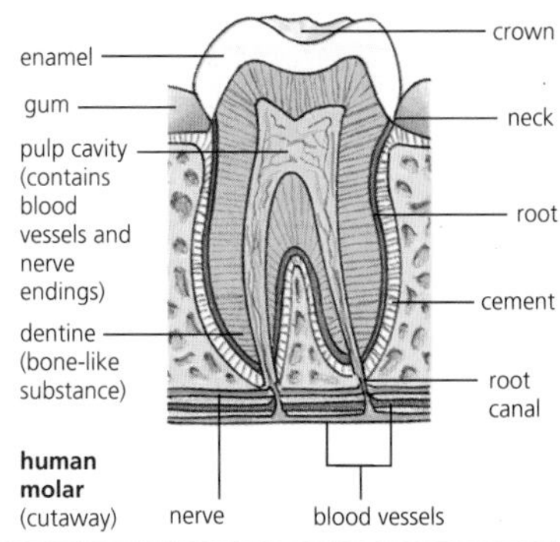


**human molar** (cutaway)

**top** **topping** **topped** **1** *(n)* the highest point of something. **2** *(adj)* very good, or best. *A top singer.* **3** *(n)* a covering, or a lid. **4** *(n)* a piece of clothing for the upper part of your body. **5** *(v)* to be the best, or to lead. *Fred topped the class in spelling.*

**top-heavy** *(adj)* If something is **top-heavy**, it is heavier towards the top, and therefore likely to fall over.

**topic** 1 *(n)* the subject of a discussion, study, lesson, etc. **2** *(n)* an extended study of a subject, usually in a primary school.

**topical** *(adj)* relevant now, or in the news at present.

**topple** **toppling** **toppled** *(v)* to fall over, usually from a height.

**Torah** *(n)* the sacred scroll in a Jewish synagogue, on which is written in Hebrew the books of Genesis, Exodus, Leviticus, Numbers, and Deuteronomy.

**torch** **torches** **1** *(n)* a battery-powered light that you can carry with you. **2** *(n)* a piece of wood dipped in wax or fat, used to light buildings in medieval times.

**toreador** *(toh-ree-a-dor) (n)* a bullfighter mounted on a horse.

**torment** **tormenting** **tormented** **1** *(tor-**ment**) (v)* to upset or annoy someone deliberately. **2** *(**tor**-ment) (n)* great pain.

**tornado** **tornados** *or* **tornadoes** *(n)* a windstorm that swirls in a circle.

**torpedo** **torpedoes** *(n)* an underwater missile that explodes when it hits something.

**torrent** *(n)* a large mass of flowing or falling water. **torrential** *(adj).*

**torso** *(n)* the part of your body between your neck and your waist.

**tortoise** *(n)* a slow-moving reptile with a shell and thick, scaly skin. *This tortoise is allowing finches to search for parasites on its body.*

**giant tortoise**

**totem pole**

**torture** **torturing** **tortured** *(v)* to cause someone extreme pain. **torture** *(n).*

**Tory** **Tories** *(n)* a nickname for a member of the Conservative Party. **Tory** *(adj).*

**toss** **tosses** **tossing** **tossed** **1** *(v)* to throw something upwards. *Matt tossed the pancake and caught it in the pan.* **2** *(v)* to throw something away casually. *Janet tossed the letter in to the bin.*

**total** 1 *(n)* the result of an addition or multiplication sum. *Add up these figures and give me the total.* **total** *(v).* **2** *(adj)* complete and utter. *The birthday party was a total surprise.* **totally** *(adv).*

**totem pole** *(n)* a carved pole that acts as a sacred emblem for a tribe or family of Native Americans. *The painted totem pole shown here is in Stanley Park, Vancouver, Canada.*

**totter** **tottering** **tottered** *(v)* to sway and stagger.

**toucan** *(too-kan) (n)* a brightly coloured tropical bird which has a huge beak.

**toucan**

**touch** **touches** **touching** **touched** **1** *(v)* to make contact with something, using your hands or other areas of your body. **2** Your **sense of touch** is your ability to feel things with your fingers or other parts of your body. **3** If you **keep in touch** with someone, you contact them regularly.

**touching** *(adj)* Something that is **touching** appeals to your emotions.

**touchy** **touchier** **touchiest** *(adj)* irritable and easily annoyed. **touchiness** *(n).*

**tough** *(tuff)* **tougher** **toughest** **1** *(adj)* strong and difficult to damage, either physically or mentally. **2** *(adj)* difficult. *A tough decision.*

**tour** **1** *(n)* a journey round a set route, often for sightseeing. **tour** *(v).* **2** When a band or team go **on tour**, they go to different places to play.

**tourist** *(n)* someone who travels and visits places for pleasure. **tourism** *(n).*

**tournament** 1 *(n)* a competition for players of sports, chess, cards, etc. 2 *(n)* In the Middle Ages, **tournaments** were events where knights jousted. *See* **joust**.

**tow** **towing towed** *(v)* to pull something behind you, usually with a rope, chain, etc. *The truck towed the car away.*

**towards** *or* **toward** *(prep)* in the direction of. *Oswin marched towards the door.*

**towel** *(n)* a thick, soft, absorbent cloth for drying yourself.

**tower** **towering towered** 1 *(n)* a tall structure that is thin in relation to its height. *The picture shows the Leaning Tower of Pisa in Italy.* 2 *(v)* to be very tall and dominant. *The skyscraper towered over the houses.*

**tower**

**town** *(n)* a place with houses, shops, offices, schools, etc. where many people live.

**towpath** *(n)* a path beside a canal or river.

**toxic** *(adj)* poisonous.

**toy** **toying toyed** 1 *(n)* an object that children play with. 2 *(v)* If you **toy** with something, you play with it in a half-hearted, unenthusiastic way.

**trace** **tracing traced** 1 *(v)* to find out where something or somebody is. 2 *(v)* to draw over the outline of a shape. 3 *(n)* a visible sign that something has happened or that someone has been somewhere. *Traces of blood.*

**track** **tracking tracked** 1 *(n)* the marks left by a moving animal or person. 2 *(n)* a path, or a route. 3 *(n)* a course for races. *A greyhound track.* 4 *(v)* to follow someone or something.

**tracksuit** *(n)* loose trousers and a top, usually worn for sports.

**tractor** *(n)* a powerful vehicle used on a farm. Tractors are often used to pull farm machinery or heavy loads. *See* **farm**.

**trade** **trading traded** 1 *(n)* the business of buying and selling things. **trader** *(n).* 2 *(n)* a particular job or craft. *Bob's trade is thatching.* 3 *(v)* to exchange one thing for another. *We traded computer games.*

**trademark** *(n)* a name, sign, or design that shows that a product is made by a particular company.

**trade union** *(n)* an organized group of workers, set up to help improve work conditions and pay. **trade unionist** *(n).*

**tradition** *(n)* a custom, ceremony, or activity that is passed from generation to generation. **traditional** *(adj).*

**traffic** **trafficking trafficked** 1 *(n)* moving vehicles. *There was heavy traffic in the city centre.* 2 *(v)* to buy and sell drugs or other goods illegally.

**traffic warden** *(n)* someone whose job is to check that vehicles are parked legally.

**tragedy** **tragedies** 1 *(n)* a serious play with a sad ending. 2 *(n)* a very sad event.

**trail** **trailing trailed** 1 *(n)* a track or path for people to follow. 2 *(v)* to follow someone, in order to check up on them. 3 *(v)* to follow slowly behind others. *Marcus was trailing a long way behind.*

**trailer** 1 *(n)* a vehicle that is towed by a car or truck and used to carry things. 2 *(n)* a short piece of film used to advertise a film or programme.

**train** **training trained** 1 *(n)* a string of railway carriages pulled by an engine. 2 *(v)* to learn how to do something, such as a job. **training** *(n).* 3 *(v)* to teach a person or animal how to do something. 4 *(v)* to practise and prepare for a sports event. **training** *(n).* 5 *(n)* the long piece of fabric that trails behind a bride's dress.

**trainer** 1 *(n)* someone who helps a person or animal become fit enough to compete in a sport. 2 *(n)* a light shoe with a thick sole, designed for sport.

**traitor** *(n)* someone who betrays their country or friends.

**tram** *(n)* a large vehicle that carries passengers and runs on rails in the road.

**tramp** **tramping tramped** 1 *(v)* to go for a long walk. *We tramped through the countryside.* 2 *(v)* to walk or tread with heavy steps. 3 *(n)* someone who does not have a permanent home.

**trample** trampling trampled *(v)* to damage something by walking all over it.

**trampoline** *(n)* a piece of canvas attached to a frame by elastic rope or springs. Trampolines are used for jumping on, either for sport or for pleasure.

**trance** *(n)* If you are in a **trance**, you are conscious, but not really aware of what is happening around you.

**tranquil** *(tran-kwil) (adj)* calm and peaceful. **tranquillity** *(n).*

**tranquillizer** *(n)* a pill or other medication prescribed to calm someone who is very agitated. **tranquillize** *(v).*

**transatlantic** 1 *(adj)* crossing the Atlantic Ocean. *A transatlantic telephone call.* 2 *(adj)* on or from the other side of the Atlantic. *A transatlantic fashion.*

**transfer** transferring transferred 1 *(trans-**fur**) (v)* to move a person or thing from one place to another. *I transferred the ball to my left hand.* **transfer** *(**trans**-fur) (n).* 2 *(**trans**-fur) (n)* a small picture or design that can be stuck to another surface by rubbing or ironing.

**transform** transforming transformed *(v)* to make a great change in something. *Meeting Alphonso has transformed my life.* **transformation** *(n).*

**transfusion** *(n)* the injection of blood from another person into the body of someone who is injured or ill.

**transient** *(adj)* lasting for a short time only. **transience** *(n).*

**transit** *(n)* If goods are **in transit**, they are being moved from one place to another.

**transition** *(n)* a change from one situation to another.

**translate** translating translated *(v)* to put something into another language. **translation** *(n),* **translator** *(n).*

**translucent** *(n)* A **translucent** substance is not clear, like glass, but will let the light through. *Frosted glass is translucent.* **translucency** *(n).*

**transmit** transmitting transmitted 1 *(v)* to send something from one place or person to another. **transmission** *(n).* 2 *(v)* to send out radio or television signals. *The programme will be transmitted next Friday.* **transmission** *(n),* **transmitter** *(n).*

**transparency** transparencies *(n)* a photographic slide.

**transparent** 1 *(adj)* A **transparent** substance is clear, like glass, and lets light through. 2 *(adj)* obvious, or clear. *The woman was a transparent liar.*

**transplant** transplanting transplanted 1 *(trans-**plant**) (v)* to remove something, like a plant, and put it somewhere else. 2 *(**trans**-plant) (n)* a surgical operation in which a diseased organ, such as a kidney, is replaced with a healthy one.

**transport** transporting transported 1 *(trans-**port**) (v)* to move people and goods from one place to another. 2 *(**trans**-port) (singular n)* all types of vehicles that carry people or goods.

**trap** trapping trapped *(v)* to capture a person or an animal by using some sort of trick or bait. **trap** *(n).*

**trap door** *(n)* a horizontal door in a floor or ceiling.

**trapeze** *(trap-**eez**) (n)* a bar hanging from two ropes, used by circus performers and gymnasts.

**trash** 1 *(singular n)* an American word for rubbish that you throw away. 2 *(singular n)* an American word for nonsense.

**traumatic** *(adj)* If something is **traumatic**, it is shocking and very upsetting. **trauma** *(n).*

**travel** travelling travelled *(v)* to go from one place to another. **travel** *(n).*

**travel agent** *(n)* a person or company that organizes travel and holidays for its customers. **travel agency** *(n).*

**traveller** 1 *(n)* someone who is travelling or who travels regularly. 2 *(n)* someone who lives in a van or mobile home and travels around, often in a group.

**trawler** *(n)* a fishing boat that drags a large, bag-shaped net through the water.

**tray** *(n)* a flat board used for carrying food and drinks.

**treacherous** *(**tretch**-er-uss) (adj)* dangerous, or not to be trusted. *A treacherous character. A treacherous path.*

**treacle** *(n)* a sweet, sticky syrup made from sugar.

**tread** **treading trod trodden 1** *(v)* to put your foot down on the ground. *Watch where you tread!* 2 *(n)* the ridges on a car tyre or on the sole of a shoe that help to prevent slipping.

**treason** *(n)* the crime of betraying your country, for example, by spying for another country.

**treasure** **treasuring treasured 1** *(n)* very precious and valuable objects, such as gold and jewels. 2 *(v)* to love and value highly something that you have or own.

**treasurer** *(n)* the person who looks after the money for an organization, club, etc.

**treasury** **treasuries 1** *(n)* a place where treasure is stored. 2 *(n)* the funds of an organization, government, etc.

**treat** **treating treated 1** *(v)* to deal with people or things in a certain way. *In China, old people are treated with great respect.* **treatment** *(n).* 2 *(v)* Doctors **treat** people to try to cure them of illness. **treatment** *(n).* 3 *(v)* to process something in order to change it in some way. *The scientists treated the substance to make it harmless.* **treatment** *(n).* 4 *(v)* to give someone a special gift, or take someone somewhere special. *Bonzo treated us to tea.* **treat** *(n).*

**treaty** **treaties** *(n)* a formal agreement between two or more countries.

**treble** 1 *(adj)* three times as big, or three times as many. 2 *(adj)* high-pitched. *A treble recorder.*

**tree** *(n)* a large, woody plant with a trunk, roots, branches, and leaves.

**trek** **trekking trekked** *(v)* to walk a long way, often in difficult conditions. **trek** *(n).*

**tremble** **trembling trembled** *(v)* to shake, especially from fear or excitement.

**tremendous** 1 *(adj)* huge, or enormous. *A tremendous explosion.* 2 *(adj)* very good, or excellent. *A tremendous party.*

**tremor** *(n)* a shaking movement. *Earth tremors are very common in California.*

**trench** **trenches** *(n)* a long, thin channel dug in the earth.

**trend** 1 *(n)* the general direction in which things are changing. *Recently, there has been a trend towards smaller families.* 2 *(n)* the latest fashion. *The trend this season is for shorter skirts.* **trendy** *(adj).*

**trespass** **trespasses trespassing trespassed 1** *(v)* to enter someone's private property without permisssion. **trespasser** *(n).* 2 *(n) (old-fashioned)* a sin.

**trial** 1 *(n)* a test. 2 *(n)* the examination of someone who appears in court accused of a criminal offence.

**triangle** 1 *(n)* a three-sided shape. **triangular** *(adj).* 2 *(n)* a triangular percussion instrument.

**tribe** *(n)* a group of people who share the same ancestors, customs, etc. **tribal** *(n).*

**tributary** **tributaries** *(n)* a stream or river that flows into a larger stream or river. *See* **river**.

**tribute** If you **pay tribute to** someone or something, you praise them.

**trick** **tricking tricked 1** *(v)* If you **trick** someone, you make them believe something that is not true. **trick** *(n).* 2 *(n)* a clever, entertaining act. *A magic trick.*

**trickle** **trickling trickled** *(v)* to flow very slowly in small quantities. **trickle** *(n).*

**tricky** **trickier trickiest** *(adj)* difficult, or awkward. *A tricky situation.*

**trifle** 1 *(n)* a dessert made from layers of sponge cake, fruit, jelly, custard, and cream. 2 *(n)* something that is not very important. **trifling** *(adj).*

**trigger** **triggering triggered 1** *(v)* the lever on a gun that you pull to fire it. 2 *(v)* to cause something to happen, as a reaction. *The man's arrest triggered riots in the streets.*

**trim** **trimming trimmed 1** *(v)* to cut small pieces off something in order to improve its shape. **trim** *(n).* 2 *(adj)* slim and shapely. *A trim waistline.*

**trio** *(n)* a group of three things or people.

**trip** **tripping tripped 1** *(v)* to stumble, or to fall over. 2 *(n)* a journey, or a visit. *A trip to the zoo.*

**triple** **tripling tripled 1** *(v)* to make something three times as big or three times as many. **triple** *(adj).* 2 *(adj)* made up of three parts. *The triple jump involves a hop, a step, and a jump.*

**triplet** *(n)* one of three children born to the same mother at almost the same time.

**tripod** *(n)* a three-legged stand used to support something, such as a camera.

**triumph** *(n)* a great achievement, or a victory. **triumph** *(v)*, **triumphant** *(adj)*.

**trivial** *(adj)* not very important. *Don't bother me with such trivial questions.*

**trolley** 1 *(n)* a two or four-wheeled cart used for carrying things. *A shopping trolley.* 2 *(n)* a table on wheels.

**troop trooping trooped** 1 *(n)* an organized group of soldiers, etc. 2 *(v)* to move in a group. *Sid and his friends trooped through the house.*

**trophy** *(troh-fee)* **trophies** *(n)* a prize, or an award.

**tropic** 1 *(n)* one of the lines of latitude that are 23.5° north and south of the equator, and are called the Tropic of Cancer and the Tropic of Capricorn. 2 **the tropics** *(plural n)* the extremely hot area between the Tropic of Cancer and the Tropic of Capricorn.

**tropical** *(adj)* to do with, or living in, the hot, rainy area of the tropics.

**tropical fish tropical fish** *(n)* fish that originally come from the tropics. Tropical fish are often kept as pets in aquariums.

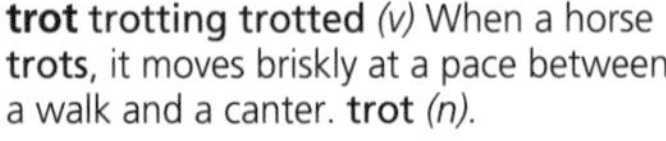

**trot trotting trotted** *(v)* When a horse **trots**, it moves briskly at a pace between a walk and a canter. **trot** *(n)*.

**trouble troubling troubled** 1 *(n)* a difficult or dangerous situation. 2 *(v)* If you **trouble** someone, you disturb or worry them. *The letter troubled Perdita.* 3 If you **take the trouble** to do something, you make an effort to do it. *James always takes the trouble to send me a card.* 4 *(v)* to bother someone by asking them for help.

**trough** *(troff)* *(n)* a long, narrow container from which animals can drink or feed.

**trousers** *(plural n)* a piece of clothing with two legs that covers the lower part of your body.

**trout trout** *(n)* an edible, freshwater fish.

**trowel** 1 *(n)* a tool with a small, curved blade used for planting and other light garden work. 2 *(n)* a tool with a flat, diamond-shaped blade, used for laying cement, filling holes in plaster, etc.

**truant** 1 *(n)* a pupil who stays away from school without permisssion. **truancy** *(n)*. 2 If pupils **play truant**, they stay away from school without permission.

**truce** *(n)* a temporary agreement to stop fighting.

**truck** 1 *(n)* a large motor vehicle used for carrying goods by road. *An articulated truck.* 2 *(n)* a large container used for carrying goods by rail.

**trudge trudging trudged** *(v)* to walk slowly and heavily. *We trudged through the mud in search of the farmhouse.*

**true truer truest** *(adj)* accurate, or correct. **truly** *(adv)*.

**truncheon** *(n)* a thick, rounded stick that is used by the police in violent situations.

**trundle trundling trundled** 1 *(v)* to move along on wheels or rollers. *The trucks trundled along the track.* 2 *(v)* to walk without hurrying. *Marcus trundled to school.*

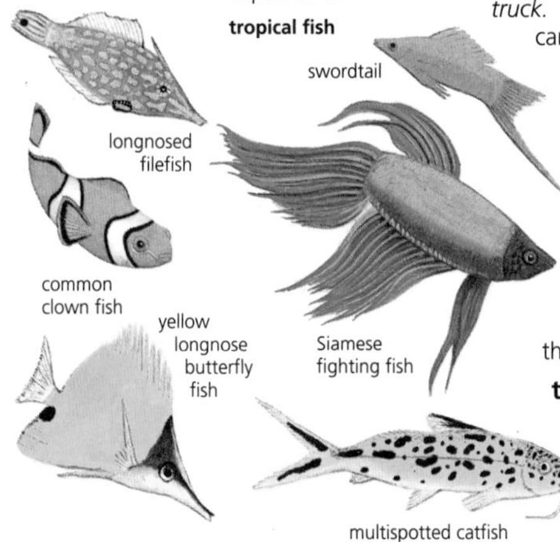


**tropical fish**

**trunk** 1 *(n)* the main stem of a tree. 2 *(n)* a large case or box, used for storage or for carrying clothes on a long journey. 3 *(n)* the long nose of an elephant. 4 **trunks** *(plural n)* close-fitting shorts worn by men or boys for swimming.

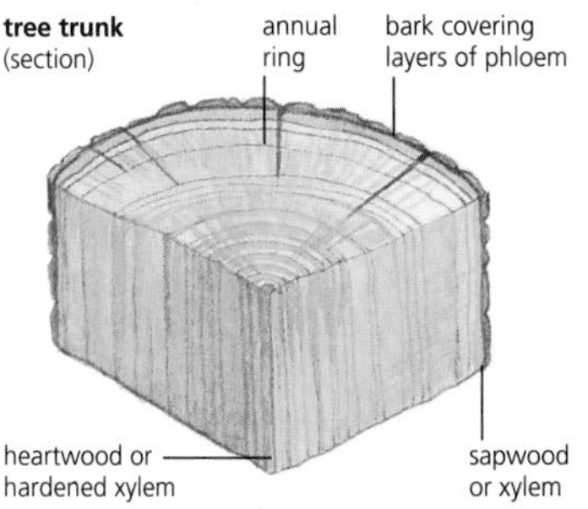


**trust** trusting trusted *(v)* If you **trust** someone, you believe that they are honest and reliable. **trust** *(n)*.

**trustworthy** *(adj)* honest, reliable, and able to be trusted. **trustworthiness** *(n)*.

**truth** *(n)* the real facts. **truthful** *(adj)*, **truthfully** *(adv)*.

**try** tries trying tried 1 *(v)* to attempt to do something, or to do the best you can. **try** *(n)*. 2 *(v)* to examine someone accused of a criminal offence in a court of law.

**trying** *(adj)* If a person is **trying**, they make you feel annoyed and impatient.

**tub** 1 *(n)* a plastic container used for storing foods. 2 *(n) (old-fashioned)* a large, wide container, used for bathing in, or for washing clothes.

**tubby** tubbier tubbiest *(adj)* Tubby people are short and slightly fat. **tubbiness** *(n)*.

**tube** 1 *(n)* a long, hollow cylinder. 2 **the tube** *(n)* the nickname for London's underground railway system.

**tuck** tucking tucked 1 *(v)* to fold or push something into a restricted space. *Tuck in your shirt.* 2 *(n)* a small fold sewn in material. 3 *(v) (informal)* If you **tuck in** to your food, you eat it enthusiastically. 4 **tuck shop** *(n)* a shop where sweets, crisps, chocolate, etc. are sold.

**tuft** *(n)* an upright bunch of hair, grass, feathers, etc. **tufted** *(adj)*.

**tug** tugging tugged 1 *(v)* to pull hard. **tug** *(n)*. 2 **tug** *or* **tug boat** *(n)* a small, powerful boat that tows large ships. 3 **tug of war** *(n)* a contest between two teams, each at one end of a rope, who try to pull each other over a centre line.

**tuition** *(tew-**ish**-un) (n)* training or teaching, often given to a single person or to a small group.

**tumble** tumbling tumbled 1 *(v)* to fall, often with a rolling motion. 2 **tumble dryer** *(n)* a machine which dries clothes by tossing them around in hot air.

**tumbler** *(n)* a tall glass with straight sides.

**tumour** *(n)* a swelling or lump caused by the abnormal growth of a mass of cells.

**tummy** tummies *(n) (informal)* your stomach.

**tumult** *(n)* loud noise and confusion. *The tumult of the battle.* **tumultuous** *(adj)*.

**tuna** tuna *or* tunas *(n)* a large, edible sea fish.

**tune** tuning tuned 1 *(n)* a series of musical notes, arranged in a pattern. 2 *(v)* to adjust a radio, the pitch of a musical instrument, etc. 3 **in tune** producing the right notes. *Can you sing in tune?*

**tunic** *(n)* a loose, sleeveless garment.

**tuning fork** *(n)* a piece of metal with two prongs, which always makes the same note when struck.

**tunnel** *(n)* an underground passage.

**turban** *(n)* a man's headdress, made from a long cloth wound round the head.

**turbine** *(n)* an engine driven by water, steam, wind, or gas which passes through the blades of a wheel and makes it turn.

**turbulent** *(adj)* wild, confused, or unpredictable. *Turbulent waters.*

**turf** *(n)* the surface layer of grass and earth on a lawn or sports pitch.

**turkey** *(n)* a large, flightless bird, usually reared for its meat.

**wild turkey**

**turmoil** *(n)* violent confusion. *The class was in turmoil.*

**turn turning turned 1** *(v)* to change direction. *Turn left at the junction.* **turn** *(n).* **2** *(v)* to spin, or to revolve. *Turn the wheel.* **3** *(v)* to change appearance or state. *Liquid turns into a vapour when it is heated.* **4** *(v)* to move a switch, tap, etc, in order to control the supply of something. *Turn up the volume.* **5** *(n)* If it is your **turn** to do something, it is your chance or duty to do it. **6** *(n)* A **good turn** is a helpful action. **7 turn down** *(v)* If you **turn something down**, you refuse it. **8** *(v)* If someone **turns up**, they appear.

**turnip** *(n)* a round, white root vegetable.

**turnstile** *(n)* a revolving gate that only turns one way, and controls admission to a sports ground, theme park, etc.

**turntable** *(n)* a circular, revolving surface.

**turquoise** *(tur-kwoyz)* *(n)* a bluish-green colour. **turquoise** *(adj).*

**turtle** *(n)* a water reptile with flippers and a large shell.

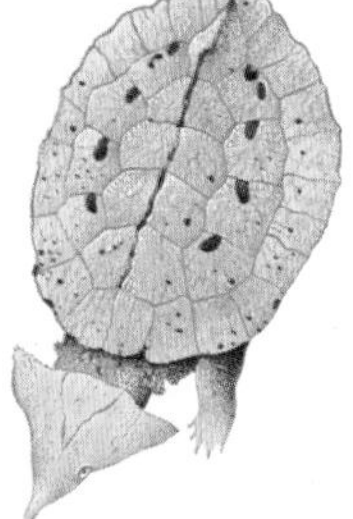
**matamata turtle**

**tusk** *(n)* one of the pair of long, curved, pointed teeth of an elephant, walrus, etc.

**tussle tussling tussled** *(v)* to fight or wrestle vigorously. **tussle** *(n).*

**tutor** *(n)* a teacher, usually one who teaches people individually or in small groups. **tutorial** *(n).*

**tutu** *(n)* a short ballet skirt made of several stiff layers of net.

**TV** *short for* **television**.

**tweezers** *(plural n)* small pincers used for pulling out hairs or for picking up very small objects.

**twice** *(adv)* two times.

**twig** *(n)* a small, thin branch.

**twilight** *(n)* the time of day when the Sun has just set and it is getting dark.

**twin 1** *(n)* one of two children born to the same mother at almost the same time. **2** *(adj)* one of a matching pair. *Twin beds.* **3** If a town is **twinned** with a town in another country, the two towns exchange visits and organize events together.

**twinge** *(twinj)* *(n)* a sudden pain or unpleasant feeling. *A twinge of arthritis. A twinge of regret.*

**twinkle twinkling twinkled** *(v)* to shine and sparkle. *The stars twinkle in the sky.* **twinkle** *(n).*

**twirl twirling twirled** *(v)* to turn or spin round and round. **twirl** *(n).*

**twist twisting twisted 1** *(v)* to turn, or to bend. *Rod twisted the top off the jar. The road twisted through the mountains.* **2** *(v)* to wind two strands of something together.

**twitch twitches twitching twitched** *(v)* to make small, jerky movements.

**type typing typed 1** *(n)* a kind, or a sort. *What type of car do you have?* **2** *(v)* to write something using a typewriter or computer. **typist** *(n).*

**typewriter** *(n)* a machine that prints letters and numbers when you press keys with your fingers.

**typhoon** *(ty-foon)* *(n)* a violent, tropical storm.

**typical 1** *(adj)* Something that is **typical** has the usual features that you associate with that kind of thing. *A typical English village.* **2** *(adj)* If someone does something that is **typical**, they behave in their usual way. *It's typical of Toby to be late!*

**tyrant** *(n)* someone who rules other people in a cruel and unkind way.

**tyre** *(n)* a circle of rubber around the rim of a wheel. Tyres are usually filled with air.

**bicycle tyre**
(cutaway)

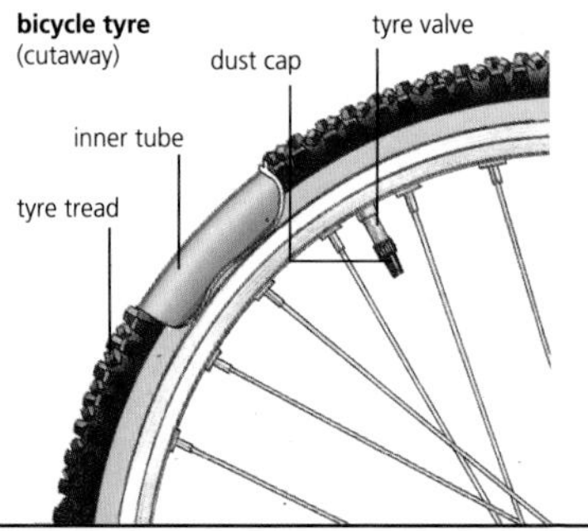

# Uu

**udder** *(n)* the bag-like part of a cow, sheep, etc. that hangs down near its back legs and produces milk.

**UFO** *(n)* a strange object in the sky, that some people believe is an alien spaceship. UFO is short for unidentified flying object.

**ugly** **uglier** **ugliest** *(adj)* unattractive and unpleasant to look at.

**ulcer** *(ul-ser)* *(n)* a sore area on your skin, or inside your mouth or stomach.

**ultimate** **1** *(adj)* last, or final. **2** *(adj)* original, or basic. *The Sun is the ultimate source of Earth's energy.* **3** *(n)* the greatest, or the best. *The ultimate in style.*

**ultimatum** *(n)* a final warning.

**ultraviolet light** *(n)* light which is given off by the Sun and makes your skin tan.

**umbrella** *(n)* a frame covered in cloth that you use to protect you from the rain.

**umpire** *(n)* someone who makes sure that a cricket or tennis match is played according to rules.

**unable** *(adj)* If you are **unable** to do something, you cannot do it.

**unacceptable** *(adj)* not good enough to be accepted or allowed.

**unaccustomed** *(adj)* If you are **unaccustomed** to something, you are not used to it.

**unaided** *(adj)* without any help.

**unanimous** *(you-nan-im-uss)* *(adj)* agreed by everyone. *A unanimous decision.*

**unapproachable** *(adj)* Someone who is **unapproachable** is not friendly, or is not easy to get to know.

**unauthorized** *or* **unauthorised** *(adj)* done without official permission.

**unavoidable** *(adj)* impossible to prevent.

**unaware** *(adj)* If you are **unaware** of something, you do not know that it exists or is happening.

**unbalanced** **1** *(adj)* Something that is **unbalanced** cannot balance and falls over. **2** *(adj)* slightly mad.

**unbearable** *(adj)* If something is **unbearable**, it is so bad or unpleasant that you cannot stand it.

**unbelievable** *(adj)* If something is **unbelievable**, it is so strange, surprising, or wonderful that you find it hard to accept that it is true.

**unburden** **unburdening** **unburdened** *(v)* If you **unburden** yourself, you get rid of a load or a worry.

**uncanny** *(adj)* very strange, and difficult to explain or understand. **uncannily** *(adv).*

**uncertain** *(adj)* not sure.

**uncivilized** *or* **uncivilised** **1** *(adj)* not yet civilized or educated. *An uncivilized tribe.* **2** *(adj)* rude and rough.

**uncle** *(n)* the brother of your father or mother, or the husband of your aunt.

**uncomfortable** **1** *(adj)* not feeling relaxed in your body or your mind. **2** *(adj)* making you feel uneasy or unhappy. *An uncomfortable situation.*

**unconscious** *(adj)* not awake, or unable to see, hear, think, etc. because you have fainted or been knocked out.

**uncontrollable** *(adj)* impossible to stop or control. **uncontrollably** *(adv).*

**uncooperative** *(adj)* refusing to help people or do things for them.

**uncouth** *(adj)* rough or rude.

**uncover** **uncovering** **uncovered** **1** *(v)* to take a cover off something. **2** *(v)* to reveal something. *Zak uncovered a wicked plot.*

**undecided** *(adj)* If you are **undecided** about something, you have not made up your mind about it.

**undeniable** *(adj)* Something that is **undeniable** is certainly true.

**under** **1** *(prep)* below or beneath something. *The key is under the doormat.* **2** *(prep)* less than a number or amount. *Children under 12 will not be admitted.*

**underarm** *(adv)* throwing with your arm swinging under your shoulder.

**underdog** *(n)* a person or team that is expected to be the loser.

**underestimate** **underestimating** **underestimated** *(v)* to think that something is not as good or as great as it really is. *Jonathan underestimates his sister's talents.*

**underfoot** *(adv)* under your feet, or on the ground. *It's slippery underfoot.*

**undergo** undergoes undergoing underwent undergone *(v)* to experience or suffer something. *Dan underwent a serious operation.*

**underground** 1 *(adj)* below the ground. 2 *(adj)* secret and often illegal. *An underground organization.* 3 *(n)* a railway system with trains that travel through tunnels. *The London Underground.*

**undergrowth** *(n)* bushes and plants that grow in a thick mass under trees.

**underline** underlining underlined *(v)* to draw a line under a word or sentence.

**undermine** undermining undermined *(v)* to weaken something gradually.

**underneath** *(prep)* under or below something. **underneath** *(adj).*

**underpass** underpasses *(n)* a road or path that passes underneath a road.

**underprivileged** *(adj)* poor and lacking the opportunities that most people have.

**understand** understanding understood 1 *(v)* to know what something means or how something works. *Luke understands engines.* 2 *(v)* to know what someone is like and why they behave in the way that they do.

**understandable** 1 *(adj)* easy to grasp or understand. 2 *(adj)* easy to sympathize with. *It's understandable that Jo is upset.*

**undertake** undertaking undertook undertaken *(v)* If you **undertake** something, you agree to do it. **undertaking** *(n).*

**undertaker** *(n)* someone whose job is to arrange funerals.

**underwater** *(adj)* living or happening under the surface of water.

**underworld** 1 *(n)* the secret world of criminals. 2 *(n)* In legends, the **Underworld** is the place where the spirits of dead people live.

**undeveloped** 1 *(adj)* An **undeveloped** country is poor and does not have many industries. 2 *(adj)* **Undeveloped** land does not have buildings on it.

**undo** undoes undoing undid undone 1 *(v)* to untie or unfasten something. 2 *(v)* to remove or destroy something's effects.

**undress** undresses undressing undressed *(v)* to take off your clothes.

**unearth** unearthing unearthed *(v)* to dig something up.

**uneasy** *(adj)* slightly worried or unhappy.

**unemployed** *(adj)* Someone who is **unemployed** does not have a paid job. **unemployment** *(n).*

**uneven** 1 *(adj)* not flat, or not smooth. 2 *(adj)* not regular, or not consistent. *An uneven essay.* **unevenly** *(adj).*

**uneventful** *(adj)* not interesting, or not exciting.

**unexpected** *(adj)* Something that is **unexpected** is surprising because you did not think it would happen.

**unfair** unfairer unfairest *(adj)* not reasonable, or not right. **unfairly** *(adv).*

**unfamiliar** 1 *(adj)* not well known, or not easily recognized. *Unfamiliar people.* 2 If you are **unfamiliar with** something, you do not know it well.

**unfit** 1 *(adj)* not healthy, or not strong. 2 *(adj)* not suitable, or not good enough.

**unfold** unfolding unfolded 1 *(v)* to open something that was folded. *I unfolded the letter.* 2 *(v)* When a story or plan **unfolds**, more of it becomes known.

**unforgettable** *(adj)* so good, bad, etc. that you will never forget it.

**unforgivable** *(adj)* impossible to forgive.

**unfortunate** *(adj)* unlucky. *An unfortunate accident.*

**unfriendly** unfriendlier unfriendliest *(adj)* unkind, or unhelpful.

**ungrateful** *(adj)* If you are **ungrateful** for something, you are not thankful for it and do not appreciate it.

**unhappy** unhappier unhappiest *(adj)* miserable, or upset. **unhappiness** *(n).*

**unhealthy** unhealthier unhealthiest 1 *(adj)* unfit, or not well. 2 *(adj)* bad for your health. *An unhealthy diet.*

**unhygienic** *(adj)* unclean, and not free from germs. *An unhygienic kitchen.*

**unicorn** *(n)* an imaginary animal like a horse with a horn on its forehead.

**unicycle** *(n)* a cycle with only one wheel.

**unidentified** *(adj)* If something is **unidentified**, no one knows what it is.

**uniform** *(n)* a special set of clothes worn by all the members of a school, army, or organization. **uniformed** *(adj).*

**unimportant** *(adj)* Something that is **unimportant** will not have a great effect and does not need to be taken seriously.

**uninhabited** *(adj)* If a place is **uninhabited**, no one lives there.

**unintelligible** *(adj)* impossible to understand. **unintelligibly** *(adv).*

**unintentional** *(adj)* done by accident, or not deliberate. **unintentionally** *(adv).*

**uninterested** *(adj)* If you are **uninterested** in something, you do not want to know about it.

**union** *(n)* an organized group of workers set up to help improve work conditions.

**unique** *(you-**neek**)* *(adj)* If something is **unique**, it is the only one of its kind.

**unisex** *(adj)* able to be used by both men and women. *Unisex clothing.*

**unison** *(n)* If people say or do something **in unison**, they say or do it together.

**unit** 1 *(n)* a single, complete thing. 2 *(n)* an amount used as a standard of measurement. *A gram is a unit of weight.*

**unite uniting united** *(v)* to join together or work together to achieve something.

**universal** *(adj)* applying to everyone or everything. *This film has universal appeal.*

**universe** *(n)* everything in space, including the Earth, Sun, Moon, and stars.

**university universities** *(n)* a place where people study for degrees and do research.

**unjust** *(adj)* not fair, or not right.

**unkind unkinder unkindest** *(adj)* unfriendly, unhelpful, and not generous.

**unknown** *(adj)* unfamiliar, or not known about. *An unknown planet.*

**unless** *(conj)* except, or if not. *I can't come unless someone gives me a lift.*

**unlike** *(prep)* If one thing is **unlike** another, the two things are very different.

**unlikely unlikelier unlikeliest** *(adj)* not probable.

**unlimited** *(adj)* If there is an **unlimited** amount of something, you can have or use as much of it as you want.

**unload unloading unloaded** *(v)* to remove things from a container or vehicle.

**unlock unlocking unlocked** *(v)* to unfasten something with a key.

**unlucky unluckier unluckiest** 1 *(adj)* Someone who is **unlucky** is unfortunate and bad things seem to happen to them. 2 *(adj)* Something that is **unlucky** happens by chance and is unfortunate.

**unmistakable** *(adj)* very individual and impossible to confuse with someone or something else.

**unnatural** 1 *(adj)* unusual, or not normal. *An unnatural sound.* 2 *(adj)* false, or not sincere. *Stan sounded unnatural.*

**unnecessary** *(adj)* not needed.

**unofficial** 1 *(adj)* not approved by someone in authority. *An unofficial report.* 2 *(adj)* informal. *An unofficial visit.*

**unpack unpacking unpacked** *(v)* to take objects out of a box, case, etc.

**unpleasant** *(adj)* horrible, or not likable.

**unpopular** *(adj)* not liked or enjoyed by many people.

**unpredictable** *(adj)* If something or someone is **unpredictable**, you do not know what they will do or say next.

**unprepared** *(adj)* not ready for something.

**unprovoked** *(adj)* not caused or encouraged by anyone.

**unravel unravelling unravelled** 1 *(v)* to unwind a tangled mass of string, wool, etc. 2 *(v)* to search for and discover the truth about a complex situation.

**unreasonable** *(adj)* not fair.

**unrecognizable** *or* **unrecognisable** *(adj)* If someone or something is **unrecognizable** they have totally changed so that you do not immediately know who or what they are.

**unreliable** *(adj)* impossible to trust or depend on.

**unrest** *(n)* disturbance and trouble.

**unrestricted** *(adj)* without rules or restrictions. *Unrestricted use of the pool.*

**unripe** *(adj)* not yet ready to be harvested, picked, or eaten.

**unrivalled** *(adj)* better than anything else.

**unruly unrulier unruliest** *(adj)* badly-behaved and disobedient.

**unscathed** *(adj)* not hurt. *The driver survived the crash unscathed.*

**unscrupulous** *(adj)* **Unscrupulous** people have few principles and are not concerned whether their actions are right or wrong. **unscrupulously** *(adv).*

**unseen** *(adj)* hidden, or not able to be seen.

**unsettle unsettling unsettled** *(v)* to disturb someone, or make them uneasy.

**unskilled** *(adj)* An **unskilled** worker has no particular skill or training.

**unstable** 1 *(adj)* not firm, or not steady. 2 *(adj)* An **unstable** person has rapid changes of mood and behaviour.

**unsteady** *(adj)* shaky, or wobbly.

**unstuck** *(adj)* no longer glued together.

**unsuccessful** *(adj)* If you are **unsuccessful**, you do not do well, or do not get what you want.

**unsuitable** *(adj)* not right for a particular purpose. *Unsuitable shoes for climbing.*

**unsure** *(adj)* not certain, or not definite.

**unthinkable** *(adj)* If something is **unthinkable**, it is out of the question and cannot be considered.

**untidy untidier untidiest** *(adj)* not neat.

**untie untying untied** *(v)* to undo knots and bows.

**until** *(conj)* up to the time that. *You can stay until tomorrow.*

**untold** *(adj)* too great to be counted or worked out. *Untold damage.*

**untouched** 1 *(adj)* not handled by anyone. 2 *(adj)* left alone, or ignored. *The thieves left the jewellery untouched.*

**untrue** *(adj)* false, or incorrect.

**unused** *(adj)* An **unused** item has never been used.

**unusual** *(adj)* strange, abnormal, or odd.

**unwanted** *(adj)* If something is **unwanted**, you do not need or want it.

**unwelcome** *(adj)* not gladly received or accepted.

**unwell** *(adj)* ill, or poorly.

**unwieldy** *(adj)* difficult to hold, or hard to manage. *An unwieldy parcel.*

**unwilling** *(adj)* reluctant, or not keen to do something. **unwillingly** *(adv).*

**unwind unwinding unwound** 1 *(v)* to undo something that has been wound up. 2 *(v)* to relax and become less worried.

**unworthy** *(adj)* not deserving, or below standard. *An unworthy gift.*

**unwrap unwrapping unwrapped** *(v)* to take the packaging or outer layer off something.

**upbeat** *(adj) (informal)* optimistic and cheerful.

**upbringing** *(n)* the way that a child is brought up or raised.

**update** *(n)* the latest information about something. **update** *(v).*

**upheaval** *(n)* a big change or disturbance.

**uphill** *(adj)* sloping upwards.

**uphold upholding upheld** *(v)* to support something that you believe to be right. *The appeal court upheld the verdict.*

**upholstery** *(n)* the stuffing, covering, etc. that is put on furniture.

**upon** *(adv)* on. *Look upon me as a sister.*

**upper** *(adj)* higher. *An upper window.*

**upper case** *(adj)* **Upper case** letters are capital letters.

**upright** 1 *(adj)* standing up, or standing straight. 2 *(adj)* honest and fair.

**uprising** *(n)* a rebellion, or a revolt.

**uproar** *(n)* shouting, noise, and confusion. *The lesson ended in uproar.*

**uproot uprooting uprooted** 1 *(v)* to take a plant out of the earth. 2 *(v)* to move someone from where they are settled in their home or work.

**upset upsetting upset** 1 *(v)* to make someone unhappy or distressed. **upset** *(adj).* 2 *(v)* to overturn something. *Sinead upset the milk.* 3 *(v)* to make someone feel ill. *Oysters always upset me.*

**upside down** 1 *(adv)* the wrong way up. 2 *(adv)* in a confused or untidy condition. *The thieves turned the place upside down.*

**upstairs** *(adv)* to or on a higher floor.

**up-to-date** *(adj)* containing the most recent information, or in the latest style.

**urban** *(adj)* to do with, or living in towns or cities. *Urban wildlife.*

**urge urging urged** 1 *(v)* to encourage or persuade someone strongly. *Joni's father* *urged her to try hard.* 2 *(n)* a strong wish or need to do something.

**urgent** *(adj)* If something is **urgent**, it needs very quick or immediate action. **urgency** *(n).*

**urine** *(yoor-in) (n)* the liquid waste that people and animals pass out of their bodies.

**urn** 1 *(n)* a vase used as an ornament or as a container for the ashes of a dead person. *The picture shows an urn made in Ancient Greece.* 2 *(n)* a large, insulated container used for serving tea or coffee.

**urn**

**usage** 1 *(n)* the way that something is used or treated. *Careless usage.* 2 *(n)* the way that a language is spoken and written. *English usage.*

**use** **using** **used** 1 *(yooz) (v)* to do a job with something. *I used a penknife to cut the string.* 2 *(yooce) (n)* the action of using something. *Put away the tools after use.* 3 **use up** *(yooz) (v)* If you **use something up**, there is nothing left of it.

**used** 1 *(yoozed) (adj)* already made use of. *A used car.* 2 *(yoost)* If you are **used to** something, you know it well. 3 *(yoost)* If you **used to do** something, you did it in the past.

**useful** *(yooce-ful) (adj)* Something that is **useful** is helpful and can be used a lot.

**useless** *(yooce-less)* 1 *(adj)* Something that is **useless** cannot be used or is not helpful. 2 *(adj) (informal)* not very good. *I'm useless at French.*

**usual** *(adj)* normal, or regular. **usually** *(adv).*

**utensil** *(n)* a tool or container, often one used in the kitchen.

**utmost** *(adj)* the most, or the greatest possible. *I'll do my utmost to help.*

**utter** **uttering** **uttered** 1 *(v)* to speak, or to make a sound with your mouth. *Petra uttered a moan.* 2 *(adj)* complete, total, or absolute. *An utter disaster.* **utterly** *(adv).*

**U-turn** 1 *(n)* a U-shaped turn made by a vehicle, to change its direction. 2 *(n)* a complete reversal of policy or attitude.

# Vv

**vacant** 1 *(adj)* empty, or not occupied. *A vacant house.* 2 *(adj)* available. *This job is vacant.* 3 *(adj)* If someone looks **vacant**, they have a blank expression on their face.

**vacate** **vacating** **vacated** *(v)* to leave, or to make somewhere empty. *Hotel guests should vacate their rooms by 10 a.m.*

**vacation** 1 *(n)* a break between university or college terms. 2 *(n)* an American word for a holiday.

**vaccinate** **vaccinating** **vaccinated** *(v)* to protect someone against a disease, usually by giving them an injection.

**vacuum** *(vak-yoom) (n)* a sealed space from which all air or gas has been emptied.

**vacuum cleaner** *(n)* a machine that sucks up dirt from carpets, furniture, etc.

**vacuum flask** *(n)* a container that keeps liquids hot or cold.

**vagina** *(vaj-eye-na) (n)* the passage leading from the womb, through which babies are born.

**vague** *(vayg)* **vaguer** **vaguest** *(adj)* not clear, or not definite. *Vague memories.*

**vain** **vainer** **vainest** 1 *(adj)* too proud of yourself, especially of the way that you look. 2 *(adj)* unsuccessful, or futile. *Bik made a vain attempt to stop the bus.*

**valiant** *(adj)* brave, or courageous.

**valid** 1 *(adj)* sensible and acceptable. *A valid reason.* **validity** *(n).* 2 *(adj)* acceptable, or legal. *A valid ticket.*

**valley** *(n)* an area of low ground between hills, usually containing a river.

**valour** *(n) (poetic)* bravery, or courage.

**valuable** 1 *(adj)* worth a lot of money or very important in some other way. *A valuable jewel. Valuable information.* 2 **valuables** *(plural n)* possessions that are worth a lot of money.

**value** **valuing** **valued** 1 *(n)* what something is worth. *What is the value of this watch?* 2 *(v)* to think that something is important. *I value Polly's friendship.*

**valve** *(n)* a type of tap that controls the flow of fluid, air, etc.

**vampire** *(n)* In folk tales and horror stories, a **vampire** is a corpse with fangs that rises from its grave to drink the blood of human victims.

**van** *(n)* a closed vehicle used for carrying goods. *A delivery van.*

**vandal** *(n)* someone who needlessly damages or destroys other people's property. **vandalism** *(n),* **vandalize** *(v).*

**vane** 1 *(n)* A **weather vane** is a pointer that swings around to show the direction of the wind. 2 *(n)* the flat part of a bird's feather.

**vanish vanishes vanishing vanished** *(v)* to disappear suddenly.

**vanity** *(n)* a feeling of extreme pride and conceit.

**vapour** *(n)* a gas, usually one that has been changed from a liquid or solid. *Water vapour is visible as clouds or steam.*

**variable** *(adj)* likely to change. *Variable weather.* **variability** *(n).*

**variation** *(n)* a change in something.

**variety varieties** 1 *(n)* a selection of different things. 2 *(n)* a different type of the same thing. *A new variety of rose.*

**various** 1 *(adj)* several. *I have various hobbies.* 2 *(adj)* different. *The cakes were many and various.*

**varnish varnishes** *(n)* a clear coating that you paint on wood to protect it and give it a shiny finish. **varnish** *(v).*

**vary varies varying varied** 1 *(v)* to change or be different. *Mimi's writing varies depending on her mood.* 2 *(v)* If you **vary** something, you make changes to it.

**vase** *(n)* an ornamental container, often used for flowers. *The picture shows an Art Deco vase.*

**vase**

**vast vaster vastest** *(adj)* huge in area or extent. *A vast desert. A vast fund of jokes.*

**VAT** *(n)* a tax added to the cost of many types of goods. The initials VAT stand for value-added tax.

**vault vaulting vaulted** 1 *(v)* to leap over something, using your hands or other support. **vault** *(n).* 2 *(n)* an underground burial chamber.

**VDU** *(n)* the screen of a computer and the keyboard connected to it. The initials VDU stand for visual display unit.

**veer veering veered** *(v)* to change direction. *The wind veered from east to north-east.*

**vegan** *(vee-gan)* *(n)* someone who does not use or eat any animal products.

**vegetable** *(n)* a plant grown to be used as food, usually eaten with savoury foods.

**vegetarian** *(n)* someone who does not eat meat or fish. **vegetarian** *(adj).*

**vegetation** *(n)* plant life of all types.

**vehement** *(vee-er-ment)* *(adj)* If you are **vehement** about something, you express your feelings about it very strongly.

**vehicle** *(vee-ik-ul)* *(n)* something in which people or goods are carried from one place to another.

**veil** *(vale)* *(n)* a fine piece of material worn by women to hide their faces.

**vein** *(vane)* *(n)* one of the tubes through which blood is carried back to the heart from other parts of the body.

**velocity** *(vel-oss-it-ee)* **velocities** *(n)* speed. *The rocket's velocity is 3,000mph.*

**velvet** *(n)* a soft, thick fabric made from cotton or silk. **velvety** *(adj).*

**vendetta** *(n)* a long-running feud between two families, gangs, etc.

**vending machine** *(n)* a coin-operated machine from which you can buy food, drink, or other products.

**venetian blind** *(n)* an indoor blind made from thin strips that can be tilted to alter the amount of light coming in.

**vengeance** *(n)* action that you take to pay someone back for harm they have done to you or your friends or family.

**venom** *(n)* poison produced by some snakes and spiders and injected through their fangs into their victims' bodies.

**ventilate ventilating ventilated** *(v)* to allow fresh air into a place and to send stale air out. **ventilation** *(n).*

**ventriloquism** *(n)* the art of speaking without moving your lips so that your words seem to come from somewhere else, such as a dummy. **ventriloquist** *(n).*

**venture** **venturing** **ventured** *(v)* to put yourself at risk by doing something daring or dangerous. **venture** *(n).*

**venue** *(ven-yoo) (n)* a place where an event is held.

**veranda** *or* **verandah** *(n)* a raised platform around the outside of a house, often with a roof.

**verb** *(n)* a word that describes what someone or something does, thinks, or feels. "Run", "have", and "dream" are all verbs. *See* page 3.

**verbal** 1 *(adj)* to do with words. *A verbal reasoning test.* 2 *(adj)* spoken. *Verbal abuse.* 3 *(adj)* to do with verbs.

**verdict** *(n)* the decision of a judge or jury on whether someone is guilty or not.

**verge** 1 *(n)* the land at the side of a road 2 If you are **on the verge** of doing something, you will do it soon.

**verify** **verifies** **verifying** **verified** *(v)* to confirm, or to back up. *Roberta verified what the witness said.* **verification** *(n).*

**verruca** *(ver-oo-ker)* **verrucae** *or* **verrucas** *(n)* a small, sometimes painful growth, usually on the sole of the foot.

**versatile** *(adj)* talented or useful in many ways. *A versatile person. A versatile tool.*

**verse** 1 *(n)* one part of a poem or song, made up of several lines. 2 *(n)* a general name for poetry.

**version** 1 *(n)* one way of expressing something. *Holly gave her version of the story.* 2 *(n)* a revised form or model of a book, car, piece of software, etc.

**versus** *(prep)* against. *Today's match is USA versus Canada.*

**vertebra** **vertebrae** *(n)* one of the bones that make up your spine.

**vertical** *(adj)* upright and perpendicular to the ground. *A vertical post.*

**very** 1 *(adv)* to a great extent, much, or most. *I am very pleased.* 2 *(adv)* exact. *You're the very person I wanted to see.*

**vessel** 1 *(n)* a general name for a ship. 2 *(n) (old-fashioned)* a container for liquids.

**vet** *(n)* someone trained to treat sick animals. Vet is short for veterinary surgeon.

**veteran** *(n)* someone with a lot of experience of something.

**veterinary** 1 *(adj)* to do with the treatment of animals. 2 **veterinary surgeon** *see* **vet**.

**veto** *(vee-toe)* **vetoes** **vetoing** **vetoed** *(v)* If someone **vetoes** a plan, they use their power to put a stop to it. **veto** *(n).*

**via** *(prep)* by way of. *This train goes to Edinburgh via York.*

**viable** *(adj)* workable, or capable of succeeding. *A viable plan.* **viability** *(n).*

**viaduct** *(n)* a large bridge that carries a railway or road across a valley.

**vibrant** *(adj)* bright, or lively. *Vibrant colours. A vibrant personality.*

**vibrate** **vibrating** **vibrated** *(v)* to shake rapidly. **vibration** *(n).*

**vicar** *(n)* a priest in the Church of England.

**vicarage** *(n)* a vicar's house.

**vice** *(n)* immoral or criminal behaviour.

**vice captain** *(n)* a deputy who helps the captain and takes over duties when the captain is unable to act.

**vice president** *(n)* a deputy who helps the president and takes over duties when the president is unable to act.

**vice versa** *(adv)* a Latin phrase meaning "the other way round". *You help me and vice versa.*

**vicinity** *(vis-in-it-ee)* **vicinities** *(n)* the area near a particular place. *Police sealed off all the roads in the vicinity of the robbery.*

**vicious** *(adj)* bad-tempered, aggressive, and violent. **viciousness** *(n).*

**victim** *(n)* someone who suffers or is killed because of something or someone else.

**victimize** *or* **victimise** **victimized** **victimizing** *(v)* to pick someone out for unfair treatment. **victimization** *(n).*

**victor** *(n)* the winner.

**victory** **victories** *(n)* a win in a battle or contest. **victorious** *(adj).*

**video** **videoing** **videoed** 1 *(v)* to record sound and pictures on to a tape. 2 *(n)* a machine for playing video tapes. 3 *(n)* a pre-recorded video tape.

**vie** **vying** **vied** *(v)* If you **vie with** someone, you compete with them. *The brothers vied for attention.*

**view** **viewing viewed** 1 *(n)* what you can see from a certain place. *The view from my window.* 2 *(n)* what you think about something. *My views on whaling.*

**vigilant** *(adj)* watchful and alert.

**vigorous** *(adj)* energetic, lively, or forceful. *Vigorous exercise.* **vigour** *(n).*

**Viking** *(n)* one of the Scandinavian peoples who invaded England and parts of northern Europe between the 8th and 11th centuries.

**vile** **viler vilest** *(adj)* horrible and disgusting. **vileness** *(n).*

**villa** 1 *(n)* In Ancient Roman times, a **villa** was a country house, usually built around a courtyard and including farm buildings. 2 *(n)* a large house set in a garden, usually in Mediterranean countries.

**village** *(n)* a small group of houses and other buildings in the countryside.

**villain** *(n)* a wicked person, often an evil character in a play. **villainous** *(adj).*

**vindictive** *(adj)* unforgiving, and wanting revenge. **vindictiveness** *(n).*

**vine** *(n)* a climbing plant on which grapes grow.

**vinegar** *(n)* a sour-tasting liquid, used to flavour food.

**vineyard** *(vin-yard)* *(n)* an area of farmland where grapes are grown.

**violate** **violating violated** 1 *(v)* to break a promise, a rule, or a law. 2 *(v)* to treat a person or a place with no respect.

**violence** *(n)* the use of physical force to hurt or kill. **violent** *(adj),* **violently** *(adv).*

**violin** *(n)* a musical instrument with four strings, played with a bow.

**VIP** *(n)* a famous or important person. VIP stands for very important person.

**viper** *(n)* an adder.

**virgin** *(n)* someone who has never had sexual intercourse.

**virtually** *(adv)* nearly, or almost. *We have virtually finished.* **virtual** *(adj).*

**virtual reality** *(n)* an environment created by a computer which seems real to the person who experiences it.

**virtue** *(n)* a good quality. *Patience is a virtue.* **virtuous** *(adj).*

**virulent** *(adj)* very severe or harmful.

**virus** **viruses** 1 *(n)* an organism that multiplies in body cells, often causing disease. *See* **AIDS**. 2 *(n)* the disease caused by a virus. 3 *(n)* hidden instructions within a computer program, designed to damage data or destroy a system.

**visa** *(vee-zer)* *(n)* a document allowing someone to enter a foreign country.

**visible** *(n)* able to be seen. **visibility** *(n).*

**vision** 1 *(n)* sight. 2 *(n)* something you see in a dream or a trance, which is often strange or beautiful.

**visit** **visiting visited** *(v)* to go to see people or places. **visit** *(n),* **visitor** *(n).*

**visual** *(adj)* to do with seeing. *A visual guide.* **visually** *(adv).*

**visualize** *or* **visualise** **visualizing visualized** *(v)* to picture something, or to see something in your mind.

**vital** *(adj)* essential, or absolutely necessary. **vitally** *(adv).*

**vitality** *(n)* energy and liveliness.

**vitamin** *(n)* one of the substances in food that is necessary for good health.

**vivid** *(adj)* very bright, clear, or realistic. *A vivid dream. Vivid colours.* **vividly** *(adv).*

**vivisection** *(n)* the use of live animals for scientific and medical research.

**vocabulary** **vocabularies** *(n)* the range of words that a person uses and understands. *Caspar has a very wide vocabulary.*

**vocal** 1 *(adj)* to do with the voice. 2 *(adj)* If someone is **vocal** they are outspoken and often express their opinions. **vocally** *(adv).* 3 *(plural n)* On a tape, CD, etc. the **vocals** are the parts that are sung.

**vocalist** *(n)* a singer.

**vocation** 1 *(n)* a strong feeling that you want to do a particular job. 2 *(n)* a job or profession, especially one that needs special training. **vocational** *(adj).*

**vociferous** *(vo-**sif**-er-us)* *(adj)* If someone is **vociferous**, they are noisy and talkative and insist on being heard.

**voice** 1 *(n)* the power to speak and sing. 2 *(n)* the sound produced when you speak and sing. *A high voice.*

**void** 1 *(n)* an empty space. *The spaceship careered into the void.* 2 *(adj)* If a result is **void**, it does not count.

**volcano** volcanoes *(n)* a mountain with vents through which molten lava, ash, cinders, and gas erupt, sometimes violently. *The picture shows a cutaway view of an erupting volcano.*

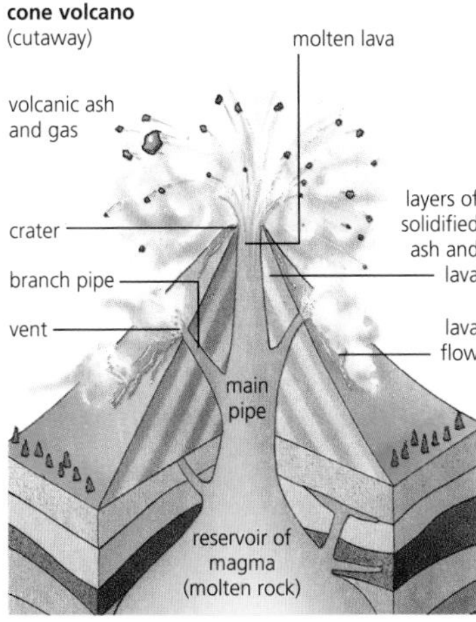


**volume** 1 *(n)* the amount of space taken up by a three-dimensional shape, such as a box or room. 2 *(n)* the degree of sound produced by something. 3 *(n)* a large book, often one of a series.

**voluntary** *(adj)* willing and unforced. *A voluntary decision.*

**volunteer** volunteering volunteered *(v)* to offer to do a job. volunteer *(n).*

**vomit** vomiting vomited *(v)* When you **vomit**, you bring up food from your stomach through your mouth. **vomit** *(n).*

**vote** voting voted *(v)* to make a choice in an election or other poll, usually by marking a paper or raising your hand. **vote** *(n).*

**voucher** *(n)* a piece of paper which can be exchanged for goods or services.

**vowel** *(n)* one of the letters a, e, i, o, and u. Y is also a vowel in words like gym, but a consonant in words like yo-yo.

**voyage** *(n)* a sea journey. **voyager** *(n).*

**vulgar** *(adj)* rude, or coarse.

**vulnerable** *(adj)* If someone or something is **vulnerable**, they are in a weak position and likely to be hurt or damaged in some way.

**wad** *(wod) (n)* a thick pad, or bundle. *A wad of banknotes.*

**waddle** waddling waddled *(v)* to walk awkwardly, swaying from side to side.

**wade** wading waded *(v)* to walk through water.

**wafer** *(n)* a thin, light, crispy biscuit.

**waffle** waffling waffled 1 *(n)* a type of square pancake. 2 *(v) (informal)* to speak in a long-winded, rambling way.

**wag** wagging wagged *(v)* to move something from side to side.

**wage** waging waged 1 wage *or* wages *(n)* the money someone is paid for their work. 2 *(v)* If you **wage** a campaign or war, you start it and carry on with it.

**waggle** waggling waggled *(v)* to move from side to side.

**wagon** 1 *(n)* a horse-drawn cart. 2 *(n)* a railway truck.

**wail** wailing wailed *(v)* to let out a long cry of sadness or distress. **wail** *(n).*

**waist** *(n)* the middle part of your body, between your hips and your ribs, where your body narrows.

**waistcoat** *(n)* a short, light, sleeveless jacket, worn over a shirt.

**wait** waiting waited 1 *(v)* to pause, or to stop doing something for a period of time. 2 *(v)* If you **wait** on someone, you serve them food and drink in a restaurant.

**waiter** *(n)* a man who serves people with food and drink in a restaurant or bar.

**waitress** *(n)* a woman who serves people with food and drink in a restaurant or bar.

**wake** waking woke woken 1 *(v)* to become fully conscious after being asleep. 2 *(v)* to rouse someone from their sleep.

**walk** walking walked 1 *(v)* to move along on your feet. **walker** *(n).* 2 *(n)* a journey on foot.

**walkover** *(n) (informal)* a very easy victory in a sports match.

**wall** *(n)* a solid structure that separates two areas or supports a roof.

*Some words that begin with a "w" sound are spelt with a "wh".*

**wallaby** wallabies *(n)* a small type of kangaroo.

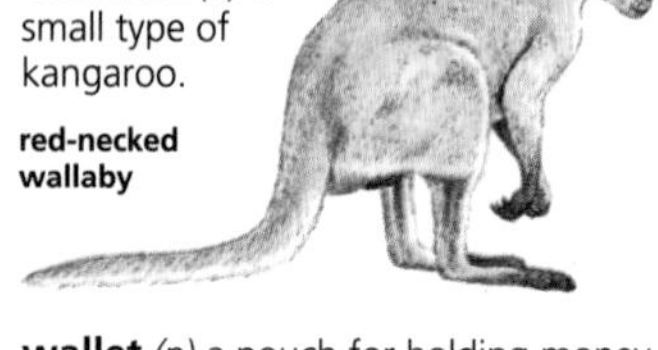
**red-necked wallaby**

**wallet** *(n)* a pouch for holding money, usually made of leather.

**wallop** walloping walloped *(v)* *(informal)* to hit someone very hard.

**wallow** wallowing wallowed 1 *(v)* to roll about in mud or water. 2 *(v)* If you **wallow** in something, you enjoy it a lot.

**walrus** walruses *(n)* a large sea animal from the Arctic, with tusks and flippers.

**walruses**

**wand** *(rhymes with pond)* *(n)* a thin stick that is supposed to have magical powers.

**wander** wandering wandered 1 *(v)* to walk around without going in any particular direction. **wander** *(n)*. 2 *(v)* to move around. *Don't let your eyes wander.*

**wane** waning waned 1 *(v)* to get smaller or less. *Jem's enthusiasm is waning.* 2 *(v)* When the Moon **wanes**, it appears to get smaller. *See* **moon**.

**wangle** wangling wangled *(v)* *(informal)* to gain something by crafty or dishonest methods. *I wangled free tickets.*

**want** wanting wanted 1 *(v)* to feel that you would like something. *I want a chocolate.* 2 *(v)* to need something. *You want a good meal.*

**war** 1 *(n)* fighting between opposing forces. 2 *(n)* a struggle against something. *A war against hunger.*

**ward** *(n)* a large room in a hospital where patients are looked after.

**wardrobe** 1 *(n)* a tall cupboard used for storing clothes. 2 *(n)* a collection of clothes or theatrical costumes.

**warehouse** *(n)* a large building used for storing goods.

**warfare** *(n)* a general term for the fighting of wars. *Jungle warfare.*

**warlike** *(adj)* hostile, aggressive, or likely to start a war.

**warm** warmer warmest 1 *(adj)* fairly hot. **warmth** *(n)*. 2 *(v)* to increase the temperature of something. 3 *(adj)* very friendly. *A warm welcome.* **warmth** *(n)*.

**warm-blooded** *(adj)* **Warm-blooded** animals have a body temperature that remains approximately the same, whatever their surroundings.

**warn** warning warned *(v)* to tell someone about a danger or a bad thing that might happen. **warning** *(n)*.

**warp** warping warped *(v)* to twist or bend because of heat or damp.

**warrant** *(n)* an official piece of paper that gives permission for something.

**warren** *(n)* a group of underground tunnels where rabbits live.

**warrior** *(n)* a soldier, or someone who fights.

**wart** *(rhymes with port)* *(n)* a small, hard lump on your skin. **warty** *(adj)*.

**wary** warier wariest *(adj)* cautious and careful. *Desmond is always very wary of dogs.* **wariness** *(n)*.

**wash** washes washing washed 1 *(v)* to clean something with water, soap, etc. **wash** *(n)*. 2 *(v)* When you **wash up**, you clean the plates, cutlery, etc. after a meal.

**washable** *(adj)* If a material is **washable**, you can wash it without damaging it.

**washer** *(n)* a plastic or metal ring that fits under a bolt or screw to give a tighter fit or to prevent a leak.

**washing** 1 *(n)* clothes that are going to be washed, or have been washed. 2 **washing-up** *(n)* the plates, cutlery, etc. that need cleaning after a meal.

**wasp** *(n)* a flying insect that has black and yellow stripes and can sting.

**waste** wasting wasted *(v)* If you **waste** something, you use it wrongly or throw it away when you do not need to. *Don't waste your time.* **waste** *(n)*.

**wasteful** *(adj)* If you are **wasteful**, you use things up needlessly and do not think about saving them. **wastefulness** *(n)*.

*Some words that begin with a "w" sound are spelt "wh".*

**wasteland** *(n)* land that is not used for anything.

**watch** watches watching watched 1 *(n)* a small clock, usually worn on your wrist. 2 *(v)* to look at something. 3 *(v)* to notice, or to be careful about something. *Watch what you're doing with that knife!*

**water** watering watered 1 *(n)* a colourless liquid that you can drink. 2 *(v)* to pour water on something. *Water the plants.* 3 *(v)* If your mouth **waters**, you see or smell food and feel hungry. 4 *(v)* If your eyes **water**, tears come from them.

**watercolours** *(plural n)* paints that are mixed with water, not oil.

**water cycle** *(n)* the constant movement of the Earth's water. Water evaporates from rivers, oceans, and plants, making water vapour. The vapour rises, forms clouds and falls as rain, hail, or snow. Some water enters plants and soil and the rest runs off into rivers and oceans.

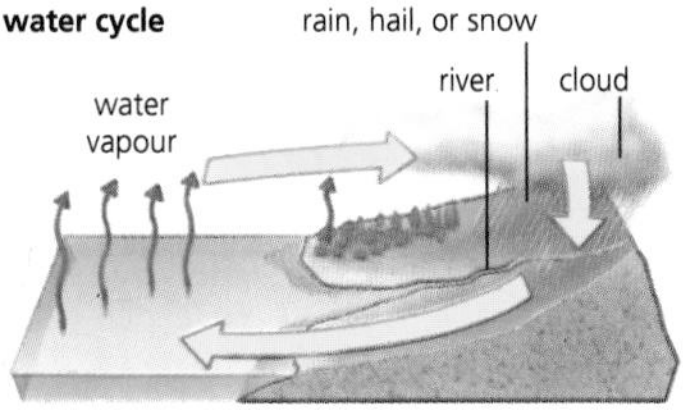

**waterfall** *(n)* water from a stream or river that falls down over rocks.

**waterlogged** *(adj)* completely flooded or filled with water. *Waterlogged ground.*

**water main** *(n)* a large supply pipe that carries water under the ground.

**watermark** *(n)* a mark in paper that you can see when you hold it up to the light.

**waterproof** *(adj)* keeping water out. *A waterproof coat.*

**water-ski** water-skiing water-skied *(v)* to travel on skis over water, towed by a boat. **water-skier** *(n)*, **water-skiing** *(n)*.

**watertight** *(adj)* completely sealed so that water cannot enter or escape.

**water vapour** *(n)* the gas produced when water evaporates.

**wave** waving waved 1 *(v)* to move your hand, for example when you are saying hello or goodbye to someone. **wave** *(n)*. 2 *(v)* to move something from side to side in the air. *The fairy godmother waved her wand.* **wave** *(n)*. 3 *(n)* a moving ridge on the surface of water, especially the sea. 4 *(n)* a curl in your hair. **wavy** *(adj)*. 5 *(n)* a vibration of energy that travels through air or water, for example, sound waves or radio waves.

**wavelength** 1 *(n)* the distance between one wave of light, sound, etc. and another. 2 *(n)* the size of wavelength that a radio station uses to transmit its programmes.

**waver** wavering wavered *(v)* to be uncertain or unsteady.

**wax** waxes waxing waxed 1 *(n)* a substance made from fats or oils, and used to make crayons, polish, and candles. 2 *(v)* When the Moon **waxes**, it appears to get larger. *See* **moon**.

**WC** *(n)* a toilet. The initials WC stand for water closet.

**weak** weaker weakest 1 *(adj)* not powerful, or not having much force. **weakness** *(n)*. 2 *(adj)* easy to break. 3 *(adj)* lacking taste. *Weak tea.*

**weakling** *(n)* a weak person or animal.

**wealthy** wealthier wealthiest *(adj)* Someone who is **wealthy** has a lot of money or property. **wealth** *(n)*.

**wean** weaning weaned 1 *(v)* When you **wean** babies, you start giving them other food instead of milk. 2 **wean off** *(v)* If you **wean someone off** something, you help them to give it up gradually.

**weapon** *(n)* something that can be used for fighting, such as a sword or gun.

**wear** wearing wore worn 1 *(v)* to be dressed in something, or have something attached to you. *Max wore a blue badge.* 2 **wear out** *(v)* If an activity **wears you out**, it makes you very tired. 3 *(v)* If you **wear out** your clothes, you make them ragged and useless. 4 **wear away** *(v)* to destroy something slowly, bit by bit.

**weary** wearier weariest *(adj)* very tired, or exhausted. **weariness** *(n)*.

**weather** *(n)* the state of the atmosphere, for example, how hot or cold it is and whether it is raining, snowing, etc.

**weather-beaten** *(adj)* damaged or worn by the weather.

**weave** **weaving** **wove** *or* **weaved** **woven** *or* **weaved** 1 *(v)* to make cloth, baskets, etc. by passing threads or strips over and under each other. 2 *(v)* to move from side to side in order to get through something. *Tim wove through the crowd.*

**web** *(n)* a very fine net of sticky threads, made by a spider to catch insects.

**webbed** *(adj)* Animals with **webbed** feet have skin connecting their toes.

**wedding** *(n)* a marriage ceremony.

**wedge** *(n)* a piece of food, wood, etc. that is thin at one end and thick at the other. *A wedge of cake.*

**wee** *(adj)* very small, or tiny.

**weed** **weeding** **weeded** 1 *(n)* a wild plant, growing in a garden or field. 2 *(v)* If you **weed** your garden, you pull the weeds out.

**week** *(n)* a period of seven days, usually from Sunday to Saturday. **weekly** *(adj).*

**weekday** *(n)* one of the five working days of the week, from Monday to Friday.

**weekend** *(n)* Saturday and Sunday.

**weep** **weeping** **wept** *(v)* to cry because you feel very sad or very emotional. **weepy** *(adj).*

**weigh** **weighing** **weighed** *(v)* to measure how heavy or light someone or something is.

**weight** 1 *(n)* how heavy someone or something is. 2 *(n)* a heavy object.

**weightlifting** *(n)* a sport in which people lift weights to show how strong they are. **weightlifter** *(n).*

**weir** *(rhymes with fear) (n)* a wall built across a river to control the flow of water.

**weird** *(weerd)* **weirder** **weirdest** *(adj)* strange, or mysterious. **weirdness** *(n).*

**welcome** **welcoming** **welcomed** 1 *(v)* to greet someone in a friendly way. 2 *(adj)* If something is **welcome**, you like it or are glad to have it. **welcome** *(v).*

**welfare** *(n)* Someone's **welfare** is their state of health, happiness, and comfort.

**welfare state** *(n)* a government system that uses money from taxes to pay for education, health and social services.

**well** **better** **best** 1 *(adv)* If you do something **well**, you do it successfully. 2 *(adv)* thoroughly. 3 *(adj)* healthy. *You look well.* 4 *(n)* a hole from which you can draw water or oil from under the ground.

**well-off** *(adj)* wealthy or rich.

**west** 1 *(n)* one of the four main points of the compass, the direction in which the Sun sets. 2 *(adj)* A **west** wind blows from the west.

**western** 1 *(adj)* to do with the west of a country or the west of the world. *Western France. Western civilization.* 2 *(n)* a cowboy film, set in the western part of the USA.



**wet** **wetting** **wet** *or* **wetted**; **wetter** **wettest** 1 *(adj)* covered with, or full of liquid. 2 *(v)* to make something wet.

**whack** *(n)* a hard hit. **whack** *(v).*

**whale** *(n)* a large sea mammal.

**whaler** 1 *(n)* someone who hunts whales for their meat and oil. **whaling** *(n).* 2 *(n)* a boat used to catch whales.

**wharf** *(worf)* **wharfs** *or* **wharves** *(n)* a place where boats and ships can be loaded or unloaded.

**wheel** *(n)* a circular object which turns on an axle, used to work machinery or move a vehicle.

**wheelchair** *(n)* a chair on wheels for people who are ill, injured, or disabled.

**wheelie** *(n) (informal)* If you do a **wheelie** on a bicycle or motorcycle, you ride with the front wheel off the ground.

*Some words that begin with a "w" sound are spelt "wh".*

**wheeze** wheezing wheezed *(v)* to breathe with difficulty, making a whistling noise in your chest. **wheezy** *(adj).*

**whereabouts** 1 *(adv)* roughly where. *Whereabouts in New York was it?* 2 *(n)* the place where someone or something is. *Do you know Billy's whereabouts?*

**whereas** *(conj)* but. *My parents eat meat, whereas I am a vegetarian.*

**whether** *(conj)* if. *I wonder whether it will rain.*

**whey** *(n)* When you separate milk to make cheese, the watery part is **whey**.

**whichever** *(pronoun)* any, or no matter which. *Choose whichever book you want.*

**whiff** *(n)* a smell in the air.

**while** 1 *(n)* a period of time. *It was a long while before I ate noodles again.* 2 **while** *or* **whilst** *(conj)* during the time that. *Can you feed my cat while I am away?* 3 *(conj)* in contrast to. *Hannah likes skating while I prefer skiing.*

**whim** *(n)* a sudden idea or wish, which is often rather silly.

**whimper** whimpering whimpered *(v)* to make weak, crying noises.

**whine** whining whined 1 *(v)* to make a long, drawn-out sound that is sad or unpleasant. 2 *(v)* to complain or moan about something in an irritating way.

**whinge** whingeing whinged *(v)* *(informal)* to whine, or to complain.

**whip** whipping whipped 1 *(n)* a long piece of leather used for hitting people or animals. **whip** *(v).* 2 *(v)* to beat cream, eggs, etc. until they are stiff.

**whirl** whirling whirled 1 *(v)* If something **whirls**, it moves around quickly. **whirl** *(n).* 2 *(informal)* If you **give something a whirl**, you try it.

**whirlwind** 1 *(n)* a wind like a cyclone, that moves in a tall column and goes round and round very fast. 2 *(adj)* very quick or sudden. *A whirlwind tour.*

**whisk** *(n)* a metal implement that you use for beating eggs or cream. **whisk** *(v).*

**whisker** *(n)* one of the long, stiff hairs near the mouth of some animals.

**whisper** whispering whispered *(v)* to talk very quietly, or to make a soft sound. **whisper** *(n).*

**whistle** whistling whistled 1 *(n)* an instrument that makes a high, loud sound when you blow it. 2 *(v)* to blow air through your lips to make a sound.

**white** whiter whitest 1 *(n)* the colour of snow. 2 *(adj)* If your skin is **white**, it is pale in colour. 3 *(n)* The **white** of an egg is the part around the yolk.

**whizz** whizzes whizzing whizzed *(v)* to move very fast.

**whole** 1 *(adj)* the total amount of something. *A whole loaf of bread.* 2 *(adj)* complete, or not broken. *I'd rather have a whole biscuit than a broken one.* 3 *(n)* the entire thing, or all the parts of something. *Two halves make a whole.*

**wholefood** *(n)* food that has been processed as little as possible, such as brown rice.

**wholemeal** *(adj)* **Wholemeal** flour has all the grain left in it.

**wholesale** *(adv)* When shopkeepers buy things **wholesale**, they buy them cheaply in large quantities, in order to sell them in their shops.

**wholesome** *(adj)* healthy, or good for you. *A wholesome diet.*

**wholly** *(ho-lee)* *(adv)* completely. *Joshua was wholly responsible for the accident.*

**whoop** *(n)* a loud cry. *A whoop of joy.*

**whooping cough** *(n)* an infectious disease that makes you cough violently.

**why** *(adv)* The word **why** is used to ask about the reason for something.

**wick** *(n)* the twisted cord running through a candle, which you light.

**wicked** wickeder wickedest *(adj)* very bad, cruel, or evil. **wickedness** *(n).*

**wide** wider widest 1 *(adj)* from one side to the other, or from edge to edge. *The room is seven metres wide.* 2 *(adj)* large from side to side. *A wide tunnel.* 3 *(adj)* covering a large number of things. *A wide range of magazines.* **widely** *(adv).*

**widespread** *(adj)* happening in many places, or among many people. *There is widespread concern about pollution.*

**widow** *(n)* a woman whose husband has died, and who has not married again.

**widower** *(n)* a man whose wife has died, and who has not married again.

**width** *(n)* the distance from one side of something to the other.

**widthways** *(adv)* in the direction of the widest side. *Fold the paper widthways.*

**wife** **wives** *(n)* the female partner in a marriage.

**wig** *(n)* a covering of false hair, made to fit someone's head.

**wiggle** **wiggling** **wiggled** *(v)* to make small movements from side to side or up and down. **wiggly** *(adj).*

**wild** **wilder** **wildest** **1** *(adj)* natural and not tamed by humans. *Wild flowers.* **2** *(adj)* uncontrolled, often in an angry way. *Dad went wild when he saw the mess.*

**wilderness** **wildernesses** *(n)* an area of wild, uninhabited land, such as a desert.

**wildlife** *(n)* wild animals and plants.

**will** **1** *(n)* written instructions stating what should happen to someone's property and money when they die. **2** *(n)* determination. *A will to succeed.*

**willing** *(adj)* eager and pleased to offer help. **willingness** *(n),* **willingly** *(adv).*

**willow** *(n)* a tree with thin, hanging branches, often found near water.

**wilt** **wilting** **wilted** *(v)* If a plant **wilts**, it begins to droop.

**wimp** *(n) (informal)* a feeble or cowardly person. **wimpish** *(adj).*

**win** **winning** **won** **1** *(v)* to come first in a contest. **2** *(v)* to gain or deserve something. *Julius won Sally's respect.*

**wince** **wincing** **winced** *(v)* to twitch or flinch because you are in pain. **wince** *(n).*

**winch** **winches** *(n)* a cable wound around a rotating drum, that you use for pulling or hoisting things. **winch** *(v).*

**wind** **winding** **wound** **1** *(winned) (n)* moving air. **windy** *(adj).* **2** *(wined) (v)* to wrap something round something else. *Val wound a scarf around her neck.* **3** *(wined) (v)* to twist and turn. *The road wound up the mountain.* **4** *(wined) (v)* to turn the key of a clock, toy, etc.

**windfall** **1** *(n)* fruit that has been blown off a tree. **2** *(n)* a sudden piece of good fortune, usually some unexpected money.

**wind instrument** *(n)* an instrument played by blowing, for example, the trombone, harmonica, or clarinet.

**windmill** *(n)* a machine for grinding grain to make flour, worked by the wind turning a set of sails.

**window** *(n)* an opening in a wall or roof to let in light and air.

**windpipe** *(n)* the tube that links your lungs with your nose and mouth.

**windscreen** *(n)* the strong glass window in front of the driver of a vehicle.

**windsurfing** *(n)* the sport of sailing by standing on a board with a flexible mast and a sail. **windsurfer** *(n).*

**windsurfing**

**windswept** *(adj)* exposed, and blown by the wind.

**wind turbine** *(n)* a machine that uses energy from the wind to make electricity.

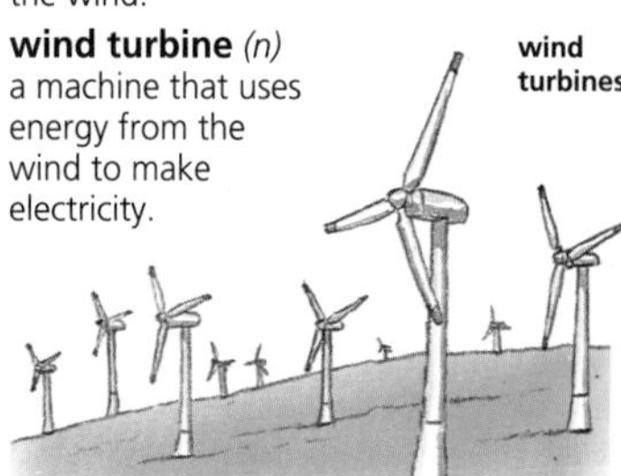

**wind turbines**

**wing** **1** *(n)* one of the feathered limbs of a bird, that it uses to fly. **2** *(n)* an outer part or extension of something. *A hospital wing.* **3** *(n)* a wing-like structure on an aircraft that makes it able to fly.

**wingspan** *(n)* the distance between the outer tips of something's wings.

**wink** **winking** **winked** *(v)* to close one eye briefly as a signal or friendly gesture.

**winner** *(n)* a person or team that wins a contest.

**wipe** **wiping** **wiped** **1** *(v)* to clear or clean a surface with your hand or a cloth, using a sweeping motion. **2** *(v)* to rub something in order to clean it or dry it. **3** *(v)* to remove something. *Wipe that smile off your face!* **4** **wipe out** *(v)* to destroy something totally. *The earthquake wiped out the village.*

**wire** wiring wired 1 *(n)* a long, thin, flexible piece of metal. 2 **wire up** *(v)* to connect electrical wires to equipment.

**wiry** wirier wiriest 1 *(adj)* tough and stiff. *Wiry hair.* 2 *(adj)* A **wiry** person is thin but tough.

**wisdom** *(n)* knowledge, experience, and understanding.

**wise** wiser wisest *(adj)* **Wise** people know what is right to say and do in different situations.

**wish** wishes wishing wished 1 *(v)* to think or say that you would like something. **wish** *(n)*. 2 *(v)* to hope for something for someone else. *I wish you a happy New Year!*

**wisp** *(n)* a small and delicate piece of something. *A wisp of smoke.* **wispy** *(adj)*.

wombat

**wit** 1 *(n)* the ability to say clever and funny things. 2 *(n)* someone who can say clever and funny things. 3 *(n)* the ability to think quickly and clearly.

**witch** witches *(n)* a woman who claims to have magic powers.

**withdraw** withdrawing withdrew withdrawn 1 *(v)* to remove, or to take away something. *Alex withdrew his support.* 2 *(v)* to drop out, or to go away. *Lee withdrew from the team.*

**withdrawn** *(adj)* very shy and quiet.

**wither** withering withered 1 *(v)* When something **withers**, it shrivels up because it has lost moisture. 2 *(adj)* A **withering** look or remark is a very scornful one.

**within** *(prep)* inside. *Within the cave was a dragon. Come back within ten minutes.*

**witness** witnesses *(n)* someone who sees something happen and may be called to give evidence in court. **witness** *(v)*.

**witty** wittier wittiest *(adj)* Someone who is **witty** says humorous things. **wittily** *(adv)*.

**wizard** 1 *(n)* a man who claims to have magical powers. 2 *(n)* someone who is very good at something. *A computer wizard.*

**wobble** wobbling wobbled *(v)* to move from side to side in an unsteady manner.

**woe** *(n)* great sadness or grief.

**wolf** wolves *(n)* a wild, flesh-eating mammal, that looks like a large dog.

Asiatic wolf

**woman** women *(n)* an adult, female human being. **womanhood** *(n)*, **womanly** *(adv)*.

**womb** *(woom)* *(n)* the part of a woman in which a baby develops before it is born. See **pregnant**.

**wombat** *(n)* a short-legged marsupial that makes burrows.

**wonder** wondering wondered 1 *(v)* to think about something in a casual or curious way. *I wonder whether it is time for tea.* 2 *(v)* to be amazed at something.

**wonderful** 1 *(adj)* amazing, splendid, or magnificent. 2 *(adj)* extremely pleasant.

**wood** 1 *(n)* the substance that forms the trunk and branches of a tree. 2 *(n)* an area of trees that is smaller than a forest.

**wooden** 1 *(adj)* made out of wood. 2 *(adj)* stiff and unnatural. *Wooden movements.*

**woodpecker** *(n)* a brightly coloured bird that lives in woodland and can drill through bark and wood with its bill.

**woodwind** *(adj)* The **woodwind** section of an orchestra is made up of instruments that you blow into, that were originally made of wood.

**woodwork** 1 *(n)* things made of wood. 2 *(n)* the craft of making wooden things.

**wool** *(n)* the hair of a sheep which can be spun into thread for knitting, weaving, etc. **woollen** *(adj)*.

**word** 1 *(n)* **Words** are spoken or written sounds that have a meaning. 2 *(n)* an order. 3 *(n)* news, or a message. *Is there any word from Sue?* 4 If you **give your word**, you promise something.

*Some words that begin with a "w" sound are spelt "wh".*

**word processing** *(n)* the use of a computer and software to type and print documents. **word processor** *(n)*.

**work** **working** **worked** 1 *(v)* to study, or to do a job. **work** *(n)*. 2 *(v)* to function properly. *Does your computer work?* 3 **works** *(singular n)* a factory. 4 *(v)* If you **work out** a puzzle, you solve it by thinking hard. 5 *(v)* When you **work out**, you do physical exercise. **work-out** *(n)*.

**workable** *(adj)* If a plan is **workable**, it can be carried out.

**worker** 1 *(n)* someone who is employed to do a job. 2 *(n)* someone who works hard. *Nat's a real worker!*

**workman** **workmen** *(n)* a man who does manual work.

**workshop** *(n)* a room, shed, etc. where things are made or mended.

**world** 1 *(n)* the planet Earth. 2 *(n)* an area of activity. *The world of sport.*

**worldly** **wordlier** **worldliest** 1 *(adj)* concerned with the world of money and possessions, rather than spiritual or religious matters. 2 *(adj)* used to the way that people behave.

**worldwide** *(adj)* to do with, or reaching most parts of the world.

**worm** *(n)* a small creature that lives in the soil. Worms have long, thin, soft bodies and no backbone.

**worn** *(adj)* Something that is **worn** has been used so much that it has become old and damaged.

**worry** **worries** **worrying** **worried** 1 *(v)* to be anxious or uneasy about something. 2 *(n)* something that makes you anxious.

**worse** *(adj)* less good.

**worship** **worshipping** **worshipped** *(v)* to express your love and devotion to God or a god. **worship** *(n)*.

**worst** *(adj)* worse than anything else.

**worth** 1 *(adj)* having a certain value. *This vase is worth a fortune.* 2 *(adj)* deserving, or good enough for. *It's worth going to the sales for the bargains.*

**worthless** *(adj)* useless, or having no value. **worthlessness** *(n)*.

**worthwhile** *(adj)* useful and valuable.

**worthy** **worthier** **worthiest** *(adj)* deserving. *A worthy cause.*

**wound** *(n)* an injury in which the skin is cut. **wound** *(v)*.

**wrangle** **wrangling** **wrangled** *(v)* to argue or debate in a noisy or angry way.

**wrap** **wrapping** **wrapped** *(v)* to cover something in paper, material, etc.

**wrapper** *(n)* the protective material in which something is wrapped.

**wrath** *(roth)* *(n)* anger.

**wreath** *(reeth)* 1 *(n)* an arrangement of flowers, leaves, etc. in memory of the dead. 2 *(n)* a circle of flowers or leaves worn on the head. *A laurel wreath.*

**wreck** **wrecking** **wrecked** 1 *(v)* to destroy or ruin something completely. 2 *(n)* something that has been ruined, for example, a ship.

**wreckage** *(n)* the broken remains at the site of a crash or explosion.

**wrench** **wrenches** **wrenching** **wrenched** *(v)* to pull something suddenly and forcefully. *Firemen had to wrench open the car door.*

**wrestle** **wrestling** **wrestled** *(v)* to fight by gripping your opponent and trying to throw them to the floor.

**wrestling** *(n)* a sport in which you fight according to rules. *The picture shows the ancient Japanese sport of Sumo wrestling.* **wrestler** *(n)*.

**Sumo wrestling**

**wriggle** **wriggling** **wriggled** *(v)* to twist and turn.

**wring** **wringing** **wrung** *(v)* to squeeze the water from wet material by twisting it.

**wrinkle** *(n)* a crease or line in someone's skin, or in material.

**wrist** *(n)* the joint that connects your hand and your arm.

**write** **writing** **wrote** **written** 1 *(v)* to put down letters, words, or numbers on paper or another surface, using a pen, pencil, etc. 2 *(v)* to compose poetry, prose, music, etc. **writer** *(n)*.

**writing** 1 *(n)* anything that has been written. 2 *(n)* literature, stories, etc.

**wrong** 1 *(adj)* incorrect, or not right. *Wrong answers.* 2 *(adj)* bad and sinful. *It is wrong to steal.* **wrong** *(n)*.

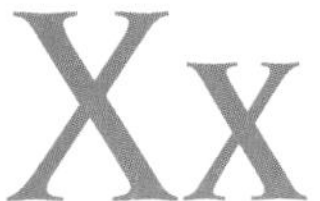

**Xmas** *see* **Christmas**.

**x-ray** 1 *(n)* a beam of energy that can pass through solid things. 2 *(n)* a photograph of the inside of a person's body, taken using x-rays. **x-ray** *(v)*.

**xylophone** *(zy-ler-fone)* *(n)* a musical instrument with wooden bars of different sizes, which are struck to give notes.

# Yy

**yacht** *(yot)* *(n)* a large sailing boat, used for pleasure or for racing. **yachting** *(n)*.

**yap** yapping yapped *(v)* to bark repeatedly, with short, high-pitched sounds.

**yard** *(n)* an enclosed area with a hard surface, usually next to a building.

**yarn** *(n)* a very long strand of wool or cotton, used for sewing, knitting, etc.

**yawn** yawning yawned *(v)* to open your mouth wide and breathe in, often because you are tired or bored. **yawn** *(n)*.

**year** *(n)* a period of 365 days, or 366 days in a leap year, which is the time that it takes the Earth to circle the Sun once.

**yeast** *(n)* a yellow fungus used to make bread and to ferment alcoholic drinks.

**yell** yelling yelled *(v)* to shout or scream very loudly. **yell** *(n)*.

**yes** *(interject)* a word used to show agreement.

**yesterday** *(n)* the day before today.

**yet** 1 *(adv)* so far, or up to now. *I haven't seen the baby yet.* 2 *(adv)* still, or even. *Yet more people came.* 3 *(conj)* but. *Celia passed her exams yet couldn't find a job.*

**yield** yielding yielded 1 *(v)* to produce something. *The field yielded 90 tons of potatoes.* **yield** *(n)*. 2 *(v)* to surrender.

**yogurt** *or* **yoghurt** *(n)* a slightly sour-tasting food prepared from curdled milk.

**yoke** *(n)* a wooden frame attached to the necks of oxen to link them for ploughing.

**yolk** *(yoke)* *(n)* the yellow part of an egg.

**Yom Kippur** *(n)* a Jewish holy day when Jews fast to mark the Day of Atonement.

**young** younger youngest 1 *(adj)* Someone or something that is **young** has lived or existed for a short time. 2 *(plural n)* the offspring of an animal.

**youngster** *(n)* a young person.

**youth** 1 *(n)* the time of life when a person is young. 2 *(n)* a young male person, usually aged between 13 and 18.

# Zz

**zany** zanier zaniest *(adj)* humorous in an unusual, crazy way. **zanily** *(adv)*.

**zap** zapping zapped *(v)* *(slang)* to shoot someone, usually in a game.

**zeal** *(zeel)* *(n)* enthusiasm and eagerness.

**zebra** *(n)* an African animal, like a horse, with black and white stripes on its body.

**zebra crossing** *(n)* a pedestrian crossing marked by flashing orange lights and broad white stripes painted on the road.

**zero** *(n)* nothing, nought, or nil.

**zigzag** *(n)* a line with sharp, diagonal turns. **zigzag** *(v)*.

**zip** *(n)* a fastener for clothes, made of linking metal or plastic teeth. **zip** *(v)*.

**zone** *(n)* an area that is used for a special purpose. *A conservation zone.*

**zoo** *(n)* a place where animals are kept for people to see or study them.

**zoom** zooming zoomed *(v)* to move very fast. *Pod zoomed off on her bike.*

## Numbers

| | |
|---|---|
| 1 - one | 16 - sixteen |
| 2 - two | 17 - seventeen |
| 3 - three | 18 - eighteen |
| 4 - four | 19 - nineteen |
| 5 - five | 20 - twenty |
| 6 - six | 21 - twenty-one |
| 7 - seven | 30 - thirty |
| 8 - eight | 40 - forty |
| 9 - nine | 50 - fifty |
| 10 - ten | 60 - sixty |
| 11 - eleven | 70 - seventy |
| 12 - twelve | 80 - eighty |
| 13 - thirteen | 90 - ninety |
| 14 - fourteen | 100 - hundred |
| 15 - fifteen | 1000 - thousand |

## Days of the week

Monday
Tuesday
Wednesday
Thursday
Friday
Saturday
Sunday

## Months of the year

| | |
|---|---|
| January | August |
| February | September |
| March | October |
| April | November |
| May | December |
| June | |
| July | |

## Measurements

### Length

METRIC

1 millimetre (mm)
1 centimetre (cm) = 10mm
1 metre (m) = 100cm
1 kilometre (km) = 1,000m

IMPERIAL

1 inch (in)
1 foot (ft) = 12in
1 yard (yd) = 3ft
1 mile = 1,760yd

### Volume

METRIC

1 millilitre (ml)
1 centilitre (cl) = 10ml
1 litre (l) = 100cl
1 kilolitre (kl) = 1,000l

IMPERIAL

1 fluid ounce (fl oz)
1 pint (pt) = 20fl oz
1 quart = 2pt
1 gallon (gal) = 8pt

### Weight

METRIC

1 milligram (mg)
1 gram (g) = 1,000mg
1 kilogram (kg) = 1,000g
1 tonne (t) = 1,000kg

IMPERIAL

1 ounce (oz)
1 pound (lb) = 16oz
1 stone = 14lb
1 hundredweight (cwt) = 112lb
1 ton = 20cwt

### Area

METRIC

1 square cm ($cm^2$)
1 square m ($m^2$) = 10,000$cm^2$
1 hectare = 10,000$m^2$
1 square kilometre ($km^2$) = 100 hectares

IMPERIAL

1 square inch ($in^2$)
1 square foot ($ft^2$) = 144$in^2$
1 square yard ($yd^2$) = 9$ft^2$
1 acre = 4,840$yd^2$
1 square mile = 640 acres

## Shapes

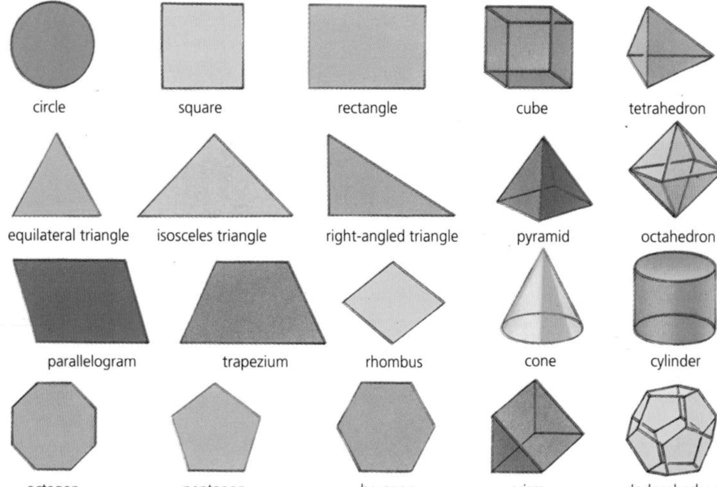


The publishers are grateful to Mitsui Machinery Sales (UK) Ltd. for supplying photographic material (158).

This is an abridged version of The Usborne Illustrated Dictionary, first published in 1994 by Usborne Publishing. This edition first published in 1995 by Usborne Publishing Ltd, 83-85 Saffron Hill, London EC1N 8RT, England. 
Printed in Great Britain